# HISTORICAL DICTIONARIES OF AFRICA
**Edited by Jon Woronoff**

1. *Cameroon,* by Victor T. Le Vine and Roger P. Nye. 1974. *Out of print. See No. 48.*
2. *The Congo,* 2nd ed., by Virginia Thompson and Richard Adloff. 1984. *Out of print. See No. 69.*
3. *Swaziland,* by John J. Grotpeter. 1975.
4. *The Gambia,* 2nd ed., by Harry A. Gailey. 1987. *Out of print. See No. 79.*
5. *Botswana,* by Richard P. Stevens. 1975. *Out of print. See No. 70.*
6. *Somalia,* by Margaret F. Castagno. 1975. *Out of print. See No. 87.*
7. *Benin (Dahomey),* 2nd ed., by Samuel Decalo. 1987. *Out of print. See No. 61.*
8. *Burundi,* by Warren Weinstein. 1976. *Out of print. See No. 73.*
9. *Togo,* 3rd ed., by Samuel Decalo. 1996.
10. *Lesotho,* by Gordon Haliburton. 1977. *Out of print. See No. 90.*
11. *Mali,* 3rd ed., by Pascal James Imperato. 1996. *Out of print. See No. 107.*
12. *Sierra Leone,* by Cyril Patrick Foray. 1977.
13. *Chad,* 3rd ed., by Samuel Decalo. 1997.
14. *Upper Volta,* by Daniel Miles McFarland. 1978.
15. *Tanzania,* by Laura S. Kurtz. 1978.
16. *Guinea,* 3rd ed., by Thomas O'Toole with Ibrahima Bah-Lalya. 1995. *Out of print. See No. 94.*
17. *Sudan,* by John Voll. 1978. *Out of print. See No. 53.*
18. *Rhodesia/Zimbabwe,* by R. Kent Rasmussen. 1979. *Out of print. See No. 46.*
19. *Zambia,* 2nd ed., by John J. Grotpeter, Brian V. Siegel, and James R. Pletcher. 1998. *Out of print. See No. 106.*
20. *Niger,* 3rd ed., by Samuel Decalo. 1997.
21. *Equatorial Guinea,* 3rd ed., by Max Liniger-Goumaz. 2000.
22. *Guinea-Bissau,* 3rd ed., by Richard Lobban and Peter Mendy. 1997.
23. *Senegal,* by Lucie G. Colvin. 1981. *Out of print. See No. 65.*
24. *Morocco,* by William Spencer. 1980. *Out of print. See No. 71.*
25. *Malawi,* by Cynthia A. Crosby. 1980. *Out of print. See No. 84.*
26. *Angola,* by Phyllis Martin. 1980. *Out of print. See No. 92.*
27. *The Central African Republic,* by Pierre Kalck. 1980. *Out of print. See No. 51.*
28. *Algeria,* by Alf Andrew Heggoy. 1981. *Out of print. See No. 66.*
29. *Kenya,* by Bethwell A. Ogot. 1981. *Out of print. See No. 77.*
30. *Gabon,* by David E. Gardinier. 1981. *Out of print. See No. 58.*
31. *Mauritania,* by Alfred G. Gerteiny. 1981. *Out of print. See No. 68.*

32. *Ethiopia,* by Chris Prouty and Eugene Rosenfeld. 1981. *Out of print. See No. 91.*

33. *Libya,* 3rd ed., by Ronald Bruce St John. 1998. *Out of print. See No. 100.*

34. *Mauritius,* by Lindsay Riviere. 1982. *Out of print. See No. 49.*

35. *Western Sahara,* by Tony Hodges. 1982. *Out of print. See No. 55.*

36. *Egypt,* by Joan Wucher King. 1984. *Out of print. See No. 89.*

37. *South Africa,* by Christopher Saunders. 1983. *Out of print. See No. 78.*

38. *Liberia,* by D. Elwood Dunn and Svend E. Holsoe. 1985. *Out of print. See No. 83.*

39. *Ghana,* by Daniel Miles McFarland. 1985. *Out of print. See No. 63.*

40. *Nigeria,* 2nd ed., by Anthony Oyewole and John Lucas. 2000. *Out of print. See No. 111.*

41. *Côte d'Ivoire (The Ivory Coast),* 2nd ed., by Robert J. Mundt. 1995.

42. *Cape Verde,* 2nd ed., by Richard Lobban and Marilyn Halter. 1988. *Out of print. See No. 62.*

43. *Zaire,* by F. Scott Bobb. 1988. *Out of print. See No. 76.*

44. *Botswana,* 2nd ed., by Fred Morton, Andrew Murray, and Jeff Ramsay. 1989. *Out of print. See No. 70.*

45. *Tunisia,* 2nd ed., by Kenneth J. Perkins. 1997.

46. *Zimbabwe,* 2nd ed., by Steven C. Rubert and R. Kent Rasmussen. 1990. *Out of print. See No. 86.*

47. *Mozambique,* by Mario Azevedo. 1991. *Out of print. See No. 88.*

48. *Cameroon,* 2nd ed., by Mark W. DeLancey and H. Mbella Mokeba. 1990.

49. *Mauritius,* 2nd ed., by Sydney Selvon. 1991.

50. *Madagascar,* by Maureen Covell. 1995. *Out of print. See No. 98.*

51. *The Central African Republic,* 2nd ed., by Pierre Kalck, translated by Thomas O'Toole. 1992. *Out of print. See No. 93.*

52. *Angola,* 2nd ed., by Susan H. Broadhead. 1992. *Out of print. See No. 92.*

53. *Sudan,* 2nd ed., by Carolyn Fluehr-Lobban, Richard A. Lobban Jr., and John Obert Voll. 1992. *Out of print. See No. 85.*

54. *Malawi,* 2nd ed., by Cynthia A. Crosby. 1993. *Out of print. See No. 84.*

55. *Western Sahara,* 2nd ed., by Anthony Pazzanita and Tony Hodges. 1994. *Out of print. See No. 96.*

56. *Ethiopia and Eritrea,* 2nd ed., by Chris Prouty and Eugene Rosenfeld. 1994. *Out of print. See No. 91.*

57. *Namibia,* by John J. Grotpeter. 1994.

58. *Gabon,* 2nd ed., by David E. Gardinier. 1994. *Out of print. See No. 101.*

59. *Comoro Islands,* by Martin Ottenheimer and Harriet Ottenheimer. 1994.

60. *Rwanda,* by Learthen Dorsey. 1994. *Out of print. See No. 105.*

61. *Benin,* 3rd ed., by Samuel Decalo. 1995.

62. *Republic of Cape Verde,* 3rd ed., by Richard Lobban and Marlene Lopes. 1995. *Out of print. See No. 104.*

63. *Ghana,* 2nd ed., by David Owusu-Ansah and Daniel Miles McFarland. 1995. *Out of print. See No. 97.*

64. *Uganda,* by M. Louise Pirouet. 1995.

65. *Senegal,* 2nd ed., by Andrew F. Clark and Lucie Colvin Phillips. 1994.

66. *Algeria,* 2nd ed., by Phillip Chiviges Naylor and Alf Andrew Heggoy. 1994. *Out of print. See No. 102.*

67. *Egypt,* 2nd ed., by Arthur Goldschmidt Jr. 1994. *Out of print. See No. 89.*

68. *Mauritania,* 2nd ed., by Anthony G. Pazzanita. 1996. *Out of print. See No. 110.*

69. *Congo,* 3rd ed., by Samuel Decalo, Virginia Thompson, and Richard Adloff. 1996.

70. *Botswana,* 3rd ed., by Jeff Ramsay, Barry Morton, and Fred Morton. 1996. *Out of print. See No. 108.*

71. *Morocco,* by Thomas K. Park. 1996. *Out of print. See No. 95.*

72. *Tanzania,* 2nd ed., by Thomas P. Ofcansky and Rodger Yeager. 1997.

73. *Burundi,* 2nd ed., by Ellen K. Eggers. 1997. *Out of print. See No. 103.*

74. *Burkina Faso,* 2nd ed., by Daniel Miles McFarland and Lawrence Rupley. 1998.

75. *Eritrea,* by Tom Killion. 1998.

76. *Democratic Republic of the Congo (Zaire)*, by F. Scott Bobb. 1999. (Revised edition of *Historical Dictionary of Zaire*, No. 43)

77. *Kenya,* 2nd ed., by Robert M. Maxon and Thomas P. Ofcansky. 2000.

78. *South Africa,* 2nd ed., by Christopher Saunders and Nicholas Southey. 2000.

79. *The Gambia,* 3rd ed., by Arnold Hughes and Harry A. Gailey. 2000.

80. *Swaziland,* 2nd ed., by Alan R. Booth. 2000.

81. *Republic of Cameroon,* 3rd ed., by Mark W. DeLancey and Mark Dike DeLancey. 2000.

82. *Djibouti,* by Daoud A. Alwan and Yohanis Mibrathu. 2000.

83. *Liberia,* 2nd ed., by D. Elwood Dunn, Amos J. Beyan, and Carl Patrick Burrowes. 2001.

84. *Malawi,* 3rd ed., by Owen J. Kalinga and Cynthia A. Crosby. 2001.

85. *Sudan,* 3rd ed., by Richard A. Lobban Jr., Robert S. Kramer, and Carolyn Fluehr-Lobban. 2002.

86. *Zimbabwe,* 3rd ed., by Steven C. Rubert and R. Kent Rasmussen. 2001.

87. *Somalia,* 2nd ed., by Mohamed Haji Mukhtar. 2002.

88. *Mozambique,* 2nd ed., by Mario Azevedo, Emmanuel Nnadozie, and Tomé Mbuia João. 2003.

89. *Egypt,* 3rd ed., by Arthur Goldschmidt Jr. and Robert Johnston. 2003.

# Historical Dictionary of Nigeria

Toyin Falola
Ann Genova

*Historical Dictionaries of Africa, No. 111*

The Scarecrow Press, Inc.
Lanham, Maryland • Toronto • Plymouth, UK
2009

# SCARECROW PRESS, INC.

Published in the United States of America
by Scarecrow Press, Inc.
A wholly owned subsidiary of
The Rowman & Littlefield Publishing Group, Inc.
4501 Forbes Boulevard, Suite 200, Lanham, Maryland 20706
www.scarecrowpress.com

Estover Road
Plymouth PL6 7PY
United Kingdom

British Library Cataloguing in Publication Information Available

**Library of Congress Cataloging-in-Publication Data**

Falola, Toyin.
  Historical dictionary of Nigeria / by Toyin Falola and Ann Genova.
      p. cm. — (Historical dictionaries of Africa ; 111)
  Includes bibliographical references.
  ISBN 978-0-8108-5615-8 (cloth : alk. paper) — ISBN 978-0-8108-6316-3
(ebook)
  1. Nigeria–History–Dictionaries. I. Genova, Ann. II. Title.
  DT515.15.F35   2009
  966.9003—dc22                                    2009006158

⊗ ™ The paper used in this publication meets the minimum requirements of
American National Standard for Information Sciences—Permanence of
Paper for Printed Library Materials, ANSI/NISO Z39.48-1992.
Manufactured in the United States of America.

# Contents

# Editor's Foreword

Geographically, Nigeria is one of the largest countries in Africa, and by far the biggest in West Africa, which it dominates. Nigeria's population, is gigantic and constantly growing. The land, although not exceptionally rich, does provide the basis for agriculture and mining, and the production of oil has been a godsend or curse, depending on your perspective. Still, it does generate wealth, which could be used to power the economy. Moreover, Nigeria has masses of educated and hardworking people, eager to get ahead, and it has finally returned to an almost-democratic political system, which should theoretically allow its elected officials to chart more promising paths than the series of military dictators.

But these positives are apparently more than counterbalanced by negatives—a varied and often fractious national community divided by ethnic groups, religion, and political goals, birth rates that are too high for its educational and health infrastructure, and a meddling military. Thus, after about half a century of independence, Nigeria remains a land of promises that are inadequately fulfilled.

This completely new edition of the *Historical Dictionary of Nigeria* is particularly welcome because it covers such a wide variety of topics over such an extensive time frame. The core of the book is obviously the dictionary section, which includes specific entries on the most crucial aspects of the country, its past and present, its population and geography, its economic endowment and policies, its confusing and often disappointing politics, its religions and culture. Many of these are on persons, others on significant events, and yet others on ethnic groups, or religions, or political parties. Because they are amply cross-referenced, one easily leads to another and cumulatively they do impart of better understanding of the overall situation. A general overview is also provided in the introduction, which highlights many of the successes and, alas, also the failures. The chronology allows readers to follow this over time, from the earliest days to the present. The list of acronyms is an indispensable tool in reading the literature about Nigeria, of which there is a great deal. Many of the better works, on a wide range of subjects, are included in the bibliography.

Writing such a book from scratch was clearly an impressive task, all the more so in that it was accomplished by two authors, Toyin Falola and Ann Genova. Dr. Falola is a Nigerian who was born in Ibadan and studied at the University of Ife, Nigeria. At present, he is the Frances Higginbotham Nalle Centennial Professor at the University of Texas in Austin, where he is also a Distinguished Teaching Professor. He is a fellow of the Nigerian Academy of Letters and a Fellow of the Historical Society of Nigeria, and has written extensively, including his memoir *A Mouth Sweeter than Salt* and *Christianity and Social Change in Africa.* Dr. Ann Genova, who received her doctorate from the University of Texas at Austin, is particularly interested in such key areas as petroleum, nationalism, and development in Nigeria. She is presently assistant professor of African history at Roanoke College. Among other works, she coauthored *Politics of the Global Oil Industry* and coedited *Yoruba Identity and Power Politics.* Between them, they cover the essentials, and provide a steady and helpful foundation for those who want to know more about what remains one of Africa's most important countries.

Jon Woronoff
Series Editor

# Reader's Note

The dictionary includes standard transliteration of terms and names, without diacriticals. Personal names, particularly Muslim ones, have been placed in the dictionary as they are commonly used. Most Muslim, Hausa, and Fulani names do not conform to the Western structure of given/middle/family. That said, however, some individuals have used their names in the Western style. "Usman dan Fodio," for example, appears as it is written while General Alhaji Abdulsalami Abubakar appears as "Abubakar, General Alhaji Abdulsalami." The name Muhammad appears in the spelling used by the individual who bears the name. All personal names appear in full as entries, with the person's preference mentioned within an entry. For example, the popular musician Fela Kuti appears in full as "Anikulapo-Kuti, Olufela" and the artist dele jegede as "Jegede, Omodele."

Readers will notice that the titles of chief and king appear regularly. They represent European attempts starting in the 16th century to categorize the political systems and role of leaders within them. A chief held political and, possibly, religious power within his village or town prior to the early 20th century. The title of chief during colonial rule became largely ceremonial. Today, it is given by a community to an outstanding individual as a way to honor their achievements. It is not uncommon for Nigeria's political and cultural leaders, then, to be a chief of several different locations. Like chief, king applies to Nigerian rulers prior to the early 20th century who held political and, perhaps, religious power. It differs from chief in that it is no longer used. The title of *alhaji* for men, and sometimes *alhaja* for women, is for those Muslim men and women who went on *hajj* (spiritual pilgrimage) to Mecca. In some instances, an individual's place of origin or title has become part of his or her name, which is reflected in the entries. King Jaja of Opobo and Queen Amina of Zaria appear as "Jaja of Opobo, King" and "Amina of Zaria, Queen."

The dictionary lists entries alphabetically in the language most used in the secondary literature on Nigeria. Thus, *jangali* appears rather than "cattle tax," and *hajj* rather than "pilgrimage" when discussing Islam. Cross-references to relevant dictionary entries are indicated in **bold** within an entry. Entry titles not mentioned in that entry but that are closely related may appear in the *See also*. In addition, entries with alternate spellings or related terms direct readers to the relevant entry. *See* cross-references.

# Acronyms and Abbreviations

| | |
|---|---|
| ABN | Association for Better Nigeria |
| AC | Action Congress |
| AD | Alliance for Democracy |
| AG | Action Group |
| AIDS | Acquired Immunodeficiency Syndrome |
| AP | African Petroleum Company |
| APP | All People's Party |
| ANTUF | All-Nigeria Trade Union Federation |
| AU | African Union |
| BBC | British Broadcasting Corporation |
| BDPP | Benin Delta People's Party |
| BP | British Petroleum |
| Brig. | Brigadier |
| BYM | Bornu Youth Movement |
| CMS | Church Missionary Society |
| Col. | Colonel |
| Com. | Commodore |
| ECOMOG | Economic Community of West African States Monitoring Group |
| ECOWAS | Economic Community of West African States |
| EUG | Egba United Government |
| FCT | Federal Capital Territory |
| FESTAC '77 | World Black and African Festival of Arts and Culture |
| FMG | Federal Military Government |
| GDP | Gross Domestic Product |
| Gen. | General |
| GNI | Gross National Income |
| GNPP | Great Nigerian People's Party |

| | |
|---|---|
| HDI | Human Development Index |
| HIV | Human Immunodeficiency Virus |
| ICJ | International Court of Justice |
| IMF | International Monetary Fund |
| INEC | Independent National Electoral Commission |
| ING | Interim National Government |
| Insp. Gen. | Inspector General |
| IYC | Ijaw Youth Council |
| JAC | Joint Action Committee |
| JAMB | Joint Admissions and Matriculation Board |
| KNC | Kamerun National Congress |
| KPP | Kano People's Party |
| Lt. Col. | Lieutenant Colonel |
| LYM | Lagos Youth Movement |
| Maj. Gen. | Major General |
| MAMSER | Mass Mobilization for Self Reliance, Social Justice, and Economic Recovery |
| MBPP | Middle Belt People's Party |
| MDF | Mid-West Democratic Front |
| MEND | Movement for the Emancipation of the Niger Delta |
| MPC | Mid-West People's Congress |
| MOSOP | Movement for the Survival of the Ogoni People |
| NAC | National Africa Company |
| NADECO | National Democratic Coalition |
| NAP | Nigeria Advance Party |
| NBA | National Basketball Association |
| NCNC | National Council of Nigeria and the Cameroons |
| NCNC | National Council of Nigerian Citizens |
| NCTUN | National Council of Trade Unions of Nigeria |
| NDC | Niger Delta Congress |
| NEC | National Electoral Commission |
| NEC | National Economic Council |
| NECON | National Electoral Commission of Nigeria |
| NEPA | National Electric Power Authority |
| NEPA | Northern Elements Progressive Association |
| NEPAD | New Partnership for African Development |
| NEPU | Northern Elements Progressive Union |
| NGO | Nongovernmental Organization(s) |

| | |
|---|---|
| NIIA | Nigerian Institute of International Affairs |
| NIP | National Independence Party |
| NISER | Nigerian Institute of Social and Economic Research |
| NLC | Nigerian Labour Congress |
| NNA | Nigerian National Alliance |
| NNDP | Nigerian National Democratic Party |
| NNFL | Nigerian National Federation of Labour |
| NNOC | Nigerian National Oil Corporation |
| NNPC | Nigerian National Petroleum Corporation |
| NPC | Northern People's Congress |
| NPF | Northern Progressive Front |
| NPN | National Party of Nigeria |
| NPP | Nigerian People's Party |
| NRC | National Republican Convention |
| NSEC | Nigerian Securities and Exchange Commission |
| NSM | National Solidarity Movement |
| NTUC | Nigerian Trade Union Congress |
| NUT | Nigerian Union of Teachers |
| NYM | Nigerian Youth Movement |
| NYSC | National Youth Service Corps |
| OAU | Organization of African Unity |
| OIC | Organization of the Islamic Conference |
| OMPADEC | Oil Mineral Producing Areas Development Commission |
| OPC | O'odua People's Congress |
| OPEC | Organization of Petroleum Exporting Countries |
| PDP | People's Democratic Party |
| PPA | Progressive Parties Alliance |
| PRC | Provisional Ruling Council |
| PRP | People's Redemption Party |
| RBDA | River Basin Development Authorities |
| RNC | Royal Niger Company |
| RWU | Railway Workers' Union |
| SAP | Structural Adjustment Programs |
| SDP | Social Democratic Party |
| SMC | Supreme Military Council |
| SWAFP | Socialist Workers and Farmers Party |

| | |
|---|---|
| TAC | Nigerian Technical Aid Corps |
| TUCN | Trade Union Congress of Nigeria |
| UAC | United African Company |
| UDP | United Democratic Party |
| ULC | United Labour Congress |
| UMBC | United Middle Belt Congress |
| UN | United Nations |
| UNESCO | United Nations Educational, Scientific, and Cultural Organization |
| UNICEF | United Nations Children's Fund |
| UNIP | United National Independence Party |
| UPE | Universal Primary Education |
| UPF | United Progressive Front |
| UPGA | United Progressive Grand Alliance |
| UPN | United Party of Nigeria |
| UPP | United People's Party |
| WAFF | (Royal) West African Frontier Force |
| WAI | War Against Indiscipline |
| WB | World Bank |
| WHO | World Health Organization |

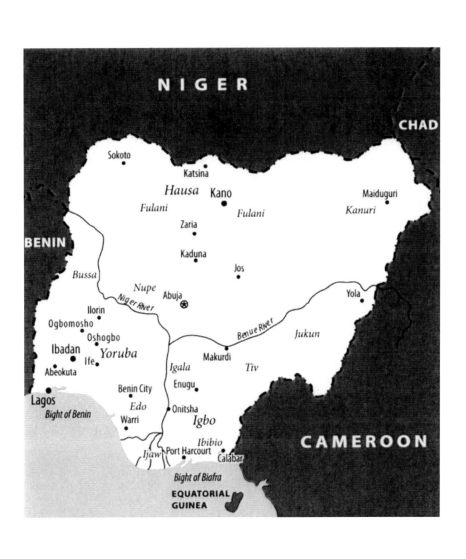

# Chronology

**600 BCE–200 CE**   Evidence of Nok civilization.

**900–1000 CE**   Islam introduced in northeastern Nigeria. Establishment of Hausa Kingdoms, Benin Kingdom, Kanem–Bornu Empire, and the Oyo Empire.

**1300–1600**   Height of the trans-Saharan trade, Oyo Empire, and the Sefawa Dynasty in northeastern Nigeria.

**1472**   Portuguese traders visit the Bight of Benin.

**1485**   Joao Alfonso d'Alveiro visits Benin Kingdom and invites the King Ozolua to Portugal.

**1789**   The first printing of Olaudah Equiano's narrative.

**1797–1806**   Mungo Park explores the Niger River.

**1804**   Usman dan Fodio leads a jihad in the Hausa Kingdoms.

**1807**   The British abolish the slave trade in England.

**1822–1826**   Hugh Clapperton travels across Nigeria and records his encounters with royalty.

**1830**   Legitimate trade begins in the hinterland by way of the Niger River.

**1833**   Final collapse of the Oyo Empire.

**1841**   The first (Anglican) Church Missionary Society members arrive in Nigeria during an expedition on the Niger River.

**1842**   The Wesleyan Methodist Missionary Society establishes the first Christian mission at Badagry.

**1846**   The Anglican Church Missionary Society establishes a Christian mission at Abeokuta.

**1851**   John Beecroft establishes the first British diplomatic outpost at Lagos.

**1859**   The circulation of Nigeria's first newspaper, *Iwe Ihorin*, which was written in Yoruba.

**1859–1893**   The Yoruba Wars, including the Ijayi War.

**1861**   The British seize Lagos from King Dosumu and establish the Lagos Colony.

**1879**   George Goldie starts the United African Company.

**1882**   The United African Company changes its name to the National Africa Company.

**1884**   Oil Rivers Protectorate is established.

**1886**   The National Africa Company becomes the Royal Niger Company upon receipt of a royal charter from the British government.

**1890**   The British claim territories in northern Nigeria through the Anglo–French Agreement.

**1892**   The Gallwey Treaty between the British and the King of Benin is signed.

**1893**   The Oil Rivers Protectorate becomes the Niger Coast Protectorate.

**1895**   The Akassa Massacre in the Niger Delta involving the people of Brass and the Royal Niger Constabulary. The founding of the Hope Waddell Training Institute at Calabar.

**1897**   The name "Nigeria" is officially adopted.

**1899**   **December:** The establishment of the Protectorate of Northern Nigeria and the Protectorate of Southern Nigeria.

**1900**   The British revoke the Royal Niger Company's charter and combine the Niger Coast Protectorate with nearby areas to form the

Protectorate of Southern Nigeria. Likewise, areas in the North become the Protectorate of Northern Nigeria.

**1903**   The British conquer and take the Sokoto Caliphate.

**1909**   The Niger Traders' Association forms. **September:** The founding of King's College.

**1912**   Sir Frederick Lugard is appointed governor of the protectorates.

**1914**   The amalgamation of the protectorates.

**1914–1918**   The British recruit Nigerian troops during World War I.

**1915**   Coal mining begins at Enugu.

**1917**   The Lagos Town Council is established.

**1922**   The Clifford Constitution is implemented.

**1925**   Ladipo Solanke forms the West African Students' Union in London.

**1926**   **June:** The *Daily Times*, Nigeria's first English-language newspaper, begins circulation.

**1929**   Aba Riots occur in southeastern Nigeria.

**1932**   The advent of the Aladura churches and Yaba Higher College.

**1934**   The Lagos Youth Movement is formed.

**1936**   The Nigerian Youth Movement is founded.

**1937**   Shell–D'Arcy Exploration Company begins oil exploration in the Niger Delta.

**1938**   Sir Alhaji Ahmadu Bello receives the ceremonial title of *sardauna*.

**1939**   Southern Nigeria is divided into Eastern and Western provinces.

**1939–1945**   The British recruit troops during World War II.

**1940** **January:** Chief Michael Imoudu forms the Railway Workers' Union.

**1944** The National Council of Nigeria and the Cameroons is created.

**1945** **June–August:** General Strike by Nigeria's labor unions.

**1946** **January:** Implementation of the Richardson Constitution and the creation of three regions.

**1947** University College of Ibadan is founded.

**1949** The Northern People's Congress is created.

**1950 March:** Chief Obafemi Awolowo creates the Action Group.

**1951** The Macpherson Constitution is implemented.

**1952** Nigeria holds its first general elections.

**1953** Nigeria's three major political parties attend a constitutional conference to discuss the adoption of a federal constitution and allowance of self-government for any region desiring it.

**1953** **January:** The Eastern Regional government crisis occurs.

**1953** **May:** Kano Riots take place in the midst of intense political campaigning.

**1954** The Lyttleton Constitution is implemented.

**1955** Chief Obafemi Awolowo launches the Universal Primary Education program in Western Region.

**1956** The Shell–BP Petroleum Company discovers commercial quantities of petroleum in the Niger Delta. The Mid-West Movement agitates for the creation of the Mid-Western Region.

**1957** *Black Orpheus* begins publication. **September**: The British launch the Willink Commission on minority groups. The Eastern and Western Regions declare self-rule. **April:** The establishment of the Nigerian Broadcasting Corporation.

**1958** The first batch of petroleum is exported. Susanne Wenger and her colleagues start the New Sacred Art Movement.

**1959** The Northern Region declares self-rule. The Central Bank of Nigeria is established.

**1959 December:** Nigeria holds its elections in preparation for independence.

**1960 October:** Nigeria becomes independent. **May:** Nigeria joins the British Commonwealth.

**1961** The University of Ife is established.

**1962** University of Lagos and Ahmadu Bello University in Zaria are established. The Action Group Crisis erupts in the Western Region. The creation of the Jama'atu Nasril Islam to promote Islam and unify Muslims.

**1963** Nigeria's first population census is held, but the results are not released. **August:** A portion of the Western Region is made into the Mid-Western Region. **September:** Chief Obafemi Awolowo is imprisoned on charges of felony. **October:** Nigeria becomes a republic.

**1964 December:** Nigeria holds elections, which many people from the Western and Eastern Regions boycotted.

**1965 October:** The Western Region holds elections, which result in violence.

**1966 January:** The first military coup d'état occurs, placing Major General Johnson Aguiyi-Ironsi as the head of state. **24 May:** Aguiyi-Ironsi abolishes regions, creating a centralized administrative structure. **May:** Northerners reject Aguiyi-Ironsi's removal of regions and engage in violent attacks on southerners, mainly Igbo, living in north. **29 July:** Northern officers launch the second military coup d'état and place General Yakubu Gowon as the head of state. **August:** Chief Chukwuemeka Ojukwu, governor of the Eastern Region, rejects Gowon's authority.

**1967 January:** The Aburi Conference is held, but is not successful. **May:** Gowon transforms Nigeria's four regions into 12 states. In response, Ojukwu declares the Eastern Region independent and renames it the Republic of Biafra. **July:** The civil war begins. **19–21 September:** The Mid-Western Region is declared independent and named the Republic of Benin.

**1969 June:** Ojukwu presents the Ahiara Declaration, declaring the Republic of Biafra a socialist state. The Petroleum Decree is issued. **August:** Peace talks are held in Kampala.

**1970  7 January:** Owerri is seized by federal forces. **11 January:** Ojukwu leaves Biafra for Ivory Coast. **12 January:** Biafra surrenders, ending the civil war.

**1971  April:** Creation of the state-owned Nigerian National Oil Corporation. **July:** Nigeria joins the Organization of Petroleum Exporting Countries.

**1973**  The Nigerian Supreme Council of Islamic Affairs is established to unify and represent all Muslims. **January:** The national currency is switched to the naira. **June:** Gowon sets up the National Youth Service Corps program to promote unity.

**1974**  The second population census is taken, but the results are not released.

**1975  May:** The Economic Community of West African States is formed. **July:** A third military coup d'état takes place, making General Murtala Mohammed head of state.

**1976 February:**  Mohammed creates seven new states, bringing the number of states to 19. He also selects Abuja as the future site of Nigeria's new capital. **13 February:** Mohammed was assassinated and General Olusegun Obasanjo becomes head of state. **September:** A Universal Primary Education program is launched nationwide.

**1977  January–February:** Nigeria hosts the World Black and African Festival of Arts and Culture. **April:** The Nigerian National Petroleum Corporation replaces the Nigerian National Oil Corporation as the state oil company.

**1978**  The unification of all major trade unions into one national union, called Nigerian Labour Congress.

**1979**  The formation of the Okigbo Commission to assess revenue allocation. **August:** Aspects of British Petroleum's operations are nationalized. **October:** Alhaji Aliyu Usman Shagari is elected as president, marking the start of Nigeria's Second Republic. **December:** Shagari launches the Green Revolution.

**1980** **December:** The Maitatsine Riots erupt in the North.

**1982** **12 February:** Pope John Paul II of the Catholic Church makes a visit to Nigeria.

**1983** Nigeria starts a Structural Adjustment Program. **December:** The fourth military coup d'état takes place, removing Shagari and installing Major General Muhammadu Buhari as head of state. This transfer of power marks the end of the Second Republic.

**1984** Buhari launches his War Against Indiscipline program.

**1985** **August:** The fifth military coup d'état ejects Buhari and installs General Ibrahim Babangida.

**1986** Wole Soyinka wins the Nobel Prize for Literature. Nigeria joins the Organization of the Islamic Conference.

**1987** Babangida creates two new states, making the total number of states 21. **March:** The Kafachan Riots erupt in Kaduna State. **July:** The founding of the Mass Mobilization for Self Reliance, Social Justice, and Economic Recovery program.

**1989** **October:** Babangida allows only two political parties— (the Social Democratic Party and the National Republican Convention) to operate in Nigeria, giving the appearance of democracy.

**1990** **August:** The Economic Community of West African States Monitoring Group (ECOMOG) is created.

**1991** The third population census is taken, placing Nigeria's population at 88.5 million people. **August:** Babangida creates several new states, increasing the number of states to 30. **December:** Abuja replaces Lagos as Nigeria's capital.

**1992** The Movement for the Survival of the Ogoni People is formed. **July:** The Oil Mineral Producing Areas Development Commission is established to improve the economic situation for the inhabitants of the Niger Delta.

**1993   12 June:** A failed presidential election takes place, which would have marked the start of a Third Republic. Chief M. K. O. Abiola, who many identify as the winner, is accused of treason and imprisoned. **August:** Babangida passes power to the Interim National Government.

**1994   May:** The National Democratic Coalition is formed. **November:** The sixth military coup d'état ends the Interim National Government and places General Sani Abacha as the new head of state.

**1995   **The National Human Rights Commission is established. **March:** Abacha unfairly tries and imprisons several prominent politicians. **August:** The Oduduwa People's Congress is formed in response to the annulled presidential elections of 1993. **1 October:** Abacha declares the transition to a civilian government in three years. **November:** Ken Saro-Wiwa, along with eight other Ogoni leaders, is hanged by Abacha. Nigeria's membership in the Commonwealth Secretariat is suspended until 1999.

**1996   June:** Abacha lifts the bans on political associations, allowing for the organization of political parties. **September:** Abacha unveils his Vision 2010 plan. **October:** Abacha creates six new states, making a total of 36 states.

**1998   **The emergence of the Ijaw Youth Council. **January:** The second wave of violent clashes between the Modekeke and Ife (a Yoruba subgroup) occurs in Ile-Ife. The Independent National Electoral Commission is created to oversee elections. **8 June:** Abacha dies and General Abdulsalami Abubakar replaces him as head of state. **7 July:** Abiola dies in prison. **20 July:** Abubakar facilitates Nigeria's transition to a democratic state and allows nine registered parties to promote candidates.

**1999   **The Universal Primary Education program is replaced by the Universal Basic Education program. Nigeria's membership in the Commonwealth Secretariat is reinstated. **May:** Obasanjo becomes Nigeria's democratically elected, civilian president, ushering in the Fourth Republic.

**2000   **Zamfara State is the first state to incorporate aspects of Shari'a into its criminal law. The vigilante Bakassi Boys emerge in Anambra State.

**2001**   A series of clashes between the Jukun and Tiv in Taraba State over land rights. **October:**   A massacre of an estimated 100 civilians is carried out by Nigerian soldiers in Benue State. Nigeria participates in the launching of New Partnership for African Development.

**2002**   Twelve states, predominantly in the North, implement Shari'a into their criminal law. The International Court of Justice rules in favor of Cameroon regarding the disputed Bakassi Peninsula. **February:** Violence between Yoruba and Hausa youths erupts in Lagos over religion. **March:** Safiya Husseini is acquitted of adultery, which saves her from the sentence of death by stoning. **October:** *Phantom Crescent*, a play by the Nigerian playwright Shehu Sani, is banned by a Shari'a court in Kaduna State. **November:** Miss World Pageant riots take place in Kaduna.

**2003**   **May:** Obasanjo wins a second term as president. **July:** A strike lasts nine days over the government's increase in fuel prices. **August:** ECOMOG sends a military force (dominated by Nigerian soldiers) to end Liberia's civil war. To facilitate this, Nigeria offers Liberia's President Charles Taylor asylum. **September:** With Russian assistance, Nigeria launches its first telecommunications satellite called Nigeria-Sat-1.

**2004**   A series of national strikes over the rising price of fuel takes place. Transparency International ranks Nigeria the second most corrupt country in the world. **February:** Amina Lawal is acquitted of adultery, which saves her from the sentence of death by stoning. **May:** A state of emergency is declared in Plateau State as a way to stop violence between Muslims and Christians.

**2005**   **July:** Nigeria receives debt relief of $18 billion by the Paris Club lenders. The much criticized National Electric Power Authority company is renamed the Power Holding Company of Nigeria.

**2006**   **January:** The emergence of the Movement for the Emancipation of the Niger Delta (MEND). The kidnapping of foreign oil workers in the Niger Delta becomes a frequent occurrence. **February:** Riots over caricatures of the Prophet Muhammad in a Danish newspaper erupt in northern Nigeria. **March:** The fourth population census is taken, placing Nigeria's population at 140 million. Nigeria agrees to hand Charles Taylor over to the Liberian government. **May:** Nigeria's Senate rejects Obasanjo's constitutional amendment that would allow him to stand for a third term as president. **August:** Nigeria releases the Bakassi Peninsula to Cameron, as called for by the International Court of Justice. **October:** Alhaji Muhammadu Maccido, the 19th sultan of Sokoto, dies in a plane crash. **November:** Alhaji Colonel Muhammed Sa'adu Abubakar III is installed as the 20th sultan of Sokoto.

**2007** A *hisbah* emerges in northern Nigeria. **April:** A round of general elections takes place, tainted by flagrant fraud and corruption. **May:** Alhaji Umaru Yar'Adua is sworn in as president, marking Nigeria's first successful transfer of power from one elected president to another. **September:** MEND threatens to end a cease-fire and return to its disruptive activities.

**2008** Transparency International ranks Nigeria as the 59th most corrupt country in the world. **June:** Nigeria's loss of oil production, caused by instability in the Niger Delta, reaches a record high of one-third.

# Introduction

In Nigeria, Christians declare "trust in Jesus" and Muslims say "if Allah wills it." Although the speakers of these ideas might clash over legal jurisdiction and political representation, they agree that success in their daily lives in Nigeria is uncertain and that outside intervention, spiritual or human, is long overdue. Their faith-based statements identify their feelings of lost hope in the government and their reliance on cultural and religious institutions to improve their lives. A look at Nigeria's culture, history, and economy helps to explain why these declarations are so commonplace.

Nigeria was under British colonial rule for nearly a century. British colonial rule not only defined Nigeria's present-day boundaries, but also incited ethnic and religious friction. Nigeria gained its independence in 1960 only to slide into a three-year civil war. Since 1970, Nigeria's political past has been comprised of alternating periods of democratic and military rule and its economic history has been shaped by petroleum exports, foreign debt, and mismanagement of government funds. Observers are quick to assign Nigeria's problems to its high population, geographic features, and ethnic and religious pluralism. Although these factors do pose challenges, they alone are not the cause of the degree of economic frailty and political instability. Nigeria has had a long history of religious tolerance, democracy, and fluid ethnic interaction. Many scholars attribute Nigeria's current situation to the universal issues of uneven development, financial mismanagement, and manipulation of religious and ethnic affiliations for the purpose of political gain. Despite these challenges, Nigeria shows great potential as a leading oil exporter, promoter of diversity and transnational cooperation, and supporter of entrepreneurship.

## LAND AND PEOPLE

### Geography

Nigeria is one of Africa's largest and most populated countries. Situated in West Africa, it covers 923,768 square kilometers and is roughly twice the size of California. Nigeria shares its northern border with Niger and Chad, western with Benin, and eastern with Cameroon. To the south is a coastal stretch on the Gulf of Guinea and the Bights of Benin and Biafra. The natural boundaries include the Lake Chad basin in the northeastern corner of Nigeria and Mandara mountains on the eastern boundary. The geographic coordinates of Nigeria are 3° to 15°E longitude and 4° to 14°N latitude. Nigeria stretches roughly 1,046 km from north to south and 1,126 km from east to west. The country holds the distinction of being called the "Giant of West Africa" because of its size, population, and political presence.

The Nigeria of today, however, is a relatively new creation, dating back to the early 20th century. Boundaries prior to that time included numerous chieftaincies and empires that expanded and contracted geographically without regard to modern Nigeria's boundaries. For the early peoples of Nigeria, only geographic boundaries, such as the Sahara Desert or Atlantic Ocean, might have kept them in place. Western European powers competing for territory and political control in Africa during the late-19th century determined Nigeria's boundaries to suit their needs. Much of Nigeria's western, eastern, and northern borders are the results of rivalry and compromise by European powers. As a result, ethnic groups and former kingdoms straddle boundaries. The Hausa, for example, live not only in Nigeria, but also Niger, Cameroon, and Chad. The Sokoto Caliphate, which was established by Fulani jihadists in the 19th century, was dismantled by the British and geographically divided between Nigeria and Niger. Modern-day Nigeria is a conglomeration of hundreds of ethnic groups, spanning across different geographical zones.

### Terrain

The climate and landscape of Nigeria changes as one travels south to north. Nigeria has diverse geographical zones, ranging from tropical wet to dry semiarid. Along the coast, Nigeria has both freshwater and mangrove swamps. The Niger Delta, particularly, is a 36,000-sq. km area of creeks and tributaries lined with dense vegetation. It is home to numerous species of fish, birds, and other animals. Otters, hippopotamus, manatee, and an estimated 150 kinds of fish live in the Niger Delta. The ecology of the delta is fragile and is being threatened by environmental destruction. Moving northward from the coast, Nigeria's landscape becomes a dense tropical forest and woodland. Here, tropical fruits, such as mangoes and bananas, and various palm trees grow easily. The rich soil of this region also allows for the cultivation of numerous vegetables. Moving toward the Middle Belt region of Nigeria, the terrain is primarily woodland and tall grass savanna. This landscape covers the majority of Nigeria. The Niger and Benue Rivers meander through this region, meeting at the Niger–Benue confluence at the town of Lokoja. The final geographical zone is situated in the North. Here is short grass savanna and marginal savanna. This region is part of the *sahel*, a grassy edge of the Sahara Desert that stretches across most West African countries.

In terms of Nigeria's climate, there are two major seasons: wet and dry. The wet season lasts from about May to October, particularly in the South. In the North, the wet season is much shorter, lasting from about July to September. In general, southern Nigeria has more cloud coverage and experiences more rain than northern Nigeria. During January and February, the *harmattan* brings high winds and dust from the Sahara southward. Nigeria's annual rainfall varies by zone. The coastal city of Lagos, for example, has about 28 mm of rain in January, while Kano in the North has almost none. People living along the coast endure an average daily temperature of 25°C with high humidity, while their northern counterparts experience 30°C daily with mild to low humidity.

## Peoples

To identify a single Nigerian culture is difficult. Nigeria is home to between 200 and 250 ethno-linguistic groups. Three main ethnics groups, however, make up the majority of the country's population. They are the Hausa, Yoruba, and Igbo. The Hausa live in northern Nigeria and make up about 21 percent. Cities with a significant Hausa population include Kano, Sokoto, and Kaduna. The Yoruba live in southwestern Nigeria and make up about 20 percent of the population. The cities with the largest concentration of Yoruba people are Ile-Ife, Lagos, and Ibadan. The Igbo live in southeastern Nigeria and make up about 17 percent of Nigeria's total population. This ethnic group is concentrated in Enugu and Owerri. Most of the major cities in Nigeria, however, have significant populations of all three ethnic groups. An estimated one-third of Nigerians belong to minority groups, which include the Tiv, Nupe, Igala, and Jukun in the Middle Belt and the Ijo, Itsekiri, Urhobo, and Ibibio in the Niger Delta. The minority groups have protested over the past several decades for greater political representation and a larger monetary share in federal revenue allocation schemes.

Although more than 200 languages are spoken in Nigeria, the official language is English. Most schools and businesses operate in English. Outside of these settings, however, most Nigerians prefer to speak an indigenous language or pidgin English. Nigeria's indigenous languages belong to the Bantu, Chadic, and Niger–Congo language families. The Niger–Congo languages include Edo, Igbo, Ijaw, Itsekiri, and Yoruba. Similarly, many languages spoken in Nigeria are dialects of another language. For example, Yoruba is the root language for the dialects of Igala and Itsekiri. The development of pidgin and mingling of different language families in Nigeria indicates the extent to which Nigerian communities and kingdoms interacted with their African neighbors and Europeans traders. Much of this blending also comes from a long history of urban centers and migration patterns.

## Religion

The religious practices in Nigeria overlap closely with ethnic or cultural affiliation. Most ethnic groups developed their own religion and cosmology over at least a century based on their environment and survival needs. Many of the religions, such as that of the Nupe, involved not only worship and ancestor veneration, but also contact with supernatural forces through divination. The Yoruba pantheon of deities in this culture's religion is well known within Nigeria and across the African Diaspora. Several modern towns and states in Nigeria in southwestern Nigeria are named after their gods. Since the mid-19th century, however, indigenous religions have been losing popularity. Many of the festivals and components of the religions, such as divination, masquerades, and traditional medicine, have been preserved as cultural practices. The majority of Nigerians are either Christian or Muslims, with an almost even split between the two in the number of adherents.

Islam first appeared between the 11th and 14th centuries, while Christianity arrived in the 19th century. Initially, Islam attracted only the elite desirous of power and trade. The emergence of the Sokoto Caliphate in the 19th century spurred the spread of Islam from royalty to the common people. The majority of Muslims in Nigeria are Sunni. The Zaria-based Islamic Movement of Nigeria, however, holds beliefs that seem closer to Shi'a doctrine than Sunni. Most Muslims live in the North and most Christians in the South; most Muslims are of Fulani, Hausa, and Kanuri descent and most Christians are of Yoruba and Igbo descent. This said, about one-third of Yoruba people are Muslim.

Christianity was first introduced by Portuguese traders in the mid-1500s, but failed to take root. In the mid-19th century, European interest in spreading Christianity and Western culture, reached Nigeria. The first missionaries were former slaves from Sierra Leone, who established missions in Abeokuta and Badagry. They were followed by British organizations, such as the (Anglican) Church Missionary Society, which set up stations in the 1840s. Nigerian converts quickly developed their own Christian churches, such as the Aladura churches in the 1930s, which blended indigenous cultural practices with Christian doctrine. The most popular forms of Christianity today are Charismatic and Pentecostal, with churches in nearly every major city across Nigeria.

In general, Christians and Muslims coexist peacefully. This is not to say that religion and politics are easily kept separate. Most protests and bursts of violence between the two groups are based on scarce resources and poor governance in the country as opposed to just religion. It is no coincidence that violent clashes between Christians and Muslims occurred in the early 1980s when Nigeria's economy took a turn for the worse. Disagreements developed in northern cities over the implementation of Shari'a (Islamic law) and the installment of Muslim leaders within the central government. To say that all Muslims in Nigeria shared the same beliefs and political views is misleading. For example, in December 1980, the Islamic fundamentalist followers of Muhammadu Marwa launched the Maitatsine Riots, terrorizing Muslims (and Christians) in Kano.

## HISTORY

### Early Nigerian History

The earliest evidence of civilizations in Nigeria dates back to the Iwo-Eleru rock shelter located near Akure in Ondo State. Inside this cave is a skeleton dated c. 9000 BCE in the Late Stone Age. Archeological evidence from the Iron Age is more abundant, particularly from the Nok. This civilization was comprised of agriculturalists skilled in iron smelting who lived between 500 BCE and 200 BCE. Miners in 1943 unearthed numerous clay pots and terracotta sculptures used by the Nok. Similarly, the Taruga flourished around 300 BCE. Several notable developments in the 11th century dramatically shaped the cultural landscape and political organization of Nigeria's early peoples.

Social groups in Nigeria did not live in isolation. Instead, they formed segmented political polities, kingdoms, and empires, particularly around 1000 CE. Even nomadic peoples, such as the Fulani, moved in clearly organized political structures. These early peoples established diplomatic and economic networks that stretched across long distances. For example, royalty from Borno in the northeastern corner of Nigeria sent 100 camels, 100 horses, and 100 articles of clothing to a king in Borgu situated in eastern Nigeria. The most studied kingdoms and empires that developed around the 11th century were the Hausa kingdoms and the Oyo Empire. According to oral tradition, the Hausa kingdoms developed from a marriage between Prince Bayajidda of Baghdad and a princess from Daura around the 10th century. One version of the story says their son, Bawo, and his sons established the first several Hausa kingdoms, which include Daura, Kano, and Katsina, to name a few.

The establishment of early political units, such as the Hausa Kingdoms, however, was not without negotiation or dispute. Land, for instance, was traded, purchased, and stolen. The founder of the town of Ilesha in southwestern Nigeria, according to oral tradition, purchased the site from a chief at Oyo for four slaves (male and female), two cows, one horse, 200 bundles of cowries, and 100 kola nuts. A kingdom at Kanem, however, was invaded and dismantled in 1389 by the nomadic Bulala people who desired the area for their own temporary settlement. The history of Nigeria between 1000 and 1800 included the rise and fall of kingdoms as well as the expansion of long distance and international trade.

A significant part of trade included the buying and selling of slaves. Nigeria played a major role in the transatlantic slave trade, with seven of West Africa's 13 major slave depots located in Nigeria. Roughly 51 percent of all African slaves traded across the Atlantic were from the Bights of Benin and Biafra. Abolishing the slave trade from the supply side (in Africa) became a major preoccupation for European humanitarians and, more specifically, missionaries. Much of the life established through peace and violence prior to the 19th century was dramatically altered, starting in the mid-19th century, by the arrival of Europeans.

## British Colonial Era: 1840s–1960

Initially, European interest was in trade and humanitarian projects. There was also a strong component of intellectual curiosity about the geography and people. In 1797, Mungo Park went to West Africa in hopes of navigating the Niger River. Another major expedition in the 1820s, led by Hugh Clapperton, included meeting Hausa royalty and trading on the Niger River. Following on the heels of those explorations were European missionaries who sought to convert the "natives" and traders who wanted to encourage legitimate commerce. The Wesleyan Methodist Missionary Society set up one of the first missions in 1842 at Badagry. Others, including the Southern Baptist Convention, followed suit.

By the 1850s, European governments became increasingly interested in not only engaging in trade in West Africa, but dominating it. This was coupled with an interest in securing territory, which was largely driven by competition among European powers. In the case of Nigeria, what territory the British did not claim and defend would be claimed by the French or the Germans. In 1861, the British deposed King Dosumu from Lagos, declaring it a colony. Eastward along the coast, the Royal Niger Company worked its way up the Niger River acquiring territory and controlling trade by force. In the North, the British focused on securing its control over the Sokoto Calipahte in 1903 to prevent it from going to the French. Resistance to colonial expansion was fierce. The northern and southern protectorates were merged to form one Nigeria in 1914. Over the remainder of the 20th century, Nigeria became a British colonial experiment amidst two world wars.

At the close of World War II, organized resistance to colonial rule escalated. Nigerians agitated for greater respect, participation in government, and independence. Anticolonial activists used a range of strategies to disrupt the system, including challenging legislation in court, protesting, and engaging in acts of violence. Two examples illustrate the intensity with which Nigerians responded to exploitation and oppression. In the 1940s, the Abeokuta Women's Union, led by Chief Olufunmilayo Ransome-Kuti, protested the taxation on women and the *alake*'s (chief) abuse of power. The union was successful in pressuring the colonial government to remove him from power. In 1945, 40,000 laborers launched a general strike that lasted more than one month. They campaigned for better pay and open government–labor relations and won.

By the late 1950s, it became clear to the British that colonial rule was becoming increasing difficult to maintain. Dialogue was established between Nigeria's anticolonial leaders and colonial officials. One of the first steps of the decolonization process included determining the date of independence and the form of government that would best suit an independent Nigeria. In 1957, the Eastern Region and Western Region gained self-government, followed by the Northern Region two years later. The general elections, which determined the structure and composition of Nigeria's First Republic, took place in December 1959. Nigeria became independent on 1 October 1960.

## Civil War: 1967–1970

From its start, the First Republic functioned on shaky ground. Tension among regions and within the central government muddled Nigeria's first stretch of independence. In January 1966, Nigeria's first military coup d'état took place. Major General Johnson Aguiyi-Ironsi's first order of business was to dismantle the regional structure. In response, the Northern Region refused to cooperate. In May, a pogrom against Igbos living in the North erupted. This massacre was followed by a mass exodus of Igbos to southeastern Nigeria. At the end of July, another coup d'état by northern soldiers took place. Some deliberations occurred before settling on General Yakubu Gowon as the new head of state. This arrangement did not please all regional leaders. Chief Chukwuemeka Ojukwu, in particular, refused to recognize Gowon's authority. As governor of the Eastern Region, Ojukwu felt a responsibility to the Igbo people to declare the region independent in May 1967.

A series of negotiations between Ojukwu and Gowon failed. To defend its independence, Ojukwu's Republic of Biafra prepared for war with the federal government. Civil war erupted in July 1967 and lasted until January 1970 between the two sides.

Nigeria's civil war was one of Africa's first. The degree of bloodshed and impact on civilians shocked the world. Scholars suggest that the duration of the war was tied to the amount of declared and undeclared assistance from such outside powers as France, Great Britain, the Soviet Union, and neighboring Francophone African countries. Ultimately, the war resulted in high casualties and starvation in Biafra. The International Red Cross responded to the crisis by attempting to supply food to starving people in Biafra. By early January 1970, Biafra had lost a significant amount of territory, including the city of Owerri, the Biafran nerve center. On 12 January 1970, Biafra surrendered. The civil war gravely damaged Nigeria's economy and reputation.

## Military Rule: 1966–1979

After the civil war, Gowon set Nigeria on a path of reconciliation and reconstruction. He promoted a vision of a united, progressive Nigeria under his leadership. A rapid transition to democratic rule, however, was not part of his plan. Nigeria entered into its second phase, which can be best described as one of intensive activism, particularly in African politics. Under Gowon, Nigeria changed its currency to the naira, engaged in large-scale indigenization and nationalization projects, and set up the Nigerian Youth Service Corps. Much of these plans were funded by Nigeria's wealth generated from high oil prices. In the early 1970s, Nigeria was awash with oil revenues.

Within the economic sector, Gowon also sought to rejuvenate Nigeria. In line with so many other military leaders in the world, he favored a nationalist vision of diversifying Nigeria's economy. He sought to replace the long-standing formula of British investment in Nigeria as a development strategy and attempted to find alternate methods and trading partners. In this spirit, Nigeria initiated the formation of the Economic Community of West African States (ECOWAS), which created a special economic relationship with its West African neighbors. Gowon saw relative success in his plans for Nigeria and remained in power until removed through a coup d'état in July 1975.

Nigeria's new regime, under the leadership of General Murtala Mohammed, lasted until his assassination in February 1976. Although Mohammed's rule was short, he set Nigeria on an extreme path of activism. He provided financial and military assistance to liberation movements, while engaging in a vigorous campaign to jumpstart Nigeria's economy. Mohammed's successor, General Olusegun Obasanjo, continued on the path set by Mohammed. Under his leadership, Nigeria implemented a nation-wide universal primary education program and hosted the World Black and African Festival of Arts and Culture (also known as FESTAC '77). Obasanjo differed from his predecessors in his commitment to transitioning Nigeria to democratic rule, which happened in October 1979.

## Second Republic: 1979–1983

The Second Republic started with the election of Alhaji Aliyu Usman Shagari as president. One key feature of this new government included the abandonment of the British-style parliamentary constitution for an American one. In December 1979, Shagari launched Operation Feed the Nation. As part of his Green Revolution program, Shagari encouraged Nigerians to focus on agricultural productivity in an effort to reduce the importation of basic foodstuffs. But, the wealth generated from crude oil sales in the early 1970s was poorly invested, leaving Nigeria vulnerable to the bust in oil prices. Virtually overnight, Nigeria's revenue from oil sales dropped and the country slid into a recession. All over Nigeria, people struggled to make a living, while its leaders squandered and hoarded money. In search of community support and answers to their problems, many Nigerians turned to their ethnic and religious communities. During the 1980s, violence between Christians and Muslims erupted in Nigeria's northern cities and ethnic groups clashed over scarce resources.

After a year or two, it became evident to the Nigerian public that the Second Republic was less than perfect. Shagari's government operated with corruption, ineptitude, and financial mismanagement. The National Party of Nigeria (NPN) dominated politics during the Second Republic. Shagari's regime was criticized for focusing on building patronage networks within the party. Members of the NPN channeled state and federal revenue to development projects in their own districts to bolster their political positions. In building the Federal Capital Territory, the federal government awarded contracts to its party supporters and members. After hitting financial rock bottom, Shagari's administration turned to the International Monetary Fund (IMF) for assistance and underwent Nigeria's first structural adjustment program. In December 1983, Nigeria's fourth coup d'état took place, deposing Shagari and installing Major General Muhammadu Buhari as the military head of state.

## Military Rule: 1983–1998

Nigeria's return to military rule marked a distinct move toward becoming a pariah state. The military regimes of the 1980s and 1990s pushed the meaning of authoritarian rule to a new level. Concepts of accountability and civil rights did not registered for leaders like General Ibrahim Babangida and General Sani Abacha. The goal of returning Nigeria to democratic rule was simply lip service. Nigeria's military rulers focused on economic reform and personal job security by any means necessary. They censored journalists and imprisoned political agitators. The economy continued to decline, depriving Nigerians of basic human needs. Nigerians struggled with high inflation and unemployment.

Under Buhari, Nigeria underwent corrective reforms designed to undo the problems created by the Second Republic. One of Buhari's signature programs was the War Against Indiscipline, which encouraged Nigerians to become personally invested in improving daily life. He asked people to stop throwing trash on the ground and start standing in organized queues while waiting for a bus. Buhari also promised to remove corrupt politicians and promote ethical ones. Like his predecessors, Buhari did not present a timetable for transferring power to an elected head of state. He also failed to improve Nigeria's failing economy and pacify a demanding military.

In August 1985, the military launched the fifth coup d'état and installed General Ibrahim Babangida. Facing a collapsing economy, Babangida returned to the IMF for financial assistance. He decided to adhere to the IMF's recommended structural adjustment program, but not to take the accompanying loan. Babangida's reconstruction plan included the Mass Mobilization for Self Reliance, Social Justice, and Economic Recovery program, privatization of public corporations, and creation of several new states. In October 1989, political parties received the green light to regroup and apply for official recognition to give the impression of a democracy. Babangida allowed the formation of only two political parties (the Social Democratic Party and the National Republican Convention). He maintained a strict hold on the press and stifled any public disapproval of his leadership. In fear of losing northern Muslim support, he made Nigeria a member of the Organization of the Islamic Conference, which incensed Christian southerners. Babangida's handling of the election of 12 June 1993 convinced the world of his disregard for accountability and reliability. He annulled the election and imprisoned Chief M. K. Abiola when preliminary results suggested that Abiola might win . Had the elections succeeded, Nigeria would have started its Third Republic. Under severe pressure, Babangida formed the Interim National Government to take power and guide Nigeria toward democratic rule.

Abacha, who was part of the Babangida regime, became impatient with the interim government and decided to take power through Nigeria's sixth coup d'état. Abacha's reign has been characterized as the worst in Nigeria's history because of his predatory style of governing. He ran an oppressive state, not tolerating dissension. To implement his development plan and show sensitivity to the poor, he launched Vision 2010. He focused on privatization and trade liberalization, while draining the state coffers for his personal use.

Nigeria's economy was in a terrible shape. Its education system barely operated and its external debt crossed $100 million. The austere structural adjustment programs eroded much of Nigeria's social welfare network, leaving many to rely on their communities. Across Nigeria, hometown associations (private, voluntary organizations rooted in Nigerian local communities) focused on promoting cultural and social support appeared. These ethnic-based associations are designed to maintain a sense of community, even when away from home, as well as provide financial and social support in ways that Nigeria, as a failed state, has not done.

Some of Nigeria's worst human rights violations occurred during Abacha's reign. Abacha became infamous around the world for conducting a biased trial and sentencing Ken Saro-Wiwa and other members of the Movement for the Survival of the Ogoni People to death by hanging in November 1995. After this flagrant abuse of human rights,

Abacha launched the National Human Rights Commission in a weak attempt to improve his and the country's reputation. In June 1998, Abacha died under mysterious circumstances; his death was welcomed by many Nigerians.

## Fourth Republic: 1999–

After a brief period of recovery and transition under the leadership of General Abdulsalami Abubakar, Nigeria was put on a new political and economic path. Nine political parties were formally allowed to run candidates for the presidential elections. In May 1999, Obasanjo became Nigeria's civilian president, marking the start of the Fourth Republic. He served two four-year terms and attempted to change the constitution to allow him to run for a third term, but failed. Obasanjo restored a moderate level of trust in government by the people of Nigeria. He focused on privatization and the reduction of Nigeria's external debt. He secured debt relief of $18 million by Paris Club lenders and paid off $4.6 billion. He revamped the Universal Primary Education program, changing its name to the Universal Basic Education. One of Obasanjo's greatest accomplishments was reintegrating Nigeria into the global diplomatic scene and trade system. He worked closely with the United Nations on projects ranging from malaria eradication to nuclear energy.

During his leadership, several complicated issues have tested the strength of the government's commitment to democracy and human rights. One major issue has been the resurgence of faith-based tension that first appeared in the 1980s between Christians and Muslims. In 2000, Zamfara State became the first northern state to incorporate Shari'a into its criminal law. Non-Muslim communities saw this as a major step toward Islamizing the country and restricting their religious freedom. Although Shari'a is only for Muslims, non-Muslims are concerned that this exception may disappear. Human rights groups have criticized Shari'a, and the informal *hisbah* group that enforces it, for applying inhumane and humiliating punishments that violate international standards of civil rights. Eleven other northern states have since followed Zamfara's lead. Another major issue that escalated during Obasanjo's presidency was the Niger Delta Conflict. A series of violent attacks on oil facilities and kidnapping of oil workers has turned the Niger Delta into a war zone. Who is committing such acts is unclear.

One group, Movement for the Emancipation of the Niger Delta, has claimed responsibility for some of the activities, particularly in 2007, as a way to pressure the oil companies to leave and the government to offer tangible benefits for living amidst the country's oil industry. On both issues, Obasanjo received criticism for responding with human rights violations. Thus far, no substantial action has been taken to address Shari'a in the North or the crisis in the Niger Delta.

In April 2007, Nigeria held its third round of democratic elections of the Fourth Republic. The inauguration of Umaru Musa Yar'Adua as president marked the first time Nigeria's government has successfully transitioned from one elected, civilian leader to another. Yar'Adua has expressed his commitment to continue economic reform and the country's fight against corruption. The second promise seemed a total farce considering the blatant rigging and manipulation of the presidential elections by the People's Democratic Party, to which both Yar'Adua and Obasanjo belong. The tradition of cronyism, so rampant during the Second Republic, has continued in the current one. In selecting his new cabinet, Yar'Adua appointed Obasanjo and three of Obasanjo's ministers. Despite this, Yar'Adua was recognized as one of Nigeria's only governors to publicly declare his assets and hold an advanced degree. Only a few months into his presidency, Yar'Adua has given a sobering message to Nigerians that the country is in dire financial straits. His approach and policies are generally regarded to be slow, earning him the comical but critical nickname of "Baba Go Slow." Nonetheless, after three rocky election cycles, Nigeria is still enjoying the relative tranquility of the Fourth Republic.

# Dictionary

## – A –

**ABA RIOT.** Also referred to as the Aba Women's War, this was an important protest by the **women** of Aba in southeastern Nigeria that took place in 1929. Aba is a town northeast of **Port Harcourt** and southeast of Owerri in the **Niger Delta**. Men had been taxed in the **Eastern Region** since 1926, but women had not. A rumor, which lated proved to be false, circulated that the **warrant chief**, Okugo of Oloko, was going to start taxing them. The women protested against **taxation** and other forms of exploitation, attacking Nigerian and European administrators and property. The **police** responded by shooting at the female protestors, killing 30 and wounding 30. After the riot, colonial officials set up two commissions of inquiry. They inaccurately concluded that the men of Aba had organized the women's protest, and that it was simply a protest by farmers over low prices. The protest made evident the necessity for democratizing local government operations.

**ABACHA, GENERAL SANI (1943–1998).** Born in September 1943 in **Kano**, as a young man Abacha studied at the City Senior Primary School and Provincial Secondary School in Kano (1957–1962). He started his military career in 1962. He attended the Nigerian Military Training College in **Kaduna** (1962–1963) and was promoted to the rank of major general in 1984 and to chief of army staff one year later. Abacha played key roles in the 1983 and 1985 military **coups d'état**. He was promoted to chief of defense staff as well as to chairman of the joint chiefs in 1990. In November 1994, Abacha overthrew the **Interim National Government** and declared himself president. His regime had a poor **human rights** record, stifling the press and any form of opposition. He maintained his power through violence and **corruption** until 1998.

During his stint as supreme military commander of Nigeria, Abacha attempted to settle Nigeria's turbulent political climate and improve his image. He sought short-term approval for his leadership by minimizing the **petroleum** price increase as requested by the **Nigerian Labour Congress**. Abacha set up a governing council that included an array of individuals from previous military governments to give the appearance of popular representation. He promoted French as a potential official **language**. But he lacked support both within and outside Nigeria. Under Abacha, Nigeria's economic situation steadily declined as the naira weakened and inflation rocketed. Foreign investment diminished, Nigeria's external **debts** went unpaid, and the money borrowed was poorly used. His government imprisoned several notable political figures, including **Chief M. K. O. Abiola** and **General Shehu Musa Yar'Adua**, and executed **Kenule Saro-Wiwa**. In 1996, he launched **Vision 2010**, which promised change to the despondent population. Critics complained that he spent more time maintaining power in destructive ways than improving the lives of his people. Abacha died under mysterious circumstances in June 1998 and was succeeded by **General Abdulsalami Abubakar**. *See also* ARMED FORCES; NATIONAL ELECTORAL COMMISSION OF NIGERIA.

**ABAYOMI, SIR KOFOWOROLA ADEKUNLE (1896–1979).** Born in July 1896 in **Lagos,** Abayomi was an eye doctor as well as a politician. He attended the Methodist Boys' High School, University of Edinburgh in Scotland, and Moorfield Eye Hospital in London. After completing his studies, he returned to Nigeria in 1930 and started a private practice. In 1934, he became involved in politics as an active member of the **Lagos Youth Movement**. In 1938, he became president of the **Nigerian Youth Movement** and was elected its representative to the **Legislative Council**. Two years later, Abayomi resigned from the Legislative Council and returned to Great Britain as a Rhodes Scholar in ophthalmology. Later, he served on the Yaba Higher College Advisory Board as well as the Board of Medical Examiners. Abayomi was also a member of the University College of Ibadan Council. In 1948, he became the president of Nigeria's Society for the Blind and chairman of the Federal Electoral Commission in 1964. His wife, **Lady Oyinka Morenike Abayomi**, was also politically active in the decades leading up to **independence**. He received the honorary title of Knight Commander of the Order of the British Empire. Abayomi died in January 1979.

**ABAYOMI, LADY OYINKA MORENIKE (1897–?).** Abayomi was the daughter of Sir Kitoye Ajasa II, the first Nigerian to be knighted by the British Empire. She attended the Girl's Seminary of the (Anglican) **Church Missionary Society** in **Lagos** and also the Ryeford Hall College in England. Abayomi was the *lika* (**chief**) of Ijemo, **Abeokuta**. She served as president of the Women's Party in 1946. She also created the Girl's Guides of Nigeria and led the Young Women's Christian Association of Nigeria. Abayomi is considered one of Nigeria's most important female grassroots activists because of her dedication to social work and the improvement of **women**. She received the honorary title of member of the Order of the British Empire and was a recipient of the Medal of Merit.

**ABDULLAHI MAJE KAROFI (?–1882).** Abdullahi was the fourth **emir** of **Kano**, ruling from 1855 to 1882. He was of **Fulani** descent and part of the **Sokoto Caliphate**. His sons also served as emirs in the late 19th and early 20th centuries. His reign saw a period of political expansion. Abdullahi used royal **slaves** to extend political control over Kano. The royal slaves increased their influence in government and gained new rights. They also began marrying free Fulani **women** during his reign.

**ABEOKUTA.** The city of Abeokuta is located north of **Lagos**. **Oral tradition** dates **Yoruba** settlement in Abeokuta to 1830. The **Egba**, a Yoruba subgroup, made Abeokuta their capital and thus home of the *alake* (**chief**). In the **Yoruba language**, Abeokuta means "beneath the rock." In the first half of the 19th century, the **Yoruba Wars** displaced thousands of people. Abeokuta and other cities saw an influx of refugees. As a result, Abeokuta has distinct towns, such as Ibara and Owu, within it, and various chieftaincy titles are used in Abeokuta. The town was one of the first locations for European **Christian** missions, such as the (Anglican) **Church Missionary Society**. Notable Nigerian Christians like **Bishop Samuel Ajayi**

**Crowther** were sent to Abeokuta to do missionary work. As a result, Abeokuta produced many Western-educated individuals. For example, **Olufunmilayo Ransome-Kuti**, born in 1900, led the Abeokuta Women's Union in a protest against a **corrupt** *alake* and the **taxation of women**. In 1914, the *alake* became the **paramount chief** of the Egba, to fit into the colonial administrative structure of **indirect rule**. Abeokuta is known for *adire* cloth, which is made by resist-dyeing using wax and indigo. Today, it is the capital of **Ogun State** and its **population** is approximately 700,000.

**ABIA STATE.** Located in southeastern Nigeria, Abia is one of Nigeria's current 36 states. The capital is Umuahia. It was carved out of **Imo State** in 1991. The name Abia is an acronym for the state's four most populated regions: Aba, Bende, Isuikwuato, and Afikpo. Abia State is home to Abia State University and Abia State Polytechnic. Its inhabitants are primarily of **Igbo** descent. Economic activity in the state includes **petroleum**, cashews, tubers, and **bananas**. **Christianity** is the dominant religion of the state. *See also* STATE CREATION.

*ABIKU.* A **Yoruba** term meaning "children of the spirit world" or "ancestral soul being reborn." It refers to the belief that *abiku* children are those who died in one life and continually return in succeeding ones. In a study conducted in **Ondo State** and **Ekiti State**, over 50 percent of women interviewed believed in *abiku*. The existence of *abiku* is addressed in both **Akinwande Oluwole Soyinka**'s *Ake* (1983) and **Chinua Achebe**'s *Things Fall Apart* (1958). **John Pepper Clark** published a poem in 1962 that encourages *abiku* to "step in, step in and stay." *Abiku* does not desire to stay on earth, but to live out its life in heaven with the freedom to travel as it pleases between heaven and earth. Yoruba mothers of an *abiku* may join Egbe Ogba, which is a cult designed to conciliate the spirit through a ceremony. These members fashion iron rattles for the children to wear around their ankles. Upon the death of the child, a mother may shave a spot on its head or cut a notch in its ear as a future identifier should the child return.

**ABIODUN (?–1789).** The *alaafin* (**king**) of the **Yoruba Oyo Empire** between 1770 and 1789. He was the first *alaafin* to rule after defeating Dahomey (in present-day **Benin**). Under his leadership, Oyo grappled with being a fragile but peaceful state. He deposed Gaha, the *basorun* (head of the council of notables). In 1783, Oyo was attacked by **Borgu** warriors, which started a period of decline in Oyo. Abiodun is portrayed as an autocratic leader in **Femi Osofisan**'s play *The Chattering and the Song* (1977).

**ABIOLA, CHIEF MOSHOOD KASHIMAWO OLAWALE (1937–1998).** Born in August 1937 in **Abeokuta**, Abiola attended the University of Glasgow to study accounting. After completing his degree in 1965, he worked for the Lagos University Teaching Hospital, Pfizer Pharmaceuticals, and International Telephone and Telegraph, where he became vice president of its Africa/Middle East operations. His company secured telecommunications contracts with military regimes during the 1970s. He also served as chairman and chief executive for the company in Nigeria. Abiola was a member of the **National Party of Nigeria** from 1978 until he resigned in 1982, after the party prevented him from taking part in the primary **elections** for the presidency. He received more than a hundred honorary chieftaincy titles, including *basorun* of **Ibadan**. He was a major financial supporter of national sports and a crusader for reparations from the colonial government. In the 1990s, at the age of 56, he returned to national politics as the presidential candidate of the **Social Democratic Party**. He took part in the controversial **election of 12 June 1993**, which **General Ibrahim Babangida** annulled when it appeared that Abiola had won.

Abiola was a popular choice for many Nigerians, particularly among the **Yoruba**, because of his philanthropy. **Baba Gana Kingibe** was his running mate. In addition to annulling the election results, Babangida imprisoned Abiola, who died in detention in July 1998. His wife, Kudirat Olayinka Abiola, was killed on 4 June 1996 while actively campaigning for the release of her husband and the reinstatement of the 1993 election results. She had earned the affectionate title of the "Mother of the June 12 Struggle" in the media.

**ABORTION.** Nigeria does not have a law explicitly declaring abortion illegal in all circumstances. The Criminal and Penal Codes of Nigeria, however, call for the punishment of any **woman** who acts "with the intent to procure a miscarriage." The law does allow for abortion if necessary to save the mother's life. Nigeria's criminal code, however, only applies to those southern states that have not implemented aspects of **Shari'a**. Under Islamic law, abortions are punishable by death. Many women desiring an abortion consult "backstreet abortionists." The majority of abortions performed in Nigeria are conducted under unsafe and unsanitary conditions.

People calling for legalized abortion in Nigeria make the argument that due to delivery complications, 704 out of 100,000 live births result in the death of the mother. If abortion were legalized, they argue, the number of deaths would drop. In 1981, the Nigerian Society of Gynecology and Obstetrics sponsored a bill to legalize abortion, but it was rejected. A similar bill was proposed and rejected in 2004. An estimated 610,000 abortions are performed in Nigeria annually, 60 percent of which are conducted by nonphysicians. In Nigeria's conservative culture, open discussions about sex, contraception, and abortion are avoided. Women often feel they have few resources to protect themselves from unwanted sexual advances, disease, and children.

**ABOYADE, OJETUNJI (?–1994).** Aboyade became a major political figure while serving as chairman of the Department of Economics at the **University of Ibadan**. He served as the vice chancellor of the University of Ife (present-day **Obafemi Awolowo University**). In 1977, he headed the Aboyade Technical Committee on Revenue Allocation (also referred to as the Aboyade Commission), which was charged with reviewing Nigeria's **revenue allocation** scheme. The committee's recommendations were rejected in 1979. Aboyade was also the head of an ad hoc Presidential Advisory Committee, which was created in October 1985 to improve the federal bureaucracy, and a member of the Commission on Economic Reform. He published several works on **industrialization** in Nigeria. He died in December 1994. A collection of essays, *Footprints of the Ancestor: The Secret of Being Ojetunji Aboyade* (1999), was published in his honor.

**ABTI AMERICAN UNIVERSITY OF NIGERIA.** Founded and owned by **Atiku Abubakar**, a wealthy businessman and former vice president of Nigeria, the school received funding and advice from American University in Washington, D.C. It opened in 2005 as a private institution, providing high-quality **education**. The university offers courses primarily in the natural sciences and mathematics. It is located in Abubakar's home state of **Adamawa**, in the town of **Yola**. *See also* HIGHER EDUCATION.

**ABUBAKAR, GENERAL ALHAJI ABDULSALAMI (1942– ).** Born in Minna, in **northern Nigeria**, Abubakar joined the air force in 1963 and transferred to the army after three years. He was promoted to the rank of major general in 1991. In 1993, he became the chief of defense staff. Abubakar was the eighth military leader of Nigeria, serving from June 1998 to May 1999. He took over from **General Sani Abacha**, who died in June 1998. Abubakar's first speech lauded the leadership of Abacha, which worried those who desired change. Under his leadership, Nigeria became the 13th poorest country in the world, despite being one of the world's largest **petroleum** producers. Abubakar has the distinction of overseeing a successful transition of power from military to civilian rule in May 1999. In April 2007, Abubakar tried to run as a civilian for president, but failed. *See also* ARMED FORCES; INDEPENDENT NATIONAL ELECTORAL COMMISSION.

**ABUBAKAR, ATIKU (1946– ).** Born in November 1946, Abubakar is a **Fulani** Muslim from **Adamawa State**. He has four wives and numerous children. He was a founding member of the **People's Democratic Party (PDP)**. He worked as a customs officer at the Murtala Mohammed Airport in **Lagos** for 20 years before serving as vice president to **General Olusegun Obasanjo** (1999–2007). Abubakar is a multibillionaire with business interests in **petroleum**, media, publishing, and **education**. In 2007, Obasanjo accused him of diverting $125 million from the country's Petroleum Development Trust Fund into his personal business. In the months leading up to the April 2007 **election**, Abubakar split with the PDP and launched his own **political party**, the **Action Congress**, placing himself as a presidential candidate. However, the embezzlement charges, which the Supreme Court later dropped, prevented him from receiving the **Independent Electoral Commission**'s approval to run until the last minute. Complications with the printing of ballots days before the election resulted in the omission of his name. Abubakar owns **ABTI American University of Nigeria**. *See also* CORRUPTION.

**ABUBAKAR III, SULTAN SIDDIQ (1903–1988).** Born in **Sokoto** in March 1903, Abubakar was the 17th **sultan** of Sokoto, from 1938 until his death in 1988. When he died, the princes of Sokoto engaged in a bitter contest over the position of sultan. He is remembered as being an austere but honest sultan. *See also* MACCIDO, SULTAN ALHAJI MUHAMMADU.

**ABUJA.** On 12 December 1991, Abuja replaced **Lagos** as Nigeria's capital. It is located in the **Federal Capital Territory**, which was deliberately created in the middle of the country to emphasize the central government's commitment to ending regional favoritism. The location was also chosen in 1976 for its mild climate and low **population** density, which would allow for territorial expansion in the future. Abuja is Nigeria's first planned city and is ranked among Africa's fastest growing cities. Although initially planned for a population of 258,000 people, it has continued growing and presently has a population of about 740,000. Abuja is located just north of the **Benue River** and **Niger River** confluence and occupies 8,000 square kilometers. It is divided into the government district, or Three Arms Zone (**National Assembly**, Presidential Complex, and Supreme Court), and the commercial district, where its citizens can live, shop, and relax. Many of the nation's government offices and international embassies, however, are still located in **Lagos**.

The Nigerian government has made the new capital's appearance and accessibility its top priority. Although the rest of the country suffers from a lack of reliable running **water** and **electricity**, Abuja does not. Within Abuja is the natural landmark Aso Rock, which is a 396-meter high, rounded rock that sits at the north end of the city. Aso Rock has become a colloquial reference when referring to the federal government or president, similar to Capitol Hill in the United States. Aside from serving as the home of Nigeria's national government, Abuja has other notable features. During the mid-20th century, the **Ladi Kwali** Pottery Centre was the premier location for Nigerian ceramicists to teach, create, and display their **art** work. *See also* AIRLINES.

**ABURI CONFERENCE.** After **General Yakubu Gowon** became Nigeria's new head of state in July 1966, ethnic-based tension threatened to pull the federation apart. He called a meeting at a town about 48 kilometers outside **Ghana**'s capital, Accra, to diffuse tension between his federal military government and **Chief Chukwuemeka Ojukwu**'s secessionist group in the **Eastern Region**. The conference was held on 4–5 January 1967; it was tense and those involved displayed little ideological overlap. The conclusions of the conference included an agreement not to use force to resolve the conflict, a reorganization of the **armed forces** to grant the military governors more power, the repeal of any decrees that centralized government, and assistance to **Igbo** refugees who fled from the North. But Ojukwu was extremely dissatisfied with the conference, and ultimately it only fueled the tensions that resulted in **civil war**. The conference marked the transition point from tension to war.

**ACHEBE, CHINUA (1930– ).** Born in Ogidi, in **Anambra State**, Achebe was baptized **Albert** Chinualumogu. He is one of Nigeria's most renowned English-language novelists. He received his bachelor's degree in **literature** from the University College (present-day **University of Ibadan**). Achebe worked for the Nigerian Broadcasting Corporation (1954–1967). In 1967, he joined the faculty of the University of Nigeria at **Nsukka** as a literature professor. During the **civil war**, Achebe worked for the **Republic of Biafra**. In 1967, he cofounded a publishing company with **Christopher Okigbo**, who died during the civil war. Many of Achebe's works touch on Nigerian political issues. His famous works include *Things Fall Apart* (1958), *Anthills of the Savannah* (1987), and *No Longer at Ease* (1960). After the war, he worked as the director of African Studies at the University of Nigeria at **Enugu**. During the 1970s, he taught at several different universities in the United States. He spent the next 20 years living in both the United States and Nigeria, holding various positions such as director of Heinemann (Nigeria). Achebe was a member of the **People's Redemption Party**. In 1990, he was paralyzed from the waist down by a serious car accident in Nigeria. Achebe has received numerous awards, including the Margaret Wong Prize, the New Statesman "Jock" Campbell Prize, and the Commonwealth Poetry Prize (1972). He has also received several honorary doctorates from international universities. *See also* HIGHER EDUCATION.

**ACHUZIE, COLONEL JOE "HANNIBAL"** (1935– ). Born in 1935 in the **Niger Delta**, Achuzie was never a member of the **armed forces**. He lived for some time in England, where he met his British wife, Ethel. In Nigeria, he ran an electricity business in **Port Harcourt**. During the **civil war**, Achuzie served as a key field commander for the **Republic of Biafra**. He led Biafran forces toward **Onitsha** and recaptured Owerri. After the war, Achuzie was imprisoned. During his incarceration, he wrote his memoir, *Requiem Biafra* (1986), which described his role in the war and his views on the fate of the federal structure in Nigeria. He has been involved with the **Igbo** cultural organization **Ohaneze Ndigbo** since 1990. Achuzie has been criticized by hard-line nationalists for abandoning the Igbo presidential vision and supporting former president **General Oluse-gun Obasanjo**.

**ACTION CONGRESS (AC).** A **political party** created by **Atiku Abubakar** in 2006 to rival the **People's Democratic Party** in the April 2007 **election**. It resulted from the merging of several political parties, including **Alliance for Democracy**, created to run Abubakar as its presidential candidate.

**ACTION GROUP (AG).** A **political party** formed by **Chief Oba-femi Awolowo** in March 1950. The name was supposed to convey the idea that this party was about action, not words. It emerged out of a **Yoruba** cultural organization, **Egbe Omo Oduduwa**. It was led by Awolowo, who drew heavily on Yoruba cultural symbols to promote the party. The AG's members were largely drawn from Yoruba professionals and intelligentsia, many representing local organizations, such as Ilorin Parapo of the **Northern Region**. The party dominated the political scene in the **Western Region**. It promoted the idea of "democratic socialism." Opposition to the AG in southwestern Nigeria came largely from the **National Council of Nigeria and the Cameroons** (NCNC), which attracted support in **Ibadan** and Oyo. In 1952, the AG was elected into the regional government, which placed Awolowo as the region's **premier**. In 1962, the AG's solidarity was threatened by the **Action Group Crisis**, which resulted in the fracturing of the party and some members joining the NCNC. The AG, like all other political parties, was banned in 1966.

**ACTION GROUP CRISIS.** In 1962, the **Action Group** was divided and losing power. **Chief Obafemi Awolowo**, the founder of the **political party** and former **premier** of the **Western Region**, did not like the premier, **Chief Samuel Akintola**. A crisis developed, resulting in the national government declaring a state of emergency in the region. In May 1962, Chief Samuel Akintola was removed from his post as premier of the Western Region. In Akintola's absence, **Alhaji Dauda Adegbenro** held the position. There was a great deal of debate about Akintola's removal. Members of other **political parties** weighed in on the conflict. For example, **Michael Okpara** of the **National Council of Nigeria and the Cameroons** supported Akintola. Exacerbating the crisis, **Chief Obafemi Awolowo** was accused of treason and imprisoned in 1963. The crisis spread beyond the Western Region, disrupting the 1962 and 1963 censuses and weakening North–East unity. In January 1963, Akintola was returned to his premiership through the support of the federal government. He eventually broke from the Action Group and formed a new **Nigerian National Democratic Party**, in honor of **Sir Herbert Macaulay**'s party of the same name, active in the 1930s. Akintola aligned his party with the **Northern People's Congress** to form the **Nigerian National Alliance**. The crisis marked the start of the **First Republic**'s steady decline and the beginning of a series of military **coups d'état**. The first order for the coup d'état was to end the use of the federal army to suppress political opposition in the Western Region. *See also* MAJEKODUNMI, CHIEF MOSES ADEKOYEJO.

**ADAMA, MORDIBO (?–1848).** Born in the Verre Hills, Adama received an Islamic education from Mallam Kiari. He became an Islamic teacher, earning the Fulani title *mordibo* (an educated individual exhibiting piety). When he heard of the **jihad** being led by **Usman dan Fodio**, he traveled with a friend to **Sokoto** to offer his services. During the **Fulani** jihad that established the **Sokoto Caliphate**, Adama was one of the flag bearers who assisted in the conquest and territorial expansion across present-day northeastern Nigeria. In 1806, he received a flag and a small army to establish Adamawa and Gurin, where he resided for over 20 years. In 1809, he continued the jihad as far as Gongola, where he met **Buba Yero**. Together, Yero and Adama continued the conquest. In 1831, Adama moved the capital of his territory from Gurin to Ribardo, in 1839 to Jobalio, and in 1841 to **Yola**, where Adama died in 1848. It is believed that he never stopped fighting from the start of his jihad until his death. From each place he settled he received tribute in **slaves** and horses, which he in turn used to pay tribute to the caliph of Sokoto. *See also* ADAMAWA STATE; GONGOLA STATE.

**ADAMAWA STATE.** Situated in northeastern Nigeria on the border with **Cameroon**, its capital is **Yola**. Adamawa State was formed in 1991 out of **Gongola State**. It is one of Nigeria's current 36 states. The state is named after **Mordibo Adama**, the 19th-century jihadist. The **population** is primarily **Hausa** and **Fulani**, who are Muslim. Economic activity in the state centers on **kolanut**, maize, and rice production. Adamawa State is the home of **ABTI American University** and Sukur Cultural Landscape, which became a UNESCO World Heritage site in 1995. Sukur comprises a chief's palace, terraced fields, remnants of sacred spaces, and a once-flourishing iron smelting industry. *See also* STATE CREATION.

**ADE, SUNNY (1946– ).** Born in Osogbo, Ade was the son of a Methodist **Christian** minister. At a young age, Ade joined a touring **Highlife music** band and played the guitar. His greatest inspirations were I. K. Dairo and Tunde Nightingale. In 1966, Ade formed his own band, the Green Spots, with whom he recorded 12 albums. He was given the affectionate title "King" because by 1967 he dominated the **Juju music** style. In 1974, he started recording albums under his own label and changed the name of his band to the African Beats, which had over 16 members. He is known internationally for his brand of mellow Juju music that incorporated **Yoruba** and Western styles, which he dubbed "Synchro Systems." His music had broad appeal, while still attracting Yoruba listeners through his use of Yoruba idioms. His songs are primarily in Yoruba and English. In the late 1990s, he began working solo with an American producer. His 1998 album *Odu*, a compilation of Yoruba folk songs, won a Grammy Award. He runs a nonprofit, the King Sunny Ade Foundation. His latest album is *Glory of God* (2007).

**ADEBAYO, MAJOR GENERAL ROBERT ADEYINKA (1928– ).** Born in **Ile-Ife**, in **Oyo State**, Adebayo attended the Eko Boys'

School in **Lagos** as a young man and later the University of London (1966). He joined the army in 1948 and attended various military schools. He served in Central Africa as part of a United Nations peacekeeping force and was the chief of staff of the army (1964–1965). Adebayo served as military governor of the **Western Region** from August 1966 to July 1967. During the **civil war**, he served on the federal side. He was responsible for reviewing each soldier who fought for the **Republic of Biafra** and determining whether he could rejoin the federal **armed forces**. In 1971, Adebayo ran the Nigeria Defence Academy in **Kaduna**. In 1975, he was forced to retire from the military. Three years later, Adebayo became a member of the **National Party of Nigeria** and served as its deputy chairman.

**ADEBO, SIMEON OLAOSEBIKAN (1913–1994).** Born in **Abeokuta**, Adebo attended grammar school in Abeokuta and **King's College** in **Lagos**. He received a law degree in London and was a barrister-at-law in England. In Nigeria, he worked as a clerk for the Nigerian Railway from 1933 to 1942. In 1948, he worked as a senior civil servant for the colonial government. He was promoted to the position of head of the **civil service** and chief secretary of the **Western Region** (1961). Adebo served as a permanent representative to the United Nations. Six years later, he became the undersecretary-general of the United Nations and executive director of the United Nations Institute for Training and Research. Adebo is most known for heading the Adebo Salary Review Commission, which reviewed the salaries of civil service workers. In 1979, he worked in the National Institute of Policy and Strategic Studies in addition to several other appointments. Adebo died in October 1994.

**ADEBOLA, ALHAJI HAROUN POPOOLA (1916– ).** Born in October 1916 in Ijebu-Ode, in **Ogun State**, Adebola attended primary and secondary school in **Abeokuta** and Ijebu-Ode. He worked for the Nigerian Railway from 1941 until 1949. He was a member of the Ijebu Constitution Review Committee in 1949. Between 1946 and 1952 he acted as the secretary-general of the Nigeria Union of Railway Staff. Between 1951 and 1954 he was a member of the **Western House of Assembly**. Adebola served as president of the **United Labour Congress** from 1962 to 1969. He served as a member in the **Western House of Chiefs** from 1963 to 1965. Adebola was vice president of the International Confederation of Free Trade Unions from 1965 to 1970. Adebola was a part of the **constitution** committee in 1977. At the height of his political participation, he acquired the nickname "Horse Power." *See also* TRADE UNIONS.

**ADEDEJI, ADEBAYO (1930– ).** Adedeji was born in Ijebu-Ode and received his primary and secondary schooling in Ijebu-Ode and **Ibadan**. He earned several advanced degrees, including a Ph.D., from the University of London and Harvard University. Adedeji has also received numerous honorary degrees from institutions such as the University of Zambia and Dalhousie University in Canada. He was a full professor at **Obafemi Awolowo University** and director of the Institute of Administration at the university (1966 and 1971). Between 1971 and 1975, Adedeji was the federal commissioner for economic development and reconstruction for **General Yakubu Gowon**'s regime. He assisted in the creation of the **National Youth Services Corps** in 1973. In the United Nations, Adedeji served as undersecretary-general from 1978 to 1991. He also contributed to the African Alternative Framework to Structural Adjustment Programmes plan in 1989 and the African Charter for Popular Participation, drafted in 1990. He currently heads the African Centre for Development and Strategic Studies in Ijebu-Ode. He is the author of several books on development and democracy in Africa.

**ADEDOYIN, PRINCE ADELEKE (1912– ).** Born in March 1912 in **Lagos**, Adedoyin was the son of the *akarigbo* (**chief**) of Ijebu-Remo. As a young man, he studied at Methodist schools. He received a law degree and was called to the bar in 1940. He worked as court magistrate in Lagos and Ikot-Ekpene and served as commissioner of the Supreme Court. Adedoyin entered Lagos politics in 1947 as a member of the **Lagos Town Council** and **Legislative Council**. He was a member, and briefly secretary, of the **National Council of Nigeria and the Cameroons**. In 1951, he was a member of the **Western House of Assembly**, and in 1952 of the Western House of Representatives. Also in 1952, Adedoyin replaced his father briefly as the *akarigbo*, but was removed by the people of Ijebu-Remo. In 1956, he switched his affiliation to the **Action Group**. With the support of that **political party**, he served as speaker of the Western House of Assembly. During the **Action Group Crisis** of 1962, he supported **Chief Samuel Akintola** and joined the **Nigerian National Democratic Party**. Two years later, he became a member of the **Federal House of Representatives**. In 1978, he was an active member of the **National Party of Nigeria**.

**ADEGBENRO, ALHAJI DAUDA SOROYE (1909–1975).** Born in **Abeokuta**, in **Ogun State**, as a young man Adegbenro attended Baptist Day School and Baptist Boys' High School there. He worked as a **civil servant** for the Nigerian Railway and as a storekeeper for the **United African Company**. He was a member of the Egba Central Council and **Western House of Assembly** during the 1950s. He then served as minister of lands and labor for the **Western Region** and as **premier** of the region briefly, from May to December 1962, during the **Action Group Crisis**. Adegbenro was a member of the House of Representative (1951–1954). He served as minister of justice and local government from 1954 and 1956 and as the commissioner of the Ministry of Trade and Industry from 1967 to 1971. He then withdrew from politics and died in 1975 in Abeokuta.

**ADEKUNLE, BRIGADIER GENERAL BENJAMIN MAJA ADESANYA (1936– ).** Born in **Kaduna**, **Adekunle** completed his primary and secondary schooling in Nigeria and then went to **Great Britain** to attend the Sandhurst military academy. He joined the British army in 1958 and was sent to Central Africa two years later. In 1962, he was appointed camp assistant to **Sir Akanu Ibiam**, governor of the **Western Region**. One year later, he was again sent by the army to Central Africa. After completing his tour of duty, Adekunle went to India to attend the Defence Services Staff College. During the **civil war**, he led two federal battalions into battle against the secessionist **Republic of Biafra**, including a major attack on **Bonny**. Many attribute the federal government's victory over Biafra to him. His successes during the war earned him the rank of colonel and brigadier general. Adekunle also earned a reputation as a ruthless "bloodhound of Nigeria" and "black scorpion" for the killing of thousands of **Igbos** during the war. He retired from the **armed forces** in 1974. In 1978, he joined the **Nigerian People's Party**. His son,

Abiodun Adekunle, wrote about his father's participation in the civil war and compiled his father's letters in *The Nigeria Biafra War Letters: A Soldier's Story* (2003).

**ADELABU, ALHAJI ADEGOKE ODUOLA AKANDE (1915–1958).** Born in September 1915 in **Ibadan**, Adelabu attended Church Missionary Society schools (1925–1931) and **Yaba Higher College** (1932–1937). He then worked as an inspector and manager for the **United African Company** (1937–1946). In 1953, Adelabu founded the **Mabolaje Grand Alliance political party** in Ibadan. He was the first vice president of the **National Council of Nigeria and the Cameroons** in 1955. He served as an elected member of the **Western House of Assembly** in 1956 as an opposition leader. He was a member of the Egbe Omo Ibile, a cultural organization based in Ibadan. Adelabu also served as the chairman of the Ibadan District Council in the mid-1950s. He died in March 1958 in a car accident. His supporters suspected foul play. An author known for writing **Onitsha Market Literature** wrote a drama about Adelabu's last years.

**ADELE II, SIR ADENIJI (1893–1964).** A **Yoruba** born in November 1893, Adele II was the grandson of Adele I, the *oba* (**chief**) of **Lagos** (ca. 1775–ca. 1837). During his youth, Adele II attended Holy Trinity School in Ebute Ero and the Church Missionary Society Grammar School in Lagos. He then worked as a surveyor for the colonial government between 1913 and 1914. For a brief time, Adele II served as president of the **Lagos Town Council**. He saw active military service during **World War I**. Between 1916 and 1937, Adele II worked as an assistant clerk to the colonial treasury office. He then worked as secretariat (1937–1939) and acting assistant secretary in the Inland Revenue Department (1939–1940). He was also an accountant and treasurer for the colonial government in Lagos and Kano. In 1949, Adele II was installed as the *oba*. In 1952, he was a member of the **Western House of Chiefs**. He was awarded the honorary titles Commander of the Order of the British Empire (1956) and Knight of the Order of the British Empire (1962).

**ADEMOLA, SIR ADETOKUNBO ADEGBOYEGA (1906–1993).** Born in **Abeokuta**, Ademola was the son of **Chief Sir Ladipo**

Ademola II. He contributed to the political transformation of Nigeria from colony to country through his involvement in the judicial system. As a child, he studied as St. Georgory's Grammar School and **King's College** in **Lagos**. Between 1928 and 1931 he studied at Cambridge University for his bachelor's degree. In 1934, he was called to the bar in London. He returned to Nigeria one year later and worked in the colonial attorney-general's office. Ademola also worked as the assistant secretary of the colonial secretariat in **Enugu** (1935–1936). In 1939, he was appointed to the post of magistrate in the colonial protectorate **court**. Ten years later, he became the first Nigerian to serve as a judge. He worked as chief justice for the **Western Region** (1953) and then for the entire country (1955). In 1957, he received the honorary title Knight Commander of the British Empire, and in 1963 became one of Queen Elizabeth's II privy councilors. In September 1966, Ademola joined several other prominent politicians to bring **General Yakubu Gowon** and **Chief Chukwuemeka Ojukwu** together in a dialogue. During his career, he served on the United Nations Public Service Advisory Board and the International Commission of Jurists. He also acted as president of the Nigerian Red Cross International and the Reformed Ogboni Fraternity. He was a founder of several social clubs, including the Yoruba Club, Metropolitan Club, and Island Club.

**ADEMOLA II, CHIEF SIR LADIPO SAMUEL (1872–1962).** Born in September 1872 in the *alake's* (**chief**) palace in **Abeokuta**, Ademola II completed secondary school at St. Paul's School in **Lagos**. He was the *alake* of the **Egba** people from 1920 until 1962. Ademola II faced a great deal of opposition, particularly from female cloth dyers and traders of the Abeokuta Women's Union. The colonial government did not initially trust him because he had been previously accused of **corruption**. He ran the **Native Authority** and the Egba Native Council between 1920 and 1962. The Abeokuta Women's Union, led by **Chief Olufunmilayo Ransome-Kuti**, vehemently protested the *alake*'s tax collection methods and mismanagement of funds. For this, he was temporarily stripped of his title and sent into exile from 1948 to 1949. He received the honorary title Commander of the Order of the British Empire (1934) and attended the coronation of King George IV in England.

**ADEREMI, SIR CHIEF ADESOJI TADENIAWO (1889–1980).**
Born in November 1889 in **Ile-Ife**, Aderemi attended the Church
Missionary School there. After completing his studies, he worked as
a **civil servant** for the Railway Department from 1909 to 1921. He
then worked as a produce merchant from 1921 to 1930. In August
1930, he became the *ooni* (**chief**) of Ile-Ife. In 1932, he established
Oduduwa College. In 1937, he received the King's Medal for African
Chiefs. He was a member of the **Legislative Council** (1946) and the
**marketing board** for **cocoa** trading (1947). He also worked as the
director of the Nigeria Produce Marketing Board in 1947. His political activities increased in the early 1950s when he served as president
of the **Western House of Chiefs** in 1954 and as the first Nigerian
governor of the **Western Region** from July 1960 to December 1962.
He collected an array of honors, including the honorary titles of
Knight Commander of the Order of the British Empire and Companion of St. Michael and St. George. He died in July 1980.

**ADETILOYE, ARCHBISHOP JOSEPH ABIODUN (1929– ).** Born
in December 1929 in Odo-Owa, in **Ondo State**, as a young man, Adetiloye studied in Ijebu-Ekiti. In England, he studied **Christianity** between
1954 and 1961. He was ordained as an Anglican priest and deacon in
1954. Adetiloye established the Church of Nigeria and developed internal provinces of the church within Nigeria to cover the three geographical areas. These steps contributed to the Church of Nigeria expanding
rapidly across Nigeria. In 1970, he became the bishop of Ekiti. He was
ordained as the sixth primate of the Nigerian Anglican Communion at
the Cathedral Church of **Lagos**. In 1988, he became archbishop. Adetiloye created 10 missionary dioceses in 1990. He retired in 1999.

**ADUBI WAR.** Often called the Egba Uprising, this revolt occurred in
June 1918 in **Abeokuta**. The **Egba** people, from outside of Abeokuta,
were involved in the struggle against the British over the termination of
Egba independence in 1914. The uprising was also in response to the
introduction of colonial **taxation** and **indirect rule** in 1918. The "war"
concluded with the death of a British official and an Egba **chief**.

**ADVANCED FEE FRAUD.** Scams run via e-mail that started in
the late 1990s and are considered **criminal** activities. They are also

referred to as "419 scams" after Nigeria's legal code that prohibits fraud. Victims are attracted to these e-mails because they offer large cash returns. Common features include specific references to events, individuals, or organizations that have been mentioned in international **newspapers**. The solicitor typically asks the recipient to pay an "advance fee," or "transfer tax," or to pay for specialists to "clean" money. Many of the e-mails, particularly in the early years of the scams, were written in all capital letters and included numerous typographical errors. These e-mails often begin with a generic salutation of "Dear Sir" and include religious phrases and references to personal tragedy. There is major disagreement about whether these scams actually originate in Nigeria and are committed by Nigerians. Investigations by foreign governments have exposed clear linkages. Victims all over the world, but particularly in Europe and the United States, have lost hundreds of millions of dollars. Economic analysts have factored advanced fee fraud into the country's many sources of revenue. Today, any fraudulent action in Nigeria is colloquially referred to as "419."

**AFENIFERE.** A **Yoruba** social organization with political interests that formed in February 1993. It had similar goals to the **Egbe Omo Oduduwa** of 1945. Afenifere was created to support **Chief M. K. O. Abiola** in the **election of 12 June 1993**. **Chief Michael Adekunle Ajasin** acted as the leader of the organization until his death in 1997. Afenifere became closely aligned with the **Alliance for Democracy** political party. In 2007, the organization found itself in opposition to another Yoruba social organization, the **O'odua People's Congress**. In some circumstances, Afenifere has acted as a pressure group. It has been described as the Yoruba equivalent to the **Ohaneze Ndigbo**, an **Igbo** cultural organization.

**AFONJA (?–1823).** Afonja was the ruler of the **Yoruba** city of **Ilorin** in the 19th century. He was posted at Ilorin by the *alaafin* (**king**) of the **Oyo Empire** to run the defensive outpost. Afonja was the *are ona kakanfo* (the Old Oyo commander-in-chief). In 1817, Afonja declared Ilorin's independence by sending an empty calabash to the *alaafin*. He relied upon **Hausa** soldiers from Oyo to resist any attacks. He was killed by his own soldiers in 1823.

**AFRICAN CHURCH MOVEMENT.** European **Christian** missionaries set up stations and attracted African converts starting in the mid-19th century. Within a few decades, however, the African Church Movement was started by Africans seeking a religious vocation. The founders called for the separation and establishment of African independent churches. For example, in 1888, Reverend W. J. David broke away from the Lagos Baptist Church and formed the United Native African Church. *See also* RELIGION.

**AFRICAN PETROLEUM COMPANY (AP).** The African Petroleum Company emerged as a national **petroleum** company to take over British Petroleum's marketing and distribution operations in Nigeria in August 1979. It is a subsidiary of the **Nigerian National Petroleum Corporation**. In 1998, African Petroleum became a private company, selling shares on the **Nigerian Stock Exchange**.

**AFRICAN UNION (AU).** The African Union grew out of the Organization of African Unity (OAU) in 2002. The OAU was created in May 1963 by **Sir Alhaji Abubakar Tafawa Balewa** and other African heads of state. OAU members were divided on Nigeria's **civil war**. The Biafrans appealed to the OAU for assistance. Much to their dismay, the OAU responded by assuring **General Yakubu Gowon** that it respected Nigeria's sovereignty and saw the conflict as a Nigerian problem. The OAU tried to organize peace talks in Addis Ababa, Ethiopia, and Kampala, Uganda, which failed. Several OAU member states offered vocal support to each side of the conflict independently. Less than 40 years later, the AU took over the responsibilities of the OAU. The AU, based in Addis Ababa, acts as a governing body to promote peace, prosperity, and solidarity among independent African nations. Nigeria has played a major role in the AU in leadership and soldier commitment. Of the 9,000 AU peacekeeping troops currently in Darfur (a region of Sudan), Nigerians make up one-third. **Baba Gana Kingibe** was head of the AU's special mission in Sudan from 2002 to 2006. Like the OAU, the AU has been criticized for its lack of action toward oppressive heads of state, **human rights** violations, **HIV/AIDS**, and Africa's economic problems. While president, **General Olusegun Obasanjo** served as chairman of the AU from 2004 to 2006. *See also* ECONOMIC COM-

MUNITY OF WEST AFRICAN STATES; NEW PARTNERSHIP
FOR AFRICAN DEVELOPMENT.

**AFROBEAT.** A **music** style popularized by **Olufela Anikulapo-Kuti**
in the music halls of **Lagos**. It is the fusion of jazz rhythms with African instruments and prose. The songs are typically over 10 minutes in
length, with a driving, danceable beat, and are peppered with instrumental solos and lyrical moments. It is not uncommon for Afrobeat
bands to have several female dancers and backup singers providing
entertainment and variations to the pulse of a song.

**AGBEBI, MOJOLA (1860–1917).** Born in April 1860 in Ilesha,
Agbebi was born David Brown Vincent, but changed his name in
the late 1880s. As a young man, he studied at a **Church Missionary
Society** (CMS) school in **Lagos** and a CMS teacher training school.
Agbebi then worked as a schoolmaster. He also acted as leader of
the Native Baptist Church in Lagos between 1888 and 1903. A few
years later, he founded Ebenezer Baptist Church in Lagos. Agbebi
also worked as an editor for several major **newspapers**, such as the
*Lagos Times* and *Lagos Weekly Record*. He received several honorary degrees. *See also* CHRISTIANITY.

**AGE-GRADE (AGE-GROUP) SYSTEM.** The concept refers to the
organization of a society based on age. Children are organized into
groups, or associations, by their age and given, for boys, economic,
political, and military training. Among the **Yoruba**, an age-grade
of young individuals provided a reliable source of labor on farms.
Many **Urhobo** communities were governed by and organized into
age-grade systems. Urhobo **women** were organized into three age-
grades: *ekwokweya* (women 50 years old and above), *eghweya* (married women aged 15 to 50), and *emete* (unmarried girls under age
15). The last group was responsible for running errands, looking after
young children, and keeping the public spaces clean.

Almost all **Nupe** boys and young men belong to an age-grade association. Although participating in an age-grade system is not always
compulsory, not joining would be unusual and perhaps regarded with
suspicion. By joining an association, a young man agrees to protect
the land, culture, and citizens. Members take part in collective farm

work, training sessions on warfare, and organized recreation. The system serves as a bonding experience for the young men, with an emphasis on **education**. These young men are often the focus and organizers of annual festivals.

**AGRICULTURAL CREDIT GUARANTEE SCHEME FUND.** A funding scheme created in 1977 under Decree No. 20 and implemented in 1978. The federal government contributes 60 percent and the Central Bank of Nigeria 40 percent. The latter also manages the fund. The capital base of the scheme was originally ₦100 million. In March 2001, that amount was increased to ₦3 billion. The point of the fund is to have a pool of capital available for local banks to extend credit to farmers at a beneficial interest rate. As the name of the fund indicates, it is publicized as a guaranteed place for farmers to seek financial assistance. *See also* AGRICULTURE; ECONOMY.

**AGRICULTURE.** Nigeria depends heavily on its agriculture and is among Africa's largest producers of **cassava** and **oil palm**. Much of Nigeria's agricultural production is done without sophisticated irrigation systems or mechanized farming tools, making its annual yields highly dependent on the weather. In **northern Nigeria**, people grow crops in areas known as *fadama* ("wetlands" in the **Hausa language**), which are lowlands situated along the flood plains of rivers. In these areas, farmers can grow valuable foodstuffs such as tomatoes, onions, and peppers in a largely dry part of the country. Beyond the *fadama*, people in northern Nigeria mainly grow cereals and herd cattle. In **southern Nigeria**, fruit, vegetable, and tuber cultivation are the dominant agricultural activities. Along the coast, oil palm production, processing, and export are a major cornerstone of the **economy**.

At the start of **legitimate commerce**, the British had a great interest in the already existing trade of oil palm. During colonial rule, the British designated certain areas for specific cash crops. The North became the colony's **groundnut** center, and the Southwest specialized in **cocoa**. Many people from the Southeast also became migrant workers or artisans in the other regions. In addition to the cash crops, Nigerian farmers grew a variety of fruits and vegetables to sell locally and internationally. Until the mid-1970s, agriculture was responsible for the majority of Nigeria's exports and foreign exchange earnings. Agriculture made up 85 percent of Nigeria's exports in 1960, but by 1974 it was only 5 percent. Of particular interest in local markets were **kolanuts, bananas**, peppers, **yams**, maize, rice, and **cotton**.

The majority of Nigeria's citizens are farmers or traders selling local foodstuffs. Although **petroleum** dominates Nigeria's **foreign trade** today, agricultural products still dominate domestic **trade**. Successive governments have attempted to correct this imbalance and promote agricultural production by offering farmers low-interest loans, setting up irrigation programs, and providing modern tools and fertilizers. *See also* AGRICULTURAL CREDIT GUARANTEE SCHEME FUND; MARKETS.

**AGUDA COMMITTEE.** *See* FEDERAL CAPITAL TERRITORY.

**AGUIYI-IRONSI, MAJOR GENERAL JOHNSON THOMAS UMUNANKWE (1924–1966).** Born in March 1924 in Umuahia, Aguiyi-Ironsi joined the army in 1942. He trained at a series of military schools in Nigeria and Great Britain. In the (Royal) **West African Frontier Force**, he served as second lieutenant. In 1960, he was promoted to lieutenant colonel. He led a Nigerian division of a United Nations peacekeeping force in Central Africa in the early 1960s. After Nigeria's first military **coup d'état** on 15 January 1966, he became the head of state for seven months. He was assassinated during a military countercoup in July 1966. **General Yakubu Gowon** replaced Aguiyi-Ironsi as Nigeria's new head of state. *See also* ARMED FORCES; UNIFICATION DECREE.

**AHIARA DECLARATION.** After almost two years of fighting in Nigeria's **civil war, Chief Chukuemeka Odumegwu Ojukwu** issued the Ahiara Declaration on 1 June 1969. It stated that the **Republic of Biafra** would undergo an economic revolution, whereby all property would be distributed for the benefit of all people. This revolution emphasized egalitarianism as well as private investment. In short, Ojukwu applied his own brand of socialism in the secessionist state.

**AHMADIYYA.** One of several **Islamic** Sufi *tariqahs* (brotherhoods or orders) that gained popularity in Nigeria. This mystical form of Islam was established in India by Mirza Ghulam (b. 1836–1906). It reached **Lagos** in 1916. Young Muslim intellectuals in Lagos were attracted to it and turned it into a sort of religious and political movement. Alhaji Jubril Martin led in conjunction with the **Nigerian Youth Movement**. The order had weakened significantly by the late 1950s. *See also* QADIRIYYA; TIJANIYYA.

**AHMADU BELLO UNIVERSITY.** Founded in October 1962 as the University of Northern Nigeria, it was the first university in the region. It is located in **Zaria**, in **Kaduna State** and is named after **Sir Alhaji Ahmadu Bello**. The university was transferred to federal control in 1975. Ahmadu Bello University is well known among historians for its Center for Historical Documentation and Research, or Arewa House, which houses a rich collection of Arabic manuscripts and correspondence. *See also* HIGHER EDUCATION.

**AIDS.** *See* HIV/AIDS.

**AIKHOMU, VICE ADMIRAL AUGUSTUS AKHABUE (1939– ).** Born in October 1939 in Irrrua-Ishan, in **Edo State**, Aikhomu attended Irrua Government School and Yaba Technical Institute (1954–1958). He also attended **Yaba Higher College** in **Lagos**. He joined the navy in 1958. In England, he attended the Britannia Royal Naval College and Royal Naval Engineering College. Aikhomu also studied at the Long Gunnery Training Course in India (1969–1970) and Defence Services Staff Institute for Policy and Strategic Studies (1982). He worked in the Federal Ministry of Works for the **Western Region** and as an architect-in-training at Yabe Higher College. In 1986, he achieved the highest ranking of chief of naval staff. In the mid-1980s, Aikhomu became almost exclusively involved in the federal government. He served as vice president to **General Ibrahim Babangida**. He was the chief executive behind Decree No. 2, which allowed for the detention of individuals without being charged. He retired from the **armed forces** and government service in 1993. In 2003, he formed the Fourth Dimension of Nigeria organization to unite people of the South. He is currently a member of the newly created United Nigeria Democratic Party. In 2007, Aikhomu was stopped from leaving the country when traveling to London for a wedding based on government suspicion of the Fourth Dimension.

**AIR FORCE.** *See* ARMED FORCES.

**AIRLINES.** Nigeria's airline industry has undergone significant restructuring in the past 20 years. The country maintained its own airline, Nigerian Airways, from 1958 to 2003. It started as a joint venture between the Nigerian government and the British Overseas Airways Corporation and Elder Dempster & Co. In 1961, the Nigerian government took full ownership. Nigeria's leaders promoted Nigerian Airways as a symbol of the country's progress and independence. The airline carried between a half million and two million passengers a year to European and North American destinations, making it the largest African airline. It also ran domestic flights to all the major cities in Nigeria. However, it was troubled by poor management, fatal crashes, and financial decline. Communication between air traffic control and approaching planes in Nigeria was not reliable. By 1979, this national airline was being run by employees of KLM Royal Dutch Airlines. In the mid-1980s, Nigeria temporarily lost its membership in the International Air Transport Association because it failed to settle its debt. Nigerian Airways owed $20.8 million to three major European airlines, and its management faced accusations of illegal financial dealings. A series of fatal crashes and safety cancellations gave the airline a bad reputation. It ceased operations in 2003 and three years later struck a joint venture agreement with Virgin Atlantic, creating Virgin Nigeria Airways as part of a **privatization** project.

For domestic travel, Nigeria maintains 22 airports in large cities with paved runways. All of Nigeria's airports are operated and regulated by the Federal Airport Authority of Nigeria. For international travel, there are three major airports: Nnamdi Azikiwe International Airport in **Abuja**, Mallam Aminu Kano International Airport in **Kano**, and Murtala Muhammed International Airport in **Lagos**. In 2008, the government began construction of the Gombe Lawanti International Airport in **Gombe**, to facilitate the annual *hajj* (**pilgrimage**) of Muslims to Mecca from northeastern Nigeria. The National Hajj Commission currently airlifts around 80,000 Muslims from 11 designated airports across the country. In past years, Nigeria has struggled to provide a successful journey for its pilgrims and has repeatedly failed to meet the strict arrival time assigned by Saudi Arabia, disappointing the country's pilgrims. In 2006, Nigeria left 4,000 pilgrims waiting in Kano while it begged Saudi Arabia for a new arrival time. Since privatization, Nigeria's airline industry has improved, providing more safe and reliable flights. *See also* ISLAM; RAILROADS; ROADS.

**AJASIN, CHIEF MICHAEL ADEKUNLE (1908–1997).** Born in November 1908 in Owo, in **Ondo State**, Ajasin attended St. Paul's Anglican School (1914–1921) in Owo and St. Paul's Anglican College (1924–1927) in Oyo. He attended Fourah Bay College in Sierra Leone. In London, he attended the University of London and graduated in 1928. After receiving his bachelor's degree in **education**, he returned to Nigeria and became the schoolmaster of St. Andrew's Anglican School at **Warri** for two years. He also worked as the headmaster of St. Luke's Anglican School in Sapele from 1941 to 1943 and was the principal at Imade College in Owo from 1947 to 1962. He was the founder of Owo High School in 1963 and its first principal until 1975. He was an active member of **Egbe Omo Oduduwa**. He served as a member of the **Federal House of Representatives** in **Lagos** in 1954. Ajasin was an active member of the **Unity Party of Nigeria** in 1978. During the **coup d'état** of 1983, Ajasin, **Chief Bola Ige**, and **Chief Victor Onabanjo** were accused of **corruption**. In the early 1990s, Ajasin joined other politicians in the creation of the **National Democratic Coalition** and remained an active member until his death in October 1997. *See also* POLITICAL PARTIES.

**AJULUCHUKU, CHIEF MELIE CHEKELU KAFUNDU (1924–2003).** Ajuluchuku was born in February 1924 in Nnwei, in **Anambra State**. As a young man, Ajuluchuku attended the Church Missionary Society Central School in Nnewi, Government College in Umuahia, and **Yaba Higher College** in **Lagos**. After completing his studies in Nigeria, he relocated to the United States. Ajuluchuku studied at Bethune-Cookman College (1947) and Brooklyn College (1947–1949). In Nigeria, he worked as an editor for **newspapers** such as the *Daily Comet* (1946–1947, between his educational adventures), *West African Pilot* (1951–1953), and *Nigerian Outlook*

(1954–1960). From 1960 to 1970, he served as the general manager for the Eastern Nigeria Information Service as well as director of the federal government's Post Group of Newspapers, which published the *Sunday Post*. From 1961 to 1978, he was the chairman and managing director of One Nigeria Press, and from 1971 to 1976 for Herwa Press. He also worked as the general manager of Concord Press of Nigeria from 1984 to 1986.

In the arena of national politics, Ajuluchuku was a founding member of the **Zikist Movement** and assistant national secretary of the **National Council of Nigeria and the Cameroons** (1947–1950). He worked as the director of research and publicity for the **United Party of Nigeria** in 1978. He was a member of the **People's Democratic Party** from 1998 until his death in 2003.

**AKASSA MASSACRE.** A violent clash between the **Brass**, a subgroup of the **Ijaw**, and the **Royal Niger Constabulary**, the native police force of the **Royal Niger Company**, in 1895 in the **Niger Coast Protectorate** in the **Niger Delta**. The Brass people formed a 1,500-man army and attacked the company's trading post at Akassa. The **Niger Coast Constabulary** retaliated with violence. *See also* TRADE.

**AKENZUA II (1899–1978).** Born in **Benin**, Akenzua II was the *oba* (**chief**) of Benin from 1933 to 1978. He attended Government School in Benin and **King's College** in **Lagos** (1918–1921). He acted as the president of the Benin Divisional Council and was a member of the **Western House of Chiefs**, starting in 1952. In 1953, he formed the **Benin Delta People's Party**. He also served as the chancellor of **Ahmadu Bello University** in **Zaria** from 1966 to 1972. He received the honorary title Commander of the Republic of Nigeria. He died in 1978.

**AKINJIDE, CHIEF RICHARD OSUOLALE ABIMBOLA (1931– ).** Born November 1931 in **Ibadan**, as a young man, Akinjide attended St. Peter's School in Ibadan, Oduduwa College in **Ile-Ife** (1943–1949), and the University of London (1952–1956). He worked as a clerk for the Cooperative Department in Ibadan and **Benin** in 1952. In 1956, he started practicing law in Nigeria. He was briefly held in political detention in 1962. From 1959 to 1966, Akinjide served as a member of the Ibadan South-East Constituency in Nigeria's Parliament. In 1960, he was a member of the Nigerian Delegation to the United Nations. He also held the positions of federal minister of education (1965–1966) and minister of justice (1979–1983). From 1970 to 1973, he was president of the Nigerian Bar Association and a member of the editorial board of *Nigerian Monthly Law Reports*. From 1975 to 1976, he was a member of the governing council for the University of Ife (present-day **Obafemi Awolowo University**) and, in 1976, pro-chancellor and chairman of the University of Jos. In the late 1970s, he was a member of the **National Party of Nigeria**. He went into self-imposed exile from 1984 to 1992. When he returned to Nigeria in 1992, he resumed practicing law. In 1999, he was a member of and presidential hopeful for the **People's Democratic Party**. *See also* COURTS; LEGAL SYSTEM; POLITICAL PARTIES.

**AKINRINADE, CHIEF LIEUTENANT GENERAL IPOOLA ALANI (1939– ).** Born in October 1939 in Yakoyo of **Yoruba** descent, Akinrinade studied at Offa Grammar School, the Royal Nigerian Military Training College in **Kaduna** (1960), the Royal Military Academy at Sandhurst in Great Britain (1960–1962), the U.S. Army Infantry School (1965–1966), the Royal College of Defence Studies in Great Britain (1978), and the Command and Staff College in Jaji. From 1959 to 1960, he worked for the Ministry of Agriculture of the **Western Region**. He moved through the ranks of the army, becoming lieutenant colonel in 1968, major general in 1975, and lieutenant general in 1980. Akinrinade retired from the **armed forces** in 1981. From 1982 to 1985, he was chairman of Nigerfeeds and Agriculture Operations Company. He returned to the government as minister of agriculture, water resources, and rural development (1985–1986), minister of industries (1986–1989), and minister of transport (1989). In 1994, Akinrinade went into self-imposed exile. In 1996, while he was in Europe, armed men burned down his house in **Lagos**. One year later, he was formally charged with treason by **General Sani Abacha**. Akinrinade has received several honorary titles and decorations, including *jagunmolu* (**chief**) of **Ile-Ife**, Grand Commander of the Order of the Nigeria, and Commander of the Order of the Federal Republic.

**AKINSANYA, SAMUEL (1898–1985).** Born in August 1898, Akinsanya received his early education from Ishara Anglican School. He worked as a shorthand note taker and typist from 1916 to 1931. Between 1932 and 1940, Akinsanya was the organizing secretary of the Nigerian Produce Traders. He was president of the Nigerian Motor Transport Union, a **trade union**. He also served as the secretary and later vice president of the **Nigerian Youth Movement** from 1933 to 1940. Akinsanya was the *odemo* (**chief**) of Ishara starting in 1941. He was an active member of the **Action Group**, a prominent **political party**. He served in the **Western House of Chiefs**. Akinsanya died in January 1985.

**AKINTOLA, CHIEF SAMUEL LADOKE (1910–1996).** Born in July 1910 in Ogbomoso, Akintola completed his primary and secondary schooling there. He worked for a few years for the Baptist mission in **Lagos**, the Nigerian Railway, and the *Daily Service* **newspaper**. He was an active member of the **Nigerian Youth Movement**. In 1946, he went to Oxford University for a law degree. Three years later, Akintola returned to Nigeria and worked as a legal advisor to **Egbe Omo Oduduwa**, a **Yoruba** cultural association. He was also an active member of the **Action Group** (AG), a **political party**. In May 1953, he led a group of AG members to **northern Nigeria** to campaign, which sparked the **Kano Riots**. He was also the deputy leader of the AG in 1955. During the 1950s, he held several positions in various branches of government, including the **Legislative Council** and **Federal House of Representatives**. He served as **premier** of the **Western Region** twice during the **First Republic** (December 1959 to May 1962 and January 1963 to January 1966). His second term as premier was during the **Action Group Crisis** of 1962, in which he was heavily involved. Tension between Akintola and **Chief Obafemi Awolowo** (the previous premier of the Western Region) escalated over whether the AG should align itself with the **Northern Region**'s dominant party, the **Northern People's Congress**.

In 1963, Akintola left the AG and formed the **United People's Party**. A year later, the United People's Party aligned itself with several minor political parties (and former members of the **National Council of Nigeria and the Cameroons**) to form the **Nigerian National Democratic Party**. Later that year, this new party merged with the Northern People's Congress to form the **Nigerian National Alliance**. Akintola's critics accused him of rigging the regional **elections**. He was killed in

January 1996 during the first military **coup d'état**. The Ladoke Akintola University of Technology in Ogbomoso is named after him.

**AKINTOYE (?–1853).** Akintoye was installed as *oba* (**chief**) of **Lagos** by the *oba* of **Benin**. He served as the *oba* from 1841 to June 1845 and again from February 1852 to September 1853. **Kosoko**, Akintoye's nephew, resented Akintoye's rule and focused on undermining his authority. In 1845, Kosoko ejected Akintoye from the throne, and Akintoye sought refuge in **Badagry** and alliances in **Abeokuta**. The British, under the leadership of **John Beecroft**, saw him as a potential ally and sent him to the island of **Fernando Poo** for protection. While on the island, Akintoye agreed to end the **slave trade** in Lagos. The British removed Kosoko from the throne and reinstalled Akintoye; in exchange, Akintoye agreed to provide support for **Christian** missionaries and British traders. Akintoye died in 1853 and was succeeded by his son, **Dosunmu**.

**AKWA IBOM STATE.** Located in southeastern Nigeria, in the **Niger Delta**, Akwa Ibom State is the home of Akwa Ibom State University of Technology and Akwa Ibom State Polytechnic. It is the second largest **petroleum**-producing state in Nigeria. It was created in 1987 out of **Cross River State**. Its capital is Uyo. Akwa Ibom has a multiethnic composition, including **Ibibio**, Anang, Oron, Eket, Ibeno, and Mbo. The major **religions** are indigenous and **Christianity**. Akwa Ibom is one of Nigeria's current 36 states. *See also* STATE CREATION.

**ALADURA CHURCHES.** A Christian-based religious movement that has many similarities to Nigeria's current **Charismatic Christian** and **Pentecostal Christian** movements. The name comes from the **Yoruba language** and has been translated as "owners of prayer" or "praying hands." The practice of healing during a prayer at an Anglican church in Ijebu-Ode marked the start of healing prayer groups such as the Precious Stone Society and Diamond Society in the 1920s. **Joseph Ayo Babalola**, for example, established the **Christ Apostolic Church** in the early 1930s. Collectively these churches were known as Aladura churches. They attracted thousands of people to **Christianity**, particularly in southwestern Nigeria among the **Yoruba**. The Aladura focused on healing to rid Christians of evil, unexplained sickness, and family problems afflicting communities. Members of Aladura Churches are interested in prayers, visions, and healers far more than in baptisms and miracles, which are of great interest to Charismatic Christian churches. Leaders of the Aladura churches were prophets who served their congregations as diviners, healers, and social leaders. Worship services tended to last over two hours and include a great deal of singing, dancing, and clapping. Today, some Aladura churches are identified as Pentecostal or Charismatic. *See also* RELIGION.

**ALAKIJA, SIR ADEYEMO (1884–1952).** Born in May 1884, Alakija completed his primary and secondary education in **Lagos**. He worked as a clerical officer from 1900 to 1910. He studied law in London and was called to the bar in 1913. Alakija worked closely with **Sir Herbert Macaulay**, but disagreed with him over a court case involving a **chief**. As an independent candidate, Alakija ran for the colonial government's legislative council in 1923 and 1926 and lost. However, he was appointed to the **Legislative Council** as a representative of the Egba Division (1933–1941). With Richard Barrow and a few others, Alakija cofounded the ***Daily Times* newspaper** in 1926. He is also remembered for his contribution to the creation of **Egbe Omo Oduduwa**, a **Yoruba** cultural organization. In 1945, he received the honorary title Knight Commander of the British Empire. Alakija died in May 1952.

**ALCOHOL.** A variety of alcoholic beverages are produced and consumed in Nigeria. For the most part, alcohol consumption is a male activity, and the production of local drinks is a female activity. **Palm wine**, for example, is made from the sap of an **oil palm** tree, which is low in alcohol. It is particularly popular in the rural areas among **Yoruba** men. The relaxed atmosphere of palm wine drinking sessions was complemented in the first half of the 20th century with palm wine **music**. Prior to the 20th century, those living outside Bida (in **Niger State**) preferred *burukutu* (sorghum beer) to palm wine, while those living in Bida preferred to import palm wine from southwestern Nigeria. Another popular drink in Nigeria is *ogogoro* (in the **Yoruba language**) or *akpetashi* (in the **Tiv language**), which is a locally produced gin with a high alcohol content. It is frequently mixed with medicinal herbs, including marijuana, to produce what is called *paraga*, *oosa*, or "hot drink." These concoctions are particularly popular among **Lagos** men and are believed to increase virility.

Although **Islam** forbids the consumption of alcohol, some Muslim men argue that they can drink palm wine. Today, consumption of alcohol in **northern Nigeria** is punishable by flogging under the **Shari'a criminal** code. In areas of the country that have a mixture of Muslims and non-Muslims, alcohol consumption has prompted mixed responses. In **Kano State**, for example, a law was passed in 2004 banning alcohol consumption, even for non-Muslims. The consumption of grape-fermented wine is popular only among elite Nigerians; beer is popular among the majority of non-Muslims. Nigeria is home to one of Africa's largest beer companies, Nigerian Breweries, which was established in 1946. The company sold its first bottle of Star lager in July 1949 in Lagos. Today, it has a network of breweries and distributors across the country. The company sponsors television shows and art competitions, and promotes public safety. In 2008, Nigerian Breweries launched a **Nollywood** film scriptwriting contest.

Since the 1990s, **health** experts have been concerned about the significant increase in alcohol consumption in Nigeria. As in most countries, there is a direct relationship between alcohol and high **unemployment**, poverty, and domestic abuse. Indeed, many poor men will substitute a heavy alcoholic beverage such as *burukutu* for a proper meal. In recent years, health researchers have been looking at the relationship between **HIV/AIDS** prevalence and alcohol consumption in Nigeria.

**ALHAJI, SIR ALHAJI ABUBAKAR (1938– ).** Born in November 1938 in **Sokoto**, Alhaji attended primary and secondary school there, Katsina Government College, Bournemouth College of Commerce and Technology (England), and the University of Reading (England). He also studied at the Hague Institute of Social Sciences (Netherlands) in 1970 and the International Monetary Fund Institute (United States) in 1974. In Nigeria, Alhaji was the executive director of the African Development Bank (1972–1974) and executive secretary of the **World Black and African Festival of Arts and Culture** (FESTAC '77). In the government, Alhaji served as the deputy permanent secretary of the Ministry of Finance. He also worked as the permanent secretary of the Ministry of Trade (1975–1978) and Ministry of Finance (1979–1984). From 1984 to 1988, he was the director-general of the Ministry of National Planning and, from 1988 to 1990, minister of state for budget and planning (special assistant to the president). He was also the minister of finance and economic development (1990–1991). Outside the political arena, he served as chairman and director for a wide range of Nigerian businesses, such as the Nigerian Hotels, Nigerian Produce Marketing Company, and Ajaokuta Steel Company. He also served as a board member for a variety of private and public businesses, such as the **Nigerian National Petroleum Oil Corporation** and Nigerian Telecommunications. He received the honorary title Knight Commander of the Order of the British Empire in 1989 and a honorary doctoral degree from Sokoto State University. *See also* BANKING; ECONOMY.

**ALI BABBA BIN BELLO (?–1859).** The son of **Muhammad Bello** and grandson of **Usman dan Fodio**, Ali Babba is also identified as Aliyu Babba in historical texts. He served as the ruler of the **Sokoto Caliphate** from 1842 to 1859. He successfully protected the caliphate against revolts from **Kebbi**, Dendi, and **Zamfara**. In 1853, he signed a treaty with Henry Barth of Great Britain, which gave British **traders** permission to operate.

**ALI GHAJI DUNAMAMI.** Ruler of the **Kanem-Bornu Empire** during the **Sefawa Dynasty** from 1472 to 1503. Ali Ghaji faced intense rivalry for the throne at the same time that **Bulala** nomads were threatening to take **Bornu**. He settled first at Wudi and Yamia before founding the city of Birni N'gazargamu as the new capital in 1472, which lasted until it was sacked by **Fulani jihadists** in 1808.

**ALL PEOPLE'S PARTY (APP).** A right-of-center organization based in **northern Nigeria**. It included supporters of the late **General Sani Abacha** and was one of nine **political parties** allowed by **General Alhaji Abdulsalami Abubakar**'s regime to present candidates for the 1999 **elections**. Initially, **Chief Emmanuel Iwuanyanwu** was the party's presidential candidate, and **Alhaji Umaru Shinkafi** was its vice presidential aspirant. In January 1999, the APP joined with the **Alliance for Democracy** to run **Chief Samuel Oluyemisi Falae**

as a presidential candidate. **Major General Muhammadu Buhari** was the party's presidential candidate in the 2007 elections.

**ALLIANCE FOR DEMOCRACY (AD).** One of nine **political parties** approved by **General Alhaji Abdulsalami Abubakar**'s government to field candidates for the 1999 **election**. The party promoted a welfare program. Its membership included opponents of the late **General Sani Abacha** and supporters of the **Afenifere**, a **Yoruba** cultural organization. Critics accused the party of promoting ethnic-based politics. In January 1999, the AD joined with the **All People's Party** to run **Chief Samuel Oluyemisi Falae** as a presidential candidate. In 2006, it merged with the **Action Congress** party.

**ALL-NIGERIA TRADE UNION FEDERATION (ANTUF).** A **trade union** formed in 1953. Like other trade organizations, it served as a lobbying group on behalf of workers across Nigeria. **Chief Michael Imoudu** was its president. This federation did not last long because of disagreements over which unions it should affiliate with. The **National Council of Trade Unions of Nigeria** (NCTUN) grew out of it in 1957. Two years later, ANTUF joined NCTUN to reform the **Trade Union Congress of Nigeria**.

**AMALGAMATION OF NIGERIA.** Unification of the **Protectorate of Northern Nigeria** and the **Protectorate of Southern Nigeria** in January 1914 by **Sir Frederick Lugard**, who became the colony's first **governor general**.

**AMINA OF ZARIA, QUEEN (ca. 1533–1610).** Daughter of Queen Bakua Turuku of **Zaria**. According to **oral tradition**, Amina built a walled camp, from which she launched attacks on neighboring states such as **Kano** and **Katsina**. Her conquests extended as far as **Nupe** territory. She began ruling the town of Zaria, previously called Zazzau, in 1576. Zaria was named after one of Amina's daughters. Amina died in Attagara. *See also* HAUSA KINGDOMS.

**ANAMBRA STATE.** Located in southeastern Nigeria on the **Niger River**, Anambra State was created in 1976 out of **East-Central State**. Between 1976 and 1991, Anambra State included other states.

The capital is Awka. The state's name comes from the Anambra River, a tributary of the Niger River. The people of Anambra State are primarily of the **Igbo ethnic group**. Anambra is one of Nigeria's current 36 states and is home to the federal Nnamdi Azikiwe University and Anambra State University. **Christianity** and indigenous are the primary forms of **religion**. Economic activity includes the cultivation of **yams** and fishing. In early times, people living near the Anambra River specialized in canoe-building. *See also* BAKASSI BOYS; STATE CREATION.

**ANGLICAN CHURCH.** *See* CHURCH MISSIONARY SOCIETY.

**ANGLO–FRENCH AGREEMENT.** The Anglo–French Agreement arose out of a series of negotiations over the Nigeria–**Benin** border, which started in 1863 and ended in 1914. The British and French expanded the boundary starting at the coast and moving northward. In 1889, the **Lagos**–Dahomey boundary was determined. In the process, major kingdoms, such as **Borgu**, located in northwestern Nigeria, were split between the British and French. By 1906, an agreement was made over the boundary between the coast and the **Niger River**. This agreement underwent minor modifications before becoming the final Anglo–French Agreement of 1914. Although basically the same, minor changes were made to the Nigeria–Benin border during and after colonial rule.

**ANIKULAPO-KUTI, OLUFELA (1938–1997).** Born in October 1938 in **Abeokuta**, Anikulapo-Kuti was the son of the famous **Chief Olufunmilayo Ransome-Kuti** and her husband, Canon Josiah Ransome-Kuti. He was the brother of **Bekolari Ransome-Kuti** and **Olikoye Ransome-Kuti**. He changed his surname to Anikulapo-Kuti, which means "death in my pocket" in **Yoruba**. After completing his primary and secondary education in Abeokuta, he studied at the Trinity College of Music in England (1959–1963). Fela Kuti, as he preferred to be called, worked for the Nigerian Broadcasting Corporation from 1964 to 1967. He played the saxophone, composed songs, and sang in a series of bands, including Koola Lobito, Africa '70, and Egypt '80. Fela is considered the creator of the **Afrobeat music** style, which blends indigenous African instruments and **music**

sensibility with American jazz. At any one time, Fela's performances on stage included 10 or more musicians, dancers, and singers. His musical influences include James Brown. His political influences include the Black Panthers, whom he encountered during as visit to the United States.

Fela was Nigeria's best known musician and political pundit. His songs often criticized Nigeria's military regimes and the embrace of Western culture by individual Nigerians. "Suffrin' and Smilin'" and "Colonial Mentality" are among the songs that most clearly articulate his political views. For his activism, he was harassed by the Nigerian **police**. In 1978, they stormed his compound, which resulted in injuries to his family, particularly his mother. It is believed that the assault contributed to her death later that year. That same year, Fela formed the Movement of the People political organization. He was well known outside of Nigeria, and he toured extensively in Europe and the United States. He opened his own music club in **Lagos**, The Shrine, in which he played regularly. He also married 28 women, in response to public outcry about the indecency of the singers and dancers in his band in 1978. Eight years later he divorced them. Between 1984 and 1986, Fela was imprisoned for obstructing a governmental decree. He died in August 1997 of complications of AIDS. His son, Femi Kuti, has continued his musical legacy as the singer and saxophone player of a large jazz band, playing regular shows in Lagos at The Shrine. Femi Kuti has posed for billboards that raise awareness about **HIV/AIDS**. In 2003, the New Museum in New York City hosted an **art** exhibit dedicated to Fela.

**ANYAOKU, CHIEF ELEAZAR CHUKWUEMEKA (1933– ).** Born in January 1933 in Obosi, Anyaoku studied at the Merchants of Light School, **University of Ibadan**, and Institute of Public Administration (London). In Nigeria, Anyaoku worked as the executive assistant to the Commonwealth Development Corporation (London and **Lagos**) from 1959 to 1962. He worked for the Nigerian Foreign Service in 1962. Anyaoku was a member of Nigeria's Permanent Mission to the United Nations from 1963 to 1966. He was the assistant director of the International Affairs Division of the Commonwealth Secretariat from 1966 to 1971 and director of the Commonwealth Secretariat from 1971 to 1975. In 1983, he was the minister of external affairs. Anyaoku served as secretary-general of the Commonwealth from 1990 to 2000. He received a number of advanced degrees, from the **University of Ibadan** (1990), **Ahmadu Bello University** (1991), and the University of Nigeria at **Nsukka** (1991), and the honorary titles *ichie adazie* (**chief**) of Obori and Commander of the Order of the Niger (1982).

**ARCHITECTURE.** The architecture of Nigeria reflects the diversity of its people, history, and culture. Much of the structural variation is shaped by Nigeria's climate and access to materials. In the dry heat of rural **northern Nigeria**, mud homes and places of business are made with small windows to help protect families from the intense sun and keep the interior cool. Because trees are scarce in the North, building with wood is limited to frames and doors. The roofs are typically made of grass or mud spread flat. In rural **southern Nigeria**, homes and places of business are made of brightly colored concrete walls and are often two stories high. In forested areas, people build their homes of mud with a thatched roof. Buildings constructed during the colonial period, although a bit run down today, have ornate designs in the porch and balcony walls.

European **Christian** missionaries of the 19th century made the construction of buildings a high priority. The (Anglican) **Church Missionary Society** imported brick makers and carpenters to teach the local people how to use new methods and tools. Under the direction of **Harry Townsend**, the first stone building was constructed in **Abeokuta**. Typical examples of this architecture can be seen on Victoria Island in **Lagos**. In the **Niger Delta**, many homes and buildings are constructed on raised platforms to protect them from the swampy, saturated ground. Builders use whatever materials are at their disposal, including bamboo and raffia palm. The Jos Museum Complex includes 50 acres of life-sized reproductions of buildings unique to Nigeria's major regions.

Postcolonial architecture displays a combination of the colonial style with a unique Nigerian flare. This is most evident in government offices, research institutions, and universities. Buildings on the campus of **Obafemi Awolowo University** in **Ile-Ife** are excellent examples. Each resembles a sculpture that plays with space, function, and art. In urban areas all over Nigeria, houses and shops are frequently made of manufactured cement and have corrugated iron sheets as roofs.

**AREWA PEOPLE'S CONGRESS.** *See* JAM'IYYAR MUTANEN AREWA.

**ARIKPO, OKOI (1916– ).** Born in September 1916, Arikpo was educated at the Church of Scotland School in Ugefa and **Yaba Higher College**; he was interested in laboratory sciences. He attended University College in London. From 1937 to 1938 he was the assistant master at Government College at Umuahia and assistant lecturer in chemistry at Yaba Higher College from 1939 to 1942. A year later, he was science master at **King's College** in **Lagos**. In 1949, he returned to England and was an assistant lecturer of anthropology at University College until 1951. Between 1952 and 1953, he worked for the Ministry of Lands, Survey, and Local Development. He was an independent in the **Eastern House of Assembly** and then joined the House of Representatives. Taking a break from politics, Arikpo returned to London to study law. He practiced law in **Calabar** between 1957 and 1963. In 1963, he was appointed to the National Universities Commission. Arikpo served as the federal commissioner for external affairs between 1967 and 1975. He received a Coronation Medal in 1953. Arikpo is the author of *The Development of Modern Nigeria* (1967). A business complex in Lagos is named after him.

**ARINZE, CARDINAL FRANCIS (1932– ).** Born in November 1932 in the village of Eziowelle, in **Anambra State**, Arinze has devoted his life to the **Catholic Church**. After completing his primary and secondary school studies at Catholic missionary schools, Arinze studied at All Hallows Seminary in **Onitsha** (1947–1952) and Bigard Memorial Seminary in **Enugu** (1953–1955). He went to Rome and obtained his D.D. at Urban University in 1960. From 1960 to 1962, he taught at Bigard Memorial Seminary. He also attended the Institute of Education at the University of London from 1963 to 1964. In 1965, he returned to Nigeria as the world's youngest bishop. Two years later, he became the first black archbishop of Onitsha, a position he held until 1985. From 1979 to 1984, he served as president of the Catholic Bishops' Conference of Nigeria. Much of his focus while in Nigeria was on the traditional religious practices among the **Igbo**. To attract more followers, he sought to incorporate aspects of those practices into the Nigerian Catholic Church's services.

Arinze's religious work earned the respect of the late Pope John Paul II, who asked him to join the Vatican in 1982. Cardinal Arinze devoted his work in Rome to bridging the gap between Catholicism and other faiths, as the president of the Pontifical Council for Inter-religious Dialogue from 1984 to 2002. While in Rome, he became a cardinal in 1985. His success in the Catholic Church, coupled with the death of Pope John Paul II, launched Cardinal Arinze into the international spotlight. In April 2005, he became one of the possible choices as John Paul's successor. In comparison to other cardinals, his stance on social issues, such as birth control and **abortion**, was considered quite conservative. However, his experience of living in Nigeria, where the **population** is almost evenly split between **Christians** and Muslims, set him apart from other conservative cardinals because of his acceptance of **Islam**. In April 2005, Pope Benedict XVI awarded him the position of Cardinal Bishop of Velletri-Segni in Italy. He received an honorary degree from the University of Nigeria at **Nsukka** (1986) and the title *ochudouwa* (**chief**) of Eziowelle (1985). He is the author of several books about interfaith dialogue and peace. *See also* RELIGION.

**ARMED FORCES.** Nigeria has three branches of the armed forces: army, navy, and air force. Its armed forces were created out of the (Royal) **West African Frontier Force** (WAFF) of colonial times. The WAFF became the Nigerian Regiment in 1956. The Royal Nigerian Army formed in 1960 out of the Nigerian Regiment. In 1963, the Royal Nigerian Army became simply the Nigerian Army. Most of Nigeria's military leaders came out of army barracks.

Nigeria's navy and air force have histories similar to that of the army. The origin of the navy dates to 1914, with the creation of the Nigerian Marine Department. In 1958, the British formed the Royal Nigerian Navy. In 1963, the name was simplified to Nigerian Navy, with bases in **Calabar** and **Lagos**. The air force became an independent branch in 1964 through Nigerian Act No. 11, with great assistance from the German air force. In 1990, Nigeria claimed the largest naval force in West Africa. Major conflicts in which the armed forces have been involved include the **civil war** in Liberia and Nigeria's own civil war from 1967 to 1970.

Most men involved in a branch of the armed forces attended military school and training programs in Great Britain and Nigeria.

**General Yakubu Gowon, Major General David Akpode Ejoor, Major General Shehu Musa Yar'Adua,** and **Major Patrick Chukwuma Nzeogwu,** for example, attended the Royal Military Academy at Sandhurst. Most distinguished army generals after 1960 attended the Nigerian Defence Academy in **Kaduna,** the Nigerian Military School in **Zaria,** and the National Institute for Policy and Strategic Studies in **Jos.** The Nigerian Defence Academy was established in January 1964. It replaced the Royal Nigerian Military Training College in **Kaduna,** which was established in April 1960 to provide six-month training prior to overseas training. The establishment of the Defence Academy meant that all military training could be done in Nigeria. The Defence Academy was designed to train potential officers for the three branches of the armed forces. It became a degree-awarding institution in 1985 as a five-year program. **General Ibrahim Babangida** taught at the academy in the early 1970s. One of its cadets was **Lieutenant General Donaldson Oladipo Diya,** who attended from 1985 to 1987.

Since independence, the armed forces have gone from being defenders of the nation to being controllers of it. Nigeria's six **coups d'état** were all led by members of the armed forces. These power grabs were made by the military because they have the communication networks, skills, and weaponry needed. Members of the military also have the best access to the head of state they want to remove. The first coup d'état took place in 1966 and was led by army **Major General Johnson Aguiyi-Ironsi.** Aguiyi-Ironsi made himself the head of the short-lived **National Military Government.** A counter-coup took place in July 1966, ending with army **General Yakubu Gowon** as the new head of state. He ran the country through the **Supreme Military Council,** which served as the governing structure until 1985.

The third coup d'état happened in July 1975 and was organized by army **General Murtala Mohammed** and **General Olusegun Obasanjo,** who both fought on the federal side of the **civil war. Major General Muhammadu Buhari** of the army led a coup d'état in December 1983, ending the Second Republic. In August 1985, army General Ibrahim Babangida, who fought on the federal side during the civil war and taught at the Nigerian Defence Academy, seized power and proclaimed himself the new head of state. Babangida created the

**Armed Forces Ruling Council** and **Armed Forces Consultative Assembly** to govern Nigeria. Army **General Sani Abacha,** a graduate of the Nigerian Military Training College, launched Nigeria's sixth coup d'état in November 1993. In 1999, Obasanjo returned to the political arena as a civilian president. Nigeria's current president, **Umaru Musa Yar'Adua**, is one of only three heads of state not affiliated with the armed forces.

**ARMED FORCES CONSULTATIVE ASSEMBLY.** Established in June 1989 to facilitate cooperation among the **armed forces**, the **police**, and the **Armed Forces Ruling Council**, the assembly's role was to advise the council and, more specifically, **Major General Ibrahim Babangida**. It was disbanded in 1993.

**ARMED FORCES RULING COUNCIL.** From 1985 to 1993, under the leadership of **General Ibrahim Babangida**, the council was the highest governing body in Nigeria, charged with creating and enforcing national policies. It was based on the **Supreme Military Council** (1966–1979 and 1983–1985), with some modifications. It served as the country's legislative body, with the president as chairman. Notable political figures, such as **Major General Joshua Nimyel Dogonyaro**, were members. *See also* NATIONAL DEFENCE AND SECURITY COUNCIL.

**ARMY.** *See* ARMED FORCES.

**ARO PEOPLE.** The origin myth of the Aro people claims descent from Nna Uru, an **Igbo** man who settled on a tract of land located in the present-day Obinkita village of **Arochukwu**. This settlement emerged as a strong economic force in Igbo territory in the mid-17th century. The Aros' rise to power is often linked to the rise in the **slave trade**, which operated out of Arochukwu. The slaves who moved through Arochukwu were destined for the transatlantic slave trade from 1650 to the 1850s. It is believed that many of the slaves were Igbo. For this reason, the Aro are often vilified in Igbo history. The British conquest of **eastern Nigeria** included the Aro Expedition. The Aro people were the keepers of the **oracle**, *Chukwu Ibinokpabi*. The British attacked the Aro, forcing them to end their slave trade and destroying their oracle in 1901. **Mary Mitchell Slessor** acted as an arbiter in postconflict negotiations. The Aro had a kingship political system, as opposed to the more commonly recognized segmentary system most associated with Igbo society. Within the kingdom, societies such as the male-dominated Ekpe/Okonko played a key political role in settling internal disputes. Aro settlements can still be identified today in **Anambra State** and **Enugu State**.

**AROCHUKWU.** Home of the famous *Chukwu Ibinokpabi* **oracle**, of which the **Aro** people were custodians. The oracle settled disputes between villages. The success and good reputation of the oracle attracted other ethnic groups in southeastern Nigeria, such as the **Efik**. Large numbers of votaries and pilgrims would travel to the shrines of *Ibinokpabi* to worship and receive answers to their personal and spiritual questions. Because of this sacred power, Arochukwu also wielded control over regional trading. It was the capital of the Aro people and a major trading center for **slaves**.

**ART.** Art in Nigeria embodies the beauty and dissonance that makes up daily life in Nigeria. Much of the art produced in Nigeria is functional, with pockets of artist communities and schools producing art for sale and display in homes and galleries. As Nigeria's economy has weakened, its art production has suffered. Prior to the 19th century, Nigeria's communities developed distinct art styles. For example, the **Nok** created terracotta pottery and iron jewelry.

The era of modern art and formal artistic instruction began in the 1920s. It began when Kenneth C. Murray from Great Britain traveled to Nigeria in 1927 and taught art in secondary schools. He was the first formal art teacher to integrate art training into a classroom. In 1953, the Nigerian College of Arts, Sciences, and Technology was established in Ibadan. Three years later, it was moved to **Zaria** and became Nigeria's first formal art school. In 1955, **Yaba Higher College** opened its first art department. In 1961, **Ahmadu Bello University** was established in Zaria and took over the Nigeria College of Arts, Sciences, and Technology's art department. In 1973, the University of Ife (present-day **Obafemi Awolowo University**) launched a fine arts degree program; two years later, the University of Benin did the same. With the establishment of art schools came the founding of art journals and galleries to promote and display the works produced by Nigerian students.

The first art journal, *Nigerian Teacher* (later *Nigeria Magazine*), was launched in 1933 by the Education Department and specialized in promoting art and culture. The Exhibition Centre (referred to today as the Old Exhibition Centre) in **Lagos** was opened in 1943 and served as the headquarters for *Nigeria Magazine*. That same year, the Lagos Museum and the Department of Antiquities were opened. In 1963, the Museum of Popular Art was established at the *ataoja*'s (**chief** or **king**) palace in Osogbo. The New Exhibition Centre replaced the previous one in 1967. In 1977, Nigeria hosted the second **World Festival of Black and African Arts and Culture** (FESTAC '77). During the festival, several art exhibits introduced Nigerian modern art. In 1979, the long-awaited National Gallery of Modern Art was opened in Lagos, attached to the National Theatre complex. It houses artwork that was featured during FESTAC '77. Modern art from Nigeria, particularly during the 1970s, was often featured in European museums and private art galleries. In the past 20 years, Nigeria's art communities, galleries, and schools have been in steady decline and have become isolated. Young artists have found some assistance from small organizations, such as Terra Kulture in Lagos.

Most Nigerian artists are painters or sculptors. There are, however, several notable artists who produce impressive political cartoons and ceramics. Political cartoons are a popular form of art in Nigeria. Akinola Lasekan was Nigeria's first published political cartoonist. His work was regularly featured in the *West African Pilot*. Well-known sculptors include **Lamidi Olonade Fakeye**, George Bamidele, Ben Osawe, and **Benedict Chuka Enwonwu**. Nigeria's well-known painters include **Chief Aina Onabolu**, Ovia Idah, **Omodele Jegede**, and Yusef Grillo, to name a few. Ovia Idah was a well-known painter who created numerous relief murals and cement plaques between 1948 and 1968. **Susanne Wenger** and other artists, such as **Chief Muraina Oyelami**, were interested in celebrating **Yoruba** deities through art. Wenger started the New Sacred Art Movement in 1958. **Ladi Kwali** is one of Nigeria's best-known ceramicists. Nigeria's artists, regardless of medium or subject, have made significant contributions to modern art.

**ASHBY COMMISSION.** *See* HIGHER EDUCATION.

**ASIKA, ANTHONY UKPABI (1936–1994).** Born in June 1936 in **Jos,** as a young man Askia studied at St. Patrick's College in **Calabar** (1949), Edo College in **Benin** (1951), University College (present-day **University of Ibadan**) (1956–1961), and the University of California at Los Angeles (1961–1965), where he received his Ph.D. in political science. He worked as a clerk for the Onitsha Town Council and the Department of Marketing and Exports in **Lagos** during the early 1950s. From 1965 to 1967, he taught political science at the University of Ibadan. In 1967, his career aspirations turned toward national politics. Asika was as an administrator for **East Central State** (1967–1975) and a member of **General Yakubu Gowon's Supreme Military Council** (1970–1975). During the **civil war**, he publicized his desire to see Nigeria remain unified, which was not common for someone with ethnic ties to the East. Many people in **eastern Nigeria** praised him for ensuring that pensions and salaries were paid and international relief organizations arrived to repair the East after the civil war ended in 1970. Asika served as chairman of the Technical Committee on the Review of the National Population Census of 1973 and commissioner for Economic Development and Reconstruction in East Central State. In the private sector, he was chairman of Sigma Systems and Communications (1975), director of ORS Hospital Projects Nigeria, director of Guardian Press and Guardian Newspapers (1983), and chairman of the board for Industry Skoda (1985). Asika received a number of honorary degrees, awards, and titles, including honorary degrees from **Ahmadu Bello University** (1970) and the University of Nigeria at **Nsukka** (1971). He was a Rockefeller Foundation Scholar (1961–1965) and recipient of the Canada Council Non-Resident Fellowship in Economics (1961). Askia received the honorary title *ajie* (**chief**) of **Onitsha** (1985). *See also* CENSUS.

**ASMA'U, NANA (1793–1864).** A celebrated poet, Asma'u was a respected **Fulani** public figure. She was active in politics, **education**, and social reform. One of 40 children born to **Usman dan Fodio**, her name indicates that she was a twin. Her twin brother was Hassan. Instead of naming her Husseina, however, dan Fodio named her after a famous Muslim's daughter (Asma bint Abu Bakar). Asma'u also means "beautiful" or "noteworthy" in Arabic. "Nana" is an honorific that served to deepen her respectability. Asma'u managed a household of several hundred in an age when technology was limited. During times of war, she witnessed battles and recorded them. She was quadrilingual (Arabic, **Fula**, **Hausa**, and Tamachek) and a devoted member of the Islamic **Qadiriyya** order. She had six sons with her husband, Gidado.

In her writings, Asma'u focused heavily on the *Sunna*, which is writing on the exemplary way of life set forth by the Prophet Muhammad. As a young woman, she did the standard rote memorization of the **Koran** and was tutored by her family in **Islamic** philosophy, texts on prayer, mysticism, and legal matters. Asma'u set up educational programs for **women**, particularly those living in *purdah*. She sent elderly women to do in-house teaching. Many of her poems were mnemonic devices for literacy training. She wrote 19 elegies and didactic works for her students in whatever language was most comfortable for them. In her work, she demonstrates her respect for the realities of building an Islamic state and living a blameless life. Readers may also find several key features of Islamic poetry from **northern Nigeria**. Asma'u incorporated Sufi Islamic recitation, **Koranic** commentary, and praises of the Prophet Muhammad. She also wrote acrostic poetry (quite unique for the time), where the first letter of each line forms its own message, which relates to the message contained in the verses of the whole work. In her poem "So Verily," the last letters of each line spell out the Koranic line "so verily with every difficulty there is relief." She wrote about her brother, **Muhammad Bello**, and father, Usman dan Fodio, as well as other notable descendants of Usman lost to the historical record. Asma'u died in 1864 and was buried close to her father in **Sokoto**. *See also* LITERATURE.

**ASQUITH COMMISSION.** A committee established to report on the development of **higher education** in Nigeria in 1945. The Asquith Commission built on the work of the 1943 **Elliot Commission**. Members of the committee emphasized the importance of universities for creating a pool of educated Nigerians for colonial service. The focus was on preparing these individuals to serve as future leaders when the country achieved self-rule. What came out of the commission was the establishment of the first university in Nigeria, which was University College at Ibadan (present-day **University of Ibadan**) in 1948.

**ASSOCIATION FOR BETTER NIGERIA (ABN).** A **political party** formed in 1992 and led by Chief Francis Arthur, a wealthy businessman. ABN called for the extension of **General Ibrahim Babangida**'s military rule for at least four more years and the post-ponement of the slated **election of 12 June 1993**.

**ATIBA (?–1859).** Ruler of the **Oyo Empire** from 1836 until his death, Atiba was the son of **Abiodun** and is remembered for abolishing the practice of the eldest son dying with his father in 1858. He was the first *alaafin* (**king**) of Oyo to be succeeded by his son, Adelu. This change in tradition caused conflict within **Yoruba** territory. The Ijaye, for example, refused to recognize Adelu as the new *alaafin*. **Ibadan**, on the other hand, recognized him. This disagreement fractured the Oyo Empire and resulted in the **Ijaye War**. *See also* KURUNMI.

**ATTAHIRU I, MUHAMMADU (?–1903).** Also referred to as *Sarkin Musulmi* (chief of Muslims), Attahiru I was a great-grandson of **Usman dan Fodio** and son of Ahmad bin Abu Bakr Atiku. He was the last caliph of the **Sokoto Caliphate**, ruling from October 1902 to March 1903. The British attacked the Sokoto Caliphate and seized it, but not without a fight. Attahiru I led a Mahdist rebellion against British rule, which was based on the desire to forge a path for the arrival of the liberating religious leader. He emigrated eastward through **Zamfara** from **Kano** in search of this liberator, or *mahdi*. Tens of thousands of people followed him. In July 1903, the British defeated the Mahdist rebellion at Bormi, and Attahiru I was among those killed. Those who survived continued their travels to the Sudan.

**ATTAHIRU II, MUHAMMADU (?–1915).** Great-grandson of **Usman dan Fodio** and son of **Ali Babba bin Bello**, Attahiru II was the first **sultan** of **Sokoto** under British colonial rule. He held the position from 1903 to 1915. During his reign, Sokoto assisted the British colonial government in squashing a Mahdist rebellion in Satiru in 1906. Sokoto forces, led by Mallam Isa, marched to Satiru with 300 horsemen and foot soldiers and joined forces with the (Royal) **West African Frontier Force**. In general, Attahiru II faced the difficult challenge of retaining his subjects' respect as well as British approval.

**AWOKOYA, CHIEF STEPHEN OLUWOLE (1913–1985).** Born in July 1913, Awokoya attended Sagun United Primary School in Oro, St. Andrew's College in Oyo, and **Yaba Higher College** in **Lagos**. Awokoya was the first Nigerian to obtain a bachelor's degree in chemistry from the University of London, which he earned in 1946. For his advanced degree in science, he attended University College in London. He was the senior schoolmaster at Abeokuta Grammar School (1941–1943) and principal at Molusi College in Ijebu-Igbo (1949–1951). He served as minister of education for the **Western Region**, resigning in 1956. Awokoya was an active member of the **Action Group**. He worked with the United Nations Educational, Scientific, and Cultural Organization from 1967 to 1968 on improving science **education**. In 1973, Awokoya was a researcher for the University of Ife (present-day **Obafemi Awolowo University**). The Stephen Oluwole Awokoya Foundation of Science Education was founded in his honor. Awokoya received the honorary titles *aseto* (**chief**) of Awa and Commander of the Order of the British Empire.

**AWOLOWO, CHIEF OBAFEMI (1909–1987).** Awolowo was born in Ikenne, in **Ogun State**. To the **Yoruba** people, he was a magnetic political leader. In 1948, Awolowo formed **Egbe Omo Oduduwa**, a cultural organization, which became the **Action Group political party** in 1951. In this political party, he called for the end of colonial rule and Yoruba solidarity. He invoked Yoruba origin myths and cultural distinction to draw support. Awolowo also used his **newspaper**, the *Nigerian Tribune*, as a mouthpiece for his ideas. From October 1954 to December 1959, he served as the first **premier** of the **Western Region**. As premier, he introduced the **Universal Primary Education** program.

In 1963, he was accused of treason and imprisoned until 1966, when he was released by **General Yakubu Gowon**. That same year, the **Coker Commission** also found Awolowo guilty of **corruption**. In September 1966, Awolowo joined several other prominent Nigerian politicians to form the **National Conciliation Committee** in hopes of easing tension between **Chief Chukwuemeka Ojukwu** and Gowon. In 1977, he formed the **Unity Party of Nigeria**. In 1979 and again in 1983, he ran unsuccessfully for the presidency. Over the course of his political career, he received the title chief and national honors. He wrote several works laying out his hope and vision for not only Nigeria as a state, but also the Yoruba as a nation, including *Path to Nigerian Freedom* (1947) and *Thoughts on the Nigerian Constitution* (1966). In 1960, he published his autobiography, *Awo: The Autobiography of Chief Obafemi Awolowo*. The University of Ife changed its name to **Obafemi Awolowo University** in his honor. His picture is on the ₦100 bill. *See also* FIRST REPUBLIC.

**AZIKIWE, NNAMDI (1904–1996).** Born in **Zungeru** in present-day **Niger State**, Nnamdi Azikiwe, also known as "Zik," was one of Nigeria's most distinguished **Igbo** political figures. As a child he attended Church Missionary Society Central School in **Onitsha**. His career as a nationalist thinker and leader began in 1925 when he left Nigeria to pursue his postgraduate studies in the United States. He attended Storer College, Howard University, Lincoln University, the University of Pennsylvania, and Columbia University. Between 1934 and 1937, he was the editor-in-chief of the *African Morning Post* in **Ghana**. After returning to Nigeria, he started his **newspaper**, *West African Pilot*, as the voice of the nationalist movement in 1937, and worked as its editor-in-chief until 1947. In 1943, he drafted a memo entitled "Atlantic Charter and British West Africa," which called for **educational** and political reform as well as the end of colonial rule in 15 years. Several major newspaper editors signed it. Azikiwe also participated in the influential **Lagos Youth Movement** and set up one of Nigeria's major **political parties**, the **National Council of Nigeria and the Cameroons** (NCNC), in 1944 to represent his **ethnic group**.

When the NCNC's president, **Sir Herbert Macaulay**, passed away in 1946, Azikiwe replaced him. Between 1948 and 1951, he was a member of the **Legislative Council**. From 1952 to 1953, he was also a member of the **Western House of Assembly**. He was also the first **premier** of the **Eastern Region** (1954–1959). Azikiwe was also involved in the **Ibo State Union**. After his stint as premier, he served as president of the Senate in the Nigerian Federal Parliament in 1959 and 1960. On 1 October 1960, Azikiwe became the first indigenous **governor general** and Nigeria's first ceremonial president, a post he held until 1966. Throughout his life he remained active in politics, running for president in 1979 and again in 1983. He was the **Nigerian People's Party** candidate in 1979 and the **Progressive Parties Alliance** candidate in 1983. He received an honorary law degree and a doctorate in literature. Azikiwe was honored with the title chief. The international airport in **Abuja** is named after him, and his picture is engraved on the ₦500 bill. *See also* FIRST REPUBLIC.

## – B –

**BABALOLA, APOSTLE JOSEPH AYO (1904–1959).** Babalola was born in Ilofa, in **Kwara State**. After completing his primary education, he worked as a civil servant for the colonial Public Works Department. In 1930, after receiving a holy message telling him to go out and preach the word of God, he devoted himself to **Christian** missionary work in southwestern Nigeria. He spent the rest of his life traveling around West Africa, preaching and healing people. He saw indigenous **religions** as idolatrous and would destroy non-Christian religious objects. Babalola was the founder of the **Christ Apostolic Church**, earning him the title apostle. In 1955, he established the Christ Apostolic Church Teacher Training College at Efon Alaye in **Ondo State**.

**BABANGIDA, GENERAL IBRAHIM BADAMASI (1941– ).** Babangida was born in 1941 in Minna, in **Niger State**, and is of **Gwari** descent. He completed his primary and secondary schooling in Minna and Bida. He joined the army in 1963 and studied at the Nigerian Military Training College in **Kaduna** and the Indian Military Academy in India. He also studied at the National Institute of Policy and Strategic Studies in Kuru. During the **civil war**, Babangida led a battalion on the federal side. In the early 1970s, he taught at the Nigerian Defence Academy and commanded the Armoured Corps. He rose to the rank of major general and gave himself the title general when he became Nigeria's head of state. In 1984, he served as army chief of staff. Babangida came to power in August 1985 through a military **coup d'état** and remained in office until he was ousted in August 1993. One of Babangida's most disappointing actions as head of state was to annul the **election of 12 June 1993** and stop Nigeria's transition to democratic rule. From January 1993 to August 1993 he served as the chairman of the **National Defence and Security Council**.

Many saw the Babangida years as a period of economic decline and social division. Under his rule, **structural adjustment programs** were introduced. He abolished the **marketing board** structure of **foreign trade** in favor of trade liberalization and **privatization**. He made Nigeria a member of the Organization of the Islamic Conference in 1986 in an attempt to appease northern Muslims. Non-Muslims saw this as a sign of his attempting to turn Nigeria into an **Islamic** state. After leaving office, Babangida maintained a low profile until recruited by **General Alhaji Abdulsalami Abubakar** to act as an informal adviser. During the 1999 **elections** he offered financial support to **General Olusegun Obasanjo**'s campaign. In 2006, Babangida expressed his intention of running in the 2007 presidential election as a candidate for the **People's Democratic Party**, but he did not succeed in running.

**BABARI, SARKIN.** A *sarki* (ruler) who led **Gobir**, a **Hausa Kingdom**, from 1742 to 1770. He was the son of the previous ruler, Uban Iche. Babari launched military campaigns against **Katsina**, **Kano**, and **Borgu**. To facilitate the expansionist efforts south of Gobir, Babari offered his sister in marriage to the king of **Zamfara**. He encouraged the peaceful settlement of the **Hausa** from Gobir in Zamfara. In 1764, however, the peace was broken by Babari's army sacking Zamfara. His critics saw him as a harsh ruler who levied high *jangali* on **Fulani** herders. *See also* YUNFA.

**BADAGRY.** One of seven major ports in Nigeria used for the trading of slaves during the transatlantic **slave trade**. It was the first location of several European **Christian** missions, such as the (Anglican) **Church Missionary Society**. Prior to colonial rule, Badagry was a major **Yoruba** town near **Lagos**. Its current **population** is approximately 241,000.

**BAFYAU, PASCHAL MYELERI (1947– ).** Bafyau was born March 1947 in Lamude, in **Gongola State**. As a young man, Bafyau attended St. Patrick's School, St. Rita's School, and Villanova Secondary School. He also attended the School of Agriculture (1966) at Kabba, the Railway Permanent Way Training School (1967–1969) in **Zaria**, and the National Institute for Policy and Strategic Studies in **Jos**. Outside Nigeria, he studied at the International Centre for Advanced Technical and Vocational Training in Italy. He held several different posts in Nigeria's **trade union** structure. He was general secretary for the Northern Nigeria Agricultural Students Union (1966–1967) and chairman (school branch) of the Railways Permanent Way Workers' Union (1969–1973). In the following decade, he was district secretary for the Nigerian Union of Railwaymen (1972–1973), vice president of the Railway Permanent Way Workers' Union (1974–1978), general secretary of the Nigerian Union of Railwaymen (1978–1979), and vice president of the **Nigerian Labour Congress** (1988–1989). From 1989 to 1994, he served as president of the Nigerian Labour Congress. In the political arena, he was a member of the National Constitutional Conference (1995) and the Political Bureau (1986–1989). He was also a member of the Constituent Assembly in **Abuja** (1988–1989) and chairman of the Nigeria Committee in Defence of Nicaragua (1988–1989).

**BAGAUDA.** A name from **Hausa oral tradition** with various meanings. In some instances, it is the name of a migrating group led by a man named Bagauda, who settled in **Kano** between the 10th and 11th centuries. Another version of the story has Bagauda as the grandson of **Prince Bayajidda** of Baghdad and a princess from **Daura**. Bagauda has also been credited as the founder of the **Hausa Kingdoms**, an accomplishment usually attributed to Prince Bayajidda. In short, the identity and achievements of Bagauda are not entirely clear in the historical record. Nonetheless, the story of Bagauda fits into a common practice in West Africa of assigning the origin of an **ethnic group** to a *kisra* (**king**), a Muslim man from the Middle East who spread **Islam** and established dynasties across the region sometime between the 7th and 11th centuries. The *Song of Bagauda* bears his name. This precious written work in Hausa tracks the history of Hausa kings with artistic flair and was recited by peasants in public forums. Like the *Kano Chronicle*, it provides a rare glimpse of early Hausa history.

**BAIKIE, WILLIAM BALFOUR (1825–1864).** The Scottish captain of the ship *Dayspring*, which made an expedition to research the political situation and economic prospects at the Niger–Benue confluence. Baikie made reports in the 1850s that encouraged British **trade**

and, later, territorial claims to the region. He is also most associated with articulating the British interest in favoring northern Muslims over non-Muslims (and non-Christians) in **northern Nigeria**. After the *Dayspring* crashed near Jebba, Baikie and others settled in **Lokoja**.

**BAKASSI BOYS.** A primarily male vigilante group armed with guns that patrols local neighborhoods in southeastern Nigeria. Such groups have formed in response to **police** shortages and failures. The Bakassi Boys began their activities in Abia and **Onitsha** in **Anambra State**. In 2000, they were officially recognized by Anambra State. The Bakassi Boys have been accused of extrajudicial killings. Citizens of the region also complain that these men are recruited for political purposes and receive support from state and local governments. They have detained and tortured hundreds of people in makeshift head-quarters and prisons without regard for **human rights**.

**BAKASSI PENINSULA.** A **petroleum**-rich area of some 1,000 square kilometers on the coastal border of Nigeria and **Cameroon**. Both countries claimed it as part of their territory. The dispute over the region dates back to the rivalry between European powers over territory in West Africa. In the late 19th century, **Great Britain** and Germany agreed to the delimitation. This placed the peninsula under British control as part of Nigeria. In 1913, however, a new boundary agreement placed the peninsula in Cameroon. After 1960, the poten-tial for lucrative petroleum development in the region became clear to both Nigeria and Cameroon. In the early 1990s, Nigeria asserted its claim as the rightful authority, and Cameroon responded by send-ing troops to the peninsula. France also sent armed reinforcements to Cameroon. The dispute escalated to the point that international arbitration was necessary. In 2002, the International Court of Justice (ICJ) ruled in favor of Cameroon. In December 2003, Nigeria and Cameroon withdrew their military forces from the region and began the process of transferring authority. It took until August 2006, how-ever, for Nigeria to release the peninsula to Cameroon as required by the ICJ. Tension over the region continues. In November 2007, Cameroonian soldiers were killed by Nigerian men in uniform. Those claiming Nigerian allegiance in the region have expressed displea-sure with living in Cameroon. *See also* FOREIGN POLICY.

**BALEWA, SIR ALHAJI ABUBAKAR TAFAWA (1912–1966).** Born in December 1912 in the town of Tafawa Balewa, in **Bauchi State**, Balewa attended secondary school at Katsina Higher College. He also studied at the University of London's Institute of Education. When he returned to Nigeria, he worked as a teacher and school administrator at Bauchi Middle School. Balewa became involved in politics in the late 1940s, serving as a member of the **Legislative Council** and **House of Assembly**. In 1949, he and others, such as **Sir Alhaji Ahmadu Bello**, founded a cultural association, **Jam'iyyar Mutanen Arewa**, which later became the **Northern People's Congress**. He served as the deputy leader of the party. Between 1951 and 1966, Balewa held several government positions, including minister of works (1951–1954), minister of transport (1954–1957), and prime minister (1957–1966). In 1962, he declared a state of emergency in the Western Region and accused **Chief Obafemi Awolowo** of the **Action Group** of treason. Balewa's critics described him as a puppet of Bello. Balewa was assassinated during Nigeria's first military **coup d'état** in January 1966. The British found him a beneficial political ally and agreeable individual, which they showed by awarding him several honors in the 1950s, including Knight Commander of the Order of the British Empire. Balewa also acquired the affectionate nickname "Balewa the Good." His picture is on the ₦5 bill.

**BALOGUN, CHIEF KOLAWOLE (1922–2002).** Born in April 1922 in Osogbo, in **Osun State**, Balogun attended the Government College in **Ibadan** and also the University College in London, where he received a law degree. He also earned an M.A. and Ph.D. He was called to the bar in 1951. He worked as a **radio** announcer and editor for the *West African Pilot* **newspaper**. Balogun also served as a member of the **Lagos Town Council** (1953–1955), Oshun Divisional Council (1954–1955), **Western House of Assembly** (1953–1954), and House of Representatives in **Lagos** (1954–1958). In 1958, Balogun cofounded the **Democratic Party of Nigeria and the Cameroons** as a splinter group of the **National Council of Nigeria and the Cameroons**. He served as the federal minister of labor and welfare in 1955. During the 1960s, he was the high commissioner to **Ghana** (1960–1961), chairman of the Nigerian National Shipping Line (1962–1965), commissioner of economic planning and social development for the **Western Region** (1967), and commissioner of education for the Western Region (1968–1970). He was a cofounder of the **Nigerian People's Party** in 1978 and the **Great Nigerian People's Party** in the late 1970s. Balogun was ejected from the latter and subsequently joined the **National Party of Nigeria**. He received the honorary title *jagun* (**chief**) of Otan. Balogun died in December 2002.

**BANANAS.** Bananas are found in an array of types that vary in color (yellow or red), size, and taste. They are native to southeastern Asia. In general, bananas have a short shelf life, which requires localized production and marketing. Nigeria grows a range of bananas, mostly for domestic consumption. Most Nigerians consume bananas in their simplest form, removing the peel and eating them when ripe. Plantains, a type of banana, are prepared primarily by frying. In the **Yoruba language**, fried plantains are called *dodo* and grilled plantains are called *booli*. When visiting **Hausa** territory, British officials documented the use of banana leaves in making soap. For at least a century, the people of **Brass** enjoyed the *idu pele olali* festival ("feast of banana cutting"), which includes the cutting of a banana tree. The direction the banana tree falls reveals whether the creator god accepts their offerings. Bananas are one of Nigeria's most valuable **agricultural** products. *See also* MARKETS; TRADE.

**BANJO COMMISSION.** A commission created to review the **education** system in the **Western Region** in 1955. It focused on the weaknesses of the primary and secondary curriculum. The commission isolated teaching as a major flaw. It recommended to the regional government the funding of teacher training programs and the recruitment of skilled teachers. *See also* UNIVERSAL PRIMARY EDUCATION.

**BANKING.** In addition to having a national bank that handles the government's revenue and investment, Nigeria also has an array of local and international banks. The Central Bank of Nigeria was established in 1959, which the **World Bank** had recommended doing in 1954. The central bank is charged with regulating and controlling Nigeria's monetary and financial activities, including issuing **currency**, maintaining national reserves, acting as the nation's bank, and advising the federal government on financial issues. It also has the authority to grant and cancel licenses of independent banks operating in Nigeria. Since its formation it has undergone several changes in the level of control it can exercise over other banks and financial institutions. The central bank enjoyed a great deal of autonomy in 1991, much of which it lost in 1997 when it returned to the Ministry of Finance. The central bank was separated from the Ministry of Finance by **General Ibrahim Badamasi Babangida** in the mid-1980s as part of Nigeria's **structural adjustment program**.

Nigeria also has specialized banks, such as the Nigerian Bank for Commerce and Industry and the Federal Mortgage Bank. The Nigerian Bank for Commerce and Industry was created in April 1973 to provide loans for Nigerian-run businesses, particularly manufacturers. It was also designed to identify serious entrepreneurs and assist them with the loan and repayment process. The Nigerian Agricultural Bank was created in 1973 to advance agricultural production in rural areas by creating accessible loans for **agricultural** development. The federal government created the People's Bank of Nigeria in 1989 to offer banking to low-income families and small business owners. By the 1980s, Nigeria's banking system had undergone few substantial changes and comprised about 28 commercial banks, a handful of development banks, and 12 merchant banks. Financial instability during the 1990s caused many banks to collapse.

All of Nigeria's banks face hardship with regard to the strength of Nigeria's financial sector and currency exchange. Nigerian banks find themselves in vigorous competition with private, unofficial exchanges run from a simple storefront or on the street. These informal exchanges often give a better rate of exchange, which attracts tourists and locals alike. Although this practice is illegal, it continues unabated. *See also* ECONOMY; NATIONAL ECONOMIC RECONSTRUCTION FUND.

**BAPTIST CHURCH.** The Nigerian Baptist Convention, based in **Ibadan**, is one of the largest Baptist organizations in the world. It is one of many Christian churches that sent missionaries to Nigeria in hopes of spreading **Christianity**. Baptists in Nigeria today number an estimated three to six million. The Baptists started their proselytizing in the 1850s as part of an overseas mission by the Southern

Baptist Convention of the United States. For example, in 1853, a Baptist missionary was established in Ijaye. The civil war in the United States forced a hiatus in their work until 1875. The Nigerian Baptist Convention was formally established in 1912 and today operates nine theological schools for pastors, hospitals in Ogbomoso and Eku, and primary and secondary schools. Bowen University in Iwo is named after **Reverend Thomas J. Bowen**, a missionary from the United States. Baptist churches were also established by Nigerians. For example, **Mojola Agbebi** founded the Ebenezer Baptist Church and was a leader of the Native Baptist Church in **Lagos** in the late 19th and early 20th centuries.

**BASORUN.** A title given to the leader of the council of notables, or *oyomesi*, in the **Oyo Empire**. The council comprised seven nonroyal **chiefs** of each capital city, who advised the **king** of Oyo, the *alaafin*. The *basorun* often demonstrated power that went beyond that of the king. **Gaha** was a notable *basorun* who forced the suicide of several *alaafin* in the mid-18th century. The nomination of a new *alaafin* required the final approval of the *basorun*. The *basorun* exercised authority between the death of one *alaafin* and installation of another. During a period of political instability, the *basorun* served as ruler in the mid-18th century while waiting for the next *alaafin*, Ayibi, to become old enough to hold the post. The *basorun* also served as commander-in-chief.

**BAUCHI.** The capital of **Bauchi State**, it was one of the towns founded during the **Fulani jihad** that established **the Sokoto Caliphate** in **northern Nigeria**. It was founded in 1753. In the mid-20th century, Bauchi served as one of the locations where followers of the radical Muslim **Muhammadu Marwa** were located. Today, Bauchi is home to the Abubakar Tafawa Balewa University, and its **population** is approximately 300,000.

**BAUCHI GENERAL IMPROVEMENT UNION.** A union formed in 1943 by **Sa'adu Zungur, Alhaji Muhammed Aminu Kano**, and **Sir Alhaji Abubakar Tafawa Balewa** from the disbanded Bauchi Discussion Circle. The purpose of the organization was to agitate for reforms in the **Native Authority** system. The **emir** of **Bauchi**, however, saw the union as undermining his authority and banned it from using public spaces for its meetings. Although the union was short lived, it prompted the formation of similar pressure groups in the North. It has been heralded by many as the first **political party** to form in **northern Nigeria**. Several of its founders and supporters later formed the **Northern People's Congress**.

**BAUCHI STATE.** Bauchi State was created in 1976 out of **North-Eastern State**. Its population is predominantly Muslim. In 1996, Bauchi was reduced in size by the creation of **Gombe State**. It has a fairly heterogeneous **population**, including **Hausa**, **Fulani**, Gerawa, Ningawa, and Tangale. The capital is the town of **Bauchi**. It is one of 12 states that have incorporated **Shari'a** into their criminal codes. It is also one of Nigeria's current 36 states. Since 1928, it has been home to Teacher's College at Toro, which was the second **higher education** institution in **northern Nigeria**. Bauchi State is also home to Abubakar Tafawa Balewa University and Bauchi State Polytechnic. Economic activity in the state includes the production of maize, rice, and **groundnuts**. In the northern corner of Bauchi State lies the Hade Jia Nguru Wetlands, which provide moisture and fertile soil for **agricultural** development and suitable grazing land for herding. *See also* STATE CREATION.

**BAYAJIDDA, PRINCE.** Bayajidda (also referred to as Abu Yazid and sometimes **Bagauda**) was believed to be a Muslim leader from Baghdad who rode a horse and maintained a large military force sometime between the 7th and 10th centuries. At the town of **Daura,** he reportedly killed a dangerous snake, which had prevented people from collecting water at a well. He married a princess from Daura (another version of the story connects her to the the **Kanem-Bornu Empire**) and became the descendant of the seven founders of the first **Hausa Kingdoms** in the 10th century. The life of Bayajidda is unclear, and scholars have linked him to a common **oral tradition** in Nigeria that identifies him as a *kisra* (**king**), a Muslim man from the Middle East who spread **Islam** and established kingdoms across West Africa. A variant on the story is that Bayajidda's son, Bawo, is the founder of the Hausa Kingdoms.

**BAYELSA STATE.** Created in 1996 out of **Rivers State**, Bayelsa is an acronym of three former local governments, **Brass**, Yenagoa, and Sagbama. Its capital is Yenagoa. Bayelsa State is located in southeastern Nigeria on the coast, and its eastern border is the **Niger River**. It is one of Nigeria's current 36 states and part of the **Niger Delta** region. **Christianity** and indigenous are the major forms of **religion**. The people of Bayelsa represent four **ethnic groups**: Izon, Nembe, Ogbia, and Epie-Atissa. Bayelsa's main economic activities are fishing and **oil palm** cultivation. *See also* STATE CREATION.

**BAYERO, ALHAJI ABDULLAHI (1881–1953).** Bayero was born in **Kano**, the son of Muhammadu Abbas, the **emir** of Kano from 1903 to 1919. Bayero served as a district head in Bichi, located in **Kano State**. He was the tenth emir of Kano, from 1926 until his death in December 1953. As the emir, he made development a high priority for Kano and was successful. In 1934, he visited King George V in England. He was the first emir of Kano to travel to Mecca by car during his *hajj* (**pilgrimage**). Bayero encouraged Muslim students in **northern Nigeria** to attend Western-style schools. In 1964, Ahmadu Bello College changed its name to Bayero University to honor him.

**BAYERO, ALHAJI ADO (1930– ).** Born in June 1930 in **Kano**, Bayero studied at Kwaru Koranic School (1934–1939), Kofar Kudu Elementary School (1939–1942), and Kano Middle School (1942–1947). He also attended the School of Arabic Studies (1947–1949) and Zaria Clerical Training College (1951–1952). After completing his studies, Bayero worked as a clerk for the Bank of British West Africa in Kano (1949–1955) and for the Kano City Council. He also worked for the Kano Native Authority. Bayero is credited with recognizing the need for and initiating people-oriented reforms. He was a member of the **Northern House of Assembly** in **Kaduna** (1955–1957), Northern Region Development Corporation, and Northern Board of Nigerian Broadcasting. From 1957 to 1962, he worked as the chief of **police** for the Kano Native Authority. He was ambassador to Senegal (1962–1963), chancellor of the University of Nigeria at **Nsukka** (1966–1975), and vice president of the International Association of University Presidents (1978). Muslims admire his commitment to the maintenance and purity of **Islam** in Nigeria. He received the honorary title **emir** of Kano in 1963 and Commander of the Order of the Federal Republic of Nigeria. He was Kano's longest serving emir. *See also* NATIVE AUTHORITY.

**BEECROFT, JOHN (1790–1854).** Born in England, Beecroft served as the British consul for the coastal territories of Nigeria. When he visited **Abeokuta** in 1851, Chief Ogubonna presented him with locally produced gifts such as **cotton**, ginger, and pepper. In 1851, deposed king **Akintoye** of **Lagos** requested his assistance in restoring him to the throne. Beecroft agreed on the condition that Akintoye abolish the **slave trade** and trade exclusively with British merchants in other commodities. Beecroft died on the island of **Fernando Poo**.

**BEKEDEREMO-CLARK, JOHN PEPPER.** *See* CLARK, JOHN PEPPER.

**BELLO, SIR ALHAJI AHMADU (1909/1910–1966).** Bello was born in June 1910 (many sources say 1909) in Rabah, a town near **Sokoto**. He was the great-great-grandson of the famous **Usman dan Fodio**. As a young man, Bello studied at Sokoto Provincial School and Katsina Training College. He taught English and mathematics at Sokoto Middle School from 1931 to 1934. Following in his family's footsteps, he devoted himself to politics. Starting in 1934, Bello served as the district chief of Rabah for four years. In 1938, he became the *sardauna* (leader of war) of Sokoto, a lifelong position, and a member of the Sokoto Native Authority. When he went up against Abubakar for the position of **sultan** of Sokoto and lost, Abubakar appointed him *sardauna* as a conciliatory gesture. In 1949, Bello was a member of several political bodies: the Nigeria Coal Board, Northern Regional Production Development Board, and Northern Regional Development Board. That same year, Bello and others, including **Sir Alhaji Abubakar Tafawa Balewa**, founded the **Northern People's Congress**. Between 1952 and 1954, he was a member of the **Northern House of Assembly**, Northern Region Ministry of Works, and Northern Region Ministry of Local Government and Community Development. In October 1954, he became the first **premier** of the **Northern Region**.

When Nigeria gained its **independence** in 1960, Bello maintained a great deal of influence from his post in **northern Nigeria** over the entire country through his colleague, Balewa. He was the first chancellor of the University of Northern Nigeria, which later changed its name to **Ahmadu Bello University** to honor him. He was murdered in January 1966 during a military **coup d'éta**t that ended Nigeria's **First Republic**. In his poetry, **Christopher Okigbo** described Bello affectionately as "the elephant." Bello received the honorary title Knight Commander of the Order of the British Empire. His image is on the ₦200 bill.

**BELLO, MUHAMMAD (1781–1837).** Bello was the son of **Usman dan Fodio**, the leader of a **Fulani jihad** in **northern Nigeria**. As one of the jihadist flag bearers, he led an attack on the town of Birnin Gwari (located south of **Zaria**) in 1810. He and his brother, Abdullahi ibn Muhammed, were rewarded with territory as part of the newly established **Sokoto Caliphate**. After his father's death in 1817, Bello became the caliph. It was he who made Sokoto the capital of the caliphate. He is also remembered for successfully protecting Sokoto from the **Kanem-Bornu Empire**. Bello was succeeded by Abu Bakr Atiku. His sister, **Nana Asma'u**, described him in her poetry as valiant and politically influential.

**BENDEL STATE.** Created in 1976 out of **Mid-Western State**, Bendel State was located in the **Niger Delta** region. The southwestern boundary of the state was the Gulf of Guinea and the eastern boundary was the **Niger River**. In 1991, it was broken into two states, **Edo** and **Delta**. *See also* STATE CREATION.

**BENIN.** Benin was the center of a great **Benin Kingdom**. Today, it is the modern capital of **Edo State**, located in the **Niger Delta**. A thousand years ago, the people of Benin used the complicated method of lost-wax casting when forging iron tools and adornments. Ancient Benin is particularly known for its bronze statues and masks, which are displayed in museums around the world. It was one of Nigeria's seven major slave trading ports during the era of the transatlantic **slave trade**. It was also a major center for the trade of ivory and metal works. During the 15th century, Benin was a strong kingdom. According to **oral tradition**, the Benin people are of **Yoruba** descent. **Oranmiyan**, the son of Oduduwa, married the daughter of a Bini chief. When Oranmiyan left Benin and returned to **Ile-Ife**, he left the throne to his son, Eweka I. During the **First Republic**, Benin served as the capital of the **Mid-Western**

**Region**. Today, it is home to the University of Benin, and its **population** is approximately one million.

**BENIN DELTA PEOPLE'S PARTY (BDPP).** A **political party** formed in October 1953 by **Akenzua II** of **Benin**. The primary goal of the organization was to promote the idea of creating a new region out of Benin and Delta provinces called the **Mid-Western Region**. It also served as an alternative party to the **Action Group** in the region. It obtained its goal in August 1963. *See also* MID-WEST STATE MOVEMENT.

**BENIN KINGDOM.** The Benin Kingdom existed between roughly the 11th and 16th centuries. Its history is divided into two phases, the first being the *ogiso* (**king**) dynasty of the Edo-speaking people (also referred to as Bini). According to **oral tradition**, the second phase was marked by the arrival of **Oranmiyan**, a **Yoruba**, from **Ile-Ife** in the 14th century. After some time, Oranmiyan decided to return to Ile-Ife and left his son, Eweka I, as the ruler. In the 15th century, Benin thrived and expanded, especially under the leadership of **Ewuare**. Ewuare constructed walls around Benin for protection. **Ozolua**, one of Ewuare's sons, traveled with Joao Alfonso d'Aveiro to Portugal and returned to Benin with luxury items from the Portuguese king. Some of Benin's people converted to **Christianity** and established a few churches, such as Holy Cross Cathedral. **Islam** was introduced in the 19th century. By that time the British had become interested in dismantling Benin's authority for their own territorial interests. This process started with the British forcing the **Gallwey Treaty** of 1892 on Benin. In 1897, the British attacked Benin and sent Ovonramwen into exile for refusing to comply with the terms of the treaty. Ovonramwen was deposed and sent to **Calabar,** where he died in 1914. *See also* BENIN; ESIGIE; IDIA.

**BENIN, REPUBLIC OF.** Nigeria's eastern neighbor. It is not to be confused with the city of **Benin** or the early **Benin Kingdom**. It is also different than the very short-lived Republic of Benin that existed under the authority of the secessionist **Republic of Biafra** from 19 to 21 September 1967. Several of Nigeria's **ethnic groups** straddle the Nigeria–Benin border established by the British and French in the late 19th century. Much of present-day Benin was claimed by the Dahomey Empire between the 17th and 19th centuries. The Dahomey Empire's dominant ethnic group was the **Yoruba**, who were divided during colonial demarcation in the 1880s. The French took control of Dahomey. The **Oyo Empire** included a substantial portion of Dahomey territory until 1818. In return, Dahomey terrorized Yoruba towns during the second half of the 19th century. They also attacked and were defeated by kingdoms in **Borgu**. *See also* ANGLO–FRENCH AGREEMENT.

**BENSON, CHIEF THEOPHILUS OWOLABI SHOBOWALE (1917–2008).** Born in July 1917, Benson attended the Church Missionary Society Grammar School in **Lagos** and the University College in London, where he received a law degree. From 1937 to 1943 he worked as a customs officer in Nigeria. He was called to the bar in 1947. After returning to Nigeria, he served as chief party whip, financial secretary, and legal adviser to the **National Council of Nigeria and the Cameroon**. He was a member of the **Lagos Town Council** (1950–1952) and acted as deputy mayor of Lagos (1952–1953). He also served as the federal minister of information, broadcasting, and culture (1959–1960) and was elected to represent Lagos in the **Western House of Assembly** (1951–1954) and to the House of Representatives (1954). Benson also acted as the whip in the House of Representatives from 1954 to 1959. In 1966, he was a member of the Federal Cabinet of the Prime Minister. He received several honorary titles from the city of New Orleans (1984) and borough of West Chester (1997) as well as the titles Commander of the Order of the Federal Republic (1983) and Knight Grand Commander of the Liberian Humane Order of African Redemption. Benson died in February 2008.

**BENUE-PLATEAU STATE.** A state that existed from 1967 to 1970, located in south-central Nigeria. It was one of six states created out of the **Northern Region**. The capital was **Jos**. *See also* BENUE STATE; STATE CREATION.

**BENUE RIVER.** One of Nigeria's two largest and most historically significant rivers. It flows from the Adamawa Mountains in **Cameroon** northwest toward **Yola** and then southwest to **Lokoja**, where it meets the **Niger River**. It is the longest tributary of the Niger River. Prior to the 20th century, the Benue served as a "water highway" for regional and **foreign trade**. A variety of goods was transported along the river. Heinrich Barth, a German explorer, encountered the Benue River in 1851 and a year late, announced in Europe that it connected to the Niger River at Lokoja.

**BENUE STATE.** A state located in southeastern Nigeria that shares a short border with **Cameroon**. It is named after the **Benue River**, which runs through the northern part of the state. Benue State is one of Nigeria's current 36 states. The major **ethnic groups** residing in the state are the **Tiv**, Idoma, and Igede. The capital is Makurdi. Economic activity in the state includes cultivating **cassava** and **yams** and mining natural gas and **coal**. Benue produces a substantial portion of Nigeria's soy beans. Benue State was created in 1976 from **Benue-Plateau State** and a portion of **Kwara State**. *See also* STATE CREATION.

**BIAFRA, REPUBLIC OF.** A country located on the Bight of Biafra that emerged out of the **Eastern Region**. It was established in 30 May 1967 when the Eastern Region seceded. This move marked the start of the **civil war**. The Republic of Biafra collapsed and was reintegrated into the federal republic of Nigeria in January 1970. The republic developed its own flag and **currency**, the Biafran pound. To promote and defend the republic, **Chief Chukwuemeka Ojukwu** implemented special fighting forces and propaganda campaigns. The Biafran Organization of Freedom Fighters served as a paramilitary unit. **Colonel Joe "Hannibal" Achuzie** was its strongest field commander. The Biafran Overseas Press Service, launched in 1968, served as the republic's public relations exchange. It was based in Geneva to reach European sympathizers and was run by William Bernhardt, an American publicist. The propaganda campaign focused on the starvation and ill health suffered by Biafrans. During the war, **Chief Arthur Nwankwo** wrote for the Propaganda Directorate of Biafra and edited the *Biafra Newsletter*. *See also* AHIARA DECLARATION; POLITICAL ORIENTATION COMMITTEE.

**BIG MAN.** A colloquial term for a man who has advanced in age and acquired wealth. These men are influential members of a community, providing advice and financial loans. A Big Man is often associated with a particular church or mosque and will often fund development projects. These individuals also frequently hold a political post. A **Yoruba** proverb highlights what makes a big man: "I have money, I have people, what else is there that I have not got?" *See also* COR-RUPTION; ECONOMY; HOMETOWN ASSOCIATIONS.

**BINNS FISCAL REVIEW COMMISSION.** *See* REVENUE AL-LOCATION.

***BLACK ORPHEUS.*** A literary journal that was run out of **Ibadan** and published irregularly between September 1957 and August 1967. It was started in 1957 by Ulli Beier (husband of the artist **Susanne Wenger**) and Janheinz Jahn. From 1960 to 1964, **Akinwande Olu-wole Soyinka** acted as coeditor. The full name of the journal was *Black Orpheus: A Journal of African and Afro-American Literature*, which was taken from Jean-Paul Satre's famous "Orpheus Noir" introduction published in 1948. The focus of *Black Orpheus* was on celebrating and showcasing a range of literary styles written by peo-ple from Africa and the African Diaspora. Well-known Nigerian con-tributors to the journal included Soyinka and **Christopher Okigbo**. It was the primary venue for cutting-edge Nigerian **literature**.

**BONNY.** A coastal city on the Bonny River, an estuary of the **Niger River**. For centuries, Bonny's wealth was based on the **oil palm** trade. It was one of Nigeria's major **slave trading** ports during the era of the transatlantic slave trade. The (Anglican) **Church Mission-ary Society** set up a **Christian** mission at Bonny in 1861. Along with missionaries came European traders. In the 18th and 19th centuries, Bonny was organized into trading houses representing each powerful clan. For example, the Anna Pepple House was run by Opubu until he passed it to Alali, who was not of the royal clan. Upon Alali's death, the house elected **Jaja**, also not of the royal clan. In 1868, the Anna Pepple House, under the leadership of Jaja, was attacked by a rival trading house. Jaja decided to relocate his trading house to Opobo instead of engaging in war. Some of the earliest written records in **southern Nigeria** include correspondence from Jaja of Opobo and the papers of the *amanyanabo* (**chief**) of Bonny dating to the mid-1800s. Today, Bonny is one of Nigeria's most important centers for **trade** and processing **petroleum**. In fact, Nigeria's high-quality crude oil is named Bonny Light. Economic activities in the city include petroleum and fishing. Bonny has a **population** of approximately 215,000.

**BORGU.** The region within which a series of dynasties and kingdoms created a shared history for its inhabitants. The origin of the name Borgu is unclear. Europeans used the term to refer to the people who lived along what is now the westernmost edge of the **Niger River**. Scholars have concluded, however, that the people did not live as one Borgu **ethnic group**. The people of this region speak six related languages: Bissa, Tienga, Boko, Kamberi, Batonu, and Bokobaru.

According to **oral tradition**, Borgu was established in the 10th century by a *kisra* (a dynastic founder claiming a linkage to a particular Persian leader). This settlement caused migration and political reconfiguration. A series of groups that inhabited Borgu after the 10th century appear to have a shared disdain for the spread of **Islam**. In the 16th century, Muslim missionaries from the Songhay Empire (in present-day Mali) went to Borgu and were sent away. The area of Borgu consisted of three kingdoms—Bussa, Illo, and Nikki—located between the **Yoruba** to the South and the **Hausa** to the North at various times between the 1st and 19th centuries. Bussa was considered the oldest and most prosperous because of its location on the Niger River. Borgu was a major producer of shea butter (used for cooking and lighting), which was sold to the **Nupe**, Hausa, and Yoruba. When members of the **Royal Niger Company** arrived in Borgu in 1824, they saw Bussa as the largest kingdom in the region and assumed that a treaty with Bussa gave the British full claim to the area. The French, however, made the same conclusion about their agreement with Nikki. In the 1890s, the French colonized Nikki, while the British claimed Illo and Bussa. These claims were resolved by the **Anglo–French Agreement**. Today, the Borgu are considered part of the **Middle Belt** region. The people of Borgu cultivate vegetables, maize, and beans. *See also* TRADE.

**BORNO STATE.** Created in 1976 out of **North-Eastern State**, it contained **Yobe State** until 1991. It is located in northeastern Nigeria, sharing a border with **Cameroon**, **Chad**, and **Niger**. It is one of

Nigeria's current 36 states and one of 12 states to incorporate aspects of **Shari'a** into their criminal law. The capital is **Maiduguri**. **Islam** is the dominant **religion**. The northeastern corner of the state is advantageously located in the Lake Chad basin. The **Kanuri** are the major **ethnic group** in Borno State. Borno was the location of the great **Kanem-Bornu Empire** until the mid-19th century. During colonial rule and the first seven years of Nigeria's **independence**, Borno remained relatively autonomous. Today, economic activity in the state includes farming, herding livestock (such as cattle and goats), and mining (such as limestone and iron ore). **Agricultural** products cultivated in the state include **groundnuts**, maize, beans, and onions. *See also* BORNU KINGDOM; STATE CREATION.

**BORNU KINGDOM.** This was a kingdom that was situated in the Lake Chad basin, in present-day **Borno State**. In the 14th century, the kingdom of Kanem, of the **Kanuri** people, fell, forcing its relocation to Bornu. This marked the start of the great **Kanem-Bornu Empire**.

**BORNU YOUTH MOVEMENT (BYM).** Created in June 1954 by a group of **Kanuri** men, led by Alhaji Ibrahim Imam, the movement sought change within the **Native Authority** and the **Northern People's Congress political party**. They campaigned for the end of **corruption** and the creation of a **North-Eastern State**. The Northern People's Congress responded by reducing corruption. Imam aligned the Bornu Youth Movement with the **Northern Elements Progressive Union** for four years. In 1958, he shifted the movement's alliance to the **Action Group**. By **independence**, the movement had dissolved.

**BOUNDARY ADJUSTMENT COMMISSION.** Part of the continual project of **state creation** aimed at appeasing ethnic demands for access to national revenue and ethnic representation, the commission was chaired by Muhammadu Nasir (it is often referred to as the Nasir Commission). In February 1976, the commission was charged with identifying boundary disputes and suggesting the demarcation of new states. It was also responsible for examining a concern voiced by the **Irikefe Commission** in December 1975 about whether Andoni and Nkoro of **Cross River State** should go to **Rivers State** and whether Ndoni should go to Rivers State or **Imo State**. The **Niger Delta** figured prominently. After a preliminary review, the Boundary Adjustment Commission identified 55 disputes and the need for seven more states. The commission's primary goal was to clarify boundaries to assist in settling interstate disputes.

**BOWEN, REVEREND THOMAS JEFFERSON (1814–1875).** The first American Baptist missionary from the **Southern Baptist Convention** (United States) to work in Nigeria. He set up several **Christian** missions in the interior at locations such as Ijaye and Ogbomoso during the mid-1800s. One of his greatest contributions was his *Grammar and Dictionary of the Yoruba Language* (1858), which was one of the earliest written recordings of a strictly spoken **language**. Bowen University, located in Iwo and founded in 2002, is named after him.

**BRASS.** A coastal city of the Nembe (or Brass), Okpoama, and Eweama people, Brass is located in the Bight of Biafra in the **Niger Delta**. The (Anglican) **Church Missionary Society** established a **Christian** missionary station at Brass in 1861. It was one of Nigeria's major slave trading ports during the era of the transatlantic **slave trade**. In the 1890s, the people of Brass were considered foreigners, living outside the British territory. The financial implications of this were severe. Brass traders were required to pay the **Royal Niger Company** £50 annually for a trading license and £10 for the use of a trading center. Participation in the **trade** of **alcohol** cost an additional £100 annually. In 1889, **Frederick William Koko Mingi VIII** became the *amanyanabo* (**king**) of Brass. In 1895, the Brass people revolted by raiding Akassa (the Royal Niger Company's trade port), demanding unrestricted access to markets. Brass fighters destroyed the company's trading stores, killed 43 of its traders, and captured 60 of them. This is referred to as the **Akassa Massacre**. In 1896, the British responded by forcing the *amanyanabo* into exile and burning down Nembe. Brass is the home of the *idu pele olali* festival (meaning "feast of **banana** cutting"), which used to be celebrated every seven years. It celebrates the Nembe (Brass) creator god and ends with the cutting down of a banana tree. The direction in which the tree falls reveals whether the creator god accepted the offerings. Today, Brass is a quiet fishing and farming island. It is the site of Nigeria's liquefied natural gas project, which was launched in 2007.

**BRIDE PRICE.** A payment in cash or kind by the bridegroom to the family of the bride-to-be. It is also referred to as bridewealth. It is an important part of the pre-wedding ritual for many societies in Nigeria. In the **Yoruba language**, the phrase literally translates into "money to carry the wife." Bride price varied across location and time period. During the colonial period, a bride in Ondo, for example, went for £10.12 and some gifts. By the 1950s, **cocoa** growing regions in southwestern Nigeria estimated marriage costs at around £50. Bride price only represented a portion of the total marriage cost. As part of the courting ritual, the man was expected to visit the bride's family and offer small gifts. If a divorce took place, the man could demand a refund of the bride price. *See also* YORUBA.

**BUBA YERO (1762–1841).** Born near the town of Mada, Yero completed his Koranic studies with **Usman dan Fodio** at **Gobir**. In 1804, he received a flag from **Usman dan Fodio** to take part in the **Fulani jihad** that established the **Sokoto Caliphate**. He was one of 14 flag bearers. He led his fighters to the **Benue River**, where he was stopped by Usman dan Fodio because he had disobeyed orders and started fighting without being instructed to do so. Nonetheless, he was the founder of Gombe, earning the title *lamido* (**king** in the **Fula language**). He was killed by a former fellow student, Hamarua, in 1841. *See also* ADAMA, MORDIBO. GOMBE STATE

**BUHARI, MAJOR GENERAL MUHAMMADU (1942– ).** A **Fulani**, Buhari was born in 1942 in **Daura**, in **Katsina State**. He joined the army in 1962 and was the military governor of the **North-Eastern State** in 1975 and **Borno State** in February 1976. He was commissioner of petroleum and energy between March 1976 and 1979. Buhari served as the military head of state from December 1983 to August 1985. He ran the **War Against Indiscipline** campaign and passed the **Exchange Control Decree** in 1984. Buhari was viewed by many as incorruptible; however, he had a poor **human rights** record. He was ousted in a **coup d'état**. He retired from the **armed forces** in September 1985. In 2003, Buhari ran against **General Olusegun Obasanjo** for president and lost. He ran again in April 2007 as the **All People's Party**'s candidate. In March 2008, Buhari appealed to the Supreme Court to overturn the **election** of **Umaru Musa Yar'Adua** as president because of the flawed electoral process.

**BUKAR D'GIJIAMA (?–1828).** A **Kanuri** ruler of Mandara, which was a province of the **Kanem-Bornu Empire** between 1773 and 1828. Mandara is located in present-day **Cameroon**. Under the leadership of Bukar, Mandara struggled to maintain its independence. Bornu attempted to reclaim it, but failed. Bukar relied on **slaves** in his royal court. In 1809, the **Fulani jihad** led by **Usman dan Fodio** also tried to claim Mandara. After a stalemate, the Fulani tried to negotiate with Bukar, but he had the emissaries beheaded. Bukar instead aligned himself with **Muhammed al-Amin al-Kanemi**, the leader of the Kanem-Bornu Empire, and successfully fought the Fulani jihadists. Al-Kanemi married his daughter. Bukar died in 1828. In the historical literature, he is also referred to as Bukar Jama and Bukara Gyama.

**BULALA.** A nomadic people from around Lake Fitri, in present-day **Chad**. They fiercely defended their migration pattern southwest through the **Kanem-Bornu Empire** in the 13th century. They claim to be descendants of a **Kanuri king**'s daughter. Around 1389, the Bulala took the kingdom of Kanem and drove out its ruler. The Bulala conquest of Kanem led to the establishment of the Kanem-Bornu Empire. The Bulala posed a continual threat to the Kanuri people until the 16th century. In 1507, they were forced out of their capital, Njimi. What is known of Njimi comes from a text written in Arabic from Bornu. Its exact location has not yet been identified.

## – C –

**CALABAR.** One of Nigeria's historic coastal cities, is situated in the Bight of Biafra. For a long time, Calabar's wealth was derived from a lucrative **oil palm** trade. It is mainly inhabited by the **Efik** people. In the late 19th century, Calabar was split and referred to as Old Calabar and New Calabar. Old Calabar was the kingdom of the Efik, whereas New Calabar referred more to Ijo territory. Old Calabar and New Calabar were two of Nigeria's seven major slave trading ports during the era of the transatlantic **slave trade**. One of Nigeria's well-documented slave traders, Antera Duke, conducted his business from Old Calabar. In 1846, the **Church of Scotland Mission** established a **Christian** church in Calabar. During the early years of colonial rule, Calabar served as an administrative center for the **Niger Coast Protectorate** and the **Oil Rivers Protectorate**. Nigeria's first public hospital, St. Margaret Hospital, was located in Calabar. It was also home to **Hope Waddell Training Institute**. Calabar is one of several cities in Nigeria that has a sizable number of **Charismatic Christians**. It is the birthplace of notable Nigerians such as **Eyo Ita** and home of the University of Calabar. It is the capital of **Cross River State**. Finally, Calabar is known as the origin of the Calabar bean, which is the poisonous seed of a *physostigma venenosum*. The bean has been used to uncover guilt. The **population** of Calabar is approximately 400,000. *See also* NIGER DELTA.

**CALIPHATE.** A caliph is an **Islamic** leader and political head of state. This is an Arabic word meaning "successor to the messenger of God." The first caliph of the **Sokoto Caliphate** was **Usman dan Fodio**. After 1903, the title of caliph was changed by the British to **sultan**. Other titles related to the Sokoto Caliphate are **emir** and *sardauna*.

**CAMEROON, REPUBLIC OF.** The country east of Nigeria. For several decades, parts of Cameroon were under British colonial authority and were governed as an appendage of Nigeria starting in 1914. In 1951, northern Cameroon was part of the **Northern Region** and southern Cameroon was part of the **Eastern Region**. In 1954, the status of northern Cameroon remained the same, but southern Cameroon became a semifederal territory of Nigeria. In 1957, a **constitutional conference** declared southern Cameroon as its own region, warranting its own **premier**. Citizens of this region had political representation in the **National Council of Nigeria and the Cameroons**. In 1961, southern Cameroon split from Nigeria. Since the 1970s, Nigeria and Cameroon have engaged in a border dispute over the **Bakassi Peninsula** in the Gulf of Guinea. Cameroon and Nigeria both claimed this area because they believed it contained large **petroleum** reserves. The dispute resulted in military clashes and the detention of war prisoners by both sides. Sporadic clashes continued mixed with peace efforts for 20 years. The case was heard by the International Court of Justice, which awarded the peninsula to Cameroon in 2002.

**CARR, HENRY RAWLINSON (1863–1945).** Born in **Lagos**, the son of manumitted parents from England who returned to Nigeria from Sierra Leone, Carr was among the first Nigerians to complete a Western **education** and graduate from Fourah Bay College in Sierra Leone. For a short time, he taught at the Church Missionary Society Grammar School. Carr served on the **Legislative Council** and acted as the resident of the **Lagos Colony** (1918–1924). Throughout his career, he pushed for educational reforms in the colonial structure as opposed to calling for the end of colonial rule entirely. He earned the title Commander of the Order of the British Empire.

**CASSAVA.** An edible tuberous root that grows well in tropical and semitropical regions. It is a starchy food, high in antioxidant vitamins. Its preparation varies from region to region. It is a staple in the Nigerian diet because it can be grown in soil of poor quality and can remain in the ground long after it has matured. Thus, sophisticated irrigation and harvesting technology is not essential. Nigeria produces roughly 20 percent of the world's annual cassava yield. Among the **Yoruba** of southwestern Nigeria, cassava is typically prepared as a semi-solid food called *fufu* and served with an **oil palm**- and pepper-based stew with meat. Cassava is also ground and fermented into *gari*, which can be eaten in a porridge form when mixed with cold water or in a semisolid form when mixed with hot water called *eba*. The **Igbo** vary the preparation by adding oil palm during the processing of cassava, giving the finished *gari* a yellow color. *See also* AGRICULTURE; YAMS.

**CATHOLIC CHURCH.** The Roman Catholic Church, through the French Catholic Society of African Missions, set up **Christian** missionary stations in **Lagos, Abeokuta**, Oyo, and **Ibadan** in the mid-19th century. The first missionaries arrived in 1867, but they stayed only briefly because of a war in France. The Holy Ghost Fathers arrived in **eastern Nigeria** in 1885, setting up a mission at **Onitsha**. An estimated 15 percent of Nigerians today are Roman Catholic, with the largest concentration in the southeast. The cardinal archbishop, currently **Anthony Olubunmi Okogie**, resides in Lagos. There are nine archbishoprics in Nigeria, located in all major cities across central and **southern Nigeria. Cardinal Francis Arinze**, of southeastern Nigeria, is one of Nigeria's most famous clergymen, because in 2005 he was a candidate for the late Pope John Paul II's position. *See also* RELIGION.

**CENSUS.** Census-taking in Nigeria is a major point of contention and is overlaid with tension over **revenue allocation**, religious rights, and international prominence. For this reason, Nigerians have resisted a formal, national census-taking project. The first census was taken in 1962, but the results were not released. The same happened with the 1974 census results compiled by the National Census Board. In 1991, a national census was conducted and placed Nigeria's population at 88.5 million people. This number served as the basis for **population** projections until recently. Despite the burden of a large population, Nigeria is proud of its size and believes its population gives it political clout, especially within West Africa. The census of March 2006 confirmed that Nigeria is Africa's most populated country, with an estimated 140 million people. Census details from Nigeria are used by scholars with caution because of fraud and procedural discrepancies. The counting process required a million enumerators and 42,000 monitors, supplied by the Nigerian Civil Liberties Organisation to ensure fair treatment. Several states called for a recount. *See also* ECONOMY; RELIGION.

**CENTRAL BANK OF NIGERIA.** *See* BANKING.

**CHAD, REPUBLIC OF.** Nigeria's northeastern neighbor, it shares the Lake Chad basin with Nigeria's northeasternmost states. Many kingdoms and cities in **northern Nigeria** were settled by migrants from present-day Chad, particularly in the Lake Fitri region. Evidence of this early history lies in the fact that both **Hausa** and Bolawa are Chadic **languages**.

**CHARISMATIC CHRISTIANITY.** The term "charismatic" was first used in the 1960s to identify those focused on the baptism of the Holy Spirit while maintaining memberships in their respective churches (Anglican, Methodist, etc.). Differences between Charismatic and **Pentecostal Christian** churches are few, with the exception that the former is much more transdenominational and transnational than the latter.

Charismatic Christianity started as a significant **Christian** religious movement in Nigeria in the early 1980s, gaining momentum in the 1990s. It has been largely contained within southwestern Nigeria. Its popularity came from an effort by some Christians to revitalize existing churches. The Deeper Life organization, for example, had around 350,000 members in 1994. In 1997, Nigeria had an estimated 2,000 Charismatic churches located in Nigeria's major cities, such as **Lagos, Ibadan, Kaduna, Jos,** and **Abuja**. Charismatic churches founded in **northern Nigeria** were frequently started by members of the **National Youth Services Corps** during the 1970s. Key features of Charismatic churches include being born again, prophecies, Pentecostal baptism, speaking in tongues, miracles, and physical healing. The movement is found primarily in urban areas because it relies on printed pamphlets and posters. Religious services often last longer than three hours and include a great deal of clapping, singing, and dancing.

Charismatic Christians in Nigeria are concerned with helping people through their personal problems arising from a contemporary, urban lifestyle. They emphasize baptism of the Holy Spirit over prayers, visions, and healings. The charismatic churches of Nigeria are connected to the global activities of Pentecostal churches all over the world. Adherents tend to be literate and English speaking. Charismatic churches in Nigeria tend not to use sacred symbolism (e.g., palm fronds) outside of the baptism ritual. Leaders of Charismatic churches act as founders and teachers. Popular Charismatic churches in Nigeria include the **Aladura Churches**, Deeper Christian Life Ministry, and Redeemed Christian Church of God, to name a few. *See also* KUMUYI, WILLIAM FOLURUNSO; RELIGION.

**CHIEF COMMISSIONER.** Within the British colonial administrative structure, the chief commissioner answered to the **lieutenant governor** of each portion of the British Nigeria Colony. The chief commissioner was of British descent and worked for the British colonial administration. The use of chief commissioners in **northern Nigeria** began in 1932; in the **Western Region** the position opened in 1939. After October 1954, the positions of chief commissioner and lieutenant governor were replaced by a governor. In some cases, the chief commissioner replaced the lieutenant governor as the sole British colonial authority in a region.

**CHIEFS.** The term "chief" is often used interchangeably with **king** with regard to early African societies. However, the European use of the word tends to indicate one having less power than a king, which is inaccurate. How one becomes a chief varies from one village or **ethnic group** to another. For many societies in Nigeria the succession of a chief based on heredity or election is not rigidly fixed. In the case of the **Nupe**, the chief of Jebba and Mokwa was likely to be promoted from among the elders, regardless of their family lineage. Colonial rule dramatically changed the status and authority of chiefs. Many chiefs with legitimate, popular support saw their power diminish at the behest of unpopular individuals without previous authority. Colonial rule effectively dismantled most of the kingdoms. The powerful, often spiritually appointed, kings were assassinated, exiled, or appointed as merely local chiefs supervised by colonial officials.

Every **language** in Nigeria has its own term for chief. In **Igbo** it is *eze*; in **Yoruba** it is *oba*, with regional variations. The head chief of Oyo, for example, was the *alaafin*, while his contemporary in **Ibadan** was called *olubadan*. The people of Ijebu-Ode refer to their chief as *awujale*, and the people of Ekpon use *onogie*. The level of authority and the area under a chief's control also varies considerably within Nigeria. During colonial rule, the British frequently appointed a chief to act as a mediator, tax collector, and labor recruiter. Not all societies in Nigeria, however, had one person with ultimate authority who acted as a **paramount chief**. In such cases, the British government selected someone they saw as loyal and appointed him as the new chief. In **southern Nigeria** among the Igbo, these chiefs were regarded as **warrant chiefs**.

In most cases, chiefs chosen or preferred by the colonial government lacked legitimacy and trust among their own people and found ways to abuse their power for personal gain. Scholars looking at the role of chiefs contend that the British created a kind of super chief, with unprecedented power. Today, receiving the title of chief based on social or political contributions to a community is relatively commonplace for a man. Nearly all men who made their mark in Nigerian history, for example, acquired the title of chief in their adult years.

**CHILD LABOR.** As in many other developing nations, Nigerian parents depend on the contributions of their children to the family business. It is not uncommon to see children working in **trade**, transportation, or **agriculture**. However, children in Nigeria have also been targeted by human traffickers for the foreign sex trade and hard labor. In the past 10 years, **human rights** organizations have drawn international attention to children caught up in **human trafficking**.

**CHRIST APOSTOLIC CHURCH.** Founded by **Joseph Ayo Babalola** in 1930 as the United Apostolic Church. Babalola changed the name of the church to Christ Apostolic Church in 1943. The church broke away from European **Christian** missions and joined the **Aladura Church** movement. Intense worship and prayer were common features of the church. Christ Apostolic Church is also considered a **Pentecostal Christian** church. Its popularity reached its height between 1930 and 1960. The church established numerous religious training colleges in **southern Nigeria**. *See also* RELIGION.

**CHRISTIAN ASSOCIATION OF NIGERIA.** An organization designed to unify **Christian** churches, it was formed in 1976 largely as a response to national discussions about the legalization of **abortion** and the implementation of **Shari'a** (**Islamic** law) that was taking place in the North. During the 1980s, it served as a crucial representative of Christian interests in Muslim-dominated **northern Nigeria**. It included representatives of **Charismatic**, **Catholic**, and **Pentecostal Christian** churches. The president of the association is the Catholic Archbishop of **Abuja**, John Onaiyekan. The association was particularly vocal in 2000 regarding the implementation of Shari'a in several northern states. *See also* RELIGION.

**CHRISTIANITY.** One of the most popular **religions** in Nigeria, it was first introduced by Portuguese traders in the mid-1500s, but failed to take root. Sustained missionary activity in Nigeria started in the mid-19th century. Among the first missionaries were former slaves from Sierra Leone proselytizing in Nigeria. These individuals established missions in **Badagry** and **Abeokuta** in southwestern Nigeria. British missionary organizations such as the Wesleyan Methodist Missionary Society and the (Anglican) **Church Missionary Society** also set up stations in the 1840s. The **Wesleyan Methodist Missionary Society** set up its first missionary station at Badagry in 1842. Also present were the United Presbyterian **Church of Scotland Mission**

in **Calabar** and the Southern Baptist Convention in Ijaye. The Catholic Society of African missions, representing the **Catholic Church**, reached **Lagos** and Abeokuta in 1863. William de Graft was a prominent Methodist missionary who assisted in the establishment of the first Western-style school in Badagry. **Mary Mitchell Slessor** was a Scottish missionary who worked in the **Niger Delta** from ca. 1890 to 1915. Although she was committed to spreading Christianity, the first baptism among the local community didn't take place until 1903 and included only seven adults. This "conversion rate" was not uncommon among missionaries working in Nigeria. Ebute Metta, a neighborhood in Lagos, was started as a settlement in the 19th century by Christian refugees from **Abeokuta**.

By the late 19th century, Christianity had a stable following in **southern Nigeria**. Decades later, several independent Nigerian Christian churches emerged as part of a broad **African Church movement**. **Mojola Agbebi**, for example, was a leader of the Native Baptist Church in Lagos (1888 and 1903) and founder of the Ebenezer Church. The **Aladura Churches**, which were established in the 1920s, and the Deeper Christian Life Ministry contributed to the establishment of a uniquely Nigerian Christian movement. Notable Nigerian Catholic clergy of the 20th century include **Cardinal Francis Arinze**, **Cardinal Dominic Ekandem**, and **Cardinal Archbishop Anthony Okogie**. notable Nigerian Protestant clergy include **Archbishop Joseph Adetiloye** and **Bishop Adolphus Howells**.

Today, Christians make up roughly 40 percent of Nigeria's population. They live primarily in the **Middle Belt** and southern Nigeria. The most popular forms of Christianity are **Charismatic** and **Pentecostal**, particularly in the South. The Christ Army Church and **Christ Apostolic Church** are major Pentecostal churches. Since 1928, the **Jehovah's Witness** movement has been active in Nigeria. *See also* BAPTIST CHURCH; BOWEN, REVEREND THOMAS JEFFERSON; CHRISTIAN ASSOCIATION OF NIGERIA; NATIONAL CHURCH OF NIGERIA.

**CHURCH OF SCOTLAND MISSION (CSM).** The United Presbyterian Church of Scotland Mission established a mission in **Calabar** in 1846. It focused heavily on people living along the Cross River. **Mary Mitchell Slessor** was a prominent member of this mission.

The mission sent several Presbyterian groups, particularly in the 19th century, to focus on convincing the **Igbo** to accept **Christianity** and the **Aro** to cease their participation in the **slave trade**. *See also* CHURCH MISSIONARY SOCIETY; RELIGION; WESLEYAN METHODIST MISSIONARY SOCIETY.

**CHURCH MISSIONARY SOCIETY (CMS).** The (Anglican) Church Missionary Society (CMS) set up its first missions in Nigeria in the southwestern towns of **Badagry** in 1845 and **Abeokuta** in 1846. This mission was by far the most active and influential in Nigeria prior to the 20th century. Several CMS missionaries were part of the first **Niger River** expedition in 1841. In 1851, the CMS established a mission in **Ibadan**. The mission served as an overseas extension of the Anglican Church of England. Some attribute the abolition of the transatlantic **slave trade** and the development of the antislavery movement in Nigeria to the tireless efforts of the CMS. Missionaries devoted much of their time to establishing **legitimate commerce**. The CMS in Abeokuta, for example, saw **cotton** as the ideal legitimate good to replace slaves. In 1856, the CMS established an Industrial Institution in Abeokuta, and later in **Onitsha** and **Lokoja**. The institutions' primary purpose was to encourage and oversee the cultivation of cotton for export, which involved teaching people how to process cotton using a cotton gin. The CMS placed Abeokuta at the center of its operations, with the plan of spreading **Christianity** outward to neighboring towns. The society also established a presence and a following in **Lagos** and Ilesa. *See also* CHURCH OF SCOTLAND MISSION; WESLEYAN METHODIST MISSIONARY SOCIETY.

**CIVIL SERVICE.** The civil service in Nigeria has undergone a number of changes since its establishment by the British colonial government. The British found that the most economically feasible way to carry out the necessary administrative duties of the colony was to train and hire people from the indigenous population. The civil service sector during the colonial period was organized into departments (i.e., **agriculture**, medical, **education**). When the ministerial structure was introduced in the 1950s, new positions were created to close the communication gap between the regional governors, ministers, and civil servants. This meant that secretarial positions in the ministry were often filled by a man younger than people filling the positions below him, which went against Nigerian culture, in which age determined the importance and rank of a person. **Chinua Achebe** dealt with this issue in his novel *No Longer at Ease* (1960).

After **World War II**, the British government initiated reforms of the salaries, benefits, and conditions for African civil service workers. European civil servants in Nigeria organized themselves into the Association of European Civil Servants in Nigeria in 1919. In 1936, the Lagos Women's League formed to pressure the colonial government to hire more **women** into the civil service. The Federal Public Service Commission was created by the **Macpherson Constitution** in 1954. This commission was charged with appointing and influencing civil servants. It was slightly modified and renamed the Federal Civil Service Commission in 1979.

Many notable figures in Nigeria's history worked as civil servants during colonial rule, and most anticolonial activists started their careers as civil servants. **Chief Henry Fajemirokun**, for example, served as president of the Nigeria Civil Service Union after a career in the (Royal) **West African Frontier Force** in the 1940s. **Chief Samuel Oluyemisi Falae** held numerous civil service positions in the 1970s prior to working as a secretary in **General Ibrahim Babangida**'s government. Nigeria's civil servants have always struggled for adequate pay and provisions. In 1972, the **Udoji Commission** suggested a new pay scale for civil servants, which was accepted. In postcolonial times, the civil service sector has been seen as an exclusive club of individuals whose activities have been based on self-interest. Many members of the civil service, particularly in the 1970s and 1980s, appeared to dislike public interference. The civil service has become the focus of **corruption** scandals and **election** fraud. *See also* FOOT COMMISSION; GORSUCH COMMISSION; HARRAGIN COMMISSION; MORGAN COMMISSION.

**CIVIL WAR.** Nigeria's civil war, between the federal government of Nigeria and the secessionist **Republic of Biafra**, began in May 1967 and lasted until January 1970. Much of the fighting took place along the southeastern coast of Nigeria, referred to as the Bight of Biafra. In September 1966, rioting erupted over the succession of **General Yakubu Gowon** as the new head of state, and a massacre (some say genocide) of **Igbo** people in the North followed. Many Igbo fled to the **Eastern Region** for protection. In response, **Chief Chukuemeka Ojukwu**, the governor of the Eastern Region, launched plans for secession. The newly placed Gowon called for the **Aburi Conference** between himself and Ojukwu in Aburi, Ghana. Gowon then proceeded to issue a decree dividing Nigeria's four regions into 12 states. Unsatisfied, Ojukwu declared the secession of the Eastern Region and establishment of the **Republic of Biafra** on 27 May 1967.

Less than two months later, fighting broke out between federal and Biafran forces. With a combination of declared and undeclared assistance from outside powers such as France, **Great Britain**, the Soviet Union, and neighboring Francophone African countries, the war resulted in high casualties and starvation in Biafra. The then young Organization of African Unity (OAU) tried to end the bloodshed and establish lasting peace in Nigeria by organizing peace talks. In August 1968, the two sides agreed to meet in Addis Ababa, Ethiopia. The meeting failed to secure peace. On 1 June 1969, Ojukwu issued the **Ahiara Declaration**, which called for Biafra to become a socialist state. The fighting continued, with high casualties on the Biafran side. The International Red Cross responded to the crisis by attempting to supply food to starving people in Biafra. On the Biafran side, **Colonel Joe "Hannibal" Achuzie** was the strongest field commander. On the Nigerian side, **Brigadier General Benjamin Adekunle** was the hero.

Two months later, representatives of the federal government and Biafra attempted another round of peace talks sponsored by the OAU in Kampala, Uganda. The **Kampala Peace Talks** collapsed over the federal government's proposed handling of former rebel Igbo troops. In the last months of the war, Biafra gradually lost almost all control of its region to the federal government. On 7 January 1970, Owerri fell to federal troops, and four days later Ojukwu left Biafra for Ivory Coast. On 12 January, Biafra, in the absence of Ojukwu, surrendered over the radio, marking the end of Nigeria's brutal civil war.

The civil war has been the subject of novels, plays, and poems. **Akinwande Oluwole Soyinka**'s *Madmen and the Specialists* (1971) deals with the maddening effects of war on soldiers, and **Kenule Saro-Wiwa**'s *Soza Boy* (1985) highlights the measures people in Biafra took to survive. **John Pepper Clark**'s *Casualties: Poems*

(1966–1968) explores the impact of civil war on Nigerian society. **General Olusegun Obasanjo** wrote *My Command: An Account of the Nigerian Civil War* (1980); Achuzie also wrote about his role in the civil war. During the war, many artists from **eastern Nigeria** went to Enugu and created political posters and illustrations for various Biafra publications. In 1969, several artists were featured in a traveling exhibition of Biafran **art** that went to three German cities. *See also* NWANKWO, CHIEF ARTHUR AGWUNCHA; OPERATION BIAFRAN BABY; VON ROSEN, COUNT CARL GUSTAF.

**CLAPPERTON, HUGH (1788–1827).** A Scottish explorer who went to Nigeria to identify the course of the **Niger River**. In the 1820s, he traveled from North Africa to **northern Nigeria**. He recorded his travels in a series of journals, including *Journal of a Second Expedition into the Interior of Africa from the Bight of Benin to Soccattoo* [Sokoto] (1829). Although colored by a Western bias, his accounts provide eyewitness evidence of regional and local **trade** patterns in the 19th century. He traveled in Nigeria between 1822 and 1826. While visiting Kaiama in the **Borgu** region, he saw the arrival of an impressive **Hausa** caravan that carried goods from as far away as present-day **Ghana** and **Bornu** in northeastern Nigeria. The caravan included approximately a thousand men and **women**. He also discussed in one of his journals the activities of a wealthy female **slave trader** named Zuma in the town of Wawa on the Niger River, who owned about a thousand slaves and hired them out to local traders. Clapperton visited a plantation cultivated by slaves in **Kano** in 1823. He witnessed a ceremony involving guns carried out by royal slaves in the 1820s. Clapperton traveled with **Richard Lander** through **Yoruba** from **Badagry** in 1826.

**CLARK, JOHN PEPPER (1935– ).** Clark was born in April 1935 in Kiagbodo, in **Delta State**. As a young man, he studied at the Native Administration School (1948–1954); University College (present-day **University of Ibadan**) (1955–1960), earning a degree in English; and Princeton University (1962–1963). While a student, he edited several magazines, including *The Horn*. He also worked as a clerical officer for the Office of the Chief Secretary (1954–1955) and information officer for the Ministry of Information of Western

Nigeria (1960–1961). For the latter, he worked as a feature editor for the *Daily Express*, based in **Lagos**. Clark also taught English courses at the University of Lagos between 1965 and 1980. He was a distinguished fellow at several prestigious institutions.

In 1982 Clark and his wife, Ebun Odutola, founded the Pec Repertory Theatre in Lagos. He is one of Nigeria's distinguished poets and playwrights. In his works, Clark focuses on African nature, such as the capturing the beauty of a first rain. His works also exhibit his interest in reincarnation. Since his retirement from the University of Lagos, he has been a visiting lecturer at several universities in the United States, including Yale University. His notable works include *Casualties: Poems 1966–68* (1970), which explores Nigeria's **civil war**, and *A Reed in a Tide* (1965), covering his foreign travels and African identity. *See also* LITERATURE.

**CLIFFORD CONSTITUTION.** Named after the British colonial governor of Nigeria, Sir Hugh Clifford, this constitution was enacted in 1922. It allowed for the **election** of four Western-educated Nigerian men (three from **Lagos** and one from **Calabar**) to the 46-person **Legislative Council**. This constitution prompted **Sir Herbert Macaulay** to form the **Nigerian National Democratic Party** in 1923. The Clifford Constitution is one of several constitutions implemented after colonial rule. *See also* CONSTITUTIONAL CONFERENCES; LYTTLELTON CONSTITUTION; MACPHERSON CONSTITUTION; RICHARDS CONSTITUTION.

**COAL.** Commercial quantities of coal were identified in 1909. The first coal mine was opened at Ogbete in **Enugu** in 1915. Enugu's colliery produced 600,000 tons of coal annually in the mid-20th century. (The Udi and Iva mines produced over 200,000 tons of coal in 1935.) Nigeria's main coal deposits are located in south-central Nigeria, with the majority in **Enugu State**, **Edo State**, and **Kogi State**. Coal mining in Nigeria reached its peak in the late 1950s, at 900,000 tons per year. The mining was run by the Nigerian Coal Corporation, which was created in 1950. Today, coal is largely used as a source of energy for Nigeria's cement and brick factories. The largest coal reserve is the Ogboyoga Mine in Kogi State. Nigeria's coal mines are in the process of being **privatized** and revitalized, with a goal of returning production levels to 900,000 tons annually. However, the Nigerian Coal Corporation is on the verge of bankruptcy and has already sold off many of its shares. In 2003, Nigeria and China entered into an agreement on technical assistance. *See also* ECONOMY; PETROLEUM.

**COCOA.** In southwestern Nigeria, cocoa cultivation began in **Ibadan** in the 1890s and spread to towns such as **Ile-Ife** and Ondo by the 1930s. Cocoa production encouraged the **migration** of individuals and families into the cocoa farming region of southwestern Nigeria. The **trade** of cocoa was done through a **marketing board**. Nearly 90 percent of Nigeria's cocoa goes to European markets. Until the 1960s, Nigeria was the second largest cocoa producer in the world. Like other **agricultural** commodities, cocoa production and exports took a dive in the 1970s. In 1974, cocoa exports accounted for 50 percent of Nigeria's foreign exchange earnings. At its peak, Nigeria produced 400,000 tons per year. In 2005, Nigeria launched a subsidies scheme to boost cocoa production. *See also* ECONOMY; FOREIGN TRADE.

**COKER COMMISSION.** Set up by G. B. A. Coker, a colonial official, in 1962, the commission's purpose was to investigate the financial dealings of the **Western Region** to expose **corruption**. The Coker report found **Chief Obafemi Awolowo** guilty of using the Western Region's money to finance the promotion and activities of the **Action Group** political party through an investment corporation. The Coker Commission created an opportunity for **Chief Samuel Akintola** to be reinstalled as the region's **premier**.

**COLONIZATION.** In the context of Africa, colonization was the process by which European powers expanded their empires through territorial claims. It included the exploitation of African labor and appropriation of raw materials such as **cocoa, cotton,** and **oil palm**. It also involved interference with existing cultural practices and political structures. For Nigeria, British colonization began in the mid-19th century with the takeover of **Lagos** in 1861. The process of colonization for the British in Nigeria was not without vigorous resistance to this loss of sovereignty. The push for decolonization and **independence** in Nigeria escalated after **World War II**.

**CONSTITUTIONAL CONFERENCES.** As part of the process of drafting, implementing, and revising each new **constitution**, leaders of Nigeria (British and Nigerian) set up numerous constitutional committees and conferences within and outside Nigeria. In several instances, the conferences were convened with the specific purpose of amending an already existing constitution. Several of the conferences were simply identified as Ad Hoc Constitutional Conferences, created to review the constitution active at the time. One major conference is highlighted here. Three years after the **Lyttlelton Constitution** of 1954 was implemented, a constitutional conference was held in London to begin work on revising it. Ten Nigerian regional representatives and the British **governor general** made several major changes. First, they decided to allow the **Eastern** and **Western Regions** to become independent at an unspecified date; the **Northern Region** would become independent in 1959. Second, the queen would continue to select a regional governor; in turn, the governor would continue to appoint the deputy governor in the Western and Eastern Regions. Third, the Eastern Region, like the other regions, would have a **House of Chiefs**. Fourth, southern **Cameroon** would be considered a region, requiring the appointment of a **premier**. Finally, a committee would consider the division of Nigeria into a 320-electoral-seat constituency. By **independence** in 1960, several of these decisions had faded away as the demands of the **First Republic** reconfigured the political landscape. Other notable constitutional conferences took place in 1995, in an effort to revise the 1979 constitution, and in 2005, to improve **revenue allocation** among the 36 states. *See also* NATIONAL DEMOCRATIC COALITION.

**CONSTITUTIONS.** The drafting and ratification of a fair and representative constitution has been a major issue for Nigeria since the mid-1950s. Thus far, the drafting and approval process has largely excluded **women**. Since the end of British colonial rule, this all-encompassing composition of fundamental laws has been written and discarded numerous times. Nigeria has had six constitutions: the **Clifford** (1922), **Richards** (1946), **Macpherson** (1951), **Lyttlelton** (1954), 1979 Constitution, and 1999 Constitution. For each of the constitutions, formal conferences were held in London (during the colonial period) and **Lagos** (after 1960). Committees, comprising

Western-educated Nigerian elite men, were also formed to comment on and recommend revisions to the drafts. The first four constitutions were named after the colonial governor serving at the time. The first two were drafted by the British colonial government and applied to colonial Nigeria without consultation. The Macpherson and Lyttlelton Constitutions included some level of negotiation and review by appointed Nigerians.

The major points of debate centered on the structure of government (federation versus republic) and ethnic representation. A great deal of fragmentation along ethnic and regional lines emerged in the decade leading up to **independence** in 1960. The Lyttlelton Constitution, for example, placed Nigeria on the path of regional autonomy, which failed to please all political groups. Nigeria's first military regime moved the country toward a federal structure. Between 1957 and 1999, Nigeria's leaders convened several **constitutional conferences** and organized committees in attempts to implement a new constitution. The last two constitutions coincided with Nigeria's two major transitions from military to civilian rule, in 1979 and 1999. The 1979 constitution was written by a drafting committee of 49 men. The 1999 constitution was composed by a constitution debate coordinating committee and reviewed by the Presidential Technical Committee, which included male representatives from the major **political parties**. The technical committee was also referred to as the Tobi Committee, after Justice Nikki Tobi, the head of its activities. Both constitutions confirmed Nigeria's federal structure, the number of states, and the role of the federal government.

**CORRUPTION.** Individuals and social groups define corruption differently. In general, a corrupt action has taken place if an individual or official within the government or private sector has required an additional payment, in cash or kind, to perform a service for personal gain. A related corrupt act involves an individual or official deliberately subverting protocol regarding employment (i.e., hiring, wages, or duties) for personal gain. Corrupt actions include the maintenance of a patronage system, cronyism, and sustaining a kleptocracy (a political system in which corruption is institutionalized). Corruption is one of the most difficult types of **crime** to prevent, particularly in the context of underdevelopment.

Nigeria's political, economic, and social situation provides a breeding ground for corruption. Since 1960, it has struggled with collapsed states, regional rivalry, and mounting **debt**. Some scholars argue that strong cultural bonds, which facilitate a patronage system, have been another reason for rampant corruption in Nigeria. The high **unemployment** rate has also been a contributing factor. A nonprofit organization, Transparency International, ranked Nigeria the second most corrupt country in the world in 2004. Since the late 1990s, Nigeria has acquired the dubious distinction of being the originator of **advanced fee fraud** e-mail scams. In the 1990s, Nigeria's military leaders stole over $2.2 billion from the government coffers for personal use.

Corruption in Nigeria is a daily annoyance. The **police** regularly set up roadblocks to allegedly inspect public and private vehicles for safety and stolen goods. In reality, they harass innocent people and bus drivers for cash handouts and provide no security. Each new head of state since the mid-1960s has promised to crack down on corruption and improve the safety of the citizens, but in point of fact, has done the opposite. In addition to financial extortion, Nigeria's leaders have shamelessly engaged in subverting democratic **elections**. The April 2007 presidential election sadly confirmed the extent to which powerful individuals would and could manipulate the process, even with the world watching. The legacy of corruption deeply tarnished what should have been a celebratory moment in Nigeria's history. *See also* ECONOMY.

**COTTON.** The soft, white material spun and woven from the fruit of a cotton plant has played an integral role in the **economy** and culture of Nigeria. Even before colonial rule, cotton was grown, woven, and dyed in **Kano** and then exported across the Sahara Desert to North African markets. Cotton was used in the production of regionally distinct **textiles**. The spinning of cotton into thread was typically considered women's work. European visitors to **Abeokuta** during the 19th century commented on the importance of this commodity. Cotton produced in Abeokuta was sold on the Manchester exchange starting in 1853. In Abeokuta, several hundred cotton gins were in use by 1861. Cotton ginneries opened along the **railroad** lines at several other major towns, including as **Ilorin**, Kano, and **Sokoto**.

The British Cotton Growing Association (BCGA) experimented with the growing and processing of cotton in Nigeria. It was responsible for establishing the Moore Plantation at **Ibadan**. After the BCGA introduced a high-yield variety of cotton from the Americas, Nigeria's cotton production reached 30,000 bales per year. Cotton production also thrived in the North, in part because the BCGA provided free seeds. Cotton farms located on the Sokoto and Gongola Rivers produce the majority of the North's cotton.

Since **independence**, Nigeria has struggled to keep its cotton cultivation efficient and lucrative. Investment in modernizing technology and soil maintenance has been the focus of the government since the 1970s, but with little success. The North produces between 200,000 and 300,000 tons per year, with around 80 percent consumed domestically. The number of textile mills has dropped, from 175 in 1980 to 20 in 2007. Cotton growers find it difficult to get a fair price for their goods, and textile producers face the challenge of competing with inexpensive imported cloth and ready-made clothing from Asia. Before leaving office, **General Olusegun Obasanjo** committed ₦70 billion to reviving Nigeria's textile industry. *See also* AGRICULTURE; FOREIGN TRADE; MARKETING BOARDS.

**COUNCIL OF CHIEFS.** A governing body that included chiefs and spiritual leaders. It was responsible for checking the authority of a king during colonial times. Today these councils operate primarily on a local level and have a symbolic presence.

**COUP D'ÉTAT.** Nigeria's history is primarily segmented by one military ruler failing to promote democracy, who was then swept aside by a new military leader, who also made empty promises. Government takeovers in Nigeria have been conducted primarily by members of the **armed forces** because they have the strongest skills, resources, and communication networks. They also have better access to the president or military leader they want to remove. In most cases, the military coups d'état (coups) are bloodless, meaning that they take advantage of a moment when the head of state is out of town.

Since **independence**, Nigeria has experienced six military coups. The first took place in January 1966 and was carried out by seven military officers, of whom six were **Igbo**. It was led by **Major Gen-**

eral **Johnson Aguiyi-Ironsi**, who lacked the skills and objectives to act effectively as the new head of state. During the coup, Prime Minister **Alhaji Abubakar Tafawa Balewa**; the **premier** of the **Northern Region, Alhaji Ahmadu Bello**; and the premier of the **Western Region, Chief Samuel Akintola**, were killed. A counter-coup took place in July 1966, which made **General Yakubu Gowon** the new head of state. A third coup occurred in July 1975, while Gowon was in Uganda. It was orchestrated by **General Murtala Mohammed** and **General Olusegun Obasanjo**. The **Second Republic** was ended by a military coup that installed **Major General Muhammadu Buhari** in December 1983. A fifth military coup took place in August 1985 and made **General Ibrahim Babangida** head of state. After the failed **election of 12 June 1993**, Nigeria was ruled by the **Interim National Government**. **General Sani Abacha** grew impatient and displeased with the transition process and launched Nigeria's sixth military coup, usurping power in November 1993. Currently, Nigeria is enjoying a stretch of democracy known as the **Fourth Republic**, although its integrity has been questioned.

**COURTS.** Today there are three types of courts operating in Nigeria: **Shari'a**, Customary, and Federal. Prior to **independence**, Nigeria's court system focused on **native courts**, or customary courts. As outlined in Nigeria's 1999 **constitution**, Nigeria's judicial system is organized into a series of tiers that move from the customary to federal level. The Supreme Court is the highest court. Under the Supreme Court is the Federal Court of Appeal, which hears cases from the lower courts and special tribunals. The Federal Court of Appeal has approximately 15 judges, with no less than three trained in Shari'a. The next level includes the High Court and Shari'a Court of Appeal. The fourth level includes the Magistrate and District Court, which operate on a state level. The final, lowest level includes the Shari'a Court, Customary Court, and Area Court.

In the North, Shari'a Court has been separated from Customary Court. Customary law is based on ethnic culture and values and designed primarily to handle cases regarding individuals, families, marriage, and guardianship of children for each **ethnic group**. In most of **northern Nigeria**, Shari'a Courts are separate from Customary Courts and are based strictly on Islamic law. Nigeria's court system has struggled to maintain legitimacy and respectable outcomes despite chronic understaffing and the practice of special settlements. Judges in these courts are selected through a series of commissions that operate on a national and state level. The **Judicial Service Commission** advises the **National Judicial Council** on the nomination of qualified members to Nigeria's court system. *See also* FATAYI-WILLIAMS, ATANDA; IBEKWE, DAN ONUORA; LEGAL SYSTEM; MBANEFO, SIR LOUIS MWACHUKWU; WILLIAMS, CHIEF FREDERICK ROTIMI ALADE.

**COWRY SHELLS.** Small, white shells with a high gloss, they were used as **currency** prior to colonial rule. Traders acquired them from the Indian Ocean at the Maldive Islands and Zanzibar Island. They were used in West Africa, especially coastal Nigeria, as a form of currency around the 11th century. They reached **Hausa** territory in the 18th century, primarily through European traders. **Sir Frederick Lugard** even participated in the transportation of cowry shells, carrying them by donkey in west central Nigeria. In a **Kano** market in 1851, cloth carried by 300 camels was worth 60 million shells. Among the **Yoruba**, cowry shells were used to pay taxes and tribute as well as for financing trade. Cowries were used in the **oil palm** trade in southeastern Nigeria. The buying and selling of slaves in the **Sokoto Caliphate** was done using cowry shells. Cowry shells also had a role in spiritual activities, as in the case of the Urhobo water spirit shrines. Tracing the use of cowries across Nigeria has been done by looking at how these shells were bundled and counted. For example, neither the Yoruba on the coast, nor the Hausa inland, strung their cowry shells on a string. The **Igbo** counted their cowries in groups of six not strung, which is not replicated elsewhere in Nigeria. In the 20th century the British systematically replaced the cowry with the British pound sterling. *See also* DIVINATION; SLAVERY/SLAVE TRADE.

**CRIME.** Crime has ranked high among concerns related to slow development and high **unemployment** in Nigeria. Crimes in Nigeria range from petty theft to large-scale embezzlement from the state coffers, with the money channeled into foreign bank accounts. In the 1980s, Lawrence Anini became a notorious criminal, who posed a threat to **General Ibrahim Babangida**'s regime. He was accused of being not only a common criminal, but also a "hit man" for anti-Babangida activity in the city of **Benin**. The press named him the "Outlaw King of Benin." **Corruption** among political leaders is one of the state's most damaging crimes. Since 1999, Nigeria's government has promised to end corruption by sniffing out suspects and punishing them. Also marring Nigeria's global reputation in the 21st century is the wave of **advanced fee fraud** e-mail scams allegedly originating from Nigeria, which has robbed victims all over the world of millions of dollars.

Much of the crime in Nigeria is the result of people attempting to create a reliable income for themselves and their families in a country where the average person lives on $1.20 per day. Smuggling of used vehicles, petrol, and illegal **drugs** in and out of the country is not uncommon. Nigeria has not been able to reduce criminal activity. It suffers from the inability to maintain a reliable **police** force that will uphold the law instead of profiting from its position of power. Instead of pulling over dilapidated buses, directing traffic, and catching thieves in stolen cars, many police set up checkpoints along major **roads** in order to collect tips from drivers. It is not uncommon to encounter these checkpoints every 10 or 20 kilometers on the Lagos–Ibadan Expressway. Nigerians often complain about the dilemma of who is policing the police. *See also* BANKING; ECONOMY; HUMAN TRAFFICKING; PROSTITUTION; SMUGGLING.

**CROSS RIVER STATE.** Located in southeastern Nigeria on the coast, its capital is **Calabar**. The state is named after the Cross River and was created in 1976 out of **South-Eastern State**. It is one of nine states situated in the **Niger Delta**. The **population** is predominantly **Efik**. Cross River State is home to the University of Calabar and the Leboku Festival. It is also the site where the late missionary **Mary Mitchell Slessor** worked on behalf of the United Free Church of Scotland. It is one of Nigeria's current 36 states.

**CROWTHER, BISHOP SAMUEL AJAYI (1806/1809–1891).** Born in 1809 (some sources say 1806) in **Abeokuta**, Crowder was the first African Bishop of the Anglican Church in Nigeria. In 1821 he was captured and enslaved, but his slave ship was stopped, and those on board were released in Sierra Leone. It was there that he converted to **Christianity** and received a formal **education** from the (Anglican)

**Church Missionary Society** (CMS). Crowther became an ordained minister in 1844 and was sent to Nigeria to serve as a missionary in Abeokuta. He translated the New Testament into the **Yoruba language**, which earned him an honorary doctoral degree from Oxford University. In 1864, he was consecrated as the first bishop of the Niger Territories by the Church of England, but in 1890, he was forced to resign from his position as bishop. In Abeokuta, Crowther and his wife were put in charge of the CMS's **cotton** project. His son took over the project in 1854. Crowther traveled to **Hausa** territory with **Henry Townsend**, a fellow Christian missionary, in the mid-1800s. He was also part of a British expedition up the **Niger River** on the *Dayspring* during the 1850s, which was led by **William Balfour Baikie**.

**CURRENCY.** From time immemorial, **trade** has necessitated the standardization of exchange. Prior to the 20th century, a variety of items served as acceptable media of trade across Nigeria. Purchases of land, slaves, and major commodities were made using a single or combination of currencies such as **kolanuts**, stamped gold coins (*mithqal*), and **cowry shells**. The *mithqal* was made from gold imported from Bonduku (in present-day Ivory Coast) and minted. It was used extensively along trade routes between central Nigerian kingdoms and the **Hausa Kingdoms**. The **Nupe** used cowry shells in their trade. Even after the introduction of British currency, cowry shells were used for some time for select exchanges in which the symbolism was almost more important than the amount. These included the payment of **bride price** and symbolic, traditional gifts. **Sir Frederick Lugard** commented on the use of hoes as a form of currency in **Borgu** during the 19th century.

The British actively sought to shift the usage of currency away from such forms toward the exclusive use of the British pound sterling (£). They made this change by requiring **taxes** to be paid in cash, not kind; by pushing Nigerians into wage labor; and by requiring capital advances in the form of cash. By 1887, the trade in **oil palm** kernels and oil was conducted using British currency. For a time, sterling silver and Maria Theresa dollars were circulating along with cowry shells. European observers in the mid-1800s commented on the use of Maria Theresa dollars in **Bornu**. During colonial rule, Nigerians used the British West African pound, which was equivalent to one British pound. This form of currency was introduced in 1907.

Starting in 1912, it was issued and controlled by the West African Currency Board. Paper forms of this currency became available in 1916 for shillings and in 1918 for one pound.

In 1958, Nigeria transitioned to using the Nigerian pound (N£). Since 1 January 1973, Nigeria has used the naira (₦) as its form of currency. As part of a **structural adjustment program**, Nigeria devalued its currency to stimulate **foreign trade**. In July 2007, ₦118 was worth $1. Nigeria's currency has been relatively unstable on the international foreign exchange markets for most of its existence. Nigeria has also grappled with a thriving black market in foreign currency. Although a structural adjustment program in the mid-1980s reduced black market trading, it did not eradicate it. In 2007, the Central Bank of Nigeria decided to remove the Arabic script from the bank notes. Supporters argued that Arabic is not one of Nigeria's spoken languages and that its removal would allow the use of other languages such as **Igbo** or **Yoruba**. This change went into effect in February 2007. *See also* BANKING; EXCHANGE CONTROL DECREE.

**CUSTOMARY COURTS.** *See* COURTS.

# – D –

**DAHOMEY.** *See* BENIN, REPUBLIC OF.

***DAILY TIMES.*** Nigeria's first daily **newspaper** published in English, it began circulation in June 1926 in **Lagos**. This historic paper was started by Richard Barrow, **Sir Adeyemo Alakija**, and others as an independent newspaper. It has frequently been the news source that first unveils political scandals. **Alhaji Ismail Jose** was the editor (1957–1962) and managing director (1962–1976). In 1977, the federal government took ownership of it. Even today, it is still one of Nigeria's top-selling newspapers for political and economic news.

**DANJUMA, LIEUTENANT GENERAL THEOPHILUS YAKUBU (1937– ).** Born in December 1937 in Takum, in **Taraba State**, Danjuma studied at Takum Elementary School (1944–1950), St. Bartholomew's Primary School (1950–1952), Benue Provincial

Secondary School (1953–1958), and the Nigerian College of Arts, Science, and Technology in **Zaria** (1959–1960). After completing his general studies, he turned to military service. In 1960, he attended the Nigerian Military Training Centre in **Kaduna**. He worked at military training schools in **Great Britain** and later joined the army (1960). He served as company commander for United Nations and Nigerian army operations in several different African countries. In the army he held a number of leadership positions and achieved the rank of lieutenant general. In 1966, he assisted in a counter-**coup** that removed **Major General Johnson Aguiyi-Ironsi** and installed **General Yakubu Gowon**.

After retiring from the army in 1979, Danjuma pursued a career in politics. He was the director of the National Institute for Policy and Strategic Studies in **Jos** (1979–1982) and served in various executive positions in the private sector. For instance, he was the director of Nigerian Eagle Flour Mills and Michelin Motor Tyre Services. In 1996, he chaired a subgroup of the main committee to develop **General Sani Abacha**'s **Vision 2010**. Under the presidential leadership of **General Olusegun Obasanjo**, Danjuma served as the minister of defense. He received several honorary titles, including Grand Commander of the Order of the Nigeria in 1979, *abonta* (**chief**) of Wukari, and *ochiagha* (chief) of Obowu. *See also* ARMED FORCES.

**DANTATA, ALHAJI ALHASSAN (1880–1955).** Born in Bebeji, Dantata was a wealthy Muslim trader. As a young man, he assisted his family in the trading of **kolanut** and **groundnut**. The trading network extended from **Kano** to Kumasi, **Ghana**. Whereas most traders moved their goods by camel across the land, Dantata moved kolanuts by sea. He was a prosperous trader, especially during the groundnut boom of 1912. By 1918, the **Royal Niger Company** was receiving the majority of its groundnuts from him. While traveling on *hajj* (**pilgrimage**) to Mecca, Dantata visited **Great Britain** and met King George V. Over the span of a few decades, Dantata established himself as the primary middleman in groundnut and kolanut trading. In 1950, he cofounded the Kano Citizens' Trading Company, which set up Nigeria's first **textile** mill in Kano. He also served as the director of the Nigerian Railway Corporation. He died in October 1955. *See also* TRADE.

**DASUKI, SULTAN IBRAHIM (1923– ).** Born in December 1923 in Dogondaji, in **Sokoto State**, Dasuki studied at a **Koranic school** in Dogondaji (1928–1930) and at Sokoto Elementary and Middle Schools (1931–1935), Kaduna College (present-day Barewa College) in **Zaria** (1940–1944), and Oxford University in England (1955–1956). During his early years, he worked as a clerk for the Sokoto Native Authority Treasury (1943–1945) and as a clerical officer for the Gaskiya Corporation (1945–1953). Starting in 1953, Dasuki worked almost exclusively in Nigeria's colonial and independent governments. He held numerous positions, including deputy secretary of the Northern Nigeria Executive Council (1957–1958), first secretary for the Nigerian Embassy in Sudan (1960–1961), permanent secretary of the Northern Nigeria Ministry of Local Government (1962–1965), and member of the Ministry of Trade and Industry (1965–1968). He was also director of the Nigerian Produce Marketing Company (1966–1969), United Arewa Stores (1969), Gusau Oil Mills (1969), and Zamfara Textile Industries (1971). During the 1970s, he was a member of the Governing Council for the **Nigerian Institute of International Affairs** in **Lagos**, chairman of the Federal Government Commission on Local Government Service Reforms, and a member of the Constituent Assembly (1977–1978). His dedication to **Islam** led him to be an active member of **Jama'atu Nasril Islam** and the **Nigerian Supreme Council of Islamic Affairs** in the early 1970s.

Dasuki was a cofounder of the **National Party of Nigeria** in 1978. He was also the chairman (and major shareholder) of the Bank of Credit and Commerce International (BCCI). He was the **sultan** of **Sokoto**, through a controversial turn of events, from November 1988 to April 1996. A dispute over the position of sultan emerged in 1986 involving the previous sultan's son, **Sultan Alhaji Muhammadu Maccido**. In general, the Nigerian government, military or civilian, is not involved in selection of a new sultan, but in 1988 **General Ibrahim Babangida** installed Dasuki as the new sultan. The response was widespread violence, targeting places such as Dasuki's BCCI in Sokoto. Dasuki was a longtime business associate of Babangida. In 1991, Dasuki and Babangida were exposed for fraudulent investments. In 1996, Dasuki was deposed by **General Sani Abacha**. Between 1996 and 1998, Dasuki lived in seclusion in the town of

Jalingo and rarely appeared in public. He received the honorary titles Commander of the Order of the Niger (1965), *baraden* (**chief**) of Sokoto (1973), and sultan of Sokoto (1988–1996).

**DAURA.** One of the oldest **Hausa Kingdoms**, Daura was established around the 10th century. **Oral tradition** has it that **Prince Baya-jidda** from Baghdad killed a dangerous snake (referred to as *sarki*) in Daura, which had prevented the locals from collecting water at a well. In gratitude the king of Daura offered his daughter to Baya-jidda in marriage. Daura fell to **Fulani jihadists** in 1809. As part of the **Sokoto Caliphate**, Daura was divided into three provinces. As in the other emirates, **slaves** were used to staff the military and government.

**DAVID-WEST, TAMUNOEMI SOKARI (1936– ).** Born in August 1936 in Buguma, in **Rivers State**, David-West studied at St. Michael's School, Kalabari National College, and University College (present-day **University of Ibadan**). Outside Nigeria, he attended Michigan State University (1958–1960); Yale University (1960–1962); and McGill University (1964–1966), where he received his Ph.D. David-West taught at the University of Ibadan's College of Medicine. His specialty was virology. He was also the commissioner of education and a member of the Executive Council for Rivers State (1975–1979). He assisted in the drafting of the 1979 **constitution**. From 1984 to 1986, David-West was the federal minister of petroleum energy. At the same time, he continued working for the University of Ibadan, serving on the university's senate and governing council in the mid-1970s. He was a member of the World Health Organization's (WHO) Expert Panel on viral diseases and director of the WHO's National Influenza Centre. David-West received a medical research fellowship from the WHO, a postdoctoral fellowship from a Canadian institution, and a visiting research fellowship with the British National Institute of Medical Research. He was also a member of **General Sani Abacha**'s **Vision 2010** committee from 1996 to 1997. He received several awards from foreign institutions and governments, including Liberia. In the 1999 **elections**, he sought unsuccessfully to be the presidential nominee of the **People's Democratic Party**.

**DAVIES, CHIEF HEZEKIAH OLADIPO (1905–1988).** Born in April 1905, as a young man Davies attended the Methodist Boys' High School and **King's College** in **Lagos**. He worked as an administrator at King's College (1924–1925) and as a clerk for the Northern Province secretariat in **Kano** (1925–1928) and the Survey Department (1928–1933). Between 1934 and 1937, he attended the London School of Economics, where he received a degree in law. When he returned to Nigeria, he became heavily involved in the anticolonial movement. In 1934, he cofounded the **Nigerian Youth Movement**. In 1937, he founded and ran the *Daily Service Press*. In 1941, Davies switched jobs and worked for the Agricultural Department for a couple of years. In 1944, he went to London, returning to Nigeria in 1947. He then served as the secretary and later chairman of the Nigerian Youth Movement in Lagos (1947–1949). After that he worked as the legal advisor to the **Action Group** and the Colony State Movement in Lagos. In 1958, he was chosen to act as a counsel to the queen of England. Davies was a member of the **Nigerian National Democratic Party** in 1964. He served as the minister of state in the Ministry of Industries from 1964 to 1966. Davies also worked for several multinational corporations in Nigeria, including Total.

**DEBT (RELIEF).** For decades, Nigeria received government-to-government loans in addition to multilateral loans (loans from international financial institutions such as the **World Bank**). Nigeria's total outstanding debt was an estimated $488.6 million in 1970. Nigeria's first major loan to service its debt, for $1 billion, was taken in 1978. By 1985, Nigeria was devoting over 33 percent of its export earnings to paying accrued debt. Nigeria's debt became a serious problem as a result of the growing import–export gap. Most experts at the time agreed that the way to handle the large debt was to restructure Nigeria's economy. Thus, Nigeria underwent a **structural adjustment program** designed and recommended by the International Monetary Fund (IMF) starting in the mid-1980s. However, Nigeria continued to take foreign loans to address immediate problems and failed to reach a balanced account system. It stopped taking foreign loans in 1992. In 2005, Nigeria received debt relief of $18 billion from the Paris Club lenders. In 2006, Nigeria paid off $4.6 billion of its debt, but it still owes $35 billion. *See also* ECONOMY.

**DELTA STATE.** A state created in 1991 out of **Bendel State**. It is one of nine states considered part of the **Niger Delta**. Its southeastern boundary is the Gulf of Guinea and its eastern boundary is the **Niger River**. It is one of Nigeria's current 36 states. It is home to Delta State University. Economic activities in Delta State include **petroleum** production; fishing; and cultivation of fruit (mango, pineapple, and **bananas**), rice, **yams**, **oil palm**, and rubber (the state's major export crop). The major **ethnic groups** in the state are the **Itsekiri**, **Igbo**, Urhobo, Izon, and Isoko. The most prominent **religions** in the state are **Christianity** and indigenous ones. The capital is the town of Asaba. Delta State, and particularly the town of **Warri**, has suffered from violent clashes and ongoing tension between the oil corporations and local communities. *See also* MINORITY GROUPS; NIGER DELTA CONFLICT.

**DEMOCRATIC ADVANCED MOVEMENT.** A **political party** led by Tunji Braithwaite, a lawyer. It was one of only nine political parties that received authorization by **General Alhaji Abdulsalami Abubakar** to field candidates for the 1999 **election**.

**DEMOCRATIC PARTY OF NIGERIA AND THE CAMEROONS.** A splinter group from the **National Council of Nigeria and the Cameroons**, which formed as a rival **political party** in 1958. It was led by **Kingsley Mbadiwe** and **Chief Kolawole Balogun**. The party focused on campaigning for a federal structure of government based on the principles of socialism. Two years after its formation, the party was disbanded after it performed poorly in the federal **elections**.

**DEVELOPMENT PLANS.** Nigeria underwent several development plans after 1960. In general, they overlapped in the vision to revive the agricultural sector, expand transportation and **electricity** networks, and create schools and training programs for skilled jobs. The first three development plans focused heavily on, and received public praise for, their efforts to transfer foreign business operations to Nigerian ownership, as well as for placing skilled Nigerian workers in positions previously held only by foreigners. These plans exemplified Nigeria's commitment to the establishment of a mix of state-owned industries and private enterprise.

The first plan (1962–1968) focused on economic growth. The second plan (1970–1974) was launched by **General Yakubu Gowon**. He projected a cost of ₦3 billion, but after several revisions ended up spending ₦5.3 billion. Like previous development plans, it sought to stimulate Nigeria's **economy** in the areas of **agriculture**, **education**, **health**, industry, **telecommunications**, defense, and transportation. More specifically, the plan was focused on rebuilding Nigeria, particularly in the East, after the **civil war**. The third plan (1976–1980) started with the recognition of several problems, including a shortage of indigenous skilled labor, poor condition of **roads**, and low returns from the agricultural sector. It was implemented by **General Olusegun Obasanjo** and focused on rural electrification and agricultural development.

Since 1980, Nigeria has increasingly moved toward reducing the number of state-owned industries and following a program of **privatization**. The fourth and fifth plans worked within the framework of a **structural adjustment program**, which involved the management of loans. As a result, the emphasis was opposite in many ways to that of the first three development plans. The fourth plan (1981–1985) emphasized the involvement of local and state governments in identifying and expediting development programs. The fifth plan (1988–1992), introduced by **General Ibrahim Babangida**, was based on continual assessment and revision as opposed to one plan executed over several years. The goals of the fifth plan included conservative expansion of infrastructure and stabilizing Nigeria's **currency**. *See also* AIRLINES.

**DIKE, KENNETH O. (1917–1983).** Dike was born in December 1917 in Awka, in **Anambra State**. He left Nigeria and attended Fourah Bay College in Sierra Leone. He received his advanced degrees from the University of Durham. Dike was a major contributor to the revision and expansion of historical works on Africa. One of his pioneering works is *Trade and Politics in the Niger Delta, 1830–1885* (1956). He taught at the **University of Ibadan** and invested many years in setting up Nigeria's National Archives. He was a research fellow at the West African Institute of Social and Economic Research (1952–1954). At the University of Ibadan, he served as vice chancellor (1960) and as the director of the Institute of African Studies (1962–1967).

**DIKKO, RUSSELL ALIYU BARAU (1912–1977).** Born in June 1912 in **Zaria**, Dikko studied at the Church Missionary Society School in Zaria and **King's College** in **Lagos**. He was one of the few **Fulani** people to convert to **Christianity**. To further his education, he went overseas and studied medicine at the University of Birmingham in England. Upon returning to Nigeria, he worked as a junior medical officer (1940–1941), medical officer (1941–1953), and senior medical officer. In 1948 he assisted in the formation of the **Jam'iyyar Mutanen Arewa**. When the organization became the **Northern People's Congress political party** in 1951, he served as its head for two years. He was minister of health of the **Northern Region** (1962–1967) and commissioner for mines and power in the **Federal Executive Council** (1967–1971). From 1971 to 1975, he served as the commissioner of transport.

**DINA COMMITTEE.** A committee convened in 1968 by the federal military government to evaluate **revenue allocation** among the 12 states. The committee was led by Chief Isaac Dina. Ultimately, the committee suggested that a new allocation scheme be devised, which would include an allocation schedule for state and federal governments. It also recommended a uniform income tax and a federally funded **education** system. The committee's recommendations were not accepted.

**DIPCHARIMA, ZANNA BUKAR SULOMA (1917–1969).** Born in 1917 in **Maiduguri**, Dipcharima studied at Maiduguri Middle School and Katsina Higher College. After earning his teaching certification in 1938, he taught at various grammar schools. In 1946, he became heavily involved in national politics. He was an active member of the **National Council of Nigeria and the Cameroons**. He worked briefly for John Holt Company. When he returned to national politics, he joined the **Northern People's Congress**. He also worked for the Borno Native Authority. In 1954, he was a member of the **Federal House of Representatives** in **Lagos**. In 1964, he worked for the Ministry of Transport and later served as the minister of transport (1964). During the first military **coup d'état**, he was a member of the cabinet that oversaw the transition from civilian to military rule. Dipcharima died in a plane crash in 1969.

**DIVINATION.** Many **ethnic groups** in Nigeria engage in the practice of divination, which is carried out by a trained individual to obtain information from gods and ancestors that is not available to people through ordinary empirical means. The practice was more common prior to colonial rule among both Muslim and non-Muslim people than it is today. Information collected through divination is used for things such as finding a guilty person, diagnosing and healing an illness, calling for rain, solving social problems, and determining the succession of **kings**. Divination is used to guide people, individually or communally, into the future. Diviners are typically men who have gone through rigorous training. In order to receive messages from ancestors and gods, the diviner must go into an altered state of consciousness. Diviners tend to draw conclusions about **health** more from a perceived societal and spiritual imbalance than a physical, internal one.

For the most part, the purpose, social role, and principles of interpretation are the same across groups. The interpretation, tools (and related paraphernalia), and methods of invocation often differ. The **Nupe** practice *eba*, which involves the throwing of **cowry shells**, and *hatí* (the word is a derivative of the Arabic word *hatim*, meaning magic square), which involves the drawing of patterns in the sand. The **Yoruba** also throw cowry shells, **kolanuts**, or **oil palm** nuts when practicing *ifa* divination. For example, a Yoruba divination priest, or *babalawo*, would give 16 cowry shells to the client, who in turn would whisper his or her problem to the shells and throw them into a wooden tray covered in sand. The *babalawo* relies on a sacred text (which comprises 16 books and 800 verses) to interpret the client's throw and draw his conclusion. Before colonial rule, it was not uncommon for a **chief** or **king** to keep a trusted diviner close to the palace and consult him. Divination is often associated with **traditional medicine** because of its use in healing the sick. *See also* ORACLE; RELIGION.

**DIYA, LIEUTENANT GENERAL DONALDSON OLADIPO (1944– ).** As a young man, Diya studied at Yaba Methodist Primary School in **Lagos**, the Odogbolu Grammar School, and the Nigerian Defence Academy in **Kaduna**. In 1971, he left Nigeria for further military training in the United States. Diya served as the military governor of **Ogun State** from 1984 to 1985 and as a member of the **Armed Forces Ruling Council** from 1985 to 1987. Diya was brought into **General Sani Abacha**'s **Federal Executive Council** as chief of general staff. Many saw Diya as strategically placed in that position to give the effect of fair and equal representation among the different **ethnic groups** in Nigeria in the military, because he was a **Yoruba**. In 1997, Abacha accused Diya of plotting a **coup d'état** and sentenced him to prison. Two years later he was released. *See also* ARMED FORCES.

**DOGONYARO, MAJOR GENERAL JOSHUA NIMYEL (1942– ).** Dogonyaro was born in September 1942 in Dakan-Kuka, in **Plateau State**. As a young man, he studied at the Boys' Secondary School in Gindiri, Nigerian Defence Academy in **Kaduna** (1964–1967), Nigerian Army School of Infantry, and the National Institute for Policy and Strategy Studies. He enlisted in the army in 1964 and was promoted to major general in 1988. He held numerous positions in the army, particularly during the **civil war**. His notoriety came from his announcing on 27 August 1985 the replacement of **General Muhammadu Buhari** by **General Ibrahim Babangida** in a military **coup d'état**. Dogonyaro served as a member of the **Armed Forces Ruling Council**. In the 1990s he served in Liberia. After retiring from the **armed forces** in 1993, he received the Forces Service Star.

**DOSUNMU (?–1885).** Dosunmu ruled **Lagos** from 1853 to 1885. His father, **Akinoye**, died in 1853. The British supported his ascension to the throne, but in August 1861 they took Lagos from him by force. Dosunmu refused to cooperate and placed his life at risk. Although he maintained his title as **king** of Lagos, it was largely symbolic. Dosunmu was viewed by some as a weak ruler, who required regular assistance from the British to maintain order. Under pressure from the British, he interdicted trade between Lagos and Ekpe and sent **Madam Tinubu** out of Lagos.

**DRUG CONTROL.** In 1966, the Nigerian government passed Indian Hemp Decree No. 19, which stipulated that the possession of hemp would result in no less than 10 years' imprisonment and hard labor. In 1975, an amendment to the Indian Hemp Decree reduced the prison sentence to no less than six months or a fine for possession. Decree No. 20 (1984) imposed punishment or death for the possession, use, and selling of narcotics. It also established the Miscellaneous Offences Tribunal to try drug offenders. If someone were caught using, selling, or possessing cocaine (or other hard drugs), the punishment was to be death by firing squad. After the public execution of three men under the stipulations of Decree No. 20, the law was relaxed. Decree No. 22 (1986) determined that the punishment for involvement with hard drugs would no longer be death, but imprisonment. In the 1980s, Nigeria stepped up its efforts to secure its borders and keep drugs out of the country. It set up a National Drug Unit at the border in 1988. In 1989, Nigeria signed the Mutual Legal Assistance Treaty with the United States. A similar treaty was signed with **Great Britain**.

Nigeria created the National Drug Law Enforcement Agency in 1990. However, **corruption** undermined the legitimacy and effectiveness of the agencies and the decrees. In 2007, Nigerian law enforcement made over 200 arrests at the **Lagos** airport for drug trafficking. Nigerian drug couriers are moving drugs from outside West Africa to Europe. For example, cocaine moves from South America to West Africa en route to Western Europe. On Nigeria's streets, drugs are circulated by gangs, or "area boys." Drug trafficking and abuse are on the rise in Nigeria, but nowhere near the levels seen in the United States and Europe. *See also* CRIME; LEGAL SYSTEM.

**DUAL MANDATE.** *See* LUGARD, SIR FREDERICK.

**DUNAMA DIBBALEMI (?–1259).** Dunama was the ruler of the **Kanuri** people in the **Kanem-Bornu Empire** between 1221 and 1259 (some sources have 1203–1242 or 1210–1248). He focused on expanding his territory and strengthening the empire. This ruler of the **Sefawa Dynasty** was able to gain control of trade flowing north of Lake Chad. Many of his commanders broke away and established their own states. Dunama was one of the earliest Kanuri leaders on record to have contact, possibly conflict, with the **Bulala** people. He is also credited with setting up a religious school in Cairo for Kanuri students.

**DUNAMA IBN AHMAD LEFIAMI (?–1820).** Dunama was ruler of the **Kanem-Bornu Empire** from 1808 to 1809 and again from 1813 to 1820. He assisted **Muhammed al-Amin al-Kanemi** against the **Fulani,** who occupied Birni N'gazargamu. Together they protected

Kanem-Bornu from Fulani control. In gratitude, Dunama gave al-Kanemi a tract of land. In 1809, the **Kanuri** people deposed Dunama and placed Muhammed Ngileruma on the throne. Dunama was killed in 1820 during a conflict with al-Kanemi.

## – E –

**EAST-CENTRAL STATE.** A state created in 1967 as one of Nigeria's 12 states. In 1976, East-Central State was divided into **Imo State** and **Anambra State**. East-Central State was located in the **Niger Delta**, with the **Niger River** as its western boundary. *See also* STATE CREATION.

**EASTERN HOUSE OF ASSEMBLY.** Created by the **Richards Constitution** in 1946, the assembly included the **chief commissioner**, official and unofficial members, and men nominated by the regional governor. It served as a moderator between the local **Native Authorities** and the **Legislative Council** in **Lagos**. As a result of the 1966 **coup d'état**, the Eastern House of Assembly was dissolved. *See also* HOUSES OF ASSEMBLY; NORTHERN HOUSE OF ASSEMBLY; WESTERN HOUSE OF ASSEMBLY.

**EASTERN HOUSE OF CHIEFS.** Unlike the other two regions (**Northern** and **Western**), the **Eastern Region** did not have a House of Chiefs until 1959, when it was created by the ruling party of the region, the **National Council of Nigeria and the Cameroons**. The Eastern House of Chiefs was dissolved after the 1966 **coup d'état**. *See also* CHIEFS; HOUSE OF CHIEFS; NORTHERN HOUSE OF CHIEFS; WESTERN HOUSE OF CHIEFS.

**EASTERN NIGERIA.** Eastern Nigeria is the area primarily east of the Niger–Benue confluence and south of the states that border the **Benue River**. States considered part of eastern Nigeria include **Bayelsa**, **Delta**, **Rivers**, **Enugu**, **Anambra**, **Ebonyi**, **Abia**, **Cross River**, and **Akwa Ibom**. Important cities in eastern Nigeria include **Port Harcourt**, **Enugu**, **Warri**, and **Calabar**. The **Igbo** are the ethnic majority in eastern Nigeria; among the other groups present are the **Ibibio**,

Ijaw, and **Ogoni**. Eastern Nigeria encompasses the same territory as the **Eastern Region** during colonial rule and the **First Republic**. Today, eastern Nigeria receives a great deal of international attention due to turmoil taking place in the **Niger Delta** over poverty, environmental destruction, and **petroleum** development. *See also* ETHNIC GROUPS; MIDDLE BELT; MINORITY GROUPS; NORTHERN NIGERIA; SOUTHERN NIGERIA; WESTERN NIGERIA.

**EASTERN REGION.** One of the three regions, along with the **Northern Region** and **Western Region**, developed during British colonial rule that were established under the **Richards Constitution** of 1946. This region attained self-government within Nigeria's federal structure in 1957. The governors from October 1954 through May 1960 were British colonial officials: Sir Clement Pleass (October 1954–November 1956) and Sir Robert Stapledon (November 1956–May 1960). After May 1960, the governors of the Eastern Region were Nigerian. In addition to a governor, the Eastern Region also had a **premier**. **Nnamdi Azikiwe** was the region's first premier (October 1954–December 1959), and **Michael Okpara** was the second (January 1960–January 1966). The regional divisions were retained after **independence** in 1960, during the **First Republic**.

The Eastern Region includes the area from east of the **Niger River** to the border of **Cameroon** and south of the **Benue River**. Its **population** is largely **Igbo**; other **ethnic groups** present are **Ibibio, Ijaw,** and **Tiv**. When **General Yakubu Gowon** reconfigured the four regions into 12 states in 1967, the Eastern Region was turned into three states (**Eastern-Central, South-Eastern**, and **Rivers**). Gowon's decision to divide Nigeria into 12 states largely stemmed from his desire to weaken eastern unity. During the **civil war** (1967–1970) the Eastern Region, under the leadership of **Chief Chukwuemeka Ojukwu**, seceded from the federation and formed the **Republic of Biafra**. Today, the name Eastern Region indicates the same area as during the First Republic, but emphasizes the cultural aspects that make the area unique. It is used interchangeably with **eastern Nigeria**. *See also* MINORITY GROUPS.

**EASTERN REGIONAL GOVERNMENT CRISIS.** In January 1953, turmoil associated with the **National Council of Nigeria and**

the **Cameroons** (NCNC) developed in the **Eastern Region**. The region's Parliamentary Committee called for the resignation of nine members to reinforce **Nnami Azikiwe**'s authority over the party and region. The goal was to reshuffle members of the Parliamentary Committee and regional Executive Council. One month later, six ministers were given a vote of no confidence by the **Eastern House of Assembly**. Arguments developed over the **election** process. The colonial **lieutenant governor** became involved in the crisis and called for the temporary disbanding of the Eastern House of Assembly. In a new round of elections, Nnamdi Azikiwe and the NCNC took control of the Eastern Region's government. *See also* FOSTER-SUTTON COMMISSION OF INQUIRY.

**EASTERN STATES INTERIM ASSETS AND LIABILITIES AGENCY.** The federal military government set up this agency in 1970 under Decree No. 39. The purpose of the agency was to assess and administer all assets and liabilities of the former **Eastern Region**. It was also charged with distributing the assets equally among the three new states: **East-Central**, **South-Eastern**, and **Rivers**. The agency was dissolved in 1975 by Decree No. 19.

**EBONYI STATE.** Located in the **Niger Delta** region in **southern Nigeria**, Ebonyi State was created in 1996 out of parts of **Enugu State** and **Abia State**. Ebonyi State is one of Nigeria's current 36 states. The **Igbo** make up the majority of the ethnic **population** of the state. Ebonyi State is located inland from the Bight of Bonny in southeastern Nigeria. Economic activities in the state include the cultivation of **yams** and beans. It also produces its own brand of rice, named after the state's capital, Abakiliki. Located in Ebonyi State are two major **salt** water deposits, earning the state the nickname "Salt of the Nation." The state is named after the Aboine River. *See also* STATE CREATION.

**ECONOMIC COMMUNITY OF WEST AFRICAN STATES (ECOWAS).** A regional body established to promote accelerated and sustained economic development and to create a more homogenous society, leading to unity. To make this happen, all 14 West African member countries agreed to eliminate customs and other duties on **trade** and implement a regionwide tariff. The Economic Community of West African States is somewhat like a mini-version of United Nations and was inspired by the United Nations Economic Commission for Africa, which held a conference in the mid-1960s that divided Africa into regions for the purposes of economic development. The creation of ECOWAS was slow, developing through a series of meetings over several years. In 1972, Nigeria and Togo launched the community and encouraged others to join. A treaty was formally signed among the West African countries in **Lagos** on 28 May 1975.

ECOWAS is not without its problems. Influence in the organization is based on **population**, geographic size, and economic strength. There was little to no preexisting trade among the members, making any trade agreements weak. The former French colonies in the community continue to share the Franc **currency**, which is more stable. The memory of a being colonial states has prevented each member country from sacrificing any sense of sovereignty for the good of the community. Nonetheless, ECOWAS has developed funds for cooperation and development. It has set aside resources for compensating member states that suffered major economic losses. ECOWAS has also engaged in the development of projects that link member states in the sharing of resources such as **electricity** and natural gas.

In August 1990, ECOWAS created the Economic Community of West African States Monitoring Group (ECOMOG) to intervene in Liberia's civil wars. ECOMOG requires the pooling of national **armed forces**. Thus far, Nigeria has supplied the most soldiers and equipment. At the same time, Nigeria has been accused of using its strength to push its own agenda. ECOMOG has received credit for providing a positive force in the Liberian and Sierra Leone civil wars. Nigeria, in particular, has been praised for ending Liberia's second civil war by offering Charles Taylor asylum in August 2003, which effectively stopped the bloodshed. *See also* AFRICAN UNION; ECONOMY; FOREIGN TRADE; NEW PARTNERSHIP FOR AFRICAN DEVELOPMENT.

**ECONOMY.** One of Nigeria's biggest challenges has been its economy. Every head of state has promised a dramatic economic turnaround, the end to **corruption**, and the cure for high **unemploy-**

**ment**. At independence, Nigeria's economy was relatively strong, but dependent on foreign consumers, with a burgeoning oil export industry and stable cash crop production. Between 1966 and 1980, Nigeria's rate of economic growth increased significantly as its annual oil exports went from almost 140 million barrels (bbl) in 1966 to a little over 800 million bbl in 1979. However, although Nigeria's gross national income (GNI) may have risen, its standard of living and **agricultural** sector declined.

Nigeria's leaders implemented a series of **development plans, price controls**, and **revenue allocation** schemes designed to stimulate nationwide economic development. These programs included a mixture of **industrialization, indigenization**, and nationalization. Poor management of finances, global economic downturns, and corruption prevented these plans from spurring development. By the mid-1980s, Nigeria's economy was in such bad shape that **General Ibrahim Badamasi Babangida** changed course and placed the country in an austere **structural adjustment program**. By 2000, nearly all of Nigeria's nationalization plans had been repealed and replaced with **privatization**. In 2004, **General Olusegun Obasanjo** implemented his National Economic Empowerment and Development Strategy to improve government spending and the process of privatization. In 2007, the annual salary for a doctor was $6,720 and for a teacher, $1,920.

Overall, minor improvements have been made to Nigeria's economy, but over 54 percent of Nigerians are surviving on $2 or less a day. Nigeria has a low GNI of $930 and a poor human development index (HDI) ranking of 158 out of 177, which takes into account literacy and life expectancy to accurately measure the country's chance of sustainable development. *See also* NATIONAL ECONOMIC RECONSTRUCTION FUND.

**EDET, INSPECTOR GENERAL LOUIS OROLA (1913–1979).** Edet was born in August 1913 in **Calabar**. After completing his primary and secondary education in **Bonny** and Calabar, he joined the **police** force. During **World War II**, he worked for the Immigration Department. After serving as a member of the United Nations peacekeeping force in Central Africa, Edet became police commissioner in **Abuja**. In 1964, he was promoted to the rank of inspector general, making him the first African to hold the title. He retired from the police force in 1966 after the first military **coup d'état**. He later worked for the Nigerian High Commission in London and the government of **South-Eastern State** after the **civil war**. He received the honorary titles Commander of the Order of the British Empire and member of the Order of the Federal Republic of Nigeria. Edet died in January 1979.

**EDO.** An **ethnic group** spread across **Edo State** and **Delta State** in the **Niger Delta**. The name refers not only to an ethnic group, but also to a **language** shared by the people of **Benin**, Ishan, and **Itsekiri**, to name a few. **Oral tradition** credits Edo speakers with founding the **Benin Kingdom** and establishing the first ruling dynasty. After the *ogiso* (meaning "**king**") was driven out of Benin, a **Yoruba** Dynasty ruled the kingdom. This explains why the Edo and Yoruba share cultural and artistic features, but not language. *See also* MINORITY GROUPS.

**EDO STATE.** One of nine states in Nigeria located in the **Niger Delta**, Edo was created in 1991 out of **Bendel State**. It is one of Nigeria's 36 current states. Its capital is **Benin**. The people of Edo trace their history back to members of the first **Benin Kingdom**, and many are ethnic Edo. The primary **language** spoken in the state is Edo (also called Bini). Economic activities in Edo include the cultivation of **yams**, rice, fruits, **oil palm**, and rubber and the mining of quartz, gold, and **coal**. *See also* STATE CREATION.

**EDUCATION.** Education in Nigeria has assumed a variety of forms. Among Nigeria's precolonial societies, life lessons and skills were imparted through **oral traditions**, apprenticeship systems, and **Koranic schools**. Oral traditions involved the telling of family history, teaching of cultural and religious practices, and enforcing a moral code and social conduct. They combined memorization of details with creative expression. For agricultural skills and craft production, early societies relied on the apprentice system, in which young people would spend time with family members, learning their trades. Typically, gender determined the skills that would be learned. Young girls could learn agricultural and domestic skills (this would often include a craft, depending on the culture), and boys could learn about

**trade**, a craft, **agriculture**, and raising livestock. The apprenticeship system was particularly popular for young artists. For communities that practiced **Islam**, studying the **Koran** was an important part of a young person's education. Attending a Koranic school involved reading and memorizing part or all of the Koran and studying aspects of Islamic doctrine. The Koranic school model, however, declined during colonial rule. Isolated efforts were made to maintain this form of education. For example, the Young Unsar-Ud-Deen Society formed in 1923 to develop Muslim schools in major towns across Nigeria.

Educational systems changed under colonial rule. The arrival of Christian missionaries in the region involved the establishment of missionary schools, which were to train young people in the fundamentals of **Christianity** and (Western) social conduct as well as to provide them with a basic Western education. Nigeria is home to several of Africa's oldest primary/secondary schools. The Baptist Academy in **Lagos** was founded in 1854; the **Church Missionary Society** Grammar School in Bariga in 1859; the Methodist High Schools for boys and girls of Yaba in 1878 and 1879, respectively; and **King's College** in Lagos in 1909. Under colonial rule, Nigeria's educational development became geographically lopsided between the North and South. Islamic institutions in **northern Nigeria** continued to operate without significant meddling by British administrators and Christian missionaries. As a result, the North did not experience the establishment of missionary schools. In the South, however, missionary schools established a foundation of Western formal education in the region. Scholars attribute this to the recommendations of colonial inquiries on education, such as the Phelps-Stokes Commission and the **Memorandum on Education Policy in British Tropical Africa**. The Phelps-Stokes Commission of 1924 recommended the cooperation of colonial administration and Christian missions in providing education for Nigerian youth. In independent Nigeria, the lack of formal, Western education was viewed as a hindrance to the country's development that had to be addressed. The **Elliot Commission** (1943) and the **Asquith Commission** (1945) called for establishment of universities in Nigeria.

In contemporary Nigeria, all levels of government contribute to the educational system. For example, local governments may run primary and secondary schools, while state and federal governments operate universities and technical institutes. The need for the latter was raised by the Thorp and Harlow Commission in April 1949. Three years later, the Nigerian College of Arts, Science, and Technology was established, with its first branch in **Zaria**. In the late 1950s, the **Eastern** and **Western Regions** implemented **universal primary education**, guaranteeing a free education to all children in their regions. Attendance was compulsory for all school-aged children. The regional governments were charged with constructing schools and covering the cost. In 1961, the **Northern Region** appointed the **Oldman Commission** to examine universal primary education for its children. In 1976, the idea, conceptualized by **Chief Obafemi Awolowo**, was implemented on a national level.

The number of universities and specialized education programs increased substantially between 1960 and 1980. The Nigerian Defence Academy for the **armed forces** was established in 1964 and trained many of Nigeria's prominent leaders. From 1964 to 1976, the federal government covered all of the expenses incurred by the University of Lagos and the **University of Ibadan**. At one point, Nigeria had the most advanced and prestigious institutions of **higher education** in West Africa. By the 1990s, however, economic turmoil and political instability had taken their toll. The scheme of universal primary education was dismantled, and higher education was no longer completely, or even partially, free for students. Nigeria's leaders saw this decline happening and struggled to find ways to prevent the impending crisis. Periodically, since 1960, the federal government has set up commissions, such as the Nigerian Educational Research Council and the Curriculum Conference of 1969, to examine Nigeria's educational system and suggest ways to improve it. Ultimately, the conclusions of these commissions were shelved due to financial constraints across the country. Yet even as Nigeria's public schools lurch forward with limited funds, tools, and skilled teachers, its private schools are thriving. The private schools are run by secular and religious institutions. Christ the King College in **Onitsha**, for example, is currently considered one of Nigeria's best secondary schools.

An estimated 66 percent of adults were identified as literate in 2004. The enrollment of students in primary school in 2004 broke down to 74 percent of boys and 60 percent of girls. Today, the government's primary concern is funding and quality. Students struggle to pay their fees, only to encounter dilapidated classrooms, rundown computer labs, and empty libraries. As a result, strikes on university campuses by faculty, staff, and students are not uncommon. Bright Nigerian students with financial resources are forced to complete their education abroad. Many complain that the draining of Nigeria's most talented and resourceful people is caused by a failing educational system. *See also* BANJO COMMISSION; JOINT ADMISSIONS AND MATRICULATION BOARD; MONGUNO, ALHAJI CHIEF ALI; NOMADIC SCHOOLS.

**EFIK.** An **ethnic group** that lives primarily in **Cross River State**, in the **Niger Delta**. They are culturally and linguistically connected to the **Ibibio**. The Efik engaged heavily in **trade** from the 17th to the 19th centuries. In 1846, the **Church of Scotland Mission** set up a station in **Calabar** to spread **Christianity** among the Efik. The Efik, like many other ethnic groups, have tried to preserve and maintain a sense of cultural pride and community. The Esop Ndito Efik Efut Ye Qua is a **hometown association** created to maintain ties between the Efik outside Calabar and Nigeria and the Efik in Calabar. The Efik are known for developing the Ekpe (meaning "leopard") secret society, which was introduced to Calabar in the 19th century from **Cameroon**. The secret society facilitated trade and ensured peace and unity among the segmented Efik communities. *See also* MINORITY GROUPS.

**EGBA.** The Egba people live in southwestern Nigeria and are a subgroup of the **Yoruba**. The **paramount chief** of the Egba is called the *alake*. In the 18th century, **Lishabi** broke the Egba away from the **Oyo Empire**. Egba independence was threatened again later. The Egba left **Ibadan** in 1830, led by Sodeke, and settled in **Abeokuta**. Prior to colonial economic dominance, the Egba engaged in blacksmithing, carpentry, and cloth dyeing. During the **Yoruba Wars**, the Egba offered protection to refugees fleeing from the fighting. The Ijaye and Owu, for example, sought protection and settled among the Egba. A treaty signed by the governor of **Lagos** and Egba **chiefs** in 1893 granted the Egba semiautonomy under the **Egba United Government**. In 1914, the Egba demonstrated against the incarceration of Adegboyega Edun, who died in prison. Egba authorities were not able to contain the protests and invited troops from Lagos to assist, which caused the Ijemo Massacre. This violent outburst resulted in the Egba losing their independence to the British colonial government. Four years later, the Egba fought in the **Adubi War** against British colonial forces over their loss of sovereignty and the introduction of **indirect rule**. *See also* EGBA UNITED GOVERNMENT; ETHNIC GROUPS.

**EGBA UNITED GOVERNMENT (EUG).** This system of semiautonomous government existed from 1893 to 1914 specifically for the **Egba** in **Abeokuta**. The *alake* (**paramount chief** of the Egba people) had central authority. The eight-member Egba Central Council (EUG) assisted the *alake*. The council included a Muslim and a Christian **chief**. It is most associated with Gbadebo, the *alake* from 1898 to 1920. The EUG controlled the collection of export **taxes** as well as tariffs on imported **alcohol**. The administration was small, numbering about 350 by 1908. Under the EUG's political authority, a prison was built, **roads** were constructed, and vaccinations were distributed. The EUG included a customs department, police department, public printing office, education department, and post office. In 1918, Egba autonomy ended, but not without great resistance. In June 1918, the Egba engaged in a war with the British called the **Adubi War**. *See also* TRADE.

**EGBA UPRISING.** *See* ADUBI WAR.

**EGBE OMO ODUDUWA.** A cultural organization created by **Chief Obafemi Awolowo**. One of its founding members was **Akinola Maja**, who later became president. The organization's name means "descendents of Oduduwa." It drew its support from traditional rulers as well as the Western educated elite. It was designed to create an appearance of political neutrality by traditional Yoruba leaders. In 1950, the organization's secretary, Isaac Delano, traveled around Nigeria promoting the organization and inducting new members. *See also* EGBE OMO OLOFIN; EGBE OMO YORUBA.

**EGBE OMO OLOFIN.** A pan-**Yoruba** organization that formed in January 1964, it was similar to **Egbe Omo Oduduwa** in that it was also a cultural organization designed to promote Yoruba political interests. Founders saw this group as the "true" name of their Yoruba ancestor and hoped to merge it with Egbe Omo Oduduwa. Members of Egbe Omo Oduduwa, however, refused to join. *See also* EGBE OMO YORUBA.

**EGBE OMO YORUBA.** A cultural organization based outside of Nigeria, but with a focus on the maintenance of **Yoruba** culture and ties to Nigeria. It is also referred to as the National Association of Yoruba Descendants in North America and is based in Washington, D.C. The organization formally came into being when its constitution was ratified in 1995. There are chapters across the United States in many of the major cities, especially in the southeast. In the past, it has made public statements about political developments in Nigeria. For example, it acted as a pressure group for the release of Yoruba political prisoners being detained by **General Olusegun Obasanjo** in 2005. The organization is concerned with the well-being of the Yoruba in Nigeria and North America. Egbe Omo Yoruba holds national conventions and quarterly meetings for the executive council. It is similar to a **hometown association**, but differs in that it is focused on an **ethnic group** as opposed to a specific town of that ethnic group. In brief, it is a contemporary and globalized version of the **Egbe Omo Oduduwa**. *See also* EGBE OMO OLOFIN.

*EGUNGUN.* A plural word meaning "ancestral spirits masquerading," which usually takes place during a festival. *Egungu* is a masked god who returns to the living world from the spiritual world. Although *egungun* originated among the Yoruba, it spread to neighboring **ethnic groups**. The **Nupe** for example, practiced *egungun* and introduced it into **Borgu**. The *egungu*'s dress includes bright colors, feathers from different kinds of birds, or skins of various animals. The body of the *egungu* is concealed from head to foot. The *egungu*'s vision is restricted through a small mesh cloth over the eyes. The masquerades were used to collect money for **women**. However, they have also been described as a lucky time for men, because women paid for the food. Also, men could call on the *egungun* if they wanted to reinforce their dominance, in the form of punishment, over their wives. The punishment for revealing the secret of *egungun* to women is death. In ancient times, the *egungun* were in charge of killing women who were practicing witchcraft. The annual festival to worship the *egungun* typically occurs in February and overlaps with the end of the bean harvest. The anniversary of the *egungun* comes in either May or June. The *egungun* also appear at funerals.

**EJOOR, MAJOR GENERAL DAVID AKPODE (1932– ).** Born in January 1932 in Ovu, in **Delta State**, as a young man Ejoor studied at the Church Missionary Society School and Baptist School in Ovu. He also attended the Native Administration School in Isiokolo (1946–1947) and Government College in Ughelli (1948–1952) before focusing on his military career. He attended military training centers in **Ghana** and **Great Britain**. Like many notable military leaders in Nigeria, Ejoor attended the Royal Military Academy at Sandhurst (1955–1956) and the Royal College of Defence Studies (1971). He started his career as an officer cadet in the (Royal) **West African Frontier Force**. In the army, he held several leadership positions. He served as company commander in the Congo for United Nations from 1960 to 1963 and was governor of the **Mid-Western Region** from January 1966 to August 1967. The Mid-Western Region was occupied by Biafran forces from August to September 1967, forcing Ejoor to side with them out of expediency.

In 1971, he was promoted to major general. Ejoor served as chief of staff for the army (1972–1975), after which he formally retired. In the 1980s, he was chairman of the board of directors for the West African Provincial Insurance Company and chairman of the Nigerian–Belgian Chamber of Commerce. Ejoor received several honorary titles, including Officer of the Order of the Federal Republic (1982), Grand Commander of the Order of the Niger (1984), and Grand Commander of the Republic of Togo. He also acquired the chieftaincy titles *olorogun* of Olomu, *okakuro* of Agbon, and *ohovwore* of Ovu. In recent years, Ejoor has been publicly honored as a distinguished member of the Urhobo community. *See also* ARMED FORCES.

**EKANDEM, CARDINAL DOMINIC (1917–1995).** Born in Ibiono, in **Cross River State**, Ekandem was baptized in 1928. He was the first **Catholic** priest in the Calabar Diocese. In 1952, he served as rector at the Queen of Apostles Seminary. Two years later, he became a bishop, making him the youngest religious official in British West Africa. In 1963, he relocated to Ikot Ekpene. After the **civil**

**war**, he acted as an administrator in the Port Harcourt Diocese. He was president of the Catholic Bishops Conference of Nigeria for two terms in the 1970s. He was the first archbishop of **Abuja**, and in 1976 he rose to the rank of cardinal. Ekandem died in Abuja.

**EKE, IFEGWU (1935– ).** Born in May 1935 at Abiriba, in **Abia State**, Eke lived and studied in **eastern Nigeria** until he finished secondary school. He completed his postgraduate studies at Harvard University. After a variety of jobs in the field of economics in the United States and Canada, he returned to Nigeria to work for the federal government. He served as the commissioner of information for the **Republic of Biafra** during the **civil war**. He was the senior economist for the Ministry of Finance and Economic Planning Commission in **Enugu**. He also provided information within and outside the Republic of Biafra. After the **civil war**, Eke withdrew from public life.

**EKITI STATE.** A state created in 1996 out of **Ondo State**, located in southwestern Nigeria, with its capital at Ado-Ekiti. It is one of Nigeria's current 36 states. In the **Yoruba language**, *ekiti* means "hill," which is indicative of the landscape. The state is largely populated by the Ekiti, a **Yoruba** subgroup. The Ekiti are primarily practitioners of **Christianity** or **Islam**. Economic activities in the state include the cultivation of **cocoa**, rubber, and **oil palm** as well as the mining of quartzite and granite. *See also* STATE CREATION.

**EKWENSI, CYPRIAN ODIATU DUAKA (1921–2007).** Born in September 1921 in Minna, in **Niger State**, as a young man Ekwensi attended Government School in **Jos**, Government College in **Ibadan**, and **Yaba Higher College**. He also studied at the School of Pharmacy at Yaba (1947–1949) and University of London, where he received his doctorate (1956). Focusing his career solely on writing, he attended the International Writing Program at the University of Iowa. He taught at Igbobi College (1947–1949) and School of Pharmacy (1949–1951). He then worked for the Nigerian Medical Services (1956–1957), Nigerian Broadcasting Corporation (1957–1961), and Federal Ministry of Information (1961–1967). During the **civil war**, he worked for the Broadcasting Corporation of the **Republic of Biafra** (1967–1970). By the 1970s, his activities centered more on politics and the media than on pharmaceuticals. He became managing director of Star Printing and publisher and consultant for the *Weekly Trumpet*, the *Daily News*, and the *Weekly Eagle* **newspapers** (1980–1981). Ekwensi is attributed with coining the concept **War Against Indiscipline**. In 1985, he was a member of the board of governors of the Federal Broadcasting Corporation. He died in November 2007.

Throughout his career, Ekwensi devoted a great deal of time to writing novels and short stories. He also chronicled oral folktales. His first novel was *People of the City* (1954), and his most notable works include *Burning Grass* (1962) and *Gone to Mecca* (1991). Many of his stories have been translated into foreign languages. *African Night's Entertainment* (1962), for instance, was translated into Swahili. He received the Dag Hammarskjold International Award for Literary Merit in 1968 and was inducted into the Nigerian Academy of Letters in 2006. *See also* LITERATURE.

**EKWUEME, ALEX IFEANYICHUKWU (1932– ).** Ekwueme was born in October 1932 in Oko, in **Anambra State**. After completing grammar school, he attended **King's College** in **Lagos** (1945–1950), the University of Washington in Seattle (1952–1957), the University of London (1976–1978), and the University of Nigeria at **Enugu** (1988–1989). He also attended the Nigerian Law School at Lagos from 1990 to 1991. Upon completion of his studies he earned a doctorate in law. He worked as a clerk for Nigerian Railways, as a teacher at King's College, as an architect for a private firm in London, and as a coordinator for Esso. In 1958, he formed the Ekwueme Associates (Architects and Town Planners). He also worked closely with the Nigerian Institute of Architects. During the 1970s, Ekwueme was a member of the East Central State Development Authority and East Central State Advisory Committee on the Prerogative of Mercy.

Ekwueme served as vice president of the Federal Republic of Nigeria from 1979 to 1983. A military **coup d'état** ejected him from the position. On 1 December 1983, he was arrested and was detained for three years. In 1994, he was an elected member of the National Constitutional Conference. In the political arena, he was an executive member of the **National Party of Nigeria** (1979–1983) and a member of the **People's Democratic Party**. In 1999, he was the presidential hopeful for the People's Democratic Party. He also received several honorary titles, including *ide* (**chief**) of Aguata, Oko, and Orumba, and Grand Commander of the Order of the Niger (1988). He received honorary degrees from Abia State University (1996) and the Federal University of Technology (1997).

**ELECTION OF 12 JUNE 1993. Alhaji Bashir Tofa**, a northern **Hausa** Muslim, and **Chief M. K. O. Abiola**, a southern **Yoruba** Muslim, were the strongest opposing candidates in this **election**. Sylvester Ugoh was Tofa's running mate and **Baba Gana Kingibe** was Abiola's. Tofa was the **National Republican Convention**'s candidate; Abiola was the **Social Democratic Party**'s candidate. These two **political parties** were established by **General Ibrahim Babangida**. The election was supposed to mark the start of the **Third Republic** and a new **constitution**, which had been drafted in 1989. However, Babangida meddled with the election process and ultimately canceled it. After the majority of the election returns were tallied, the results from 14 states and the **Federal Capital Territory** indicated that Abiola would win. Babangida annulled the results. A crucial factor in disrupting the democratic process was the creation of the **Association for Better Nigeria** by supporters of Babangida. The association focused on campaigning for the continuation of the Babangida regime through propaganda and the judicial system. Aside from the unfortunate annulment, many Nigerians remember this election as being the fairest in Nigeria's history. Many attribute this fairness to the chairman of the **National Electoral Commission, Humphrey Nwobu Nwosu**.

**ELECTIONS.** The topic of elections is a sensitive one for Nigerians. Few elections in Nigeria's history have been fair and democratic. **Women** in Nigeria have complained that they are used by male politicians to get votes instead of being included in politics directly. Most important, Nigerians complain that their elections are rife with **corruption**. Nominal attempts have been made since independence to make elections transparent and fair. The open ballot system, used sometimes until the mid-1990s, did not prevent corrupt activities. This system allowed people to vote in public by acclamation, which required all voters to participate within a narrow time frame. It was used first in 1951 in the **Western Region**. But the open ballot system revealed a voter's decision and exposed him or her to coercion. It was abandoned and replaced by the secret ballot system. The secret ballot system was used during the **First** and **Second Republics**. It lent itself to corruption because people could buy ballots and stuff election boxes behind closed doors. In 1993, Nigeria started using the open secret ballot system, which allows voters to mark their choice secretly and deposit the ballot in the election box in a public space. Election officials are charged with counting the ballots and recording the results in front of a public audience. For every major election, a so-called independent commission was appointed to register **political parties**, run the election, and ensure fair voting practices. These commissions, however, were not truly independent of government influence, because many of their members were appointed by the head of state.

The Federal Electoral Commission was appointed in 1978 to oversee the 1979 election process. Only five registered political parties ran candidates in the 1979 general election: the **Great Nigerian People's Party**, **Nigerian People's Party**, **National Party of Nigeria**, **Unity Party of Nigeria**, and **People's Redemption Party**. The FEC had strict regulations, which prevented parties such as the **Nigeria Advance Party** from running. One of the darkest moments in Nigeria's election history was the **election of 12 June 1993**, which was annulled by **General Ibrahim Babangida** because he did not approve of **Chief M. K. O. Abiola**'s lead. This happened in spite of his appointment in 1987 of the **National Electoral Commission** to ensure fair and free elections. Critics argue that the commission actually ran the fairest elections in Nigeria's history. In 1996, **General Sani Abacha** created the **National Electoral Commission of Nigeria** to oversee a democratic election that never took place. The first and second term elections for **General Olusegun Obasanjo** in 1999 and 2003, respectively, went relatively smoothly. Accusations of fraud and coercion, however, did circulate. Since 1999, Nigeria has turned into an essentially one-party country dominated by the **People's Democratic Party** (PDP). In recent history, the most blatantly dysfunctional election happened in April 2007 under the watch of the **Independent National Electoral Commission**, which was created in 1998. The election process was riddled with violence and voting irregularities. **Atiku Abubakar** accused the PDP of deliberately keeping his name off the ballot. Hours before polling was to begin, Nigeria was missing 60 million ballot papers, which were allegedly delayed in South Africa. Nonetheless, the election of President **Umaru Yar'Adua** is the first time that Nigeria has seen a transfer of power from one elected, civilian head of state to another.

**ELECTRICITY.** The production and distribution of electricity in Nigeria has been a thorny problem since colonial rule. A steady supply of electricity determines a country's level of economic development as well as **health** and **educational** systems. Without electricity, factories and hospitals cannot run effectively. Students of the 21st century are studying in the dark and losing ground in the Internet revolution. In Nigeria, whether a person has access to a steady supply of electricity or not reveals information about his or her political clout and socioeconomic standing. For most Nigerians, electricity does not run regularly, and blackouts are a daily occurrence. The Electricity Corporation of Nigeria was in charge of Nigeria's electricity from 1950 to 1972. Several notable Nigerians worked for the company, including **Chief Frank Kokori** (1966–1971). Between 1972 and 2005, the country's electricity was administered by the **National Electric Power Authority**, which Nigerians referred to as "Never Electric Power Always." In 2005, the Bureau of Public Enterprises renamed the company the Power Holding Company of Nigeria in a step toward **privatizing** the entire electricity system. One of Nigeria's sources of electricity is the hydroelectric Kainji River Dam, located in southwestern Nigeria, which was built in 1968. Since 2000, Nigeria has worked with multinational companies, such as Siemens and ExxonMobil, to construct turbine stations and distribution networks. *See also* ECONOMY; TELECOMMUNICATIONS.

**ELIAS, TASLIM OLAWALE (1914–1991).** Born in **Lagos**, Elias completed his primary and secondary schooling in Lagos. He earned a Ph.D. in law from the University of London (1949) and taught law at Manchester University in England (1951–1953). In Nigeria, Elias served as Nigeria's first attorney general (1960–1972) and minister of justice (1960–1966). He was also chief justice of the Supreme Court (1972–1975). Elias was an expert at international law. He served as dean of the law school at the University of Lagos for several years and was a member of the drafting committee for the charter of the Organization of Africa Unity in 1964. Elias held several positions at the International Court of Justice (ICJ) in The Hague. He became a judge of the court in 1975, was its vice president from 1979 to 1981, and served as its president from 1981 to 1985. Elias published several works on law and development in West Africa before his death in August 1991. He earned more than 16 honorary doctorates from universities in North America, Africa, and Europe.

**ELLIOT COMMISSION.** A commission formed in 1943 that, in conjunction with the **Asquith Commission** (1945), called for the establishment of the first universities in Nigeria. The Elliot Commission clearly articulated the need for universities in Nigeria for the expansion of a skilled, educated class to run the country. *See also* EDUCATION; HIGHER EDUCATION.

**EMECHETA, BUCHI (1944– ).** A well-established novelist, Emecheta was born in **Lagos**. She completed her primary and secondary education in Lagos. At age 16, she married and moved to London with her husband. After her marriage ended, she began writing novels in English. Her fictional works are primarily autobiographical, particularly *In the Ditch* (1972) and *Second Class Citizen* (1974), and address the complexity of being an African **woman**. One of her most popular novels, *The Rape of Shavi* (1983), deals with the interplay of Western and African culture in the life of an African woman. Emecheta is one of Nigeria's most famous female writers. *See also* LITERATURE.

**EMIR.** An Arabic term that means someone of high military or political ranking. Emirs exercise their power through a religious mandate and are accountable to the caliph. In the **Sokoto Caliphate**, the emirs carried out the **jihad** in a specific place. In the Sokoto Caliphate, the emir candidates had to impress the caliph's senior royal **slaves** in addition to the caliph. An emir or sultan may also be referred to as a *sarki* (*sarakuna* as plural). *See also* ISLAM; RELIGION.

**ENAHORO, CHIEF ANTHONY ERONSELE (1923– ).** Born in July 1923 in Uromi, in **Edo State**, Enahoro was a member of the Ishan **ethnic group**. As a young man, he attended government schools in Uromi and Owo as well as **King's College** in **Lagos**. During the 1940s, he worked as an editor for several different **newspapers** in Nigeria, including *Southern Nigeria Defender*, *Daily Comet*, and *West African Pilot*. He was editor-in-chief of the *Nigerian Star* newspaper from 1950 to 1953. While working as a journalist, he also participated in politics as a member of the House of Representatives (1951–1954). He was also the general secretary of the **Action Group** in the mid-1950s.

Enahoro served as the federal minister of information and was a key leader for the Ishan people during **General Yakubu Gowon**'s regime. Along with other members of the Action Group, Enahoro became involved in what has been called the **Action Group Crisis**. In 1963, Enahoro and other party leaders were tried and imprisoned for treason. In 1966, he was released by the federal military government. He was arrested again on 4 June 1967 for misuse of power and **corruption**, but he was later released on bail. He was president of the second **World Black and African Festival of Arts and Culture** from 1972 to 1975. Enahoro was part of a mass dismissal of corrupt **civil servants** by **General Murtala Mohammed** in 1975. Enahoro was a member, and later chairman, of the **National Party of Nigeria** from 1978 to 1980. He was later a member of the **National Democratic Coalition**. He received an honorary doctoral degree from the University of Benin (1972) as well as the titles *adolo* of Uromi and Commander of the Order of the Federal Republic (1982). Enahoro was again arrested and detained in 1994, this time by **General Sani Abacha**. After his release, he went into exile in the United States. In 2000, he returned to Nigeria. He is the author of *Fugitive Offender* (1965).

**ENGLISH LANGUAGE.** English is the official **language** of Nigeria. It is primarily used for official business and coursework in schools and universities. Informal communication between Nigerians of like **ethnic groups** is largely conducted in an indigenous language. The English spoken in Nigeria blends indigenous terms and draws from a local variant, creating a unique form of pidgin English. The lyrics of the musical legend **Olufela Anikulapo-Kuti** provide excellent examples of pidgin English.

**ENUGU.** A city established in 1912 as a small **coal**-mining town during British colonial rule. By 1960, Enugu was a large, bustling city. It was the capital of the former **East-Central State** from 1967 until 1976, when that state became part of **Anambra State**. In 1991, Anambra State was divided to form **Enugu State**, taking with it the city of Enugu. Enugu has earned the nickname "coal city." In 1949 during a conflict with colonial **police**, Enugu coal miners were shot. The **National Emergency Committee** was formed by several prominent Nigerians to look into the matter and ensure a just conclusion. It was chaired by **Akinola Maja**. Enugu was the capital of the short-lived **Republic of Biafra** during the **civil war**. It is also one of several cities in Nigeria that has a sizable **Charismatic Christian** population. Enugu is the location of one of Nigeria's first three technical colleges, founded in 1952. The **population** of Enugu is approximately 689,000.

**ENUGU STATE.** A state located in southeastern Nigeria, created in 1991 out of **Anambra State**. The capital is the city of **Enugu**. The **Igbo** are the dominant **ethnic group**. Economic activities in Enugu include mining **coal**; manufacturing cars; producing steel; and cultivating rice, **oil palm**, fruit, and **yams**. *See also* STATE CREATION.

**ENWONWU, BENEDICT CHUKA (1921–1994).** Enwonwu was born in July 1921 in **Onitsha**. As a young man, he attended primary and secondary schools in **Ibadan**, **Port Harcourt**, and Umuahia. He studied **art** with Kenneth C. Murray, Nigeria's first formal modern art teacher, between 1934 and 1937. He attended Ruskin College (1944–1946) and Slade School of Fine Art (1946–1948) in London. Enwonwu was a graphic artist, painter, and sculptor. He was the art master at Government College in Umuahia (1938–1940), Mission School in **Calabar** (1940–1941), and Edo College in **Benin** (1941–1943). He also worked as the art supervisor for the Public Relations Department in **Lagos** from 1948 to 1954. In 1950, he lectured and showed his work in the United States. He was as an editor for *Nigeria Magazine* in 1966. Between 1966 and 1968, he was a fellow at the University of Lagos.

Enwonu taught art classes at the University of Ife (present-day **Obafemi Awolowo University**) from 1971 to 1975. He acted as an artistic consultant for the second **World Black and African Festival of Arts and Culture** in 1977. His first major international art show with other new artists was at the Zwemmer Gallery in London in 1937. In 1942, Enwonwu held his first solo show in Lagos. In 1948, he was appointed the art adviser to the colonial government. In 1969, he received an honorary doctorate from **Ahmadu Bello University**. He received numerous commissions for his work, including a bronze statue of Queen Elizabeth II (located in Lagos), a stone statue of **Nnamdi Azikiwe**, a bronze statue for the United Nations (located in New York), a ceramic mural for the Nigerian Port Authority, and a sculpture of **Sango** for the **National Electric Power Authority**. He also illustrated **Amos Tutuola**'s book, *The Brave African Huntress* (1958). Enwonwu died in February 1994 in Lagos.

**EQUIANO, OLAUDAH (1745–1797).** An **Igbo** ex-slave who wrote *The Interesting Narrative of the Life of Olaudah Equiano*, which was first published in 1789. Based on the information provided in his second chapter, historians have confirmed that he was indeed of Igbo descent from the **Benin Kingdom**. His work is characterized as a "spiritual autobiography" because of its **Christian** appeal for the abolition of the **slave trade**. Living a tranquil life in **southern Nigeria**, he was kidnapped at age 11 along with his sister, whom he never saw again. Equiano was taken on board a ship destined for Barbados and then to Virginia. He was purchased by a British naval officer, Michael Henry Pascal, who took him to England. While in England Equiano was baptized Gustavus Vassus, a name Equiano seemed to prefer and used in daily life. Equiano traveled with Pascal around the world during periods of peace and war. He was sold to another owner and ultimately earned enough money to purchase his freedom. During his youth, Equiano had converted to Anglicanism. He wrote extensively about the social and religious urgency of abolishing the slave trade. He died in March 1797.

**EREDIAUWA I, CHIEF SOLOMON AKENZUA (1923– ).** Akenzua was born in June 1923 in **Benin**. Erediauwa I is a chieftaincy title, meaning "Ere has come to set things right," which he acquired in 1979. He is the 38th *oba* (**chief**) of **Benin**. As a young man, he studied at the Government Primary School in Benin, Edo College in Benin, Government College in **Ibadan**, **Yaba Higher College** (1940–1947), and Cambridge University (1948–1951). He worked as an administrator for the Nigerian Public Service (1952–1954) and Eastern Region Public Service at **Enugu** (1954). He worked in several ministries of the **Eastern Region** from 1954 to 1965. He was also the deputy permanent secretary for the Federal Civil Service (1965–1968) and permanent secretary for the Federal Ministry of Mines and Power and Federal Ministry of Health (1965–1968). In the private sector, he held several positions, including representative of Gulf Oil and chairman of the Tate and Lyle Sugar Company. He also served on the board of directors/governors for the University of Lagos Teaching Hospital and University College Hospital in Ibadan. Akenzua was also on the board of management of the **National Electric Power Authority**.

**ESIGIE.** The ruler of the **Benin Kingdom** in the 16th century (ca. 1514 to ca. 1550). His father was **Ozolua**, who ruled Benin from ca. 1480 to 1514. He engaged in extensive **trade** and extended diplomatic ties with Portuguese traders. He created a post within his royal administration for his mother, **Idia**, called *iyoba* (queen mother). Portuguese representatives urged Esigie to purchase arms from them for future military campaigns, on the condition that he convert to **Christianity**. To prove his might, Esigie attacked and defeated Igala to the North in 1516 without Portuguese artillery. This campaign was in retaliation for a failed attack on Benin by Igala. Esigie is known for his conversion to Christianity and his literacy in Portuguese. He was baptized in 1516. He associated with the cross of the Order of Christ because, as the legend goes, he commissioned a crucifix to be made as a gift for the king of Portugal. Furthermore, **slaves** sent by Esigie to Portugal were branded with a cross on their right arms.

**ETHNIC GROUPS.** More than 250 **languages** are spoken in Nigeria, which means that for each language, there is a distinct **ethnic group** speaking it. Each ethnic group maintains a unique religious, cultural, and political tradition. For example, the majority of the **Hausa** and **Fulani** are Muslims, and the majority of Igbo are Christians. The **Yoruba** have a long history of being city dwellers; the Fulani are historically nomadic cattle herders in the *sahel*. The **Kanuri** in the North rely on grain and **groundnut** cultivation, and the **Ogoni** in the South rely on fishing. Nigeria's ethnic groups fall into two basic categories: dominant groups and **minority groups**.

The dominant ethnic groups in Nigeria are the Hausa, **Igbo**, and Yoruba. The Hausa number 10–15 million, the Igbo 19 million, and the Yoruba over 15 million. Many of the other ethnic groups are subgroups of these three politically dominant groups. For example, the **Egba** and **Ijebu** are subgroups of the Yoruba, and the **Nri** are a subgroup of the Igbo. Each ethnic group maintains a regional dominance, but rarely has a state dominance. For example, the Yoruba claim the majority presence in southwestern Nigeria and the Igbo do the same in southeastern Nigeria. But in **Kano State** or **Kaduna State** in the North, these two groups are minorities. In fact, one of the catalysts of the **Republic of Biafra** seceding in 1967 was the massacre of Igbo in **northern Nigeria**. The experience of the dominant groups differs significantly from the minority groups in Nigeria.

The most vocal minority groups of the 20th century have been the **Ijaw**, **Jukun**, Ogoni, and **Tiv**. Minority groups are significantly smaller in number than the Hausa, Igbo, or Yoruba. The Tiv, for example, are considered the largest minority group, with a population of four million. Other notable minority groups are the **Efik**, **Edo**, **Gwari**, **Itsekiri**, **Ibibio**, **Igbirra**, **Igala**, **Nupe**, **Urhobo**, and **Modekeke**. Minority groups rarely have regional or state dominance. They have regularly clamored for political representation and access to economic opportunities since 1960. *See also* CHRISTIANITY; ISLAM; NORTHERN REGION; RELIGION; SOUTHERN REGION; SCARIFICATION; STATE CREATION.

**EWEKA I.** *See* BENIN KINGDOM.

**EWUARE.** Leader of the **Benin Kingdom** in the 15th century (ca. 1440 to ca.1473). **Ozolua** was his third son. **Oral tradition** has it that Ewuare wrestled with Olokun, god of the sea and wealth, for possession of coral beads and that this is how he became ruler of Benin. He is known for expanding the territory of Benin to control parts of **Yoruba** and **Igbo** territory. For instance, he launched a campaign against more than 200 towns across **southern Nigeria**. He captured the **chiefs** and required the townspeople to pay tribute. Ewuare also constructed major **roads** and a protective wall around the capital, **Benin**. During his reign, he declared that every year he would sacrifice a leopard. Over time, the leopard came to symbolize the strength of Benin and Ewuare. *See also* ESIGIE; OZOLUA.

**EXCHANGE CONTROL DECREE.** A decree passed in 1984 by the regime of **Major General Muhammadu Buhari** to facilitate the federal government's control over foreign exchange transactions. He implemented it with the intention of strengthening the Exchange Control Decree of 1962. This decree made importing or exporting without declaration a criminal act. It also made illegal maintaining a foreign bank account and holding foreign **currency**. Those with foreign currency were required to declare it and convert it into naira, Nigeria's national currency. The Exchange Control Decree is often paired with antisabotage decrees. Complementing this law was a revised Counterfeit Currency (Special Provisions) Decree (1974), which called for death by firing squad for anyone caught making or trading counterfeit money.

**EXECUTIVE COUNCIL.** Throughout Nigeria's history, the Executive Council has gone in and out of use as a central part of the country's administration. During the colonial period, it comprised British members of the colonial government. The executive council included the **governor general** and colonial advisors. The **Macpherson Constitution** of 1952 called for replacement of the Executive Council with a council of ministers. During the **First Republic**, the Executive Council was reintroduced as the cabinet. Between 1966 and 1999, there were various versions of the Executive Council, for example, the **Federal Executive Council** and **National Executive Council**. Today, Nigeria's cabinet is called the Federal Executive Council.

– F –

**FADAHUNSI, SIR JOSEPH ODELEYE (1901–1986).** Born in Ilesha, in **Osun State**, Fadahunsi studied at Osu Methodist School and Wesley Teacher Training College in **Ibadan**. He worked as a schoolteacher, storekeeper, and salesperson in the 1920s and 1930s. In 1948, he founded and ran the Ijesha United Trading and Transport Company. He worked for the **marketing board** for **cocoa** trading from 1948 to 1953. He also worked as the director of the Nigeria Produce Marketing Company from 1952 to 1953. From 1955 to 1960, he was the chairman of the Ijesha Divisional Council. He was briefly the chairman of Nigeria Airways in 1961. He was an active member of the **National Council of Nigeria and the Cameroons political party**. Fadahunsi was governor of the **Western Region** from January 1963 to January 1966. He received the honorary title Knight Commander of the Order of the British Empire in 1963.

**FAGUNWA, DANIEL OLORUNFEMI (1903–1963).** As a child, Fagunwa attended **Christian** missionary schools in southwestern Nigeria. In the 1920s and 1930s, he worked as a schoolteacher. He is best known as one of the premier **Yoruba** novelists, writing between 1939 and 1961. He published six novels in the **Yoruba language**, in which he draws heavily from Yoruba folktales and proverbs. His best known work is *Ogboju Ode Ninu Igbo Irunmale* (1939), which was translated into English by **Akinwande Oluwole Soyinka**. *See also* LITERATURE.

**FAJEMIROKUN, CHIEF HENRY OLOYEDE (1926–1978).** Born in July 1926 in Ile-Oluji, in **Ondo State**, as a young man Fajemirokun studied at St. Peter's School and at St. Luke's between 1937 and 1940. He also attended Ondo Boys' High School. He enlisted in the (Royal) **West African Frontier Force** in 1944 and served in India. After World War II, he studied accounting and worked for the **civil service**. In 1948, he acted as president of the Post and Telecommunications Ex-servicemen's Union. He was also president of the Nigerian Civil Service Union. In 1956, he shifted his career focus away from **trade union** activity toward business, taking an active interest in the Lagos Chamber of Commerce. He received an honorary chieftaincy title from his community and a doctoral degree from the University of Ife (present-day **Obafemi Awolowo University**). He died in Ivory Coast while on business, in March 1978.

**FAJUYI, LIEUTENANT COLONEL ADEKUNLE (1922–1966).** Fajuyi was born in June 1922 in Ado-Ekiti, in **Ondo State**. He joined the army in 1943. In 1954, he was the first African to become an officer in the British Army of the Rhine. For his military contributions during **World War II**, the British government awarded him a medal of honor. Like many of his peers in the army, he served as a member of a United Nations peacekeeping force in Central Africa in the early 1960s. During the military **coup d'état** of 1966, he was serving as the commanding officer of the Abeokuta Garrison. That same year, he was appointed military governor of the **Western Region** (January 1966–July 1966). The renowned poet **Akinwande Oluwole Soyinka** portrays Fajuyi as a martyr in his poem "For Fajuyi," because Fajuyi sacrificed his life to refute the idea that the Western Region colluded with the **Northern Region**. He died, along with **Major General Johnson Aguiyi-Ironsi**, in July 1966.

**FAKEYE, LAMIDI OLONADE (1928– ).** Born in Ila-Orangun, in **Osun State**, Fakeye learned how to carve wood sculptures from his father. He apprenticed for three years with George Bandele. He was also a member of the **Western House of Assembly**. He toured the United States, running workshops and giving lectures between 1963 and 1966. For a year, he was an artist-in-residence at Western Michigan University, the University of Ile-Ife (present-day **Obafemi Awolowo University**), and the **University of Ibadan**. He was best known for his wood sculptures and had several solo **art** exhibitions in Nigeria, the United States, and **Great Britain**. He was also part of an art movement, started by **Susanne Wenger**, among southwestern Nigerian artists that made carvings of important gods and goddesses of the **Yoruba religion**. In 1947, he was commissioned to do **Christian** works of art for the Society of African Missions. He was also commissioned to make carved doors for the Kennedy Center for the Performing Arts in Washington, D.C. In 1987, he created a four-meter-tall statue of Oduduwa, which is today housed at Obafemi Awolowo University. Fakeye received the honorary title of member of the Order of the Federal Republic of Nigeria (1960).

**FALAE, CHIEF SAMUEL OLUYEMISI (1938– ).** Falae was born in September 1938 in Ilu-Abo, in **Ondo State**. As a young man, he studied economics at the **University of Ibadan** and Yale University (1972). He worked in the **civil service** from 1963 to 1981. In 1989, he worked on a political transition scheme. In the 1990s, he served as minister of finance, during which time he took part in the planning and implementation of Nigeria's **structural adjustment program**. He ran for the presidential nomination for the **Social Democratic Party** and lost. When the **election of 12 June 1993** was annulled, Falae agitated for the recognition of **Chief M. K. O. Abiola** as the winner. **General Sani Abacha** sent him to prison from January 1997 until June 1998. Falae became an active member in the **Alliance for Democracy** in preparation for the 1999 **elections**. Again, he ran as the presidential candidate for the party, but he lost. He challenged the results of the election in federal **court** and lost in April 1999.

**FANI-KAYODE, CHIEF REMI ADE (1921–1995).** Born in December 1921 in England, Fani-Kayode received his primary and secondary schooling from the Church Missionary Society Grammar School and **King's College** in Lagos. He also went overseas to receive bachelor's and law degrees from Downing College and Cambridge University. He was called to the bar in 1945. After returning to Nigeria, he became involved in politics and served as the assistant federal secretary for the **Action Group** from 1954 to 1955. He also worked as the central chairman of the Action Group Youth Association from 1953 to 1955. Fani-Kayode was a member of the **Western Regional House of Assembly** and the House of Representatives. He was also a member of the **National Council of Nigeria and the Cameroons**. In January 1963, he became deputy **premier**. In 1966, he withdrew from national politics and practiced private law. In 1978, he joined the **National Party of Nigeria**.

**FATAYI-WILLIAMS, ATANDA (1918–2002).** Born October 1918 in **Lagos**, Fatayi-Williams studied at the Methodist Boys' High School in Lagos (1929–1938) and at Cambridge University (1943–1947). He was called to the bar in 1948 and had a private legal practice from 1948 to 1950. He was a member of the Crown Council in Lagos (1950–1955). He held numerous positions in Nigeria's government. For the **Western Region**, he served as legal advisor and judge. He was a judge for the High Court of the Western Region (1960–1967), justice of appeal for the Western State Court of Appeal (1967–1969), and justice on the Supreme Court (1969–1979). From 1979 to 1983, he was the chief justice of Nigeria. He also served as chairman of the National Archives Committee in 1979. During the 1980s, he was a member of several organizations, including the International Commission of Jurists, World Council of Judges, and Royal Society of Arts (London). Fatayi-Williams retired in 1983. He received the honorary titles Commander of the Order of the Federal Republic (1980) and Grand Commander of the Order of the Niger (1983). *See also* COURTS; LEGAL SYSTEM.

**FAWEHINMI, CHIEF ABDUL-GANIYU OYESOLA (1938– ).** Fawehinmi was born in April 1938 in Ondo. As a young man, he studied at the Ansar Ud-Deen School (1946–1953), Victory College in Ikare (1954–1958), the University of London (1961–1964), and Nigerian Law School in **Lagos** (1964). He was called to the bar in 1965, after which he started a private legal practice. He also worked as a columnist for the *Nigerian Tribune* and the *Chronicle* **newspapers**. He worked closely with university student unions. He received awards from **Obafemi Awolowo University** and the American Bar Association. He was the founder of the National Conscience Party (1978). Fawehinmi has written several published works on Nigeria's **court** system. He has been a vocal critic of the government, with a particular focus on **human rights**. He was head of the Joint Action Committee for Democracy in the early 1990s, which was briefly involved with the **O'odua People's Congress**. Fawehinmi has been arrested and detained by federal security forces about 34 times since 1969. In September 2001, Fawehinmi received the title Senior Advocate of Nigeria. *See also* LEGAL SYSTEM.

**FEDERAL CAPITAL TERRITORY (FCT).** In 1975, **General Murtala Ramat Mohammed** assembled the Aguda Committee, named for Timothy Aguda, to assess whether **Lagos** should remain the nation's capital. After the review, Mohammed decided to create a new capital and move all the nation's government offices. The first step involved the reconfiguring of the country's states to create the FCT in 1976. The purpose of establishing the territory was to locate the nation's capital in the middle of the country as a symbol of the government's commitment to national unity. Its central location meant that the government was not seated in one dominant ethnic region. Also, the territory was chosen for its mild climate and small **population**, which would allow for territorial expansion in the future. The final step was the government's official move from Lagos to **Abuja**, which took place on 12 December 1991. Thus far, the FCT is roughly 8,000 square kilometers in size. It is the least populated state in Nigeria. A portion of the territory has also been designated as an arboretum to protect indigenous plant and animal life. It is the site of Nigeria's Nnamdi Azikiwe International Airport and National Mosque. *See also* MIDDLE BELT.

**FEDERAL COUNCIL OF MINISTERS.** An organ of the federal government that existed from 1954 until 1966. It developed out of the Council of Ministers, which was created in 1951. The Federal Council of Ministers included the **governor general**, ex-officio members, and ministers from each region (including southern **Cameroon**). After 1960, the council's composition changed to include a prime minister and cabinet members.

**FEDERAL EXECUTIVE COUNCIL.** The executive advisory body of Nigeria's government, which was deliberately created to enforce the federalist structure. In May 1966, it was transformed into the **National Executive Council**. In July 1966, it was reinstated with the previous title. Members included **Chief Josiah Okezie**. In 1999, it was reinstituted as the cabinet and is still in use today. *See also* EXECUTIVE COUNCIL.

**FEDERAL HOUSE OF REPRESENTATIVES.** One of two legislative chambers in the federal government that was active during the **First** and **Second Republics**. The number of seats allocated to each region was determined by **population**. The House of Representatives had 312 seats during the First Republic and 450 during the Second Republic. Its power was equal to that of the Senate.

**FEDERAL PARLIAMENT.** Nigeria's legislative body during the **First Republic**. It was divided into two chambers, the **Federal House of Representatives** and the Senate. The Federal House of Representatives had 312 members and the Senate had 12 senators and 8 members selected by the president. The Federal Parliament was disbanded in January 1966.

**FEDERAL PUBLIC SERVICE COMMISSION.** *See* CIVIL SERVICE.

**FEDERAL RADIO CORPORATION OF NIGERIA.** *See* RADIO BROADCASTING.

**FEDERAL REPUBLIC OF NIGERIA.** Shortly after gaining its **independence**, Nigeria became the Federal Republic of Nigeria. Maintaining unity and a balanced federal system has been a challenge. The number of states in the federation has changed significantly from its inception. To reduce tension over **revenue allocation** and representation, Nigeria has engaged in the perilous program of **state creation**.

**FERNANDO POO.** A fertile island off the coast of Nigeria, which changed colonial hands several times. The Portuguese claimed it in 1471 and established sugar plantations, which depended on African slave labor. In 1778, Spain received control of it from Portugal and turned the island into a province of Spanish Equatorial Guinea. At that time, the island was used for large-scale **cocoa** cultivation. In 1807, Spain allowed **Great Britain** to use the island as a strategic location to suppress the **slave trade** and resettle liberated Africans from Sierra Leone. For a brief time, Fernando Poo was the location of a British consul. The British were interested in overseeing the **trade** in **oil palm** from this location. The island also served as a place of punishment. **John Beecroft**, on behalf of the British, sent **Akintoye** of **Lagos** to the island as punishment in 1845. The island was seized by the Spanish in 1848 and remained under Spanish control until 1968. A majority of the labor on the plantations was provided by Nigerians in the 20th century. Out of a population of 64,000 in 1960, 40,000 were Nigerian. In the mid-20th century, the British attempted to protect Nigerian laborers from harsh working conditions and treatment, which included sending fewer Nigerian laborers to the island. Today, Fernando Poo is part of Equatorial Guinea.

**FESTAC '77.** *See* WORLD BLACK AND AFRICAN FESTIVAL OF ARTS AND CULTURE.

**FILM.** *See* NOLLYWOOD.

**FIRST REPUBLIC.** Nigeria's First Republic lasted from October 1960 to January 1966, although technically it did not exist until October 1963. During this period, Nigeria was run as a parliamentary democracy. The president was **Nnamdi Azikiwe** and the prime minister was **Sir Alhaji Abubakar Tafawa Balewa**. During the First Republic, the three major regions aggressively competed for control of the federal government. The republic also survived the **Action Group Crisis** of 1962. Ultimately, Nigeria's first attempt at democracy ended prematurely through a military **coup d'état** by **Major General Johnson Thomas Umunankwe Aguiyi-Ironsi**. *See also* BELLO, SIR ALHAJI AHMADU; FOURTH REPUBLIC; SECOND REPUBLIC; THIRD REPUBLIC.

**FLAG.** The current Nigerian flag was designed by a student in **Ibadan** in 1959 and has not been modified. It has three vertical bands of color, with two green bands on the outside and one white band on the inside. The green represents Nigeria's **agricultural** endowment, and white represents peace and unity. *See also* NATIONAL ANTHEM.

**FODIO, USMAN DAN.** *See* USMAN DAN FODIO.

**FOOT COMMISSION.** Named for Sir Hugh Foot, chief secretary of the colonial government, the commission was appointed by Sir John Macpherson in June 1948 to address the need for recruiting Nigerians into senior **civil service** positions. The commission suggested the necessary steps required for recruiting and training Nigerians for these posts. It also called for the training and placement of Nigerian **women**. Macpherson agreed with the Foot Commission's findings and followed its recommendations. *See also* MACPHERSON CONSTITUTION.

**FOREIGN POLICY.** Nigeria's foreign policy has undergone significant changes from **independence** to the present day. Like other countries, Nigeria's foreign relations are based on its own immediate interests (i.e., sovereignty, end of colonial rule, and diplomatic integrity). Scholars divide its development into several broad phases. It is no coincidence that these phases coincide with Nigeria's changes in leadership, although none of the **coups d'état** was driven by the failings of Nigeria's foreign policy. Generally speaking, Nigeria's foreign policy underwent a deliberate expansion away from an exclusive political and economic relationship with **Great Britain** toward a more diverse one. Nigeria toyed with fostering trade relations, albeit weak ones, with Japan, the Soviet Union, and, with great success, its West African neighbors. **Sir Alhaji Abubakar Tafawa Balewa** adhered to a policy of nonalignment, whereby Nigeria maintained an intentionally pragmatic and nonideological policy, placing it in a neutral position. Nonalignment, however, did not prevent Nigeria from maintaining a minimal membership in the Organization of African Unity (present-day **African Union**) since its formation in 1962.

Nigeria entered into a new phase during the 1970s, best described as intensive activism, particularly in African politics. In 1971, for example, Nigeria joined the **Organization of Petroleum Exporting Countries**, which was a bold move. Nigeria also assisted with the creation of the **Economic Community of West African States** in 1975. **General Murtala Ramat Mohammed** set Nigeria on a path of extreme activism, promising direct military assistance to African resistance forces in Southern Africa in the mid-1970s. **General Olusegun Obasanjo** built on his predecessor's commitment to the liberation of Southern Africa, but was described as "soft-pedaling" because of his connections to the United States and Great Britain in the second half of the 1970s. During the 1980s, Nigeria maintained its foreign policy course, although distracted by its own political upsets. Nigeria's reputation turned sour due to flawed **elections**, military coups, and economic collapse. Over the past 10 years, Nigeria's leaders have focused on improving Nigeria's image. In 2001, Nigeria joined other major African countries to form the **New Partnership for African Development**. Nigeria also played a significant role in ending civil war in Liberia. *See also* BAKASSI PENINSULA; BENIN, REPUBLIC OF; CAMEROON, REPUBLIC OF; FOREIGN TRADE; GHANA, REPUBLIC OF; NIGERIAN INSTITUTE OF INTERNATIONAL AFFAIRS.

**FOREIGN TRADE.** Prior to the 20th century, **trade** extending beyond the various regions of present-day Nigeria involved moving luxury goods, slaves, and nonperishable foodstuffs through the **trans-Saharan trade**, across West Africa, to European traders. In the mid-19th century, Nigeria's foreign trade underwent a transition away from an **economy** dominated by the **slave trade** to one of **legitimate commerce**. Since **independence**, Nigerian leaders have struggled to set and maintain a policy on foreign trade. During the colonial period,

Nigeria's foreign trade involved exporting raw materials to Europe and importing manufactured goods from Europe. Foreign trade was dominated by European trading companies, with little investment in local industry. Not surprisingly, independent Nigeria's first leaders saw this as an exploitative relationship and sought to overhaul Nigeria's role in the global economy. During the 1970s, Nigeria's foreign trade model relied heavily on exports, particularly **petroleum**, with a reduction in imports in hopes of expanding Nigeria's manufacturing of basic goods. Poor fiscal planning over the span of several decades, however, made Nigeria heavily reliant on revenue from its petroleum exports. Starting in the late 1980s, Nigeria underwent a **structural adjustment program** to stimulate economic development. One of the conditions included liberalizing its foreign trade.

In recent years, Nigeria has made great strides in diversifying and liberalizing its foreign trade and, more important, has seen quantifiable improvements in its economy as a result. In 2006, 50 percent of Nigeria's exports (i.e., petroleum) went to the United States, and 10 percent of its imports came from the People's Republic of China.

**FOSTER-SUTTON COMMISSION OF INQUIRY.** A commission named for the chair of the committee, Sir Stafford Foster-Sutton, who was the chief justice in 1956. The purpose of the commission was to investigate the relationship between **Nnamdi Azikiwe**, the **Eastern Region**'s government, and the African Continental Bank. Azikiwe had been accused of fraud. The report was published in July 1957 and stated that the way in which Azikiwe set up the bank was dishonest. In response, the **Eastern House of Assembly** dissolved itself and held new **elections**. Azikiwe ran on behalf of the **National Council of Nigeria and the Cameroons** and won. But he was required to transfer his control of the bank to the Eastern Regional government. *See also* EASTERN REGIONAL GOVERNMENT CRISIS.

**FOURTH REPUBLIC.** A period of democratic rule in Nigeria that began with the **election** of **General Olusegun Obasanjo** as a civilian president in May 1999. After three rocky but completed election cycles, Nigeria is still enjoying the relative tranquility of the Fourth Republic. President **Umaru Musa Yar'Adua** is the current president. *See also* FIRST REPUBLIC; SECOND REPUBLIC; THIRD REPUBLIC.

**FULA LANGUAGE.** The Fula **language** comes from the Atlantic branch of the Niger–Congo language family. Because the **Fulani** people historically were pastoralists, the language spread across West Africa from Senegal and east to **Chad** and northern **Cameroon**. Several dialects of Fula exist, for example, Pulaar and Fulfulde. When written, Fula can be expressed using the Latin alphabet, with some alterations to better suit the language and Arabic script.

**FULANI.** The Fulani are primarily pastoralists who, according to **oral tradition**, reached **northern Nigeria** by the 12th century. The Fulani have embraced **Islam** since the ninth century and acted as disseminators of that **religion** across West Africa. Oral tradition also suggests that the Fulani claim descent from Ukuba, a relative of the Prophet Muhammad. Ukuba was sent by one of Muhammad's grandsons to an area where the Fulani had settled for a time. The semiconverted Fulani, living in a pagan land, decided to return to Mecca. As they traveled, families refused to proceed. This story explains the diffusion of Fulani people across the *sahel* of West Africa. For this reason, the Fulani are called different names throughout the region. In the Senegal, the Fulani are called Peul, and toward the eastern edge of West Africa, they are called the Fulfulde. The Fulani, led by **Usman dan Fodio**, engaged in a **jihad**, sacking **Hausa Kingdoms** in 1804. By 1812, Usman and his followers had established the **Sokoto Caliphate**. **Nana Asma'u**, a daughter of Usman dan Fodio, wrote beautiful poetry about Islam and her father. Today, the Fulani of Nigeria speak **Fula** and practice Islam. **Alhaji Shehu Shagari**, **Major General Muhammadu Buhari**, and **Alhaji Muhammed Aminu Kano** are three prominent Fulani politicians. The Fulani are the second largest non-**Hausa** group living in northern Nigeria. *See also* ETHNIC GROUPS.

**FUNTUWA, BILKISU AHMED (?– ).** A popular **Hausa** author writing in the **Hausa language**, whose works contribute to the **Kano Market Literature** body of fiction. Her novels exemplify the mainstay features of Kano Market Literature, the exploration of love and passion. Her first novels, published in the 1980s, were *Wa Ya San Gobe? (Who Knows the Future?)* and *Allura Cikin Ruwa (A Needle in the Water)*. Through the characters in her novels she offers advice on attaining happiness in a polygamous household and the value of **education** for females. In Hausa society, Funtuwa is "a conservative in revolt," because she supports some Hausa conservative ideals while rejecting others. The resolution of her novels typically involves the female protagonist attaining a new level of **Islamic** religious devotion and success in her career through education. In recent years, Funtuwa has worked in **film** production to reach her illiterate audience. *See also* LITERATURE; POLYGAMY; WOMEN; YAKUBU, BALARABA RAMAT.

## – G –

**GAHA (?–1774).** Gaha acted as *basorun*, or leader of the council of notables, for the **Oyo Empire** from 1754 to 1774. As *basorun*, Gaha wielded a tremendous amount of political influence. **Oral tradition** attributes the ejection of several *alaafin* (**kings**) to Gaha. He quarreled with the *alaafin* over whether to expand the empire and take advantage of the **slave trade**. Gaha supported the expansion; the *alaafin* did not. It is believed that Gaha orchestrated the murder of Alaafin Awonbioju only 130 days after his reign began. One *alaafin* hired magicians to kill Gaha, but the magicians only succeeded in paralyzing his legs. After 1754, Gaha succeeded in placing his supporters in the royal court, exposing him to political animosity. In 1774, **Abiodun** conspired with neighboring rulers to kill Gaha's sons and attack the capital. Gaha was captured and executed.

**GALLWEY TREATY.** A treaty between Captain Henry Gallwey, the commissioner and vice-consul of the Benin River District in the **Oil Rivers Protectorate**, and Ovonramwen, King of **Benin**, in March 1892. Under British persuasion, Ovonramwen agreed to become part of the Oil Rivers Protectorate. The treaty called for British protection of Benin and an exclusive trading relationship, but not the abolition of the **slave trade** or practice of human sacrifice. The treaty was translated from **English** into the **Yoruba language** and then into **Edo**. The ruler of Benin argued that his council signed under duress and that the true meaning of the document was lost in translation. In fact, Ovonramwen did not sign the treaty himself, but allowed his council to mark an "X" on his behalf. Five years later, Ovonramwen was forced into exile for not complying with the terms of the Gallwey Treaty.

**GAMBARI, IBRAHIM AGBOOLA (1944– ).** Born in November 1944 in **Ilorin**, in **Kwara State**, as a young man, Gambari studied at **King's College** in **Lagos** (1963–1964), the London School of Economics and Political Science (1965–1968), and Columbia University (1968–1974). He received a Ph.D. in political science. He taught at the State University of New York at Albany (1974–1977) and **Ahmadu Bello University** (1986–1989) in addition to several visiting terms at universities in the United States. In the political arena, Gambari was director-general of the **Nigerian Institute of International Affairs** (1983–1984) and served as the minister of external affairs (1984–1985). In 1999, he served as president of the United Nations International Education Fund. Gambari has published several books on Nigerian **foreign policy**.

**GANA, JERRY (1945– ).** Gana was born in November 1945 in Busu, in **Niger State**. He studied at Government College in Bida (1960–1964), Okene Secondary School (1965–1966), **Ahmadu Bello University** in **Zaria** (1968–1970), and the University of Aberdeen (1974). He received his Ph.D. in geography. Gana taught and conducted research at Ahmadu Bello University for several years. He worked as the consulting director for the Food, Roads, and Rural Infrastructure project. He was minister of information in the mid-1980s and again from 1999 to 2004. He was chairman of **Mass Mobilization for Self Reliance, Social Justice, and Economic Recovery** (1987 and 1992). He was the minister of information again for **General Sani Abacha**'s government from 1993 to 1995. He has been a member of the **People's Democratic Party** since 1998. He also worked as special advisor to **General Olusegun Obasanjo** from 2004 to 2007. Gana had presidential aspirations in 2007 and sought support from the People's Democratic Party, but was unsuccessful.

**GARBA, MAJOR GENERAL JOSEPH NAUVEN (1943–2002).** Born in July 1943 at Langtang, in **Plateau State**, Garba studied at Sacred Heart School in Shendam (1952–1957), Nigerian Military School in **Zaria** (1957–1961), and officer training academies in **Great Britain**. He also studied at the National Defence College in India (1980) and Harvard University (1982–1983). Garba earned a master's degree in public administration. He joined the army in 1962 and held several positions in it until he retired in 1980. He served in a United Nations force in Kashmir in 1966. During the **civil war**, he led the Federal Guards into battle. He was a close friend of **General Yakubu Gowon**, but became disillusioned with him and played a leading role in the **coup d'état** that removed Gowon from power. It was Garba who announced the 1975 coup d'état in the early morning hours over national radio. He was the commissioner of the Federal Ministry for External Affairs (1975–1978) and member of the **Supreme Military Council** (1975–1979). Garba was a research fellow at the J. F. Kennedy School of Government and Harvard University between 1980 and 1981. In 1989, he was elected president of the United Nations General Assembly. He received the honorary titles Commander of the Order of the Federal Republic (1979) and *dan iya* (**chief**) of Langtang. He was a member of the **All People's Party** (1998). Garba died in June 2002 in **Abuja**. *See also* ARMED FORCES.

**GENERAL STRIKE.** The General Strike of 1945 was a response to the restricted life Nigerians endured during **World War II**. Three years prior to the strike, workers pressured the colonial government for an appropriate cost-of-living allowance to counter rising inflation. Workers wanted either an increase in their wages or an increase in their individual shares of the allowance. When neither demand was met, the **trade unions** called for a strike. It lasted from 22 June to 6 August and included around 40,000 people. Those most vocal in the strike worked as civil servants and railway operators across southwestern Nigeria. The strikers refused to go to work, facing risks of hunger and abuse. The significance of the strike is that it marks a turning point in Nigeria's labor history. For the first time, workers united and successfully appealed to the general **population**. The Tudor-Davies Commission was created in October 1945 to discuss government–labor relations and the cost-of-living allowance. In March 1946, the commission presented its recommendations, which included a 50 percent increase in the allowance and the creation of a new wage scheme. It was a powerful moment in Nigeria's history of openly resisting colonial rule.

**GENOCIDE.** According to the United Nations (UN) Convention on Genocide (1948), genocide is the deliberate killing of one social group by another. Critics argue that this definition fails to clearly address two issues. First, it does not clarify how many deaths have to occur before genocide can be declared. One of the contributing factors to Nigeria's **civil war** was the massacre of **Igbos** living in **northern Nigeria** that took place between May and October 1966. **Chief Chukwuemeka Ojukwu** accused the federal military government, under the leadership of **General Yakubu Gowon**, of genocide. When the **Republic of Biafra** seceded to ensure Igbo liberty, Gowon responded by blocking food, aid, and military supplies from reaching Biafra. Ojukwu used this as further evidence of genocide. Scholars, however, have argued that if a pogrom occurred, it was conceptualized and executed locally and not by Gowon. Second, the UN definition only discusses physical attacks on people, not on their environment.

What about attacks on the environment on which people rely so heavily? This was a question posed in the 1990s by the **Ogoni** people, whose community has suffered greatly from the environmental destruction caused by **petroleum** production in the **Niger Delta**. In the case of the Ogoni, the Nigerian government was accused of conspiring with the Shell Petroleum Development Company in the destruction of the environment and indirect extermination of the Ogoni people. Accusations of genocide are difficult to prove because of a lack of statistics on deaths and evidence of intent by Nigeria's national and community leaders. This does not, however, dilute evidence that ethnic-based murder and environmental destruction have been committed.

**GHANA, REPUBLIC OF.** Since ancient times, people from present-day Nigeria have interacted with those from present-day Ghana. Ghana is located to the east of Nigeria along West Africa's coastline. Between Nigeria and Ghana are the two small states of Togo and **Benin**. The British claimed colonial control in West Africa over Ghana and Nigeria, and much of the colonial policies and laws emerged from their handling of one or the other. During **Great Britain**'s years of **legitimate commerce** and colonial rule, present-day Ghana was called the Gold Coast. When the Gold Coast received its independence from the British in 1957, the country's first president, Kwame Nkrumah, changed its name to Ghana after the ancient empire of Ghana. During Nigeria's **civil war**, Ghana attempted to facilitate the peace process by hosting the **Aburi Conference** on 4–5 January 1967. Nigeria and Ghana have both been members of the **Economic**

**Community of West African States** since 1975. Today, Nigeria and Ghana have a close economic relationship through the construction of a natural gas pipeline that will supply natural gas from Nigeria to its West African neighbors at discounted rates. Construction on the project began in 2005, and it is expected to come fully on line by early 2009. *See also* FOREIGN POLICY; FOREIGN TRADE.

**GOBIR.** One of the **Hausa Kingdoms** that was established sometime between the 10th and 18th centuries. **Babari** (the *sarki* of Gobir) attempted to expand his territory by seizing **Zamfara** in the 18th century. To achieve this goal, Babari offered his sister in marriage to Mairoki, the **king** of Zamfara. What started as a peaceful settlement in 1764 in Zamfara turned into a conquest by Gobir warriors. Gobir is famous for being the birthplace of **Usman dan Fodio**, the **Fulani jihadist** who established the **Sokoto Caliphate**. In the late 18th century, Usman dan Fodio was training Babari's son, **Yunfa**, in **Islam**. When Babari died, Yunfa became king and saw his former Muslim teacher as a political threat. Yunfa attempted to kill Usman dan Fodio; in response, Usman launched a jihad in 1804. Four years later, this Fulani jihad sacked Gobir and killed Yunfa and his advisers. Gobir then became part of the Sokoto Caliphate.

**GOLDIE, SIR GEORGE TAUBMAN (1846–1925).** Goldie was born in May 1846 on the Isle of Man. Following a family tradition, George Goldie attended the Royal Military Academy at Woolwich. He did not take to military life, and after two years of military service went to Egypt. He married in 1871. His family sent him to Nigeria to look after their interests in 1875, providing him with an opportunity to explore the **Niger River**. In 1879, he created the **United African Company** (UAC), the result of a four-company merger of British trading companies in the **Niger Delta**. In 1886, he participated in the formation of the **Royal Niger Company** to secure territory and trade routes from the encroaching French and Germans. The Royal Niger Company (previously the **National Africa Company**) also faced resistance from the **Fulani** in the North. In 1887, Goldie dropped "Taubman" from his name and became known as simply George Goldie. In 1900, the British government took over the responsibilities of the Royal Niger Company. Goldie felt liberated because he was more interested in trading than in British conquest. Between 1905 and 1908, Goldie served as president of the Royal Geographical Society. He died in August 1925.

**GOMBE STATE.** Created in 1996 out of **Bauchi State**, Gombe State is located in the northeast corner of Nigeria. Its predominantly Muslim **population** is composed of **Hausa** and **Fulani** peoples. Gombe has acquired the nickname "Jewel of the Savannah" because it is a major service hub for northeastern Nigeria in terms of tailoring, hairdressing, transportation, and entertainment. Other economic activities include the herding of livestock, leather-working, and growing of cereal crops. Its capital is the town of Gombe, which has historical significance as an emirate within the **Sokoto Caliphate** during the 19th century. **Yero Buba** was its founder and **emir**. Today, Gombe State is one of the 12 states that have incorporated **Shari'a** into their criminal law. It is one of Nigeria's current 36 states. *See also* STATE CREATION.

**GOMWALK, JOSEPH DESHI (1935–1976).** Born in April 1935 in Sudan, Gomwalk studied zoology at the Nigerian College of Arts, Science, and Technology in **Zaria** (1955–1958) and University College (present-day **University of Ibadan**). After graduation, he briefly worked at the Kaduna Veterinary Clinic. In the 1960s, he worked as an administrator for the Mapilla local government. In 1966, he joined Nigeria's national **police** force. He served as the military governor of **Benue-Plateau State** from 1967 to 1975. Among Muslim elites in the North, Gomwalk was considered the "black sheep" because he promoted institutions that allegedly undermined those of the Interim Common Service Agency. In 1976, he was accused of taking part in the **coup d'état** attempt that resulted in the assassination of **General Murtala Mohammed**. Gomwalk, along with several others, was put to death by firing squad in May 1976.

**GONGOLA STATE.** A state was created in 1976 out of **North-Eastern State** and then split into two states, **Adamawa** and **Taraba**, in 1991. The capital was **Yola**. It was located in northeastern Nigeria. *See also* STATE CREATION.

**GORSUCH COMMISSION.** In 1954, the **Western Region** decided to raise **civil service** wages by five shillings a day (an increase of nearly 100 percent). Seeing this, the British colonial government organized a committee to review the public services to ensure a balance between regional and federal governments. The chairman of the commission was L. H. Gorsuch. The commission specifically examined civil service wages and made recommendations. It reported its findings and encouraged the government to raise wages to be on a par with the Western Region across the country in 1956. This structure came under review again in 1972 by the **Udoji Commission**.

**GOVERNOR GENERAL.** The standard British colonial structure placed a governor general at the head of each colony. In the case of Nigeria, the first governor general, **Sir Frederick Lugard**, was appointed in January 1914. The governor general, situated in **Lagos**, would acquire information from the **lieutenant governors** across the colony. This position was often held for several years. Several of Nigeria's **constitutions**, for example the **Macpherson, Lyttleton**, and **Richards**, were named for former governor generals. In 1957, the colonial structure was modified to include a prime minister, which made the governor general a ceremonial figure. Sir James Wilson Robertson experienced this transition as governor general from 1954 to 1960. As Nigeria's first president, **Nnamdi Azikiwe** essentially replaced Robertson. The position of governor general was officially abolished in 1963. *See also* INDEPENDENCE.

**GOWON, GENERAL YAKUBU (1934– ).** Born in the **Middle Belt** region in October 1934, Gowon was Nigeria's youngest head of state. As a young man, he studied at St. Bartholomowo's School in Wusasa (1939–1949) and Government College in **Zaria** (1950–1953). He joined the army in 1954 and attended several training schools in Nigeria and elsewhere (e.g., the Royal Military Academy at Sandhurst, 1955–1956). He was promoted to the rank of major in 1963. From July 1966 to July 1975, he was the head of the federal military government and commander-in-chief of the **armed forces**. He became a major general in 1967 and a general in 1971.

Gowon led the federal government through the **civil war** and the **petroleum** boom years. Believing that Nigeria was not ready for civilian rule, he extended his term as head of state for an unspecified length of time. He also took the colonial regional divisions of Nigeria and divided them into 12 states. The military objected and organized a **coup d'état**. After he was overthrown by **General Murtala Mohammed**, Gowon went into exile in **Great Britain**. In 1983, he returned to Nigeria and continued his political career as a senator. He received a doctoral degree in political science from the University of Warwick in 1987. He also received numerous honorary titles and degrees. He is the *aare ajagunla* (**chief**) of Ile-Ife, Officer of the Federal Republic, and Grand Commander of the Federal Republic (1996). He received an honorary doctorate in law from **Ahmadu Bello University**, University of Lagos, University of Ife, River State University for Science and Technology, and Shaw University. He also received honorary doctoral degrees from the University of Benin, University of Nigeria at **Nsukka**, and Cambridge University. *See also* NATIONAL COMMISSION FOR REHABILITATION; NATIONAL YOUTH SERVICE CORPS.

**GRAHAM-DOUGLAS, NABO BEKINBO (1926–?).** Born in July 1926 in Abonnema, in **Rivers State**, Graham-Douglas studied at Nyemoni School and Kalabari National College before completing his advanced studies in law in England. He returned to Nigeria and established a private legal practice in **Port Harcourt**. In 1966, Graham-Douglas served as the attorney general for the **Eastern Region**. He strongly advised **Chief Chukwuemeka Ojukwu** against secession, but his advice was disregarded. After the Eastern Region seceded and became the **Republic of Biafra**, Graham-Douglas was detained. Federal troops freed him in 1968. To show his appreciation, he engaged in pro-federal military government tours around Europe during the remainder of the civil war. From 1972 to 1975, he served as the federal military government's attorney general. In 1975, he earned the title Senior Advocate of Nigeria. *See also* CIVIL WAR; COURTS; LEGAL SYSTEM.

**GREAT BRITAIN.** The United Kingdom of Great Britain and Northern Ireland, or Great Britain for short, has a long and complicated history with Nigeria. Regular contact between Britain and the west coast of Africa began in the 18th century. British traders traveled along the coast in search of luxury items and slaves. After the abolition of the **slave trade** in 1807, British traders became involved in **legitimate commerce**.

In the second half of the 19th century, a combination of European rivalry, economic pressures, and religious zeal prompted Great Britain to expand its trade and territorial claims across West Africa. Great Britain claimed **Lagos** in 1861 as its first piece of territory, naming it the **Lagos Colony**. British explorers spent a great deal of energy tracking the path of the **Niger River**. On their heels were missionaries and traders setting up camp along the Niger River, starting at the **Niger Delta**. Colonial Nigeria was constructed by the British piecemeal, establishing and merging colonies: **Oil Rivers Protectorate** (1884), **Niger Coast Protectorate** (1893), **Protectorate of Northern Nigeria** (1899), **Protectorate of Southern Nigeria** (1899), and Colony of Nigeria (1914). Weakened by **World Wars I and II** and growing African resistance, London began the process of decolonization by allowing Nigerians to organize **political parties** and prepare for the transfer of power through an **election** in 1959.

Nigeria became independent on 1 October 1960, marking the starting point of a new relationship between Nigeria and its former colonizer. During the 1970s, Nigeria focused on moving away from its diplomatic and economic reliance on Britain. For example, Nigeria publicly criticized Britain's handling of white supremacist governments in southern Africa and nationalized British businesses. Today, Nigeria maintains close ties with Britain through **trade**, diplomatic relations, and business. Nigerians tend to study, live, and holiday in Britain more than in any other Western country. At 5.7 percent, Great Britain is Nigeria's fifth largest source of imported goods. Nigeria is also a member of the Commonwealth. *See also* INDIGENIZATION.

**GREAT NIGERIAN PEOPLE'S PARTY (GNPP). A political party** was formed by **Alhaji Waziri Ibrahim** and **Chief Kolawole Balogun** in 1978. Its focus was on fulfilling Ibrahim's presidential ambitions and desire to serve as party chairman. The party was a splinter party from the **Nigerian People's Party**. After the conclusion of the 1979 **elections**, in which Ibrahim did not win, he aligned his party with the **Unity Party of Nigeria**. The GNPP was one of only five officially registered political parties to run in the 1979 election. After many initial successes in the 1979 general elections, the party began to fall apart. Ultimately, the party, along with all others, was banned in 1983. *See also* NATIONAL PARTY OF NIGERIA; PEOPLE'S REDEMPTION PARTY.

**GREEN REVOLUTION. Alhaji Shehu Aliyu Shagari** launched the Green Revolution in December 1979. It was an **agricultural** program designed to increase food production and reduce hunger and poverty in the country. The scheme included an increase in imports of agricultural supplies and encouraged all Nigerians to maintain large and small plots of crops. The goal was to make Nigeria self-reliant in food supplies. The plan was designed to improve upon **General Olusegun Obasanjo**'s **Operation Feed the Nation**, developed in May 1976. In February 1980, Shagari replaced Operation Feed the Nation with the National Council on Green Revolution, which included the federal minister of agriculture and state commissioners of agriculture, and the president, to oversee the scheme. Although the phrase has fallen out of usage, the idea of boosting agricultural production is still prevalent. *See also* RIVER BASIN DEVELOPMENT AUTHORITIES.

**GROUNDNUTS.** Also referred to as peanuts, groundnuts are a staple in Nigerian cuisine and foreign trade. They are grown primarily in **northern Nigeria** by **Hausa** farmers and traded through **Kano**. During the colonial period, Nigeria was a major producer and trader. Soil depletion and drought, however, have reduced groundnut production and **trade** to a regional activity. In the 1980s, the government tried to promote groundnut cultivation outside of northern Nigeria. Today, most groundnuts are destined for the domestic market.

**GUMI, SHEIKH ABUBAKAR MAHMOUD (1922–1992).** Gumi was born in November 1922 in Gumi, in **Zamfara State**. As a young man, he studied the **Koran** and memorized it. He completed his primary and secondary education in **northern Nigeria**. In 1942, he studied Arabic and **Islam** in **Kano**, and in 1943 he studied at the Shari'a Law School in Kano. He taught **Shari'a** (Islamic law) in **Sokoto** in the late 1940s. Gumi also studied Islamic doctrine in Sudan and Saudi Arabia. Upon his return to Nigeria, he served as a West African pilgrims' officer. He also served as a deputy and, later, full Muslim judge (or *grand khadi*) in the Shari'a Court of Appeal (1960–1976). Dissatisfied with the organization's commitment to Islamic principles, he left. Gumi was an outspoken critic of **General Yakubu Gowon**, which earned him the position of religious legal adviser to the **Supreme Military Council**. He was the leader of the

Jama'atu Nasril Islam from 1962 to 1970. In 1976, he acquired the title grand mufti of Nigeria. His critique of Nigerian politics and religious direction inspired the **Izala** association in 1978. He retired from the **civil service** in 1986. He has been considered a member of the illusive **Kaduna Mafia**. One of his major contributions to the study of Islam in northern Nigeria was the translation of the Koran from classical Arabic into the **Hausa language**. He also encouraged Muslim men in northern Nigeria to allow their wives and daughters to vote in federal **elections**. Gumi gave numerous public lectures and published written works criticizing mystical Islam. He died in September 1992. *See also* COURTS; *HAJJ*; KORANIC SCHOOLS.

**GWARI.** One of Nigeria's many **ethnic groups**, they live primarily in **Niger State**. They derive from one of the **Hausa Kingdoms** that existed from roughly the 10th to the 18th centuries. **Oral tradition** suggests that the Gwari people arrived from **Bornu**. The construction of a **road** from Zungeru to Kuta by the British colonial government in November 1907 unearthed the remains of a former Gwari town, called Ajugbai. The road passed through a burial ground of the old town, where construction workers unearthed earthenware pots and various metal objects used when burying the dead. Ajugbai served as a stopping-place for traders, but was destroyed by a neighboring kingdom. Notable members of the Gwari people are **General Ibrahim Babangida** and **Ladi Kwali**.

## – H –

**HABE KINGDOMS.** *See* HAUSA KINGDOMS.

*HAJJ.* Muslims are required to go on a spiritual journey to Mecca (referred to in Arabic as the *hajj*) at least once in their lives if they are financially and physically able. Performing this **pilgrimage** is one of the Five Pillars of **Islam**. The *hajj* includes, but is not limited to, seven circumambulations of the Kaaba and throwing pebbles at a stone pillar to reenact Abraham's rejection of Satan, over a roughly six-day span. Because about half of Nigeria's **population** is Muslim, the government of Nigeria has attempted to orchestrate this annual event. **Alhaji Abubakar Imam**, for example, served as pilgrim commissioner in the 1970s. Currently, the National Hajj Commission airlifts some 80,000 Muslims from 11 designated airports across the country. *See also* KORAN; RAMADAN.

**HARMATTAN.** A cold, dry wind that blows south and southwest off the Sahara Desert between November and March. As it passes over the desert, especially between December and February, it picks up dust particles. In **northern Nigeria**, the harmattan dust can create a lingering haze in the air and reduce visibility. In Nigeria, several universities divide their academic year into the harmattan semester and the rain semester. The harmattan is felt most strongly in the North, but can sometimes be felt along the coast.

**HARRAGIN COMMISSION.** At the close of **World War II**, the British attempted to maintain control of their colonies by reforming their administrative policies. In particular, they reviewed colonial Nigeria's **civil service**. African protest about unequal pay for work also done by expatriate workers and a general economic slump during World War II prompted the survey. The colonial government appointed Sir Walter Harragin, chief justice of the Gold Coast (present-day **Ghana**), to review and make recommendations about the salaries and working conditions of civil servants in British West Africa. The commission (Harragin and his administrative staff) spent the majority of their time in Nigeria. The report was submitted in September 1946. It contained recommendations for salary increases and improved working conditions. The Harragin Commission set the standards of pay, benefits, training, and pensions for civil service workers that lasted in Nigeria until the 1970s, when new attempts at reform were made.

**HAUSA.** The most well-known northern social group in Nigeria. Today, they are estimated to number 10–15 million people. Although referred to as an **ethnic group**, the Hausa are a community of different ethnic backgrounds who speak a common **Hausa language** and, for the most part, adhere to **Islam**. Hausa territory is a model of cultural absorption and territorial expansion, particularly with the **Fulani** and **Kanuri** peoples, over several centuries. The Hausa live primarily in northwestern Nigeria toward **Borno State** and southwestern **Niger State**.

The Hausa did not live in isolation, but engaged in expansive **trade** and diplomatic relations, with varying success. The **Yoruba**, for example, used Hausa **slaves** in commerce and military service, particularly under **Sir Adeniji Adele II** in **Lagos**. Hausa traders regularly traveled south to **Abeokuta** to purchase **kolanuts**. Much of what we know about pre-19th-century Hausa royalty comes from the *Kano Chronicle* and the *Song of Bagauda*. In 1804, **Usman dan Fodio**, a **Fulani**, led a series of **jihads** that subsumed the **Hausa Kingdoms** in the **Sokoto Caliphate**. During this period, the Hausa established a literary tradition of recording royal history, praising leaders through poetry, cataloging commercial activity, and celebrating Islam. In 1903, the British and French dismantled the caliphate.

The Hausa have made significant contributions to the vibrant, creative culture of Nigeria. **Alhaji Mamman Shata** is a famous Hausa musician, Naram-bad a well-known praise-singer, and **Bilkisu Ahmed Funtuwa** a major contributor to the **Kano Market Literature**. **Alhaji Bashir Tofa** and **Alhaji Abubakar Imam** were major cultural and political figures.

**HAUSA KINGDOMS.** Hausa **oral tradition** is quite varied. A popular theory about the founding of the Hausa Kingdoms says that they descend from Baghdad royalty. The Hausa Kingdoms developed from a marriage between **Prince Bayajidda** of Baghdad and a princess from **Daura** around the 10th century. The people were tormented by a *sarki* (snake, but also **king**), and Bayajidda saved them, earning the hand of the princess. Their son, Bawo, and his sons established the first seven Hausa Kingdoms: **Kano, Daura**, Rano, **Katsina**, Zazzau, **Gobir**, and Garutt Gabas (different sources will offer variations of this list, such as including **Zamfara** and excluding Garutt Gabas). These kingdoms were linked by lineage, **language**, and **trade**. Islam was introduced sometime in the 11th century, but there were few devout adherents until the 18th century. Non-Muslims living in **Hausa** territory were referred to as *maguzawa*. Another version identifies **Bagauda**, a grandson of Bayajidda, as the founder of the Hausa Kingdoms, or at least of Kano. Both of these stories build on the idea of **Kisra**, a Muslim from the Middle East who introduced Islam and established Muslim dynasties in West Africa, with some local variance. In any case, each kingdom was under the leadership of a *sarki*.

The Hausa Kingdoms were organized under a hereditary chief, or **emir**, who was advised by a council of title-holders. The kingdom, or emirate, was divided into districts, with each under a district head. The Hausa kingdom, or emirate, structure, for the most part, remained unaltered during the 19th century. These first seven kingdoms are referred to as the *Hausa bakwai* ("Hausa states") or Habe kingdoms. Of these seven, the most influential were Kano and Zazzau. Hausa oral tradition also says that Bayajidda had several illegitimate children, who founded seven kingdoms: Gwari, **Kebbi**, Kwararafa, **Nupe**, **Zamfara**, **Yoruba**, and **Jukun**. These kingdoms are referred to as the *banza bakwai* ("bastard states"). Some oral sources identify these kingdoms as being not of blood relation to Bayajidda or the Hausa. Much more evidence exists for this version. Scholars may exclude Zamfara and Kwararafa and include Yauri and **Borgu** in the list of seven states. Historians often describe these Hausa Kingdoms as city-states. Almost all of these Hausa Kingdoms became part of the **Sokoto Caliphate** in the 19th century. *See also* HAUSA LANGUAGE; MUHAMMADU, KANTA.

**HAUSA LANGUAGE.** Hausa is considered a Chadic **language**. Today, Hausa speakers are estimated to total about 40 million. The language is primarily spoken in **northern Nigeria** and Niger, but can also be heard in neighboring countries such as **Chad**, Burkina Faso, northern **Cameroon**, Togo, **Benin**, and **Ghana**. Several dialects are used, for example, **Kano** and **Sokoto**, across northern Nigeria. Since the 17th century, Hausa has been written in a version of Arabic script called *ajami* that, like Arabic, is written and read left to right. Hausa is a tonal language, signifying that the meaning of a word depends on the high, medium, or low tone assigned to the vowels. The spellings of words, however, have not been standardized, and variations exist. Many of the written works in Hausa, especially prior to the mid-20th century, are based on Islamic themes. A version of Hausa using the Latin alphabet was developed by Europeans in the 20th century. The BBC World Service, for example, called *boko*, provides international news in the *boko* form of Hausa. In **northern Nigeria**, Hausa is considered the primary language of government, **education**, and commerce. *See also* HAUSA KINGDOMS.

**HEALTH.** Health and well-being in Nigeria have been of serious concern, especially with the explosion of **HIV/AIDS** in Africa. The most prevalent illnesses affecting Nigeria include, but are not limited to, **polio**, guinea worm, HIV/AIDS, **malaria**, sickle cell anemia, sleeping sickness (carried by a tsetse fly), typhoid, cholera, and yellow fever. Nigeria is ranked fourth in Africa for cases of tuberculosis. Nigerians seek medical consultation from not only Western-style doctors, but also healers who practice **traditional medicine**. Despite these diseases, Nigeria has seen an increase in life expectancy, from 35 years in 1960 to 51 years in 2008.

In recent years, the government has supported public health campaigns. In 2003, Nigeria committed over $3 million to the "Roll Back Malaria" campaign, launched globally by the World Health Organization (WHO). In 2007, religious leaders in **Sokoto State** publicly united to encourage communities to vaccinate their children against a "wild" polio virus. In 2006, Nigeria pledged over $3 million for the training of health workers, testing stations, and treatment of basic illnesses.

Overall, there has been more emphasis on preventative medicine than on treatment and cure. This is because Nigeria's health services are considered very poor by international standards. In 2004, the WHO determined that 20 percent of children die between birth and age five. The two most cited causes were malaria (26 percent) and neonatal complications (24 percent). Basic medical supplies, such as clean needles and other hygienic instruments, are in short supply. Without a steady supply of **electricity**, Nigeria's health industry can only marginally improve. *See also* LAMBO, CHIEF THOMAS ADEOYE; MAJEKODUNMI, CHIEF MOSES ADEKOYEJO; MANUWA, SIR SAMUEL LAYINKA AYODEJI; OKEZIE, CHIEF JOSIAH ONYEBUCHI JOHNSON.

**HICKS-PHILLIPSON COMMISSION.** A commission that collected data and reviewed the existing formula for **revenue allocation** and reported back in 1951. The Hicks-Phillipson Commission essentially amended the **Phillipson Commission** report of 1946 by proposing that 50 percent of the revenue earned from exports be returned to the region of origin. All the regions (including the region of origin), would receive 35 percent to share, and the central government would get 15 percent. *See also* RAISMAN COMMISSION.

**HIGHER EDUCATION.** In the early 1960s, Nigeria saw a flurry of tertiary institutions established to make the country a center for **education**. **Southern Nigeria** is home to several historically significant universities, including the **University of Ibadan**. The University of Nigeria at **Nsukka** was created in response to a law requiring establishment of a university in the **Eastern Region** in 1955. It was opened in 1960 and started with an enrollment of 220 students and 13 faculty members. Its slogan is "restoring the dignity of man." **Northern Nigeria** is home to Bayero University and **Ahmadu Bello University**.

The **Asquith Commission** of 1945 and the Ashby Commission of 1959 reviewed Nigeria's higher education system. The Ashby Commission recommended the expansion of teacher training and technical education and the creation of a university in **Ile-Ife** to better meet demand in southwestern Nigeria. In 1962, the National Universities Commission was created to administer Nigeria's five universities, located in **Ibadan**, **Lagos**, Nsukka, Ile-Ife, and **Zaria**. It was also charged with guiding the federal government on the appropriate funding and development of the universities. In the 1990s, Nigeria's economic crisis hit its higher education system very hard. Universities today face a chronic shortage of faculty and teaching tools and facilities. Strikes implemented by the faculty or students occur regularly, and can take several months to resolve.

The lack of government funding has prompted the emergence of private universities. For example, American University opened a jointly operated university in **Yola** in 2005, called **ABTI-American University**. In response to the growing need for skilled labor and technological advancements, Nigeria has also established **agricultural** and technical tertiary institutions. In contemporary Nigeria, universities and technical schools are run by state and federal governments. Almost every state in Nigeria has a university in it. Several universities in Nigeria are known internationally and respected as national symbols. *See also* OBAFEMI AWOLOWO UNIVERSITY; YABA HIGHER COLLEGE.

**HIGHLIFE MUSIC.** A uniquely West African creation, which developed out of the **Palm Wine** music style. Highlife music, as first identified in the 1920s, is best described as Palm Wine music with a large band. This **musical** style incorporates swing, jazz, and Latin rhythms by combining multiple guitars with a brass band. The name refers to the European upper classes living a "high life." The characteristics of highlife music include using written (as opposed to memorized) music, salaried performers, incorporation of Western instruments, dressing in European clothing, substantial singing in English or pidgin, and members of the band being ethnically heterogeneous. Nigeria's most famous highlife artists include Bobby Benson and Rex Lawson. A unique Nigerian variation of Highlife is **Juju music**.

**HIP-HOP MUSIC.** Probably the most popular **musical** style, particularly among young adults in Nigeria. Historically, it includes break dancing, graffiti art, and rap music. In short, hip-hop is not simply a musical style, but a way of life. It is a means of creative expression that gives voice to young, urban populations. Hip-hop was developed in the Bronx neighborhood of New York City in the 1960s and 1970s by residents living in poverty. It helped ameliorate the hard conditions of inner-city life. This musical style reached Africa in the 1980s.

Many hip-hop songs in Nigeria include cultural proverbs and references to **Islam** or **Christianity**. Musicians of this genre express a desire for cultural pride, economic self-sufficiency, and collective survival. In Nigeria, the hip-hop community (through music, videos, and websites) functions almost parallel to the state. This is reflected by followers talking about being residents of "Naija," a variation on "Nigeria." Nigerians identify their own brand of this music style as Naija hip-hop. Just as in the United States, some lyrics are thought-provoking, whereas others are simplistic, sexist, and violent. There are few female hip-hop artists in Nigeria. In Nigeria, hip-hop performers and fans are not necessarily poor, because they need some wealth and global exposure to even be exposed to American rap. Scholars argue that hip-hop's popularity comes in part from its shared qualities with **oral tradition**. At present, some of the most popular hip-hop artists originating and performing regularly in Nigeria are P Square from **Anambra State**, Amplifyd Crew from **Lagos**, and 9ice from Lagos, who raps in **Yoruba**.

**HISBAH.** The *hisbah* are as a policing force designed to maintain the tenets of **Shari'a** in **northern Nigeria**. The word *hisbah* means "a good deed performed to improve humankind and earn a reward from God." Members of this group enforce bans on **alcohol** sales and public gender segregation. Although members of the *hisbah* adhere to Shari'a, they violate the federal government's civic code. For this reason, they are regarded as violators of **human rights** and merely a vigilante group. The *hisbah* are most visible in **Kano** and **Zamfara States**, because they receive state government support. The *hisbah* have emerged as a public answer to the failings of the **police** and government.

Membership is on a volunteer basis. The *hisbah* are largely composed of young men with little formal education or background in law or law enforcement. The men patrol the streets armed with sticks and, based solely on their own judgment, administer punishment to violators. They have flogged and beaten people as well as dragged them into Shari'a **courts**. In May 2007, the *hisbah* demolished four theaters in Kano State as part of a campaign to eradicate immoral behavior. In recent years, state governments have attempted to regulate the *hisbah* and standardize their duties.

**HIV/AIDS.** One of the major **health** concerns for Nigeria in the past two decades has been the spread of the human immunodeficiency virus (HIV), which causes acquired immunodeficiency syndrome (AIDS). It has been a global pandemic since the 1990s, with African countries the hardest hit. The first reported case of AIDS in Nigeria was in 1986. It is spread primarily through heterosexual transmission, but has affected **women** more than men. The recorded percentage of adults living with HIV/AIDS in Nigeria, based on a 2008 study by the World Health Organization (WHO), is 2.3 to 3.8 percent. The WHO 2008 study indicated that about 198,000 people were receiving antiretroviral therapy out of the 750,000 who qualified for it. In 2005, an estimated 20 percent of women and 25 percent of men understood how to prevent the spread of HIV. Education about HIV/AIDS has included the use of billboards, commercials, public lectures and seminars, and pamphlets. For example, **music** and television celebrities, such as Femi Kuti and Fati Muhammed, have appeared on billboards in Nigeria reminding people that you cannot determine who is HIV-positive by their looks. The government promised in 2004 to develop a scheme for local manufacturing of affordable antiretroviral drugs (the current cost of antiretroviral therapy is roughly $3,000 per year). *See also* MALARIA.

**HOMETOWN ASSOCIATIONS.** Private, voluntary organizations in Nigerian local communities that focus on promoting culture and support. For example, the Esop Ndito Efik Efut Ye Qua is an organization for the **Efik**, Efut, and Qua people from the **Calabar** area who live outside **Cross River State**. The members of these organizations are predominantly male and pay regular dues. These associations are important features of Nigerian society and are largely organized by ethnicity. They are designed to maintain a sense of community when away from home. They also pick up the financial and social slack within a failed state. Hometown associations promote the development of towns and villages as well as meeting the welfare needs of those living away from home. For example, the Asaba hometown association has branches in **Ibadan** and **Lagos**. The forms of assistance that these organizations provide include legal and financial aid, employment, and hosting of social events. They also commit funds to the construction of **roads** and building of schools and **health** centers. In sum, hometown associations emphasize social and ethnic unity as well as development. *See also* BIG MAN; ECONOMY; ETHNIC GROUPS.

**HOPE WADDELL TRAINING INSTITUTE.** Founded in 1895 as a school for girls and boys in **Calabar**, the institute was established to honor the late **Reverend Hope Masterton Waddell** from Dublin, Ireland. Many of its graduates became notable political figures in Nigeria. Alumni include **Sir Chief Alvan Ikoku, Eyo Ita**, and **Kingsley Mbadiwe**. *See also* EDUCATION.

**HOUSE OF CHIEFS.** A House of Chiefs was first set up in the **Northern Region** by the **Richards Constitution** in 1946. The **Western Region** assembled a House of Chiefs through the **Macpherson Constitution** of 1952. The **Eastern Region** acquired one in 1959. The purpose of the regional houses of chiefs was to provide an opportunity for direct involvement by traditional rulers and leaders. These houses worked in tandem with the regional **House of Assembly**. A House of Chiefs could recommend a legislative bill be ratified by the House of Assembly. The system was dismantled after the 1966 **coup d'état**. *See also* CHIEFS; EASTERN HOUSE OF CHIEFS; NORTHERN HOUSE OF CHIEFS; WESTERN HOUSE OF CHIEFS.

**HOUSES OF ASSEMBLY.** The **Richards Constitution** of 1946 not only organized the colony into three regions, but also endowed each with a House of Assembly. These houses were also simply referred to as regional councils. Each House of Assembly had three head **chiefs** and three traditional rulers appointed by the **governor general** as well as 11 representatives from the **Native Authorities**. The purpose of creating regional-level Houses of Assembly was to bridge the regional and central legislative organs. More specifically, the Richards Constitution found this a solution to incorporating the North into the central **Legislative Council**. A regional House of Assembly could recommend a bill be ratified by the regional **Houses of Chiefs**. The system was dismantled after the 1966 **coup d'état**. *See also* EASTERN HOUSE OF ASSEMBLY; NORTHERN HOUSE OF ASSEMBLY; WESTERN HOUSE OF ASSEMBLY.

**HOWELLS, BISHOP ADOLPHUS WILLIAMSON (1866–1938).** Howells was born in August 1866 in **Abeokuta**. As a young man, he attended Ake School and the Christian Missionary Society's Training Institute in **Lagos**. He began teaching in the mid-1880s in **Badagry** and Lagos. In 1891, he traveled to Sierra Leone to study at Fourah Bay College. He also studied in England. In 1894, he taught at the Church Missionary Society Grammar School in Lagos. Three years later, he became deacon of a church. He became an ordained priest in 1897. In 1919, he became the first African vicar of the Pro-Cathedral Church of Christ. One year later, he became a bishop at St. Paul's Cathedral in London. He served in the Niger Diocese from 1920 to 1933. Howells returned to Abeokuta in 1933 and served there until his retirement as resident bishop. His son, A. W. Howells, carried on his father's legacy as a pastor in **Enugu** and provost at a **Catholic** church in Lagos.

**HUMAN RIGHTS.** As humans we expect to have certain rights, which include the freedom to pursue personal and communal goals as well as the guarantee of being treated fairly by others. In a modern context, the maintenance of human rights happens through customs, laws, and **courts**. Most people cherish freedom of speech and the right to due process of law. In the late 1970s, attempts were made to incorporate human rights directly into Nigeria's **constitution**. Ironically, amid some of the gravest human rights violations committed by **General Sani Abacha**'s regime, he created the National Human Rights Commission in 1995. The purpose of the commission was to investigate human rights violations and develop a national human rights policy. The commission is run by a council, which is chaired by a former justice of the Supreme Court. The council includes members of the government, nongovernmental organizations (NGOs), and lawyers. Among the more prominent human rights NGOs are Human Rights Watch and Amnesty International.

**HUMAN TRAFFICKING.** In Nigeria, human trafficking has taken several different forms. People in present-day Nigeria have engaged in human trafficking as captors, **traders**, and **slaves** for centuries. These slaves served as concubines, soldiers, servants, and low-level political administrators for Muslim leaders. The practice of human trafficking continues in the 21st century. Recently, European police and journalists have exposed the trafficking of children, especially young girls, from West African countries such as Nigeria to work as prostitutes in Europe. The United Nations estimates that 60 to 80 percent of trafficked children are females being forced into a foreign sex trade. The common route of travel is from Nigeria northward through Mali and Morocco to Spain or Saudi Arabia.

There are three general categories of child trafficking. Girls are desired for domestic help and prostitution and boys for working as scavengers, drug peddlers, and farmers. Both boys and girls are sold for menial jobs. An estimated 15 million children are involved in forced **child labor** in Nigeria. In 2003, Nigeria passed the Trafficking in Persons Prohibition and Administration law, which assigned law enforcement officers the power to arrest traffickers and rescue victims. The law also called for the creation of the National Agency for Prohibition of Traffic in Persons, which receives financial and logistical assistance from the United Nations Children's Fund. *See also* MIGRATION; PROSTITUTION.

**HUSSEINI, SAFIYA (1971– ).** The first Nigerian **woman** to be sentenced to death by stoning for adultery under **Shari'a**. Husseini was accused of adultery in 2001 in **Sokoto State** at the age of 30. After getting divorced, Husseini had become involved with Yahaya Abubakar and did not get remarried. When she became pregnant, she was accused of adultery. Abubakar admitted to having sexual relations with her to the **police** on three different occasions during the ordeal, but he was released by the **court** on the grounds of there not being four male witnesses to his **crime**. **General Olusegun Obasanjo** intervened, pleading for Husseini's acquittal. She was acquitted in March 2002 by a court in **Sokoto** because she had become pregnant just prior to the implementation of Shari'a in Sokoto State. The same year that Husseini was acquitted, another woman, **Amina Lawal**, was also accused of adultery and acquitted. *See also* ISLAM; LEGAL SYSTEM.

– I –

**IBADAN.** A city in southwestern Nigeria. During the **Yoruba Wars** of the 19th century, thousands of people fled and settled new towns such as Ibadan. Oral history describes Ibadan as having emerged from an **Egba** village. Through a series of wars the village was destroyed, and the Egba relocated to **Abeokuta**. Subsequently, a warrior from **Ile-Ife** by the name of Lagelu founded Ibadan. In 1851, the (Anglican) **Church Missionary Society** established one of its first missions in Ibadan. In the mid-19th century, the population of **slaves** outnumbered free people. Starting in the 1940s, it was a major center of the Student Christian Movement in Nigeria and **Charismatic Christians**. Ibadan was home to one of Nigeria's first three technical colleges, founded in 1952. Today, it is a commercial and administrative center, with a largely **Yoruba population**. It is the site of the historic **University of Ibadan** and is the capital of **Oyo State**. Ibadan is Nigeria's third largest city, with a population of approximately 3.6 million.

**IBEKWE, DAN ONUORA (1919–1978).** Ibekwe was born in June 1919 in **Onitsha**, in **Anambra State**. He completed his primary and secondary schooling in Onitsha before studying law in London. He was called to the bar in 1951 and had a private legal practice for about six years. Ibekwe served as the legal advisor to the **premier** of the **Eastern Region** (1956) and solicitor general to the Eastern Region (1958–1964). In 1965, he became involved in Commonwealth relations. During the **civil war**, he was detained by the secessionist **Republic of Biafra**. Upon his release in 1970, he became the commissioner for works, housing, and transport in **East-Central State**. Two years later, he served as justice of the Supreme Court. He was also the federal attorney general and commissioner for justice in 1975 and president of the Federal Court of Appeal in 1976. He served as chairman of the **Nigerian Institute of International Affairs** in the mid-1970s. Ibekwe died in March 1978. *See also* COURTS; LEGAL SYSTEM.

**IBIAM, SIR FRANCIS AKANU (1906–1995).** Born in November 1906 in Unwana, in **Anambra State**, Ibiam studied at the **Hope Waddell Training Institute** in **Calabar** and **King's College** in **Lagos**. He received his postgraduate degrees in medicine in England and Scotland. In 1935, he returned to Nigeria to practice medicine. A year later, he founded the Abiriba Hospital at Itu. He worked as a medical missionary for the **Church of Scotland Mission** from 1936 until the outbreak of the **civil war** in 1967. He also sat on the board of governors for the Hope Waddell Training Institute and as a member of the Unwana Clan Council. In 1951, he was decorated as a Knight Commander of the British Empire. He declared his retirement from politics after a crisis in 1953 within the **Eastern House of Assembly** and assumed the directorship of the Nigerian Printing and Publishing Company. Between 1958 and 1962, he served as chairman of the Christian Council of Nigeria. In 1961, he was copresident of the World Council of Churches. But his withdrawal from national politics did not last long. Between December 1960 and January 1966, he was governor of the **Eastern Region**. He served as **Chief Chukwuemeka Odumegwu Ojukwu**'s special adviser for the **Republic of Biafra** during the civil war. In the 1980s, the **University of Ibadan** and the University of Ife (present-day **Obafemi Awolowo University**) presented him with honorary degrees. He died in July 1995.

**IBIBIO.** An **ethnic group** that lives in **Cross River State** and numbers roughly one million people. The Ibibio are closely related to the **Efik**. Unlike the Efik, however, they lived in a decentralized political configuration, relying on secret societies to maintain law and order and protect the villages from natural disasters. The Ibibio cultivate **oil palm** in the **Niger Delta**. The largest concentrations of Ibibio are in Ikot Ekpene and Itu. The Ibibio are identified in the narrative of

**Olaudah Equiano** by their practice of teeth-filing. *See also* MINORITY GROUPS; NIGER DELTA.

**IBO FEDERAL UNION.** One of the prominent cultural organizations that made up the membership of the **National Council of Nigeria and the Cameroons** (NCNC). It was founded in 1944 to focus on **Igbo** unity and development. In 1948, it changed its name to the **Igbo State Union**.

**IBO STATE UNION.** In 1948, the **Ibo Federal Union** was renamed the Ibo State Union. The union's membership included representatives from local Igbo-dominant unions and supporters of the **National Council of Nigeria and the Cameroons** (NCNC). The union focused on **Igbo** political solidarity under the leadership of the NCNC. **Nnamdi Azikiwe** served as president from 1948 to 1952. In 1953, Christopher C. Mojekwu acted as the organization's legal adviser. The union was banned in 1966, along with all other **political parties**.

**IBRAHIM, ALHAJI SIR KASHIM (1910–1990).** Born in 1910 in **Maiduguri**, in **Borno State**, Ibrahim completed his education at Borno Provincial School and Katsina Training College. Starting in 1939, he worked as a teacher, then as an **education** officer from 1949 to 1952. He was a cofounder of the **Northern People's Congress** (NPC) in 1952. Ibrahim also worked as the central minister of social services in **Lagos** (1952–1955) and as an administrator in the Borno Native Authority Administration (1955–1962). He returned to his work in education for several years, serving as chairman of the Nigerian College of Arts, Sciences, and Technology (1958–1962) and chairman of the provisional council for **Ahmadu Bello University** (1960–1966). He was the first Nigerian governor of the **Northern Region** (January 1962–January 1966). Between 1966 and 1977, Ibrahim served as chancellor of the **University of Ibadan** and University of Lagos. He received numerous awards, including Member of the Order of the British Empire, Commander of the Order of the British Empire, and Grand Commander of the Order of the Niger. He also received honorary degrees from the University of Nigeria at **Nsukka**, **University of Ibadan**, University of Lagos, and **Ahmadu Bello University**. Ibrahim died in July 1990.

**IBRAHIM, ALHAJI WAZIRI (1926–1992).** Born in February 1926 in Yerwa, in **Borno State**, Ibrahim studied at Maiduguri Middle School and Kaduna College. Between 1953 and 1954, he worked for the **United African Company** in the **Benue River** region in various capacities. In 1959, he became a member of the House of Representatives. He also served as the federal minister of health and minister of economic development in the 1960s. During the **civil war**, he sided with the federal military government. He returned to his business activities during the period of military rule. In 1978, he created the **Nigerian People's Party**, but then left it to form the **Great Nigerian People's Party** (GNPP) because of a dispute over his role as presidential candidate and party chairman. He lost the 1979 presidential **election**, but within his home state, Ibrahim received 54 percent of the votes, largely from the **Kanuri** people. After the election, he aligned the GNPP with the **Unity Party of Nigeria** (UPN) until 1982. This shift stemmed from a rift within the GNPP, which involved resistance to Ibrahim. He ran for president again in 1983 as the GNPP candidate, receiving just over 2 percent of the votes. Ibrahim died in July 1992. He is most associated with the inspiring words "politics without bitterness."

**IBRAHIM BEN AHMED (?–1846).** Ibrahim ben Ahmed was the younger brother of **Dunama ibn Ahmed Lefiami** of the **Sefawa Dynasty**. He was ruler of the **Kanem-Bornu Empire** from 1820 to 1846. He held court in the town of Birni Kafela and launched several military campaigns from there. After the death of **Muhammed al-Amin al-Kanemi** in 1837, Ibrahim became largely a figurehead, while al-Kanemi's son, **Umar ibn al-Amin al-Kanemi**, ascended to the throne. Ibrahim tried to reestablish the **Sefawa Dynasty**, but did not succeed. Ibrahim also attempted to have Umar removed, but failed and was killed by Umar in 1846 at Kukawa.

**IDIA.** Queen mother of **Esigie**, the ruler of the **Benin Kingdom** in the early 1500s. Esigie created the political title *iyoba* to include her in his administration. Idia has been described as a valiant warrior. She is credited with Esigie's successful conquest of the neighboring **Igala** Kingdom. Esigie built her a palace outside **Benin** and gave her territory over which to rule. In Bini oral tradition, Idia has several praise names, such as *Idia ne ekonorhue* (meaning "Idia, the womb of Orohue"). An ivory carving of her face was adopted in 1977 as the emblem of the **World Black and African Festival of Arts and Culture**.

**IDIAGBON, MAJOR GENERAL TUNDE (1943–1999).** Idiagbon was born in September 1943 in **Ilorin**, in **Kwara State**. After completing his primary and secondary schooling in Ilorin, he studied at the Nigerian Military School in **Zaria** (1958) and joined the **army**. He earned the rank of secondary lieutenant in 1965. He also received military training overseas. During the **civil war**, he fought for the federal military government as a commanding officer. He served as an administrator for **Borno State** from 1978 to 1979. He was also secretary of the army (1981–1983) and chief of staff (1984–1985). Idiagbon is associated with the creation and enforcement of State Security (Detained Persons) Decree No. 2, which allowed the federal military government under the leadership of **Major General Muhammadu Buhari** to detain people indefinitely and without a trial. After the 1985 military **coup d'état**, Idiagbon was imprisoned for about three years. After his release, he maintained a low profile. Idiagbon died in March 1999.

**IDRIS BEN ALI ALOMA (?–ca. 1603).** When Idris was young, his mother, Queen Amsa, built the royal complex of Gambaru to separate Idris from the royal court. His reign from ca. 1570 to ca. 1603 marked a revival of the **Kanem-Bornu Empire** at a time when it was under attack by **Bulala** and **Hausa** peoples. Idris placed territories outside Bornu under the administration of trusted individuals instead of his blood relatives. He raised money for the empire through **taxation**, **slave trading**, and tribute collection. Idris established an **Islamic** judicial system. He is also credited with the construction of a hostel in Mecca for citizens of Kanem-Bornu on *hajj* (**pilgrimage**). A major historical text written in Bornu using Arabic script, the *Kanem Wars of Idris Aloma*, provides details not only about Idris, but also about the Kanem-Bornu Empire. After his death in ca. 1603, Kanem-Bornu went into a period of decline.

**IGALA.** The Igala live in **Kogi State** and are engaged in **agriculture**. They had a prominent kingdom at Idah as early as the 15th century.

Oral tradition says that Atah formed the Igala into a relatively decentralized kingdom, with his capital at Idah. Igala royal society divided into decentralized clans, claiming the same **Jukun** ancestry. The Igala live at the Niger–Benue confluence, exposing this group to numerous other **ethnic groups** and trade networks in Nigeria. They have exercised influence over other social groups, including the Idoma and the **Nupe**. *See also* MINORITY GROUPS.

**IGBINEDION, CHIEF GABRIEL OSAWARU (1934– ).** Born in September 1934 in Okada, in **Edo State,** Igbinedion studied at Benin Baptist Primary School (1944–1951) and Eko Boys' High School (1952–1954). He was a member of a teacher's council. He worked for the **police** in 1958 and then for several years in sales for the Leventis Company. Igbinedion launched a series of businesses under the name Okada Group, which specialized in, among other things, **airlines**, motor sales, soft drink bottling, and shipping. In the political arena, he was a member of the **People's Democratic Party** in the 1990s. He was also a major financial contributor to **General Olusegun Obasanjo**'s presidential candidacy in 1999. He has received numerous accolades, including the chieftaincy of *esama* of **Benin**. He established the Igbinedion University in Benin.

**IGBIRRA.** Considered a **minority group**, the Igbirra live near the Niger–Benue confluence in **Kogi State**. They speak the **Nupe** language, but are related to the **Edo**-speaking pople. The Igbirra are known for their Ekwechi-Anokehi festival, which includes competing masquerades. Eku, an ancestral spirit endowed with supernatural powers, plays an important role in the celebration. *See also* ETHNIC GROUPS.

**IGBO.** The Igbo live primarily in southeastern Nigeria and are united by the **Igbo language** and **religion**. It is estimated that the Igbo **ethnic group**'s **population** is roughly 19 million. They are the ethnic majority in **Akwa Ibom, Anambra, Cross River**, and **Rivers States**. The origin of the Igbo is uncertain, but some scholars have said they migrated from the Niger–Benue confluence to their present location in southeastern Nigeria. The territory dominated by the Igbo is commonly referred to as Igboland. Although the Igbo political system is most commonly described as acephalous, or segmentary, there are several instances within Igbo society of a kingship system. The **Aro, Onitsha**, and **Nri** are just a few examples.

During the colonial period, the British attempted to establish the administrative practice of **indirect rule**, which had been so successful for them in **northern Nigeria**. Indirect rule in Igboland, however, initially failed because the British could not identify a **chief** and resolved to appoint an individual to fulfill that role. The Igbo response was the **Aba Riot** of 1929. In May 1966, thousands died during a massacre resembling **genocide**, which sparked the secession of the **Eastern Region** from Nigeria and the **civil war**. Today, it is not uncommon to see Igbo war veterans sitting along the roadside in **Enugu** collecting donations. The Igbo have developed a reputation as skilled traders and entrepreneurs, causing them to travel far from their traditional home in search of business. **Ohaneze Ndigbo** was an important Igbo cultural association. Notable Igbo cultural and political figures include **Chinua Achebe, Michael Okpara, Nnamdi Azikiwe**, and **Chief Chukwuemeka Ojukwu**.

**IGBO LANGUAGE.** The **Igbo** language is part of the Kwa language, which is part of the Niger–Congo family. It is primarily spoken in **eastern Nigeria** and in the **Niger River** basin. There are an estimated 19 million Igbo speakers. When writing, the Igbo use Latin letters, with some variation, to express sounds unique to the language. Igbo is a tonal **language**, signifying that the meaning of a word depends on the high or low tone addressed to each vowel. There are several dialects of Igbo, for example, Enu-Onitsha Igbo. The translation of this **ethnic group**'s name into English has resulted in two spellings, Igbo and Ibo. Both are widely used and accepted when referring to the language or ethnic group. *See also* IGBO RELIGION.

**IGBO RELIGION.** The **Igbo** have practiced their religion since ancient times. They believe that *Chukwu* (God) created the universe and cohabited with humans. Chukwu created Eri, the progenitor of humans, and sent him to a waterlogged earth. Eri and Namaku, his wife, arrived in the town of Aguleri, located in present-day **Anambra State**. A blacksmith was also sent to dry the land with fire. Eri and Namaku had four children—Nri, Aguleri, Igbariam, and Amanuke— who are the ancestors of the Igbo people. Chukwu assigned the maintenance and protection of humans in their daily lives to a pantheon of deities. Practitioners seek assistance from gods such as Ala, Igwe, and Mbatuku, and give thanks to them through offerings and community festivals. Today, most Igbo practice **Christianity**. They believe very strongly in *agbara* (spirit), which acts as a strong force to encourage people to do good things. *See also* IGBO LANGUAGE.

**IGE, CHIEF BOLA (1930–2001).** Born in September 1930 in Esa-Oke, in **Oyo State**, Ige attended St. Joseph's Catholic School in **Kaduna** (1936–1941), St. John's School in Ilesha (1942), Ibadan Grammar School (1943–1948), and University College (present-day **University of Ibadan**) (1956–1959). For several years between educational programs, Ige taught at Ibadan Grammar School. Ige got his law degree at the University of London (1956–1959) and was called to the bar in February 1961. He set up his own private legal practice in 1961. From 1967 to 1970, he was the commissioner for **agriculture** and natural resources for **Western State**. Ige was also the governor of Oyo State (1979–1983). In 1983, he was arrested, with several others, for allegedly receiving kickbacks from a contract. He was acquitted but later sentenced to 21 years in prison. Ige was a member and then leader of the UPN (1979–1983). During the 1983 military **coup d'état**, **Chief Victor Onabanjo**, **Chief Michael Ajasin**, and Ige were accused of **corruption** involving the **Unity Party of Nigeria** (UPN). Ige was a strong advocate for the implementation of the results of the **election of 12 June 1993**. He was a member of **Afenifere**, a pan-**Yoruba** social group. He was also a member of and presidential aspirant from the **Alliance for Democracy**. In 2000, he served as attorney general. He received the chieftaincy titles of *asiwaju* of Esa-Oke, *jagun* of Ilesha, *odofinojuwa* of Ila-Orangun, *apesin* of Irewole, and *maiyegun* of Aiyete. Ige died in **Ibadan** in December 2001 from gunshot wounds.

**IJAW.** The Ijaw are one of the largest **ethnic groups** to inhabit the **Niger Delta**, numbering 8 million. They are the fourth largest ethnic group in the country. Nigeria's current vice president, **Goodluck Jonathan**, is of Ijaw descent. **Oral tradition** describes the Ijaw as a migratory group that arrived in the Niger Delta in the 15th century from a northeastern location. The Ijaw rely on fishing and scattered farmlands in the swampy terrain. Their houses are built on stilts over the water. The Ijaw, like many other groups along the southern coast, participated in the transatantic **slave trade** during the 18th century. Since the mid-20th century, the Ijaw have struggled with having the center of Nigeria's **petroleum** in their community. Like others in the Niger Delta, the Ijaw have complained of pollution, unemployment, and financial neglect caused by oil production. The Ijaw youth participated in protests, acts of resistance, and **crime**, contributing to the broadly labeled **Niger Delta Conflict**. The **Ijaw Youth Council** emerged in 1998 to create a unified voice of resistance.

However, the line between gang activity and sincere protest is blurred. Many young men of the Ijaw ethnic group are involved in militia, or gang, wars against rival groups over control of the Niger Delta. These groups have kidnapped oil workers and stolen oil from pipelines to sell on the black market. The militia activities of the Ijaw rely not only on weapons and intimidation, but also on the supernatural. By tying or carrying a particular kind of leaf close to his body, a militia member believes he is protected from bullets and machetes. These young men place faith in their god of war, Egbisu, to protect and guide them. *See also* MINORITY GROUPS.

**IJAW YOUTH COUNCIL (IYC).** A confederation of **Ijaw**-based youth organizations formed in 1998. Its development was prompted by the Kaiama Declaration, which called for the consolidation of Ijaw youth movements in Nigeria against **petroleum** companies. This council is heavily involved in the **Niger Delta Conflict**. At the founding meeting in Kaiama (located in **Bayelsa State**), 5,000 young men and women represented 500 communities. The Ijaw Youth Council stated that all petroleum in their region belongs to the people and all exploration/production must cease. The council has also called for the creation of a national conference to equally represent **ethnic groups** in the country. Since 1998, numerous outbursts of violence have been attributed to the council. In response, the federal military government declared a state of emergency in Bayelsa State and sent in troops in 2005.

**IJAYE WAR.** A conflict between **Ibadan** and Ijaye over the succession of the *alaafin* (**king**) of the **Oyo Empire** from 1859 to 1861. The war was part of the **Yoruba Wars**. The origin of the war dates back to 1836, when **Kurunmi**, the ruler of Ijaye, assisted in making **Atiba** the new *alaafin* of Oyo. When Atiba died in 1859, Ibadan called for Atiba's first son, Adelu, to become the new *alaafin*, rejecting the tradition of the *alaafin*'s first son following his son to the grave. Kurunmi was outraged and refused to accept Adelu. The ruler of **Ibadan** responded by sending people to persuade Kurunmi to recognize him. Instead of agreeing, Kurunmi waged war against Adelu, which prompted an attack on Ijaye by Ibadan. The **Egba** supported Ijaye militarily. In 1861, Kurunmi died in battle along with thousands of Ijaye who died of starvation. In 1862, the Ijaye kingdom collapsed, prompting many of its people to settle in **Abeokuta**.

**IJEBU.** A subgroup of the **Yoruba**, totaling an estimated 8 percent of Yoruba speakers. **Oral tradition** cites the Ijebu and Awori people as the ancient inhabitants of **Lagos**. Prior to colonial rule, the Ijebu were organized into a kingdom, which was ruled by the *awujale* (**king**) and located in the town of Ijebu-Ode. In 1891, the Ijebu and the British signed a treaty abolishing human sacrifice and ensuring free trade. After the Ijebu refused to comply with the treaty, the British attacked them in 1892. Today, the Ijebu are one of the dominant **ethnic groups** in **Ogun State**.

**IJEMO MASSACRE.** *See* EGBA.

**IKOKU, SIR CHIEF ALVAN AZIMWA (1900–1971).** Born in August 1900 in **Arochukwu**, in **Abia State**, Ikoku was the son of a successful merchant. He completed his primary education at Government School in **Calabar** and his secondary at **Hope Waddell Training Institute**. In 1920, he started teaching for the Presbyterian Church of Scotland. Two years later, he began teaching at St. Paul's Teacher Training College and at the same time earned advanced degrees through correspondence. He is considered a pioneer of formal **education** in Nigeria. Between 1921 and 1931, he worked as a schoolmaster, tutor, and teacher at schools such as Hope Waddell and Church Missionary Society Training College. In 1928, he received his Ph.D. in philosophy from the University of London. Three years later, he started Aggrey Memorial College (named after a famous Ghanaian educator), a private secondary school in Arochukwu.

In addition to his career as a teacher, Ikoku was also involved in government. He served on the Board of Education for the **Eastern Region House of Assembly** (1947) and the **Legislative Council** (1947–1951) in **Lagos** representing the Eastern Region. Starting in 1955, he was an active member and later president of the **Nigerian Union of Teachers**. In 1966, he was part of a committee assessing the feasibility of a national education program. Ikoku was the honorary chief of Obosi and recipient of the honorary title Officer of the Order of the British Empire. He also received an honorary law degree from the **University of Ibadan**. He died in November 1971. Ikoku's picture is on the ₦10 bill.

**IKOLI, ERNEST SESEI (1893–1960).** Ikoli was of **Ijaw** descent, born in March 1893 in **Brass**, in **Rivers State**. As a young man, he attended mission schools in Brass and **Onitsha** as well as Bonny Government School in **Bonny** and **King's College** in **Lagos**. He worked as a journalist and editor for a number of **newspapers**, including the *Daily Times* and *Lagos Daily Record*, between 1919 and 1943. He also served as the head of King's College. In 1921, he started his own newspaper, the *African Messenger*, which ran for five years. He was a member of the **Legislative Council** from 1941 to 1946 as well as a member of the Board of Education. He was one of the founding members of the **Lagos Youth Movement** and editor of the organization's *Daily Service* newsletter. One writer affectionately remembered Ikoli as having a "rasping voice" and "sardonic wit." He received the honorary title Officer of the Order of the British Empire in 1953. Ikoli died in October 1960.

**ILE-IFE.** The sacred city of the **Yoruba** people, located in **Osun State**. According to **oral tradition**, Ile-Ife was the cradle of human civilization. It was the final home of Oduduwa, the ancestor of Yoruba *oba* (**kings**). In the center of town today is a large statue honoring Oduduwa. Archeological evidence, including bronze head and terra cotta sculptures, dates the occupation of Ile-Ife as far back as the 11th century. Ile-Ife had lost its status as the center of Yoruba politics to the **Oyo Empire** by the 14th century. During the 1980s, Ile-Ife was home to the Ona Artists, who popularized the Yoruba concept of *ona* (reverence for decoration and ornamentation). Today, the population of

Ile-Ife is estimated at 300,000 and includes the **Modekeke** and Ife sub-groups of the Yoruba. In 1997 and 1998, Ile-Ife was the site of violent clashes between the Modekeke and Ife inhabitants. Ile-Ife is the home of **Obafemi Awolowo University**. *See also* YORUBA RELIGION.

**ILORIN.** A **Yoruba** town in **Kwara State** and the state's capital. Today, Ilorin has a **population** of approximately 778,000. Prior to the 20th century, Ilorin was one of the **Oyo Empire**'s military posts, until **Afonja** tried to declare independence. Ilorin was seized by **Fulani jihadists** and Afonja was killed. A long war took place between the Fulani and Yoruba of Oyo in Ilorin (1817–1837). Neighboring **Borgu** kings sided with Oyo to prevent the spread of **Islam**. Involved in this war were Yoruba provincial chiefs, such as Onikoyi and Solaberu, who wanted to break away from Oyo control. During the colonial period, Ilorin was in the **Protectorate of Northern Nigeria** and the **Northern Region**. Much of its early history was documented in Reverend Samuel Ojo's work, *Short History of Ilorin* (1957).

**IMAM, ALHAJI ABUBAKAR (1911–1981).** Imam was born in 1911 in Kagara, in **Niger State**, and was of **Hausa** descent. As a young man, he studied at Katsina Training College. Imam held several different positions in the colonial **civil service** in the **Northern Region**. He dedicated his life to **literature** and politics in Nigeria. He wrote exclusively in the **Hausa language** and published several novels. In 1934, the colonial government published on his behalf *Ruwan Bagaja* (*The Water of Cure*) (1971). His most famous work is a three-volume collection of stories, *Magana Jari Ce* (*The Ability to Speak Money*) (1960). He also worked as an editor for *Gaskiya Ta Fi Kwabo*, a Hausa **newspaper**, from 1939 to 1954. As a major newspaper editor, he was invited to travel with other editors, such as **Nnamdi Azikiwe**, to England in 1943. Azikiwe drafted a memo, "Atlantic Charter and British West Africa," which called for reform and the end of colonial rule. Imam was among the few who did not sign the memo.

In the political arena, Imam cofounded the **Jam'iyyar Mutanen Arewa** cultural association, which became the **Northern People's Congress**. He also served as treasurer of the Northern People's Congress. In the 1950s, he was a member of the **Northern House of Assembly** and House of Representatives. From 1959 to 1966, he worked for the Public Service Commission of the North. Imam is credited with the creation of a Nigeria Office in Jeddah and the assignment of a *hajj* (**pilgrimage**) commissioner to facilitate travel to Mecca. Imam died in June 1981.

**IMO STATE.** A state named for the Imo River in southeastern Nigeria, with the **Niger River** serving as its western boundary. **Christianity** is the major **religion** in the state. Imo State is considered part of the **Niger Delta** region. Economic activities in the state include the cultivation of rice, **oil palm**, rubber, and various fruits, as well as fishing. The capital is Owerri. *See also* STATE CREATION.

**IMOUDU, CHIEF MICHAEL OMINUS (1902–2005).** Imoudu was born in September 1902 in the town of Ora, in **Edo State**. As a young man, he studied at the Government School in Ora, Catholic School in **Onitsha**, and Agbor Government School. He was an assertive trade unionist and dedicated politician. His first job was with the Department of Post and Communications. In 1928, he worked as a laborer on the **railroads**. In January 1940, Imoudu submitted the paperwork that officially established the **Railway Workers' Union**, the first recognized **trade union** in Nigeria. The individual originally assigned with the task lost his courage and asked Imoudu to do it. This courageous act earned Imoudu the nickname "Nigeria's Labor Leader Number 1." For the next 20 years, he was a committed trade union leader. Between 1943 and 1945, he was detained by the federal government. In 1945, he led 3,000 railway workers demanding better wages and safer working conditions from the colonial government. That same year, he led Nigeria's longest lasting **general strike** (six weeks).

From 1947 to 1958, Imoudu was president of various trade unions, including the **All-Nigeria Trade Union Federation**. He was also the first president of the first **Nigerian Labour Congress**, which formed in 1950. Imoudu's political activities often landed him in direct confrontation with the British colonial government. During the 1970s, he was involved in politics as a vocal member of the **People's Redemption Party**. He received an honorary law degree from **Obafemi Awolowo University** in 1978. He held the title of **chief** as well as the national honor of Commander of the Federal Republic. The former National Institute for Labour Studies changed its name to Michael Imoudu Institute for Labour Studies in 1992 in honor of his achievements. He died at the age of 103 in July 2005 at his home in Edo State.

**INDEPENDENCE.** Nigeria gained its independence from **Great Britain** on 1 October 1960. The final years of the 1950s, devoted to seeking independence, appeared promising, with the organization of **political parties** and the holding of **elections**. At the London Constitution Conference in 1957, the three major political parties—**Action Group**, **National Council of Nigeria and the Cameroons**, and **Northern People's Congress**—were united as the National Unity Government, with **Sir Alhaji Abubakar Tafawa Balewa** as the prime minister of the Federation of Nigeria. The British government passed the Nigerian (Constitution) Order in Council on 12 September 1960, which called for independence. The order came into effect on 1 October 1960. Since independence, however, Nigeria's political situation has remained shaky, making the concept of political freedom and independence, to some Nigerians, a farce. *See also* FIRST REPUBLIC; SELF-GOVERNMENT MOTION CRISIS.

**INDEPENDENT NATIONAL ELECTORAL COMMISSION (INEC).** A permanent government body created by **General Alhaji Abdulsalami Abubakar** in 1998 to organize and oversee state and federal **elections** in 1999. INEC's goals include improving the levels of transparency, credibility, and integrity of the election process in Nigeria. The current commission has received a great deal of criticism for its handling of the severely flawed 2007 presidential election. Similar political bodies were created, including the **National Electoral Commission**, which was intended to oversee the failed **election of 12 June 1993**.

**INDIGENIZATION.** A program of economic transformation, first launched by **General Yakubu Gowon** in the late 1960s. It called for the replacement of foreign employees with indigenous Nigerian ones. It also called for the transfer of foreign ownership to indigenous Nigerian owners. As part of this economic overhaul, Gowon issued a specific law, called the Nigerian Enterprise Promotions Decree, which outlined timetables and guidelines to assist in carrying out his vision. This included the creation in 1972 of the Nigerian Enterprise

Promotions Board to oversee this transition and promote Nigerian businesses. Successive regimes after Gowon's continued to work on this vision until the mid-1980s. The overall goals of the indigenization program were to reduce **unemployment**, limit foreign control over Nigeria's **economy**, and unite a fractured Nigerian society behind a promising economic ideology. Indigenization also included the creation of state-owned companies such as Nigerian Airways and the **Nigerian National Petroleum Corporation**. Today, indigenization has been shelved in favor of **privatization**. *See also* DEVELOPMENT PLANS; INDUSTRIALIZATION.

**INDIRECT RULE.** The administrative pattern of ruling a colony indirectly through local African authorities was used to the same extent by all European powers throughout Africa. It was the British, however, who announced it as formal policy. It is the system of colonial governance that facilitates ruling of an indigenous **population** through **chiefs**, **emirs**, and **Native Courts**. These local leaders would be responsible for enforcing laws, presiding over Native Courts, collecting **taxes**, and recruiting labor for public works projects. Ultimately, they were charged with carrying out colonial policy. **Sir Frederick Lugard** formally recorded and justified the use of indirect rule as an administrative method in the early 20th century. He explained the function and purpose of indirect rule in *The Dual Mandate in Tropical Africa* (1922). Before Lugard promoted indirect rule in Nigeria, he tested it in India and the Sudan in the late 19th century.

Lugard first promoted indirect rule as a unique British strategy in the **Protectorate of Northern Nigeria** before applying it to the rest of the colony. In **southern Nigeria**, the British tried to implement indirect rule between 1914 and 1916. In many cases, the British looked for a leader to instill with power, even if that person lacked legitimacy among his people. They ignored historical events that had shaped the regional strength of **ethnic groups**, fostering hostility among a leader's subjects. For example, the British conferred leadership upon the *alaafin* (**king** in the **Yoruba language**) of Oyo despite the fact that in the 19th century the great **Oyo Empire** had collapsed and **Ibadan** was the new regional power. In southern **Borgu**, the British made the Mora Tasude of Kaima **paramount chief**, elevating him in status and expanding his regional authority immensely.

In **eastern Nigeria**, "paramount" chiefs did not exist. As a result, the British actually appointed **warrant chiefs**. Although their position was often recognized, and enhanced, by the British, these chiefs faced growing opposition from their subjects. It was not long before the traditional method of checks and balances crumbled and rulers became despotic.

**INDUSTRIALIZATION.** This aspect of economic development came relatively late to Nigeria in comparison to other British colonies in Africa. Since the mid-20th century, before the end of colonial rule, Nigeria has undergone a series of industrialization programs. However, Nigeria has always struggled with a lack of indigenous skilled labor and capital to launch new industries. As a result, factories usually only last a short time before closing, and most manufactured products are imported. By 1940, only a few privately owned industries operated in Nigeria: four **cotton** granaries, a cigarette manufacturer, a drum-making factory, six sawmills, a soap manufacturer, and two **oil palm** processing plants. After **World War II**, a few factories opened in Nigeria to manufacture cement, rubber tires, and glass. Since **independence**, Nigeria's government has grappled with the dilemma of how to industrialize without being overrun by foreign companies. This explains the use of subsequent **development plans**, few of whose industrial goals were achieved. In 1958, Nigeria launched its **petroleum** production, which quickly became Nigeria's largest and most lucrative industry. In the late 1960s, the federal military government began an **indigenization** program, which sanctioned the replacement of foreign business owners, shareholders, and managers with Nigerians. The idea was that Nigerians could take over important industries in the country piecemeal. The government also launched new industrial activities such as fertilizer plants, steel manufacturing, and soap production. The Federal Institute for Industrial Research was established in 1966 to provide technical advice to Nigerian entrepreneurs and assistance with setting up new industries. The vision of increasing Nigeria's industrial output has not disappeared, but the formation of formal industrialization plans has. *See also* PRIVATIZATION.

**INTERIM ADMINISTRATIVE COUNCIL.** A council created in May 1967 to administer the former **Northern** and **Eastern Regions**, which had been carved into states. The council was charged with determining the allocation of assets and **civil servants** of the regions to each new state. **Major General Hassan Katsina** served as chairman of the committee for one year. The **civil war** interrupted its research in the East. The council was replaced by the Interim Common Services Agency and the Interim Assets and Liabilities Agency in 1968 and 1970, respectively. The former became a forum for northern interests.

**INTERIM NATIONAL GOVERNMENT (ING).** A temporary government from August 1993 to November 1994, composed of representatives from both of the major parties—**Social Democratic Party** and **National Republican Convention**—to replace the **Transitional Council**. It was cobbled together to transition Nigeria from military rule after **General Ibrahim Babangida** annulled the **election of 12 June 1993**. This interim government created stability and was headed by **Chief Ernest Shonekan**. The only military representative in the ING was **General Sani Abacha**, who acted as defense secretary. The ING was criticized for its short-term focus as a political entity created to simply fill a void in state control. It pledged to stamp out **corruption**, reduce **petroleum** price subsidies, and balance the government's budgets. In reality, it lasted less than one full year and failed to meet its objectives. The activities of the ING ended abruptly in November 1994, with Abacha forcing Shonekan to resign and installing himself as the new head of state for Nigeria.

**IRIKEFE COMMISSION.** A commission established by the federal military government in August 1975 to examine the creation of new states. Ayo Irikefe, a Supreme Court judge, headed the commission. It was charged with determining not only if new states were necessary, but also where they and their capitals could be located. In December 1975, the Irikefe Commission recommended the redrawing of boundaries in the **Niger Delta** and the establishment of new states. *See also* BOUNDARY ADJUSTMENT COMMISSION; STATE CREATION.

**ISLAM.** A form of **religion** dating back to the seventh century, introduced by the Prophet Muhammad into present-day Saudi Arabia. Exactly when Islam reached Nigeria is a subject of debate. Some scholars identify Berbers from North Africa as the main group to introduce Islam into **Borno**, around the 11th century. Others disagree, saying it did not come through Borno, but arrived via Mali to **Kano**, west of Borno. The introduction of Islam brought new sociopolitical systems and literacy in Arabic. For example, Islam restricted **slavery** to the enslavement of only non-Muslims living outside Muslim rule and offered spiritual reward for manumission. For several centuries, Islam remained the religion of the **Hausa** elite in **northern Nigeria**. In the early 19th century, a **Fulani jihad** led by **Usman dan Fodio** spread Islamic reform to the general populous.

At present, Muslims make up roughly 50 percent of the population in Nigeria and live primarily in northern and southwestern Nigeria. Muslims in Nigeria adhere as strictly as possible to the principles of the **Koran** and Five Pillars of Islam, including going on *hajj* (**pilgrimage**) to Mecca and fasting during **Ramadan**. The majority of followers adhere to the Sunni branch of Islam. But many Nigerians are also members of an Islamic *tariqah* (brotherhood or order), such as **Ahmadiyya**, **Tijaniyya**, or **Qadiriyya**. Young Nigerians learn Arabic and the values and principles of Islam in **Koranic schools**. Muslims in Nigeria are united in their reverence for the **sultan of Sokoto**, who acts as the spiritual head of all Muslims in Nigeria.

For the most part, **Christians** and Muslims coexist peacefully. This is not to say that religion and politics are separated in Nigeria. For example, in 1924 the Islamic Society of Nigeria was created in **Lagos** to serve as a nonpartisan voice for Muslims. Outbursts of protest and violence between the two groups are based more on scarce resources and poor governance in the country than on religion. The primary catalysts for clashes, particularly in the 1980s in cities such as **Kaduna**, were the implementation of **Shari'a** (Islamic law) and the installment of Muslim leaders. Shari'a had been in use, in full or part, well before the 19th century. In recent years, northern states have reinserted aspects of it into their legal systems, which frightens the Christian **population**. In addition, having a Muslim as head of state (achieved through a **coup d'état** or **election**) raises concerns for Christians about Nigeria becoming an Islamic theocracy. For example, in 1986 **General Ibrahim Babangida** brought Nigeria into the Organization of the Islamic Conference without consulting the public. Muslim individuals and organizations, including the **Jam'iyyar Mutanen Arewa, Islamic Movement of Nigeria, Jama'atu Nasril**

**Islam**, and **Izala**, thus far have focused more on protecting and preserving Islamic culture than on making Nigeria a Muslim state. In the 1980s, however, the South expressed concern over the plans of an alleged **Kaduna Mafia** of elite Muslims in the North to control Nigeria. *See also* PURDAH.

**ISLAMIC MOVEMENT OF NIGERIA.** An organization based in **Zaria**, with its headquarters at the Fudiyyah Islamic Center since 2002. It was founded and led by **Sheikh Ibrahim al-Zakzaky**. The Islamic Movement of Nigeria is also referred to as the Nigerian Muslim Brothers. Inspired by Iran's Shi'a groups during the 1970s, this movement is often referred to in the Nigerian media as "Shi'ites." Members of the movement, however, identify themselves as Sunni. A main goal of the movement is to enlighten Muslims about their individual and communal duties. The movement owns and operates several hundred schools, known as Fudiyyah Schools, throughout **northern Nigeria**. It also owns *Al Mizan*, a widely distributed **Hausa-language newspaper**. The Islamic Movement of Nigeria has expanded its activities into the field of **health**, putting together a medical team for its community. The organization boasts over a million members. Activities of the organization include mass demonstrations about national issues that concern Muslims, workshops, and intense study sessions. *See also* ISLAM.

**ITA, EYO (1902–1972).** Born in **Calabar**, Ita studied at the **Hope Waddell Training Institute** and Columbia University, starting in 1931, where he studied **education** and **religion**. He taught at the Baptist Academy in **Lagos**. In 1933, he returned to Nigeria and joined the **Nigerian Youth Movement**. Ita published several works that expressed his views on the **independence** struggle and the role of youth in the West African People's Institute. He refused to allow an expatriate to work as his private secretary. He was an active member of the **National Council of Nigeria and the Cameroons** (NCNC) and served as its first vice president in 1948. He was a member of the **Eastern Nigeria House of Assembly** (1951) and minister of national resources for the Eastern Region. In 1953, after being ejected from the NCNC, he formed the **National Independence Party**. During the **civil war**, Ita sided with the secessionist **Republic of Biafra**. He died in 1972.

**ITSEKIRI.** An **ethnic group** that resides in the **Niger Delta.** Their neighbors include the **Urhobo** and the Ijo. The Itsekiri **language** is a dialect of the **Yoruba language** with a **Benin** influence. The Itsekiri organized themselves into a kingdom around the 15th century under a Benin prince who settled in **Warri** and married a **Yoruba woman.** In 1848, the king died and a power struggle erupted between two lineages. Prior to the 20th century, the Itsekiri were most identified with their economic activity of acting as middlemen between traders of the interior region and European traders on the coast. **Chief Nana Olomu**, for example, made his wealth through **trade.** *See also* MINORITY GROUPS.

**IWUANYANWU, CHIEF EMMANUEL CHUKWUEMEKA (1942– ).** Born in September 1942 in Atta, in **Imo State**, as a young man Iwuanyanwu studied at St. Patrick's School in **Port Harcourt** (1948–1954), New Bethel College in **Onitsha** (1955–1959), and University of Nigeria at **Nsukka** (1963–1971). As a civil engineer and industrialist, he worked for a number of private firms, such as Magil Industries and Benhol Farms. He was the chairman and founder of the Iwuanyanwu Foundation and a council member of the Nigerian Association of Chambers of Commerce, Industry, Mines, and Agriculture. In the political arena, he was a member of the Nigerian Youth Council. Iwuanyanwu ran unsuccessfully to be a presidential candidate of the **National Republican Convention** in 1993 and the **All People's Party** in 1999. Frustrated with the All People's Party, he decided to join the **People's Democratic Party.** He has received more than 40 honorary chieftaincy titles. He was also a member of the Order of the Niger (1981) and Knight of the Order of St. Christopher. Iwuanyanwu has received several honorary doctoral degrees, from Shaw University (1989), University of Jos (1989), and University of Calabar (1990). He has published several works that highlight his interest in **industrialization** and development in Nigeria.

**IZALA.** Since the late 1970s, this Muslim northern organization has been a vocal opponent to the established **Qadiriyya** and **Tijaniyya** *tariqahs* (brotherhood or order). Izala is the simplified, popular name for Jama'at Izalatil Bid'a wa Iqatamus Sunnah (Movement against Negative Innovations), which formed in 1978 from the **Jama'atu**

Nasril Islam cultural organization. The Izala is an **Islamic** revivalist movement and proponent of **Shari'a** (Islamic law). Members of the Izala refused to pray in the presence of other orders and accused them of being unbelievers. The organization was led by Mallam Ismai'la Idris, who was inspired by **Sheikh Abubakar Gumi**. The Izala, along with the **Maitatsine** movement, was linked to a number of violent clashes in the 1980s. In more recent years, the Izala has transformed itself into a respected voice for Islamic reform.

## – J –

**JAJA OF OPOBO, KING (?–1891).** King Jaja was a freed slave who ruled near **Bonny** and acquired his wealth and power through **trade**. He was head of the Anna Pepple trading house and had a monopoly trade, working as a middleman in the **oil palm** trade. In 1868, his trading post was attacked by a rival trading house. Instead of fighting, Jaja relocated his trading house to Opobo. This new location cut Bonny off from oil palm being produced and traded in the interior. In 1884, Jaja signed a treaty with the British placing his territory under British protection (with freedom of trade omitted). Jaja was suspicious of the word "protectorate," but he was assured that it did not mean loss of sovereignty. In the meantime, the British declared his territory part of the **Oil Rivers Protectorate**. Jaja signed a treaty with the British ensuring free trade; however, he did not honor it. He was a staunch opponent of free trade and refused to allow the **Royal Niger Company** to squeeze him out. The British became frustrated with him. Both sides engaged in acts of sabotage. In 1887, Jaja was invited onboard a British ship by **Henry Hamilton Johnston**, who threatened him and the security of his empire. Jaja was deported and sent to the West Indies (he was allowed to return in 1891, but died en route). King Jaja of Opobo is one of the best examples of resistance in the **Niger Delta** during the 19th century, matching violence and might with violence and might.

**JAKANDE, ALHAJI LATEEF KAYODE (1929– ).** Born in July 1929 in **Lagos**, Jakande studied at Lagos Public School (1937–1939), Banham Memorial Methodist School in **Port Harcourt**

(1939–1943), **King's College** in Lagos (1944), and Ilesha Grammar School (1949–1950). Before becoming involved in national politics full time, Jakande worked as a journalist and editor for several **newspapers** during the 1960s, including the *Daily Service* and *Nigerian Tribune*. He was an honorary lecturer at the Nigerian Institute of Journalism from 1985 to 1990. He was also the founder and president of the Nigerian Guild of Editors. Jakande was a member of the **Action Group**, which included serving as its publicity secretary and general secretary in Lagos. He was a deputy chairman of the **Federal Executive Council** and federal commissioner of finance in the 1970s. He was also a member of the **United Party of Nigeria** and the **All People's Party**. He was governor of Lagos in 1979 and won a second term in 1984. From 1993 to 1995, he was the minister of public works and housing as well as chairman of the finance and economic committee. He received an honorary doctorate from Lagos State University (1994) and the Best Reporter of the Year from the *Sunday Times* (1977). He received the honorary titles of *baba adinni* from the Muslim communities of Ekpe and **Badagry**.

**JAMA'ATU NASRIL ISLAM.** An organization created in 1962 by Muslim leaders in **northern Nigeria**. Its name means "Group for the Victory of Islam." From 1962 to 1970, **Sheikh Abubakar Gumi** was the organization's leader. **Sultan Ibrahim Dasuki** was a prominent member. The purpose of the organization was to promote **Islam** and unify Muslims. However, the assassination of **Sir Alhaji Ahmadu Bello**, the *sardauna* of **Sokoto**, in 1966 put a strain on inter-Muslim relations. After some time, Gumi criticized the organization for lack of commitment to strict Islamic principles and encouraged his students to form the **Izala**. The organization became more vocally opposed to the **Tijaniyya** and **Qadiriyya** *tariqahs* (brotherhood or order). Its activities included promoting Islamic **education** and the publication of *Haske*, a weekly **newspaper**. By the late 1970s, Jama'atu Nasril Islam had been eclipsed by the Izala. *See also* KORANIC SCHOOLS.

**JAM'IYYAR MUTANEN AREWA.** A cultural association based in **northern Nigeria**, comprising several groups that formed in the late 1940s. Its name means "Arewa People's Congress." **Alhaji Muhammed Aminu Kano, Sir Alhaji Ahmadu Bello**, Yahaya Gusau, and **Sir Alhaji Abubakar Tafawa Balewa** were active members of the organization. Many of its members came from the Kaduna College Old Boys' Association, established in **Kaduna** in 1939. **Russell Aliyu Barau Dikko** assisted in the formation of Jam'iyyar Mutanen Arewa in **Zaria** between 1948 and 1949. It was created in conjunction with the Kaduna-based Mutanen Arewa, a Yau organization, meaning "People of the North Today." It transformed into the **Northern People's Congress** in 1951. Dikko was head of the organization until it became a **political party**. Some scholars see this organization as the beginning of the **Kaduna Mafia**. Jam'iyyar Mutanen Arewa, like other organizations of its kind, was banned in 1966.

*JANGALI.* Prior to the colonial period, **Fulani** pastoralists paid a cattle tax, which was called *jangali* in **northern Nigeria**. It was tribute paid to local rulers as a "payment to pasture" and was often accompanied with gifts of livestock. When this **taxation**, even during the life of the **Sokoto Caliphate**, became burdensome, the Fulani would relocate. *Jangali* was typically collected during the rainy season, from July to October. Colonial officials adopted and modified this system through the Nigeria Land Revenue Ordinance of 1904 and Native Revenue Proclamation of 1906. The *jangali* was collected by a British-appointed Fulani leader in a district as part of the **indirect rule** system. The tax was per cattle, requiring the district officer and the Fulani representative to physically go and count them. The Fulani paid a flat rate per cattle until 1916, when goats and sheep were included in the *jangali* tax.

**JEGEDE, OMODELE (1945– ).** Born in April 1945 in Ikere-Ekiti, Jegede is one of Nigeria's most prominent artists. He signs his work dele jegede. He studied at Yaba College of Technology (previously **Yaba Higher College**) in **Lagos** and **Ahmadu Bello University** in **Zaria**. He received his bachelor of arts degree in 1973. In the United States, he earned his master's and doctoral degrees from Indiana University in 1981 and 1983, respectively. In the early 1970s, he drew cartoons for a variety of **newspapers** and worked as the graphic arts officer for the North Eastern State Ministry of Education. From 1974 to 1977, he was the art editor for the *Daily Times* newspaper. Jegede also taught part time at Yaba College of Technology from 1977 to 1979 and 1984 to 1986. At Indiana University, he taught in the African Studies Department from 1980 to 1982. At the University of Lagos, he was a research fellow in the Centre for Cultural Studies from 1977 to 1986. Jegede's artwork (paintings, political cartoons, and drawings) has been displayed numerous times in Nigeria and elsewhere. He has been commissioned to do several prominent projects, including the alumni crest of the University of Lagos, the logo for the Nigerian Institute for Advanced Legal Studies, and the emblem of the Nigeria Deposit Insurance Corporation. His work has appeared in the National Gallery of Modern Art in Lagos and on the cover of a memoir, *A Mouth Sweeter Than Salt* (2005). He is also the author of several academic works on African **art**.

**JEHOVAH'S WITNESSES.** A **Christian**-based **religious** movement that was started in the 19th century by Charles Taze Russell in the United States. Jehovah's Witnesses are known for doing door-to-door proselytizing. They believe that Jesus Christ was destined to rule God's kingdom, which only individuals who have worked hard and have been baptized may inhabit. The religion first arrived in Nigeria in 1928. There are an estimated 6.5 million active "witnesses" throughout the world. In 2002, Nigeria has claimed the largest **population** of Jehovah's Witnesses in Africa.

**JEMIBEWON, MAJOR GENERAL DAVID MEDAIYESE (1940– ).** Born in July 1940 in Iyah-Gbedde, in **Kogi State**, as a young man Jemibewon studied at the Church Missionary Society Primary School in Burutu (1949), Community Primary School in Iyah-Gbedde (1954–1954), Offia Grammar School (1955–1959), and the School of Radiography in **Lagos** (1960). After expressing an interest in joining the **army**, Jemibewon attended numerous military schools and training colleges in Nigeria and elsewhere. He also attended **Ahmadu Bello University** (1978–1980), University of Lagos (1983–1985), and Nigerian Law School (1985–1986). During the **civil war**, he fought for the federal military government as a company commander and commanding officer. He was the military governor of **Western State** (1971–1972) and military governor of **Oyo State** (1976–1978). He retired from the **armed forces** in 1983. For the next four years, Jemibewon studied law at the University of Lagos. In 1998, he supported **General Olusegun Obasanjo** as a presidential candidate in the 1999 **elections**, which earned him the appointment of minister of police affairs. He received the honorary titles *jagunmolu* (**chief**) of **Ibadan** and *majeobaje* (chief) of Idanre as well as Officer of the Order of the Federal Republic (1981).

**JIGAWA STATE.** One of Nigeria's current 36 states, Jigawa State is located in **northern Nigeria**, sharing a border with **Niger**. It was created in 1991 out of **Kano State**. The **Hausa** and **Fulani ethnic groups** dominate the state. **Islam** is the major **religion**. Jigawa is one of 12 northern states that incorporated aspects of **Shari'a**. The capital is Dutsi. Spanning the northeastern corner of Jigawa and extending into the neighboring states of **Yobe** and **Bauchi** are the Hade Jia Nguru Wetlands. Farmers in the state grow **groundnuts** and **cassava**; herders tend to their cattle. Economic activity in Jigawa State relies heavily on **water** and surrounding fertile land. *See also* STATE CREATION.

**JIHAD.** An Arabic word literally meaning "striving in the path of God." This aspect of **Islamic** doctrine is open to interpretation, which has led to some confusion over its meaning. It can mean the struggle within a person against sinful thoughts or an exceptional act by someone for the improvement and religious strengthening of a Muslim community. The most notable expression of jihad takes the form of a holy war, which is considered an exceptional act. Several jihads have occurred in Nigeria, with the most notable leading to the establishment of the **Sokoto Caliphate** in 1804 by **Usman dan Fodio**, a **Fulani**. Among the different applications of jihad, war has figured most prominently, giving the term a negative connotation.

**JOHNSON, SAMUEL (1846–1901).** Born in 1846 in Sierra Leone, Johnson moved with his parents to **Lagos** in 1857. He spent much of his life in **Ibadan**, becoming an Anglican priest and working as a **Christian** missionary. Although born in Sierra Leone, he claimed descent from a **chief** of the **Oyo Empire**. Johnson received his education from the Church Missionary Society's Training Institute in **Abeokuta** in 1865. A year later, he became a deacon. In the 1870s, Johnson assisted in negotiating peace between the warring **Yoruba** groups and became a catechist. In 1888, he became an ordained priest. He is best known in Nigerian studies as the author of *History* *of the Yorubas*, which he completed in 1897. Johnson died in 1901, and 20 years later his brother cleaned up the manuscript and published it. Johnson's work is one of the first African-authored books to document an African **ethnic group**'s cultural practices, **oral traditions**, and history.

**JOHNSTON, SIR HENRY HAMILTON (1858–1927).** Born in England, Johnston was a British explorer and colonial administrator. In October 1886, the British government made him vice-consul of the **Cameroons** and the **Niger Delta**. A year later, he became acting consul and was responsible for the banishment of **King Jaja of Opobo**. Johnston left Nigeria in 1888 to pursue other British expansionary efforts elsewhere in Africa. He coauthored *The History of a Slave* (1889), which discussed in detail the use of non-Muslim **slaves** in the **Hausa cotton** garment industry in **Kano**.

**JOINT ACTION COMMITTEE (JAC).** A committee created in September 1963 during a meeting of the **United Labour Congress**. The focus of the committee was to agitate for a wage increase for Nigerian workers. Its activities prompted the government's formation of the **Morgan Commission**, which examined the wage structure and working conditions.

**JOINT ADMISSIONS AND MATRICULATION BOARD (JAMB).** Nigeria's official examination board for male and female students planning to apply to Nigeria's public universities after completing their secondary school **education**. It was created in 1978 to facilitate the recruitment of Nigerians from all over the country and reduce competition for students between universities. Today, the board has a negative reputation for designing weak exams that demand little academic rigor and for tolerating cheating among exam takers.

**JONATHAN, GOODLUCK (1957– ).** Born in November 1957 in Otuekeke, in **Bayelsa State**, Jonathan is of the **Ijaw ethnic group** in the **Niger Delta**. He completed his primary and secondary school **education** in Bayelsa State at **Christian** schools. He received his doctorate in zoology from the University of Port Harcourt in 1995 and taught at the Rivers State College of Education (1983–1993). He worked for the **Oil Mineral Producing Areas Development Commission** (1993–1998). Jonathan was deputy governor (1993–2005) and governor of Bayelsa (2005–2007). He is a member of the **People's Democratic Party**. Since April 2007, Jonathan has been Nigeria's vice president. He was invited to take this prominent position in an effort to resolve the **Niger Delta Conflict**, but the job has not been easy for him. He has been attacked by rebel forces in the Niger Delta twice, once just days before the election. In May 2007, rebels attacked and destroyed his home while he was away.

**JOS**. The capital of **Plateau State**. It is named for its location on the northern edge of the Jos Plateau. It has a sizable number of **Charismatic Christians**. It is also the location of Nigeria's major deposits of **tin** and tin mining activities. The current **population** of Jos is approximately 820,000.

**JOSE, ALHAJI ISMAIL BABATUNDE (1925– ).** A Muslim, Jose was born in December 1925 in **Lagos**. As a young man, he studied at the Lagos Government School, Yaba Methodist School, and Saviour's High School in Lagos. He worked in several different positions for several various Nigerian **newspapers** between the 1940s and 1970s. He was the editor (1957–1962) and managing director (1962–1976) of the *Daily Times*. He served as a member of the Board of Governors for the Nigerian Broadcasting Corporation from 1965 to 1966. In 1976, he resigned from the *Daily Times* in protest against the federal military government's desire to restrict freedom of the press. He also served as chairman for several private companies, such as the Naira Properties, and government organizations, such as the National Drought Relief Fund Committee (1973–1976). Jose was a member of the Constituent Assembly (1977–1978) and chairman of the Nigerian Television Authority (1977–1980). He was president of the **Ahmadiyya** Movement in Islam (also known as the 'Anwar-Ul-Islam) from 1960 to 1973. During the 1980s, he worked almost exclusively in the private business sector. He later wrote about his life in *Walking a Tight Rope* (1987). He received the honorary chieftaincy titles *bameso* of Lagos (1973), *bobatolu* of Ikare, and *seriki musulumi* of Ikare (1974), as well as an honorary doctorate from the University of Benin. In 1973, he received the Pope Pius Medal for promoting religious tolerance in Nigeria.

**JUDICIAL SERVICE COMMISSION.** A commission created in 1966 by the federal military government to facilitate the appointment of judges to the **courts**. Starting in 1979, recommendations for judges made by the commission required approval from the Senate. Since 1999, the Judicial Service Commission has been charged with advising the **National Judicial Council** on nominating qualified members to Nigeria's court system on a national and state level. The Judicial Service Commission includes chief judges as well as legal and non-legal practitioners appointed by the attorney general. It can also discipline members of the federal courts. *See also* LEGAL SYSTEM.

**JUJU MUSIC.** It is generally agreed that this unique **musical** style was developed in southwestern Nigeria by **Yoruba** musicians. It incorporates new instruments into a traditional style and has a strong presence of traditional praise music. It started as the rural adaptation of **Highlife music** in the 1940s and spread to urban audiences. After **World War II**, electric instruments were added to the collection of banjos, tambourines, and gourds covered with beads. In the cities, Juju bands play at elite parties, lower-class bars, weddings, and funerals. Popular Juju music performers were Tunde Nightingale in the early 1940s and I. K. Dairo in the 1950s. The latter incorporated an accordion (as opposed to a guitar) in his music. Other famous musicians of this style are Ebenezer Obey, Segun Adewale, and **Sunny Ade**.

**JUKUN.** A **minority group** that lives in northeastern Nigeria in **Taraba State**. **Oral tradition** says they came from Yemil, east of Mecca in Saudi Arabia, led by Agugu, who traveled across the Sudan. According to **Hausa** tradition, the progenitor of the Jukun people was Kororofa. This version explains why the Jukun kingdom's capital is named Kororofa. Their military prowess has been recorded in 14th-century texts. At its height in the 18th century, the Jukun Kingdom extended from Cross River to **Bornu** and included the towns of **Zaria** and **Kano**. The **Fulani jihad** of 1804 that established the **Sokoto Caliphate** destroyed the city of Kororofa. In 2001, the **Tiv** and the Jukun clashed over land rights in Taraba State. The Jukun identify themselves as the original inhabitants and the Tiv as settlers; however, the Tiv disagree, arguing that they lack equal rights and political representation.

## – K –

**KADUNA.** The capital of **Kaduna State**, with a **population** of approximately 1.5 million, making it the fourth largest city in Nigeria. Historically, Kaduna was one of the **Hausa Kingdoms** that existed sometime between the 10th and 18th centuries. The British designated Kaduna as the administrative center of the **Protectorate of Northern Nigeria** in 1900. It also served as the seat of government for the **Northern Region**. In the late 1950s, it was the home base for the **Northern People's Congress**. It became home to Nigeria's Defence Academy in the 1960s. In 1980, Kaduna became the site of one of Nigeria's four **petroleum** refineries. It was constructed to refine heavy crude oil and expected to even out the distribution of petroleum products throughout the country. Kaduna has significant **Christian** and Muslim populations. There is a sizable number of **Charismatic Christian** churches. In the past 20 years, this city has been the site of faith-based conflict. In 2001 and 2002, violent clashes between Christians and Muslims erupted over the implementation of a modified version of **Shari'a**. The traditional chief, Alhaji Ahmadu Yakubu, and the chairman of the local government, Frank Bala, were arrested for inciting the riot. The violence left 10 people dead and hundreds wounded. Kaduna is also home to Kaduna Polytechnic.

**KADUNA MAFIA.** Some scholars have traced this group's origins to colonial times, but most assign it to the late 1970s and 1980s. The Kaduna Mafia is allegedly a group of powerful, elite Muslims based in **Kaduna** who wield a great deal of political power. The term may have been coined by Mvendaga Jibo, a journalist for the *New Nigerian* **newspaper**. The exact members of this mafia are unknown, and the extent to which they operated as a mafia is unclear. The ambiguity of the term suggests that it came from an anti-Northern perspective. Those who speak of a Kaduna Mafia are liable to have overstated the influence northern elites had in national politics. Members may have included **Major General Shehu Musa Yar'Adua** and others who supported the **Social Democratic Party** in the failed **election of 12 June 1993**. The Kaduna Mafia has also been accused of controlling the Bank of the North, the New Nigerian Development Corporation, and the *New Nigerian* **newspaper**.

**KADUNA STATE.** In the **Hausa language**, *kaduna* means crocodiles, referring to those living in the Kaduna River. Kaduna was one of the seven original **Hausa Kingdoms** established between the 10th and 18th centuries. It was created in 1976 out of **North-Central State** and in 1991 was separated from **Katsina State**. Kaduna is located in **northern Nigeria**. It is one of a dozen states in Nigeria to incorporate **Shari'a** in the past 10 years. Half the **population**, however, is **Christian**. The ethnic composition of Kaduna State is relatively heterogeneous, including Kamuku, Gwari, Kadara, Hausa, and Kurama peoples. It is one of Nigeria's current 36 states. The capital is the city of **Kaduna**. Economic activities in the state include the growing of **cotton**, rice, and chili peppers. Kaduna State is known for its "southern Kaduna ginger." It is the center of an alleged **Kaduna Mafia**, which controlled national politics through coercion and manipulation during the late 1970s. It was also the location of the **Kafanchan riots** in the late 1980s. *See also* STATE CREATION.

**KAFANCHAN RIOTS.** A series of clashes in March 1987 between **Christians** and Muslims at the Kafanchan College of Education in **Kaduna State**. The riots started with a dispute between the Fellowship of Christian Students and Muslims Students Society over the college's hosting of the Christian religious meeting Mission '87, which was organized by the Christian organization. A banner describing the campus as a "Jesus Campus" was prominently displayed until the Muslim organization complained and the college removed it. A second issue arose over the speeches given at Mission '87. Comments about the **Koran** and the Prophet Muhammad inflamed the Muslim students. Violence ensued, paralyzing the state for a week. When the violence died down, 12 people were dead and several churches and mosques had been damaged. The Kafanchan incident was the first in a chain of clashes between the two religious groups in cities such as **Kano** and **Zaria** that occurred in the late 1980s. *See also* RELIGION.

**KAMERUN NATIONAL CONGRESS (KNC).** A **political party** that emerged in the early 1950s and was led by Emmanuel Endeley in southern **Cameroon**. It was formed through the merger of the Cameroons National Federation and the Kamerun United National Congress in 1953. The convergence resulted in the expulsion of N. N. Mbile, who went on to form the Kamerun People's Party. The Kamerun National Congress initially campaigned for the separation of the northern and southern Cameroons (connected to present-day Cameroon) from Nigeria. In the 1954 federal **elections**, the seats allocated to the southern Cameroon were all occupied by the Kamerun National Congress. In 1961, the party assisted in the transfer of southern Cameroon to Cameroon. Northern Cameroon, however, remained part of Nigeria.

**KAMPALA PEACE TALKS.** A series of peace talks held from 23 May to 31 May 1968. They were convened by Milton Obote of Uganda to broker peace during Nigeria's **civil war**. Both sides of the war—the federal military government and the **Republic of Biafra**—sent delegates to the peace talks. Obote encouraged both sides to consider a cease-fire and reconciliation. The talks were tainted and largely unsuccessful. Johnson Banjo, a federal government delegate, was kidnapped and killed by unknown persons during the talks. Both sides left the meeting displeased, and the war continued for another two years. *See also* AFRICAN UNION.

**KANEM–BORNU EMPIRE.** An empire located northeast of Lake Chad that lasted from the 11th to the 19th centuries. Kanem was the kingdom of the **Kanuri** people, who speak Kanembu. The Kanuri people were led by Saef Ben Dhu Yasan, the founder of the **Sefawa Dynasty**, who established the empire. This empire started as the Kanem Kingdom until it collapsed in the 14th century. A combination of environmental deterioration and dynastic disputes exposed Kanem to outside attacks. The kingdom was invaded and occupied by the nomadic **Bulala** people in 1389. The Kanem Kingdom became a Muslim kingdom between the 11th and 13th centuries. Its primary exports were **slaves** and ivory. Kanem reached the pinnacle of its territory and power in the 13th century, under the leadership of *Mai* (**king**) **Dunama Dibbalemi**. In 1389, Kanem's leaders fled to Bornu, which had been a tribute-paying town, and founded the Kanem-Bornu Empire. Bornu became a major center of trade and scholarship in **northern Nigeria**. Kanem-Bornu's power came from its involvement in the **trans-Saharan trade** and an army of horsemen. **Idris ben Ali Aloma** ruled in the 14th century. Between the 15th and 18th centuries, the Kanem-Bornu Empire covered present-day **Borno** and **Yobe States**.

The **Fulani jihad** that established the **Sokoto Caliphate** in the early 19th century destabilized Kanem-Bornu, providing an opportunity for **Umar ibn Muhammed al-Amin al-Kanemi** to eject the Sefawa Dynasty in 1861 and start his own dynasty, based in Kukawa. Kanem-Bornu fiercely defended its autonomy and did not collapse during Fulani expansion. However, British colonialism posed a serious threat. In the mid-1800s, **Hugh Clapperton** arrived with a trading party, met al-Amin al-Kanemi, and received permission to establish a British consulate in Kukawa. At the Berlin Conference (1884–1885), **Great Britain** laid claim to the region through negotiation with other European powers. In 1893, the empire was attacked and occupied by a Sudanese conqueror. Rivalry for territory between the British and French further weakened Kanem-Bornu. Through complex bargaining, the British installed Abubakar Garbai on the throne and established a British garrison. The British also moved the capital of the empire to Yerwa (present-day **Maiduguri**). *See also* IBRAHIM BEN AHMED; AL-KANEMI, MUHAMMED AL-AMIN.

**AL-KANEMI, MUHAMMED AL-AMIN (?–1837).** The son of Sheikh Ninga, al-Kanemi was a scholar, warrior, and religious leader. Through a series of political maneuverings, al-Kanemi positioned himself as one of the most powerful figures in the **Kanem-Bornu Empire**. Al-Kanemi assisted in protecting the Kanem-Bornu Empire from a **Fulani jihad** in the 19th century. The jihadists reached Bornu around 1808. Al-Kanemi successfully drove out the jihad flag bearer, Ibrahim Zaki, sending him back to Katagum. In preparation for his battle with the jihadists, al-Kanemi spent days praying. He also made a special charm out of verses from the **Koran** written on a small calabash. According to **oral tradition**, when the two sides met at Birni Gazargamu, al-Kanemi threw the charm to the ground, shattering it, which caused the Fulani to flee. In 1814, al-Kanemi established his own dynasty, based at Kukawa, and took the title *shehu* (**king**). *See also* BUKAR D'GIJIAMA; DUNAMA IBN AHMAD LEFIAMI.

**AL-KANEMI, UMAR IBN MUHAMMAD AL-AMIN (?–1881).** The "son of Muhammad al-Amin al-Kanemi." He became the *shehu* (**king**), of the **Kanem-Bornu Empire** after his father died in 1837. Al-Kanemi is most remembered for overthrowing the **Sefawa Dy-**

nasty in 1846, which had ruled Kanem-Bornu from the 11th to the 19th centuries. Aside from unseating the Sefawa Dynasty, al-Kanemi appears to have been a largely ineffective ruler. He supported the Bukhari revolt against the **Sokoto Caliphate** to protect his own empire. In 1853, his advisors staged a **coup d'état** and put his brother, Adburrahman, on the throne. Al-Kanemi, however, returned to power and negotiated peace with the caliph of Sokoto in 1880.

**KANO.** The capital of **Kano State** and Nigeria's second largest city, located in **northern Nigeria**. It was one of the seven original **Hausa Kingdoms** from roughly the 10th to the 18th centuries. Hausa is the dominant **language**. By the 15th century, Kano had earned a reputation as an intellectual and politically influential Islamic city. During the **trans-Saharan trade**, Kano was an important stop. In the 17th century, Kano engaged in warfare with the neighboring Hausa Kingdoms of **Katsina** and **Kebbi**. It was taken over through a **Fulani jihad** in the early 19th century and brought into the newly established **Sokoto Caliphate** by Dan Zabuwa, a flag bearer of the jihad, in 1807. Dan Zabuwa made himself the **emir**. Kano was one of the most populous and economically active cities in the **caliphate**. Much of what scholars know about Kano before the 20th century comes from the *Kano Chronicle.*

During the 19th century, Kano was a center for large-scale **trade** and farming. The workers and supervisors on plantations in Kano were **slaves**, who also staffed the emirate's military and government. **Abdullahi Maje Karofi** was a notable emir in the 19th century. In 1893, Kano's citizens endured a civil war over an emir's successor, which continued to simmer until 1903 during the reign of Emir Aliyu. In 1903 the British conquered Kano and incorporated it into the **Protectorate of Northern Nigeria**. Notable emirs of the 20th century include Muhammadu Abbas, **Alhaji Abdullahi Bayero**, and **Alhaji Ado Bayero**. Kano was described by Europeans as the "London of the Soudan" because of its economic, political, and intellectual importance in West Africa. Kano's **population** today is approximately 3.5 million. It is home to a sizable number of **Charismatic Christians**. It was the site of the **Kano Riots** (1953) and the **Maitatsine Riots** (1980).

**KANO, ALHAJI MUHAMMED AMINU (1920–1983).** Born in August 1920 in **Kano**, Kano was a **Fulani** Muslim. As a young man, he completed his preliminary studies in **Zaria** and **Bauchi**. He received his teaching certificate and an advanced degree in **education** from the University of London (1947). **Kano** dedicated his political career to improving the lives of northerners, particularly the *talakawa* (commoners). He criticized the colonial **Native Authority** system. His political career started in the 1930s with his cofounding of the **Bauchi General Improvement Union** in 1943. He worked closely with **Sa'adu Zungur** and **Sir Alhaji Abubakar Tafawa Balewa**. From 1948 to 1953, Kano was a member of the Northern Teacher's Association. While working at a teaching center in **Sokoto**, he became involved with the **Jami'yyar Mutanen Arewa**, a cultural association. That organization became the **Northern People's Congress** (NPC). In 1950, Kano formed the **Northern Elements Progressive Union** (NEPU) and served as its leader from 1950 to 1966. He was a member of the House of Representatives from 1959 to 1966. Between 1959 and 1964 he was the deputy government chief whip. When the NEPU and **National Council of Nigeria and the Cameroons** (NCNC) formed a coalition in 1954, Kano became vice president of the NCNC. He was the minister of health from 1967 to 1974 and a member of the Constituent Assembly between 1977 and 1978. He formed the **People's Redemption Party** in 1978 and was its presidential candidate. Kano died in April 1983. The international airport in Kano is named after him.

**KANO CHRONICLE.** A valuable document for historians because it provides the most detailed information available on early **Hausa** society, with an emphasis on **Kano**. It is an annotated list of **kings** written in classical Arabic script. British colonial officials in the early 20th century circulated several copies to gain an understanding of Hausa politics and history dating back to the 14th century. The *Kano Chronicle* was also of particular interest to colonial administrators because it explains in great detail the **Islamic** system of governance. For all of the information it does provide, however, important details of its publication date, authorship, and purpose are unclear. Some scholars have dated its first appearance to the 17th century, while others move the date to the late 19th century. Comparing it to other sources, such as those by African and Arab travelers, scholars have confirmed its accuracy and authenticity. The *Kano Chronicle* records the activities of Muslims and non-Muslims alike. It was translated from the **Hausa language** into English by **Sir Herbert Richard Palmer**, a British official in the early 1900s.

**KANO MARKET LITERATURE.** A body of popular fiction written in the **Hausa language** and sold in the northern cities of **Kano**, **Zaria**, **Kaduna**, **Katsina**, and **Sokoto**. These novels are a common sight in market areas. This genre is similar to the **Onitsha Market Literature** that became so popular in southeastern Nigeria from the 1940s to the 1960s. In the Hausa language, this genre is called Littattafan Soyayya ("Books of Love") because these stories address love and romance, flirting with the conservative Muslim culture of **Hausa** society. Common topics are **polygamy**, *purdah* (**women** living in seclusion), and female **education**. Although these works appear light and sensational, they are commenting on Hausa gender relations and social change. It is no surprise that the most recognized authors of Kano Market Literature are female. Notable authors include **Bilkisu Ahmed Funtuwa** and **Balaraba Ramat Yakubu**. Conservative Hausa individuals see these novels as encouraging liberal behavior by young female Hausa readers. The authors, however, see their works as supporting Hausa ideals and morals. *See also* LITERATURE.

**KANO PEOPLE'S PARTY (KPP).** A **political party** that grew out of the **Northern People's Congress** in response to the removal of Alhaji Sir Muhammadu Sanusi, the **emir** of **Kano** in 1963. The party's primary focus was on the 1964 **elections** in the Kano State. It was a pro-**Tijaniyya** *tariqah* (brotherhood or order) organization. The KPP, along with many others, was banned in 1966.

**KANO RIOTS.** In May 1953, a fierce debate ensued over the target year for **independence**. Two southern-based **political parties**, the **Action Group** and the **National Council of Nigeria and the Cameroons**, campaigned in the House of Representatives for independence in 1956, but their northern counterparts did not agree. Delegates from the two southern parties, including **Chief Samuel Akintola**, toured **northern Nigeria** campaigning for 1956 as the best option. Northerners resented their visit, and a four-day riot ensued in the **sabon gari** of **Kano**. By its conclusion, 36 people (21 southerners and 15 northerners) had died and 277 were injured. At the end of

the month, another **constitutional conference** in London convened
to address the **Self-Government Motion Crisis**.

**KANO STATE.** One of Nigeria's current 36 states, created in 1967,
but reduced in size in 1991 with the formation of **Jigawa State**. Its
northern border is shared with **Niger**. It is one of the 12 northern
states that introduced aspects of **Shari'a** into their criminal codes.
Enforcing moral order in Kano, the *hisbah* are in full operation and
receive state government support. The capital is the city of **Kano**.
Kano has been well known for its large-scale **groundnut** cultivation,
but in recent years it has diversified to include the growing of millet.
Kano State is also a major cattle herding state. The dominant **religion**
is **Islam** and the major **ethnic group** is the **Hausa**. Kano State has the
largest **population** of Nigeria's states, with more than nine million
people. *See also* STATE CREATION.

**KANURI.** One of Nigeria's many **ethnic groups**, the Kanuri live primarily in **northern Nigeria** in **Borno State** near Lake Chad. They
established one of Nigeria's largest empires, the **Kanem-Bornu
Empire**. Kanuri **oral tradition** identifies Saef Ben Dhu Yasan of
Yemen nobility as their ancestor and founder of the **Sefawa Dynasty**. The Kanuri are skilled in cattle rearing and **agricultural**
production. Political authority has been based on kingdoms and
local **chiefs**, assisted by a council of elders. Ruins from precolonial
Kanuri life have been identified by their unique red brick buildings dating to the 15th century, particularly at Birni N'gazargamu.
Several prominent Kanuri leaders, such as **Dunama Dibbalemi** and
**Idris ben Ali Aloma**, ruled Kanem-Bornu. The Kanuri have continued to shape Nigeria's history. For example, **Chief Ali Monguno**
and **Baba Gana Kingibe** were well-known political figures in the
1960s and 1970s.

**KATAGUM.** A town in **Bauchi State** nestled between the Katagum
and Hadeija Rivers. Prior to the 19th century, it was a farming region
inhabited by several different groups, including the Lerewa. It became part of the **Sokoto Caliphate** through the **Fulani jihad** in 1804
led by Ibrahim Zaki. By the early 20th century, Katagum's authority
had been consumed by the British colonial administration.

**KATSINA.** Located in **northern Nigeria**, Katsina was one of the **Hausa Kingdoms**, which existed from roughly the 10th to the 18th centuries. The end of the Songhay Empire's domination in the 16th century encouraged the resettlement of scholars to Katsina, which served as a bustling center for **trade** and Islamic **education**. In the 14th century, Ali Murabus constructed a wall around Katsina for protection. Between 1570 and 1650, Katsina and **Kano** engaged in warfare. In 1807, Katsina was conquered by a **Fulani jihadist**, Umaru Dallaji, and became part of the **Sokoto Caliphate**. Today, Katsina is the capital of **Katsina State**, which was created in 1987. It has a **population** of approximately 380,000. *See also* ISLAM.

**KATSINA, MAJOR GENERAL HASSAN USMAN (1933–1995).** Born in March 1933 in **Katsina**, he studied at Kankiya Elementary School, Katsina Middle School, and Kaduna College. For his tertiary education, Katsina attended the Institute of Administration and the Nigerian College of Arts, Sciences, and Technology in **Zaria**. In 1956, he joined the **army** and participated in training programs in **Ghana** and England. He was a member of a United Nations peacekeeping force in Central Africa in 1961. He served as governor of the **Northern Region** from January 1966 to January 1967 and then as chairman of the Interim Common Services Agency (1967–1968). During the **civil war**, he was the army chief of staff. Complimentary references to him, in addition to other northern soldiers, appeared in poetry published in **Hausa language newspapers** during the civil war. In 1971, he was promoted to major general. He retired from the **armed forces** in 1975. Katsina was a member of the **National Party of Nigeria**. He died in July 1995.

**KATSINA STATE.** In 1976, **North-Central State** was renamed Kaduna State. Katsina State was created from that state in 1987. It is one of Nigeria's current 36 states. It is located in **northern Nigeria** and shares its northern border with the **Niger**. Katsina State is one of the 12 northern states that have introduced **Shari'a** into their criminal law. The **population** of Katsina State is primarily **Hausa** and **Fulani**, who are Muslim. Economic activities in the state include herding cattle and cultivating grains, **cotton**, and **groundnuts**. The capital is the city of **Katsina**. Until he was elected president in 2007, the governor was **Alhaji Umar Musa Yar'Adua**. *See also* STATE CREATION.

**KEBBI.** A historic town in **northern Nigeria** that was one of the **Hausa Kingdoms** established between the 10th and 18th centuries. Its first *kanta* (ruler) was **Muhammadu**. In the 16th century, the capital of the Kebbi Kingdom was moved from Surame to Birnin Kebbi. Both cities were protected by fortified walls. This kingdom successfully resisted the **Fulani jihad** that established the **Sokoto Caliphate**. Kebbi could not resist foreign incursion from North Africa and broke into several small kingdoms. By the late 19th century, Kebbi was under British occupation. Today, Kebbi is known as Birnin-Kebbi and is the capital of **Kebbi State**. Its **population** is approximately 268,000.

**KEBBI STATE.** Kebbi started as one of the **Hausa Kingdoms** that were established sometime between the 10th and 18th centuries. Kebbi State was created in 1991 out of **Sokoto State**. It is located in **northern Nigeria** and shares its eastern boundary with **Niger** and **Benin**. The ethnic composition of Kebbi is predominantly **Fulani** and **Hausa**, with **Islam** as the dominant **religion**. It is one of Nigeria's current 36 states. It is also one of 12 northern states that incorporated **Shari'a** into their criminal codes. The capital is Birnin-Kebbi. Kebbi State is the home of the annual Argungu Fishing Festival. Economic activities include quarrying stone (granite and quartzite) and growing crops such as **cotton**, grains, and beans. In the *fadama* areas (lowland floodplains of rivers), farmers grow tomatoes, onions, peppers, and sweet potatoes during the dry season. *See also* STATE CREATION.

**KINGIBE, BABA GANA (1945– ).** Born in June 1945 in **Maiduguri, in Borno State**, Kingibe is of **Kanuri** descent. He earned advanced degrees from the University of Sussex (1968) and the British Broadcasting Corporation Television Training School in London. He taught political science at **Ahmadu Bello University** (1969–1970) and worked for the Northern Nigeria Broadcasting Corporation (1970–1972) before becoming involved in national politics. Kingibe worked as the external affairs officer for the Ministry of External Affairs in **Lagos** (1972–1975) and senior counselor for the Nigerian High Commission in London (1975–1976). He also served as the principal political secretary of the **Supreme Military Council** in Lagos and later for the executive office of the president (1976–1981). From 1981 to 1989, Kingibe was Nigeria's ambassador to Greece and Pakistan. He worked as the secretary of the Constituent Assembly in Abuja (1988–1989). In the failed **election of 12 June 1993**, Kingibe was **Chief M. K. O. Abiola**'s running mate. He was also chairman of the **Social Democratic Party** (1992–1993). Under **General Sani Abacha**, Kingibe served as minister of external affairs (1994–1996) and minister of internal affairs (1996–1998). In 1998, he was the minister of power and steel. In recent years, Kingibe has been Nigeria's ambassador to Sudan and head of the **African Union**'s special mission in Sudan (2002–2006). From 2007 to 2008, Kingibe served as secretary to the federal government.

**KINGS.** In the literature on the history of sociopolitical systems in Nigeria, the indigenous terms for a particular ruler are often translated into European languages as simply king or **chief**. Regrettably, the terms *chief* and *king* are often used interchangeably, ignoring scales of power and wealth. Many kings, especially before the colonial period, had a divine status and served not only as heads of state, but also as spiritual leaders. A king commonly ruled with the assistance and advice of a council. In the case of the **Yoruba**, the king's authority was often checked by a council of chiefs. It is no surprise, then, that many kings in a community's historical memory take on additional spiritual qualities. As the legend goes, **Sango**, the fourth *alaafin* (king) of the **Oyo Empire**, joined the pantheon of Yoruba gods after committing suicide. It should also be noted that the reshuffling of political systems by the colonial administration caused the definition of *alaafin* to change from "king" to "chief."

Throughout Nigeria's history, kings and kingdoms have expanded and collapsed. Kingdoms in Nigeria thrived by dominating **trade** and due to strategic geographic locations such as along a river or coastline. Archeological and historical evidence indicates that most societies in Nigeria were organized into kingdoms. These kingdoms are also referred to as states, and sometimes, chiefdoms. It is common to find the terms *kingdom* and *empire* used interchangeably because most operated as tribute-paying states. The presence of kings and kingdoms disappeared under colonial rule, and many of these kings were assassinated, sent into exile, or reassigned as merely localized leaders supervised by the colonial administration. **King Jaja** of Opobo, for example, was sent into exile by the British from 1887 until 1891. **Chief Nana Olomu**, an **Itsekiri** leader on the Benin River, was deported by the British to **Ghana** in the 1890s.

**KING'S COLLEGE.** Located on Lagos Island in the city of **Lagos**, King's College was founded in September 1909 to serve as a regional secondary school for boys. It was modeled after King's College of Our Lady of Eton. It prepared students for the matriculation exam at the University of London. It has been the alma mater of **Nnamdi Azikiwe**, **Alex I. Ekwueme**, and **John Wash Pam**, among others. Chief Hezekiah Oladipo Davies, **Sir Samuel Layinka Manuwa**, and **Raymond Amanze Njoku** also attended King's College. It attracts students from several different Anglophone West African countries as well as Nigeria. When the college opened it had 10 male students, one of whom was J. C. Vaughan. Its faculty consisted of three European and two African professors. By 1914, its student **population** had increased to 67. Several of its graduates went on to establish the **Lagos Youth Movement** in 1934. King's College is still in operation today. It has been divided between two campuses in Lagos to accommodate the number of students as well as an expanding number of computer and science labs.

**KINGSLEY, MARY H. (1862–1900).** Born in England, well-known writer, explorer, **Christian** missionary, and activist Kingsley started traveling to Africa in 1893. She participated in explorations on the **Niger River** and visited the major trading posts. She cut her tour short because she was displeased with British behavior. For example, she visited **Calabar** in 1894 and witnessed the harsh business monopoly of the **Royal Niger Company** (RNC). Nonetheless, she was involved in a complicated negotiation with the RNC and traders in Liverpool over the trading of **alcohol** in 1897 and 1899. In her writings, Kingsley challenged the popular European view of Africans as inferior. She wrote *Travels in West Africa* (1897), which documented her study on African culture. She died in 1900 in South Africa while working as a nurse. *See also* TRADE.

*KISRA.* The word *kisra* is believed to be an altered form of the Persian word *khusraw*, a title of leadership. In West Africa, *kisra* typically refers to a Muslim man named Kisra who was dissatisfied with the direction of **Islam** in Mecca and left sometime between the 7th and 10th centuries. According to some **oral traditions**, this individual reached West Africa, spread Islam, and established kingdoms, only to leave after a couple of years and settle in Persia. There is also a belief that each of his followers was identified as Kisra, and they established Muslim dynasties. The primary idea behind this oral tradition was to draw a historical connection between contemporary Muslim societies and the birthplace of Islam. At one time or another, descent from these *kisra* has been claimed by the **Hausa, Nupe, Yoruba,** and **Borgu.**

**KOGI STATE.** A state carved out of **Benue** and **Kwara States** in 1991. It is considered part of the **Middle Belt** region. It is one of Nigeria's current 36 states. Kogi State has acquired the nickname "Confluence State," because within it lies the Niger–Benue confluence in the south-central part of Nigeria. The important colonial trading town **Lokoja** is the capital. Economic activities in Kogi include fishing, **coal** mining, and cultivation of crops such as coffee, **cocoa**, **oil palm**, cashews, and melons. **Ethnic groups** identified in Kogi State include the Igala (a semi-**Yoruba** subgroup) and Ebira. *See also* STATE CREATION.

**KOKO MINGI VIII, FREDERICK WILLIAM (1853–1898).** Koko was the ruler of Nembe (also known as **Brass)** in the **Niger Delta** during the late 19th century. He vacillated between **Christianity** and an indigenous **religion**. For a brief period, he was a Christian schoolteacher. He rose to power in 1889, only to face the encroaching **Royal Niger Company** (RNC), which wanted Nembe as a trading post. Koko tried to protect his territory by forming alliances with neighboring states such as **Bonny** and Okpoma. Only the latter joined Nembe fighters in an attack on the RNC's trading post at Akassa. The RNC responded with British military support and destroyed Nembe. Koko went into exile in 1896 to Etiema. *See also* TRADE.

**KOKORI, CHIEF FRANK (1944– ).** Born in December 1944 in **Warri**, in **Delta State**, Kokori studied at Urhobo College in Warri (1959–1962), Eko Boys' High School in **Lagos** (1963–1964), **University of Ibadan** (1974), and the Institute of Social Studies at The Hague (1984). Throughout his life, Kokori was heavily involved in the support of **petroleum** workers. He worked as a clerk for the Electricity Corporation of Nigeria, the predecessor to the **National Electric Power Authority**, from 1966 to 1971. He was the general secretary for the National Union of Nigerian Bank Employees (1975–1978) and the national secretary for the National Union of Petroleum and Natural Gas Workers (1978). He was also a member of the Constitution Review Committee (1987–1988) and Constituent Assembly (1988–1989). In the oil industry, Kokori served as vice president of the African Federation of Petroleum and Chemical Workers, member of the International Labour Organization, and first administrative secretary of the **Oil Mineral Producing Area Development Commission**. He worked as an administrator for the **Social Democratic Party**. In 1994, he was arrested and detained by **General Sani Abacha**. He was released in 1998 by **General Alhaji Abdulsalami Abubakar**. *See also* BANKING; ELECTRICITY; TRADE UNIONS.

**KOLANUTS.** The consumption of kolanuts in Nigeria dates back to ancient times. Kolanuts are indigenous to West Africa. Caffeine is the active ingredient in kolanuts. They became a favorite among Muslims in **northern Nigeria** because it was the only stimulant accepted in **Islam**. It was frequently used in commercial and social exchanges. For example, the founder of the town of Ilesha in southwestern Nigeria purchased the site in exchange for 100 kolanuts and other valuable items. **Hausa** consumers got their kolanuts from Gonja, in present-day **Ghana**, through an extensive **trade** network involving the Asante.

There are several types of kolanut. **Abeokuta** farmers began producing the *gbanja* variety in the 19th century, with significant expansion in 1910 as transcolony trade became restricted. The **Nupe** specialized in growing the *labozi* type. The maintenance of kolanut trees cost less and required less labor than **cocoa** trees. Kolanut trees, growing to around 9 meters tall, can grow in poor soil. Kolanut, technically a fruit, has a harvesting period that lasts from October to December. The "nuts" are nestled in a pod, which holds three to six nuts. They keep for several months. By 1918, the towns of Agege, Otta, and Abeokuta collectively exported 77 tons of kola to northern Nigeria via Hausa traders.

Kolanut became a main ingredient in Coca-Cola after using co-caine as an additive became illegal. Today, most major cola produc-ers in the West rely on artificial ingredients; however, some natural cola drinks still use kolanuts, including Blue Sky Organic Cola in the United States. The kolanut is believed to improve endurance, curb hunger, increase the ability to concentrate, and act as a mild aphro-disiac. Its side effects, however, are much like coffee, in that it can become addictive and may cause restlessness or sleeplessness.

In the **Igbo language**, the kolanut is called *oji* (same word as "heart"). In the **Hausa language**, it is *gworo*. In the **Yoruba language**, it is *obi abata*. Kolanut consumers often have preferences about ripeness and taste. Kola tends to be chewed primarily by adults. Offering kolanut to a visitor at your home is a sign of hospitality. It is also offered as a sign of good faith in negotiations (social or economic). Breaking of the kolanut, described as a "kola communion," is done among the **Igbo** as a ritual for the host and guest to honor ancestors.

**KORAN.** The book of **Islamic** scripture, literally "recitation." It is believed to be the words of God transmitted to the Prophet Muham-mad, who wrote them down. Muslims have dedicated their lives to reading, interpreting, and reciting the Koran. The Koran is the basis of **education** in **Koranic schools**. Dandawa Muslims in **Borgu** have required that men and **women** learn and memorize the Koran before getting married. **Sheikh Ibrahim al-Zakzaky**, for example, is a *hazif* (one who has memorized the Koran). The final version of the Koran was completed in the late seventh century. The Koran consists of 114 *surahs* (chapters). It is considered by radicals and liberal Muslims alike to be the ultimate authority in religious matters. The Koran is used as a guide to living a good Muslim life. For example, the Koran limits the number of wives a man can have to four, provided he can care for and protect them. It is also the basis for the **Shari'a**. *See also* *HAJJ*; RAMADAN; WOMEN.

**KORANIC SCHOOLS.** The establishment of Koranic schools in Nigeria coincided with the spread of **Islam** into West Africa start-ing around the 11th century. In the **Sokoto Caliphate**, palace Ko-ranic schools were attended by **slaves**, **women**, and children. The Koranic schools were the first type of formal **education** in Nigeria, with **Christian** missionary schools arriving in the mid-19th century. Koranic schools emphasized the principles of Islam as well as competence in classical Arab for reading, interpreting, and transcribing the Koran. The *mallams* (teachers) received payment in cash or kind based on the wealth of a child's parents. They also teach Islamic doctrine and rituals. **Usman dan Fodio** of the Sokoto Caliphate is credited with improving the status of teachers in **northern Nigeria** in the 19th century by encouraging parents to pay the teachers. **Zaria** served as a major center for Islamic studies at the time.

Today, Koranic schools often supplement a Western-style formal education, teaching in the evenings and on weekends. In 1973, northern Nigeria supported more than 20,000 Koranic schools. At the time, an Islamic education was part of the federal school system in the North, but many parents found the coverage of religious principles inadequate in that system. Nigeria maintains two forms of Koranic schools, Sufi (Islamic mysticism) and Western oriented.

**KOSOKO.** Son of Idowu Ojulari, Kosoko was the *oba* (**king**) of **Lagos** from 1819 to 1832. In 1841, Kosoko became involved in a contest for the throne with his uncle **Akintoye**. In 1845, Akintoye ascended to the throne and remained there until June 1845, which displeased Kosoko. In June 1845, Kosoko took the throne and forced Akintoye into exile in **Badagry**. The British attempted to settle this conflict and protect the favored Akintoye on the island of **Fernando Poo**. In December 1851, when it became clear to the British that Kosoko had rejected the idea of ending the **slave trade**, they used naval might to remove him from power. Kosoko was deported to Epe, and Akintoye was returned to the throne. Kosoko received permission to return to Lagos in 1862.

**KUMUYI, WILLIAM FOLURUNSO (1941– ).** Kumuyi was a member of the Anglican Church for much of his childhood. He was born again, joining the Apostolic Faith Church in 1964 at Ikenne. While lecturing at the University of Lagos in the early 1970s, Kumuyi maintained his membership in the Apostolic Faith Church and attended student prayer meetings. He was an adviser to the Lagos Variety Christian Union, a **Charismatic Christian** church in Lagos. He was also an active member of the Evangelical Christian Union. His followers believed that he had the ability to heal people simply by touching them.

He began his own ministry in 1973 while teaching at the University of Lagos. Kumuyi was a member of the Apostolic Faith Church until 1975, when he left it and formed the Deeper Christian Life Ministry. Starting in 1976, his teachings were published in pamphlets and booklets sold in markets across Nigeria. In one of his publications, he declared that the most important and rewarding work of a **Christian** is "soulwinning." Today, the Deeper Christian Life Ministry has congregations in other parts of West Africa. *See also* RELIGION.

**KURUNMI (?–1861).** A **Yoruba** ruler of Ijaye who was involved in the start of the **Yoruba Wars** of the 19th century, Kurunmi used his political and military might to form and break alliances with other Yoruba kingdoms. In 1836, he helped **Atiba** become the ruler of the **Oyo Empire**. In exchange, Atiba put Kurunmi in charge of two military divisions to protect Oyo from Dahomey. Kurunmi ruled in an unusual manner. He did not appoint **chiefs** to each town; instead, he selected chiefs from each town to answer directly to him. Upon Atiba's death in 1859, Kurunmi resisted the installment of Atiba's son, Adelu, and refused to recognize him. Kurunmi led the Ijaye, with the assistance of the **Egba**, into a difficult war with **Ibadan**. **Ola Rotimi**'s play, *Kurunmi: An Historical Tragedy* (1971), presents the leader as a hero in this war. Kurunmi died in 1861. *See also* IJAYE WAR.

**KUTI, FELA.** *See* ANIKULAPO-KUTI, OLUFELA.

**KWALI, LADI (ca. 1930–1984).** Born in Kwali, in **Niger State**, Kwali was of **Gwari** descent. She learned to make pottery as an apprentice to a family member starting at the age of nine. She is one of Nigeria's best known ceramicists. In 1977, she received an honorary doctorate from **Ahmadu Bello University**. In 1952, she taught at the newly opened Abuja Pottery Training Centre. The training center was later renamed the Ladi Kwali Pottery Centre in her honor. She conducted workshops in addition to creating her own works of **art**. Her work often included Gwari symbolism. She frequently open fired her pots and used herbal glazes. Between 1958 and 1962, she toured Europe showing her work. In the United States between 1962 and 1970, Kwali ran workshops in cities such as Los Angeles, Dallas, and Washington, D.C. She also gave lectures and conducted workshops for Ahmadu Bello University's aspiring artists. In 1981, she received the honorary title Officer of the Order of the British Empire. Two of her large water jars were displayed at the National Museum of History in Washington, D.C. Kwali died in August 1984.

**KWARA STATE.** Kwara State was created in 1967 out of the **Western Region**. Since its formation, it has been reduced in size. It is one of Nigeria's current 36 states. The capital is **Ilorin**. Kwara State is located in southwestern Nigeria, with its western boundary shared with **Benin** and its northeastern border running along the **Niger River**. The ethnic composition of Kwara State includes the **Yoruba, Nupe,** and Baruba. The dominant **religions** are **Islam** and **Christianity**. Yoruba is the primary **language**. Economic activities include the cultivation of a wide assortment of fruits (**cocoa** and **bananas**), grains, and tubers (**yams** and **cassava**), as well as fishing in the Niger and Asa Rivers. *See also* STATE CREATION.

## – L –

**LADIPO, DURO (1931–1978).** Born in Osogbo, in **Osun State**, Ladipo was a famous playwright. His works include *Oba Kò So* (1968), based on the **Yoruba king**/god **Sango**, and *Moremi: A Yoruba Opera* (1967), based on a Yoruba heroine named **Moremi**. His plays were written and performed in the **Yoruba language**, with several translated into English. His father was a cleric in the Anglican Church and raised Ladipo in a devout household. Along with the imagery and meaning in Yoruba **religion**, Ladipo also wrote plays based on biblical stories. He founded and ran the Duro Ladipo Theatre Company, which performed internationally. **Muraina Oyelami** was a notable member of his **theater** troupe. Ladipo died in March 1978.

**LAGOS.** The largest city in Nigeria, it has played, and continues to play, a major role in Nigeria's history. It has a **population** of approximately 9 million. **Oral tradition** describes Lagos as an ancient city inhabited by the Awori and **Ijebu** people, both subgroups of the **Yoruba**. In the 16th century, Lagos was part of the **Benin Kingdom**. According to one story, the *oba* (**king**) of Benin appointed his son

Asipa to be the *eleko* (**chief**) of Lagos. Another story is that Asipa was a Yoruba warrior who befriended the *oba*. The Asipa Dynasty of Lagos was founded around 1550, which marked the shift in title of the Lagos ruler to simply *oba*.

Lagos was one of Nigeria's seven major slave trading ports during the era of the transatlantic **slave trade**. By 1840 the British had established a trading presence in Lagos to enforce the abolition of the slave trade and the inception of **legitimate commerce**. They deliberately diverted trade away from the largest slave ports of **Badagry**, Whydah, and Apa. The British faced great resistance to ending the slave trade by **Kosoko**, the *oba* of Lagos. In 1851, the British forced him off the throne and replaced him with a more amicable ruler, **Akintoye**, who had been *oba* prior to Kosoko. That same year, a number of European **Christian** missionaries set up posts in Lagos before moving into the interior. In 1861, the British forced **Dosunmu**, Akintoye's successor, to cede authority, which led to the establishment of the **Lagos Colony**. During the colonial period, the position of *oba* became largely ceremonial. Significant *obas* of the 20th century include **Sir Adeniji Adele II** and Adeyinka Oyekan II.

Lagos was the intellectual center and seat of anticolonial activity in the early 20th century. New religious movements developed in Lagos as well. By the 1910s, several charismatic Christian churches had been established. A decade later, the **Lagos Town Council** was established and was dominated by **Sir Herbert Macaulay**'s **Nigerian National Democratic Party**. Many of the first political organizations, such as the **Lagos Youth Movement**, and Nigerian-run **newspapers**, such as the *Lagos Weekly Record* and ***Daily Times***, started in Lagos. It was also the original site of Nigeria's first major educational institution, **Yaba Higher College**, founded in 1932.

From October 1954 until May 1967, Lagos was the Lagos Federal District because it served as the political and economic center of Nigeria. After May 1967, Lagos was simply incorporated into the 12-state structure and merged into **Lagos State**. In 1951, Lagos was an integral part of the **Western Region**. In 1954, it was separated from the region and designated as a federal capital under the rule of the federal government. In 1991, the capital of Nigeria was moved from Lagos to **Abuja**, in the newly created **Federal Capital Territory**. Although no longer the capital of Nigeria, Lagos continues to serve as the primary city for **economic** activity and international **trade**. It is one of several Nigerian cities with a sizable population of **Charismatic Christians**. It is also the home of several important centers of **art**, such as the National Gallery of Modern Art, National Theatre complex, and Didi Museum, to name a few. *See also* FIRST REPUBLIC; STATE CREATION.

**LAGOS COLONY. Lagos** is named for the Portuguese word for lagoon. To the people who lived there, it was called Eko. It was a small **Yoruba** kingdom involved in the **slave trade**. The British set up **trade** and intervened in Lagos politics in December 1851, throwing **Kosoko** off the throne. In 1861, the British established a consulate in Lagos and drove out **Dosunmu**. The colony was run by the **Lagos Town Council** starting in 1917. *See also* LAGOS STATE.

**LAGOS STATE.** A state created from the **Western Region** in 1967, it essentially encompassed the greater metropolitan area of **Lagos**. Lagos State is located on the coast of the Bight of Benin in southwestern Nigeria close to **Benin**. It is one of Nigeria's current 36 states. Although it is one of Nigeria's smallest states, it is also one of the most heavily populated. Lagos State serves as the core of Nigeria's **trade** and commerce. It is also the site of one of Nigeria's major international airports. The state has enormous cultural diversity, but the **Yoruba** are still considered the dominant **ethnic group**, and Yoruba is the main indigenous **language**. *See also* LAGOS COLONY; STATE CREATION; WESTERN STATE.

**LAGOS TOWN COUNCIL.** Established in 1917 by the British colonial government in **Lagos**, it was composed of elected councilmen representing the various wards in the city. In 1922, the council was dominated by **Sir Herbert Macaulay**'s **Nigerian National Democratic Party**. By 1938, this dominance had shifted in favor of the **Nigerian Youth Movement.** In 1951, the town council lost much of its authority when Lagos was integrated into the **Western Region** by the **Macpherson Constitution**. In 1953, the largely ceremonial *oba* (**king**) of Lagos became president of the Lagos Town Council within the regional structure. In later years, its named was changed to the Lagos City Council. The council was dissolved in 1976. *See also*

OLORUN-NIMBE, ABUBAKAR IBIYINKA; WILLIAMS, CHIEF FREDERICK ROTIMI ALADE.

**LAGOS YOUTH MOVEMENT (LYM).** This historically significant political organization was established in **Lagos** in 1934 by graduates of **King's College** and other anticolonial activists, including J. C. Vaughan, H. O. Davies, **Ernest Ikoli**, and **Chief Samuel Akinsanya**. It was the successor of the Union of Young Nigerians. The organization was formed in response to the colonial government's inadequacy in addressing student demands for a quality **education** system. The focus was on the status of **Yaba Higher College** in relationship to peer institutions abroad. After the issue of **higher education** died down, the Lagos Youth Movement focused its attention on other issues, such as the placement of Nigerians in senior **civil service** positions. In 1936, the name of the organization was changed to the **Nigerian Youth Movement**.

**LAIRD, MACGREGOR (1809–1861).** One of many European explorers who focused on tracking the **Niger River** in the mid-19th century, he was the first European to arrive at the town of **Lokoja**, located at the Niger–Benue confluence. Laird settled at Lokoja in 1852. In 1857, he set out again on the Niger River, with **Bishop Samuel Ajayi Crowther** and others, on the steamship *Dayspring*, to explore and trade along the Niger River.

**LAMBO, CHIEF THOMAS ADEOYE (1923–2004).** Born in **Abeokuta** in March 1923, Lambo took an educational journey from the Baptist Boys' High School in Abeokuta, to Birmingham University Medical School, to the University of London's Institute of Psychiatry. He worked as a surgeon at the General Hospital (1949) and as a resident house physician at the Midland Nerve Hospital (1949–1950) in Birmingham. In 1950, Lambo returned to Nigeria and worked as a medical officer for the Nigerian Medical Service. From 1952 to 1954 he was the medical superintendent at Aro Hospital for Nervous Diseases in Abeokuta. Lambo also taught psychiatry at the **University of Ibadan**, where he later was the dean of the medical faculty (1966). Two years later, Lambo was promoted to the position of president at the university.

Outside Nigeria, he had an active career as chairman of the West African Examinations Council and a founding member (and president) of the Association of Psychiatrists in Africa. From 1965 to 1968, Lambo was an executive member of the Council for International Organization for Medical Science. He also worked with the United Nations Advisory Committee for the Prevention of Crime and Treatment of Offenders from 1968 to 1971. At the same time, he was vice chancellor of the University of Ibadan. Lambo was assistant director-general (1971–1973) and deputy director-general (1973–1988) of the World Health Organization. He received the honorary titles *basegun* (**chief**) of Egbaland, Commander of the Order of the Niger (1979), and Officer of the Order of the British Empire (1962). He also received 14 honorary doctorates from universities in Nigeria, Europe, and the United States. Lambo died in March 2004.

**LAND TENURE SYSTEM.** The ownership and usage of land is an important part of Nigeria's history. The access to cultivable land and acquisition of territory for political glory was not simply a British colonial preoccupation. Prior to the colonial period, Nigeria's **ethnic groups** and kingdoms diplomatically and militarily clashed numerous times over land tenure, especially in areas where fertile soil was limited. Generally, land did not belong to the **king** or **chief**, but to the entire community. All community members had the right to land, and few demarcations of land plots existed. A king or chief did not have the authority to sell the land or restrict use of it by any particular family without good reason. This land tenure system often perplexed the British. In most cases, the British sought out the king or chief and pressured him into ceding territory, without regard for custom.

During the colonial period, the British grappled with the best method of turning Nigeria's cultivable land into commercial farms and maintaining social control. The British in **southern Nigeria** did not have the right under colonial law to simply take land, but they could purchase it from willing families. In the **Protectorate of Northern Nigeria**, land was controlled by the government for the people. Over time, the rules about land tenure became rigid. The British seized land and dislocated communities in favor of colonial infrastructure, such as **roads**, **railroads**, administrative centers, and trading posts.

After **independence**, Nigeria attempted to encourage agricultural production by implementing new land tenure systems. During the 1970s, the state acquired land tract by tract around state capitals for development as well as fertile land in the rural areas for commercial farming. Acquired land was frequently offered to wealthy businessmen and companies, with oversight by the government. In addition to these capitalist endeavors, the Nigerian government also passed a quasi-socialist decree in 1978, which declared that all land in Nigeria belonged to the state. Federal and state governments leased land to investors through the **River Basin Development Authorities** scheme. For example, the Upper Benue River Basin Authority encouraged the cultivation of land near the **Benue River** to increase crop yields by efficiently irrigating farms. The Land Use Decree of 1978 was largely abandoned in favor of a **structural adjustment program** in the mid-1980s and **privatization** in the 1990s.

**LANDER, RICHARD AND JOHN.** Richard and John Lander were brothers who traveled from **Badagry** in **southern Nigeria** to Bussa in **northern Nigeria**, where **Mungo Park** died. In the 1830s, they also learned that the **Niger River** flows into the Atlantic Ocean. They concluded that the Niger River moved southward and linked to what previous explorers had called the **Oil Rivers** at the **Niger Delta**.

**LANGUAGES.** Nigeria has an estimated 250 languages. What is considered a language in Nigeria, however, is most often a dialect of another indigenous language. **Yoruba**, for example, is the root language of the dialects of Igala and **Itsekiri** in Nigeria, Tsabe and Idaitsa in **Benin**, and Ife (Ana) in Togo. In the region of **Borgu**, six languages (Tienga, Boko, Kamberi, Bissa, Batonu, and Bokobaru) are spoken. Languages in Nigeria are considered to be Chadic, Bantu, and part of the Niger–Congo families. Chadic speakers settling in Nigeria were largely pastoralists and fishermen at Lake Chad. **Hausa, Fula,** and **Kanuri** are Chadic. The Bantu languages include **Efik, Ibibio,** and **Tiv**. The Niger–Congo languages include **Yoruba, Ijaw, Itsekiri,** Edo, and **Igbo**. The most commonly used languages in Nigeria are Yoruba, Hausa, Fula, and Igbo, which are spoken by millions of people.

Scholars looking at Nigerian societies prior to colonial rule rely heavily on language to understand the relationships between ethnic groups and the locations of empires. For example, in determining the arrival of maize in the Borgu territory, scholars concluded, based on language, that the Yoruba introduced it sometime after the first century because the people of Borgu use the Yoruba word *agbado* for maize. In fact, the word "Yoruba" is believed to be of Hausa origin.

**Newspapers** and **literature** are often written in, and state-level official business is often conducted in, one of the major languages. English is the official language used in **education** and official business. Outside of those two settings, however, most Nigerians prefer to speak an indigenous language. A form of pidgin English, which combines the convenient aspects of both English and indigenous languages, is also prevalent.

**LAR, CHIEF SOLOMON DAUSHEP (1933– ).** Lar was born in April 1933 in Pangna, in **Plateau State**. As a young man, he studied at the Sudan United Mission School in Langtang (1944–1949), Sudan United Teachers' Training College in Gindiri (1950–1953), and **Ahmadu Bello University** (1966–1970). He earned his law degree from the Nigerian Law School in **Lagos** (1971). He worked as a teacher briefly before becoming involved in Nigeria's national politics. He was an active member of several **political parties** in Nigeria, including the **United Middle Belt Congress, Northern People's Congress, Social Democratic Party**, and **People's Democratic Party**. He was a member of the Federal House (1959–1964) and the **Irikefe Commission** (1976). He was also a member of the Constituent Assembly in 1978 as well as the minister of police affairs in 1994 and 1995. Lar was one of several civilian members of **General Sani Abacha**'s **Federal Executive Council**. Like others in Abacha's government, Lar was appointed to give the impression of a functioning inclusive federal government. He was chairman of the People's Democratic Party and promoted **General Olusegun Obasanjo** as the party's presidential candidate in the 1999 **elections**. Lar received an honorary membership in the Order of the Federal Republic of Nigeria. The Solomon Lar Amusement Park in **Jos** is named after him.

**LAWAL, AMINA.** A **woman** from **Katsina State** in **northern Nigeria** who was sentenced in 2002 to death by stoning for committing adultery. Katsina State had only adopted **Shari'a** in 2000, and had only recently implemented it. Lawal had lived through two unhappy marriages and reared three children. She had a relationship with Yahaya Muhammed, who promised marriage. Lawal became pregnant and, as a result of the physical evidence, was grabbed by people in the community and taken to a Shari'a **court**. She was offered no legal counsel, and in court Muhammed denied having a sexual relationship with her; he was released. A Nigerian **human rights** group appointed a lawyer for Lawal and contested the charge on the basis that the baby was conceived before Shari'a went into effect in Katsina State. She was acquitted in February 2004. She was the second woman to be sentenced to death by stoning for committing adultery since Shari'a was implemented in several of Nigeria's northern states. The first was **Safiya Husseini**. *See also* ISLAM; LEGAL SYSTEM.

**LEGAL SYSTEM.** The legal system in Nigeria has evolved over time. As Nigerian society changes, so does its law. That said, most scholars focus on the legal systems in three simplified snapshots: before, during, and after the colonial period. In precolonial times, the legal system in Nigeria typically consisted of an open-air court that heard cases and offered solutions. This system is referred to as customary law. Those individuals with the authority to speak on legal issues may have received assistance from supernatural powers (i.e., gods and ancestors). The social institution that would hear cases often depended on the crime or nature of the problem, or on the **religion** of the community. Several communities incorporated **Shari'a**. In the **Nupe** town of Bida, for example, the Nupe **king** separated offenses into civil and criminal. For civil infractions, the local authorities—elders and **village heads**—were in charge. The criminal cases went to the royal court of the king, who consulted Shari'a.

During the colonial period, the British altered the legal systems of Nigerian communities and superimposed a colonial version of British law. Customary Courts were established to deal with infractions based on local custom, which differed from one ethnic or religious group to another. Cases heard in these courts were frequently of a personal or familial nature, such as marriage, divorce, inheritance, or custody of children. A case could move through the Customary **Courts**, or **native courts**, and end up at the judicial committee of the Privy Council in London.

Since gaining independence, Nigeria has revised its court system at the federal and state levels to better meet the demands of its citizens, particularly Muslims. The Customary Courts are still used. As articulated in the 1999 **constitution**, at the lowest level are the Customary and Magistrate Courts, which exist in every state across the country. Cases heard at a Customary Court may move up to the Magistrate Court and then to the High Court, also located in each state across the country. From the High Court, cases may go to the Federal Court of Appeal and then the Supreme Court.

In the North, cases move on a modified track that appeals to Muslims. Until 1956, Shari'a had been incorporated into the Customary Courts. At the lowest level is the Shari'a Court, which replaces the Customary Courts. In 2000, **Zamfara State** incorporated Shari'a into its criminal code, creating its own unique Islamic legal system. By 2002, 11 other states in the North had followed suit. **Kaduna State**, out of respect for its sizable Christian population, established a Shari'a Court but kept a Customary Court for non-Muslims. In these states, cases move through a series of Shari'a Courts. Cases heard in the Shari'a Court may move to the High Shari'a Court, Upper Shari'a Court, and then on to the Shari'a Court of Appeal. Particularly complicated cases may reach the Federal Court of Appeal, which is required by law to have three justices trained in Shari'a and three justices learned in customary law. From the Federal Court of Appeal, a case goes to the Supreme Court. Notable Nigerian lawyers of the 20th century include **Sir Louis Mbanefo**, **Dan Ibekwe**, **Chief Richard Akinjide**, and **Atanda Fatayi-Williams**. **Chief Frederick Williams**, **Chief Abdul-Ganiyu Fawehinmi**, **Nabo Graham-Douglas**, and many others were awarded the prestigious rank of Senior Advocate of Nigeria, which means they devoted a minimum of 10 years to the legal profession with distinction. *See also* CHRISTIANITY; ISLAM; JUDICIAL SERVICE COMMISSION; NATIONAL JUDICIAL COUNCIL.

**LEGISLATIVE COUNCIL.** A governing body created in 1922 by the **Clifford Constitution** to replace the defunct **Nigerian Council**

of 1914. Prior to 1922, the purpose of the council was to advise the governor-general on legislation. At the time of its creation, its membership included government officials. It was not designed as a representative entity for Nigerians. After 1922, the council was reorganized to include four elected Nigerian members (three from **Lagos** and one from **Calabar**). This legislative council only addressed issues in **southern Nigeria**. It was reorganized in 1946 by the **Richards Constitution**, becoming a representative council for elected Nigerians. *See also* EXECUTIVE COUNCIL.

**LEGITIMATE COMMERCE.** Also referred to as "legitimate trade," in the 19th century it replaced **trade** in **slaves** with commodities such as **cotton**, **oil palm**, and **cocoa**. Enforcing legitimate commerce, however, involved a gradual process of product replacement as well as confronting the institution of slavery in Africa. The British frequently resorted to violence and political gerrymandering. For example, the British installed an *oba* (**king**) in Lagos who was sympathetic to British **Christian** missionaries, trade, and antislavery legislation. In many ways, the enforcement of legitimate commerce created new economic avenues for **women**. In **Abeokuta**, for example, women benefited from the expansion of cotton production and a **textile** trade. The trade in slaves was effectively eliminated with the acquisition of territory by British traders and colonial officers in the second half of the 19th century.

**LIEUTENANT GOVERNOR.** After 1914, each former protectorate had a lieutenant governor of British descent working for the Colonial Office. In the former **Protectorate of Northern Nigeria**, for example, the lieutenant governor's home and office were located in **Kaduna**, and he was assisted by a chief commissioner, who was also of British descent. The lieutenant governor carried out orders given by the **governor general** of Nigeria, stationed in **Lagos. Sir Herbert Richard Palmer**, for example, served from 1925 to 1930 as the lieutenant governor in the North. In October 1954, the position of lieutenant governor was replaced by a governor in three newly created regions—**Northern Region, Eastern Region**, and **Western Region**—who answered to the governor general.

**LISHABI.** Prior to the 18th century, the **Egba** lived in segmentary political systems in the **Oyo Empire**. Lishabi, an Egba warrior, liberated his people from Oyo control between 1775 and 1780. Lishabi achieved this goal by unifying Egba farmers and creating an army. In a series of attacks, Lishabi's men killed more than 600 Oyo men. The *oba* (**king**) of Oyo, Abiodun, attempted to reconquer the Egba, but failed. After gaining independence, Lishabi served as the ruler of Egbaland. He focused on protecting the people from conquest by building walls and expanding Egba influence in the region through **trade**.

**LITERATURE.** Literature in Nigeria has roots going back to at least the 18th century. Nigeria's literary corpus includes works in a variety of **languages**, genres, and styles, with the major genres being poetry, drama, and prose. **Nana Asma'u** is a well-known **Fulani** poet from the **Sokoto Caliphate** who wrote in the 19th century. After the colonial period, more modern literature flourished, both in English and indigenous languages. Nigeria has produced many famous novelists, including **Chinua Achebe, Akinwande Oluwole Soyinka**, Chimamanda Ngozi Adichie, **Ken Saro-Wiwa, Daniel Fagunwa, Cyprian Ekwensi, Flora Nwapa-Nwakuche**, and **Buchi Emecheta**. In the realm of poetry, Nigeria is home to **Christopher Okigbo, Niyi Osundare, Tanure Ojaide**, and **John Pepper Clark**, to name a few. Several of these writers' works appeared in *Black Orpheus*, the literary magazine from **Ibadan**. **Alhaji Abubakar Imam** and **Sa'adu Zungur** are important **Hausa** Muslim writers. But more popular forms have also sprung up. Nigeria is home to the quirky but fascinating works of the **Onitsha** and **Kano Market Literatures**. Notable Kano Market Literature authors include **Bilkisu Ahmed Funtuwa** and **Balaraba Ramat Yakubu**. Their stories are full of drama, love, and flirtations with cultural taboos and are commonly written in indigenous languages. Nigeria also has a rich **theatrical** tradition that ranges from satire to drama.

**LOKOJA.** A town located at the confluence of the **Benue** and **Niger Rivers**. The British explorer **Macgregor Laird** is credited with being the first European to arrive at the town of Lokoja, in 1852. The British briefly ran a consulate in Lokoja, from 1865 to 1869. It was also a place of exile for the British-initiated disposal of **emirs**. Lokoja was the headquarters for the **Royal Niger Company** (1886–1900) and capital of the **Protectorate of Northern Nigeria** (1899–1914). To-day, Lokoja is the capital of **Kogi State** and is home to an estimated 195,000 people.

**LUGARD, SIR FREDERICK (1858–1945).** Born in India, Lugard had a long career as a British colonial administrator, which included a post of some duration in Nigeria. He served as the first high commissioner in the **Protectorate of Northern Nigeria** (1900–1907). He then left Nigeria for a post in Hong Kong (1907–1912), after which he returned. Although his work extended beyond **northern Nigeria**, he is best known for his conquests and administrative approach. In 1897, he organized the (Royal) **West African Frontier Force** to protect British interests from French incursions in northern Nigeria. This mission included the dismantling of the **Sokoto Caliphate** in 1903. Lugard is responsible for the amalgamation of the northern and southern Nigerian **protectorates** in January 1914. He served as the **governor general** of colonial Nigeria from 1914 to 1919, when he retired. Although the idea of **indirect rule** as a method of admin-istration existed in all the European empires, it was best articulated in Lugard's book, *The Dual Mandate in British Tropical West Africa* (1922). His wife is often given credit for coming up with the name "Nigeria" in 1897.

**LUKMAN, SIR ALHAJI RILWANU (1938– ).** Lukman was born in August 1938 in **Zaria**, in **Kaduna State**. As a young man, Luk-man completed his primary and secondary education in Zaria. He attended the Nigerian College of Arts, Science, and Technology (present-day **Ahmadu Bello University**) (1956–1958), Univer-sity of London (1959–1962), University of Mining and Metal-lurgy in Austria (1967–1968), and McGill University in Canada (1977–1978). He worked as an assistant mining engineer in Swe-den (1962–1964) before returning to Nigeria, where he was senior inspector for the Federal Ministry of Mines and Power in **Jos** (1964–1967) and assistant chief inspector for the Federal Ministry of Mines and Power in Jos (1968–1970). He became Nigeria's expert on **petroleum** production and trading. He also worked as general manager for the Cement Company of Northern Nigeria (1970–1974) and Nigerian Mining Corporation (1974–1984). Returning to the government, Lukman was minister of mines, power, and steel (1984–1985) and then minister of foreign affairs (1989–1990). He is well known for his years as president of the **Organization of Petroleum Exporting Countries** (1986–1989) and chairman of the **National Electric Power Authority** in **Lagos** (1993–1994). In 1999, he was a presidential adviser on petroleum and energy. Lukman is a Scientologist. He has received several honorary doctoral degrees from universities in and outside of Nigeria and the honorary title Knight Commander of the Order of the British Empire (1989). *See also* FOREIGN TRADE.

**LYTTLELTON CONSTITUTION.** Implemented in 1954, the Lyttlelton Constitution was the fourth formal **constitution** of Nigeria. Like the previous **Macpherson Constitution**, its contents were the product of both Nigerian and, to a larger extent, British colonial input. After much debate in Nigeria about the use of a unitary or a federal government structure, the Lyttlelton Constitution put the latter into law. The three regions (**Northern, Western,** and **Eastern**) created by the **Richards Constitution** in 1946 became the basis of this federation. The constitution created the **Federal House of Representatives,** which had 184 seats for elected representatives from the new regional Houses of Representatives. The Northern Region had 92, the Western, 42, the Eastern, 42, southern **Cameroon,** 6, and the federal territory of **Lagos,** 2. The constitution also created regional executives, called **premiers,** to preside over each region. **Nnamdi Azikiwe** became the premier of the Eastern Region, **Chief Obafemi Awolowo** became premier of the Western Region, and **Sir Alhaji Ahmadu Bello** became premier of the Northern Region. One of the major problems of the Lyttlelton Constitution was that each region was left to adopt its own electoral regulations. The Northern Region, for example, had direct **elections,** whereas the Western and Eastern Regions had indirect elections. Also, the lack of a central leader, such as a prime minister, resulted in a lack of unity and uniformity among the three premiers. *See also* CLIFFORD CONSTITUTION.

# – M –

**MABOGUNJE, AKINLAWON LADIPUPO (1931– ).** Born in October 1931 in **Kano**, Mabogunje studied at the United Native African Church School in Kano (1936–1941), Mapo Central School in **Ibadan** (1942), Ibadan Grammar School (1943–1948), University College (present-day **University of Ibadan**) (1949–1953), and University College in London (1955–1958). After receiving his doctoral degree in geography, he taught at University College from 1958 to 1968. He was then promoted to the position of dean at the university (1968–1970). During the 1970s, he devoted his professional attention to private businesses and national institutions. Mabogunje was chairman of the Nigerian Council for Management Development (1976–1979) and consultant for the Federal Capital Development Authority (1976–1984). In 1986, he was a member of the Directorate of Food, Roads, and Infrastructure. He served as president of the Nigerian Geographical Association (1968–1970). He was a member of the Western Nigeria Economic Advisory Council (1967–1971) and chairman of the Western State Forestry Commission (1968–1974). Mabogunje served as a special adviser for the National Census Board (1973–1975). During the same period, he acted as vice president of the Nigerian Economic Society. Mabogunje received several international awards related to his work in geography and two honorary degrees.

**MABOLAJE GRAND ALLIANCE.** A political organization formed in 1953 in **Ibadan** by **Alhaji Adegoke Adelabu** with supporters of the **National Council of Nigeria and the Cameroons** (NCNC) who expressed concern over the regional hold of the **Action Group**. The popularity of this alliance contributed to the NCNC's making inroads into the Action Group's political dominance in the **Western Region**. After Adelabu died in a car accident in March 1958, the alliance split into two factions and the NCNC's influence in the region weakened. In the early 1960s, the party was led by K. O. S. Are and aligned with the **Northern People's Congress**.

**MACAULAY, SIR HERBERT HELAS (1884–1946).** Born in November 1884 in **Lagos**, Macaulay was the grandson of **Bishop Samuel Ajayi Crowther**, a well-known **Christian** missionary. He completed his primary and secondary education in Lagos. He was one of the first Nigerians to receive a scholarship in Great Britain (1890–1893) to study civil engineering. In Nigeria, he worked as a land surveyor for the colonial government until 1899. Frustrated with colonialism, he devoted himself to the anticolonial struggle in Lagos and London. Macaulay was instrumental in the protest against a water tax bill in Lagos in 1908. He is also known for supporting a protest by market **women** in Lagos led by **Madam Alimotu Pelewura**. In 1912, he led a protest against inequitable **land tenure** policies. He also used the colonial legal code to demand compensation for land acquired by the British through force and manipulation from **Chief Amodu Tijani**. He won the case in 1921. Macaulay was the founder of the **Nigerian National Democratic Party** (NNDP) in 1923. The NNDP was the first **political party** in Nigeria to contest elections. Macaulay ran a **newspaper** called the *Lagos Daily News*, which was written in English and circulated in the 1930s. The newspaper served as a mouthpiece for the NNDP. He also participated in the formation of the **National Council of Nigeria and the Cameroons** (NCNC) in 1944. Two years later, he toured with other NCNC leaders to campaign against the **Richards Constitution** and raise funds. He became ill in **Kano** while touring. Macaulay died in May 1946 in Lagos. He is affectionately referred to as the "father of Nigerian nationalism." **Chief Hubert Ogunde** wrote a theatrical play about Macaulay in 1946. Macaulay's image is on all denominations of Nigeria's **currency**, the naira.

**MACCIDO, SULTAN ALHAJI MUHAMMADU (1926– ).** Born in Dange, in **Sokoto State**, Maccido was the eldest son of **Sir Sultan Siddiq Abubakar III**. He completed his primary and secondary schooling in Sokoto State. He first worked as a clerical assistant to Sultan Abubakar Sarkin Kudu. In 1953, Maccido became a district head. He also worked as the councilor of works (1956), councilor for rural development (1959), and councilor of **agriculture** (1960) for the Sokoto Native Authority. He was then the commissioner for the Ministry of Agriculture and Health for **Northwestern State** from 1976 to 1979 and state chairman for the **National Party of Nigeria** from 1979 to 1983. He worked as the presidential liaison officer of Sokoto State for **Alhaji Shehu Shagari**. Beginning in 1985, Maccido was a member of the Sokoto Emirate Council for several years.

After the death of his father in 1986, the position of **sultan** was open. Maccido was the popular choice within Sokoto, but he lacked the support of **General Ibrahim Babangida**. Ultimately, Babangida installed the favored **Sultan Ibrahim Dasuki** in 1988 and ignored the violence and protest that followed. Babangida sent Maccido to South Africa in a form of subtle exile. Maccido returned several years later, when **General Sani Abacha** seized power, and claimed the title of sultan from Dasuki, who had been deposed in April 1996. He received the honorary title Commander of the Order of the Federal Republic (1998). Maccido died in a plane crash in October 2006 and was replaced by **Sultan Colonel Muhammed Sa'adu Abubakar III**.

**MACPHERSON CONSTITUTION.** A **constitution** named for Sir John Macpherson, a colonial administrator. Macpherson proposed a revision of the 1946 **Richards Constitution** in addition to structural changes to the local government. Implemented in January 1952, the Macpherson Constitution was the third Nigerian constitution. It was the first to reflect the interests of the colonial administration and, to a lesser extent, the Nigerian **population**. In the drafting phase, the constitution was presented and discussed at the national, regional, and local levels. In January 1950, a conference was held in **Ibadan** and attended by representatives across Nigeria to discuss the new constitution. It called for a central **Legislative Council** to have 147 seats, of which 136 would go to elected representatives from the three regional houses of assemblies (Northern, Western, Eastern). Half of the seats, which were based on **population**, went to the **Northern Region**. Like the constitutions before it, the Macpherson constitution was disliked by many segments of Nigerian society. It neither represented a fair distribution of **ethnic groups** nor satisfied the divergent views about the form of government. Three years after it was introduced, a conference was held in London to revise it. *See also* HOUSE OF ASSEMBLY.

**MAIDUGURI.** A northeastern city on the Ngadda River, near Lake Chad. It is the capital of **Borno State**, with approximately 520,000 people. Its **population** is predominantly Muslim and of **Kanuri** descent. It has two major **markets**: Gomboru (also called Monday Market) and Kamuri (also called New Market). Maiduguri is one of the places where followers of the radical Muslim **Maitatsine** group were located. It is an industrial center and home to the University of Maiduguri. Historically, it has been a point of embarkation for Muslims of Nigeria to go on *hajj* (spiritual **pilgrimage**) to Mecca. In recent years, Maiduguri has made **newspaper** headlines because of outbursts of violence. In February 2006, riots erupted over a cartoon depicting the Prophet Muhammad that was published in a Danish newspaper. The riots resulted in the death of 16 people and the destruction of 40 churches. Maiduguri also hit the headlines because its general hospital, which was constructed in 2006, sat unused until the president was available for its opening ceremony. Unfortunately, the hospital was not available when there was a measles outbreak in **Borno State**, and hundreds of children died. Then, in February 2008 the new hospital burned down, destroying millions of dollars' worth of modern medical equipment.

**MAITATSINE RIOTS.** This burst of violence in 1980 was named after **Muhammadu Marwa**'s **Islamic** organization, the name of which means "the faithful" or "the believer." The Maitatsine were based primarily in **Kano**, but also in **Maiduguri, Yola**, and **Bauchi**. These riots were among the first of **northern Nigeria**'s major outbreaks of faith-based violence. They were the result of Islamic fundamentalism mixed with political turmoil. Marwa's followers were poor and unemployed. The Maitatsine were unique in that they developed an unusual ritual of prayer and interpretation of Islamic doctrine. They were anti-West and antimodern technology, including bicycles and radios. During the 1970s, the Maitatsine had engaged in a range of public disturbances, including stoning **police** officers, harassing nonmembers, and preaching on the streets without a permit. In December 1980, their activities culminated in the Maitatsine Riots, which lasted several days. Thousands of people (Muslim and Christian) were killed during the riots, and a great deal of property was damaged. Marwa, the leader of the group, was also killed.

**MAJA, AKINOLA.** As a young man, Maja attended a Methodist boys' school. He established the National Bank of Nigeria in 1933. Maja was a founding member of the **Nigerian Youth Movement**, serving as president from 1944 to 1951. He was the elected chairman of the **National Emergency Committee**, which looked into the killings of miners in **Enugu** in 1949. He was a founding member, and later president, of **Egbe Omo Oduduwa**, the **Yoruba** cultural organization. His active membership in the **Action Group** earned him the nickname "Father." There is a road named after him in **Ibadan**.

**MAJEKODUNMI, CHIEF MOSES ADEKOYEJO (1916– ).** Born in August 1916 in **Abeokuta**, in **Ogun State**, Majekondunmi studied at Abeokuta Grammar School, St. Gregory's College, and Trinity College in Dublin (1935–1941). He served as a physician for the National Children's Hospital in Dublin (1941–1943) and a medical officer for the federal government (1943–1949). He also worked in the Nigerian Federal Government Maternity Hospital and Massey Street Maternity Hospital. He was a senator in the Federal Parliament (1960) and minister of health (1961–1966). Majekodunmi served in an administrative position in the temporary absence of a **premier** in the **Western Region** in May 1962. He was the chancellor of Ogun State University (1986). He received several honorary chieftaincy titles, including *otun* of Egbaland and *agba akin* of Osogbo; Commander of the Order of the Federal Republic (1982); and Companion Order of St. Michael and St. George (1963). He also received honorary doctoral degrees from Trinity College in Dublin (1964), University of Lagos (1974), and Ogun State University (1986). *See also* ACTION GROUP CRISIS; HEALTH.

**MALARIA.** An infectious disease affecting people living in tropical and semitropical regions. It is transmitted through the bite of an infected mosquito and attacks the red blood cells, causing high fever, and, if untreated, death. Prior to the discovery of **quinine** as a prophylactic in 1854, Europeans saw Nigeria as a "white man's grave." Malaria is preventable and curable. Taking a quinine derivative can dramatically reduce the risk of contracting the disease and ameliorate its effect on an infected person. The southern half of Nigeria, especially along the coast, is malaria-ridden. This is considered a major **health** crisis in Nigeria. The inability to eradicate malaria has been linked to Nigeria's lack of development. Unsanitary environments serve as excellent breeding grounds for malaria-infected mosquitoes. Nigeria has the largest population at risk of infection in Africa.

Efforts to battle malaria have been on a local level, which explains their limited success. In 2003, Nigeria had over 2.5 million reported cases of malaria and around 5,400 deaths from it. Of the causes of death for children under the age of five, malaria ranked highest at 26 percent. Since 2003, the federal government has participated in the World Health Organization's "Roll Back Malaria" campaign. Nigeria committed $3.5 million for malaria control, which was matched with another $2.3 million from outside donors. Malaria control programs have included the purchase and distribution of insecticide-treated netting to protect people while they sleep, as well as mosquito repellants. *See also* ECONOMY; HIV/AIDS.

**MALIKI, ALHAJI ABDUL (1914–1969).** As a young man, Maliki studied at Okene Elementary School (1923–1927), Bida Primary School (1927–1929), and Katsina Training College (1929–1934). He worked as a teacher, clerk, and public works supervisor between 1935 and 1939. In 1950, he went to England and attended a local government training program. After his return, he joined the **Northern People's Congress political party**. He served as a member of the **Northern Regional House of Assembly**. Three years later, he was appointed Northern Region Commissioner to Great Britain. In 1960, he became Nigeria's first high commissioner to **Great Britain**. Six years later, he became Nigeria's ambassador to France. Maliki died in 1969.

*MAMLUK.* An Arabic-derived term that refers to powerful slaves and literally means "owned" (person or thing). It is part of an **Islamic** political system that incorporates the institution of **slavery**. Prior to the colonial era in **northern Nigeria**, the military and government were partially run by slaves. In 19th-century **Kano**, for example, slaves commanded armies, managed plantations, and collected taxes. Each emirate within the **Sokoto Caliphate** ran his *mamluk* system differently.

**MANUWA, SIR SAMUEL LAYINKA AYODEJI (1903–1975).** Born in March 1903, Manuwa studied at the Church Missionary Society Grammar School and **King's College** in **Lagos**. In **Great Britain**, he advanced his education and received a medical degree, a diploma in tropical medicine and hygiene, and a license in midwifery. He worked at the **University of Ibadan** as the examiner of anatomy and surgery. Between 1927 and 1948, Manuwa was the surgical and senior specialist for the Colonial Medical Service of Nigeria. In 1948, he was promoted to deputy and, later, director. In 1951, he became inspector-general of medical services, and in 1954, chief medical adviser to the federal government. While working in the medical community, he also participated in politics. He was a member of the **Legislative Council** (1951–1952) and Governor's Privy Council (1952–1954). He was also a member of the World Health Organization's advisory panel on public **health**. Manuwa published several books on mental illness and other health problems in West Africa. He acquired numerous chieftaincy titles and the honorary titles Companion of St. Michael and St. George, Officer Order of the British Empire, Officer Order of St. John of Jerusalem, and Knight of the Thistle.

**MARIERE, CHIEF SAMUEL JERETON (1907–1971).** After completing his primary and secondary education in southeastern Nigeria, Mariere worked as a storekeeper, business manager, and teacher. He also served as the secretary-general of the Urhobo Progressive Union based in **Warri**, president of the Agbor Social Club, and chairman of the Agbor Community Centre. He was the justice of the peace for Agbo and the district. Mariere served as governor of the **Mid-Western Region** from February 1964 until January 1966. In 1968, he became chancellor of the University of Lagos and chairman of the state's school board. Mariere received several honorary chieftaincy titles, as well as law degrees from the University of Nigeria at **Nsukka** and the **University of Ibadan** in 1964.

**MARKETING BOARDS.** Between 1947 and 1954, there were several Nigerian Commodity Marketing Boards, one for each major commodity: **oil palm**, **cocoa**, **groundnuts**, and **cotton**. The purpose of the marketing boards was to buy and sell **agricultural** products at the most advantageous rates through a single entity. They also set market standards of quality among like products. For Nigerian farmers, the marketing boards reduced price fluctuations but also forced them to sell their harvests at rates below global market prices. Any profits made were rarely returned to the farmers. Goods destined for export were handled by the colonial government. The marketing board scheme emerged out of the wartime need to protect raw materials required by **Great Britain**. After **World War II**, the marketing boards were retained in an effort to stabilize quantities and prices. Another primary reason for the marketing boards was to generate the savings required for economic development by the government. When Nigeria was divided into regions in January 1946, each region relied on its own marketing boards for revenue. The marketing boards of the **Eastern Region** traded primarily in oil palm, those of the **Western Region** in cocoa, and those of the **Northern Region** in cotton and groundnuts. Between 1954 and 1977, the marketing boards were organized primarily by region rather than commodity. In 1962, boards administered over 60 percent of Nigeria's exports. In the late 1980s, **General Ibrahim Babangida** abolished the marketing board structure. *See also* ECONOMY; FOREIGN TRADE; MARKETS; TRADE.

**MARKETS.** The markets in Nigeria were, and still are, thriving centers of commerce. They are typically found in town centers and organized into a maze of vendors selling their food and wares in wooden stalls. Sellers and buyers negotiate prices. The markets vary in size and days of operation. For example, to European travelers in the early 20th century, **Nupe** territory appeared to be one giant market. Almost every town or village has a market and fixed market days. A large town may have a market day every seventh day, whereas a small village may do it every fifth day.

The markets are typically administered by market unions and organized by type of product for sale. At Kutigi market (located in **Niger State**) during the colonial period, the southeastern quadrant of the market was devoted to hoes, mats, and items brought by **Hausa** traders, and the northwestern quadrant was designated as the location for fresh grains, fruits, vegetables, and spices. In the center of Kutigi market, traders sold smoked fish, cooked food, and **oil palm**. In 1942, a visitor to Kutigi recorded seeing some 400 to 500 people on market day out of about 3,000 inhabitants. In 1948, **Lagos** had 15 large markets maintained by 8,000 female traders. Within a roughly 80-kilometer radius, towns and villages consciously stagger their market days to allow for a beneficial flow of goods.

Some towns, like Bida, were important stations for trans-Nigerian **trade**, where goods produced in the South were sold and taken to the North. Also, the Nupe produced valuable foodstuffs such as rice, **kolanuts** (a favorite among the Hausa), and smoked fish. The Hausa arrived with a donkey caravan of beans in Bida and left with kolanuts. Female traders often traveled more than 48 kilometers between their homes, sources of goods, and markets. In addition to the central markets, traders also stop en route at a kind of relay station to make additional exchanges of goods.

Today, an estimated 80 to 90 percent of **women** in Nigeria are market traders. They typically sell foodstuffs (but not cash crops), cloth, and local handicrafts. The international trade of cash crop items, such as **cocoa** or oil palm, and imported foreign goods is done by men or foreign families. Men also dominate the trade in metallic items and electronics. *See also* ECONOMY; FOREIGN TRADE.

**MARWA, MUHAMMADU (?–1980).** Born in **Cameroon**, Marwa's exact birth date is unknown. His followers, called the Maitatsine, engaged in a series of violent outbursts in **northern Nigeria** in the 1980s, which are referred to as the **Maitatsine Riots**. Marwa was an Islamic teacher based in **Kano**, who was deeply concerned about the collapse of morality and dedication to **Islam** among Muslims in northern Nigeria. He was an enigmatic person who used several names (Maitatsine, Muhammadu Mai Tabsiri, and Marwa Darka). He traveled extensively, preaching and teaching along the way, and acquired thousands of followers. He was a *tariqa* leader, meaning that he presented himself as one who knows the true path to salvation. He loathed Western influence, modern technology, and the Muslim **Tijaniyya** and **Qadiriyya** *tariqahs* (brotherhoods or orders). Marwa created his own Islamic doctrine. He seems to have arrived in Kano in 1945 and worked as a Muslim missionary. He was arrested and deported in 1962 and again in 1966 for public disturbances such as preaching on the streets without a permit. In the 1970s, he returned to Kano and formed the Maitatsine. By 1975, he had accumulated over 2,000 followers. The Maitatsine engaged in throwing stones at **police**, public preaching, and other problematic acts in Kano. In December 1980, their activities culminated in the Maitatsine Riots, which left thousands of people (Muslims and Christians) dead, caused extensive property damage, and embarrassed the Kano police. Marwa was killed during the riots.

**MASQUERADE.** Many Nigerian **ethnic groups** incorporate masquerades into their religious festivals. The masquerades are designed to call dead ancestors from the world of the spirits into that of the living. The person wearing the mask and costume is typically known only by adult men. The ancestors emerge to bless their people. The masquerade festivals are usually yearly affairs, with the **oracle** identifying for the people the exact days each year on which to hold them. A **Yoruba** masquerade, for example, may last seven days. Additional masquerades are conducted during times of social disaster as a way of appeasing ancestors and warding off the evil that plagues a community. Masquerades are also used during funerals. For example, secret society members of **Arochukwu** wear masks to symbolize hope and healing. One of Nigeria's most well-known masquerades is *Egungun*, celebrated by the Yoruba. *See also* RELIGION.

**MASS MOBILIZATION FOR SELF RELIANCE, SOCIAL JUSTICE, and ECONOMIC RECOVERY (MAMSER).** A plan was created by **General Ibrahim Babangida** by Decree No. 31 in July 1987. The directorate comprised a chairman appointed by the head of state and a governing board, which included representatives from the various ministries. Babangida appointed the directorate to foster national pride in productive work and develop a forum in which the public could contribute to the shaping of a new Nigeria. However, the directorate proved largely unproductive and ineffective. The organization's tasks included assessing Nigerians' views on economic development and social justice. It was also assigned the goals of publicizing Babangida's vision for Nigeria and educating the citizens of Nigeria about the importance of **elections**. **Jerry Gana** was the chairman, with **Ken Saro-Wiwa** briefly serving as a member. The organization disappeared after the failure of the **election of 12 June 1993**. *See also* ECONOMY.

**MBADIWE, KINGSLEY OZUMBA (1915–1990).** Born in March 1915, Mbadiwe attended the **Hope Waddell Training Institute** in **Calabar** and various colleges in **Lagos**. For his advanced degrees, he studied in the United States at Lincoln University, Columbia University, and New York University. He started the *Daily Telegraph* **newspaper** in 1936. He also worked as a local representative for the *West African Pilot* in several towns across **southern Nigeria** in 1937. He became a member of the House of Representatives and the federal minister of communications and aviation. In 1943, he and three other African students formed the African Academy of Arts and Research in the United States, which was designed to educate Americans about Africa. In 1945, he was the first president of the African Students' Union in the United States. During the 1950s, he acted as a leader of the **National Council of Nigeria and the Cameroons** (NCNC). He was a member of two **constitutional** conferences during the mid-1950s as well as a member of the 1979 constitution drafting committee. In 1958, he cofounded the **Democratic Party of Nigeria and the Cameroons** as a splinter party of the NCNC. Mbadiwe was one of the earliest voices calling for **indigenization**. He served as the African affairs adviser for President **Sir Alhaji Abubakar Tafawa Balewa** in 1963. In 1979, he became a member of the **National Party of Nigeria**.

**MBAKWE, CHIEF SAMUEL ONUNAKA (1930–2004).** Mbakwe was born in Avutu, in **Imo State**. After completing his primary and secondary education, he attended the Teachers' Training College (1946–1947) and Fourah Bay College in Sierra Leone (1952–1953). In England, he studied at the University of Manchester, the University of Hull, and the University of London. He continued his education at the University of Nigeria at **Nsukka** and the University of Lagos. In 1959, Mbakwe was called to the bar. He opened a private legal practice in **Port Harcourt** the same year. He also worked as the director of the Nigerian Broadcasting Corporation (1961–1966). In the political arena, he was a member of the Constituent Assembly (1978) and executive governor of Imo State (1979–1983), and a member of the National Constitutional Conference (1995). He served a prison sentence for treason from 1983 to 1986. Mbakwe was a member of several **political parties**: the **Nigerian People's Party**, **Social Democratic Party**, Congress for National Consensus, and **All People's Party**. As a member of the Social Democratic Party, he actively supported **Chief M. K. O. Abiola** as a presidential candidate.

He earned more than 65 honorary chieftaincy titles, predominantly in **Igbo** territory. A local airport in Imo State is named after him. Mbakwe died in January 2004.

**MBANEFO, SIR LOUIS MWACHUKWU (1911–1977).** Born in May 1911 in **Onitsha**, in **Anambra State**, Mbanefo completed his primary school education in Onitsha. He then studied at **King's College** in **Lagos**, University of London, and King's College in Cambridge, where he completed degrees in history and law in the mid-1930s. In Nigeria, he had a private legal practice. He served as a member of the Onitsha Town Council in 1939. He was a member of the **Eastern House of Assembly** (1950–1952) and the **Legislative Council**. He was the first Nigerian chief justice in **eastern Nigeria**. In 1952, he served as a judge of the Supreme Court and in 1956 as judge of the High Court of eastern Nigeria. He also served on the Federal Supreme Court of Appeal in Lagos (1958) and the International Court of Justice at The Hague (1961). Mbanefo chaired a commission on the salaries of Eastern and **Northern Region civil service** workers in 1960. During the **civil war**, he supported the secessionist **Republic of Biafra**. He was one of the founders of the **Nigerian Institute of International Affairs**. Mbanefo died in March 1977. *See also* COURTS; LEGAL SYSTEM.

**MBU, CHIEF MATTHEW TAIWO (1929– ).** Born November 1929 in Ogoja, in **Cross River State**, as a young man, Mbu studied at St. Patrick's in Ogoja as well as at the Metropolitan College of Law in England. He was called to the bar in 1960. Back in Nigeria, he worked as a produce manager for John Holt and Company from 1944 to 1952. He also worked as the director of the Eastern Regional Production Development Board from 1952 to 1954. In the political arena, he was president of the Ogoja Divisional Council (1951–1954), a member of the **Eastern House of Assembly** (1952–1954), and minister of labour (1954–1955). In 1955, became minister of trade and industry. From 1960 to 1966, he was a member of the Parliament of Ogoja. Mbu was the first Nigerian chief representative to the United Nations (1959–1960). During the mid-1960s, he was heavily involved in the Organization of African Unity (present-day **African Union**). From 1961 to 1965, he was the minister of naval defense. Just prior to the **civil war**, he was the chairman of the Eastern Nigerian Public Commission. From 1977 to 1978, he served as a member of the Constituent Assembly. In the 1980s, he was chairman and/or director of several private companies operating in Nigeria. In 1993, he was the secretary for external affairs of the short-lived **Interim National Government** of Nigeria. He was also the ambassador to Germany in the late 1990s. Mbu was an active member of several **political parties**, including the **National Council of Nigerian Citizens** and the **Nigerian People's Party**. He earned the honorary titles Commander of the Order of the Federal Republic (1996) and *otu agrinya* (**chief**) of Bokiland. Mbu received an honorary doctorate from the **University of Ibadan** in 1988.

**MEDICINE, TRADITIONAL.** *See* TRADITIONAL MEDICINE.

**MEMORANDUM ON EDUCATION POLICY IN BRITISH TROPICAL AFRICA.** The Phelps-Stokes Commission issued a report on **education** in the British colonies in 1922. The report criticized the existing educational system. In 1925, an advisory committee formed in **Great Britain** to suggest ways to improve education in its tropical African colonies. Two years later, the committee offered its suggestions in this memorandum. It criticized the Phelps-Stokes Commission and urged the colonial government to administer education in cooperation with **Christian** missions. It also stressed that these educational programs should be designed to meet local needs, using local **languages** and including the education of girls. *See also* WOMEN.

**MIDDLE BELT.** A geographic designation for an area that stretches from East to West across central Nigeria. In precolonial times, numerous **ethnic groups**, such as the **Tiv**, settled in this area. They chose central Nigeria because it had not been claimed by the dominant empires of the South, such as Oyo, or of the North, such as the **Hausa**. Today, the Middle Belt is not so much known for its ethnic composition as for its **economic** importance. This region is endowed with valuable minerals such as **tin**, **salt**, iron, copper, and gold. It is believed by many that the people living in this region feel squeezed by the North and South politically and ignored economically, especially with regard to **revenue allocation**. At the same time, some of those living in the Middle Belt feel more or less of a cultural association with northerners and southerners.

The states considered part of the Middle Belt are **Federal Capital Territory (Abuja)**, **Niger, Nassarawa, Plateau, Adamawa, Kwara**, and **Taraba**. The southern portions of **Kaduna, Gombe, Borno**, and **Bauchi** are also considered part of the Middle Belt. Throughout the 1950s and early 1960s, several political groups formed to campaign for representation and the creation of a Middle Belt State. The Middle Belt League, for example, formed in 1950 and demanded the creation of a Middle Belt Region out of the **Northern Region**. Support for this idea increased and grew into a somewhat unified **Middle Belt State Movement**, with the creation of the **Middle Belt People's Party** in the mid-1950s. In 1955, the **United Middle Belt Congress** formed to address the needs of people of the Middle Belt within the colony's political arena. In the early 1960s, while the North clamored to remain a semiautonomous region, people of the Middle Belt entertained a similar idea. The creation of 12 states, however, broke up the Middle Belt. Some politicians describe the region as the "glue" that holds the North and South together as well as a "buffer" that keeps them at peace. *See also* MINORITY GROUPS; POLITICAL PARTIES; STATE CREATION.

**MIDDLE-BELT PEOPLE'S PARTY (MBPP).** A **political party** that broke away from the Middle Belt League in July 1953. Its members chose to split because they disagreed with the league's alliance with the **Northern People's Congress**. This new party, with E. G. Gundu as president, campaigned in the **Middle Belt** for the creation of a Middle Belt State. The formation of this party was part of a broad trend in Nigeria of **minority groups** setting up political parties to meet their specific needs. In this case, it represented predominantly **Tiv** interests. *See also* MIDDLE-BELT STATE MOVEMENT.

**MIDDLE-BELT STATE MOVEMENT.** A movement led by **Chief Joseph S. Tarka** and his **United Middle Belt Congress** that campaigned for the creation of a Middle Belt State out of the **Northern Region**. The movement included supporters from several **ethnic groups** in the region, notably the **Tiv**. In 1967 and again in 1976, the goal of representation within a federal structure was achieved through **state creation**. *See also* MIDDLE-BELT PEOPLE'S PARTY.

**MID-WEST DEMOCRATIC FRONT (MDF).** A political alliance between the **Mid-West People's Congress** and branches of the **United People's Party** and **Action Group** in the early 1960s. It included all of the **political parties** that opposed the **National Council of Nigerian Citizens** (NCNC). After losing in the **Mid-Western Region**'s elections to the NCNC in 1964, the MDF joined the **Nigerian National Alliance**. By 1965, most members of the party had shifted their support to the NCNC. Those who remained in the MDF faced harassment from those who sided with the NCNC. In 1966, the party was banned. *See also* MID-WEST STATE MOVEMENT; MID-WESTERN STATE.

**MID-WEST PEOPLE'S CONGRESS (MPC).** A **political party** formed in 1963 to represent the interests of people of the **Mid-Western Region**, it was a branch of the **Northern People's Congress**. Like all other political parties, the Mid-West People's Congress was banned in 1966. *See also* MID-WEST DEMOCRATIC FRONT; MID-WEST STATE MOVEMENT; MID-WESTERN STATE.

**MID-WEST STATE MOVEMENT.** A political movement of ethnic **minority groups** in the **Western Region** that demanded the creation of a **Mid-Western Region**. It formed in 1956 and was led by **Chief Dennis Osadebay**. A major proponent was the **Benin Delta People's Party**. The campaign was successful, and the region was created in August 1963. The movement eventually joined the **National Council of Nigerian Citizens** and ceased to act independently. *See also* MID-WEST DEMOCRATIC FRONT; MID-WEST PEOPLE'S CONGRESS; MID-WESTERN STATE.

**MID-WESTERN REGION.** The Mid-Western Region (also referred to as the Mid-West Region) was a political designation for the area west of the **Niger River** and south of the Niger–Benue confluence. It was created from part of the **Western Region** in August 1963. Between August 1963 and February 1964, it was administered by **Chief Dennis Osadebay**. Starting in February 1964, the Mid-Western

Region was run by a governor. Between February 1964 and January 1966 its governor was **Chief Samuel Mariere**, with Osadebay as **premier**. **Major General David Ejoor** served as governor from January 1966 until August 1967, when the region was taken over by the secessionist **Republic of Biafra**. In 1967, **General Yakubu Gowon** reconfigured Nigeria's four regions into 12 states. The Mid-Western Region, however, really only changed in name; its boundaries remained unchanged. In August 1967 it was occupied by Biafran forces, and on 19–21 September 1967 the region was declared the independent Republic of Benin. On 21 September 1967, it was reclaimed by the federal government. The region's population is composed of several different **ethnic groups**, including the Edo, **Igbo**, and **Ijaw**, which are considered **minority groups** in Nigeria. Today, the Mid-Western Region no longer exists because it has been divided into several states. *See also* MID-WEST DEMOCRATIC FRONT; MID-WEST PEOPLE'S CONGRESS; MID-WEST STATE MOVEMENT; MID-WESTERN STATE; STATE CREATION.

**MID-WESTERN STATE.** Mid-Western State was created out of the **Mid-Western Region** in 1967 by **General Yakubu Gowon**. During the 1960s, it was a political and military battleground. **Ethnic groups** such as the Edo and **Ijaw** felt underrepresented by the federal government, but instead of getting their needs met, their land became a war zone during the federal government's fighting with the **Republic of Biafra** during the **civil war**. In 1976, the Mid-Western State became **Bendel State**, and in 1990s the state was divided into several new states. *See also* MID-WEST DEMOCRATIC FRONT; MID-WEST PEOPLE'S CONGRESS; MID-WEST STATE MOVEMENT; MINORITY GROUPS. STATE CREATION.

**MIGRATION.** The movement of people, voluntarily or by force, within Nigeria and to foreign destinations. Large numbers of Nigerians were involuntarily enslaved and shipped during the transatlantic **slave trade**, which contributed to a vibrant diaspora in the Americas. Before air travel was available, waves of Muslims from Nigeria traveled over land to Mecca on *hajj* (spiritual **pilgrimage**). Many of these pilgrims faced hardships such as illness or bankruptcy and settled in places such as Sudan. Most Nigerians have relocated because of financial necessity. Nigeria has struggled to reduce **unemployment**, which is high despite the number of advanced degree holders in the country. In the early 20th century, the most documented reasons for male migration included the desire to secure wages to cover marriage and familial expenses. Cash crops, such as **cocoa** and **cotton**, encouraged men to migrate. Many Nigerians worked in **Ghana**'s gold mines until they were expelled in 1969.

Colonialism sparked a large-scale, rural-to-urban migration as young men and women flooded the cities in search of wage labor. Southwestern Nigerian towns experienced major population booms of at least 40 percent. The **population** of **Lagos**, for example, rose from 126,000 in 1931 to 267,000 in 1951–1952. But migration did not always result in the finding of jobs. In 1945, Lagos had an estimated 20,000 unemployed individuals among 220,000 inhabitants. In many cases, Nigerians take part in seasonal work. It is common, for example, for men from **Kebbi State** in northwestern Nigeria to work on farms in the state during the harvest and then migrate to nearby towns and cities in search of work for the remainder of the year. Migration to destinations outside of Nigeria, particularly to North America and Europe, increased dramatically in the 1950s. Similarly, people from **Niger** are migrating to Nigeria in search of jobs and food. Many prominent Nigerians have received university degrees and military training overseas. This has caused complaints of a "brain drain," whereby the country's most talented and skilled migrate to Europe or North America.

**MINORITY GROUPS.** More than 250 **languages** are spoken in Nigeria, which implies that for each language there is a distinct **ethnic group** speaking it. The largest and most politically dominant ethnic groups in Nigeria are the **Hausa**, **Yoruba**, and **Igbo**. In many cases, the minority groups are subgroups of these three major groups. For example, the Western Igbo joined several other groups in the **Mid-West State Movement**, which would split them from the Igbo, who dominate states in the East. Each group maintains a regional dominance, placing minority groups on the fringes. Within each region, minority groups have organized into **political parties** and movements, demanding representation in the local and federal government and fair access to financial resources.

Minority demands emerged as early as the mid-1950s, when Nigeria was preparing for its independence as a federation of states. In September 1957, the **Willink Commission** was assigned the task of interviewing minority leaders and cataloging their concerns. The commission's report, released in 1958, recommended public outreach to allay fears of exclusion instead of the creation of new states. The most vocal minority groups in the second half of the 20th century have been the **Ijaw, Ogoni, Tiv**, and **Jukun**. The Tiv called for the creation of a **Middle Belt State** in the early 1960s to provide political space for themselves and other minority groups in the **Middle Belt**. Since 1960, however, **state creation** has become the primary way of handling concerns about minority oppression and exclusion, which has yielded few tangible results in the context of **economic** instability.

**MISS WORLD PAGEANT RIOT.** The Miss World pageant slated to take place in Nigeria in 2002 became the catalyst for debate and violence in **northern Nigeria**. Muslims were distraught over Nigeria's hosting of such an event, and a flippant comment about how the Prophet Muhammad would have chosen one of the contestants to be a wife, published by a journalist at *This Day* **newspaper**, sparked violence. Clashes between **Christians** and Muslims in the northern city of **Kaduna** in November 2002 lasted four days. The riots resulted in more than 200 dead, 1,000 injured, and 11,000 displaced from their homes. Twenty churches and eight mosques were also destroyed. Ultimately, the pageant was not hosted by Nigeria. This is just one of several instances since the mid-1970s in which faith-based violence has erupted in northern Nigeria. *See also* ISLAM; KAFANCHAN RIOTS; KANO RIOTS; MAIDUGURI.

**MODEKEKE.** A **Yoruba** subgroup who settled in **Ile-Ife** as refugees during the **Yoruba Wars** of the 19th century. The Modekeke did not fully integrate with those already living in Ile-Ife, which has created tension. Numerous times during the 20th century, this tension became violent. In August 1997, violence ensued over the proposed relocation of Ile-Ife's government office out of a Modekeke-dominated area. In January 1998, another spate of violence resulted in eight people being killed, and numerous cars and dwellings being burned over local government affairs. Since that time, however, Ile-Ife has regained its reputation as a peaceful town. *See also* ETHNIC GROUPS.

**MOHAMMED, GENERAL MURTALA RAMAT (1938–1976).** A **Hausa** military leader who was born in **Kano** in November 1938. As a young man, he completed his primary education in Kano and studied at Government College in **Zaria**. Mohammed attended the Royal Military Academy at Sandhurst (1960–1961) and joined the **army** (1961). In the early 1960s, he was part of a United Nations peacekeeping force in Central Africa. He took a leading role in the January 1966 military **coup d'état**. During **General Yakubu Gowon**'s rule, he served as chief of staff. British officials described him as an intelligent but ruthless nationalist. During the **civil war**, his relationship with Gowon became strained. He disagreed with Gowon's position on minimum force and limited bloodshed during the war. He was given command of the Second Division, which had been created to retake the **Mid-Western Region** from the secessionist **Republic of Biafra** forces. Mohammed left his command without permission to gather additional supplies for his division in London. As punishment, Gowon stripped him of his command and sent him back to the barracks.

After regaining his position in the military, Mohammed was promoted to brigadier general in October 1972. In July 1975, through a bloodless coup d'état, he became head of state. In August 1975, he conducted the "Mass Purge," which removed undesired public officials within the federal government and forced them into retirement. These included a number of high-ranking military officers and senior public servants, totaling about 10,000. After serving as head of state for less than a year, Mohammed was assassinated during a failed coup d'état attempt on 13 February 1976. The murderer, Lieutenant Colonel B. S. Dimka, was tried and executed with six others by a firing squad in March 1976. Nigeria's international airport in **Lagos** was named in memory of Mohammed. His picture is also on the ₦20 bill. Mohammed's younger sister, **Balaraba Ramat Yakubu**, is a well-known novelist and coordinator for the Murtala Mohammed Foundation. *See also* ARMED FORCES; OBASANJO, GENERAL OLUSEGUN.

**MONGUNO, ALHAJI CHIEF ALI (1926– ).** Of Muslim, **Kanuri** ancestry, Monguno was born in 1926 in the town of Monguno, in

**Borno State**. As a young man, he completed his primary and secondary studies in Borno State. He also attended the College of Arts, Science, and Technology (present-day **Ahmadu Bello University**) and the University of Edinburgh (1958–1959), with an interest in **education**. Monguno worked as a schoolteacher and councilor of education. In the 1940s, he worked as education secretary for the Borno Local Authority. From 1959 to 1966, he was a member of the Federal Parliament. He also worked as the minister of defense in 1965 and the federal minister of internal affairs from 1965 to 1966. Monguno was the federal commissioner for mines and power in 1971 and the federal commissioner for petroleum and energy in 1975. For the University of Calabar and University of Nigeria at **Nsukka**, he served as a pro-chancellor.

Monguno held the distinction of being president of the **Organization of Petroleum Exporting Countries** from 1972 to 1973. He was a member of the Constituent Assembly from 1977 to 1978. He was also a member of the **Northern People's Congress** and chairman of the **National Party of Nigeria** (1980–1983). In addition, he served on the Nigerian delegation to the United Nations for several years. He received the honorary titles Commander of the Order of the Federal Republic of Nigeria (1982) and *shettima* (**chief**) of Borno (1960). He also became an honorary citizen of several major cities across Africa and the Americas. Today, he runs a foundation that provides scholarships to bright young students to cover school fees.

**MOREMI.** In the **Yoruba oral tradition**, Moremi was a **woman** with charm and wit who saved her people in **Ile-Ife** from attacks by the **Igbo** sometime prior to the 14th century. She allowed herself to be captured by Igbo warriors. The Igbo ruler was enchanted by her and told her secret information about future attacks planned on her town. When Moremi escaped, she warned the people of Ile-Ife, who then prepared for the arrival of the Igbo warriors disguised in raffia, carrying lit torches. Because her people were protected, the Yoruba gods asked for the sacrifice of her only son, Oluorogbo, to Esinmirin, a river god in the **Yoruba religion**. In Ile-Ife today, the annual Edi festival is celebrated in her honor. The Edi festival lasts seven days, and drumming, otherwise an integral part of any celebration, is forbidden. It takes place when the **yams** have been harvested in the dry season. The days' activities include driving out evil, lighting the symbolic flame, and wrestling competitions.

**MORGAN COMMISSION.** The Morgan Commission was headed by Justice Adeyinka Morgan. It was launched in 1963 to review the salaries and conditions of **civil service** workers in Nigeria and completed its work one year later. The formation of the commission was prompted by the **Joint Action Committee**'s agitation. The inquiry was prompted by a workers' strike in September of that year. The commission recommended a significant increase in wages for junior civil servants and private workers as well as a new daily wage system. The report's release was scheduled for April, but it was delayed until the **trade unions** launched a general strike. The commission suggested dividing the country into four sections and assigning a minimum wage to each. The government accepted the recommendations, but with minor changes. *See also* UNITED LABOUR CONGRESS.

**MOVEMENT FOR DEMOCRACY AND SOCIAL JUSTICE.** One of only nine **political parties** approved by **General Alhaji Abdulsalami Abubakar**'s government to run candidates for the 1999 **election**. It was led by a former police chief, Mohammed Yusuf.

**MOVEMENT FOR THE EMANCIPATION OF THE NIGER DELTA (MEND).** An organization formed in 2006 for the purpose of launching an armed campaign against **petroleum** companies operating in the **Niger Delta**. Although the structure of the movement and its membership are unclear, its demands are clear. Several men have declared themselves its founders—Henry Okah, Jomo Gbomoo, and Godswill Tamono, to name a few—which suggests that the movement is at best loosely organized across the delta. It insists that the oil companies operating in the delta must leave. It has threatened to, and been partially successful in, crippling Nigeria's petroleum export industry. Thus far, MEND has forced a reduction in production of 20 percent in 2007. It stepped up its attacks in the months leading up to the April 2007 **elections** to ensure that the pollution and poverty issues of the Niger Delta were top political priorities. In 2008, MEND declared an "oil war," renewing attacks on oil companies and their facilities. Numerous oil pipeline explosions and facility damage, in addition to the kidnapping of oil workers, have been attributed to this movement. Oil companies have paid large ransoms for the release of oil workers. Two questions about this movement still remain unanswered: Is it responsible for all the oil disruptions? Is it an honest activist movement, or a vigilante group enticed by money and control? The movement takes advantage of terrain by using the complicated network of creeks in the delta as its place of operation and refuge. The organization, or its branches, communicates via e-mail to Western media. *See also* MOVEMENT FOR THE SURVIVAL OF THE OGONI PEOPLE.

**MOVEMENT FOR THE SURVIVAL OF THE OGONI PEOPLE (MOSOP).** An activist organization based in the **Niger Delta** that represented the political and economic demands of the **Ogoni** people. It was established in 1992 and led by **Ken Saro-Wiwa**. The organization argued that **petroleum** production, namely by Shell Petroleum Development Company (SPDC), was destroying the **water**, air, and land on which they depended. Members of the movement agitated for greater access to oil revenues and political autonomy. At different times, they demanded the withdrawal of Shell and compensation for the environmental destruction it had caused. Saro-Wiwa focused on drawing international attention to the Ogoni's plight. The Nigerian government, which had a sizable stake in the company's operations, responded to the movement's protests with brute force. In November 1995, eight of its members, including Saro-Wiwa, were arrested for murder, tried by a biased military **court**, and sentenced to death by hanging. After the death of **General Sani Abacha** in 1998, MOSOP called for the release of all remaining members from prison. The organization has continued a scaled-down version of its campaign against SPDC, focusing on the company's construction of new oil facilities and pipelines. In 2008, MOSOP criticized the government for failing to support the **Niger Delta Development Commission**. *See also* MOVEMENT FOR THE EMANCIPATION OF THE NIGER DELTA.

**MUHAMMADU, KANTA (?–1556).** Muhammadu is believed to have been the founder and first *kanta* (ruler) of **Kebbi**, one of the **Hausa Kingdoms**. This *kanta* was part of the conquering force of

Askia Muhammed of the Songhay Empire in the 16th century. According to legend, Muhammadu broke from Askia over the unequal distribution of acquired treasures and pursued his own interests. Using a strong army, Kanta expanded Kebbi over several other Hausa Kingdoms. He built a fortified wall around Birkini Kebbi and fiercely defended his territory and political power. At the end of the 16th century, Moors threatened Askia Muhammed's political hold, causing him to seek refuge in Kebbi. Muhammadu, however, turned him away. Shortly after, Kebbi split into several small states.

**MUSA, ALHAJI ABUBAKAR BALARABE (1936– ).** Born in August 1936 in Kaya, in **Kaduna State**, Musa completed his primary and secondary studies in **Kaduna** and **Zaria**. He also attended several colleges in England from 1961 to 1969. In Nigeria, he worked as a clerk, schoolteacher (1955–1960), and accountant (1969–1970). He served as governor of Kaduna State for one year during the **Second Republic**. In 1981, he was impeached by the Kaduna State House of Assembly over an ideological clash. He was arrested and detained from 1984 to 1985. He was a member of the **People's Redemption Party** and the **Social Democratic Party**. In 2005, he was chairman of the Conference of Nigerian Political Parties. Musa has been openly critical of the **Independent National Electoral Commission** and fraudulent activities that occurred during the April 2007 presidential **election**.

**MUSEUMS.** Nigeria is home to several museums displaying Nigerian **art** and historical artifacts. The National Museum, located in **Lagos**, was established in 1957 and is the largest and has the finest collection of Nigerian art. On display at the National Museum is the bullet-holed car in which **General Murtala Mohammed** was assassinated. The Jos Museum Complex, which opened in 1952, has one of Nigeria's best collections of historical artifacts outside Lagos; it houses an exhibit on **tin** mining, **railroad** construction, and ancient artwork. A museum in **Zaria** has an exhibit on Nigeria's **civil war**. The Ile-Ife Museum offers a small collection of local artifacts intermixed with empty cases for valuable items currently on display in more prestigious museums in North America and Europe. Most museums in Nigeria opened in the mid-1950s and have struggled to remain open. Some of the freshest modern art being produced in Nigeria is displayed at restaurants and private shops.

**MUSIC.** Nigeria has a rich musical history, which ranges from praise poems to **hip-hop music**. Nigeria has produced several international stars and styles of music. **Oral traditions** often include not only spoken but also musical features. In **Borgu**, musical instruments such as a *kakaki* (trumpet) and *tambari* (royal drum) are incorporated as symbols of authority. **Alhaji Mamman Shata** is a famous **Hausa** musician. In religious worship, music is played to appease the gods or communally express devotion and praise in modern **religions**. A traditional Hausa band may include three *kakaki*, three *alghaita* (reed wind instrument), and several drums. Popular music styles that developed in the 20th century include **Afrobeat**, **Highlife**, and **Juju**. Hip-hop is currently probably the most popular form of music in Nigeria. *See also* NATIONAL ANTHEM.

**MUSLIMS.** *See* ISLAM.

## – N –

**NAIRA.** *See* CURRENCY.

**NASIR COMMISSION.** *See* BOUNDARY ADJUSTMENT COMMISSION.

**NASARAWA STATE.** Created in 1996 out of **Plateau State**, Nasarawa is one of Nigeria's current 36 states. It is located in central Nigeria, with the **Benue River** creating a natural southern boundary. It is considered part of the **Middle Belt** region. The capital is the town of Lafia. Its economic activity centers on the cultivation of various foodstuffs such as **yams, cassava**, beans, tomatoes, oranges, and **bananas** and the mining of **salt**, iron, and semiprecious stones such as amethyst. The people of Nasarawa are ethnically diverse and include, among others, the **Tiv, Hausa, Fulani**, and **Kanuri**. **Christianity** and **Islam** are the major **religions** in the state. *See also* STATE CREATION.

**NATIONAL AFRICA COMPANY (NAC).** The National Africa Company was started by **Sir George Taubman Goldie** in 1882 to take over the **United African Company**. The trading company operated in **southern Nigeria** along the **Niger River** at the Niger–Benue confluence and used **Lokoja** as its operations center. It also traded and secured territory in the **Oil Rivers**. The treaties and trade arrangements made by the NAC, of questionable validity, were recognized by the British government. NAC became the **Royal Niger Company** in 1886, when it received a charter from the British government. *See also* OIL RIVERS PROTECTORATE.

**NATIONAL ANTHEM.** Since **independence** on 1 October 1960, Nigeria has used two different national anthems. The first was composed at independence and started with the phrase "Nigeria we hail thee." The second anthem was developed in 1978 by a committee, which held a contest for new lyrics, open to all Nigerians. Five finalists were selected, and the lyrics were set to **music** composed by several musicians. This anthem starts with the phrase "Arise, O compatriots." *See also* FLAG.

**NATIONAL ASSEMBLY.** The official name of the legislature in the **Second Republic** and **Fourth Republic**. In the Second Republic, it was made up of a Senate with 95 seats and a House of Representatives with 449 seats. The **Third Republic** was also supposed to have a National Assembly, composed of a 91-seat Senate and a 593-seat House of Representatives, but it was annulled. The Fourth Republic's assembly includes 109 senators and 360 representatives. Nigeria is currently in its sixth National Assembly.

**NATIONAL CHURCH OF NIGERIA.** A faith-based extension of the **Zikist Movement**. It was formed in November 1948 in Aba by K. O. K. Onyioha and other supporters of **Nnamdi Azikiwe**. This church served as an alternative to European-dominated **Christian** churches. Weekly services included sermons based on liberation theology, emphasizing anticolonial sentiment through Christian scripture. Nigerian leaders, such as **Sir Herbert Macaulay** and Azikiwe, were made saints. The church had dissolved by 1960. *See also* RELIGION.

**NATIONAL COMMISSION FOR REHABILITATION.** Part of a program launched in 1969 by **General Yakubu Gowon**. The goal of the commission was to provide basic living supplies such as food and clothing to areas of the country debilitated by the **civil war** and to coordinate voluntary agencies.

**NATIONAL CONCILIATION COMMITTEE.** A committee set up in 1966 after the September massacre of **Igbo** people in **northern Nigeria**. Its members included **Chief Obafemi Awolowo, Sir Adetokunbo Ademola, Chief Samuel Mariere**, Samuel Aluko, **Alhaji Sir Kashim Ibrahim**, and others. The purpose of the committee was to restore negotiations and trust between the federal military government and **Chief Chukwuemeka Ojukwu** of the **Eastern Region**. However, the region failed to fully cooperate, and the committee collapsed. Ultimately, the committee's efforts failed and a **civil war** took place. *See also* GOWON, GENERAL YAKUBU.

**NATIONAL COUNCIL OF NIGERIA AND THE CAMEROONS (NCNC).** In August 1944, a conference was called in **Lagos** with the intention of bringing together politically conscious individuals from all of Nigeria. The inaugural meeting was held in Glover Memorial Hall by the **Nigerian Union of Students**. A variety of organizations attended, including **trade unions**, professional associations, and cultural organizations. The cultural organization **Ibo Federal Union**, for example, was well-represented, as were Cameroonian interests. Out of this conference came one of Nigeria's most important **political parties**, the **National Council of Nigeria and the Cameroons**. It was conceptualized as a national party, with the majority of its supporters being from the **Eastern Region**. At the first meeting, **Sir Herbert Macaulay** was elected as president and **Nnamdi Azikiwe** as general secretary. In 1951, it dominated the **Eastern Region**'s **House of Assembly**. The purpose of the NCNC was to promote the **independence** of Nigeria as well as social equality and **religious** tolerance, which was implemented through its **National Church of Nigeria**.

In the NCNC's early years, it rivaled the **Action Group** for the **Western Region**. In 1954, the NCNC merged with the **Northern Elements Progressive Union** (NEPU). In 1959, its name was changed to the **National Council of Nigerian Citizens** (which has also been referred to as the National Convention of Nigerian Citizens) as a result of southern Cameroon splitting from Nigeria. In 1963, the NCNC/NEPU coalition ended. In 1966, the party was banned by the military government. *See also* IBO STATE UNION; NATIONAL EMERGENCY COMMITTEE; NATIONAL INDEPENDENCE PARTY.

**NATIONAL COUNCIL OF NIGERIAN CITIZENS (NCNC).** Formed out of the **National Council of Nigeria and the Cameroons** in 1959, it is also referred to in historical works as the National Convention of Nigerian Citizens and National Congress of Nigerian Citizens. This **political party** was banned, along with all others, in 1966.

**NATIONAL COUNCIL OF TRADE UNIONS OF NIGERIA (NCTUN).** Formed in 1957 out of the **All-Nigeria Trade Union Federation**, NCTUN was a central promoter of the establishment of democratic **trade unions**. In January 1959, the National Labour Peace Committee facilitated the merging of the All-Nigerian Trade Union Federation and the NCTUN into the **Trade Union Congress of Nigeria**.

**NATIONAL COUNCIL OF WOMEN'S SOCIETIES.** Formed in 1958 in **Ibadan**, the council was the result of the merging of the **Women's Movement of Nigeria** (later, the Nigerian Council of Women), Women's Improvement Society, and Ibadan Progressive Union (Women's Section). It engaged in nonprofit activities such as celebrating Nigeria Women's Day, awarding **educational** scholarships, publishing a newsletter, and investing in development programs for **women**. Today, the council has branches in most states of the country, with its headquarters in **Lagos**. Its motto is "Service in Unity."

**NATIONAL DEFENCE AND SECURITY COUNCIL.** A council created by **General Ibrahim Babangida** in January 1993 in conjunction with the **Transitional Council** to replace the **Armed Forces Ruling Council**. Babangida served as the chairman. *See also* SUPREME MILITARY COUNCIL.

**NATIONAL DEMOCRATIC COALITION (NADECO).** A political organization formed in 1994 in response to **General Sani Abacha**'s regime and the failed **election of 12 June 1993**. It was founded by **Chief Michael Ajasin** and others. **Chief Arthur Nwankwo, Commodore Ebitu Ukiwe, and Chief Anthony Enahoro** were members of the coalition. It was composed of political organizations across the country. Members called for the cancellation of the national **constitutional conference**. Shortly after its formation, Ajasin, Enahoro, and others were detained. An attack at the airport in **Lagos** in 1996 was attributed to this organization.

**NATIONAL DIRECTORATE OF EMPLOYMENT.** A governmental organization formed in January 1987 to address Nigeria's high **unemployment** rate and **economic** decline. The Chukwuma Committee, created by **General Ibrahim Babangida** in March 1986, recommended its creation. The directorate was assigned the task of overseeing four schemes: National Youth Employment and Vocational Skills Development Programme, Small-Scale Industries and Graduate Employment Programme, Agricultural Sector Employment Programme, and Special Public Works Programme. The Graduate Self-Employment Scheme offered attractive loans to recent university graduates as a way of encouraging them to become self-employed instead of joining the saturated pool of job seekers. The programs also promoted the formation of cooperatives for craftsmen.

**NATIONAL ECONOMIC COUNCIL (NEC).** Created in 1954, the NEC included representatives from the three regions—**Western, Eastern,** and **Northern**—and held meetings to discuss the national **economy**. The membership of the council included the prime minister, **premiers** of each of the regional governments, and the minister of finance and economic development. The council proposed development projects and channeled foreign aid to them. Since the **Second Republic**, the council has advised the president on matters of economic development. The 1999 **constitution** assigned the vice president to the position of chairman of the council. In 2007, it was reinvigorated by President **Umaru Musa Yar'Adua**.

**NATIONAL ECONOMIC RECONSTRUCTION FUND.** A fund created in 1988 to serve as a national source of financing for small-scale businesses, particularly industrial ones, up to ₦10 million with a grace period of up to three years. The African Development Bank gave $230 million to the fund, which also received $50 million from the former Czechoslovakia. The Nigerian government contributed ₦300 million through the Central Bank of Nigeria. Ultimately, the reconstruction fund has achieved mixed results and progress has been slow. *See also* BANKING; ECONOMY.

**NATIONAL ELECTORAL COMMISSION (NEC).** A semi-independent organization created by **General Ibrahim Babangida** in September 1987 to organize and monitor all **elections** during the transition from military to civilian rule slated for 1993. The commission was composed of a chairman and eight members appointed by the president. All those involved in the commission were supposed to be nonpartisan men of integrity. The commission's activities also included registering two political parties to run in the elections. **Humphrey Nwobu Nwosu** served as its chairman. For the **election of 12 June 1993**, the commission was given the task of overseeing and tallying the votes. It bowed to pressure from Babangida to annul the results of the presidential election, proving it to be a tool of the regime. **General Sani Abacha** dismantled the commission in 1996 and replaced it with the **National Electoral Commission of Nigeria**. Two years later, **General Alhaji Abdulsalami Abubakar** created the **Independent Electoral Commission of Nigeria** to oversee elections as well. *See also* NATIONAL REPUBLICAN CONVENTION; SOCIAL DEMOCRATIC PARTY.

**NATIONAL ELECTORAL COMMISSION OF NIGERIA (NECON).** A commission created in 1996 by **General Sani Abacha** to prepare for the transition from military to civilian rule. It was charged with overseeing democratic **elections**. Most Nigerians viewed it as Abacha's political tool. It was dissolved and replaced with the **Independent National Electoral Commission** by **General Alhaji Abdulsalami Abubakar** in 1998.

**NATIONAL ELECTRIC POWER AUTHORITY (NEPA).** Established as a public corporation in 1972 under Decree No. 24 by **General Yakubu Gowon** to manage and develop Nigeria's **electricity** to reach all Nigerians continually, NEPA replaced the Electricity Corporation of Nigeria. Since 1996, private energy supply companies have been encouraged to supplement NEPA's activities. Because of its failure to reliably supply electricity to the majority of Nigerians, regardless of location, it acquired the critical name "Never Electric Power Always." In 2005, it was replaced by the Power Holding Company of Nigeria.

**NATIONAL EMERGENCY COMMITTEE.** A committee created in November 1949 by members of the **National Council of Nigeria and the Cameroons** and the **Nigerian Youth Movement** to foster a unified response to the shooting of 21 **coal** miners in **Enugu** by police during a strike. It was chaired by **Akinola Maja.** The committee organized public protests and a collective demand for the dismissal of the European police officer who ordered the shooting. In September 1950, the committee disbanded.

**NATIONAL EXECUTIVE COUNCIL.** In May 1966, the **Federal Executive Council** was turned into the National Executive Council through Decree No. 34. In July 1966, the National Executive Council was replaced by the restored Federal Executive Council. *See also* EXECUTIVE COUNCIL.

**NATIONAL HUMAN RIGHTS COMMISSION.** *See* HUMAN RIGHTS.

**NATIONAL INDEPENDENCE PARTY (NIP).** A **political party** formed on 23 February 1953 by **Eyo Ita** and several federal and regional ministers who had been ejected from the **National Council of Nigeria and the Cameroons** (NCNC). The NIP joined with the **United National Party** to oppose the NCNC, thereby supporting the **Action Group.** The National Independence Party attended the **constitutional conference** in London in 1953, but did not join other groups in the demand for "self-government in 1956." Overall, the party failed to gain much support. In 1954, the name of the party was changed to the United Nigeria Independent Party. *See also* SELF-GOVERNMENT MOTION CRISIS.

**NATIONAL JUDICIAL COUNCIL.** A regulatory and advisory judicial body established in 1999. The council comprises 23 members, mainly retired justices of the Supreme Court and chief justices of state **courts**. It also includes several representatives of the Nigerian Bar Association and members who are not lawyers or judges. It exercises a great deal of influence over the installment, punishment, and removal of judges at the national and state level. The **Judicial Service Commission** provides input on such procedures. The council also handles the judiciary finances. One of its strengths is its ability to review national policies and advise the president on them. *See also* LEGAL SYSTEM.

**NATIONAL MANPOWER BOARD.** A board established in 1964 in response to recommendations made by the Ashby Commission's report on **higher education**. It was designed to acquire data on the available skills and distribution of Nigeria's labor force. It identified geographic areas in need of manpower and made its recommendations to the **National Economic Council** and the Ministries of Labour and of Education. Today, the board provides statistical information and recommendations regarding **unemployment** and **education**, with a focus on vocational training. It works closely with the National Board for Technical Education.

**NATIONAL MILITARY GOVERNMENT.** An executive body established on 24 May 1966 as a result of Nigeria's first military **coup d'état**. It was declared the new governing body of Nigeria through Decree No. 24. This government began to transform Nigeria from a federation into a republic. It lasted until July 1966, when **General Yakubu Gowon** became Nigeria's new military head of state and returned Nigeria to a federal structure.

**NATIONAL PARTY OF NIGERIA (NPN).** Founded by **Alhaji Ibrahim Dasuki** and others in September 1978, this **political party** was led by **Chief M. K. O. Abiola**. It was one of five registered political parties allowed to form in preparation for the 1979 **elections**. **Major General Robert Adeyinka Adebayo** and **Chief Anthony Enahoro** served as executive members. The party's platform included social justice and national unity. **Chief Chukwuemeka Ojukwu** was a member of the party after his return to Nigeria from exile in 1982. **Michael Okpara**, **Kingsley Mbadiwe**, **Prince Adeleke Adedoyin**,

**Major General Hassan Katsina**, **Joseph Wayas**, and **Chief Kola-wole Balogun** also supported the party. At the 1979 elections, the party selected **Alhaji Shehu Shagari** from the North as president and **Alex Ifeanyichukwu Ekwueme** from the East as vice president. It also ran numerous candidates for the Senate and House of Representatives, with relative success. During the election process, the party formed an alliance with the **Nigerian People's Party**. Like all other political parties in Nigeria, in December 1983 the NPN was banned, and it eventually dissolved. *See also* GREAT NIGERIAN PEOPLE'S PARTY; PEOPLE'S REDEMPTION PARTY; UNITY PARTY OF NIGERIA.

**NATIONAL POVERTY ERADICATION PROGRAM.** The federal government developed this program to eliminate poverty in Nigeria. To launch the program, it dedicated $3.8 million in 2004. The states that received a portion of this money invested in microcredit projects facilitated through the Revolving Micro-Credit Fund Scheme. *See also* ECONOMY.

**NATIONAL PROVIDENT FUND.** A fund created by the national government in 1961 and modified by the Amendment Act of 1964 and Decree No. 40 in 1967. It was a compulsory savings scheme into which nonpensionable workers and their employers paid monthly. Retired Nigerians age 55 and up, as well as physically and mentally handicapped individuals, were eligible to draw from the National Provident Fund. In July 1994, it was replaced by the Nigeria Social Insurance Trust Fund. *See also* CIVIL SERVICE; UNEMPLOYMENT.

**NATIONAL REPUBLICAN CONVENTION (NRC).** The **National Republican Convention** was established in 1989. It was one of only two **political parties** legally allowed by the **National Electoral Commission** to operate, by order of **General Ibrahim Babangida**. The party's membership largely included former supporters of the **National Party of Nigeria** and the Nigerian People's Congress. It formed to represent the right-of-center vote. In the **election of 12 June 1993**, the NRC ran its presidential candidate, **Alhaji Bashir Tofa**, against the rival **Social Democratic Party** (SDP). Several others competed unsuccessfully to win the party's nomination, including

**Chief E. C. Iwuanyanwu** and **Alhaji Umaru Shinkafi**. When it appeared that Tofa was losing the election, Babangida annulled the election results, and the attempt to transition from military to civilian government failed. Many argue that the NRC's candidate had lost to the SDP's. In 1994, **General Sani Abacha** banned the NRC. *See also* ABIOLA, CHIEF M. K. O; THIRD REPUBLIC.

**NATIONAL SOLIDARITY MOVEMENT (NSM).** One of only nine **political parties** allowed to field candidates for the 1999 **election**. It ran candidates against the dominant **People's Democratic Party**.

**NATIONAL YOUTH SERVICES CORPS (NYSC).** Since June 1973, all Nigerians 18 years of age and older have been required to devote one year after secondary school to **civil service** work organized by the NYSC. This program was created through Decree No. 24 in October 1972 and was written into Nigeria's **constitution** in 1979. The scheme was developed by **Adedeji Adebayo**, a professor of public administration who also served as federal economic commissioner under **General Yakubu Gowon**. Some students work in the public **education** system at all levels as teachers or administrators. The civil service program assists young people in job placement. The national government also uses the NYSC as a way of exposing young people to new areas of the country and diversifying regional populations. For example, it is not uncommon for the NYSC to assign a young person from **Ibadan** to teach secondary school children in **Kano**. Several NYSC workers going from the South to the North established **Charismatic Christian** churches and organizations, such as the Fellowship of Christian Students and Calvary Ministries. Students who have graduated from universities or polytechnic schools are required to serve one year in a different state than their own. Married **women** are allowed to accompany their husbands to the state in which the men live. The scheme exposes young men and women to new aspects of Nigerian culture.

**NATIONALIZATION.** *See* INDIGENIZATION.

**NATIVE AUTHORITY.** A body of indigenous governance created by the British colonial government, particularly in **southern Nigeria**. The Native Authorities were colonial-appointed **chiefs** whose tasks included hearing minor court cases, enforcing colonial rule, managing finances (including **tax** collection), and recruiting labor when necessary. The British identified influential men and appointed them as chiefs. However, these chiefs often experienced a loss in legitimate authority. *See also* INDIRECT RULE; NATIVE TREASURIES; WARRANT CHIEFS.

**NATIVE COURTS.** Courts introduced in southeastern Nigeria by the British colonial administration in 1900. They were divided into two categories: minor courts run by local **chiefs** appointed by the district commissioner, and native councils, similar to the former but presided over by the district commissioner. Minor courts tried minor civil and criminal cases; the native council heard criminal cases and imposed large fines. These courts have been replaced by modern courts in a multi-tier structure that includes secular and **Shari'a** systems. *See also* INDIRECT RULE; WARRANT CHIEFS.

**NATIVE TREASURIES.** A governing body created by the British colonial government in 1906 by the Native Revenue Proclamation. It was designed to legitimize, but not standardize, the various forms of **taxation** collected in the **Protectorate of Northern Nigeria**. It explicitly instituted the practice of sharing tax revenue between the colonial government and the **Native Authorities**. In short, the foundation for the native treasuries was being established. One year later, a new Native Authority Proclamation conferred upon recognized **chiefs** the responsibility of not only collecting taxes, but also upholding colonial law in areas under their jurisdiction. The purpose of the native treasuries was to designate money for a chief's administration through an approved system. In 1911, native treasuries were officially created in the North. The **amalgamation of Nigeria** in 1914 prompted the expansion of native treasuries all over Nigeria. *See also* INDIRECT RULE.

**NATURAL GAS.** *See* PETROLEUM.

**NAVY.** *See* ARMED FORCES.

**NEW PARTNERSHIP FOR AFRICAN DEVELOPMENT (NEPAD).** A national partnership established in July 2001 at a summit meeting of the Organization of African Unity (present-day **African Union**). The principles and objectives of the program were developed by the presidents of Nigeria, Egypt, Senegal, South Africa, and Algeria. The goals of NEPAD include reviving Africa's economy and stimulating long-term sustainable development. Its headquarters is in South Africa. Nigeria played a significant role in its creation, with General Olusegun Obasanjo as chairman of the steering committee. *See also* ECONOMIC COMMUNITY OF WEST AFRICAN STATES.

**NEWSPAPERS.** Nigeria has a long tradition of newspaper publication. It is second only to South Africa in terms of numbers of circulating newspapers and readership. Financial circumstances, however, have substantially reduced the number of newspapers. Nigeria's newspapers are available in a number of **languages**. The first newspaper to be published in Nigeria was *Iwe Ihorin* (meaning "The Paper with the News" in the **Yoruba language**) in 1859. At the time it cost 30 **cowry shells**. The *Lagos Weekly Record* was started by John Payne Jackson, a Liberian, in 1891, and lasted until 1921. It was read by a select group of literate anticolonialists in **Lagos** and served as a vehicle for anticolonial sentiment. Newspapers expanded beyond Lagos in the early 1900s with the establishment of the Tika-Tore printing company, which maintained a network of small presses across Nigeria.

Major newspapers that circulated prior to 1960 include the *Daily Times, Daily Service*, and *West African Pilot*. The *Daily Times* of Lagos was first published in 1926. In 1937, **Nnamdi Azikiwe** established the *West African Pilot*. **Kingsley Mbadiwe** started the *Daily Telegraph* in 1936. The *Nigerian Chronicle* was established in 1908 by Christopher Kumolu Johnson and lasted until 1915. It was the first newspaper that took the bold step of placing Nigeria in its name. **Alhaji Abubakar Imam** was the editor of the **Hausa language** newspaper *Gaskiya Ta Fi Kwabo* (*The Truth Is Better Than a Penny*) from 1939 to 1954. The *Daily Express*, known as *Daily Service* in the mid-1900s, was the official newspaper of the **Nigerian Youth Movement** and, later, **Action Group**. Its first editor was **Ernest S. Ikoli**. The *Nigerian Pioneer*, established by Sir Kitoyi Ajasa and distributed from Lagos from 1914 to 1934, had little success. On the one hand, it was criticized for appearing pro-government; on the other, it was praised for thoroughly interpreting government policy to its readers.

Major newspapers that circulated after 1960 reflect a greater regional balance and included *New Nigerian* (based in **Kaduna**), *Daily Express* (Lagos), and *Nigerian Outlook* (**Enugu**). In the last 30 years, the newspaper business in Nigeria has been modified. The number of newspapers has declined, as well as the readership. Issues of ethnic polarization, prevalent in Nigeria's **economy** and political system, have also affected the newspapers. Meanwhile, **corruption** and lack of press freedom have dampened innovative and investigative journalism. During the 1990s, non-Yoruba readers complained of a **Yoruba** bias in the press. Today, the most widely circulated newspapers are the *Daily Times* and *Guardian.* Sensationalist newspapers are also quite popular in Nigeria. Several of Nigeria's newspapers, such as *Vanguard* and *This Day*, are now available online. *See also* JAKANDE, ALHAJI LATEEF KAYODE; JOSE, ALHAJI ISMAIL BABATUNDE.

**NIGER, REPUBLIC OF.** The country north of Nigeria that shares much of **northern Nigeria**'s culture and history. Over 50 percent of Niger's population is **Hausa**, with a small percentage of **Kanuri**. The **Sokoto Caliphate** of the 19th century extended into Niger. The country's current struggle with drought, famine, and poor economic performance has prompted many of its citizens to relocate to Nigeria in search of opportunities. *See also* MIGRATION.

**NIGER COAST CONSTABULARY.** A constabulary composed of Africans but with British colonial leadership, required to protect British settlement and trading in the **Niger Delta**. It replaced the **Royal Niger Constabulary** in 1894. Its headquarters was in **Calabar**. The Niger Coast Constabulary engaged in notable battles, such as the **Akassa Massacre** of 1895.

**NIGER COAST PROTECTORATE.** In 1893, the **Oil Rivers Protectorate**, established piecemeal by the **Royal Niger Company**, was renamed the Niger Coast Protectorate. It was situated in southeastern Nigeria and included the **Niger Delta** region and the cities of

Calabar and **Benin**. After the Royal Niger Company lost its charter in 1900, the Niger Coast Protectorate became the **Protectorate of Southern Nigeria**.

**NIGER DELTA.** An ecologically delicate wetland composed of small islands and mangroves at the mouth of the **Niger** and **Benue Rivers** on the coast of Nigeria. It covers an estimated 36,000 square kilometers. In 2000, **General Olusegun Obasanjo** expanded the list of states considered part of the Niger Delta from three to nine. They include **Abia**, **Akwa Ibom**, **Bayelsa**, **Cross River**, **Delta**, **Edo**, **Imo**, **Ondo**, and **Rivers**. The Niger Delta, as a region, contains over 40 **ethnic groups** and an estimated 20 million people. The most vocal ethnic groups in the area in the past 15 years have been the **Ogoni** and the **Ijaw**. The delta also includes, among others, the Urhobo and Itsekiri peoples. During the past few decades, the Niger Delta has been the center of conflict among the government, foreign **petroleum** producers, and local citizens. Several distinct clashes and political confrontations have taken place, but they are collectively referred to as the Niger Delta conflict. President **Umaru Musa Yar'Adua** has promised to make the Niger Delta a top priority, illustrated by his selecting **Goodluck Jonathan**, an Ijaw politician, as his vice president in 2007. However, people in the Niger Delta have heard this kind of rhetoric before and simply respond by saying that the government's plans are "in the pipeline." *See also* MINORITY GROUPS; NIGER DELTA CONFLICT; NIGER DELTA DEVELOPMENT BOARD; NIGER DELTA DEVELOPMENT COMMISSION; NIGER RIVER.

**NIGER DELTA CONFLICT.** People of the **Niger Delta** rely heavily on farming and fishing for their livelihood. Large-scale **petroleum** production in the region has disrupted their way of life. Several distinct clashes have taken place in the past two decades that are collectively addressed as the Niger Delta Conflict. Several different groups, primarily organized along ethnic lines, have utilized a combination of violent and peaceful means to express their grievances. The frustrations of **ethnic groups** such as the **Ogoni** and **Ijaw** include a lack of representation in government, lack of untarnished land and **water**, and lack of financial compensation for living in such poor conditions. As a result, the area has been engulfed in a series of confrontations between the oil producers, local inhabitants, and the Nigerian government.

Complaints of this nature surfaced as early as the 1970s, but it was not until the early 1990s that they received attention from the international community. The **Movement for the Survival of the Ogoni People**, led by **Ken Saro-Wiwa**, served as the voice of the Ogoni. The organization publicized the damages oil production had caused in their territory, with particular grievances directed at the Nigerian government and the Shell Petroleum Development Company. Similarly, the Ijaw coordinated a youth movement through the **Ijaw Youth Council** in 1998 to respond to the industry. Since about 2006, the kidnapping of oil workers, and family members, has been a frequent occurrence. In 2007, several kidnappings took place. The **Movement for the Emancipation of the Niger Delta** has claimed responsibility for many of the kidnappings and other violent acts, committed in hopes of disrupting production and pressuring the oil companies to leave.

A shortage of adequate investment combined with environmental destruction has left many people in the Niger Delta in serious poverty. As a result, dangerous activities such as tapping oil pipelines and siphoning have resulted in the regular occurrence of explosions and flammable oil leaks. All of these activities have turned the Niger Delta into an increasingly dangerous and volatile region. The government has attempted to build infrastructure and encourage investment in the region through various schemes such as the **Niger Delta Development Board** and the **Oil Mineral Producing Area Development Commission**, but so far these have been insufficient. *See also* GENOCIDE; MINORITY GROUPS; NIGER DELTA DEVELOPMENT COMMISSION.

**NIGER DELTA CONGRESS (NDC).** A **political party** created by Harold Dappa Biriye and others in 1959 to represent the interests of people living in the **Niger Delta**. It emerged out of the Chiefs and People's Conference in the Rivers Area. Membership comprised primarily **Ijaw** people. The congress aligned itself with the **Northern People's Congress** during the 1959 federal **elections**. One major goal of the group was to press for the **Niger Delta** to become a federal territory. For the 1964 elections, the NDC aligned itself with the **Nigerian National Democratic Party** and the **Mid-West Democratic Front** as part of the **Nigerian National Alliance**. The congress, like all other **political parties**, was banned in 1966. Since the 1990s, the party has reemerged, with strong statements about the liberation of the Niger Delta.

**NIGER DELTA DEVELOPMENT BOARD.** Agitation by organizations and **political parties**, such as the **Niger Delta Congress**, during the 1950s resulted in some special attention being paid to the **Niger Delta** just prior to independence. The **Willink Commission** recommended that a review of the situation in the Niger Delta be conducted, which led to the formation of the Niger Delta Development Board in 1961. The board was assigned the task of looking into **Ijaw** concerns about economic development in the region and proposing new **agricultural** and industrial schemes over a 10-year period. The board played a purely advisory role and was not assigned the task of assessing the impact of **petroleum** production, particularly in terms of environmental damage. It was replaced by the **Niger Delta Development Commission** in 2000. *See also* OIL MINERAL PRODUCING AREAS DEVELOPMENT COMMISSION.

**NIGER DELTA DEVELOPMENT COMMISSION.** A commission created in June 2000 by **General Olusegun Obasanjo** to review and prescribe ways in which the federal government could economically develop the **Niger Delta**. It replaced the poorly run **Oil Mineral Producing Areas Development Commission** of 1992. The chairman is Samuel Edem. Shortly after its formation, the commission was criticized for being ineffective. In 2008, **Movement for the Survival of the Ogoni People** strongly criticized the government for failing to meet its financial obligation to the commission. *See also* ECONOMY; NIGER DELTA CONFLICT.

**NIGER RIVER.** A major river that starts in present-day Guinea and flows eastward through Mali and **Niger**, traveling some 4,350 kilometers. In Nigeria, it meets the **Benue River** at **Lokoja** and flows south, forming the fertile **Niger Delta** on the coast. Within the Niger Delta, the Niger River splits into a myriad of creeks (referred to as the **Oil Rivers**). To Europeans, the Niger River was one of many mysteries of Africa. On their maps, they tried to connect it to the Nile River. In the 1790s, the African Association of Great Britain encouraged its members to find the source of the Niger River. Starting in 1795, **Mungo Park** explored the river on two separate expeditions. In 1806, he reached the Bubaru rapids at Bussa and died. **Richard and John Lander** explored the Niger River in the 1830s, linking Park's river with the Oil Rivers at the Niger Delta. The Niger River is the longest and most important river in West Africa.

**NIGER STATE.** Niger State is located in northeastern Nigeria, with its western boundary shared with **Benin** and its southern boundary on the **Niger River**. It was created in 1976 out of **North-Western State** and is named for the Niger River. It is Nigeria's largest state. The capital is the town of Minna. Within Niger State are the impressive Lake Kainji National Park (the largest of its kind in Nigeria) and the Kaduna River. It is also home to two hydroelectric dams, Kainji and Shiroro. The people of Niger State are primarily members of the **Nupe**, **Hausa**, and **Fulani ethnic groups**, making Hausa and **Fula** the dominant **languages**. **Islam** and **Christianity** are the dominant **religions**. Niger State is one of the 12 northern states that have incorporated aspects of **Shari'a** into their criminal law. It is one of Nigeria's current 36 states. Economic activities in the state include the cultivation of foodstuffs (grains, beans, **groundnuts**, and fruits), herding of livestock, and fishing. Niger State is also a producer of **cotton** and timber. *See also* STATE CREATION.

**NIGERIA ADVANCE PARTY (NAP).** A party established by Tunji Braithwaite in September 1978 to run in the 1979 general **elections**. It promised to overhaul and reinvigorate Nigeria's **educational** system and devise a communal **agricultural** system. It was prevented from running in the 1979 elections, but met the qualifications for the 1983 elections. It never won any seats. Like all other political parties, it was banned in 1983. Since the emergence of the **Fourth Republic**, however, the Nigeria Advance Party has regrouped.

**NIGERIAN AGRICULTURAL BANK.** *See* BANKING.

**NIGERIAN ATOMIC ENERGY COMMISSION.** A government body formed in August 1976 through Decree No. 46 to promote the development of atomic energy in Nigeria, with a particular interest in generating **electricity**. The commission was assigned the task of finding radioactive materials and constructing nuclear installations. It is also responsible for disposing of nuclear waste. **General Olusegun Obasanjo** reinvigorated the commission in 2006. The commission works closely with the International Atomic Energy Agency.

**NIGERIAN BANK FOR COMMERCE AND INDUSTRY.** *See* BANKING.

**NIGERIAN BAPTIST CONVENTION.** *See* BAPTIST CHURCH.

**NIGERIAN BREWERIES.** *See* ALCOHOL.

**NIGERIAN BROADCASTING CORPORATION.** *See* RADIO BROADCASTING; TELEVISION BROADCASTING.

**NIGERIAN COUNCIL.** After the **amalgamation of Nigeria** in 1914, **Sir Frederick Lugard** felt it necessary to set up a 36-member advisory council to assist the colonial governor. The council included British colonial representatives (the governor, members of his executive council, residents, secretaries, and nongovernmental Britons). It also included six Nigerian **chiefs** and Nigerian representatives from **Lagos**, **Calabar**, and **Benin**. The chiefs rarely attended the meetings due to a lack of interest. It was officially disbanded in 1922 by the **Clifford Constitution** and replaced by the **Legislative Council**.

**NIGERIAN DEFENCE ACADEMY.** *See* ARMED FORCES.

**NIGERIAN ENTERPRISES PROMOTIONS DECREE.** *See* INDIGENIZATION.

**NIGERIAN INSTITUTE OF INTERNATIONAL AFFAIRS (NIIA).** An institution created in 1961 to promote independent nonprofit research. It has a research library located in **Lagos** and, as the name suggests, it encourages research on Nigeria's role in international affairs. The NIIA publishes important works on Nigeria's **foreign policy**. It also provides facilities for the training of Nigerian diplomats and foreign service employees. The NIIA hosts lectures and conferences as well as funding research projects of national interest. It is headed by a director general and run by a management committee. Since its establishment, the institute has published several different newsletters and journals. The *Journal of International Affairs* and the *Nigerian Bulletin on Foreign Affairs* became the government's mouthpiece for its global activities. The NIIA also publishes papers from its lecture and dialogue series.

**NIGERIAN INSTITUTE OF SOCIAL AND ECONOMIC RESEARCH (NISER).** An institute established in 1962 as a nonprofit research center, replacing the colonial West African Institute of Social and Economic Research (1950). NISER's research library is located in **Ibadan**, attached to the **University of Ibadan**. Since 1977, the institute has been under federal control. It is a headed by a director general and run by a management committee. It became a research institution geared toward advising state and federal governments on social and economic development issues. It hosts conferences and seminars as well as funding research projects. *See also* ECONOMY.

**NIGERIAN LABOUR CONGRESS (NLC).** A much-needed national **trade union**, created in February 1978. It should not be confused with the first Nigerian Labour Congress of 1950, led by **Chief Michael Imoudu**, or the second Nigerian Labour Congress of 1975, which rapidly collapsed. Its present membership is four million. **Adams Aliyu Oshiomhole** has served as national president since 1999. Its headquarters is in **Abuja**. One of its major activities has been resisting any significant increase in the price of **petroleum** products that may have a crippling effect on the already fragile business and industry, when necessary calling for general strikes and the reversal of price hikes. Today, it is the main national organization that represents all laborers.

**NIGERIAN NATIONAL ALLIANCE (NNA).** A political alliance developed in preparation for the December 1964 general **elections**. It included the **Northern People's Congress**, the **Mid-West Demo-**

**cratic Front**, the **Nigerian National Democratic Party**, and the **Niger Delta Congress**. **Sir Ahmadu Bello** served as leader. This consolidation of support facilitated a majority win for seats in the House of Representatives. This alliance was formed in opposition to the **United Progressive Grand Alliance**.

**NIGERIAN NATIONAL DEMOCRATIC PARTY (NNDP).** Founded in 1923 by **Sir Herbert Macaulay** in **Lagos**, NNDP was the first **political party** of its kind to be established in Nigeria. **Abubakar Olorun-Nimbe** was an active member. The Lagos Market Women's Association, led by **Madam Alimotu Pelewura**, worked closely with the party, providing support from market **women**. It was the most powerful political party in Nigeria at the time. It won all three Lagos seats in the **Legislative Council** in 1923, 1928, and 1933. It also dominated the **Lagos Town Council**. The party focused heavily on Lagos issues, such as the return of **Dosunmu**'s royal lineage to power. The NNDP was one of several political organizations that attended a conference at Glover Memorial Hall in Lagos in August 1944, which led to the formation of the **National Council of Nigeria and the Cameroons**. In 1964, **Chief Samuel Akintola** and other political leaders created their own NNDP, which lasted one year, to rival the **Action Group**.

**NIGERIAN NATIONAL FEDERATION OF LABOUR (NNFL).** A **trade union** formed by the **Trade Union Congress of Nigeria** affiliating itself with the **National Council of Nigeria and the Cameroons political party** in 1947. Those who saw value in the affiliation broke away from the Trade Union Congress and joined other affiliated unions to form the Nigerian National Federation of Labour in March 1949. **Chief Michael Imoudu** served as the union's leader from 1947 to 1958.

**NIGERIAN NATIONAL OIL CORPORATION (NNOC).** A public **petroleum** company that was incorporated in April 1971. It was supervised by the Ministry of Mines and Power and was responsible for exploring for and trading Nigeria's petroleum. In 1972, the federal military government empowered the company to hold all oil concessions, allowing private transnational firms to operate. In April 1977, it was merged with the Ministry of Petroleum to form the **Nigerian National Petroleum Corporation**.

**NIGERIAN NATIONAL PETROLEUM CORPORATION (NNPC).** A corporation formed in April 1977 by the federal government's merger of the **Nigerian National Oil Corporation** and the Ministry of Petroleum, under Decree No. 33. It is a public company, with interests in **petroleum** and natural gas production, marketing, and trading conducted by its 12 subsidiaries. It is supervised by the Ministry of Petroleum Resources. It was responsible for the construction and maintenance of three of Nigeria's four operating refineries. It currently has joint venture arrangements with several of the major transnational oil companies.

**NIGERIAN PEOPLE'S PARTY (NPP).** A **political party** formed primarily in September 1978 by **Alhaji Waziri Ibrahim** and **Chief Kolawole Balogun**. **Chief Adeniran Ogunsanya** and **Chief Matthew Mbu** were important members. It was one of only five registered **political parties** to run in the 1979 **election**. A conflict arose within the party over whether the chairman should also be the presidential candidate. Ibrahim, the party's chairman, voted in favor of the dual role, while others opposed the idea. The party remained active, but lost several key members to other political parties. Ibrahim subsequently formed the **Great Nigerian People's Party** and ran as its presidential candidate. Without Ibrahim, the party ran **Nnamdi Azikiwe** as its presidential candidate, and Chief Olu Akinfosile acted as party chairman. The party lost the presidency, but won seats in several states. In 1980, the NPP and the **National Party of Nigeria** formed an alliance, which lasted only one year. Two years later, the NPP aligned itself with the **Unity Party of Nigeria**. These two parties also joined the Great Nigerian People's Party and the **People's Redemption Party** to form the **Progressive Parties Alliance**. Like other political parties, the NPP was banned in 1983.

**NIGERIAN RAILWAY CORPORATION.** *See* RAILROADS.

**NIGERIAN SECURITIES AND EXCHANGE COMMISSION (NSEC).** The first attempt at creating such a body was made in

1962; it was called the Capital Issues Committee. The NSEC was founded on 1 April 1978 to connect the federal government with the Nigerian capital market. The commission was required to analyze the market and determine the price of shares of companies on the **Nigerian Stock Exchange**. It also determined when and in what amount the shares could be sold. The commission comprises 12 members, including representatives from the Central Bank of Nigeria, the Nigerian Stock Exchange, and the Nigerian Enterprises Promotions Board. It is supervised by the Ministry of Finance.

**NIGERIAN STOCK EXCHANGE.** Set up in December 1977 to replace the Lagos Stock Exchange, it enforces rules and regulations on the buying and selling of stocks. It also provides public listings of securities and stock quotations. It is directed to respond to the needs and concerns of stockbrokers and report any major economic problems to the federal government. There are six branches, located in **Lagos**, **Kaduna**, **Port Harcourt**, **Kano**, **Onitsha**, **Ibadan**, **Abuja**, and **Yola**. There are over 250 securities listed on the exchange, the majority being shares in private companies. *See also* NIGERIAN SECURITIES AND EXCHANGE COMMISSION.

**NIGERIAN SUPREME COUNCIL FOR ISLAMIC AFFAIRS.** Established in 1973 to group and represent all Muslims as an umbrella organization, the council is led by the **sultan of Sokoto**, who is considered the spiritual leader of all Nigerian Muslims. It is run by an executive council of representatives from each state, a secretary general, a board chairman, and a legal adviser. It is still very active in Nigerian politics. Most recently, the council publicly rejected the creation of new bank notes that did not have an Arabic inscription on them. *See also* ISLAM.

**NIGERIAN TECHNICAL AID CORPS (TAC).** A body developed by **General Ibrahim Babangida** in January 1993 to organize and implement Nigeria's technical assistance programs among its neighbors in Africa, the Caribbean, and the Pacific. It was devised to improve Nigeria's international reputation and promote **economic** support among developing countries. Between 1987 and 2004, the technical corps sent over 1,500 Nigerian volunteers to over 30 countries to share their technical expertise. In March 2003, Nigeria signed a Memorandum of Understanding with developing countries in the Commonwealth Assistance Program, in which they expressed a mutual interest in using the TAC's services.

**NIGERIAN TRADE UNION CONGRESS (NTUC).** A **trade union** formed in April 1960 by **Chief Michael Imoudu** as an alternative to the **Trade Union Congress of Nigeria** (TUCN), which was suspended from 1960 to 1962. By 1962, NTUC and TUCN had merged into the **United Labour Congress**.

**NIGERIAN UNION OF STUDENTS.** An early anticolonial organization started by recent graduates from the Abeokuta Grammar School. In 1943, it sponsored a youth rally at Ojokoro. At the rally, students listened to encouraging words about self-government and freedom from Chief Bode Thomas and **Nnamdi Azikiwe**, among others. In August 1944, the union approached Azikiwe looking for a leader. The union organized a national conference at Glover Memorial Hall in **Lagos** that same month, which marked the start of the **National Council of Nigeria and the Cameroons** (NCNC). **Sir Herbert Macaulay** served as president and Azikiwe as general secretary. This union is most remembered as the originator of the NCNC.

**NIGERIAN UNION OF TEACHERS (NUT).** A teachers' **trade union** founded in July 1931 to represent **educators** across Nigeria and establish financial and collegial support for teachers. It emerged from the amalgamation of the Lagos Union of Teachers with smaller unions. It was started by mission schoolteachers from different ethnic backgrounds across **southern Nigeria**. At its inception, the secretary was **Efik**, the president was **Yoruba**, and the vice president was an **Igbo**. One of the union's key members was **Alvan Ikoku**, who served as president. Much of its operations were in the Western and Eastern Regions, with the Northern Teachers' Association operating in the Northern Region. In 1972, the Nigerian Union of Teachers merged with the Northern States Teachers' Union (formerly the Northern Teachers' Association). It originally started with government and mission schoolteachers, but expanded to include university graduates. It does not include university faculty. It is still in operation today, with branches of the union in nearly every town.

**NIGERIAN YOUTH MOVEMENT (NYM).** An influential organization was established in 1934 by **Samuel Akinsanya, Ernst Ikoli, Chief Hezekiah Oladipo Davies,** and J. C. Vaughan as the **Lagos Youth Movement**. Its original task was pressuring the colonial government for change in its **educational** policies. Students complained about the inferior status of **Yaba Higher College** at **Lagos**. In 1936, **Akinola Maja** and others joined the group to turn it into a political organization. To reflect this new direction, the organization changed its name to the Nigerian Youth Movement. After 1936, it was the primary political organization operating in Nigeria. Its goals included influencing people across the colony to see themselves as Nigerians instead of as part of their respective **ethnic groups**. The movement also focused on reforming colonial policy through the **Legislative Council**. In 1938, **Nnamdi Azikiwe** joined the organization, and **Sir Kofoworola Abayomi** acted as president of the organization. The movement ran candidates for the **Lagos Town Council** and won. In 1941, Abayomi resigned from the Legislative Council. Ikoli and Akinsanya competed to replace him, which split the organization. Ethnic identity also inflamed the rivalry. In disgust, Azikiwe withdrew his membership. Gradually others followed his lead, until the Nigerian Youth Movement dissolved.

**NIGERIANIZATION.** *See* INDIGENIZATION.

**NJOKU, ENI (1917–1974).** Born in November 1917, Njoku received his education from Ebem School in Ohafia, **Hope Waddell Training Institution** in **Calabar**, and **Yaba Higher College** in **Lagos**. In England, he earned his advanced degrees from Manchester University (1954). After returning to Nigeria, Njoku worked as the science master at Hope Waddell Training Institute (1940–1942) and as a civilian instructor in the Army Clerk's Training School (1942–1944). For several years, starting in 1948, he taught at University College (present-day **University of Ibadan**). Between 1952 and 1953, Njoku served as the minister of mines and power. He was a member of the **Eastern House of Assembly** and **Federal House of Representatives**. At the

University of Ibadan, he served as department head and, later, the dean of the Faculty of Science. In 1956, Njoku was the chairman of the Electricity Corporation of Nigeria, the **National Electric Power Authority**'s predecessor. He also worked as vice chancellor at the University of Lagos (1962–1965) and the University of Nigeria at **Nsukka** (1966).

**NJOKU, RAYMOND AMANZE (1913–1977).** Born in August 1913, Njoku studied at Our Lady's School in Emekuku, St. Charles College in **Onitsha**, and **King's College** in **Lagos**. From 1933 to 1943, he was a schoolmaster at King's College and a member of the King's College Law Society. To earn an advanced degree in law, he attended the University of London. He was called to the bar in January 1947. In Aba, he practiced law from 1947 until 1953. In the early 1950s, he also became involved in politics. He was president of the Aba Community League (1952–1954) and a member of the **Eastern House of Assembly** (1954). Njoku also served as the minister of commerce and industries in 1954 and as the federal minister of trade and industry in 1955. Three years later, he became the minister of transport. In 1964, he also served as the minister of communication. After the collapse of the **First Republic**, Njoku returned to practicing law and withdrew from politics. He died in September 1977.

**NOK.** The Nok people were agriculturalists who lived between 500 BCE and 200 CE in central Nigeria. This civilization has been heralded as fairly advanced because of its use of iron and stone materials. The Nok are best known today for their terra-cotta sculptures, iron bracelets, and pottery. There is also evidence that the Nok engaged in the laborious task of smelting iron. What little scholars know about the Nok people came from the discovery of their archeological remains during mining activities in 1943. Remains of this society are found in central Nigeria near the city of **Jos** in **Plateau State**. Nok **art** is considered highly sophisticated for its time because of the clay used and the level of detail and design that appears on each piece. Much of the artwork appears to be representations of people and animals. The faces of human sculptures are easily identified as Nok because of the triangular eyes, perforated pupils, nose, and mouth. Archeologists have found significant similarities between materials unearthed at Nok and **Ile-Ife** and **Benin**. This evidence suggests that neighboring groups were influenced by the Nok.

**NOLLYWOOD.** The nickname for Nigeria's flourishing film industry, which has emerged in the past 15 years. Although most of the movies are filmed in **Lagos** and are made by **Yoruba** filmmakers, they can be found all over Nigeria in numerous **languages**. The industry generates an estimated 2,000 low-budget films per year, with two-thirds of them in English, which exceeds India's Bollywood. The production of these films employs about one million people.

The origin of this distinct variety of films is unclear. One theory is that it started accidentally in 1992 when a Nigerian trader based in **Onitsha** was trying to sell a large stock of blank videocassettes he had bought from Taiwan. He decided they would sell better if something was recorded on them, so he shot a short film called *Living in Bondage*, which sold more than 750,000 copies. Today, each film costs between $15,000 and $100,000 to make, without the assistance of bank loans. The financial constraints and cultural infusion have created a unique Nollywood style. In general, these melodramatic films are long, with simple dialogue and low-quality production. They show clear symbols of wealth, modernity, and tradition. They typically deal with the themes of witchcraft, romance, and deceit. These films tend not to focus on the military, politics, or ethnic conflict, and often steer away from sexual content. Attached to this burgeoning film industry is advertising using famous actors and video rentals. A successful film may sell as many as 50,000 copies. Some viewers are concerned that these films present Nigeria poorly to the rest of the world, and critics claim that they lack artistic content and encourage ethnic and religious stereotypes. Nonetheless, they remain popular. The documentary *This Is Nollywood* (2007) provides a glimpse into the production of this up-and-coming genre.

**NOMADIC SCHOOLS.** Primary schools with some level of mobility to reach the nomadic societies in Nigeria, such as the **Fulani**. **Ekiti State**, in southwestern Nigeria, has five such schools in operation. The federal government launched this program in 1986. The goals of the program include raising the standard of living for mobile societies, involving them in the nation-building process, and increasing literacy among nomadic peoples. The National Commission for Nomadic Education, formed in 1990, oversees the program. At its inception, the federal government operated over 200 nomadic schools. Many of the schools held class sessions under trees rather than in permanent schoolhouses. The school curriculum includes English, basic mathematics and science, and social studies. This modified curriculum was developed at a university in **Sokoto**. The schools have a morning and afternoon shift, giving children who have animal herding responsibilities an opportunity to attend. But the program has suffered due to the lack of resources. Fulani families also complain about the program's failure to instruct children in topics relevant to their way of life. *See also* EDUCATION.

**NORTH-CENTRAL STATE.** One of Nigeria's 12 states from 1967 to 1976, North-Central State was located in **northern Nigeria**. It became **Kaduna State**. *See also* STATE CREATION.

**NORTH-EASTERN STATE.** One of Nigeria's 12 states between 1967 and 1976, North-Eastern State was located in **northern Nigeria**. It became **Borno, Bauchi**, and **Gongola States**. *See also* STATE CREATION.

**NORTHERN ELEMENT PROGRESSIVE ASSOCIATION.** An association formed in 1947 in **Kano** by Habib Raji Abdallah, an Igbirra from the **Middle Belt**. It served as the northern chapter of **Nnamdi Azikiwe**'s anticolonial movement, with a particular emphasis on the North. Although it was not a formal **political party**, several of its members were accused of conducting political activities and subsequently were fired from their **civil service** positions. The association faced strong opposition from the Kano Native Authority and ultimately collapsed.

**NORTHERN ELEMENTS PROGRESSIVE UNION (NEPU).** An organization formed in 1950 as an alternative to the **Northern People's Congress**. It was led by **Alhaji Muhammed Aminu Kano**. In 1954, the union aligned itself with the **National Council of Nigeria and the Cameroons**. It also aligned with the **Bornu Youth Movement** around 1954, but broke away in 1958. NEPU was an influential

**political party** in **northern Nigeria** during the 1960s. Critics saw it as the radical wing of the Northern People's Congress. In 1963, the union aligned itself with the **United Middle Belt Congress** to form the **Northern Progressive Front**. In 1966, like other political parties, NEPU was banned.

**NORTHERN HOUSE OF ASSEMBLY.** A governing body created by the **Richards Constitution** in 1946. The assembly included the **chief commissioner**, official and unofficial members, and men nominated by the regional governor. It served as a moderator between the local **Native Authorities** and the **Legislative Council** in **Lagos**. The Northern House of Assembly was disbanded in 1966 after the fall of the **First Republic**. *See also* EASTERN HOUSE OF ASSEMBLY; HOUSES OF ASSEMBLY; WESTERN HOUSE OF ASSEMBLY.

**NORTHERN HOUSE OF CHIEFS.** Also referred to as the Northern Council of Chiefs, it was created by the **Richards Constitution** in 1946. It included the chief commissioner and an array of local **chiefs** from the **Northern Region**. The **Macpherson Constitution** of 1952 modified the Northern House of Chiefs membership slightly to include an adviser on **Islamic** law. In 1966, the Northern House of Chiefs was disbanded. *See also* EASTERN HOUSE OF CHIEFS; HOUSE OF CHIEFS; WESTERN HOUSE OF CHIEFS.

**NORTHERN NIGERIA.** The area north of the **Niger** and **Benue Rivers** to the Nigeria–Niger border. During the colonial period it was called the **Protectorate of Northern Nigeria**, and during the early years of **independence** it was known as the **Northern Region**. It was incorporated into independent Nigeria in 1962. Under colonial rule and during the **First Republic**, the term was used interchangeably with Northern Region. It refers to the same area today, but focuses on the religious and cultural components that make the geographic place unique. Northern Nigeria is distinct from **southern Nigeria** not only in its strong **Islamic** culture, but also in its climate and topography. The **Hausa** and **Fulani** are the dominant **ethnic groups** in northern Nigeria. Southern Nigeria is primarily humid and tropical, whereas northern Nigeria is dry savanna. The states considered part of northern Nigeria today are **Adamawa, Bauchi, Borno, Jigawa, Kaduna,**

**Katsina, Kano, Kebbi, Niger, Sokoto,** and **Yobe.** Important cities in northern Nigeria include **Kano, Sokoto,** and **Kaduna.** Before the implementation of **Shari'a** in several of the northern states, **women** were enfranchised during the 1970s. *See also* EASTERN NIGERIA; WESTERN NIGERIA.

**NORTHERN PEOPLE'S CONGRESS (NPC).** The conservative branch of the northern anticolonial movement, the NPC emerged as a **political party** out of **Jam'iyyar Mutanen Arewa,** a cultural organization. Formed from a conference of European-educated northerners in **Kano** in 1949, the NPC was led by members of the **Bauchi General Improvement Union,** including **Sa'adu Zungur** (who named the party), **Alhaji Muhammed Aminu Kano,** and **Sir Alhaji Abubakar Tafawa Balewa.** Other key members of the congress were **Alhaji Sir Kashim Ibrahim, Russell Aliyu Dikko,** and Yahaya Gusau. This group officially became the NPC in 1951. The NPC became one of Nigeria's most influential political parties during the **First Republic.** It was rivaled by the **Northern Elements Progressive Union** during the 1960s. The goals of the party included uniting people of **northern Nigeria** combined with a strong desire to maintain regional autonomy. **Sir Alhaji Ahmadu Bello** became the party's president in 1951 and Balewa its deputy leader. In 1966, along with other political parties, the NPC was disbanded.

**NORTHERN PROGRESSIVE FRONT (NPF).** A group was created in 1963 as an alliance between the **Northern Element Progressive Union** and the **United Middle Belt Congress. Alhaji Muhammed Aminu Kano** served as the leader of the organization. Like all other **political parties,** the NPF was banned in 1966.

**NORTHERN REGION.** One of three regions (Northern, Western, Eastern) established by the **Richards Constitution** of 1946. It was created from the **Protectorate of Northern Nigeria,** which was governed as a British colony, separate from **southern Nigeria.** It is the area north of the **Niger River** to the border with **Niger** and covered one-third of present-day Nigeria. Its **population** included mostly **Hausa** and **Fulani** people. Its first two governors were British colonial officials, Sir Bryan Sharwood-Smith (October 1954–December

1957) and Sir Gawain Westray Bell (December 1957–January 1962). The region was incorporated into the Republic of Nigeria in 1962. From 1962 onward, the governors of the Northern Region were Nigerian, with Alhaji Sir Kashim Ibrahim (January 1962–January 1966) as the first and Hassan Usman Katsina (January 1966–January 1967) the second. In addition to governors, the Northern Region also had a premier. The Northern Region had only one **premier** between October 1954 and January 1966, **Alhaji Sir Ahmadu Bello**.

In 1959, the region attained self-government. It was politically dominated by the **Northern People's Congress**, under the leadership of Bello. The British governed the region through indirect rule to minimize administrative costs and preserve the Muslim political structure. After **independence**, Nigeria retained the three political regions until the collapse of the **First Republic**. In 1967, the Northern Region was divided into six states (**North-Western**, **North-Central**, **Kano**, **North-Eastern**, **Kwara**, and **Benue-Plateau**) by **General Yakubu Gowon**. It included numerous **ethnic groups**, such as the **Nupe**, **Fulani**, **Hausa**, **Tiv**, and **Gwari**. Today, the phrase is used with the same territorial designation as during the **First Republic**, but with a greater emphasis on the Muslim culture and **religion** that shape its politics and make the region distinct from the rest of Nigeria. The contemporary term "northern region" is used interchangeably with **northern Nigeria**. *See also* EASTERN REGION; WESTERN REGION.

**NORTH-WESTERN STATE.** One of Nigeria's 12 states from 1967 to 1976, North-Western State was located in **northern Nigeria**. It became **Sokoto State**. *See also* STATE CREATION.

**NRI.** One of several **Igbo** social groups that were not organized into a segmentary political structure, but into a kingdom. It was located in Igbo territory, west of the **Niger River**. The height of its political influence occurred between 1250 and 1670. Nri imposed its influence on the major Igbo towns of **Nsukka** and Owerri. It was the oldest of the Igbo kingships. The *eze Nri* (priest-king of Nri) sponsored men in their respective territories to represent Nri local authority and granted them the title *ozo*. Each *ozo* acted as an agent of the *eze Nri*, collecting tribute and important political information. *See also* ETHNIC GROUPS.

**NSUKKA.** Nsukka is located in southeastern Nigeria. It is an important commercial town in **Enugu State**, with a **population** just over 300,000. During the last several decades of the 20th century, Nsukka was home to the *uli* **art** movement, which utilized symbols of designs that **Igbo women** traditionally used to adorn their bodies and applied to the walls of shrines. It is also home to the University of Nigeria at Nsukka, which was established in 1960.

**NUPE.** An **ethnic group** that lives in the **Middle Belt** and is the dominant group in **Niger State** and **Kwara State**. During the Iron Age, the Nupe used the complicated method of lost-wax for casting when working with iron. Most claim descent from the Nupe Kingdom, which was founded in the 15th century by Tsoede. Between the 16th and 18th centuries, the Nupe Kingdom fought a series of wars against the **Oyo Empire**. It also fended off the **Fulani jihad** led by **Usman dan Fodio** in the early 19th century. Under the leadership of Mallam Dendo and his successors, the Nupe Kingdom's capital was relocated from Idah to Bida. The Nupe Kingdom lost its power and was eventually dismantled in the late 19th century by the **Royal Niger Company**. Major towns in Nupeland today include Bida and Jebba. The traditional Nupe **religion** includes not only prayers and sacrifice for a supreme being and deities, but also the manipulation of supernatural agencies through **divination**. In the Nupes' traditional political system, each town or village constituted a separate political system. A **village head,** or *zitsu,* claimed control over the town and satellite villages. Nupeland was one of the main sources of **slaves** for the Kano Emirate during the 19th century.

**NWAFOR-ORIZU, AKWEKE ABYSSINIA (1920–1999).** Born in July 1920, Nwafor-Orizu was the son of the Eze Ugbonyamba, the Igwe Orizu I. As a young man, he studied at St. Thomas Central School and Onitsha Central School. In 1938, he studied at Achimota College in **Ghana**. Eleven years later, he moved to the United States to study at Lincoln University and Howard University. He was active in numerous student, cultural, and political organizations in the United States. In 1944, he received a law degree from Columbia University. He also worked as an editor for the *Negro Digest* and *Pittsburgh Courier*. Back home, Nwafor-Orizu took part in a protest in support of **Enugu** miners and was placed under house arrest for two weeks in 1949. In 1951, he became a member of the **Eastern House of Assembly**. He was also an active member of the **National Council of Nigeria and the Cameroons**. Between 1964 and 1966, Nwafor-Orizu served as president of the Senate. He withdrew from national politics during **General Yakubu Gowon**'s rule. In 1978, he joined the **National Party of Nigeria**. Nwafor-Orizu died in March 1999.

**NWANKWO, CHIEF ARTHUR AGWUNCHA (1942– ).** Born in August 1942 in Ajalli, located in **Anambra State**, Nwankwo earned his advanced degrees from Eastern Mennonite College and Duquesne University. He worked as a consultant for Gulf Oil (1967) until the **civil war** erupted in Nigeria and he joined the secessionist **Republic of Biafra**. During the war, he wrote for the Propaganda Directorate of Biafra (1967) and edited the *Biafra Newsletter* (1967–1969). After the war, Nwankwo cofounded Nwamife Publishers, based in **Enugu**. He also worked as chairman of Fourth Dimension Publishing between 1977 and 1979. He ran as the **People's Redemption Party** gubernatorial candidate for Anambra State in the 1979 general **elections** and lost. During the 1980s, Nwankwo turned his attention to writing about politics and military rule in Nigeria. His most cited works include *Civilianised Soldiers* (1984) and *Biafra: The Making of a Nation* (1969). Through his **National Democratic Coalition**, he was a vocal opponent of the annulment of the **election of 12 June 1993**, which landed him in prison for several days. He received several honorary chieftaincy titles and an honorary doctoral degree from Shaw University (1986).

**NWAPA-NWAKUCHE, CHIEF FLORA (1931–1993).** Born in January 1931 in Oguta, in **Imo State**, Nwapa-Nwakuche completed her advanced degrees in **education** at the **University of Ibadan** (1957) and University of Edinburgh (1958). After returning to Nigeria in 1959, she taught in **Enugu**. She worked as an assistant registrar at the University of Lagos from 1962 to 1964. During the **civil war**, Nwapa left **Lagos** and settled in the secessionist **Republic of Biafra**. After the war, she remained in the region and served as the minister of health and social welfare (1970–1971), which involved resettling orphans. She also worked as the commissioner of lands, survey, and urban development (1971–1974). In addition to her **civil service** career, Nwapa established herself as one of Nigeria's leading female fiction writers. Her first novel, *Efuru*, was published in 1966. Her novel *Never Again* (1975) is set during the civil war. Nwapa created two publishing companies, Tana Press and Nwapa & Co., to showcase Nigerian fiction. She wrote an array of novels and short stories in English, which reached international audiences. (*Efuru* was translated into French and Icelandic.) Her writing career created opportunities to teach **literature** and writing at several universities outside Nigeria, including New York University and University of Michigan. She received the chieftaincy title *ogbuefi* of Oguta. Nwapa died in October 1993 in Enugu.

**NWOBODO, CHIEF JIM IFEANYICHUKWU (1940– ).** Born in May 1940 in Lafia, in **Nasarawa State**, Nwobodo attended the Nigerian College of Arts, Sciences, and Technology at **Enugu** and the University of Ibadan (1964). He taught at **King's College** in **Lagos** (1964–1965). He was a chairman and/or director of numerous companies, including Shell–BP and the Enugu Rangers International Football Club. During the **Second Republic**, Nwobodo was the governor of **Anambra State**. After the military **coup d'état**, he was imprisoned from 1984 to 1988. **General Ibrahim Babangida** then granted him a presidential pardon. He joined the **Social Democratic Party**, which again landed him in prison. From 1995 to 1998 he was the minister of youth and sports. He was a member of the **Nigerian People's Party** and **People's Democratic Party**. He was a presidential aspirant in the latter party. Through an unusual by-election, Nwobodo received a seat in Anambra State's Senate. In 2003, he ran as the presidential candidate for the United Nigeria People's Party.

**NWOSU, HUMPHREY NWOBU (1941– ).** Born in October 1941 in Ajalli, in **Anambra State**, Nwosu studied at Ajalli Government School (1948–1949), St. Michael's School in **Enugu** (1950–1952), Presbyterian School in Abakaliki (1952–1955), and McGregor College in Afikpo (1958–1959). He earned his advanced degrees, including his doctorate, in political science from the University of Nigeria at **Nsukka** and University of California at Berkeley

(1972–1976). Nwosu worked as a faculty member, associate dean, and department head at the University of Nigeria at Nsukka between 1979 and 1986. He was the commissioner for the Commission for Health in Anambra State (1988–1989) and chairman of the **National Electoral Commission** (1989–1993), which was charged with running Nigeria's **election of 12 June 1993**. When **General Ibrahim Babangida** disagreed with the results of the presidential **election**, he annulled the elections. Despite this, Nwosu is remembered for running the fairest general election in Nigeria. In the past several years, he has published a number of books on Nigerian politics and culture.

**NZEOGWU, MAJOR PATRICK CHUKWUMA (1937–1967).** Born in **Kaduna** and of **Igbo** ethnicity, Nzeogwu studied at St. John's College in Kaduna (1950–1955) before joining the **army** in 1956. He attended the Royal Military Academy at Sandhurst in **Great Britain**. Nzeogwu was one of the primary officers who staged Nigeria's first military **coup d'état**, which ended the **First Republic** in 1966. After resisting the placement of **General Yakubu Gowon** as head of state, he was detained in **Calabar** until the **civil war**, when **Chief Chukwuemeka Ojukwu** released him. Nzeogwu fought on the Biafran side during the civil war and was killed in battle in 1967. *See also* ARMED FORCES.

**NZERIBE, CHIEF FRANCIS ARTHUR (1938– ).** Nzeribe was born in November 1938 in Oguta, in **Imo State**. He studied at Holy Ghost College in Owerri, Portsmouth College of Technology, Chesterfield College of Technology, and the University of Manchester. In Nigeria, he worked as a director of several private companies. In 1983, he served as a senator. From 1984 to 1986, he was in self-imposed exile in England. After returning to Nigeria, he acted as chairman of the **Association for Better Nigeria** in 1993. In the years prior to the **election of 12 June 1993**, Nzeribe and his organization called for the continuation of **General Ibrahim Babangida**'s military leadership and the postponement of the upcoming **election**. He also became a senator, representing the **All People's Party** in 1999. He received the honorary chieftaincy title from the town of Oguta.

## – O –

**OBAFEMI AWOLOWO UNIVERSITY.** One of Nigeria's major universities, it was established in 1961 by the **Western Regional** government as the University of Ife in **Ile-Ife**. The first year's enrollment was 244 students. In 1975, the federal government incorporated it into the public university system. In 1987, its name was changed to Obafemi Awolowo University to honor **Chief Obafemi Awolowo**. *See also* HIGHER EDUCATION.

**OBASANJO, GENERAL OLUSEGUN (1937– ).** Born in **Abeokuta**, in **Ogun State**, in May 1937, Obasanjo is of **Yoruba** descent. He was educated at Abeokuta Baptist High School. After attending a series of military schools in Nigeria and **Great Britain**, he joined the **armed forces** in August 1961. Starting in 1963, he was part of the engineering corps, and later became the commander of the Engineering Unit. During the **civil war**, Obasanjo fought on the side of the federal government and commanded a division. He was promoted to brigadier in October 1972. After the July 1975 **coup d'état**, he served as chief of staff under **General Murtala Ramat Mohammed**. He also served as Nigeria's military head of state (i.e., chairman of the **Supreme Military Council**) from 1976 through 1979. He was celebrated as the first military leader in Nigeria to transfer power to a an elected leader. Obasanjo retired from the military in 1979 and participated in a select number of global organizations. He also wrote several books reflecting on his political and military career before returning to politics in the mid-1990s. His most cited work is *My Command: An Account of the Nigerian Civil War* (1980).

After the annulment of the **election of 12 June 1993**, Obasanjo campaigned for the **Interim National Government** to replace **General Ibrahim Babangida**. In 1995, he was accused of attempting to remove **General Sani Abacha** from power and spent almost four years in prison. Obasanjo was released in 1998 and ran for president the following year as a civilian candidate of the **People's Democratic Party** (PDP). He was inaugurated as president in May 1999 and served two four-year terms. He attempted to change the **constitution** to allow him to run for a third term, but failed. Ultimately, he stepped aside and let **Umaru Musa Yar'Adua** run as the PDP's candidate in April 2007. He has received numerous honorary degrees and titles, such as Grand Commander of the Order of the Federal Republic of Nigeria. *See also* NEW PARTNERSHIP FOR AFRICAN DEVELOPMENT.

**OBI, CHIKE (1921–2008).** Born in April 1921 in **Zaria**, Obi studied at St. Patrick's School in Zaria, Christ the King College in **Onitsha**, and **Yaba Higher College** in **Lagos**. For his advanced degrees, he attended schools in England, including University College of London, Pembroke College, and Cambridge University, as well as schools in the United States, including the Massachusetts Institute of Technology. In Nigeria, Obi taught mathematics at Africa College (1942–1943) and at New Bethel College (1944–1946) in Onitsha. From 1946 to 1947 he taught for the Cultural Society for the Advancement of Knowledge at Onitsha. He taught mathematics at the **University of Ibadan** (1959–1962) and the University of Lagos (1970–1985), where he also acted as dean. In the political arena, Obi served as the founder and leader of the short-lived Dynamic Party (1951–1966) and as a member of the Federal Parliament of Nigeria (1960–1961) and the **Eastern House of Assembly** (1961–1966). He taught mathematics at the University of Lagos in the 1970s. He was a member of the Nigeria Academy of Sciences and received awards for his contribution to mathematics. Obi died in March 2008.

**ODEBIYI, CHIEF JONATHAN AKINREMI OLAWOLE (1923–2002).** Born in March 1923 in Ikeja, in **Lagos State**, Odebiyi studied at St. Andrew's School in Ipaja, Church Missionary Society Grammar School in **Lagos**, and Fourah Bay College in Sierra Leone. In 1951, he attended the London University Institute of Education. From 1942 to 1944, Odebiyi worked as a clerk in the Judicial Department. He also earned his living tutoring children at the Church Missionary Society Grammar School (1949–1950). In 1951, he became the principal of Egbado College in Ilaro. Odebiyi's involvement in Nigerian politics began in 1951, when he served as a member of the Egbado Division of the **Western House of Assembly**. He also acted as chairman for the Egbado Divisional Council in 1954 and as a member of the Ministry of Education in 1956. Odebiyi was the leader of the Western House of Assembly (1960), representing the **Action**

Group, and a senator (1979–1983), representing the **Unity Party of Nigeria**. He was also a member of the **Alliance for Democracy political party**. Odebiyi earned the honorary chieftaincy titles *apena* of Iboro (1951), *apesin* of Ibeshe (1958), *basorun* of Aiyetoro (1960), *apesin* of Igbogila (1960), and *odofin* of Ilaro (1972). He died in March 2002.

**ODUTOLA, TIMOTHY ADEOLA (1902–1995).** Born in June 1902, Odutola attended Ijebu-Ode Grammar School. He was an active participant in Nigerian politics and business. He was a member of the **Legislative Council** (1945 and 1947) and the **Western House of Assembly** (1951). In the business world, Odutola was chairman of the **Western Region**'s representative committees for **oil palm**, **cotton**, and **cocoa** in 1954. One year later, he served as the chairman of the Ijebu Council. Odutola's business and political expertise also earned him the status of delegate to the African Conference in London (1948) and member of the Delegation to Festival Britain (1951). In 1954, he was installed as *ogbeni-oja* (**chief**) of Ijebu-Ode. He also earned the honorary title Officer of the Order of the British Empire.

**OGONI.** An **ethnic group** of about 500,000 people who live in the **Niger Delta** and have long depended on **agriculture** and fishing for their economic survival. Commercial quantities of **petroleum** were discovered in the 1950s in their homeland. The Ogoni have complained to the oil companies, notably Royal Dutch–Shell, and the Nigerian government that the oil production is polluting their **water**, ruining their crops, and poisoning the air they breathe. Other ethnic groups, such as the **Ijaw**, have voiced similar complaints. The Ogoni have also made a compelling argument that for all their suffering, they have seen almost no financial return. They lack representation in the state and federal governments and suffer high rates of **unemployment**. Almost no local community members hold skilled or unskilled jobs in the oil industry. Under the leadership of **Ken Saro-Wiwa**, an Ogoni author and activist, their concerns have reached the international community.

In the early 1990s, the Ogoni launched a major campaign against the Shell Petroleum Development Company (a joint venture between Royal Dutch–Shell and the **Nigerian National Petroleum**

**Company**). The government's response, under the leadership of **General Sani Abacha**, was fierce. Ken Saro-Wiwa and eight other members of the **Movement for the Survival of the Ogoni People** were detained illegally and hanged in November 1995. Their campaign against the federal government and the oil companies has been picked up by several other ethnic groups and organizations, such as the **Movement for the Emancipation of the Niger Delta**. *See also* GENOCIDE; MINORITY GROUPS.

**OGUNDE, CHIEF HUBERT ADEDEJI (1916–1990).** Ogunde was born in July 1916 at Ososa, in **Ogun State**. As a young man, he studied in Ososa, **Lagos**, and Ijebu-Ode. He was a member of an **Aladura Church** in the 1940s. Between 1941 and 1945, he worked for the **police**. In the mid-1940s, he devoted his life to **theater** and entertainment. He is considered the father of **Yoruba** operatic theater. Ogunde started dance, record, film, and theater companies that all bore his name. He was a leader of the Nigerian National Troupe. Ogunde wrote more than 50 plays, on themes of colonialism, spirituality, and moral degradation. His most performed plays include *Yoruba Ronu* (*Yoruba Should Think*) (1964) and *Herbert Macaulay* (1946). Ogunde received an honorary doctoral degree from the University of Ife (today's **Obafemi Awolowo University**). He died in April 1990.

**OGUNDIPE, BRIGADIER BABAFEMI OLATUNDE (1924–1971).** Ogundipe was born in September 1924 in **Lagos**. He studied at Wesley and Banham Memorial School in **Port Harcourt**. He joined the **armed forces** in 1943 and attended a series of military schools and training centers in Nigeria and **Great Britain**. Ogundipe fought on the British side in Burma and India during **World War II**. In the early 1960s, he commanded the Nigerian division of a United Nations peacekeeping force in Central Africa. During Nigeria's first military **coup d'état** (1966), Ogundipe served as the chief of staff in the **Supreme Military Council**. According to **Chief Chukwuemeka Ojukwu**, Ogundipe, not **General Yakubu Gowon**, should have succeeded **General Johnson Aguiyi-Ironsi** in 1966. After the coup d'état, Ogundipe was the military government's high commissioner based in London, a position he held during the **civil war**. He died in November 1971.

**OGUNMOLA, H. KOLAWOLE (1925–1973).** Ogunmola wrote and acted in numerous plays that drew from **Yoruba oral tradition**. He was one of Nigeria's best known theatrical actors in the 20th century and started the Ogunmola Traveling Theatre Company in 1947. One of his most cited and performed works is the **Yoruba language** operatic version of Amos Toutola's *The Palm-Wine Drinkard* (1952). *See also* THEATER.

**OGUNSANYA, CHIEF ADENIRAN (1918–1996).** Ogunsanya was born in January 1918 in Ikorudu, in **Lagos State**. He studied at Madasiola Private School (1920–1922), **Hope Waddell Training Institute** (1928), and **King's College** (1937–1940), among others. He also studied at Manchester University for seven years beginning in 1945. In Nigeria, he was a barrister-at-law and solicitor of the Supreme Court. From 1956 to 1959, Ogunsanya was chairman of the federal government's Industrial Board. In 1959, he was a member of Parliament. He also served as an executive member of the **National Council of Nigeria and the Cameroons** and president-general of **Chief Nnamdi Azikiwe**'s **Zikist Movement**. In 1968, Ogunsanya served as the attorney-general in the **Supreme Military Council**. Ten years later he was a cofounder and chairman of the **Nigerian People's Party**. Ogunsanya died in November 1996. The Adeniran Ogunsanya College of Education in **Lagos** is named after him.

**OGUN STATE.** A state created in 1976 out of the **Western State**. It is one of Nigeria's current 36 states. It is located in southwestern Nigerian, with its western boundary shared with **Benin**. The capital is **Abeokuta**. The dominant **ethnic groups** in the state are the **Yoruba** and its subgroups, making the most commonly spoken **languages** also Yoruba or dialects of it. The major **religions** are **Christianity** and **Islam**. The state is named after the Yoruba god of iron. Economic activities in the state include the cultivation of rubber, **kolanut**, citrus fruits, tubers, and **oil palm**. *See also* STATE CREATION.

**OHANEZE NDIGBO.** An **Igbo** social organization in the late 1970s created by Akanu Ibiam. It serves as a mouthpiece for Igbo interests in politics. The organization emphasizes the importance of justice, fairness, and mutual respect. Its influence had waned by the mid-1990s.

In the past decade, its most vocal member, **Colonel Joe "Hannibal" Achuzie**, has attracted international attention to the organization. It has been described as the Igbo equivalent of **Afenifere**.

**OIL.** *See* PETROLEUM.

**OIL MINERAL PRODUCING AREAS DEVELOPMENT COMMISSION (OMPADEC).** A commission established in July 1992 by Decree No. 23, under the direction of **General Ibrahim Babangida**, to address some of the objections raised by ethnic **minority groups**, such as the **Ogoni** and **Ijaw**, about **petroleum** production, pollution, and poverty in the **Niger Delta**. It was based in **Port Harcourt** in **Rivers State**. Oil-producing states were to receive 3 percent of the government's annual oil revenue to invest in development projects. The commission was also charged with improving public works and services (i.e., potable **water**, **roads**, **education**, and **electricity**) to people living in this oil-producing area. Within a few years, it became clear to those living in the Niger Delta that the commission was ineffective and **corrupt**. In 2000, it was replaced by the **Niger Delta Development Commission**. *See also* NIGER DELTA CONFLICT; NIGER DELTA DEVELOPMENT BOARD.

**OIL PALM.** The oil of a particular variety of palm tree. The fruits grow in large bunches and are brightly colored (red, black, yellow, or orange) depending on how ripe they are. The oil is largely produced in **southern Nigeria**. The **Oil Rivers Protectorate** was named after this valuable commodity. Oil palm was one of Nigeria's largest exports after the British abolished the **slave trade**. During the 20th century, the British used oil palm for lubricating mechanical parts in factories and military machinery and for manufacturing soap and candles. This thick, reddish-yellow oil is also a common ingredient in margarine. It is considered one of the healthiest forms of vegetable oil. *See also* AGRICULTURE; FOREIGN TRADE.

**OIL REVENUE ALLOCATION.** *See* REVENUE ALLOCATION.

**OIL RIVERS.** The British name for the network of tributaries of the **Niger River** along the coast. Today, this region is referred to as the

**Niger Delta**. These rivers were named by British traders in reference to **oil palm**, the most traded commodity of the region. Nigerian and British merchants engaged in trading oil palm in the early 19th century decades before colonial rule. In 1806, for example, British traders imported about 150 tons of palm oil into **Great Britain**. In 1885, the Oil Rivers region, through a combination of gunboat diplomacy and treaties, was claimed as a British territory by the **National Africa Company**. It was named the **Oil Rivers Protectorate** until the territory was expanded northward in 1895. *See also* COLONIZATION.

**OIL RIVERS PROTECTORATE.** A British **protectorate** was established in southeastern Nigeria by the **National Africa Company** (NAC) in 1884. It included the **Niger Delta**, which the British at the time referred to as the **Oil Rivers**. After about 1806, British traders regularly went to this region to buy **oil palm** from local traders, hence the name. The NAC, with British support, used a combination of diplomacy and military might to claim the Oil Rivers region as the British-controlled Oil Rivers Protectorate. In 1891, Major Claude Macdonald was installed as the protectorate's commissioner and consul general. The **Royal Niger Company** replaced the NAC and expanded trade and political influence northward; by 1895 it had incorporated the Oil Rivers Protectorate into the **Niger Coast Protectorate**.

**OJAIDE, TANURE (1948– ).** Born in April 1948 in Okpara Island, in **Bendel State**, Ojaide earned advanced degrees from the **University of Ibadan** and Syracuse University. He taught for several years at the University of Maiduguri before relocating to the United States. He currently teaches at the University of North Carolina at Charlotte. Ojaide's poetry is celebrated for its unique combination of traditional song and political commentary. In "Epilogue: Spoken by a Chorus," for example, he comments on the activities of the military dictatorship during the 1970s. He wrote several poems that focus on **Urhobo** culture and leaders. Ojaide has written more than five books of poetry. He has received several major awards for his poetry, including the All-Africa Okigbo Prize for Poetry (1988) and African Poetry Award. *See also* LITERATURE.

**OJIGI.** A ruler of the **Yoruba Oyo Empire** between about 1724 and 1735. During his reign, Oyo expanded, incorporating Dahomey (in present-day **Benin**) into its tribute-paying empire. Ojigi is associated with the height of Oyo's power.

**OJIKE, MAZI MBONU (1914–1956).** Born in May 1914 in **Arochukwu**, as a young man Ojike studied at Church Missionary Society School and Arondizuogu Awka Training College. He studied through correspondence at Wolsey Hall at Oxford before going to the United States to attend Lincoln University, the University of Illinois, Ohio State University, and the University of Chicago. In Nigeria, Ojike taught at various schools from 1926 to 1938. In addition to his work in **education**, he worked as a manager for the *West African Pilot* **newspaper** (1947–1948) and as managing director and founder of the African Development Corporation (1948–1954). From 1953 to 1954, Ojike worked for the Minister of Works for the **Eastern Region**. He was an active member of the **National Council of Nigeria and the Cameroons**. In 1949, Ojike was charged and fined by the colonial government for writing an anticolonial article for the *West African Pilot*. He was a member of the **Eastern Region House of Assembly** in 1954. He was also the region's minister of finance. He was a member of the **constitutional conference** that met in London in 1953. He was known for campaigning against Western cultural dominance in Nigeria and using the slogan "boycott all boycottables." The Ojike Memorial Medical Center at Arondizuogu in **Imo State** is named in his honor.

**OJUKWU, CHIEF CHUKWUEMEKA ODUMEGWU (1933– ).** Born in November 1933 in **Zungeru**, Ojukwu is the son of a wealthy businessman, **Sir Louis Odumegwu Ojukwu**. As a young man, he studied in Nigeria, then went to Oxford University for his postgraduate degree (1955). In 1957, he joined the **army** and spent two years training in **Great Britain**. In 1961, he was promoted to the rank of major. He participated in a peacekeeping force in Central Africa. In 1963, he was promoted to lieutenant colonel. In January 1966, **General Johnson Aguiyi-Ironsi** removed the four regional **premiers** and appointed military governors in their place. Ojukwu did not participate in the **coup d'état**, but he benefited from its outcome because Aguiyi-Ironsi made him military governor of the **Eastern Region**. When **General Yakubu Gowon** became head of the **Supreme Military Council**, Ojukwu was hostile and refused to recognize him.

Between May and October 1966, political and ethnic tension resulted in a massacre of **Igbo** communities living in the **Northern Region**. In response, Chief Ojukwu assumed leadership of the Igbo and began plans for the secession of the Igbo-dominated Eastern Region. In 1967, Ojukwu put his plans into motion and declared the Eastern Region as the independent **Republic of Biafra**. This declaration led to Nigeria's **civil war**, which lasted until 1970, when the Republic of Biafra surrendered. After the civil war, Ojukwu fled to neighboring Ivory Coast, and his family tried to relocate to Great Britain. Ojukwu was permitted to return to Nigeria and pardoned in 1982 by **Alhaji Shehu Aliyu Shagari**. He became an active member of the **National Party of Nigeria**, and ran unsuccessfuly for senator in **Anambra State**. After a military coup d'état led by **Major General Muhammadu Buhari** in 1983, he was seen as a security threat and was detained for several months. In 1994, he served as a member of a **constitutional conference** convened by **General Sani Abacha**. He received the honorary chieftaincy title *dim* of Ikemba.

**OJUKWU, SIR LOUIS ODUMEGWU (1909–1966).** Sir Louis was born in Nnewi, in **Anambra State**. After completing his education, he worked as a produce examiner and clerk for John Holt Company. In 1934, he resigned from John Holt and launched his own transport business. Sir Louis became one of Nigeria's wealthiest individuals. His involvement in politics began in 1951, when he joined the **National Council of Nigeria and the Cameroons** (NCNC). He represented the NCNC at a **constitutional conference** that same year. Sir Louis also served in the **Federal House of Representatives** in **Lagos**. He was chairman of the Eastern Region Development Corporation, the Eastern Nigeria Marketing Board, the Nigerian Shipping Line, and Nigerian Cement Company. Sir Louis also worked for Shell–BP, which was Nigeria's largest **petroleum** producer at the time. He was the father of Chief **Chukwuemeka Odumegwu Ojukwu**, who was head of the secessionist **Republic of Biafra** during the **civil war**. Sir Louis received the honorary title Knight Commander of the Order of the British Empire in 1960 and an honorary doctorate from the University of Nigeria at **Nsukka**.

**OKEZIE, CHIEF JOSIAH ONYEBUCHI JOHNSON (1926–2002).** Born in November 1926 in Ibeku, in **Imo State**, as a young man Okezie studied at **Yaba Higher College** in **Lagos**, Achimota College in **Ghana**, Yaba College of Medicine, and University College (present-day **University of Ibadan**). After earning his medical degree, Okezie worked in the **civil service** as a medical officer at Ibeku Central Hospital and Queen Elizabeth Hospital in Umuahia. He was secretary of the Nigerian Medical Association in the **Eastern Region** (1960–1970) and associate editor of the journal *Nigerian Scientist* (1961–1962). From 1965 to 1966, he was a member of the Nigerian Medical Council.

In the political arena, Okezie was a member of the **Eastern Region House of Assembly** (1961–1966) and leader of the short-lived Republic Party (1964–1966). He was a member of the **Federal Executive Council** in 1970. Okezie also served as the federal commissioner of **health** (1970–1971) and federal commission for agriculture and natural resources (1972–1975). He served on the governing councils of Imo State University (1991–1992) and Alvan Ikoku College of Education (1980–1982). From 1982 to 1984, Okezie was on the board of directors of the African Continental Bank. He received the honorary chieftaincy title *ezeomereoha* of Bende (1974) and the title Knight of St. Christopher in the Anglican Church (1988). Okezie died in January 2002.

**OKIGBO, CHRISTOPHER IFEKANDU (1932–1967).** Okigbo was born in August 1932 in Ojoto, in **Anambra State**. He was one of Nigeria's most celebrated poets. As a young man, Okigbo studied at Government College in Umuahia and **University College** (present-day **University of Ibadan**) (1951–1956). He worked as an assistant to the minister of research and information. He also worked as vice principal of Fiditi Grammar School. At the University of Nigeria at **Nsukka**, Okigbo worked as a librarian. He also worked for Cambridge University Press and was coeditor of *Transition* magazine. Okigbo wrote in English. He was one of three major poets of the Mbari Club to be formally recognized at Nigeria's **independence** ceremony (along with **Akinwande Oluwole Soyinka** and **John Pepper Clark**). After he began writing, Okigbo also worked in the tobacco industry, at a primary school, at a library, and for a British press. At the University of Nigeria at Nsukka, he started the African Authors Association.

Okigbo's writing has been described as "manifest postmodern-eclecticism," because he combines local myths with those of other societies in Africa. Okigbo's well-known work, *Labyrinths* (1971), touches on ritual, myth, and colonial power. Although a contributor to the pan-African literary journal *Black Orpheus*, Okigbo dismissed the notion of a shared cultural experience between Africans and African Americans. For this reason, he rejected an award offered to him by the Festival of Negro Arts in 1965. Okigbo's inspiration came from his family: his maternal grandfather was a priest of Idotu, a deity in the **Igbo religion**. Okigbo believed that he was a reincarnation of his grandfather, which he indicated in poems such as *Heavensgates* (1962). He is the younger brother of **Pius Okigbo**. Okigbo died fighting in the **civil war** on the **Biafran** side in October 1967. *See also* LITERATURE.

**OKIGBO COMMISSION.** A research council appointed by **Alhaji Shehu Aliyu Shagari** in 1979. It was named for **Pius Okigbo**, its head, and included six men. The commission was charged with assessing and reimagining Nigeria's **revenue allocation** scheme. The purpose was to lay out, in progressive but plain language, a new distribution plan that Shagari would embrace (he had rejected the conclusions of previous commissions). The commission's report had to include a greater sense of equality and economic development than what currently existed. It recommended the creation of a separate savings fund and that 30 percent of the federal government's revenue be shared evenly with the states. *See also* ECONOMY.

**OKIGBO, PIUS NWABUFO CHARLES (1924–2000).** Born in February 1924 in Ojoto, in **Anambra State**. Okigbo completed his primary and secondary education at various schools in Anambra State. He also studied at **Yaba Higher College** in **Lagos** (1941–1942), University of London (1944–1948 and 1982), Northwestern University (1952–1954, 1955–1957), and Oxford University (1954–1955, 1957–1958). He was an economic adviser for the **Eastern Region** (1960–1962), Federal Republic of Nigeria (1962–1967), and **Republic of Biafra** (1967–1970). He served on the board of the **Nigerian Institute of Social and Eco-**

nomic **Research** (1963–1966). During the **civil war**, he served as economic adviser to **Chief Chukwuemeka Ojukwu**.

In the 1970s and 1980s, Okigbo was a chairman or member of several government committees assigned to reviewing the **constitution**, the national **revenue allocation** scheme, and solid minerals development. For example, he headed **Okigbo Commission** in 1979. He was also involved in pan-African cooperation committees, panels, and advisory boards. In addition, Okigbo held the distinction of being the first Nigerian ambassador to the European Economic Community. He was the older brother of the Nigerian poet **Christopher Okigbo**. He received the honorary title Commander of the Order of the Niger (1977) and honorary degrees from several universities in Nigeria between 1966 and 1997.

**OKOGIE, CARDINAL ARCHBISHOP ANTHONY OLUBUNMI (1936– ).** Born in July 1936 in **Lagos**, Okogie completed his primary and secondary **education** there. In his youth, he committed his life to the **Catholic Church**. Okogie earned advanced degrees in theology from St. Theresa Minor Seminary in **Ibadan**, St. Peter and St. Paul's Seminary in Ibadan, and Urban University in Rome. He became an ordained Catholic priest in 1966 and worked at various cathedrals in Lagos. In the 1970s, he became involved with the Nigerian Broadcasting Corporation and Television. In 1971, he was appointed auxiliary bishop of the Oyo Diocese. Okogie was also the auxiliary bishop to the Archdiocese of Lagos (1972–1973). In 1973, he received the title Cardinal Archbishop of Lagos and still holds that position today. He also served as the vice president, and later president, of the Catholic Bishops Conference of Nigeria (1985–1996). In the early 1990s, Okogie challenged adherents of **Charismatic Christianity** to conform to Roman Catholic doctrine or quit the church. In Nigerian politics, he was a whistleblower, publicizing **corrupt** dealings, unjust **court** decisions, and abuses of power by heads of state. Okogie received the honorary title Commander of the Order of the Niger (1996) and a doctoral degree.

**OKONKWO, MAJOR ALBERT NWAZU.** Okonkwo was governor of the **Mid-Western Region** from August 1967 to September 1967, during the brief period when the **Republic of Biafra** controlled it.

From 19 September to 21 September 1967, Okonkwo acted as governor of the short-lived independent Republic of Benin. He recruited heavily among the members of the **National Council of Nigerian Citizens** for his administration.

**OKOTIE-EBOH, CHIEF FESTUS SAMUEL (1912–1966).** Born July 1912, Okotie-Eboh studied at the Baptist School at Sapele. He received advanced degrees in business administration and podiatry from tertiary institutions in the former Czechoslovakia. In Nigeria, he worked from 1930 to 1931 in the District Office and taught at the Baptist School in Sapele from 1932 to 1936. Also interested in business, Okotie-Eboh worked as an accountant and as manager of the Bata Shoe Company in Sapele (1930–1931). He served on the Sapele Township Advisory Board, Sapele Town Planning Authority, and Warri Ports Advisory Committee. He also acted as secretary for the Warri National Union and secretary-general of the Itsekiri National Society. From 1952 to 1954, he was a member of the **Western House of Assembly**. From 1954 to 1955, he served as the national treasurer of the **National Council of Nigeria and the Cameroons** (NCNC). Okotie-Eboh was appointed federal minister of labor (1955) and later, federal minister of finance. He also served as parliamentary party leader of the NCNC. Okoti-Eboh was killed during the January 1966 military **coup d'état**.

**OKPARA, MICHAEL IBEONUKARA (1920–1984).** Born in December 1920 in Umu-Egwu, in **Abia State**, Okpara studied at **Yaba Higher College** in **Lagos** and received a medical degree from the Nigerian School of Medicine in Lagos. He then worked as a physician (1948–1952). Okpara's focus shifted to national politics in the mid-1950s. He was **premier** of the **Eastern Region** (1960–1966). Under the Detention of Persons Decree established in 1966, he was detained along with many other political leaders. He served as leader of the **National Council of Nigeria and the Cameroons** after **Nnamdi Azikiwe** stepped down. In support of his **ethnic group**, the **Igbo**, he was a political adviser to **Chief Chukwuemeka Ojukwu** in the **Republic of Biafra** during the **civil war**. In the 1970s, he supported the **National Party of Nigeria**. He died in December 1984. *See also* EASTERN REGIONAL GOVERNMENT CRISIS.

**OKWEI, OMU (ca. 1872–1943).** A successful female trader in the **Niger Delta** who, like **King Jaja of Opobo** and **Chief Nana Olomu**, made her wealth as a middleman. She has been described as the "merchant queen of Ossomari." Starting in the early 1900s, Okwei's activities were based in **Onitsha**, in present-day **Anambra State**. She worked with the **Royal Niger Company**, supplying **oil palm** in exchange for various manufactured British goods. Okwei provided lines of credit to the Royal Niger Company, the first in 1910 for £400 a month. She also loaned money to other **foreign trading** companies to purchase canoes and property. Okwei died in 1943, leaving £5,000 in her bank account and property consisting of 24 houses. *See also* TRADE.

**OLAJUWON, HAKEEM (1953– ).** Born in January 1953, Olajuwon lived in **Lagos** until he finished secondary school and moved to the United States to attend the University of Houston. He made basketball history in the United States and is revered in Nigeria as one of the country's most successful athletes. Throughout the 1990s, he played center position with the Houston Rockets. In 1996, the National Basketball Association (NBA) named him one of the 50 Greatest Players in NBA history. His success in the NBA contributed to the rising popularity of basketball as a **sport** in Nigeria.

**OLDMAN COMMISSION.** A body created in 1961 by the **Northern Region**'s government to address issues related to the region's primary school system. The Northern Region was considering the implementation of **universal primary education**, for which it would be financially responsible. The commission focused on recommending a suitable administrative structure that could maintain and coordinate this new **educational** system.

**OLOMU, CHIEF NANA (1858–1916).** Born in Jakpa, in **Delta State**, Olomu was one of the wealthiest, most powerful traders in the **Niger Delta**. He came to power over the Itsekiri, along the **Benin River**, in 1883 after the death of his father and took over his father's **trade**. Olomu developed a trade network that extended over large areas and employed thousands of people. In 1884, Olomu signed a treaty with a British consul ceding sovereignty and accepting free trade. In 1891, the British started to expand the **Oil Rivers Protectorate** to include Olomu's territory. The British accused him of maintaining a trade monopoly that did not favor British interests and of trading **slaves**. They stripped him of his title, given in 1884, of governor of the Benin River. A war broke out between Olomu's people and the British, who found allies among Olomu's neighbors. Olomu fled the region and went to **Lagos**, where he hoped to surrender himself and save his people, in September 1894. He was deported to **Ghana**, where he stayed until 1906. He then returned to the region, and died in July 1916.

**OLORUN-NIMBE, ABUBAKAR IBIYINKA (1908–1975).** Born in **Lagos**, Olorun-Nimbe attended Methodist and **Koranic schools**. He also attended **King's College** in Lagos. After graduating in 1928, he moved to Scotland to earn a medical degree. Around 1937, Olorun-Nimbe returned to Nigeria and worked with the Government Medical Services. His political career began when he joined the **Nigerian National Democratic Party**. He later joined the **National Council of Nigeria and the Cameroons** (NCNC). In 1947, he was appointed to the **Legislative Council**. Three years later, he was elected mayor of Lagos. For refusing to step down from his post in the **Western House of Assembly**, he was expelled from the NCNC in 1951. He was also accused of fraudulent activities as head of the **Lagos Town Council** in 1953.

**OLUWASANMI, HEZEKIAH ADEDUNMOLA (1919–1983).** Born in November 1919, as a young man Oluwasanmi attended St. Paul's School, Ilesha Grammar School, and Abeokuta Grammar School. He went to the United States to complete his advanced studies in agricultural economics at Moorhouse College and Harvard University. Oluwasanmi returned to Nigeria around 1955 and taught at the **University of Ibadan** until 1966, when he became the vice chancellor of the University of Ife (present-day **Obafemi Awolowo University**). He held that position until 1975. The university library at Ife was named after him in 1980.

**ONABANJO, CHIEF VICTOR OLABISI (1927–1990).** Onabanjo was born in February 1927 in **Lagos**. In the early 1950s, he studied journalism in England. Between 1951 and 1964, he worked as an editor for the *Nigerian Citizen* and *Radio Times* **newspapers**. During that time, he also wrote political exposés under the pseudonym Aiyekoto. Onabanjo joined the **Action Group** and served as a member of parliament (1964–1966). In 1967, he was the civil commissioner for home affairs and information. He was also a member of the Western State Executive Council (1967–1970). In 1977, he joined the constituent assembly and, one year later, became a member of the **Unity Party of Nigeria** (UPN). He served as governor of **Ogun State** from 1979 to 1983. During the military **coup d'état** led by **Major General Muhammadu Buhari** in 1983, Onabanjo, along with **Bola Ige** and **Chief Michael Ajasin**, was accused of **corruption** pertaining to the UPN. Onabanjo was sentenced to 22 years in prison. Five years later, however, he was pardoned by **General Ibrahim Babangida**. Onabanjo died in April 1990.

**ONABOLU, CHIEF AINA (1882–1963).** Born in Ijebu, Onabolu has been regarded by many as the father of modern Nigerian **art** because of his commitment to incorporating art **education** into primary and secondary school curricula. He pressured and worked with the colonial government to make this idea a reality. As an adult, Onabolu studied drawing and painting in England and France. He returned to Nigeria in 1923 to teach art in **Lagos**. In 1920, Onabolu showed his work in Lagos at an exhibition entitled Pictures of Onabolu. He painted his first major portrait, *Portrait of Mrs. Spencer Savage*, in 1906. There is an art complex named after him in Lagos.

**ONDO STATE.** A state created in 1976 out of **Western State**. It is one of Nigeria's current 36 states. It is located in southwestern Nigeria, with the Bight of Benin as its natural southern boundary. The capital is the town of Akure. The dominant **ethnic groups** in Ondo State are the **Yoruba** and Yoruba subgroups, making Yoruba and its dialects the major **languages**. Economic activities in Ondo include the cultivation of **cocoa**, **oil palm**, **kolanut**, and rubber. **Petroleum** production offshore and bitumen extraction onshore also contribute to the state's **economy**. *See also* EKITI STATE; STATE CREATION.

**ONITSHA. Oral tradition** holds that the town was founded in the 18th century by people migrating northeast from **Benin**. Starting in

1856, Onitsha served as a trading post for European **traders**. The (Anglican) **Church Missionary Society**, under the direction of **Bishop Samuel Ajayi Crowther** and others, established a missionary station in Onitsha one year later. In 1885, a **Catholic Church** mission was also erected. Onitsha claims the first indigenous Anglican and Catholic bishops. It is the birthplace of the popular **Onitsha Market Literature** genre. It was also the home of a wealthy female trader, **Omu Okwei**, in the early 20th century. Today, Onitsha is a major center of commerce in **Anambra State** in southeastern Nigeria. It has a population of approximately 500,000. It was the site of violence against Muslims in 2006.

**ONITSHA MARKET LITERATURE.** A form of **literature** with broad, popular appeal that originated in the city of **Onitsha** in southwestern Nigeria. It was highly popular from the 1940s to the 1960s. Works in this genre were written primarily in English to cater to the Western-educated Nigerian elite. Most commonly, these works addressed the rapid social change that came with **decolonization** and **independence**. Authors of these works consciously made Onitsha Market Literature a popular voice, praising social change and encouraging a nationalist environment. **Kano Market Literature** shares themes with this genre.

**ONWUEME, OSONYE TESS (1955– ).** Born in September 1955 in the **Niger Delta**, Onwueme earned advanced degrees in drama from the University of Ife (present-day **Obafemi Awolowo University**) and the University of Benin (1988). Her plays confront cultural taboos and gender inequality. Her most notable plays include *Shakara: Dance-Hall Queen* (2001) and *Tell It to Women* (1995). Onwueme has received numerous grants and awards for her work, including from the Nigerian Association of Authors and the Ford Foundation. She currently teaches at the University of Wisconsin at Eau-Claire. *See also* THEATER; WOMEN.

**O'ODUA PEOPLE'S CONGRESS (OPC).** A political organization created in August 1994 in response to the annulled **election of 12 June 1993**. The OPC is named after Oduduwa, the collective ancestor of the **Yoruba** people. It focuses on promoting and protecting

Yoruba political interests. To achieve this goal, the OPC called for regional autonomy and the purging of **corrupt** elements within the Yoruba **ethnic group**. Its founders included Frederick Faseun and **Bekolari Ransome-Kuti**. For a brief time, it was a member of the Joint Action Committee for Democracy, which was led by **Chief Abdul-Ganiyu Fawehinmi**. The OPC clashed with **General Sani Abacha**'s forces on numerous occasions, resulting in the arrest of several members. Faseun, for example, was imprisoned for almost two years starting in 1996. The OPC is largely viewed as a vigilante group that formed in response to the nation's political failings. In 1999, a militant faction led by Gani Adams emerged, earning the congress a reputation for violence and intimidation, particularly within **Lagos**. Hundreds of civilians have been injured and killed since 1994. The congress has clashed with other ethnic-based organizations, such as the **Ijaw Youth Council**.

**OPERATION BIAFRAN BABY.** The name given to an airstrike mission on federal forces led by **Count Carl Gustaf Von Rosen** on behalf of the secessionist **Republic of Biafra** in May 1969 during the **civil war**.

**OPERATION FEED THE NATION.** A hunger eradication program launched in May 1976, based on **Ghana**'s Operation Feed Yourself. **General Olusegun Obasanjo** created this program to encourage Nigerians to "grow anything you like, but grow something." Operation Feed the Nation was part of Nigeria's **Green Revolution** and paired with the **River Basin Development Authorities** scheme. The program had two main objectives: to make Nigeria self-sufficient in food and to curb inflation. **Major General Shehu Musa Yar'Adua** was the head of the campaign. The program had limited success in curbing food shortages. In 1977, Nigeria began importing hundreds of thousands of tons of fertilizer, seeds, and chemicals to be distributed to farmers. The scheme was abolished in February 1980 and was replaced by the National Council on Green Revolution, which pursued similar goals.

**ORACLE.** Consulting an oracle involves a priest (or priestess) acting as a medium through whom gods and ancestors speak. The term also refs to a place at which advice was sought. In Nigeria, the latter is more common. An oracle is primarily identified in an object, such as a hill or rock formation, not specifically a person. The response of an oracle is typically incomplete and obscure, requiring a priest's interpretation. The presence of oracles is important for many societies in Nigeria, particularly before the 20th century. **Arochukwu**, for example, was the home of the **Aro** people's oracle, Chukwu Ibinokpabi. This oracle settled disputes between villages. *See also* DIVINATION; RELIGION.

**ORAL TRADITION.** Most societies in Nigeria did not have a written **language** before the arrival of Europeans. The introduction of **Islam** to the **Hausa** and **Fulani** of **northern Nigeria** in the 11th century was accompanied by classical Arabic, but it was not widely used outside of royal courts and **Koranic schools**. For the most part, people in Nigeria recorded and recited their history through oral transmission. Some royal families kept an individual trained as a historian and praise-giver to record the family's history. In the **Yoruba language**, these people are referred to as *arokin*. Oral tradition includes tales of origin, genealogical lists, poetry, praises, and lists of **kings**. A skilled transmitter of oral tradition may keep an audience entertained for hours, using a mixture of fantastic tales, history, and proverbs. Praise-singers are often the primary transmitters of oral tradition, because they compose and perform songs that promote rulers and royal families. Naram-bad was a famous Hausa praise-singer in the 1950s.

Historians find oral traditions both valuable and problematic. These traditions provide insight into royal history, but blur the line between fact and fiction. Some of the most well-known oral traditions are about the origin of the Yoruba and **Igbo** people. Muslim societies in Nigeria, such as the Hausa, often connect themselves to descendants of the Prophet Muhammad, or at least Muslim travelers from the Middle East, in their origin stories. **Borgu** oral tradition, for example, traces their ancestry to **Kisra**. *See also* MUSIC.

**ORANMIYAN. Oral tradition** places Oranmiyan as the son of Oduduwa, the founding father of the **Yoruba** people and the sacred town of **Ile-Ife**. The belief is that sometime between the 9th and 14th centuries, Oranmiyan left Ile-Ife in search of a new place to settle and establish a kingdom of his own. After traveling westward for some time, his horse slipped and he declared that location his new home. That place was named Oyo, which means "slippery place" in the **Yoruba language**. Oranmiyan has been credited as the founder and builder of the **Oyo Empire**. According to oral tradition among the people of **Benin**, Oranmiyan was also the founder of their kingdom, because he married the daughter of a Bini chief. When he decided to return to Ile-Ife, he left the **Benin Kingdom** to his son, Eweka I.

**ORGANIZATON OF AFRICAN UNITY (OAU).** *See* AFRICAN UNION.

**ORGANIZATION OF PETROLEUM EXPORTING COUNTRIES (OPEC).** An international organization formed in Baghdad in 1960 to influence and monitor **petroleum** production to benefit and protect oil-exporting countries. Nigeria became a member in July 1971. It benefited from an embargo against Western nations supporting Israel that was started by several (not all) OPEC members in 1973–1974. Although the embargo lasted only a few months and failed to cause major shortages, it had a tremendous impact on Nigeria's **economy**. Virtually overnight Nigeria was inundated by a rising tide of profits from oil sales. The result was an economic boom in Nigeria and an injection of oil revenue into Nigeria's ailing states. After the oil boom of the 1970s, Nigeria remained an active member of the organization. **Alhaji Chief Ali Monguno** served as president of OPEC from 1972 to 1973 and **Sir Alhaji Rilwanu Lukman** from 1986 to 1989.

**ORIZU, NWAFOR AKWAEKE (1914–1999).** Born in July 1914 in Nnewi, in **Anambra State**, Orizu completed his early education in **Onitsha** before studying in **Ghana**. He received his advanced degrees, including a doctorate, in political science from universities in the United States. During the **First Republic**, he served as senate president. For a brief time, Orizu was commander-in-chief of the **armed forces** (October 1965–January 1966). He later worked as an editor for the *West African Examiner* **newspaper**. He was a member of the **National Council of Nigeria and the Cameroons** and founded the Nigeria Secondary School in his hometown. He received honorary doctorates from Lane University (1948) and University of Jos (1982). Orizu died in March 1999 in Germany.

**OSADEBAY, CHIEF DENNIS CHUKADEBE (1911–1994).** Born in June 1911, Osadebay was raised in Asaba, in **Delta State**. As a young man, he studied at the Government School in Asaba, Sacred Heart School in **Calabar**, and **Hope Waddell Training Institute**. For his advanced degree in law, he attended the University of London. Back in Nigeria, he worked as a customs officer and supervisor for the Department of Customs and Excise (1930–1946). He served as a member of the House of Representatives (1952–1954) and **Western House of Assembly** (1951–1952). He also acted as leader of the **National Council of Nigeria and the Cameroons** and the opposition representative in the **Western House of Assembly** (1954–1956). Osadebay's involvement in regional politics also included serving as a member of the Western Region Privy Council and Western Region Scholarship Selection Board (1952). After **independence**, he worked as an administrator of the **Mid-Western Region** (August 1963–February 1964) and became the region's **premier** (February 1964–January 1966). During the 1970s, Osabeday withdrew from national politics and focused on practicing private law. He received several honorary chieftaincy titles, including *ojiba* of Asaba and *odogwu* of Ashara. He also received an honorary doctorate from the University of Niger at **Nsukka** and the title Grand Commander of the Order of the Niger. Osadebay died in December 1994.

**OSHIOMHOLE, ADAMS ALIYU (1953– ).** Oshiomhole was born in April 1953 in Iyamoh, in **Edo State**. He studied at Ruskin College in Oxford (1977–1979) and the National Institute of Policy and Strategic Studies in **Jos** (1987). He worked in textiles as a staff member and, later, union leader. He was the branch secretary of the National Union of Tailoring, Garment, and Textile Workers of Nigeria (1971–1974). Within that **trade union**, he worked as a state secretary (1974–1975), assistant national secretary (1976–1977), deputy national secretary (1980–1981), and general secretary (1987–1997). During the 1990s, he was a member of the Constitutional Debate Coordinating Committee, **Vision 2010** committee, and National Council of Nigeria Vision. Since 1999, he has been the president of the **Nigerian Labour Congress**. From 2001 to 2002, he served as chairman of the National Anti-AIDS Campaign. In April 2007, he became governor of Edo State.

**OSOFISAN, FEMI (1946– ).** Born in Erunwon, in **Ogun State**, Osofisan is a celebrated playwright, novelist, and poet. He attended primary school in **Ile-Ife** and secondary school in **Ibadan**. In the late 1960s, he studied at the University of Dakar in Senegal and at the **University of Ibadan**. In 1971, he acted in **Akinwande Oluwole Soyinka**'s *Madmen and the Specialists* (1970). He taught at the University of Ibadan in the 1970s in the Department of Modern Languages. He is currently head of the Department of Theatre Arts there. In 2006, Osofisan received the Fonlon-Nichols Award from the Research Institute for African and Caribbean Literature at the University of Alberta. He is also the recipient of an award from the Association of Nigerian Authors for poetry in 1989 and for **theater** in 1980. He was the artistic director of the Kakaun Sela Company of theatrical performance. His works focus on Nigeria as a failed state. His plays include *Aringidin and the Nightwatchmen* (1991) and *The Oriki of a Grasshopper* (1995).

**OSUN STATE.** A state created out of **Oyo State** in 1991. It is one of Nigeria's current 36 states. It is located in southwestern Nigeria, and the capital is Osogbo. The population is predominantly **Yoruba**. The dominant **religions** are **Christianity** and **Islam**. Osun State is the home of **Ile-Ife**, the sacred Yoruba town. The state is named after a goddess who reigns over love, wealth, and diplomacy and was a wife of **Sango**, in the **Yoruba religion** and **oral tradition**. Economic activities in Osun State include the cultivation of **oil palm**, tubers, **cocoa**, and citrus fruits. *See also* STATE CREATION.

**OSUNDARE, NIYI (1947– ).** Born in 1947 in Ikere-Ekiti, in **Ondo State**. Osundare studied **literature** at universities in Nigeria, England, and Canada. He is a prominent contemporary writer in Nigeria, writing poems and plays in English. He was a distinguished professor at the **University of Ibadan**. In his collection of poems, *Songs of the Marketplace* (1983), Osundare explores the neglect of rural dwellers in Nigeria by the government. He was the winner of the

Commonwealth Poetry Prize in 1986. His poems have been regularly published in local **newspapers**. He has been teaching and writing at the University of New Orleans since 1997.

**OVONRAMWEN.** *See* BENIN KINGDOM; GALLWEY TREATY.

**OYELAMI, CHIEF MURAINA (1940– ).** Born in Iragbiji, in **Osun State**, Oyelami studied painting, printmaking, and acting and acquired a degree in **theater** from the University of Ife (present-day **Obafemi Awolowo University**) in 1978. He was a member of the Duro Ladipo Theatre Company. He also worked in the Osogbo **art** workshops, famous for the Osun Sacred Grove. He taught music and dance at the University of Ife (1976–1987). Oyelami founded the Obatala Centre for Creative Arts in Iragbiji. He also worked as the curator for the University Museum at the University of Ife. He has had several solo exhibitions in **Lagos**, Washington, D.C., London, New Dehli, and Paris, among others. Oyelami also published several works on his experience as an artist, especially of Osogbo. He was commissioned to paint a mural in **Ile-Ife**. In 1992, he was the musical director for the production of **Akinwande Oluwole Soyinka**'s *Death and the King's Horsemen* (1975) in England. He was a fellow at Amherst College (2002–2003). Oyelami holds the title *eesa* (**chief**) of Iragbiji.

**OYO EMPIRE.** This great empire was situated in southwestern Nigeria and emerged sometime between the 10th and 14th centuries. In the **Yoruba language**, *oyo* means slippery place. According to Yoruba **oral tradition**, it was founded by **Oranmiyan**, the son of Oduduwa, who left **Ile-Ife** and decided to settle at Oyo. At the height of its power in the 17th century, Oyo extended its control to the Dahomey Empire (in present-day **Benin**), Asante Empire (in present-day **Ghana**), **Borgu**, and Tapas (territory of the **Nupe**). The desire to extend into Dahomey stemmed from Oyo's slave-raiding activities. Controlling Borgu was necessary to tap into the northern trade. **Sango** was the fourth *alaafin* (**king**) of Oyo, and was deified upon his death. Oyo began losing territory in the 1780s, when small Yoruba kingdoms, especially **Ilorin**, began to extricate themselves from Oyo control. **Abiodun** and **Ojigi** are notable *alaafin* from that time period. The

Oyo Empire began to decline in the early 19th century and collapsed in 1833. *See also* IJAYE WAR; SLAVERY/SLAVE TRADE.

**OYO STATE.** A state created in 1991 out of **Western State**. It is one of Nigeria's current 36 states. It is located in southwestern Nigeria, sharing its western boundary with **Benin**. It is named after the **Oyo Empire**. The capital is **Ibadan**, the site of the **University of Ibadan**. The dominant **language** and **ethnic group** is **Yoruba** (and its sub-groups and dialects). Economic activities in the state include the cultivation of tubers, **bananas**, **cocoa**, **oil palm**, and cashews. *See also* STATE CREATION.

**OZOLUA (?–1520).** A ruler of the **Benin Kingdom**, Ozolua was the third son of **Ewuare**. He ascended to the throne in 1480. Five years later, a Portuguese explorer, Joao Alfonso d'Aveiro, visited Benin. Ozolua agreed to open diplomatic relations with d'Aveiro and the Portuguese by allowing **Christian** missionaries to set up a station and educate his people. Ozolua traveled with d'Aveiro to Portugal and returned to Benin with luxury items. He is also remembered for substantially extending the boundaries of the kingdom, almost reaching **Lagos**. His son, **Esigie**, replaced him as ruler around 1514.

**– P –**

**PALM WINE.** An alcoholic beverage made from the sap of an **oil palm** tree. It is a popular locally produced drink in Nigeria. The sap is tapped from the tree, then filtered and diluted with **water**. As it ferments, the sap turns into a drinkable liquid with a low **alcohol** content. Palm wine is often distilled to create a concentrated drink with high alcohol content. Unless refrigerated, palm wine has a short shelf life and must be consumed within a few hours. It plays an important role in society as a drink for special occasions and improving health. A young man's request to marry a young woman often requires presenting palm wine to her father. It is also mixed with roots and herbs for medicinal purposes. The **Yoruba** call palm wine *emu* and a palm wine tapper *ademu*. During the colonial period, it was such an important business that merchants formed a **trade union** in 1942,

called the Palm Wine Sellers' Association, based in **Lagos**. *See also*
BRIDE PRICE; MUSIC.

**PALMER, SIR HERBERT RICHARD (1877–1958).** Born in **Great
Britain**, Palmer served as the **lieutenant governor** of **northern Nigeria** for the British colonial government from 1925 to 1930. Palmer
was one of the few individuals who owned an English version of the
*Kano Chronicle*, which he published in 1928.

**PAM, JOHN WASH (1922– ).** Pam was born in October 1922 in
Foron, in **Plateau State**. As a young man, he studied at **King's College** in **Lagos** (1961–1962) and **Ahmadu Bello University** in **Zaria**
(1963–1966). He worked as an assistant secretary to the military
governor's office in **Kaduna** (1966–1967) and as an administrative
officer of the Statutory Corporation Services Commission (1970–
1971). Pam was external affairs officer from 1967 to 1970. He was
also an administrative officer for the Ministry of Mines and Power
in Lagos (1971–1972). From 1977 to 1978, Pam served as a member
of the Constituent Assembly. He also served as a senator and deputy
president of the Senate from 1979 to 1983.

**PARAMOUNT CHIEF.** A term applied, particularly by the British, to
an indigenous ruler with nearly ultimate authority over a region and
group of people. In Nigeria, the term **chief** is often interchangeable
with **king**. *See also* WARRANT CHIEF.

**PARK, MUNGO (1771–1806).** A British explorer who went to Nigeria to determine the course of the **Niger River** between 1797 and
1806, on two separate expeditions. Park was commissioned by the
African Association of Great Britain. In 1805, he visited the town
of Birni Yawuri. He recorded his observations of the Hausaland–
Timbuktu trade. During his second expedition, Park visited Bussa
and drowned in the Bubaru rapids in 1806. *See also* LANDER,
RICHARD AND JOHN.

**PAWNSHIP.** A form of debt peonage that provided both labor and
credit for mutual benefit within a community. In the **Yoruba language**, it is called *iwofa*. It is frequently confused with **slavery**,

although it functions quite differently. The arrangement started with a creditor giving a loan to an individual. In lieu of paying interest, the borrower, or someone taking his or her place, would work for the creditor until the loan was repaid. The borrower worked for an agreed upon number of days per week. A young boy or girl, acting as the borrower's substitute, usually lived with the creditor's family until the loan was repaid. At the start of the 20th century, farmers relied on the pawnship system. Colonial officials sought to eliminate it because they saw it as a form of slavery. Child pawnship was banned in 1927, and the entire system was prohibited in 1938. This colonial proclamation hit towns like **Abeokuta** hard, because it reduced access to credit that many individuals sorely needed at the time. Established female cloth dyers in Abeokuta took in girls to work as assistants and learn the craft. These assistants were often pawns who lived with the dyers until their debt was paid, which could take several years.

**PEANUTS.** *See* GROUNDNUTS.

**PELEWURA, MADAM ALIMOTU (?–1951).** The founder and leader of the Lagos Market Women's Association, Pelewura was a **Yoruba** Muslim woman born in **Lagos**. By 1900, she had begun a career as a fish **trader**, which she learned from her mother. In 1910, she was recognized as a leader of Ereko market **women** in Lagos by the **Native Authority**. By the 1920s, she had been elected *alaga* (**chief** of market women). In response to a rumor circulating in 1932 that the colonial government intended to levy a **tax** on women in Lagos, Pelewura organized market women to protest. It is believed that because of organized and vocal opposition to such a tax, the colonial government shelved the idea for eight years. In 1932, she was appointed to a representative committee in Lagos. As a member of this committee, she represented more than eight market women's organizations. In 1938, Pelewura joined the executive committee of the Nigerian Union of Young Democrats while maintaining her loyalty to the **Nigerian National Democratic Party**. In 1940, she led market women in Lagos in a protest against the application of an income tax on women earning at least £50 per annum. With thousands of supporters behind her, Pelewura argued that this income limit would soon be altered to apply to all women. Pressure from market women and others resulted in the colonial administration increasing the taxable level income bracket for women to £200 per year. Until her death, Pelewura led market women in protests against a variety of economically restrictive measures imposed by the colonial government during **World War II**.

**PENTECOSTAL CHRISTIANITY.** Pentecostalism was founded by Charles Parham in 1900 in the United States. Pentecostal churches focus on the personal baptism of the Holy Spirit and speaking in tongues. Students of Charles Parham broke off to form their own Pentecostal churches in the United States and Europe. Pentecostalism reached Nigeria in the 1930s and has existed independent of the global movement. For example, in 1916 the Christ Army Church was founded in the **Niger Delta**. Another popular Pentecostal church in Nigeria is the **Christ Apostolic Church**, founded in 1930. In 1987, Pentecostal churches in Nigeria created an umbrella organization called the Pentecostal Fellowship of Nigeria. It is one of many kinds of Fundamentalist Christianity that are popular in Nigeria. *See also* CHRISTIANITY; RELIGION.

**PEOPLE'S DEMOCRATIC PARTY (PDP).** One of nine **political parties** authorized by **General Alhaji Abdulsalami Abubakar**'s regime to present candidates for the 1999 **election**. Since its formation, the PDP has dominated the Nigerian government. It is considered a centrist party of wealthy businessmen and retired military officers. Significant party members include **General Olusegun Obasanjo** and the current vice president, **Goodluck Jonathan**. Opponents of the party see the People's Democratic Party as guilty of turning Nigeria into a one-party state. President **Usmaru Musa Yar'Adua** was the party's presidential candidate in the April 2007 elections.

**PEOPLE'S REDEMPTION PARTY (PRP).** A leftist **political party** that formed in 1978 to run **Alhaji Muhammed Aminu Kano** as a presidential candidate in the 1979 **elections**. **Alhaji Mohammed Rimi** was a founding member. The PRP was one of only five registered political parties in that election. In 1983, it joined the **Nigerian People's Party**, and the **Great Nigerian People's Party** to form the **Progressive Parties Alliance**. In 1983, after the **coup d'état**, it was banned along with all other political parties. In 1999, it was one of only nine political parties that received authorization from **General Alhaji Abdulsalami Abubakar** to put forward candidates. Members included notable public figures such as **Alhaji Abubakar Musa, Yusufu Bala Usman, Umaru Musa Yar'Adua**, and **Chinua Achebe**, who served as deputy president of the party in 1983.

**PETROLEUM.** Nigeria is the world's 11th largest producer of oil in the world, with 42 percent of its crude oil going to the United States. It has been a member of the **Organization of Petroleum Exporting Countries** since 1971. Most of Nigeria's oil is located in the **Niger Delta**, with an estimated 37 billion barrels in reserves. Commercial quantities of oil were discovered by the Shell–BP Petroleum Company in 1956. Two years later, Nigeria exported its first batch of crude oil. Today, Nigeria produces roughly 3 million barrels per day, 2 million of which is onshore and the remainder offshore. The majority of Nigeria's oil production is done through a joint venture between **Nigerian National Petroleum Corporation** and transnational firms, such as ExxonMobil, Chevron, or Agip. The largest producer of oil is the Shell Petroleum Development Company, based in **Port Harcourt**. **Bonny** and **Warri** are also major oil towns.

Nigeria exports most of its high quality crude oil and, regrettably, imports much of the refined petroleum products it consumes. Since the late 1960s, Nigeria has struggled to balance its lucrative oil industry with other aspects of its **economy**. Oil accounts for 95 percent of the government's revenue, making Nigeria highly dependent on a finite commodity. Its **agricultural** output has dropped significantly since 1960. Nigeria has four refineries, all in fairly poor condition, and is eager to privatize them. Offers have emerged but, for reasons unknown, have not been successful. Aliko Dangote, a Nigerian billionaire, bought two of the refineries in April 2007, but found the sale canceled.

Nigerian citizens, particularly in the Niger Delta, complain that they do not see the benefits of being an oil-rich country. Indeed, life among the oil fields and facilities in the Niger Delta is dangerous. Pollution and displacement have destroyed the social fabric and left fishing villages without economic means of survival. Since the 1980s, the **Niger Delta Conflict** has attracted international attention and harsh responses from the Nigerian government. Disruptions between 2005 and 2008 by resistance groups have caused a 20 percent drop in production. Periodically, Nigeria sets up committees to review complaints from the region. For example, **General Ibrahim Babangida** appointed the **Oil Mineral Producing Areas Development Commission** in 1992 to review concerns raised by the **Ogoni** and **Ijaw**. In 2000, **General Olusegun Obasanjo** created the **Niger Delta Development Commission**. Nigeria has also struggled to train and employ Nigerians to work in the oil industry as part of an **indigenization** project. Those who do work for the oil and natural gas industry are members of **trade unions**, such as the National Union of Petroleum and Natural Gas Workers. **Frank Kokori** was the national secretary of the union in 1978.

Despite being a major producer of oil and natural gas, Nigeria regularly suffers shortages, particularly of power turbines that generate **electricity** for the country. Nigeria has also been criticized for not handling its oil revenues properly and engaging in poor planning and **corruption**. For example, in 1995 Nigeria set up the Petroleum Trust Fund to save oil revenue for the future, when the oil runs out. This fund has been accused of a lack of transparency. Inquiries have also been made over the years about the disappearance of oil revenue.

In addition to crude oil, Nigeria also has natural gas and bitumen reserves. In 2005, construction began on a transnational pipeline that allows Nigeria to sell its natural gas at discounted prices to its West African neighbors. However, Nigeria has until recently had tense relations with **Cameroon** over possession of the oil-rich **Bakassi Peninsula**. *See also* COAL.

**PHELPS-STOKES COMMISSION.** *See* EDUCATION.

**PHILLIPSON COMMISSION.** After **World War II**, Great Britain reviewed its colonial policies and made a number of changes with regard to Nigeria's **economy**. The Phillipson Commission was the first of many formed between the mid-1940s and 1964 that established a system for **revenue allocation** earned through exports. After conducting research, in 1946 the commission made its recommendations, which included a distribution structure in which 50 percent of export earnings would return to the region of origin, 35 percent would be shared by the regions, including the region of origin, and 15 percent would go to the central government. This ratio became the basic structure on which all subsequent revenue allocation proposals were based. *See also* HICKS-PHILLIPSON COMMISSION; RAISMAN COMMISSION.

**PILGRIMAGE.** Many Christians and Muslims in Nigeria go on a spiritual pilgrimage at least once in their lives. The most common form of pilgrimage is Muslims going to Mecca (referred to in Arabic as the ***hajj***) at least once in their lives if they are financially and physically able. Like **Ramadan**, *hajj* is one of the Five Pillars of **Islam**. **Christians** may also embark on their own spiritual journeys, to historic Christian sites in Jerusalem. *See also* AIRLINES.

**PLANTAINS.** *See* BANANAS.

**PLATEAU STATE.** A state created in 1976 out of **Benue-Plateau State**. It is one of Nigeria's current 36 states. It is located in north-central Nigeria in the **Middle Belt** region. It is named after its location on the Jos Plateau. The capital is the colonial mining town of **Jos**. Plateau State is considered one of the most diverse states in Nigeria, with over 40 **ethnic groups** represented. Economic activities in the state include the cultivation of potatoes and grains, herding of cattle, and fishing. In recent years, Plateau State has been the site of a series of clashes between **Christians** and Muslims. *See also* STATE CREATION.

**POLICE.** The role of the police in Nigeria has always been complicated by who is protecting whom, under whose rules and guidelines. During the colonial period, police forces (also described as military units) were composed of Nigerians with European leadership. They were charged with protecting European interests and maintaining European notions of law and order. However, they were also called upon in times of colonial expansion to assist in stripping sovereignty from a village or kingdom. The Hausa Constabulary, for example, was created in 1863 for the purpose of protecting **Lagos Colony**. This security force became the (Royal) **West African Frontier Force** in 1900. There was also a Lagos Constabulary. The **Royal**

**Niger Constabulary** was formed in 1886 to protect and defend the **Royal Niger Company** from its base in **Lokoja**. The **Niger Coast Constabulary** replaced the Royal Niger Constabulary in 1894. Much of what started as police forces became the basis of Nigeria's **armed forces**.

Europeans' ethnic bias within these security forces created lasting tension, particularly during the decades of military rule. Since **independence**, the police have been frequently accused of **corruption**, abuse of power, and ineffectiveness. The police are particularly loathed for their practice of creating bogus checkpoints along **roads** for the purpose of extracting cash from drivers. To reform the police, in 1999 the Nigerian government set up the Police Service Commission, a committee of nonpolice individuals whose mission is to restore public trust. It has the power to promote and discipline police officers. *See also* EDET, INSPECTOR GENERAL LOUIS OROLA; PREST, CHIEF ARTHUR EDWARD; SHINKAFI, AL-HAJI UMARU.

**POLIO.** Nigeria is second only to Ibdia in the number of cases of polio per year. It has worked with the World Health Organization (WHO) to reduce the number of cases and provide better care for those stricken with the disease. Polio vaccinations are available, but Nigeria struggles to supply them to all parts of the country. Nigeria has also struggled with people refusing to give their children the vaccinations because they distrust the vaccine and lack knowledge of its benefits. In 2003, the **Kano State** government refused to allow WHO workers to administer polio vaccinations. **Kaduna State** and **Zamfara State** followed suit. The government accused the WHO of giving its citizens medicine laced with antifertility drugs and **HIV/AIDS** as part of a Western ploy to eradicate the Muslim population of Nigeria. It took several years to establish trust in **northern Nigeria** to complete the vaccination project. *See also* HEALTH; MALARIA.

**POLITICAL ORIENTATION COMMITTEE.** A political organization created by Nigerian intellectuals during Nigeria's **civil war**. It was founded by **Chinua Achebe** and several others. The committee's focus was to plan the rebuilding of the **Republic of Biafra** after the war's end.

**POLITICAL PARTIES.** The role and influence of political parties in Nigeria has depended on the political climate in any given year. For example, there was a flurry of activity generated by various vibrant and vocal political parties in 1958, but virtually no action between 1966 and 1978. The first opportunity for genuine political parties to promote political candidates in a democratic system occurred in the two years running up to independence in 1960. Prior to that time, any political mobilization was done by anticolonial pressure groups that rarely identified themselves as political parties. More commonly, a political organization was called a "union," such as the **Nigerian Union of Students** and the **Bauchi General Improvement Union**, or a "movement," such as the **Lagos Youth Movement**. Between 1958 and 1960, Nigerians formed political parties along regional, religious, and ethnic lines. Out of habit, they also continued the practice of using terms such as "congress" or "council" instead of "party." The **Action Congress** appealed to predominantly Yoruba people living in southwestern Nigeria, and the **Northern People's Congress** attracted Muslim **Hausa** and **Fulani** living in **northern Nigeria**. Many scholars argue that its first **election** set Nigeria on a political crash course for the next 40 years, as sociopolitical groups competed with one another for political control of the country.

In the second half of the 20th century, there were several **coups d'état**, assassinations of major political players, and the banning and unbanning of political parties. Because of the long lapses between democratic governance in Nigeria, political parties frequently collapsed, and they rarely ran a candidate for more than one election cycle. This chaos began with a coup d'état and the banning of all existing political parties in 1966. The decree affected those parties from the first election as well as those that formed after 1960, such as the **Mid-West People's Congress** and the **United People's Party**. During this violent regime change, **Chief Samuel Ladoke Akintola** of the **Nigerian National Democratic Party** and **Sir Alhaji Ahmadu Bello** (the *sardauna* of Sokoto) of the Northern People's Congress were killed. In preparation for the **Second Republic** (1979–1983), **General Olusegun Obasanjo** allowed the formation of five political parties: **National Party of Nigeria**, **Great Nigerian People's Party**, **People's Redemption Party**, **Unity Party of Nigeria**, and **Nigerian People's Party**. During the 1980s, political parties were not allowed to form or promote candidates for any governing bodies. Any form of dissent was not tolerated.

The greatest political activity has occurred during the past 15 years, with political parties promoting candidates for democratic elections. In preparation for the **election of 12 June 1993**, **General Ibrahim Babangida** created two political parties, the **Social Democratic Party** (SDP) and the **National Republican Convention**. After people cast their ballots, Babangida annulled the election and disbanded the political parties. **General Alhaji Abdulsalami Abubakar** allowed the formation of nine political parties in preparation for a democratic election in 1999. Notable parties in this election included the **Alliance for Democracy** and the Social Democratic Party. Since 1999, political parties in Nigeria have been allowed to operate without harassment. Although there are more than 10 parties promoting candidates, the **People's Democratic Party** (PDP) has dominated the federal and state elections. The former president, General Olusegun Obasanjo, and the current president, **Umaru Musa Yar'Adua**, are PDP members.

**POLYGAMY.** The marriage of one man to multiple wives has a long history in Nigeria, among Muslims and non-Muslims alike. The **Koran** restricts the number of wives attached to one Muslim man to four, as long as he can provide and care for them equally. Among the **Yoruba**, for example, polygamy was practiced not only among Muslims, but also by adherents of the **Yoruba religion** and even **Christians**. By the 1950s, an estimated 62 percent of Yoruba men in the **cocoa** producing regions of southwestern Nigeria were polygamous, having at least two wives. *See also* ISLAM; *PURDAH*; WOMEN.

**POPULATION.** Nigeria's population has been a source of both problems and pride. In 2006, Nigeria conducted a census, which confirmed that Nigeria is Africa's most populated country, with an estimated 140 million people. There are 3.5 million more men than women. **Kano State** and **Lagos State** are Nigeria's most populated, and the **Federal Capital Territory** is the least populated. Overall, the **Northern Region** has a higher population than the **Southern Region**. The life expectancy for Nigerians is 51 years, and the median age in Nigeria is 18. Nigeria has a high infant mortality rate, with one in five children dying before the age of five. Also, the prevalence of **HIV/AIDS** in Nigeria, which is officially reported at 3.1 percent, continues to rise.

Despite these **health** crises, and others such as tuberculosis and **malaria**, Nigeria has a relatively high population growth rate of 2.8 percent. This is because of the cultural preference for large families or lack of family planning, which has resulted in an average of five children per woman. Although Nigeria boasts of being the "Giant of West Africa," having its population actually be counted in a **census** has been a very sensitive issue because the allocation of federal revenues, collection of taxes, and **election** districting are determined by population. *See also* REVENUE ALLOCATION; TAXATION.

**PORT HARCOURT.** Situated in the **Niger Delta**, it is the capital of **Rivers State**. It is the center of Nigeria's booming **petroleum** industry. The **population** of Port Harcourt is just over one million, making it Nigeria's fifth largest city. It is inhabited primarily by people of the **Ijaw** and Ikwerre **ethnic groups**. It was established in 1912 by the British as a port city for the export of **coal** and was named after Lewis Harcourt, a colonial secretary. In recent years, Port Harcourt has been the site of numerous oil pipeline explosions and kidnappings of oil workers. The city and its citizens have been engulfed in the **Niger Delta Conflict**. It is home to the University of Port Harcourt and two of Nigeria's four oil refineries.

**PREMIER.** The prominent administrative position of premier was used in Nigeria only during the **First Republic**. The role of the premier in the four regions—**Northern Region**, **Western Region**, **Mid-Western Region**, and **Eastern Region**—was to serve as an administrative bridge between the central and regional governments. While the governors changed several times in each region between October 1954 (August 1963 in the case of the Mid-Western Region) and January 1966, the **premier** did not. The premier of the Northern Region, **Sir Alhaji Ahmadu Bello**, held his position from October 1954 until he was murdered during a military **coup d'état** in January 1966. After 1966, the use of premiers was abandoned in favor of military governors. *See also* NATIONAL ECONOMIC COUNCIL.

**PREST, CHIEF ARTHUR EDWARD (1908–1976).** Born in February 1908 in **Warri**, Prest was the great-grandson of Akenzua I, the *olu* (**chief** or **king**) of **Warri**. As a young man, he studied at Government College at Warri, **King's College** in **Lagos**, Highgate School in London, and University College in London. In Nigeria, he worked as the chief inspector of **police** from 1926 to 1945 and as federal minister of communications from 1952 to 1955. During that time, Prest took a brief break from politics to study law at the University of London. He was called to the bar in 1946. He served as a member of the **Federal House of Representatives** (1952–1955), **House of Assembly** (1951–1956), and Public Service Board (1951–1952). In local politics, he was a member of the Itsekiri Native Authority (1948–1955) and president of the Warri National Union (1948–1954). He was a founding member of the **Action Group**. In 1951, he was appointed minister of communications. In the 1960s, he retired from politics and returned to his private legal practice. Prest died in September 1976.

**PRICE CONTROLS.** Nigeria has struggled to keep goods affordable for its citizens, who are largely poor and lack formal employment. Since **independence**, successive governments have implemented price controls to ensure low prices. For example, the Price Control Decree of 1970 called for price manipulation during times of emergency and reconstruction after the **civil war**. These controls were carried out by **marketing boards**. The plan was designed to stimulate **economic** activity for impoverished people and drive out black marketers. Items that have been subjected to price control include clothing, food and drinks, cement, and pharmaceuticals. Under a **structural adjustment program**, the Nigerian government reduced its control over the prices of goods. For example, the International Monetary Fund explicitly advised Nigeria to discontinue the subsidizing of **petroleum** products. The utilization of price controls went along with Nigeria's project of **indigenization**. Since the 1970s, Nigeria has slowly moved away from price controls and toward **privatization** to reduce the financial burden on the government. *See also* PULLEN SCHEME; SMUGGLING.

**PRIVATIZATION.** The process by which state-owned corporations are sold to private investors. In Nigeria, the trend toward privatization began in the mid-1980s and has progressed slowly. Nigeria has spent most of its existence as an independent state under the model of nationalization, which called for the conversion of major private (especially foreign) businesses into state ones. Thus far, Nigeria has privatized Nigerian Airways and NITEL, Nigeria's telephone company. Nigeria has put its four oil refineries and its state-owned **petroleum** company up for sale. The privatizing of NITEL has resulted in a boom in cell phone usage and sales. Critics of the privatization plan have declared that it has caused a rise in the price of basic foodstuffs, undermined the strength of **trade unions**, and contributed to **corruption**. *See also* AIRLINES; ECONOMY; INDIGENIZATION; RAILROADS; TELECOMMUNICATIONS.

**PROGRESSIVE PARTIES ALLIANCE (PPA).** An alliance of the **Great Nigerian People's Party**, the **Nigerian People's Party**, and the **People's Redemption Party** in 1983. For the 1983 **election**, the PPA ran both **Chief Obafemi Awolowo** and **Nnamdi Azikiwe** as presidential candidates. That same year, after the military **coup d'état**, it was banned along with all other **political parties**. It was originally created with the intention of countering the strength of the **National Party of Nigeria**.

**PROSTITUTION.** Although illegal in Nigeria, prostitution is widespread. Nigerian **women** and girls have also been drawn (willingly or by force) into prostitution networks outside the country. In recent years, Nigeria has come under fire, along with its West African neighbors, for not stopping the theft and selling of children, especially young girls. European governments regularly catch traffickers sending young girls to Europe, particularly Italy, to work as prostitutes. Exact numbers of Nigerian prostitutes are unavailable, but experts estimate that there were about 10,000 in Italy and one million in Nigeria in any given year between 2000 and 2006. Most women who become prostitutes in Nigeria do so out of financial need, placing their **health** and well-being at great risk to provide a basic living for their families. *See also* CRIME; HUMAN TRAFFICKING.

**PROTECTORATE.** During the late 19th century, portions of present-day Nigeria came under British protectorate status. A protectorate is a territory being protected and exploited as dictated by strictures of a treaty signed by, in the case of Nigeria, the British government or a chartered trading company and a Nigerian ruler. These treaties, however, were often signed under threat of violence and without full explanation of their contents. In practice, there was little difference between a colony and a protectorate as far as the treatment of Nigerians was concerned. In both cases, Nigerians became subjects of the Crown, with virtually no rights, and saw their social and political systems destroyed. The British agenda in the protectorates or colonies was the same: to extract raw materials for trade through Nigerian labor and know-how. Nigeria reached its present-day size as a result of agglomerating a series of protectorates acquired by the British directly or through the work of the **Royal Niger Company**. They included the **Protectorate of Northern Nigeria**, **Oil Rivers Protectorate**, **Niger Coast Protectorate**, and the **Protectorate of Southern Nigeria**. The protectorates were ultimately united into one Nigeria through an **amalgamation** in 1914.

**PROTECTORATE OF NORTHERN NIGERIA.** On 27 December 1899, the **Northern Region** of present-day Nigeria became the Protectorate of Northern Nigeria, which it remained until 1914, when it was merged with the **Protectorate of Southern Nigeria**.

**PROTECTORATE OF SOUTHERN NIGERIA.** In December 1899, the British reconfigured their rule over the southern coastal territories by merging the **Niger Coast Protectorate** and the **Lagos Colony** into the Protectorate of Southern Nigeria. This move facilitated the consolidation of British control and the removal of territorial and administrative control from the **Royal Niger Company**. In 1914, it was merged with the **Protectorate of Northern Nigeria**.

**PROVISIONAL RULING COUNCIL (PRC).** The executive military body under **General Sani Abacha** from 1993 to 1998. Its structure was borrowed from the **Supreme Military Council**, which lasted from 1966 to 1979. This council served as the highest governing body in Nigeria and was responsible for the crafting and implementation of national policies.

**PULLEN SCHEME.** In urban areas of Nigeria, such as **Lagos**, the **markets** suffered from food shortages and rampant inflation between 1914 and 1945. In an effort to address this problem, the colonial government, under the guidance of commissioner Captain A. P. Pullen, attempted to set **price controls** and curb the distribution of essential foodstuffs in February 1941 in Lagos and nearby markets. It mandated prices lower than the combined costs of production and transportation. The scheme was ineffective because market **women** refused to sell at prices that would deprive them of even meager profits. The Lagos Market Women's Association and the Oyingbo Market Women's Association organized public meetings and protests. These women argued that the Pullen Scheme ignored market trading practices. By 1944, it had become clear to the colonial government that it needed to work with the market women, including **Madam Alimotu Pelewura**, who was the leader of the Lagos Market Women's Association, to alter the scheme. *See also* TRADE.

*PURDAH.* The traditional **Islamic** practice of married **women** living in seclusion in their homes and going out only after receiving permission from a husband or father. Women are free to visit female friends and family members in their homes. While confined to their family dwelling, women living in *purdah* may also conduct **trade** and prepare food for public sale. It is believed that the great **Fulani** poet and daughter of **Usman dan Fodio**, **Nana Asma'u**, lived in *purdah*. She lived a life steeped in intellectual and social inquiry. She even visited other women living in *purdah* to teach them to read and understand the **Koran**.

# – Q –

**QADIRIYYA.** This is the largest **Islamic** Sufi *tariqah* (brotherhood or order) in Nigeria. The order emerged in the 11th century in Baghdad and was introduced in **Kano** in the 17th century. The **Fulani jihadist Usman dan Fodio** was an adherent. Usman contributed to the spread of the order across **northern Nigeria** in the 19th century. For this reason, it is most associated with the **Sokoto Caliphate**. In the 1970s, the Qadiriyya order underwent fundamental changes as it responded to its rival **Tijaniyya** *tariqah* and the **Izala** movement. *See also* AHMADIYYA.

**QUININE.** A medicine derived from the bark of a cinchona tree, quinine serves as both a partial preventive and treatment for **malaria** fever. For centuries, people have steeped crushed leaves of the tree in hot water when they came down with malaria. Although the medicinal properties of the cinchona tree have been long known in the tropical regions of South America, it was not until the 1820s that a French scientist extracted the antimalarial chemical and developed quinine. Quinine aided in the prevention of contracting malaria after being bitten by a malaria-infected mosquito. It became invaluable to European explorers and traders who traveled in tropical Africa. Until the development of quinine, Europeans viewed tropical regions, such as coastal Nigeria, as a "white man's grave." The development of quinine is often said to have aided the British in the expansion of colonial rule from the coastal regions of Nigeria into the interior. Despite the availability of quinine, malaria is still one of Nigeria's major **health** problems.

**QU'RAN.** *See* KORAN.

## – R –

**RADIO BROADCASTING.** Radio was first available in Nigeria in the 1930s, broadcasting news from the British Broadcasting Corporation (BBC). The Nigerian Broadcasting Service was established in April 1950, followed by the Nigerian Broadcasting Corporation in April 1957. These companies established broadcasting stations in **Lagos, Enugu, Ibadan, Kaduna,** and **Kano.** This marked the start of a national radio service, which is commonly referred to as "Radio Nigeria." Since **independence,** the radio has been used to disseminate important national news and information and to promote unity in Nigeria. The **Republic of Biafra** used radio to promote its cause during the **civil war** in the **Igbo language,** Portuguese, and English. After the civil war, the federal military government focused on using radio to spread positive messages about a reunified Nigeria. In

1978, the Federal Radio Corporation of Nigeria replaced the Nigerian Broadcasting Corporation. The purpose of this refashioning was to create a federal broadcasting structure as well as to upgrade the broadcasting frequencies.

There are currently 17 private radio stations and 36 state-sponsored stations. Listeners enjoy radio shows in English and a local **language** that is determined by the location. They can also listen to international news broadcasted by the BBC. Unfortunately, the problem of music pirating has resulted in disjointed **music** programs with frequent interruptions to prevent copying. Call-in shows about current events and spirituality are particularly popular in Nigeria. In rural areas and among Nigeria's poor (60 percent live below the poverty line), radio is the primary electronic source for news and entertainment. The second most popular source, particularly in urban areas, is **television broadcasting** and other forms of **telecommunication**. *See also* NEWSPAPERS.

**RAILROADS.** Nigeria has roughly 4,000 kilometers of railroad, but its operations are on the verge of collapse. The primary routes are operated by the state-owned Nigerian Railway Corporation and run from **Lagos** to **Kano**, **Port Harcourt** to **Maiduguri**, and **Zaria** to Gusau. Nigeria's railroad network does not yet extend to neighboring countries. The use of railroads began in 1896, with the clearing of land and laying of track between Lagos and **Ibadan**, which opened in 1901. This project required more than 10,000 African and West Indian workers. The majority of employees during the colonial period were **Yoruba**. By 1916, the railway network also included Port Harcourt, **Enugu**, and Kano. From 1898 to 1955, Nigeria's railroad system was run by the colonial government. Since 1955, it has been a public company.

By 1965, the railroad industry employed roughly 30,000 workers, about 5 percent of wage earners in Nigeria. Since the 1930s, Nigeria's railroad workers have been organized into **trade unions**, such as the **Railway Workers' Union**. As Nigeria's **economy** declined, its railways became dilapidated. One of the problems with Nigeria's railroad network, which has yet to be fully resolved, is that two different gauges of tracks were laid, and they now need to be standardized. The failure of the railroad system has resulted in an increase in heavy trucks on the highways, which are not well paved or maintained. The Nigerian government has drafted plans for rehabilitating its railroad system, but many have gone unrealized. The former president, **General Olusegun Obasanjo**, had pushed for the revitalization of the railroad through **privatization**. In 2003, the Bureau of Public Enterprises established the Transport Sector Reform Implementation Committee to oversee the transformation. *See also* AIRLINES; ROADS.

**RAILWAY WORKERS' UNION (RWU).** A union formed in 1931, it was among Nigeria's first national **trade unions**. In January 1940, **Chief Michael Imoudu** officially registered the **Railway Workers' Union**, making it the first publicly recognized trade union in Nigeria. The activities of the union included agitating for improved wages in reponse to rising living costs. Members also called for their pay to be based on daily rates, not hourly rates (as instituted in 1931), and for formally making certain jobs permanent. In July 1940, the union led the formation of a federation of government workers.

**RAISMAN COMMISSION.** The colonial federal government created this commission in 1957 to examine Nigeria's **taxation** and **revenue allocation** schemes. Sir Jeremy Raisman was appointed as chairman. The commission recommended the creation of a fiscal review commission and the redistribution of the federal government's revenue to ensure equality among the regions. It also recommended that the federal government levy taxes on **alcoholic** beverages and exports. *See also* HICKS-PHILLIPSON COMMISSION; PHILLIPSON COMMISSION.

**RAMADAN.** One of the Five Pillars of **Islam**. Muslims who are able are required to participate in this holy month by fasting during the daylight hours. It takes place in the ninth month of the Islamic calendar. It is observed by most Muslims in Nigeria. *See also* HAJJ; KORAN.

**RANSOME-KUTI, BEKOLARI (1940–2006).** Born in August 1940 in **Abeokuta**, in **Ogun State**, Ransome-Kuti was the son of the famous **Chief Olufunmilayo Ransome-Kuti** and her husband, Canon

Josiah Ransome-Kuti. He is the brother of **Olufela Anikulapo-Kuti** and **Olikoye Ransome-Kuti**. As a young man, Bekolari Ransome-Kuti studied at Abeokuta Grammar School (1951–1956), Coventry Technical College (1957–1958), and Manchester University (1958–1963). He worked as a physician, teacher, and administrator in the fields of **health** and medicine. He was the medical officer for the Federal Ministry of Health (1965) and Lagos State Ministry of Health (1968–1977). He was a member of the Nigerian Medical Association as well as secretary-general (1979–1982) and vice president (1984–1988). He taught at various teaching hospitals attached to Nigeria's major universities. He was president of the Committee for the Defence of Human Rights (1989–1995). In 1994, he cofounded the political organization **O'odua People's Congress**. That same year, he was wrongly accused of participating in a **coup d'état** to remove **General Sani Abacha**, which landed him in prison. Bekolari Ransome-Kuti died in February 2006.

**RANSOME-KUTI, OLIKOYE (1927–2003).** Born in December 1927 in Ijebu-Ode, in **Ogun State,** Ransome-Kuti was the son of the famous **Chief Olufunmilayo Ransome-Kuti** and her husband, Canon Josiah Ransome-Kuti. He is the brother of **Bekolari Ransome-Kuti** and **Olufela Anikulapo-Kuti**. He studied at Abeokuta Grammar School (1935–1944), **Yaba Higher College** (1946–1947), University College (present-day **University of Ibadan**) (1948), and University of Dublin (1948–1954). Like his brother, Bekolari, he devoted his career to medicine. From 1955 to 1980 he returned to Nigeria and taught pediatric medicine at the University of Lagos. Ransome-Kuti also worked as the federal minister of **health** (1985–1992). He was a consultant for organizations such as the World Health Organization. Olikoye Ransome-Kuti died in June 2003.

**RANSOME-KUTI, CHIEF OLUFUNMILAYO (1900–1978).** Born in October 1900 in **Abeokuta**, as a young woman Ransome-Kuti completed her primary and secondary education in Abeokuta. She also studied science and music at Wincham Hill College in Great Britain. After returning to Nigeria, she worked as a teacher at the Abeokuta Girls' Grammar School. Ransome-Kuti devoted her life to the anticolonial struggle as well as **women**'s rights, with a particular focus on market women. The protests of the Abeokuta Women's Union forced the *alake's* (**chief**) temporary removal. She was an active supporter of the **National Council of Nigeria and the Cameroons** and was the only female member of the **constitutional conference** held in 1947. She was married to Reverend Canon Josiah Ransome-Kuti, a pastor, and had several children. One of her sons, **Olufela Anikulapo-Kuti**, was an internationally famous musician. In the last few years before her death, she lived with Olufela in his compound, which the Nigerian **police** violently raided in 1978. Amid the chaos of the raid, Ransome-Kuti was seriously injured. People attribute her death in April 1978 to this tragic incident. Her other sons, **Bekolari Ransome-Kuti** and **Olikoyi Ransome-Kuti**, were medical doctors and activists. She received the honorary title Officer of the Order of the Niger (1962) and an honorary doctorate from the **University of Ibadan**. She also received the Lenin Peace Prize in 1968. *See also* MARKETS.

**RELIGION.** There are three broad categories of religion in Nigeria: **Christianity**, **Islam**, and traditional religions. Religion has always been an integral part of Nigerian life. Traditional religions are typically ethnic-based and not evangelical. Religion was an integral component of group identification and an instrument for reinforcing sociopolitical structures. The basic components of a traditional religion may include cosmogony, origin myth, priests, and the veneration of ancestors and gods. Some groups in Nigeria also integrate **divination** into their religious activities. They may also include building and maintaining shrines and sites of **oracles**. The most studied traditional religions in Nigeria include those practiced by the **Yoruba**, **Igbo**, and **Nupe**. Today, traditional religions have the smallest number of adherents in comparison to Islam and Christianity. In addition, their practitioners have frequently adapted aspects of Islam or Christianity to their rituals and beliefs.

Islam spread from north to south in Nigeria, possibly starting around the 11th century. Muslims account for roughly 50 percent of the population in Nigeria today and live predominantly in northern and southwestern Nigeria. Islam is the dominant faith of the **Fulani** and **Hausa** people. The majority of Muslims in Nigeria are of the Sunni branch of Islam, and many are members of an Islamic brotherhood. The two most popular brotherhoods are **Qadiriyya** and **Tijani-**

**yya**. In Nigeria, Muslims tend to adhere as strictly as possible to the principles of the **Koran** and Five Pillars of Islam, including fasting during **Ramadan** and going on *hajj* (spiritual **pilgrimage**) to Mecca. Starting in the late 1970s, Muslims pushed for the implementation of **Shari'a**, a legal system, as an integral part of national jurisprudence. By 2002, 12 states in Nigeria had adopted Shari'a into their criminal codes. There are several influential Muslim cultural and religious organizations: **Islamic Movement of Nigeria**, **Izala**, and **Jama'atu Nasril Islam**. The **sultan of Sokoto** is considered to be the spiritual head of all Muslims in Nigeria.

Christianity was first introduced in Nigeria by Portuguese traders to the **Benin Kingdom** in the 16th century. It did not, however, become a major religion in Nigeria until the mid-19th century. European, particularly British, missionaries settled in **Lagos**, **Abeokuta**, and **Lokoja**. At the forefront of missionary efforts in Nigeria was the (Anglican) **Church Missionary Society**, which established churches and Western-style schools, in which many Nigerians became deeply involved. Nigerians also established independent churches, including **Aladura churches** and **Christ Apostolic Church**. Since the 1980s, **Charismatic** and **Fundamentalist** forms of Christianity have been very popular in Nigeria. Christians account for over 40 percent of the population and live throughout **southern Nigeria**. There is also a spattering of Christian churches in **northern Nigeria**'s major cities. Most Christians are of Igbo and Yoruba ethnic extraction. Both Christianity and Islam have sought converts and political influence, which has created tension throughout Nigeria's history.

**REVENUE ALLOCATION.** The allocation to individual states of revenue acquired by the federal government through the sale of exports or receipt of loans. It has been at the core of much of Nigeria's political instability. For example, revenue allocation (and political representation) has been a major driving force in **state creation**. Communities living in the **Niger Delta**, whose environment has been dramatically altered as a consequence of **petroleum** production, argue that they receive significantly less than their share of the federal revenue generated from the oil industry.

Since the 1950s, each Nigerian government has created commissions, held conferences, and paid lip service to **minority groups** on the problem of revenue allocation, including the Aboyade Commission (1977), Chick Commission (1953), **Hicks-Phillipson Commission** (1951), **Okigbo Commission** (1979), and **Dina Committee** (1968), to name a few. Nigeria struggles with allocating scarce resources to regions/states that generate almost no revenue for themselves. As a result, federal administrations have grappled with how to stretch oil revenue across all the states. For example, the Binns Fiscal Review Commission met in June 1964 to determine the allocation of the country's oil revenues, especially with the creation of the **Mid-Western Region**. **Corruption** and embezzlement at the federal level also play a role in the problem of revenue allocation. *See also* ABOYADE, OJETUNJI; PHILLIPSON COMMISSION; RAISMAN COMMISSION.

**RIBADU, ALHAJI MUHAMMADU (1910–1965).** As a young man, Ribadu attended Yola Middle School. In 1926, he worked as a teacher at Yola Middle School. In the early 1930s, he began working in the colonial administration. Ribadu was a chief accountant for the Yola Native Authority (1931), district head of Balola (1936), and treasurer for the Yola Native Authority (1947). He acted as the minister of mines and power (1954) and federal minister of land, mines, and power (1955). Ribadu was a significant member of the **Northern People's Congress** and an elected member of the **Federal House of Representatives**. In 1960, he was appointed to the Ministry of Defence. He received the honorary title Member of the Order of the British Empire in 1952. Ribadu died in May 1965.

**RICHARDS CONSTITUTION.** Proposed in March 1945 and implemented in January 1946, the Richards Constitution was Nigeria's second formal **constitution**. It was named after the British colonial governor, Sir Arthur Richards. It expanded on the **Clifford Constitution** by incorporating 28 Nigerian men into the 44-person **Legislative Council** based in **Lagos**. Of those 28, 4 were directly elected and the remaining 24 were elected by their regional assemblies. As it had done with the Clifford Constitution, the colonial administration implemented the Richards Constitution without consulting its Nigerian colonial subjects. The constitution also called for the inclusion of the North into the central legislature. It created three regions (Northern,

Eastern, and Western) and three corresponding regional **Houses of Assembly**. The use of regions as administrative structures in Nigeria remained in place until May 1967.

**RIMI, ALHAJI MOHAMMED ABUBAKAR (1940– ).** Rimi was born in 1940 in Rimi, in **Kano State**. He studied at **Ahmadu Bello University** in **Zaria** (1961), University of London (1972–1974), and University of Sussex (1974–1975). He was an instructor at the Clerical Training Centre in **Sokoto** (1961–1962) and also worked for the Kano Local Government (1965–1966) and Federal Ministry of Information (1966–1970). For the **Nigerian Institute of International Affairs**, Rimi worked as an administrative secretary (1976–1977). He was a member of the Constituent Assembly (1977–1978). From 1979 to 1983, he served as a civilian governor for Kano State. Rimi was a founding member of the **People's Redemption Party** (1978–1983). He also worked as the minister of communications (1994–1995).

Rimi was one of several civilian members of **General Sani Abacha**'s government in the mid-1990s. Like many others, he was appointed with the express purpose of giving the appearance of an inclusionary government. In 1998, he joined an opposition group, which landed him in prison for several months. Rimi was a member of several **political parties**, including the **People's Democratic Party**, **Northern Elements Progressive Union**, and **Social Democratic Party**. In 2006, his wife and son died unexpectedly, within a week of one another.

**RIVER BASIN DEVELOPMENT AUTHORITIES (RBDA).** In 1976, the federal government created 11 governing authorities to ensure the efficient and effective use of rivers for **agricultural** irrigation and reduce pollution in lakes and rivers. This scheme was later paired with the 1978 Land Use Decree, which declared that all land in Nigeria belonged to the state. It was also implemented in conjunction with other programs committed to increasing farming and crop yields to feed Nigeria's growing population, such as **Operation Feed the Nation** and **Green Revolution**. The river basin authorities leased land to large-scale farmers with the purpose of increasing crop yields. Their activities included the construction of dams, dikes, wells, and drainage systems. They were also charged with coordinating the delivery of fresh water to farmers for year-round cultivation. By the early 1980s, the authorities were focusing their energy on irrigation. In 1982, they were brought into close coordination with the Nigerian Agricultural Cooperative Marketing Organisation. **Major General Muhammadu Buhari** expanded the number of authorities to 18 in 1984, but **General Ibrahim Badamasi Babangida** returned the number to 11 in 1986. Although still in operation, the scheme has been criticized for its prohibitive bureaucracy and failure to reduce socioeconomic divisions.

**RIVERS STATE.** A state was created in 1967 out of the **Eastern Region**. It is one of Nigeria's current 36 states. It is located in southeastern Nigeria, with the Bight of Bonny as its natural southern boundary and the **Niger River** as its western one. Rivers State is considered part of the **Niger Delta** region; its capital is **Port Harcourt**. Ethnically, Rivers State is very diverse and is home to several politically vocal groups, such as the **Ogoni** and Opobo. Economic activities in the state include cultivation of **oil palm**, fishing, and extracting **petroleum**. *See also* STATE CREATION.

**ROADS.** The construction, safety, and maintenance of roads have been a constant struggle for Nigeria. The quality of the roads varies greatly from elevated, modern structures spanning the skyline to dirt roads that are nearly impassible after a rain. Although the government recognizes its roads as a cornerstone of economic development, it does not always allocate sufficient funds to their maintenance. States such as **Lagos** have taken the initiative in hiring workers to clear the roads of debris and **police** to direct traffic.

Nigeria has roughly 200,000 kilometer of roads, only about one-quarter of which is paved. Because the **railroads** operate on a very limited basis, the roads are full of large, heavy trucks hauling large quantities of goods. Many of the roads need potholes repaired, unpaved portions paved, and lines painted to direct traffic. Several of Nigeria's expressways have made *US Today*'s list of the world's most dangerous highways. Without a reliable supply of **electricity** available in the country, many of Nigeria's stoplights do not operate. Despite this, Nigerian business and trade continue to operate, recognizing that they risk losing vehicles, goods, money, and employees because of the unsafe conditions. It is not uncommon to see a turned over truck with **bananas** or **petroleum** spilled onto the highway. In the 1990s, the Federal Road Safety Commission reported that there are roughly 20,000 collisions per year on Nigeria's highways, 25 percent of them fatal. In November 2007, Nigeria held a national candlelight vigil to remember road traffic victims and raise awareness about driver safety.

Nigeria's roads face an additional risk to their patrons in that they have become places of **criminal** activity. Policemen, hired to patrol the highways, pull over dilapidated vehicles, and assist drivers, abuse their power by setting up checkpoints and collecting tips. Instead of serving and protecting, the police increasingly are part of what makes Nigeria's roads unsafe. *See also* AIRLINES; ECONOMY; RAILROADS.

**ROSIJI, CHIEF AYOTUNDE (1917–2000).** Born in February 1917, as a young man Rosiji studied at Christ Church School in **Abeokuta** and **Yaba Higher College**, among others. In England, he studied at University College in London and received a law degree. In Nigeria, he served on the Western Region Education Advisory Board (1953) and Electricity Corporation Advisory Council (1953). One year later, he acted as the federal general secretary of the **Action Group** and legal adviser for the **Western Region**'s Action Group. In 1954, he also served as a member of the **Federal House of Representatives**. Three years later, Rosiji served as the federal minister of health. During the **Action Group Crisis**, he sided with **Chief Samuel Akintola**. In 1963, he served as the deputy leader of the **United People's Party**. From 1964 to 1966, he was the minister of information. Rosiji died in July 2000.

**ROTIMI, OLA EMMANUEL GLADSTONE (1938–2000).** Rotimi was born in April 1938 in Sapele, in **Delta State**. As a young man, he completed his primary and secondary education in **Port Harcourt** and **Lagos**. He studied fine arts at Boston University (1959–1963) and Yale University (1963–1966). Later, he worked as the executive artistic director at **Obafemi Awolowo University** (1970–1975). At the University of Port Harcourt, Rotimi served as department head, dean of faculty, and dean of student affairs between 1975 and 1984. He was a member of the **Unity Party of Nigeria** from 1979 and 1983. Rotimi wrote several plays, including *The Gods Are Not to Blame* (1971) and *Our Husband Has Gone Mad Again* (1977). *See also* THEATER.

**ROYAL NIGER COMPANY (RNC).** The Royal Niger Company was under the administration of **Sir George Taubman Goldie** and Lord Aberdare. It operated under a charter from the British government from 1886 to 1900 as a highly lucrative trading company. The RNC entered into agreements with local leaders through treaties, which is how it established the **Niger Coast Protectorate**. The company also enforced the abolition of **slave trading** and attempted to control indigenous **trade** of **alcohol**. It relied on the **Royal Niger Constabulary** as its military strength. It traded with the **Sokoto Caliphate**. The company used Forcados, at the mouth of **Niger Delta**, and **Lokoja**, at the Niger–Benue confluence, as trading posts. In 1900, the territorial and administrative duties performed by the **Royal Niger Company** were transferred to British authority.

**ROYAL NIGER CONSTABULARY.** This armed force was created by the **Royal Niger Company** to provide protection for **trade** activities and military assistance in expanding trade territory. It was created in 1886 and replaced by the **Niger Coast Constabulary** in 1894. The Royal Niger Constabulary comprised indigenous soldiers and was based in **Lokoja**. It was used to conquer Bida and **Ilorin**. *See also* POLICE.

**ROYAL WEST AFRICAN FRONTIER FORCE.** *See* WEST AFRICAN FRONTIER FORCE.

**RUMFA, MUHAMMAD.** Considered one of the greatest **Hausa kings** of **Kano**, Rumfa ruled from 1463 to 1499. During his tenure, he extended the city walls for protection and established the Kurmi Market and Juma'at Mosque. Rumfa was the first king to use eunuchs and **slaves** in his royal administration. Most notably, he instituted **Islam** as the official **religion** of Kano and improved Kano's political structure. Rumfa was inspired by Arab scholar al-Maghili, who wrote a treatise recommending an effective form of government, which included an ombudsman.

# – S –

**SA'ADU ABUBAKAR III, SULTAN COLONEL MUHAMMED (1956– ).** Born in August 1956 in **Sokoto**, as a young man Sa'adu studied in Sokoto and **Zaria**. In 1975, he attended the Nigerian Defence Academy in **Kaduna**. He earned the rank of second lieutenant in the army in 1977. In November 2006, he acquired the honored title **sultan** of Sokoto upon the death of his older brother, **Sultan Alhaji Muhammadu Maccido**, who died in a plane crash in October 2006. He was the compromise candidate of eight nominations. Sa'adu Abubakar is the 20th sultan.

**SABON GARI.** A particular sections in a major city inhabited by an ethnic or religious group considered outsiders. It means "strangers' quarters" or, literally, "new town" in the **Hausa language**. The plural form is sabon garuruwa. They are particularly prevalent in the major northern cities of **Kano, Kaduna,** and **Zaria**. In these cities, sabon gari refers to the sections inhabited by non-**Hausa**, such as the **Yoruba** and **Igbo**, with an emphasis on their not being Muslim. The introduction of **Shari'a** into the criminal code of a dozen northern states has intensified criticism of the inhabitants of sabon garuruwa. To conservative Muslims in Kano, for example, a sabon-gari is a sleazy part of the city, with **alcohol** and mixed gender social clubs. This section of town is the location of high-class hotels that cater to expatriates and the Nigerian elite. In 2001, Muslim youths attacked the sabon gari in Kano, leaving an estimated 30 people dead, in response to U.S. involvement in Afghanistan. Conversely, in cities in **southern Nigeria** such as **Ibadan** and **Lagos**, the sabon garuruwa are inhabited by Hausa and **Fulani** people.

**SALT.** One of the world's most valuable commodities, salt has been traded globally since ancient times. Humans depend on salt for regulating osmotic pressure and assisting in the functions of hormones and enzymes. Early African societies used salt to preserve meat and as an ingredient for making textile dye, soap, and medicine. Salt deposits in Africa have been known since the 12th century. Many are located in **northern Nigeria**, near Lake Chad to the east and along the **Niger River** to the west. During the 19th century, much of the salt industry was controlled by the **Sokoto Caliphate** and the **Bornu Empire**. Known as the central Sudan salt market, this **trade** network provided salt for a roughly 518-square-kilometer area. Similarly, people living in the **Niger Delta** and the Cross River estuary produced sea salt for local consumption. In the 19th century, however, European salt undermined local salt production in this coastal region.

**SANGO.** One of the best-known gods in the pantheon of deities in the **Yoruba religion**, Sango is the god of thunder and lightning, using these natural powers to remind people of his awesome strength and to punish wrongdoers. (In the written **Yoruba language**, a dot under the first letter is applied to indicate a "sh" sound, which is why it is written in English both as Sango and Shango.) What makes Sango so unique is that he appears in the historical record as the fourth king of the **Oyo Empire** sometime in the 15th century and was deified upon his death. Sango is the son of Orayan. He had three wives—Oba, Osun, Oya—who turned into rivers. Osun is a popular river goddess. Worshippers, male and female, are considered the wives of Sango.

Among the **Yoruba**, several versions of Sango's life and the circumstances in which he died exist. For some, he is the ideal man, having great strength, determination, and virility. Some stories about him indicate a sense of insecurity and arrogance, while others highlight his loyalty and love for his community. One story describes his desire to cleverly destroy two brave warriors whom he perceived as threats. Another story says that after discovering his ability to throw lightning bolts, he accidentally burned down the palace. In the former story, he was ejected from Oyo; in the latter, he left Oyo in shame. Without his community, he felt lost and saw his life as lacking meaning. This, the legend declares, led him to ultimately hang himself from an ayan tree.

Sango is an important god, recognized by the Yoruba not only in Nigeria, but also in the Americas among people of the African diaspora. In Haitian Vodou, he is known as Shango, and in Candomblé as Xangô. The legend of Sango is a common theme in Yoruba **literature**, **theater**, and **art**. **Duro Ladipo**'s *Oba Kò So* (1968), for example, dramatizes the life and power of Sango.

*SARDAUNA.* A **Hausa** word meaning "leader of war." In 1938, **Sir Alhaji Ahmadu Bello** became the *sardauna* of **Sokoto**. He is the only person in Nigeria to have received this ceremonial title. The title was given as a consolation for his losing the position of **sultan** of Sokoto to his rival, Abubakar.

**SARKI.** A **Hausa** word meaning "**chief**" or "**king**." A *sarki* is someone in a position of authority anointed with the power to appoint kings. The early **Hausa Kingdoms** were ruled by a *sarki*. An **emir** is often described as a *sarki* (*sarakuna* as plural). *Sarkin Muslumi* (Commander of the Faithful) is another name for the **sultan** of **Sokoto**. A proverb pertaining to a *sarki* states that *yawan magana ba ta tada sarki in bai tashi ba*, meaning "no amount of talking will raise a king if he himself does not get up." According to **oral tradition**, the word is derived from *makas sarki* (meaning "the snake killer"), in reference to **Prince Bayajidda** saving the **Daura** kingdom from a menacing snake in the 10th century. *See also* BABARI, SARKIN.

**SARO-WIWA, KENULE BEESON (1941–1995).** A prominent writer and political activist, born in October 1941 in Bori, in **Rivers State**. As a young man, Saro-Wiwa studied at Government College at Umuahia (1954–1961), **University of Ibadan** (1962–1966), and the University of Nigeria at **Nsukka** (1967). He taught at the University of Lagos (1967–1973). He was appointed administrator of **Bonny** under **General Yakubu Gowon**'s regime. He was a founding member and president of the **Movement for the Survival of the Ogoni People** (MOSOP) in the 1990s, defending the rights of the **Ogoni** people and the environment of the **Niger Delta**. In the early 1990s, Saro-Wiwa was imprisoned on several occasions for several months at a time for criticizing the government and disrupting oil production. He was hanged, with eight other MOSOP members, on 10 November 1995 for alleged involvement in an assassination. Saro-Wiwa made a notable contribution to Nigerian **literature** through the publication of his novel, *Sozaboy* (1985), and his journal, *A Month and A Day: A Detention Diary* (1995), written just prior to his death. He also produced a soap opera for Nigerian **television** called *Basi and Company*. *See also* NIGER DELTA CONFLICT.

**SCARIFICATION.** The practice of marking an individual with deliberate cuts and filling them with a charcoal mixture; they heal into permanent, black scars. These scars are usually on the face to easily identify ethnic and clan affiliation. The most common design is a short series of cuts in different directions across the cheek. Scars on a person's face, however, may simply indicate the application of **traditional medicine** in an open cut. Scarification is typically linked to initiation ceremonies for young men and women. In his pioneering work *History of the Yorubas* (1921), **Samuel Johnson** recorded the various scarification designs used by the **Yoruba** subgroups. Aside from group identification and healing, scarification may also be linked to times of war and the transatlantic **slave trade**. Sembene Ousmane, a Senegalese novelist, identified the use of scarification by communities as a way of protecting them against slave traders looking for physically unblemished Africans to enslave. Societies in Nigeria still practice scarification today, although it is on the decline. *See also* ETHNIC GROUPS.

**SECOND REPUBLIC.** One of Nigeria's isolated periods of democratic rule, which lasted from October 1979 to December 1983. **Alhaji Shehu Shagari** served as president and **Alex Ifeanyichukwu Ekwueme** as vice president; they were ousted and replaced in a military **coup d'état**. *See also* FIRST REPUBLIC; FOURTH REPUBLIC; THIRD REPUBLIC.

**SEFAWA DYNASTY.** The **Kanuri** people claim descent from this dynasty. It was the ruling dynasty of the Kanem Kingdom and the **Kanem-Bornu Empire** between the 11th and 19th centuries. According to **oral tradition**, Saef Ben Dhu Yasan founded the dynasty. Over time, this dynasty expanded its control across northeastern Nigeria, covering much of present-day **Borno State** and **Yobe State**. For a large part of its existence, Birni N'gazargamu was the seat of its power. The height of the dynasty was roughly from the 15th to the 19th centuries. Notable Sefawa rulers include **Ali Ghaji Dunamami**, **Dunama Dibbalemi**, and **Dunama ibn Ahmad Lefiami**. In 1846, **Umar ibn Muhammed al-Amin al-Kanemi** defeated the Sefawa Dynasty. *See also* IBRAHIM BEN AHMED.

**SELF-GOVERNMENT MOTION CRISIS.** Self-government as a final goal was envisioned in 1951 by nationalist leaders, but without a specific timetable. In March 1953, the **Action Group** canvased for national self-government in 1956. Delegates from **northern Nigeria**, representing the **Northern People's Congress**, considered 1956 too early and launched a counter-campaign for "as soon as possible." A lack of agreement resulted in a walkout by members of the Action Group and the **National Council of Nigeria and the Cameroons**. In 1954, the colonial government acted as arbiter and proposed self-government for regions on their own specific timetables. Thus, the **Western Region** and **Eastern Region** were offered self-government in 1957 and the **Northern Region** in 1959. **Independence** for Nigeria as a whole was left undecided. In 1957, the Eastern and Western Regions requested internal self-government, but the Northern Region set its sights on 1959. Several anticolonial leaders proposed April 1960 as the goal for independence. The radically different visions among the regions represented a serious roadblock for a smooth transition from colony to country.

**SHAGARI, ALHAJI SHEHU ALIYU USMAN (1924– ).** Born in 1924 in the town of Shagari, in **Sokoto State**, Shagari is of **Fulani** descent. He completed his education at Kaduna College. Before going into politics in 1949, Shagari taught at a school. He was a member of the **Northern People's Congress**. In 1954, he was elected to the **Federal House of Representatives**. Between 1971 and 1975, Shagari was the commissioner of finance. In November 1976, he was appointed by the **Supreme Military Council** under **General Olusegun Obasanjo** to be the head of Peugeot Automobile Company. Shagari served as Nigeria's elected president from October 1979 to December 1983 during the **Second Republic**. After a military **coup d'état**, he was banned from national politics.

**SHARI'A.** A system of **Islamic** law derived from the **Koran**, Sunna (describing the actions of the Prophet Muhammad), the Qiyas (commentary on the Koran and Sunna), and Ijma (conclusions made by consensus by Islamic scholars). Muslims identify Shari'a as broad, encompassing a system of guidelines and rules for living a moral life. This form of law dates back to the establishment of Islam in the seventh century. The incorporation of Shari'a into Nigerian society and customary, or **criminal**, law dates back to the 11th century. The

**Nupe**, for example, incorporated Shari'a into their criminal code (major offenses, including adultery, violence, murder, treason, and large debts or theft) prior to the 20th century.

Shari'a criminal law is composed of three categories. The *hudud* punishments are unambiguously articulated in the Koran and include amputation for theft, stoning or flogging for adultery, and death for renouncing Islam (apostasy). This category, not surprisingly, has been the most criticized by non-Muslims. Nigerian **courts**, however, do not apply the punishment for apostasy. The second category focuses on murder, calling for retaliation or compensation, to be paid to the family. The third category is where judges can chose from an array of punishments. The application of these categories is subject to interpretation and, in the case of Nigeria, is tempered by religious pluralism.

In the past few decades, Nigeria has seen an upswing in conservative Islam, particularly in the North. One of the most controversial developments has been the incorporation of Shari'a into criminal law in several northern states. Many non-Muslim communities see this as a major step toward Islamizing the country and restricting their religious freedom. Non-Muslims are not tried in Shari'a courts; however, there is concern that this exception may be eliminated. Concerned **Christians** in **southern Nigeria** organized the **Christian Association of Nigeria** to discuss Shari'a. By 2002, 12 states in Nigeria had adopted Shari'a into their criminal codes. **Zamfara State** was the first, in 2000. The other states are **Bauchi, Borno, Gombe, Jigawa, Kaduna, Kano, Katsina, Kebbi, Niger, Sokoto,** and **Yobe.**

**Human rights** groups have criticized Shari'a for implementing inhumane punishments and ignoring international standards of civil rights. More specifically, human rights groups argue that Shari'a relies too heavily on forced confessions and not on evidence. For example, rape is only considered to have happened if four men witnessed it. A man's denial of a rape, then, goes unchallenged. Since 2000, there have been numerous amputations, death sentences, and floggings for criminal behavior. Two **women** so far have been sentenced to death by stoning for adultery, but they were acquitted (**Safiya Husseini** and **Amina Lawal**). Related to Shari'a is the presence of the *hisbah*, groups of men who enforce strict Islamic social codes on a community. People caught by the *hisbah* may be taken to a Shari'a court and subjected to the ruling of the *grand khadi* (Islamic court judge). *See also* RELIGION.

**SHARI'A COURTS.** *See* COURTS.

**SHATA, ALHAJI MAMMAN (1923–1999).** Born in Musawa, in **Katsina State**, as a young man Shata traded **kolanuts**. He started his musical career as a praise-singer. In the 1970s, Shata was one of the most popular **Hausa** musicians in Nigeria. He composed more than 3,000 songs, which highlighted his eccentricities and talent. He participated briefly in local politics. Shata received honorary degrees from **Ahmadu Bello University** and the University of California at Los Angeles. He died in June 1999. *See also* MUSIC.

**SHINKAFI, ALHAJI UMARU (1937– ).** Shinkafi was born in January 1937 in Kaura, in **Zamfara State**. After completing his primary and secondary education, he studied at the Police College in **Kaduna** (1959), the Metropolitan Police Detective Training School (1961–1962), the University of Lagos (1968–1973), and the Nigerian Law School (1973–1974). He was deputy commissioner of **police** briefly before becoming the minister of internal affairs (1975–1978) and commissioner of police (1978–1979). He also worked as the director general of the National Security Organisation (1979–1983). Most important, he was a presidential aspirant from the **National Republican Convention** and vice presidential aspirant from the **All People's Party** in 1999. He received the honorary title *marafan* (**chief**) of **Sokoto** (1986) and Commander of the Order of the Niger.

**SHONEKAN, CHIEF ERNEST ADEGUNLE OLADEINDE (1936– ).** Born in May 1936 in **Lagos**, Shonekan studied at the University of London (1962) and Harvard Business School. He worked as a clerical officer for the Public Works Department. He was also a legal adviser for **United African Company** and later managing director of the company (1980–1993). In 1992, Shonekan served as chair of the **Transitional Council**. He was also chairman of the **Interim National Government** and commander-in-chief of the **armed forces** in 1993. The interim government lasted less than one full year because **General Sani Abacha** forced Shonekan to resign from his post in November 1994. Under Abacha, he was chairman of the **Vision 2010** committee in 1996. Shonekan received the honorary title *abese* (**chief**) of Egbaland (1981) and Grand Commander of the Federal Republic of Nigeria (1990).

**SLAVERY / SLAVE TRADE.** Nigeria played a major role in the continental and international slave trade and utilized various forms of slavery. Seven out of thirteen of the major slave-trading ports in West Africa were located in Nigeria: **Badagry**, **Lagos**, Old **Calabar**, New Calabar, **Brass**, **Benin**, and **Bonny**. An estimated 51 percent of all slaves traded across the Atlantic Ocean came from the Bights of Benin and Biafra. From the Bight of Biafra alone, 89 percent were transported from the ports of Bonny, New Calabar, and Old Calabar. Some 482,000 slaves were shipped from Lagos, Badagry, and Benin between 1651 and 1865.

Slaves who were supposed to become free as a result of the Abolition Act passed by **Great Britain** in 1807 were not returned to their homelands, but rather retained as domestic slaves by Africans. Prior to colonial rule, it was not unheard of for a slave to gain freedom and fully participate in politics and **trade** in a community. For example, Oko Jumbo was a former slave in Bonny who became head of a major trading house in the 1860s. He is responsible for driving the Anna Pepple trading house, run by **King Jaja**, out of Bonny and into Opobo. In an attempt to restrict the slave trade, **Sir Frederick Lugard** in southeastern Nigeria tried to ban slave trading while allowing the institution of slavery to continue. He laid out this idea in his 1901 Slave Dealing Proclamation as well as the Master and Servants Proclamation, locking slaves into their servile status.

The **Egba** of **Abeokuta** had, among others, **Hausa** slaves prior to the 20th century. The Hausa practiced an arrangement called *murgu*, which allowed slaves to work entirely on their own economic activities and pay a fixed payment monthly to their owners. Eunuch (castrated male) slaves were used by Hausa **kings** before the 19th century. In **northern Nigeria**, the use of slaves was prevalent.

Within the **Sokoto Caliphate**, **emirs** used royal slaves to expand political control over their territory. Royal slaves—numbering between 2,000 and 5,000 in **Kano**, for example—were prominent and were organized into slave households, which served as a system of recruitment and training. These slaves were usually war captives, with the emir retaining about half, bought using **cowry shells** as **currency**. There was a significant amount of trust between emirs and their appointed slaves. The royal slaves (those kept by the emir) in Kano had a great deal of power because they controlled the distribution of agricultural products as well as holding key positions in the government and military. For example, senior royal slaves of the caliph had influence in the appointing of emirs. They were able to obtain new rights, moving them closer to freedom. The use of royal slaves in the Sokoto Caliphate emerged out of governmental necessity, as opposed to Islamic doctrine. Most slaves in the Sokoto Caliphate worked on labor-intensive plantations.

The **Koran** allowed for the capturing and keeping of non-Muslim slaves, but encouraged slave owners to treat them kindly and manumit them. The threat of slave raids led communities in southeastern Nigeria to build walls and forts for protection. A system often compared (and confused) with slavery is **pawnship**. Although slavery is illegal today, Nigeria has been criticized for its failure to prevent **human trafficking**. *See also* ISLAM; TRANS-SAHARAN TRADE.

**SLESSOR, MARY MITCHELL (1848–1915).** Born in Scotland, Slessor worked with a Scottish Presbyterian mission in **Calabar**. She saw the relationship between missionary work and colonial rule as complementary, as both were perceived as beneficial to Nigerians. Her stations were located in areas outside the colonial boundaries at the time. She set up her first mission station among the Okoyong people. As a Christian missionary, Slessor spent her time suppressing cultural practices deemed socially destructive and cruel, including the killing of twins and human sacrifices. She also championed the respect of **women**, especially widows. In 1892, she became the first female vice-consul for the British among the Okoyong. In 1904, Slessor moved her mission station to Ikot Opong to introduce **Christianity** to the **Ibibio**. She died in Nigeria in January 1915 and is buried in Calabar.

**SMUGGLING.** The act of smuggling goods and people across international boundaries is a universal problem that modern states still face. In the case of Nigeria, smuggling is particularly acute. Unfortunately, the economic advantages of smuggling were heightened in an effort to stimulate legitimate economic growth. For example, the Nigerian government placed a ban on the importation of used clothing in the 1970s. Consumers, however, enjoyed the low cost of foreign fashions and encouraged the smuggling of these items. Nigeria also established **price controls** on select basic goods to stimulate the **economy** and protect its poorest citizens. Nigeria sold **petroleum** products below international market prices, which encouraged the smuggling of petroleum products across the border to consumers in **Niger** and **Benin**. During the years of the **structural adjustment program**, Nigerian food producers shifted from exporting to smuggling to avoid being forced to exchange their foreign **currency** into naira.

Otherwise law-abiding citizens in Nigeria felt compelled to smuggle goods out of the country due to government bans on select imported products. For example, for decades Nigeria banned the importation of raw materials and essential foodstuffs such as rice and wheat. Many Nigerians found the locally produced varieties to be of inferior quality and in short supply. For this reason, consumers encouraged the smuggling of such items. The Nigerian government struggles to patrol its borders and ports, but rampant **corruption** allows for easily obtained false documents and cooperative border patrols. *See also* CRIME; FOREIGN TRADE.

**SOCIAL DEMOCRATIC PARTY (SDP).** The Social Democratic Party was formed in 1989 as one of two legal **political parties** in Nigeria under the military rule of **General Ibrahim Babangida**. Its membership consisted primarily of individuals from **northern Nigeria**, more specifically the alleged **Kaduna Mafia**. It was considered a leftist party in comparison to the military government and its opposition, the **National Republican Convention**. In the scandalous **election of 12 June 1993**, which should have marked the transition from military rule to civilian rule and the start of the **Third Republic**, **Chief M. K. O. Abiola** ran as the presidential candidate for the SDP, with **Baba Gana Kingibe** as his running mate. When it became clear that Abiola had won, Babangida annulled the election results.

**SOCIALIST WORKERS AND FARMERS PARTY (SWAFP).** A **political party** founded by Tunji Otegbeye, a medical doctor, in 1963. It was based in **Enugu**. The focus of the party was to represent the interests of socialist laborers and farmers. Like all other political parties, it was banned in 1966.

**SOKOTO.** The capital of **Sokoto State**, with a **population** of approximately 500,000. It is historically significant for the **Hausa** and **Fulani** as the seat of the great **Sokoto Caliphate** between 1804 and 1903. Today, it is the home of the University of Sokoto, the **sultan**'s palace, and the Shehu Mosque. Of interest to historians are the Centre for Islamic Studies in Sokoto and the Waziri Junaidu History and Culture Bureau, which house manuscripts from **Islamic** scholars in Nigeria dating back to at least the 17th century.

**SOKOTO CALIPHATE.** The Sokoto Caliphate is considered one of Nigeria's last great empires. It stretched from Dori in present-day Burkina Faso east to Adamwa in present-day **Cameroon** and south to the town of **Ilorin** in Nigeria. The Sokoto Caliphate emerged from the amalgamation of over 30 emirates in 1812 through a series of **jihads** that began in 1804 and were led by a **Fulani** named **Usman dan Fodio**. The jihads were carried out by Usman and 14 flag bearers chosen by him. The caliphate was organized into semiautonomous emirates that ceded religious authority to the caliph, seated in Sokoto. The old **Hausa** aristocracy was replaced by a Fulani one, but with a revival of **Islam** and expansion of literacy.

In 1812, Usman dan Fodio divided the Sokoto Caliphate into two caliphates: Gwandu for his son Abdullahi ibn Muhammed, and **Sokoto** for his son **Muhammad Bello**. The establishment of the caliphate brought an end to interregional rivalry because it offered groups both independence and religious unity. The **emirs** would travel to Sokoto annually to show loyalty and pay tribute. For example, **Kano** paid around 5 million **cowries**; **Zaria** and **Katsina** 500,000–2 million cowries; and **Bauchi** and Fombina sent an estimated 1,000 slaves each as tribute. The institution of **slavery** played an important role in the caliphate. Slaves worked as domestic servants and on farms. Slavery remained an important aspect of economic life (domestic service and working on the land to feed the towns). By 1837, the **population** of the Sokoto Caliphate had reached 10 million people, with an estimated 1.25 million of the total population enslaved. Kano was one of the most populous emirates in the caliphate.

The Sokoto Caliphate lasted until 1903, when the British and French defeated it. The portion of the caliphate taken by the British became part of the **Protectorate of Northern Nigeria**. **Sir Frederick Lugard** abolished the title and power of caliph and replaced it with emir of Sokoto as well as the courtesy title of **sultan**, which held symbolic value. Although the Sokoto Caliphate no longer exists, it is still central to Islamic life in northern Nigeria. The status of sultan of Sokoto, which started with Usman dan Fodio, is still maintained. The sultan is considered the spiritual leader of all Muslims in Nigeria. In October 2006, **Sultan Alhaji Muhammadu Maccido**, the 19th sultan, died in a plane crash. The current sultan is **Colonel Muhammed Sa'adu Abubakar III**.

**SOKOTO STATE.** Sokoto State was created out of **North-Western State** in 1976 and has been reduced in size over the years. It is located in the northeastern corner of Nigeria, sharing a northern boundary with **Niger**. It is named after the great **Sokoto Caliphate**. It is one of 12 northern states that have incorporated **Shari'a** into their criminal law. The capital is the town of **Sokoto**, in which **Usman dan Fodio**'s tomb is located, as well as Usman dan Fodio University. The **Hausa** and **Fulani** are the dominant **ethnic groups** in the state. Economic activities include the cultivation of grains and beans and the herding of cattle. Farmers of Sokoto also utilize the *fadama* (floodplains of a river) to grow foodstuffs such as tomatoes and peppers. *See also* STATE CREATION.

**SOUTH-EASTERN STATE.** A state created in 1967 as one of Nigeria's 12 states. In 1976, South-Eastern State became **Cross River State**. This state was located in southeastern Nigeria on the coast, in the **Niger Delta**. *See also* STATE CREATION.

**SOUTHERN BAPTIST CONVENTION.** *See* BAPTIST CHURCH.

**SOUTHERN NIGERIA.** The portion of Nigeria south of the **Niger River** and **Benue River** to the Gulf of Guinea. It is covers roughly the area of the colonial **Protectorate of Southern Nigeria**. It includes the colonial and **First Republic**'s **Western Region** and **Eastern Region**. Southern Nigeria experienced a greater level of development (i.e., running **water, electricity**, paved **roads**, and schools) during the colonial period. The phrase is used primarily in comparison to **northern Nigeria**, which has a relatively uniform cultural and religious makeup based on **Islam**. The majority of Nigeria's **Christian population** lives in southern Nigeria. Although historically the southern **ethnic groups** such as the **Yoruba** and the **Igbo** have clashed over ethnic-based politics, they are generally recognized as more culturally similar to each other than to groups in northern Nigeria. Also, southern Nigeria is humid and tropical, whereas northern Nigeria is dry savannah with little vegetation. *See also* EASTERN NIGERIA; WESTERN NIGERIA.

**SOYINKA, AKINWANDE OLUWOLE (1934– ).** Soyinka was born in July 1934 in Ijebu-Remo, in **Ogun State**. After completing his primary education in **Abeokuta**, he studied at Government College at **Ibadan** (1946–1950), University College (present-day **University of Ibadan**) (1952–1954), and the University of Leeds (1954–1957). He is one of Nigeria's most famous playwrights, poets, and novelists. Soyinka worked for the Royal Court Theatre in London (1957). He also taught English at the University of Ife (present-day **Obafemi Awolowo University**) (1962–1963) and University of Lagos (1965–1967). He was the director of the School of Drama at the University of Ibadan (1967, 1969–1971). Between 1967 and 1969, he was arrested and detained by **General Yakubu Gowon** for openly criticizing Gowon's handling of the **Republic of Biafra** during the **civil war**. Between 1971 and 1975, he was in self-imposed exile in **Great Britain** and **Ghana**.

In the 1970s, Soyinka returned to the University of Ife to teach drama and also held several visiting professorships in drama departments outside Nigeria. He was the first African to win the Nobel Prize for Literature, in 1986. He uses his work, written in English, to both critique and educate. His plays borrow heavily from **Yoruba** cosmology and **Christianity**. His works include *A Dance of the Forest* (1963), *The Road* (1965), *Open Sore of a Continent* (1996), and *King Baabu* (1994), among others. From 1994 to 1998, he was again in self-imposed exile from Nigeria. In 2003, he formed the Citizens' Forum to lobby against government-sponsored **corruption** in Nigeria. In May 2004, he was briefly detained for participating in a demonstration that criticized the government of **General Olusegun Obasanjo**. *See also* LITERATURE; THEATER.

**SPORTS.** In Nigeria, sports are not only a pastime for youth, but also a forum for international politics. Exuberant cheers can still be heard when Nigeria wins a match against a British team, as a symbol of Nigeria defeating its former colonizer. By far the most popular sport in Nigeria is soccer, or as it is called in Nigeria, football. Nigeria's national football team, the Super Eagles, was ranked among the top 25 teams in the world in 2005. Despite divisions along ethnic and religious lines, football matches mark moments of national unity. Increasingly, Nigeria has become a source of remarkable athletes who are drafted to play on European and North American teams. In basketball, **Hakeem Olajuwon** made National Basketball Association history in the United States, and in soccer, the Super Eagles captain, Jay-Jay Okoch, has earned fame as Player of Year from the Confederation of African Football (2003 and 2004).

**STATE CREATION.** Since **independence**, Nigeria has reconfigured its states several times and altered each state's degree of autonomy. Nigeria grapples with the challenge of maintaining unity, granting fair representation to all **ethnic groups**, and providing equitable **revenue allocation** among states. Nigeria's leaders, both military and civilian, have used the strategy of state formation to ease tension, pacify regions and ethnic groups, or break-up geographic solidarity among ethnic groups. At independence, Nigeria inherited **Great Britain**'s division of the country into three regions: **Northern, Western**, and **Eastern**. When Nigeria became a republic in 1963, it expanded this regional division by adding the **Mid-Western Region**. **General Yakubu Gowon** divided the four regions into 12 states in May 1967. The goal was to fracture states in the East in order to undermine regional solidarity and reduce the influence or threat of any one region toward the central government.

For each new round of state creations after 1970, the government set up commissions to look into the value and feasibility of creating new states, particularly in the **Niger Delta**. In February 1976, **General Murtala Ramat Mohammed** took the 12 states and created 7 more, bringing the total to 19. This was done in response to a report by the

**Irikefe Commission.** One of these new states was the **Federal Capital Territory** in the middle of the country, which was to house the country's new capital, **Abuja**. In 1987, two more states were created, bringing the number of states to 21. **General Ibrahim Babangida** increased the number of states to 30 in August 1991. In October 1996, **General Sani Abacha** created 6 new states, and there are currently 36.

**STRUCTURAL ADJUSTMENT PROGRAM (SAP).** Like many African countries, Nigeria agreed to undergo a structural adjustment program to stimulate economic development and qualify for large international loans. The structural adjustment program was designed and recommended by the International Monetary Fund (IMF). The primary purpose of a structural adjustment program is to balance a country's accounts and ensure that the value of exports and imports are stable. The program typically lasts three to five years and requires many austerity measures. In the case of Nigeria, an SAP was first introduced under the leadership of **Alhaji Aliyu Usman Shagari** in 1983. Nigeria first approached the IMF for a loan of $2.3 billion, with hopes of restoring balance in its international payments. In 1986, **General Ibrahim Badamasi Babangida** allowed Nigeria to undergo structural adjustment without taking on new loans. The IMF recommended that Nigeria significantly trim its expenses, liberalize its **trade**, privatize state-owned corporations, and remove all subsidies, which were the typical conditions. Although the Nigerian government agreed with most of the IMF's recommendations, it resisted the removal of **petroleum** subsidies and alteration of its **currency** exchange rate.

In recent years, the IMF has received a barrage of criticisms for proposing a "one size fits all" set of conditions, which contributed to the loss of social safety nets. Some analysts have attributed Nigeria's severe poverty and shortage of hospitals and medical supplies to the loss of social welfare programs during the SAP. In 1994, **General Sani Abacha** ended the SAP. Since then, Nigeria has attempted to apply SAP-inspired changes, while reducing its debt to international institutions such as the IMF and **World Bank** as well as individual governments. *See also* BANKING; ECONOMY; PRIVATIZATION.

**SUFISM.** *See* AHMADIYYA; ISLAM; QADIRIYYA; TIJANIYYA.

**SULTAN (OF SOKOTO).** An **Islamic** title denoting political authority over a territory. In Nigeria, this honorific title is applied only to those individuals chosen to continue the linkage to **Usman dan Fodio** of **the Sokoto Caliphate**, after it collapsed in 1903. The first sultan was **Attahiru II**, the great-grandson of Usman. Prior to that date, the head of the Sokoto Caliphate was called the caliph. The sultan is also regarded as the *Sarkin Musulmi* (Commander of the Faithful). The sultan is considered by many Muslims to be the most important religious and cultural appointment in Nigeria, because he is the spiritual head of all Muslims in Nigeria. The process of selection involves discussions and approval by 11 Islamic elders in **Sokoto**. They decide which branch of the sultan's family is most suited for the position. It is common for the eldest son or younger brother of the previous sultan to be chosen. Selecting the sultan is considered outside the government's military or civilian jurisdiction. In 1988, it is believed that **General Ibrahim Babangida** attempted to install **Ibrahim Dasuki**, which caused widespread violence and resistance. Dasuki was deposed in 1996, and the popular choice, **Alhaji Muhammadu Maccido**, became the sultan. Another notable sultan was **Sultan Siddiq Abubakar III**. The current sultan is **Alhaji Colonel Muhammed Sa'adu Abubakar III**, who has held the title since November 2006. One of the important roles the sultan has is heading the **Nigerian Supreme Council for Islamic Affairs**.

**SUPREME COURT.** *See* COURTS.

**SUPREME MILITARY COUNCIL (SMC).** The executive military council that ruled Nigeria from 1966 to 1979, under three different military leaders. It was implemented under Decree No. 1. The council consisted of the president, the heads of the three branches of the **armed forces**, the chiefs of staff of the armed forces, the military governors of the four regions (**Northern, Eastern, Mid-Western,** and **Western**), and the attorney general of the federal military government. State officials were encouraged to attend the council's meetings. The Supreme Military Council served as the highest governing body in Nigeria, charged with enacting and enforcing national policies.

From July 1966 to July 1975, **General Yakubu Gowon** was the president of the council. A military **coup d'état** in July 1975 installed

**General Murtala Ramat Mohammed** as president until his death in February 1976, at which time **General Olusegun Obasanjo** assumed the position. Obasanjo placed himself as chairman of the council as well as head of state and commander-in-chief of the armed forces. Under Mohammed and Obasanjo, military governors were no longer members of the council, and state officials were no longer allowed to attend meetings. The 1979 elections dissolved the Supreme Military Council in favor of a democratic political structure, which lasted four years.

In 1983, the council was reinstated through a military coup d'état led by **Major General Muhammadu Buhari**. Until 1985, the Supreme Military Council consisted of the head of state, heads of military units, inspector general of **police** and his deputy, head of the **civil service**, and various other military members. In 1985, this particular council structure was dissolved and replaced with other similar structures, such as the **Armed Forces Ruling Council** and the **Provisional Ruling Council**.

## – T –

**TACTICAL COMMITTEE.** A temporary administration established in September 1960 to replace the **Action Group** and maintain unity within the party. The main goal was to avoid a state of emergency in the **Western Region**. The committee included **Chief Obafemi Awolowo** as chairman and several secret members. The secret members may have included **Chief Anthony Enahoro**, **Chief Ayo Rosiji**, and **Chief Samuel Akintola**. In March 1962, Awolowo requested the disbanding of the committee. Ultimately, the committee was not able to prevent the **Action Group Crisis**.

**TARABA STATE.** A state created in 1991 out of **Gongola State**. It is one of Nigeria's current 36 states. It is located in **eastern Nigeria**, sharing its southern boundary with **Cameroon**. The capital is the town of Jalingo. Within its territory are the **Benue River** and a chain of mountains. Its ethnic composition includes several **ethnic groups** such as the **Fulani**, Mumuye, and Chamba. It is also considered one of several states in the **Middle Belt** region. Economic activities in the state include the cultivation of citrus fruits, **cocoa**, tubers, and oil palm; fishing; herding; and logging. In recent years, it has been the site of clashes between the **Jukun** and the **Tiv**. *See also* STATE CREATION.

**TARKA, CHIEF JOSEPH SARWUAN (1932–1980).** Born in July 1932 in Igbor, in **Benue State**, as a young man Tarka studied at Benue Middle School in Katsina-Ala, Teachers Training College, and the Rural Science Centre in **Bauchi**. In the field of **education**, he worked as a headmaster at Junior Primary School in Katsina-Ala (1949–1952) and a rural science master at Benue Provincial Secondary School in Katsina-Ala (1953–1955). He also worked for the Tiv Native Authority as a rural science specialist and executive member in the mid-1950s. He formed and served as president of the **United Middle Belt Congress** (UMBC) in the 1960s. With the UMBC, he campaigned for the creation of a Middle Belt State as part of the **Middle Belt State Movement**. He was also the deputy parliamentary leader of the House of Representatives. In 1962, he was arrested along with **Chief Obafemi Awolowo** on charges of treason. Roughly ten years later, Tarka was accused of **corruption** and forced to resign from his post as commissioner of transport. In 1978, he joined the **National Party of Nigeria** and remained active in politics through his work as a senator until his death in March 1980.

**TAXATION.** Taxation has been an integral, but contested, part of Nigerian societies. Although its function has remained largely the same, the manner in which taxes are collected has changed. Prior to colonial rule, taxation benefited only royalty. Each **emir** in the **Sokoto Caliphate** during the 19th century would collect taxes, which often funded the keeping of slaves for the palace. It was common for royal slaves (slaves owned by the emir) to manage the emirate's tax system. **Village heads** also collected taxes from their communities annually and sent them to the emir. In **northern Nigeria**, **Fulani** pastoralists paid *jangali* (cattle tax) to local rulers as a "payment to pasture."

During the colonial period, Nigerians protested against paying taxes from which they did not benefit. Taxation in Nigeria has been viewed with great suspicion, given the introduction of new forms. The **Native Treasuries** were established first in the North in 1911 and then across Nigeria by 1914 to create a repository for taxation that was to be used by **chiefs** and their administration in the **Native Authority**. **Women**, especially in **southern Nigeria**, protested the implementation of a tax on them and on **water**, which women collected as part of their household duties. Women also protested against income tax. In 1940, market women in **Lagos**, with support from the Nigerian National Democratic Party, pressed for the colonial government to adjust the minimum taxable income to £100. In **Abeokuta**, taxation included a flat tax and a graduated tax in the 1920s. In the mid-1920s, a special tax was paid by men and women whose annual income exceeded £40. Anyone who earned below that level continued to pay an annual flat tax, which was set at five shillings for men and about two shillings for women. The taxes were collected by the village heads, who reported to the *oba* (**chiefs**), who in turn reported to the colonial-appointed *alake* (chief). All of the chiefs received a percentage of the total tax receipts. Throughout the period of colonial rule, the taxation structure all over Nigeria was under continual revision.

Since **independence**, Nigeria has struggled to establish and enforce a suitable tax structure without arousing too much resistance. As a result, it relies heavily on indirect taxation (tariffs and sales tax) instead of direct taxation (income tax and property tax). In 1986, indirect taxes contributed roughly 12 percent of the country's total revenue. In addition, the amount of naira that Nigerian citizens pay to **policemen** and **civil servants** daily as part of living in a severely **corrupt** country functions as a form of taxation. With the deep-seated mistrust Nigerian citizens have toward the government, the implementation of direct taxation on citizens is out of the question. *See also* INDIRECT RULE; RAISMAN COMMISSION; SLAVERY/SLAVE TRADE.

**TELECOMMUNICATIONS.** Nigeria has excelled in some areas of telecommunications and struggled in others. For example, the use of cell phones in Nigeria has taken off since the late 1990s. The booming industry is a testament to the strength of **privatization**. Nigeria has about 32 million cell phones in use. It is estimated that nearly three out of ten people have a cell phone.

During the 1970s, the federal military governments saw the improvement of telecommunications as key to economic development and security. All aspects of telecommunications in Nigeria were under federal control and ownership. In 1985, the federal government split telecommunications services from postal services, creating Nigerian Telecommunications. Still in operation today, Nigerian Telecommunications struggles to meet demand in Nigeria and faces fierce competition from private companies, such as MTN, Globacom, and Cisco. It had a monopoly on telecommunications services until 1999, when **General Olusegun Obasanjo** deregulated the system and invited private companies into Nigeria.

Cyber cafés have appeared rapidly in all sizable towns, equipped with webcams and scanners. In March 1995, the Nigeria Internet Group, a nonprofit organization, was created by the Nigerian Communications Commission to promote the responsible use of the Internet through workshops and training seminars. With Russian assistance, Nigeria launched its first telecommunications satellite, called NigeriaSat-1, in September 2003. Access to the Internet, for now, is restricted to the urban centers and Nigerians with disposable income. For most Nigerians, **radio** and **television** are the primary electronic devices that keep them in touch with the world. *See also* ADVANCED FEE FRAUD.

**TELEVISION BROADCASTING.** Television broadcasting in Nigeria began in October 1959. The Western Nigeria Television Service was not only the first in Nigeria, but in all of Africa. A year later, the **Eastern Region** developed its own television broadcasting service. The **Northern Region** joined the other regions in 1962. National television broadcasting developed in 1963 with the Nigerian Television Service. Since that time, television broadcasting has been available all over Nigeria and is provided by federal, state, and local services.

The Nigerian Television Authority, based in **Abuja**, was created in 1978 as the state-owned broadcasting company. It is responsible for providing free television in local **languages** and English. These channels provide the local news in English and local languages, with an emphasis on presidential and local government achievements. Nigerians with disposable income can pay for cable television, which offers stations such as MTV Africa, CNN, and African Independent Television. All television broadcasting requires that 60 percent of the program be locally created. For example, **Ken Saro-Wiwa**, the **Ogoni** activist, produced a television show called *Basi and Company*. This law, in part, has contributed to the popularity of Nigerian-made films (also known as **Nollywood** productions). For Nigerians abroad, there are websites that run previously aired television shows to remind them of home. *See also* RADIO; TELECOMMUNICATIONS.

**TEXTILES.** Textiles have played an integral role in Nigeria's **economy** and culture. Since earliest times, Nigerian societies have woven their own cloth out of **cotton** and other natural fibers into household items as well as fashionable clothing. Nigerians were also interested in cloth produced in places such as India. Certain cloths played an important role in society. White cotton cloth, for example, was required for burial ceremonies. During the era of the **slave trade**, human captives were often exchanged for European cloth and other luxury items. In **Arochukwu**, the Ekpe/Okonko society had the authority to place a physical barrier of white cloth around a disputed tract of land until the issue of ownership had been settled.

European traders found the textile trade in Nigeria difficult to penetrate, which is a testament to its vibrancy and strength. In 1830, a European traveler in Oyo saw royal wives whose prestige was signified by the particular cloth they carried. Followers of Obatala (considered the "king of white cloth"), a **Yoruba** deity, draped themselves in white cloth. Prior to the 20th century, **Kano** supplied cotton cloth to North Africa and coastal Nigeria. **Igbirra** and **Igbo** regions also sold cloth north as far as **Borno**. Between the 15th and 18th centuries, regional **trade** in cloth, which was predominantly produced by women, escalated. **Abeokuta**, for example, was (and still is) known for a style of cloth resist-dyed using wax and indigo by **women** called *adire*. In the 1930s, two men from present-day **Ghana** arrived at **Bonny** and began weaving the popular style of *kente* cloth for Nigerian consumers, which developed into a new Nigerian cloth style called *popo* (the surname of the Ghanaians). Similarly, the city of **Zaria** is known for the weaving of *babban riga* ("big robe" in the **Hausa language**), a royal cloth style. The designers stitch by hand the buyer's name or a personalized pattern that indicates his or her unique style.

Textile production in Nigeria has declined significantly since the 1980s, although there are still local cloth makers and dyers. Several prominent Nigerian women use textile as a medium of artistic production. For example, Kikelmo Oladepo, who was part of **Susanne Wenger**'s New Sacred Art Movement in Osogbo, created **Yoruba religion**-inspired batiks, and Chukwuanugo Okeke of **Nsukka** specialized in Igbo-inspired woven fabrics. *See also* ART.

**THEATER.** Theatrical performance has always played a unique role in Nigerian societies. The definition of theater in Nigeria is much broader than in Europe or the United States. For Nigeria, theater may include imaginative storytelling, elaborate festivals, and vibrant dances. These cultural performances are often dominated by aesthetics and are not compartmentalized as cultural productions. Many scholars also identify royal processions and ceremonies as a theatrical performance, designed to demonstrate the superior social status of the royal family. These performances affirm a **king**'s or **chief**'s power and the community's prosperity.

Since time immemorial, theater has been used to reduce social tensions and promote a sense of community. It is not uncommon for theater troupes to perform works that include live **music**, dance, folktales, and proverbs. However, performers may not play specific speaking roles or recite lines from a written script. In more recent times, theater has been used to express social discontent with national politics, poverty, and moral deterioration. In some instances, these playwrights have landed themselves and their work at the center of sociopolitical conflict in the country. For example, **Akinwande Oluwole Soyinka** spent 1967–1969 in prison for speaking out against the **civil war**, and Shenu Sani's *Phantom Crescent* was banned in **Kaduna State** in 2002. Theatrical performances are regularly held at the National Theatre in **Lagos**, which opened in 1976. Nigeria's best-known playwrights include **Amos Tutuola**, Shehu Sani, **Osonye Tess Onwueme**, Akinwande Oluwole Soyinka, **Femi Osofisan**, **Ola Emmanuel Rotimi**, and **Duro Ladipo**. Prominent theatrical actors in Nigeria include **Chief Hubert Adedeji Ogunde** and **H. Kolawole Ogunmola**. *See also* OYELAMI, CHIEF MURAINA.

**THIRD REPUBLIC.** Unlike the **First**, **Second**, and **Fourth Republics**, the Third Republic never actually existed. The **election of 12**

June 1993 was supposed to usher in this new democratic government, but the results were annulled by **General Ibrahim Babangida**.

**TIJANI, CHIEF AMODU.** The *oluwa* (**chief**) of **Lagos** in the early 20th century. Tijani was staunchly anticolonial and resisted British intrusion into the affairs of chiefs. In 1921, **Sir Herbert Macaulay** helped him get compensation for land acquired by the British through force and manipulation. The Privy Council in London ruled in Tijani's favor, a major triumphal step in securing a semblance of traditional authority. *See also* LAND TENURE SYSTEM.

**TIJANIYYA.** The second largest Sufi **Islamic** *tariqah* (brotherhood or order) in Nigeria, after the **Qadiriyya**. It was established in 1784 by Ahmad al-Tijani in Algeria and reached **northern Nigeria** in the 19th century. The **emir** of **Kano**, Abbas, switched his allegiance from the Qadiriyya to the Tijaniyya around 1918. In the 1950s and 1960s, there were clashes between the two dominant *tariqah*. This one, like the Qadiriyya, has faced strong opposition and criticism from fundamentalist Muslim associations in the North, such as **Jama'atu Nasril Islam** and **Izala**. *See also* AHMADIYYA.

**TIN.** Archeological findings indicate that tin mining occurred in Jos Plateau, **Bauchi**, and Okeri prior to the 19th century. The **Hausa**, for example used tin to coat the brass creations that they acquired through the **trans-Saharan trade**. Europeans found evidence of tin smelting in **Kano** in the 1880s that dated back centuries. In 1889, the **Royal Niger Company** acquired permission from the British government to establish trading posts and engage in tin mining. In 1910, there was a "tin rush" by European miners. Large-scale tin mining during the colonial period transformed the landscape of Jos Plateau into a network of **railroad** tracks, **roads**, and telegraph wires. Local smelting of tin was suppressed in favor of exporting all mined tin from **Port Harcourt** overseas. During **World Wars I and II**, Nigeria provided **Great Britain** with a steady supply of this important war material. Since the mid-1950s, plastics and other noncorrosive materials have replaced tin in the manufacturing of goods. Today, tin mining in Nigeria is small-scale and is combined with the collection of kaolin, the clay unearthed in the mining process, which is used in making glass and chalk. *See also* ECONOMY; JOS.

**TINUBU, CHIEF MADAM (ca. 1805–1887).** Born in **Abeokuta** of **Egba** descent, Tinubu was a businesswoman and politician who ran a lucrative **trade** in **cotton**, ammunition, **salt**, tobacco, and slaves from **Badagry**. She was the niece of **King Akintoye** and has been credited with assisting in his return to the throne in **Lagos**, which he lost in 1845. In Lagos, she acted as his unofficial advisor. When King Akitoye died in 1853, **King Dosunmu** succeeded him and, again, she was a loyal confidant. Wealthy inhabitants of Lagos, however, saw her role as evidence of King Dosunmu's weakness. Tinubu was driven out of Lagos by Dosunmu. She resettled in Abeokuta and continued her large-scale trading. In 1864, she became the *iyalode* (**chief**) of all **women** in Abeokuta. The title was in honor of her support during an invasion by Dahomey that year. She died in 1887 in Abeokuta. A plaza in Lagos is named after her. *See also* SLAVERY/SLAVE TRADE.

**TIV.** One of Nigeria's **ethnic groups**, numbering four million, located in the **Middle Belt** region. The Tiv **language** is part of the Bantu language family. The Tiv are the ethnic majority in **Benue State** and are considered a **minority group** in the neighboring states of **Nasarawa**, **Taraba**, and **Plateau**. Prior to colonial rule, the Tiv lived in a segmentary political structure and engaged in farming. Many **Hausa** communities in central Nigeria saw the Tiv as domineering settlers. The British conquest of central Nigeria was fiercely challenged by the Tiv in the late 19th century. The majority of **United Middle Belt Congress** (UMBC) members were of Tiv descent.

After **independence**, the UMBC agitated for the creation of the **Middle Belt State** out of the **Northern Region**. Part of this campaign was a Tiv-led riot in March 1960 against the **Native Authority**. The rioting spread to neighboring towns through October 1960. Four years later, the Tiv launched another riot, which was quelled by the Nigerian **armed forces**. Between 1990 and 1992, the Tiv clashed with the **Jukun** over land rights and authority. In 2001, the murder of a prominent **chief** sparked weeks of bloodshed and displacement of an estimated 35,000 people caused by Tiv vigilante groups in Taraba State. *See also* MIDDLE BELT STATE MOVEMENT.

**TOFA, ALHAJI BASHIR OTHMAN (1947– ).** Born in June 1947 in **Kano**, Tofa received an advanced degree from the City of London College. In Nigeria, he worked for companies such as Royal Exchange Insurance (1967–1968) and Abba Othman and Sons. He served as chairman of the International Petrol-Energy and Abba Othman Investments. Tofa was a member of the Constituent Assembly in 1995, and of the **National Party of Nigeria** (1979) and the **National Republican Convention** (NRC). He was the NRC's presidential candidate in the 1993 **election**. Many saw Tofa as **General Ibrahim Babangida**'s preferred candidate. Tofa has been a member of the **All People's Party** since 1998. He openly contested the results of the April 2007 election.

**TOWNSEND, HENRY (1815–1866).** A key member of the (Anglican) **Church Missionary Society** (CMS) as a reverend and teacher, Townsend successfully convinced the CMS to establish a mission station at **Abeokuta** instead of **Lagos**. In 1846, he and a group of European settlers moved to Abeokuta. Like other missionaries, he set out not only to spread Christianity, but also to end the trading and use of slaves. He tried to establish **legitimate commerce** through **cotton** production and **trade**. However, by 1856 he recognized that the promotion of cotton production actually intensified the use of slaves. Under his guidance, the **Egba** people were placed under the centralized leadership of the *alake* (**chief**) during the mid-1850s. Historians find Henry Townsend's papers useful because he recorded in detail his observations of **Yoruba** society, including dress, and his travels into **Hausa** territory with **Bishop Samuel Ajayi Crowther**. *See also* CHRISTIANITY; SLAVERY/SLAVE TRADE.

**TRADE.** Trade has played an integral role in the rise and fall of political entities in Nigeria for centuries. Well-developed trade networks for almost any major goods on the global market passed through Nigeria, including **tin, textiles, slaves, salt**, and **kolanuts**. The success of these early trade networks was due to a combination of dispersed settlements, such as the **Hausa** of **northern Nigeria**, and the centralized kingdoms, such as the **Oyo Empire**. Kolanut traders moved back and forth from Bonduku (in present-day Ivory Coast) to Gonja (in present-day **Ghana**), and to Hausaland. One major trade route moved goods from **Sokoto** in northern Nigeria to Lagos on the southwest coast. The **Niger River** served as a "water highway" on which goods were transported across Nigeria. Trade utilizing the Niger River connected local trade networks in **Borgu**, **Nupe**, and the **Niger Delta**. Nigerian traders also participated in the **trans-Saharan trade**. Common **language**, **religion**, and expansive kinship networks also aided early trade.

In market exchanges, particularly before the 19th century, the quantity and value of various items was well-defined and standardized. Nupe **markets**, for example, sold cloth by the arm's length, threshed grain by a large or small gourd, and beans by the basket. Most prices within a market were negotiable, but prepared food was not. In the Niger Delta prior to the 20th century, kingdoms traded through their respective trading houses. **King Jaja of Opobo**, for example, ran a lucrative trading house that he relocated from **Bonny** to Opobo in the 1860s. Each house was run by one individual, chosen among royalty, and had several members. Trading houses competed with and subsumed one another. **Chief Madam Tinubu** was another successful trader.

During British colonial rule, many of these trade routes changed as arbitrary boundaries divided colonies and cut off traders from their suppliers. European trading companies, such as the **Royal Niger Company**, and traders also influenced trade routes. Much of the trade that went from the coastal area to the interior of West Africa was discontinued; instead, goods went from the interior to coastal ports for international shipping. Colonial rule ensured that raw materials produced in Nigeria, such as **groundnuts** and **oil palm**, went for overseas trade. During **World Wars I and II**, agricultural goods produced in Nigeria were essential to wartime **Great Britain**. Independent Nigeria saw some new developments in trade patterns. The amount and type of goods imported and exported have been heavily regulated. For the most part, **agricultural** goods are traded regionally, whereas lucrative commodities such as **petroleum** and oil palm are exported as part of Nigeria's **foreign trade**. *See also* ECONOMY.

**TRADE, FOREIGN.** *See* FOREIGN TRADE.

**TRADE, LEGITIMATE.** *See* LEGITIMATE COMMERCE.

**TRADE, TRANS-SAHARAN.** *See* TRANS-SAHARAN TRADE.

**TRADE UNION CONGRESS OF NIGERIA (TUCN).** One of the key national **trade unions**. In 1942, the Federated Trade Union was formed to serve as a central union, representing a range of industrial workers. A year later, its name was changed to the Trade Union Congress of Nigeria. Its was the first government-approved, national trade union. By the late 1940s, the congress faced difficulties and broke up into several trade unions. TUCN was reformed in January 1959 by the merging of the **All-Nigeria Trade Union Federation** and the **National Council of Trade Unions of Nigeria**. In 1962, after a brief hiatus, the TUCN and the **Nigerian Trade Union Congress** were folded into the **United Labour Congress**.

**TRADE UNIONS.** Trade unions emerged as early as 1909 and gained strength during **World Wars I and II**. They started locally and later became national. Their organizational structures largely reflected those of precolonial craft guilds. In 1909, the Niger Traders' Association formed to pressure the colonial government into assisting traders in **Onitsha**. In 1923, Nigerian barristers formed the Nigerian Law Association and published a journal. Most of the early organizations, however, were based in **Lagos**, for example the Lagos Fishermen's Association (1937) and the Palm Wine Sellers' Association (1942). In 1939, the colonial government passed the Trade Union Ordinance, which allowed trade unions to operate if they registered. In 1931, the **Nigerian Union of Teachers** and the **Railway Workers' Union** were established. After 1940, trade unions agitated for better wages and recognition by the colonial, and later federal, governments. Numerous trade unions formed, split, aligned themselves with other trade unions, and dissolved. At the forefront of much of this union activity was **Chief Michael Imoudu**.

In 1942, the Federated Trade Union formed to serve as a central union, representing a range of industrial workers. A year later, its name was changed to the **Trade Union Congress of Nigeria**. Together, the trade unions launched the **General Strike**, which lasted six weeks and included around 40,000 workers. From 1949 to 1978, the trade union movement lost strength as unions formed and broke apart. Notable trade unions included the **All-Nigeria Trade Union**

**Federation** (1953), **National Council of Trade Unions of Nigeria** (1957), **Nigerian Trade Union Congress** (1960), and **United Labour Congress** (1962). In 1964, there were about 300,000 union members organized into roughly 300 trade unions across the country. In 1978, under the persuasion of the federal military government, more than 1,000 trade unions in Nigeria were merged into one, called the **Nigerian Labour Congress** (NLC). The 1980s and 1990s saw a significant decrease in industrial workers in Nigeria, which led to the decline of trade union activity. The NLC continues to serve as the nongovernmental representative of workers, and the public, in Nigeria. *See also* OSHIOMHOLE, ADAMS ALIYU

**TRADITIONAL MEDICINE.** Traditional medical consultation by professionals centered on social ills as well as individual **health** problems and has existed since time immemorial. In Nigeria, the use of traditional medicines was important in resolving familial and communal tensions as well as curing a person's ailments. The treatments ranged from ingestible concoctions and aroma-based solutions to charms. The infusion of ash-water, commonly found plants, and natron were frequently used. The ointments were made of **oil palm**, shea butter, or clay. Some herbal concoctions include a mixture of roots and tree bark. The **Nupe**, for example, have practiced *cigbe*, which refers to the application of remedies for an illness and the substance, or object, that has miraculous effects. The application of *cigbe* requires the invocation of deities and sacrifice as well as the preparation of natural substances. For rheumatic pain, for example, a Nupe healer may recommend an ointment made from shards of a clay pot that was found lying with the broken side up. Over time, some traditional remedies have fallen into disuse as new, more effective ones are applied.

In many cases, the diagnosis and treatment of a health problem seems to be in direct conflict with Western medicine. This is particularly true with regard to mental illness, infertility, and **HIV/AIDS**. In 2006, Nigeria began working with the World Health Organization on organizing traditional medicine and integrating it into the formal health system. The government is also interested in the contributions traditional medicine may make to the treatment of **malaria** and sickle-cell anemia. *See also* DIVINATION; RELIGION.

**TRANSATLANTIC SLAVE TRADE.** *See* SLAVERY/SLAVE TRADE.

**TRANS-SAHARAN TRADE.** One of the most important **trade** networks in the world in its time, this trade route went from the coast of West Africa to North Africa across the harsh Sahara Desert. Historians have linked the introduction of the camel around the fifth century to the start of this trade. Regular caravans of thousands of camels made the journey until the 16th century, when Europeans diverted trading to the coast. Nigerian producers and traders played an integral role in the success of this long-distance exchange of goods. Notable goods that went across the "ocean of sand" were gold, **salt, textiles,** slaves, beads, dates, perfumes, and spices. Major stops on the route included **Kano** and the **Kanem-Bornu Empire**. The trans-Saharan trade route, however, was not only about the exchange of goods, but also about the exchange of **religion**, culture, and scientific advances. Many scholars believe that **Islam** and the practice of writing were introduced in **northern Nigeria** through this trade around the 11th century. *See also* FOREIGN TRADE; SLAVERY/SLAVE TRADE.

**TRANSITIONAL COUNCIL.** A committee appointed by **General Ibrahim Babangida** in 1992, composed of civilians. Babangida created the council to prove to the public that he was committed to the democratic **elections** slated for 1993. The council was also charged with providing economic advice, particularly with regard to improving Nigeria's situation in the **structural adjustment program**. **Chief Ernest Shonekan** served as the chair of the council. Overall, the Transitional Council was unable to influence Babangida. The operations of the council were interrupted by the annulled **election of 12 June 1993**.

**TRANSPORTATION.** *See* AIRLINES; RAILROADS; ROADS.

**TUDOR-DAVIES COMMISSION.** *See* GENERAL STRIKE.

**TUTUOLA, AMOS (1927–1997).** Born in **Abeokuta**, Tutuola completed his studies in **Lagos** and Abeokuta. He joined the Royal Air Force in 1940 and served in **World War II**. After the war, he worked in the Ministry of Labour, and later, at the Nigerian Broadcasting Corporation. He was a visiting fellow at the University of Ife (present-day **Obafemi Awolowo University**). Tutuola was one of Nigeria's most famous playwrights, and played a major role in shaping Nigerian **theater**. Although he wrote primarily in English, he was heavily inspired by **Yoruba language**, folktales, and proverbs. His most famous work, *The Palm-Wine Drinkard* (1952), toys with the effect of literal translations from Yoruba to English. Tutuola died in June 1997.

## – U –

**UDOJI COMMISSION.** The Udoji Commission of 1972 built on the work of previous commissions in reviewing the pay of **civil service** workers. The chairman of the commission was Chief Jerome Oputa Udoji. The commission reported its findings and recommended substantial increases for civil service workers. For the lowest paying positions of ₦312, the commission suggested an increase to ₦720 per year, and for the highest pay rate of ₦8,400, it recommended an increase to ₦15,510. It also devised a grading system and result-oriented reward scheme. The federal military government accepted most of the commission's suggestions.

**UKIWE, COMMODORE EBITU (1940– ).** Ukiwe was born in October 1940 in Abriba, in **Abia State**. After completing his primary and secondary education in Abriba, Ukiwe attended the Nigerian Military Training College in **Kaduna** (1960–1961), Britannia Royal Naval College in Dartmouth (1961–1964), and the U.S. Naval War College (1980–1981). Ukiwe enlisted in the navy in 1963. He was a commanding officer on several different naval ships and served as the chief staff officer of the Western Naval Command (1976–1977). He was also the military governor of **Niger State** (1977–1978) and military administrator of **Lagos State** (1978–1979). Ukiwe retired from the **armed forces** in 1986 after serving as the chief of general staff for one year. He was a member of the **National Democratic Coalition** and a vocal supporter of **Chief M. K. O. Abiola** during the **election of 12 June 1993** crisis. Ukiwe earned the honorary title Grand Commander of the Order of the Niger (1989).

**UMAR, COLONEL ABUBAKAR DANGIWA (1949– ).** Born in September 1949 in Birmin Kebbi, in **Kebbi State,** Umar attended Government College in **Sokoto** (1964–1968) before joining the army. He studied at the Nigerian Defence Academy in **Kaduna** (1967–1972) and at other training schools in Nigeria and the United States. In the army, he worked as deputy general staff officer and military administrator for the Federal Housing Authority (1984–1985). He was the military governor of **Kaduna State** from 1985 to 1988. He also advanced his education at Bayero University in **Kano** (1979–1981) and Harvard University (1988–1989). Umar retired from the **armed forces** in 1993. In 1998, he joined a coalition of politicians voicing opposition to **General Sani Abacha.** In 2007, he mobilized his Movement for Unity and Progress organization to oppose **General Olusegun Obasanjo**'s attempt to run for president for a third term.

**UNEMPLOYMENT.** Unemployment in Nigeria is a complicated issue, because reliable statistics are difficult to obtain in a country with a thriving informal economy. On paper, Nigeria's unemployment rate of 5.8 percent nearly matches that of the United States, and close to 60 percent of Nigeria's population is living below the poverty line. In reality, Nigeria's unemployment rate is low because so few people are *actively* seeking employment in the *formal* sector. Much of Nigeria's economy is based on petty trade and noncommercial farming, which does not typically get factored into its employment statistics. Nigeria has a GNI (gross national income) of $930, making it among the poorest countries in the world. Formal jobs with regular paychecks, health benefits, or retirement packages are rare in Nigeria. The problem of unemployment, however, is not new. In 1945, **Lagos** had an estimated 20,000 unemployed individuals among its 220,000 inhabitants.

Since 1960, Nigeria's heads of state have tried to increase stable employment opportunities, with limited success. For example, **Sir Alhaji Abubakar Tafawa Balewa** established the **National Manpower Board** (1964), and **General Ibrahim Babangida** formed the **National Directorate of Employment** (1987) to facilitate employment opportunities. Having such a high level of unemployed and impoverished individuals has dramatic implications for the country's economy and political stability. Unquestionably, this problem is at the core of Nigeria's **crime** and **corruption** rates. Many wealthy and well-educated Nigerians have left Nigeria in search of reliable employment elsewhere. As a result, Nigeria suffers from the brain drain phenomenon, whereby those with advanced degrees and marketable skills leave the country. *See also* NATIONAL PROVIDENT FUND.

**UNIFICATION DECREE.** In January 1966, **General Johnson Agu-iyi-Ironsi** implemented Decree No. 34, which changed Nigeria's political status from a federation to a republic. The four regions—**Northern**, **Western**, **Mid-Western**, and **Eastern**—became simply provinces. The status of **Lagos** changed from federal territory to capital. The goal was to unify the country and reduce any obstacles between the head of state and local politics. The unification decree also banned **political parties** that had been operating in Nigeria. When **General Yakubu Gowon** took power in July 1966, the federal structure was reinstituted, but the ban on political parties remained.

**UNITED AFRICAN COMPANY (UAC).** Formed in 1879 by **Sir George Taubman Goldie**, this company was the result of a four-company merger of British trading companies in the **Niger Delta**. In 1882, the UAC changed its name to **National Africa Company**. A trading company using the name UAC reemerged in 1929 when the **Royal Niger Company** merged with the A&E trading company. In 1930, the UAC announced its plans to engage in continuing trade of *adire* (wax-based, resist dyed) cloth between **Abeokuta** (the site of the dyeing) and the Gold Coast (present-day **Ghana**). In effect, the UAC monopolized this trade and squeezed out African traders. The UAC established the privileged position of determining prices of high-demand goods such as **cotton** and **cocoa**. In 1931, it became a subsidiary of Unilever. By 1949, the UAC was responsible for 34 percent of goods imported into Nigeria. Although greatly modified, the company is still in operation today. *See also* TRADE.

**UNITED DEMOCRATIC PARTY (UDP).** One of only nine political organizations authorized by **General Alhaji Abdulsalami Abu-bakar** to put forward candidates for the 1999 **election**.

**UNITED LABOUR CONGRESS (ULC).** A **trade union** formed by a merger between the **Trade Union Congress of Nigeria** and the **Nigerian Trade Union Congress** in 1962. The United Labour Congress, however, lost members to the Independent United Labour Congress, a splinter union. The congress was led by **Alhaji Haroun Popoola Adebola** and L. L. Borha. It was considered one of the few trade unions in Nigeria that was not overtly political in nature. The ULC is credited with the formation of the **Joint Action Committee**, which agitated for a wage increase for Nigerian laborers. *See also* MORGAN COMMISSION.

**UNITED MIDDLE BELT CONGRESS (UMBC).** An organization formed by **Chief Joseph Tarka** in 1955 to represent the interests of people living in the **Middle Belt**. The primary goal of the organization was to campaign for the creation of a unified Middle Belt State. **Chief Solomon Lar** was an active member of this **political party**. The congress aligned itself with the **Northern Elements Progressive Union** to form the **Northern Progressive Front**. It was disbanded in 1966, along with all other political parties. Although the vision of a single Middle Belt State never materialized, the congress saw small gains in the formation of the **Benue-Plateau State** in 1967.

**UNITED NATIONAL INDEPENDENCE PARTY (UNIP).** Called the **National Independent Party** until its name was changed in 1954, the UNIP was a splinter **political party** from the **National Council of Nigeria and the Cameroons** that aligned itself with the **Action Group**. The party was led by **Eyo Ita** and received the majority of its support from inhabitants of the **Niger Delta**. The UNIP, along with other political parties, was banned in 1966.

**UNITED PEOPLE'S PARTY (UPP).** Formed by **Chief Samuel Akintola** after the **Action Group Crisis** of 1962, the party joined a coalition with the **National Council of Nigeria and the Cameroons**. The **Nigerian National Democratic Party** broke away from the United People's Party in 1964, and both were banned in 1966. The UPP reemerged as one of only nine political parties allowed to run candidates in the 1999 **election**.

**UNITED PROGRESSIVE FRONT (UPF).** The UPF was formed in 1979 as a coalition of four of the largest **political parties**—**Great Nigerian People's Party, Nigerian People's Party, Unity Party of Nigeria,** and the **People's Redemption Party**—against the **National Party of Nigeria**. The coalition assisted in placing non-National Party of Nigeria politicians in the state government, but not in the presidential seat.

**UNITED PROGRESSIVE GRAND ALLIANCE (UPGA).** The UPGA was formed in 1964 as a coalition of four of the major **political parties** and social organizations—**Action Group, United Middle Belt Congress, National Council of Nigerian Citizens,** and **Northern Element Progressive Union**—to rival the **Northern People's Congress** and the **National Democratic Party** in the December 1964 **elections**. This alliance served as the main opposition to the **Nigerian National Alliance**. Despite its efforts, the UPGA did not win many of the most prized political positions.

**UNITY PARTY OF NIGERIA (UPN).** Formed by **Chief Obafemi Awolowo** in 1978, the UPN was one of only five registered **political parties** in the 1979 **election**. To bolster its support base, members of the **Great Nigerian People's Party** aligned themselves with the UPN for a few years. The UPN's membership included notable figures such as **Chief Michael Ajasin, Chief Jonathan Odebiyi, Alhaji Lateef Jakande, Chief Victor Onabanjo,** and **Ola Emmanuel Rotimi**. In 1983, the UPN formed alliances with several political parties, creating the **Progressive Parties Alliance**, to defeat the **National Party of Nigeria**. Despite its efforts, the UPN had limited success.

**UNIVERSAL PRIMARY EDUCATION (UPE).** The idea of universal primary education was launched in 1955 by the **Western Region**'s government. It calls for free primary education for all young Nigerians, to be funded by the government. The **Action Group**, under the leadership of **Chief Obafemi Awolowo**, took a particular interest in the scheme. In the Western Region, the system remained in place until 1976. In 1957, the **Eastern Region** followed the Western Region and implemented its own version of UPE, but had to reinstate tuition fees a year later due to financial constraints. In 1961, the

**Northern Region** appointed the **Oldman Commission** to consider UPE for its children. The purpose of taking this idea to the national level was to balance the inequity between North and South regarding educational opportunities.

In September 1976, a nationwide version of UPE was launched to provide a six-year **education** to all Nigerians. To prepare, the existing 150 teacher-training institutions were expanded and equipped for a crash program, and 44,000 student teachers underwent training in August 1974. The government recruited 518 local and 316 overseas personnel to train teachers. The UPE was probably the largest single venture Nigeria ever undertook. Primary enrollment in 1972 was 4.4 million. In 1976, first-time enrollment of six-year-olds in primary schools reached 2.5 million. By the 1990s, UPE was no longer economically feasible, and the program was shelved. In 1999, **General Olusegun Obasanjo** replaced UPE with a new, similar program called universal basic education, which provides a free nine-year education to all Nigerians.

**UNIVERSITY OF IBADAN.** In December 1947, **Yaba Higher College** was moved from **Lagos** to **Ibadan** to serve as the core of University College, which later became the University of Ibadan. The plan was the result of the recommendations of the **Asquith Commission** on **higher education** in 1945. The University College opened its doors as Nigeria's first university in 1948 and became the University of Ibadan in 1962. The curriculum was initially based on University of London standards. The **Nigerian Institute of Social and Economic Research** was attached to it between 1962 and 1977. It has produced many famous scholars, artists, and politicians, and is the focal point of higher education in Nigeria.

**UNIVERSITY OF IFE.** *See* OBAFEMI AWOLOWO UNIVERSITY.

**URHOBO.** An **ethnic group** that lives in the **Niger Delta**. The towns of **Warri**, Sapele, and Ughelli are all considered part of Urhobo territory. There are an estimated 1.5 million Urhobo people. The Urhobo have roughly 21 subgroups, which include the Agbon, Ughelli, and Ogor. Their neighbors include the **Itsekiri**, Ijo, and Isoko. Of cultural importance to the Urhobo people, particularly for **women**, is the *opha* ceremony, which serves as a rite of passage for girls into adulthood.

The economic activities of the Urhobo people include fishing, **trading**, and lumbering. The primary cash crops produced in Urhoboland are rubber and **oil palm**. The main crops grown for local consumption are **cassava**, **groundnuts**, and **bananas**. Prior to colonial rule, many Urhobo communities were organized and governed by an **age-grade system**. The Urhobo poet **Tanure Ojaide** wrote several poems about life in Urhoboland and notable Urhobo leaders.

**USMAN DAN FODIO (1754–1817).** *Shehu* (equivalent to an **emir**) Usman dan Fodio was the founder of the **Sokoto Caliphate**, which expanded outward from the northwestern region of present-day Nigeria into present-day **Niger** and **Cameroon**. "Dan Fodio" means "son of Fodio." Usman was born in the **Hausa Kingdom** of **Gobir** and was a member of the **Fulani ethnic group**. He devoted his life to the spread of **Islam** through the **Qadiriyya** *tariqah* (brotherhood or order). He worked as a cleric, missionary, and writer. He is best known for leading a Fulani-based movement against **Hausa** rulers because of the persecution and excessive **taxation** of the Fulani people. He called for a return to pure Islam. By the 1790s, he had acquired a substantial following, which threatened the security of Gobir. In the early 1800s, the Hausa king, **Yunfa**, attempted to assassinate Usman and failed. The attempt spurred a battle between Usman's followers and Yunfa's military. Recognizing the Hausa weakness, Usman launched a **jihadist** movement in 1804 to remove the corrupt Hausa aristocracy from power, for which his followers appointed him "Leader of the Faithful." By 1812, the new, powerful Sokoto Caliphate was established, with Usman as its first **caliph**. Usman had many children, several of whom are well known: **Nana Asma'u**, Abdullahi ibn Muhammed, and **Muhammad Bello**. His great-great-grandson is **Sir Alhaji Ahmadu Bello**, the *sardauna* of **Sokoto**.

**USMAN, YUSUFU BALA (1945–2005).** Usman was born in Musawa, in **Katsina State**. After completing his primary and secondary education, he attended the University of Lancaster and **Ahmadu Bello University** in **Zaria**. He was a member of the Committee for the Review of Nigerian Foreign Policy and the Constitution Drafting Committee (1975–1976). He was also a correspondent for the *New Nigerian* **newspaper** and traveled to other African countries, including Mozambique, in the 1970s. Usman was a trustee for the **Nigerian Labour Congress** from 1978 to 1980. He also worked for the Kaduna State government during the **Second Republic** (1979–1982). Usman was involved in the creation of the Academic Staff Union of Nigerian Universities. He joined the **People's Redemption Party** in 1978 and remained an active member until 1999. Usman was badly injured in a car accident on the road from Zaria to **Kaduna** and died in September 2005 in Zaria.

## – V –

**VASSA, GUSTAVUS.** *See* EQUIANO, OLAUDAH.

**VILLAGE HEADS.** A village head has long been an integral part of effective governance in Nigeria, particularly before and during the colonial period. The role of a village head in the **Sokoto Caliphate** during the 19th century, for example, included supplying labor and collecting annual **taxes** for the **emirs**. The **Nupe** also had a village head, or *zitsu*, for every town (and incorporated satellite villages). The *zitsu*'s authority may have extended to figuratively "owning" the land and possessing the community. For this reason, the *zitsu* of Jebba Island on the **Niger River** has the title *gebba*.

The village head ruled over his community with the assistance of elders, who represented their families (broadly defined) in a council. Through the creation of **warrant chiefs** in the 20th century, however, the position of village head changed. A village head incorporated into the colonial system of **indirect rule** was only taken from large villages. He was responsible for collecting taxes from individuals or the entire village collectively. For the latter, the village head was often given the responsibility of determining the tax rate. The village heads were also part of the district council within the **Native Authority** system. In this context, these individuals were referred to as warrant chiefs. *See also* CHIEFS.

**VINCENT, DAVID BROWN.** *See* AGBEBI, MOJOLA.

**VISION 2010. General Sani Abacha** made Vision 2010 a major feature in his political program while he was the military dictator. It was a committee that he created in September 1996 in **Abuja** to draw up a long-term development strategy to enable Nigeria to join the middle income countries. One of the goals was to integrate Nigeria's swollen informal **economy** under the umbrella of federal regulation. **Chief Ernest Shonekan** was the chairman and worked with 172 members, ranging in background from military officers, to traditional chiefs, to professors, to businessmen. The committee was modeled after Malaysia's Vision 2020. After some research, the committee presented its report in 1997, which included a discussion of the value of **privatization** and **trade** liberalization. Abacha launched the program to show his concern for the poor. He selected the year 2010 as the year in which Nigeria would transition from military to democratic rule.

**VON ROSEN, COUNT CARL GUSTAF (1909–1977).** A Swedish aviator, Von Rosen shuttled aid for the Scandinavian Church organization NORD-CHURCHAID to the **Republic of Biafra** during the **civil war**. In 1968, he broke the federal air force's blockade, which had prevented aid from reaching Biafra. After this effort, several flights a day delivered goods to alleviate the **health** disaster. Frustrated by the worsening situation in Biafra, Von Rosen became more than simply an aid delivery pilot. He worked with the French secret service to fight on the Biafran side. With friends, he formed an air squadron to attack the federal air force. He launched an attack on **Port Harcourt** and other strategic places in May 1969, using four aircraft fitted with rockets. Von Rosen engaged in what he called **Operation Biafran Baby**, which was first conceived in 1968 during a visit to Biafra. He believed that the weakness in Biafra's military might was in the air, so he assisted in the Biafran purchase of aircraft from a subsidiary of SAAB under the guise of a purchase by the Tanzanian government. Von Rosen and his men took possession of the aircraft and mounted French-made rockets on them in Gabon.

# – W –

**WACHUKWU, JAJA ANUCHA (1918–1996).** As a young man, Wachukwu studied at St. George's School in Nbawsi and **Yaba Higher College** in **Lagos**, as well as other schools. He also attended universities abroad, including New Africa University College and Dublin University. He made his career as a barrister-in-law and as a political figure. He was a member of the **Eastern House of Assembly** and Eastern House of Representatives in the late 1940s. Wachukwu acted as deputy leader of the Government Party (1952–1953). He was a member, and first speaker, of the **House of Representatives**. He was the first ambassador, and then permanent representative, to the United Nations. He was also the minister of foreign affairs. During the **Second Republic**, Wachukwu was a senator who emphasized the economic value of **agricultural** production for the overall development of Nigeria.

**WADDELL, HOPE MASTERTON (?–1895).** Waddell was a missionary from Dublin, Ireland, of Jamaican descent who spent 29 years doing missionary work in the West Indies. He was the first missionary to arrive in Nigeria on behalf of the United Presbyterian Church in 1846 via Scotland. Waddell went to **Calabar** and opened a missionary school in Duke Town and Creek Town. He focused on spreading **Christianity** among the **Efik**. Between 1847 and 1849, he was sent to do missionary work outside Nigeria. In 1858, Waddell resigned from his travels and focused on Nigeria. In 1895, he constructed the **Hope Waddell Training Institute** for girls and boys. Waddell died just days before the opening of the institute in 1895. In 1902, the institute opened its first library.

**WAR AGAINST INDISCIPLINE (WAI).** For over a decade, Nigeria's federal military governments sought to control the unruly behavior of its citizens, which they believed stemmed from a lack of discipline. A series of "wars" against indiscipline were targeted at all aspects of public life: boarding buses, disposing of waste, collecting bribes, and rigging **elections**. The WAI was first articulated by **General Olusegun Obasanjo** in 1977 and was addressed by **Major General Muhammadu Buhari** in 1984. The phrase was believed to have been coined by the writer **Cyprian Ekwensi**. The scheme included rousing a nationalist spirit among Nigerians and getting them personally invested in improving daily life in Nigeria. States competed for a monetary reward for being the cleanest. **General Ibrahim Babangida** and **General Sani Abacha** carried out similar campaigns. In the case of Abacha's plan, "and Corruption" was added to the title. His program focused heavily on uncovering **corruption**, which critics described as a hunt for journalists and outspoken politicians.

**WARRANT CHIEFS.** Although most commonly discussed in the context of the **Igbo** colonial experience, this term can be applied to any case in which the British assigned the position of **chief** to an individual they deemed had political influence. This system is referred to as **indirect rule**. In the case of the pastoralist **Fulani**, the British created a kind of warrant chief out of the male head of a clan and made that person act as the Fulani representative (and tax collector) for many Fulani clans in a colonial district. This gave one individual, without full Fulani consensus, a great deal of authority. The job of warrant chief primarily included collecting **taxes**, distributing colonial resources, and reporting local activity to colonial officials. Within the **Native Court** system, warrant chiefs were appointed to hear minor civil and criminal cases in addition to their other duties.

Warrant chiefs lacked legitimacy among their people and yet had to extract cash and human resources as well as enforce restrictive colonial law. The *alake* of **Abeokuta**, for example, was still a "traditional" leader in that he commanded respect from the community, while also working for the colony. Among the **Nupe ethnic group**, colonial officers only appointed **village heads** from large villages. As a result, the Nupe word for village head, or chief, which was *zitsu*, changed to refer only to their traditional, legitimate chief. For the warrant chiefs, the Nupe adopted the phrase *etsu nyenkpa* (money chief) because of their role in tax collection. The colonial administration also appointed several ward-heads over specific quadrants of a town. Bida (in present-day **Niger State**) was divided into four wards in the mid-1930s, with the ward-heads having no residential affiliation to their posts. *See also* PARAMOUNT CHIEFS.

**WARRI.** Prior to the colonial period, the Warri Kingdom was located on the northern edge of the **Niger Delta**. The town of Warri was the administrative capital of the **Protectorate of Southern Nigeria** from 1899 to 1914. It was a major regional and international **trading** center, particularly in **oil palm**. Today, it is the capital city of **Delta State**. It is also Nigeria's second most important town, after

**Port Harcourt**, for the country's **petroleum** industry and home to one of Nigeria's refineries. Warri has a **population** of approximately 500,000. The **ethnic groups** most represented in Warri include the **Igbo**, **Itsekiri**, and **Ijaw**, who are predominantly **Christian**. In recent years, Warri has been the site of several violent clashes. In 1997 and again in 2003, violence broke out between ethnic groups over the "ownership" of and political authority over Warri.

**WATER.** Less than 30 percent of Nigerians have access to clean, potable water. For Nigeria, this is not simply a rural problem. Even citizens living in the major cities of **Lagos** do not have guaranteed access to safe, pipe-borne water. Selling water in jerry cans and individual servings in plastic bags has become big business for hawkers. The safety of these products, however, is not guaranteed. It is not uncommon for most water to be collected from a communal well or spigot, at which hawkers and other individuals stand in long lines. Many critics attribute the water crisis to the series of **corrupt** political leaders who have misdirected desperately needed funds. The Federal Ministry of Water Resources has received negative press for its failure to improve conditions.

Over the years, Nigeria's governments (military and civilian) have launched a number of programs, several with the **World Bank**, to make clean water accessible to citizens, including, among others, the National Water Rehabilitation Project (2006) and Small Towns Water Supply and Sanitation Pilot Project (2001). Unsanitary water exposes communities to water-borne diseases such as typhoid and cholera, causing **health** crises. In 2003, the United Nations Children's Fund concluded that with improved water quality the number of children dying from diarrhea in **Abuja** would decline by 22 percent. Efforts have been made by nongovernmental and nonprofit organizations, such as Lifewater Canada and Global Giving, to tackle the problem one village and school at a time. *See also* ELECTRICITY.

**WAYAS, JOSEPH (1941– ).** Born in May 1941 in Ogoja, near **Calabar**, Wayas completed his primary and secondary school education in **Onitsha** and Obodu. He also studied at several universities in England. He made a career balancing his knowledge of business with politics. He worked as a manager for various businesses in Nigeria and England between 1960 and 1969. For the Nigerian government, he served as the commissioner for transport in southeastern Nigeria. In the political arena, Wayas was a member of the Constituent Assembly (1977–1978) and president of the Senate (1979–1983). He went into self-imposed exile from 1984 to 1987 and, upon his return to Nigeria, was imprisoned for one year. In 1994, he was the deputy chairman of the National Constitutional Conference Commission. Wayas was also a member of the **National Party of Nigeria** and a presidential aspirant from the **All People's Party**.

**WENGER, SUSANNE (1915–2009).** Born in Graz, Austria, Wenger studied **art** at the School of Applied Arts in Austria and the Vienna Academy of Art, with a focus on pottery and frescoes. In Austria, she worked as a children's magazine illustrator. After marrying Ulli Beier, a prominent German linguist who cofounded *Black Orpheus*, she moved to Nigeria in 1950. She lived in **Ibadan** and Ede for a time before settling permanently in Osogbo in 1958. In Nigeria, she became a practitioner of the **Yoruba religion**. She acquired two **Yoruba** names, Iwinfumike Adunni and Adunni Olorisha. In Osogbo, she worked closely with local artists. During the late 1950s and 1960s, she devoted her creative talents to repairing, and later rebuilding, the shrines of Osun and other deities.

In 1958, she and her colleagues started the New Sacred Art Movement. Within a sacred grove, Wenger and other artists carved new sculptures into the landscape out of trees and vines. In 1987, the restored Osogbo shrines were declared national monuments by the Nigerian government. Wenger worked with other local artists and devotees to restore and maintain the Osun Sacred Grove, which became a UNESCO World Heritage Site in 2005. Wenger is also known for her wood carvings of Yoruba gods and goddesses and her striking batiks. Over the years, Wenger exhibited her work in **Lagos**, London, New York, and other cities. She designed several covers for *Black Orpheus* and was commissioned to paint a mural for the Bristol Hotel in Lagos. She and the New Sacred Art Movement have been the topic of many scholarly articles.

**WESLEYAN METHODIST MISSIONARY SOCIETY.** One of many **Christian** missionary societies that went to Nigeria to spread their **religion** and cultural values in the 19th century. This particular mission settled and set up a short-lived station at Egga on the **Niger River** as well as one at **Badagry** in 1842, three years before the (Anglican) **Church Missionary Society**.

**WEST AFRICAN CURRENCY BOARD.** *See* CURRENCY.

**WEST AFRICAN FRONTIER FORCE (WAFF).** The (Royal) West African Frontier Force was created in 1900 because of British concern, expressed primarily by **Sir Frederick Lugard**, over the encroaching French forces in the North. Many of its soldiers came from the Hausa Constabulary. Nigeria was one of several West African colonies from which the British recruited soldiers. In 1900, Nigerians made up five of the eight battalions, with **northern Nigeria** having three and **southern Nigeria** two. Although the WAFF was a regional operation, Nigeria's contribution dominated. The distinctive uniforms of the WAFF soldiers included khaki-colored outfits, red fezzes, red jackets with yellow trim, red cummerbunds, and a badge embossed with a palm tree. African officers wore additional yellow braiding. The WAFF participated on the British side during **World Wars I and II**. Between 1939 and 1947, the WAFF became the responsibility of **Great Britain**'s War Office instead of the Colonial Office. The WAFF was formally disbanded in 1960 after the contributing colonies became **independent**. The five battalions in Nigeria became the foundation for Nigeria's newly created national **armed forces**. *See also* POLICE.

*WEST AFRICAN PILOT.* One of Nigeria's most popular and influential **newspapers**, established in **Lagos** by **Nnamdi Azikiwe** in 1937. Azikiwe was its editor-in-chief until 1947. The paper was written in English and included a mixture of Azikiwe's political message, Lagos gossip, and a **women**'s page. Azikiwe wrote a daily column entitled "Inside Stuff." Articles in this newspaper showed a great deal of support for the emerging **trade union** movement and openly criticized the colonial government. Nigeria's first published political cartoonist, Akinola Lasekan, got his start by regularly featuring his work after 1944. The *West African Pilot* is still in circulation today.

**WESTERN HOUSE OF ASSEMBLY.** Created by the **Richards Constitution** in 1946, the assembly included the **chief commissioner**, official and unofficial members, and men nominated by the regional governor. It served as a moderator between the local **Native Authorities** and the **Legislative Council** in **Lagos**. As a result of the 1966 **coup d'état**, the Western House of Assembly was dissolved. *See also* EASTERN HOUSE OF ASSEMBLY; HOUSE OF ASSEMBLY; NORTHERN HOUSE OF ASSEMBLY.

**WESTERN HOUSE OF CHIEFS.** The **Western Region** obtained its **House of Chiefs** in 1952 under the **Macpherson Constitution**. The Western House of Chiefs was dissolved during the 1966 **coup d'état**. *See also* CHIEFS; EASTERN HOUSE OF CHIEFS; NORTHERN HOUSE OF CHIEFS.

**WESTERN NIGERIA.** Western Nigeria is the area south of the **Niger River**, east of **Benin**, and west of the Niger–Benue confluence. In terms of ethnicity, western Nigeria has a **Yoruba** majority. Western Nigeria's important cities include **Lagos, Abeokuta**, and **Ibadan**. Western Nigeria receives more foreign visitors than any other part of Nigeria because of Lagos, which serves as the country's commercial and business center. *See also* BENUE RIVER; EASTERN NIGERIA; NORTHERN NIGERIA; SOUTHERN NIGERIA; WESTERN REGION.

**WESTERN REGION.** The political designation of the area south of the **Niger River** and west of the Niger–Benue confluence to the border shared with the **Benin**. It was the political name given to the area under the **Richards Constitution** of 1946. Until 1914, the southwestern portion of Nigeria had been joined with southeastern Nigeria and collectively referred to as the **Protectorate of Southern Nigeria**. In 1939, the Protectorate of Southern Nigeria was divided into two regions, Western Region and **Eastern Region**. They remained as political zones for the remainder of the colonial period and into the early years of **independence**. From July 1960 to July 1967, several Nigerians held the position of governor, including **Sir Chief Adesoji Aderemi, Sir Joseph Fadahunsi, Lieutenant Colonel Adekunle Fajuyi**, and **Major General Robert Adebayo**. In addition to governors, the Western Region also had the office of **premier** built into the administrative structure. **Chief Obafemi Awolowo** served as the first premier (October 1954–December 1959), and **Alhaji Dauda**

**Adegbenro** was the third, serving only in May 1962. **Samuel Akintola** was premier twice, from December 1959 to May 1962 and again from January 1963 to January 1966. In 1957, the Western Region attained self-government within Nigeria's federal structure.

In 1967, **General Yakubu Gowon** reconfigured the four regions into 12 states, dividing the Western Region into **Western State** and **Lagos State**. Of the four regions, the Western Region holds particular historical significance for Nigeria because of **Lagos**. During the colonial period, Lagos was the first region to be colonized, and it remained the center of colonial **trade** and politics until independence. For this reason, the Western Region had more signs of development (i.e., running **water**, **electricity**, paved roads, sanitation, **education**) than the other regions. Much of Nigeria's anticolonial activity took place in the Western Region. Today the region is largely inhabited by the Yoruba **ethnic group** and includes a mix of predominantly **Christians** and Muslims. Although Nigeria's capital since 1991 has been **Abuja**, many of the country's government offices, commercial centers, and international embassies are still located in Lagos. *See also* BENUE RIVER.

**WESTERN STATE.** A state created in 1967 out of the **Western Region**. It was one of Nigeria's 12 states from 1967 to 1976. It was located in southwestern Nigeria. *See also* LAGOS STATE; STATE CREATION.

**WEY, VICE ADMIRAL JOSEPH EDET AKINWALE (1918–1990).** Wey was born in March 1918 in **Calabar**. He completed his primary and secondary schooling in **Lagos** and Calabar. He worked as a marine engineer (1950–1960) and a lieutenant commander and fleet engineer. In March 1964, he was promoted to commodore and head of the **navy**. Wey acted as the de facto deputy to **General Yakubu Gowon** through his membership in the **Supreme Military Council**. During the **civil war**, he led the navy into battle at the major ports of the **Republic of Biafra**. He was promoted to vice admiral in 1971. Wey was forced into retirement by **General Mortala Muhammed** in 1975. Just prior to his death, he founded the Nigerian Professional Security Association to enhance security in Nigeria. Wey died in December 1990. *See also* ARMED FORCES.

**WILLIAMS, CHIEF FREDERICK ROTIMI ALADE (1920–2005).**
Born in December 1920 in **Lagos** into a family of lawyers, as a young
man Williams attended the Methodist Olowogbowo Primary School
and the Church Missionary Society Grammar School in Lafia. He
studied at Selwyn College in England, earning a bachelor's degree in
1942. He also studied as a barrister-at-law and was called to the bar
in 1954, at which time he returned to Nigeria and practiced law for
several years. In 1958, Williams was appointed Queen's Counsel. He
served as the first chairman of the **Lagos Town Council** and secretary to the **Nigerian Youth Movement**. He was also a member of the
**Action Group**. In 1954, he was the minister of local government and
chieftaincy affairs. He was also the first minister of justice and attorney general in the **Western Region**. From 1959 to 1968, Williams
served as president of the Nigerian Bar Association. In 1960, he acted
as deputy **premier** of the Western Region. In 1975, he assumed the
position of Senior Advocate of Nigeria. He assisted in the drafting of
the 1979 **constitution**. He challenged in **court General Sani Abacha**'s suppression of the *Guardian* **newspaper**. Williams was hailed
by many as one of Nigeria's most successful and senior practicing
lawyers. He acquired the affectionate nickname, "'Timi the Law." He
received the honorary titles Commander of the Order of the Niger in
1965 as well as Commander of the Order of the Federal Republic of
Nigeria in 1978. Williams died in Lagos in March 2005.

**WILLINK COMMISSION.** Also referred to as the Willink Minority
Commission, it was appointed by the British government in September
1957 to address the concerns of **minority groups** about a new **constitution**. The commission was named for Henry Willink. Its report, released in 1958, included the commission's objection to **state creation**.
It recommended the inclusion of explicit language that guaranteed
the creation of regional advisory councils for the minority groups and
further study into the specific complaints of those living in the **Niger
Delta**. The Willink Commission was one of many efforts to address
the lack of political representation and economic support for minority
**ethnic groups**. *See also* ECONOMY; NIGER DELTA CONFLICT.

**WOMEN.** Women in Nigeria have been marginalized in the historical
record, despite their many contributions. They played diverse roles

in Nigerian politics and society from ancient times on but, for the most part, they have been excluded from politics, religious education, and large-scale **trade**. Of course, there are some notable exceptions. **Chief Madam Tinubu** was a wealthy trader in the 19th century. **Nana Asma'u**, the daughter of **Usman dan Fodio**, was well educated in **Islamic** doctrine and wrote eloquent poetry in several different **languages**. Women also endured cultural practices with mixed feelings. The **Urhobo**, prior to the 20th century, required that all girls be circumcised as part of the ceremony and rite of passage called *opha*. Most societies in Nigeria practiced **polygamy** prior to the 20th century (and some still do), which frequently involved the arranged marriage of a young woman to a significantly older man.

During the colonial period, women such as **Chief Olufunmilayo Ransome-Kuti** and **Madam Alimotu Pelewura** organized market women and voiced strong opposition to colonial rule. One of the most cited examples of women's resistance is the **Aba Riot** of 1929, which occurred in southeastern Nigeria. The Lagos Women's League was formed in 1936 to pressure the colonial government to hire more women for **civil service** positions. **Lady Oyinka Morenike Abayomi** established a grassroots movement for the improvement of women in the late 1940s. In 1958, the **National Council of Women's Societies** formed as an amalgamation of several women's organizations based in **Ibadan**. Among others, it included the **Women's Movement of Nigeria**. The National Council, now based in **Lagos**, is still active today in child welfare, adult **education**, and community development projects. Women received the vote in the **Western Region** (if they paid taxes) in 1955 and across **southern Nigeria** in 1959. But their counterparts in **northern Nigeria** did not acquire the right to vote until 1975.

Over the centuries, women have also served as keepers of history, family, and culture. Much of the art and culture associated with each **ethnic group** are crafted by women. **Igbo** women are known for adorning their bodies and decorating the walls of shrines with *uli*, a symbolic system. Women have been major contributors to the world of **art**, **theater**, and **literature**. Particularly notable are **Chief Flora Nwapa-Nwakuche**, **Buchi Emecheta**, Chimamanda Ngozi Adichie, **Bilkisu Ahmed Funtuwa**, **Osonye Tess Onwueme**, and **Ladi Kwali**. Recurring issues pertaining to women in Nigeria include polygamy, political rights, **prostitution**, circumcision, **abortion**, poverty, and **HIV/AIDS**. Women in northern Nigeria have watched their rights and equality under the law gradually disappear, especially with the application of **Shari'a** in a dozen northern states since 2000. *See also* BRIDE PRICE; HUSSEINI, SAFIYA; LAWAL, AMINA; MARKETS; POLITICAL PARTIES.

**WOMEN'S MOVEMENT OF NIGERIA.** A **women**'s political organization created and led by Elizabeth Adekogbe in 1952. The organization focused on female suffrage and the admission of women to the **Native Authority** and **Western House of Assembly**. The organization also promoted the **education** of young women in schools and called for a reduction in the rate of **bride price**. On particular issues of interest, the Women's Movement supported the **Action Group**. In 1953, the organization held a national conference in **Abeokuta**. In 1958, it became part of the **Nigerian Council of Women's Societies**. The purpose of the name change and merger was to give the women's movement a national scope and draw on women all over Nigeria.

**WOMEN'S RIOT OF 1929.** *See* ABA RIOT.

**WORLD BANK (WB).** Since its creation in 1944, the WB has provided financial and technical assistance to Nigeria in a variety of ways. It has funded numerous projects involving Nigeria's **agricultural** sector since the 1950s. After completing an economic survey in 1954, the WB recommended the expansion of infrastructure, accumulation of financial reserves, and establishment of a central **bank** over a five-year period. Nigeria received its first loan of $28 million for the construction of a **railroad** from **Bauchi** to **Borno** in 1958. Independent Nigeria also took out a loan of $13 million for the modernization of the **Lagos** port complex in 1962. The WB helped finance the establishment of an **oil palm** plantation and four oil palm mills in 1978. In more recent years, the WB has funded development programs that targeted farming in *fadama* ("wetlands" in the Hausa language) areas in **northern Nigeria**. It has also contributed to **water** improvement projects such as the National Water Rehabilitation Project, launched in 2006. *See also* DEBT (RELIEF); ECONOMY.

**WORLD WARS I AND II.** At the end of 1913, the British created the Nigeria Regiment, consisting primarily of **Hausa** and **Yoruba** soldiers armed with guns. During World War I, the British mobilized Nigerian labor and capital. The (Royal) **West African Frontier Force** (WAFF) fought during World Wars I and II on the side of **Great Britain**. During the first war, the WAFF engaged in battle with Germans in present-day **Cameroon** and Tanzania. During the second, the WAFF fought in Burma, Italian Somaliland, and Ethiopia. An estimated 16,000 Nigerians were in the army. Hundreds of thousands of Nigerians also contributed to the large-scale production of raw materials and building of infrastructure, which included military camps and **roads**. Market **women** argued that they bore the brunt of wartime hardships because they were responsible for feeding and clothing their unemployed family members as well as paying their **taxes**. The market women relied on their **trade**, which was strictly controlled during wartime. *See also* MARKETS; PRICE CONTROLS; PULLEN SCHEME.

**WORLD BLACK AND AFRICAN FESTIVAL OF ARTS AND CULTURE (FESTAC '77).** Nigeria hosted two FESTAC festivals. The second, and most popular, was held in **Lagos** in January and February 1977. The plans for the second had been temporarily canceled under **General Murtala Mohammed** in 1976, but were revived by **General Olusegun Obasanjo** in 1977. As the hosting of the festival was steeped in nationalist interests, the opening day celebration included a grandiose military salute and the release of 10,000 pigeons. The federal military government contributed ₦30 million to the festivities. The goals of FESTAC '77 included the revival and promotion of African cultural values; highlighting the contributions of black and African peoples to the fields of science, technology, and culture; and promoting interracial dialogue and understanding. The events included 12 exhibitions highlighting the origins of the human race, cultural development in Africa, and African **migration** patterns. During the festival, several **art** exhibits took place featuring Nigerian modern art. The official emblem of the festival, a replica of the ivory mask of **Idia**, was designed by Erhabor Emokpae, a Nigerian artist. The artwork featured during FESTAC '77 has been housed in the National Gallery of Modern Art since 1979.

## – Y –

**YABA HIGHER COLLEGE.** Established in 1932 and opened in 1934 as a technical institute in **Lagos**, Yaba was the first postsecondary **educational** institution in Nigeria. The number of student vacancies was contingent upon job openings in the colonial administration. In its first year, Yaba received over a hundred applications, but only admitted 18 students. The focus of the college was vocational training for jobs as technicians and clerks. Much of the college was moved from Lagos to **Ibadan** in December 1947 to become the core of University College, which later became the **University of Ibadan**. During the six years it operated, its largest class was 60 students. During the entire existence of the college, it only had two female students. Aspects of the college survived and became a new institution of **higher education**. In 1955, Yaba Higher College created an **art** department and took in its first art students. In 1969, its name was changed to Yaba College of Technology. In 1979, it was called Federal Polytechnic Yaba. Several significant Nigerians attended the college, including the novelist **Cyprian Ekwensi**, the artist **Omodele Jegede**, and politicians **Chief Solomon Erediauwa I** and **Michael Okpara**.

**YAKUBU, BALARABA RAMAT (1940s– ).** Currently one of Nigeria's most popular **Hausa** fiction writers, Yakubu is the younger sister of the late **General Murtala Mohammed**. Her stories are part of the **Kano Market Literature** genre, which focuses on love and relationships in Muslim, Hausa society. Yakubu is considered by many to be an Islamic feminist because she emphasizes through her novels the value of drawing **women** out of *purdah* (tradition of women living in seclusion), educating females, and ending gender inequality. Her stories also hint at her disapproval of **polygamy** as a tradition that has been abused and exploited by men. Her outspoken attitude has been attributed to the experience of being forced into marriage at age 13. More recently, Yakubu has been working on films in **Kano**. *See also* FUNTUWA, BILKISU AHMED; ISLAM.

**YAMS.** Edible tuberous roots that grow in Nigeria. They are a hearty, starchy food full of vitamins that can grow in difficult soil. There are several varieties, including white, yellow, and potato. Nigeria produces 70 percent of the world's white yams. They do not require sophisticated irrigation systems or farming machinery to be cultivated. Traditionally, yam harvesting among the **Igbo** was paired with a festival to venerate the gods, thanking them for the fertility of the land and **women**. Yams are a staple food for Nigerians, with preparation methods varying by region. In southwestern Nigeria, primarily among the **Yoruba**, yams are boiled, sliced into pieces, and served with a tomato and red pepper-based sauce. They are also boiled and pressed using a large mortar and pestle to make a semisolid, sticky substance, called *iyan* in Yoruba, and served with an **oil palm**–based stew. *See also* AGRICULTURE; CASSAVA; IGBO RELIGION.

**YAR'ADUA, MAJOR GENERAL SHEHU MUSA (1943–1997).** Born in March 1943 in **Katsina**, Yar'Adua studied at the Government School in Katsina before joining the **army**. He trained at the Nigerian Military Training College in **Kaduna** and the Royal Military Academy at Sandhurst in **Great Britain**. He received his first assignment as second lieutenant in the army in 1964. As of 1976, he served as chief of staff under the leadership of **General Murtala Mohammed**. He was placed in charge of **Operation Feed the Nation**. Some include Yar'Adua as a member of the alleged **Kaduna Mafia**, which dominated national politics in the late 1970s.

In 1979, Yar'Adua retired from the **armed forces** and pursued a career in business. He founded the People's Front of Nigeria, but aligned himself with the **Social Democratic Party** in preparation for the **election of 12 June 1993**. He was known for declaring, "I know neither North nor South, East nor West. What I know is Nigeria." Yar'Adua was imprisoned, along with his younger brother, **Umaru Musa Yar'Adua**, and **General Olusegun Obasanjo**, during **General Sani Abacha**'s regime, for plotting a **coup d'état** in 1994. For this, Yar'Adua was sentenced to 25 years. He died in Abakaliki Prison in December 1997. His younger brother became the president of Nigeria in April 2007.

**YAR'ADUA, UMARU MUSA (1951– ).** Born in **Katsina** in 1951, Yar'Adua earned advanced degrees from **Ahmadu Bello University** in **education** and chemistry. He taught at Katsina Polytechnic from

1979 to 1983. He subsequently left teaching and worked in the private sector until 1999. His involvement in politics started with his participation in the **People's Redemption Party**. In 1994, Yar'Adua was imprisoned, along with his older brother, **Major General Shehu Musa Yar'Adua**, for allegedly plotting a **coup d'état** against **General Sani Abacha**. In 1998, he formed the K34 political party, which later joined the **People's Democratic Party** (PDP). In 1999, Yar'Adua became governor of **Katsina State**; he was reelected in 2003. He is remembered for being the first Nigerian governor to publicly declare his assets. He is considered a quiet, reclusive political figure.

In April 2007, Yar'Adua ran and won as the presidential candidate for the PDP. His inauguration marked the first time Nigeria's government has successfully transitioned from one elected, civilian leader to another. As president, he promises to carry through steady economic reform, promote democracy, and continue the country's fight against **corruption**. When selecting his new cabinet, Yar'Adua appointed **General Olusegun Obasanjo** and three of Obasanjo's ministers. He appointed himself minister of energy. Yar'Adua is one of Nigeria's few presidents to hold an advanced degree.

**YERO, BUBA** *See* BUBA YERO.

**YOBE STATE.** A state located in **northern Nigeria**, sharing its northern boundary with **Niger**. It is one of Nigeria's current 36 states. The capital is the town of Damaturu. In the northeastern part of the state lies the Hade Jia Nguru Wetlands. Economic activities in the state include the cultivation of **groundnuts**, maize, **cotton**, and grains, as well as the herding of cattle. Farmers also grow tomatoes, onions, peppers, and carrots in small, irrigated garden plots. The people of Yobe State include the **Hausa**, **Fulani**, **Kanuri**, Kare-Kare, and Bade **ethnic groups**, with Hausa the dominant **language**. The dominant **religions** are **Islam** and **Christianity**. Yobe is one of 12 northern states that have reintroduced aspects of **Shari'a**. *See also* STATE CREATION.

**YOLA.** The capital of **Adamawa State**, located on the **Benue River** near the Nigeria–Cameroon border. Its **population** is approximately

400,000. The word "Yola" comes from the **Fula** word "Yoldi," translated roughly as a "knoll" or "a tongue of land running into a marsh." Yola is actually two cities in one: the traditional Yola Township and modern Jimeta. Yola is the site of the Gashaka Gumti National Park. It was conquered by **Mordibo Adama** during the **Fulani** jihad that was launched in 1804 by **Usman dan Fodio**. In 1901, the British sacked Yola. Later, it served as the colonial headquarters for the Adamawa province of the **Protectorate of Northern Nigeria**. Yola was one of the locations where followers of the radical Muslim **Maitatsine** group were located. In 2005, American University opened a jointly owned private university called **ABTI-American University of Nigeria** in Yola.

**YORUBA.** One of Nigeria's largest, most well-known **ethnic groups**. The ethnic group comprises several semi-independent peoples loosely linked by **language**, geography, culture, and **religion**. The Yoruba are estimated to total over 15 million people and live primarily in southwestern Nigeria, with additional small **populations** in **Benin** and Togo. The area inhabited by the Yoruba is commonly referred to as Yorubaland. The Yoruba groups stretched beyond the tropical region north into the savanna grasslands of the **Middle Belt** and east toward the Niger–Benue confluence. The center of Yorubaland has long been the Ogun River. Archeological evidence suggests that in ancient times the Yoruba lived in basically the same region that they do today. During the Iron Age, the Yoruba practiced the complicated method of lost-wax casting when making iron tools and adornment.

In precolonial times, the Yoruba groups developed into rivaling city-states, such as Oyo, **Ibadan**, and **Ile-Ife**. Oyo reached its height around the 17th century and dominated Yorubaland until the mid-19th century. The Yoruba subgroups moved away from the Ogun River, creating their own interpretations of Yoruba **oral tradition** and culture. These groups include the **Itsekiri**, Ondo, and Owo to the southeast; the Awori, Egbado, **Ijebu**, Ketu, and Shabe to the southwest; and the Ekiti and Ijesa to the northeast. Those who were forced to settle in Sierra Leone during the transatlantic **slave trade** went on record as the "Aku" people because of the starting phrase in Yoruba greetings, "E ku."

The British attempted to establish **indirect rule** through the existing political structure between 1914 and 1916. The Yoruba figured prominently in anticolonial activities. Notable Yoruba political agitators included **Chief Obafemi Awolowo** and **Chief Olufunmilayo Ransome-Kuti**. Several cultural and political organizations emerged in the 20th century dedicated to Yoruba unity, including **Egbe Omo Oduduwa, O'odua People's Congress, Egbe Omo Olofin, Egbe Omo Yoruba**, and **Afenifere**. Notable Yoruba figures include the politician **General Olusegun Obasanjo** and the playwright **Akinwande Oluwole Soyinka**.

The Yoruba also figure prominently in the African Diaspora because of the large number of individuals who were enslaved during the transatlantic slave trade and taken to the New World, particularly to Cuba and Brazil. Today, the Yoruba make up a substantial portion of Nigerian immigrants in North America and Europe. *See also* YORUBA LANGUAGE; YORUBA RELIGION; YORUBA WARS.

**YORUBA LANGUAGE.** The Yoruba **language** is spoken by one of Nigeria's largest **ethnic groups**, who inhabit primarily the southwestern region. Yoruba is part of the Benue-Congo branch of the Niger-Congo language family. It is also a tonal language, in that intonation is important to understanding meaning. For example, the word *ojo* can be someone's name, the word for rain, or the adjective "coward," depending on the high, middle, or low tone assigned to the vowels. Like many other African languages, Yoruba is steeped in proverbs to convey moral lessons and subtle opinions. In Nigeria, an estimated 30 million people speak Yoruba. In Cuba and northern Brazil, some Yoruba descendants speak a dialect of Yoruba called Nago. When written, Yoruba is based on the Latin alphabet, with additional letters used to convey the unique sounds. Increasingly, the Yoruba language is being standardized in textbooks and introduced into the university curriculum in the United States. See also YORUBA; YORUBA RELIGION; YORUBA WARS.

**YORUBA RELIGION.** In ancient times, the **Yoruba** developed a **religion** that incorporated important cultural aspects such as an origin myth, a pantheon of gods (*orisa*) representing nature, and the veneration of ancestors. The Yoruba religion is based on the story that God, Olodumare, lived in heaven and sent his son, Obatala, down on a chain to create the world. When Obatala was found drunk on **palm wine**, Olodumare's other son, Oduduwa, went ahead and finished the creation, making **Ile-Ife** the sacred town from which all life would begin. Before populating the world with humans, Olodumare commanded the *orisa*, such as Ogun, Osun, and Esu, to stay and serve as protectors of humans, each with its own connection to nature and special ability. Humans were expected to turn to their gods for assistance in life and, in exchange, to venerate them. Practitioners of the Yoruba religion, even today, show respect for the *orisa* and their ancestors through offerings, song, and festivals. An integral part of the religion is **divination**, in which communication with gods and ancestors is established to perhaps see into the future, interpret the past, or solve social problems.

Through the transatlantic **slave trade**, many enslaved Yoruba continued to practice their religion. In the Caribbean the Yoruba religion was intertwined with Roman Catholicism and transformed into the unique religion Santería. Since contact with Muslim traders starting in the 11th century, many Yoruba practice **Islam**. Likewise, many Yoruba today practice **Christianity**. Yoruba religion has formed the core artistic philosophy for many Nigerian sculptors and painters. For several decades in the 20th century, the town of Osogbo was the heart of the New Sacred Art Movement, led by **Susanne Wenger**, and of the *ona* (reverence for decoration and ornamentation) movement. Both focused on the re-creation of Yoruba religious shrines and symbols. *See also* ART; SANGO; YORUBA LANGUAGE; YORUBA WARS.

**YORUBA WARS.** On the eve of colonization in the early 19th century, the **Yoruba** of southwestern Nigeria underwent a major political transformation. The great **Oyo Empire** began to decline in the early 1800s, finally collapsing in 1833 because of political instability within the empire and outside pressure from **Islamic** jihads descending southward. This weakness allowed for the rise of **Ibadan** as a new power in 1840. Ibadan's rise, however, was accompanied by a series of wars among different Yoruba subgroups that lasted until 1893. Between 1859 and 1861, for example, Ibadan and Ijaye fought in the **Ijaye War**, over the installment of Adelu as the new ruler of Oyo. **Kurunmi**, the leader of Ijaye, refused to recognize Adelu. The **Egba** assisted Kurunmi's warriors against the Ibadan. After Kurunmi's death in 1861, the Egba and Ijaye withdrew their protective forces in **Abeokuta** and allowed it to be sacked by Ibadan. The Egba and **Ijebu** never accepted Ibadan's authority, and in 1877 they engaged in a 16-year war with Ibadan. Between 1865 and 1866, **Borgu** assisted Ibadan in an effort to reduce the war's impact on it. In short, Ibadan fought on several different fronts against shifting alliances. The wars spawned instability and mass migrations within the region.

Between 1882 and 1884, the British in **Lagos** refused to get involved. In 1886, a cease-fire was brokered, with the assistance of **Samuel Johnson**. The peace treaty included the recognition of select Yoruba towns and the removal of the **Modekeke** from **Ile-Ife**. The cease-fire, however, did not last. By 1892, the British and French were eager to resolve the conflict and establish colonial infrastructures. The French began laying **railroad** tracks, and the British imposed **trade** agreements. In 1893, the British colonial governor toured Yorubaland and signed treaties with the various warring factions. These agreements marked the end of full-scale war between Yoruba-speaking groups. *See also* YORUBA LANGUAGE; YORUBA RELIGION.

**YUNFA (?–1808). King** of **Gobir**, a **Hausa Kingdom**, from 1801 to 1808. He is best known for his conflict with **Usman dan Fodio**, who was his teacher and political supporter. The two men had a falling out, and Yunfa called for Usman's assassination. Yunfa actually tried to assassinate him, but his gun malfunctioned and only wounded Usman's hand. A year later, Yunfa expelled Usman from the town of Degel in present-day **Borno State**. Usman returned to Gobir with an army of men as part of a large-scale **jihad**. Yunfa and Usman entered into direct conflict at the Battle of Tsuntua, where Usman lost around 2,000 men. In 1808, Usman's jihadists sacked Gobir and killed Yunfa during a battle with warriors led by **Muhammed Bello**.

**YUSUF, BELLO MAITAMA (1947– ).** Born in April 1947, Yusuf received his business law degree from Northgate University in Washington and was called to the bar in 1974. He became a member of the **National Party of Nigeria**. He served as the minister of internal affairs (1979–1981) and minister of commerce (1981–1983). Yusuf was imprisoned in December 1991 for violating Decree No. 25 (1987), which banned senior politicians from participating in politics. He was part of **General Sani Abacha**'s **Vision 2010** in the mid-1990s. More recently, he has been an opposition party member within the Senate since 2003, representing a section of **Jigawa State**. In the Senate, Yusuf strongly objected to **General Olusegun Obasanjo**'s attempt to change the **constitution** to allow himself a third term as president. He also assisted in the formal accusation of Obasanjo mismanaging funds from the Petroleum Development Trust Fund. *See also* CORRUPTION; ELECTIONS.

## – Z –

**AL-ZAKZAKY, SHEIKH IBRAHIM (1953– ).** Born in May 1953 in **Zaria**, al-Zakzazy was an **Islamic** activist and cleric. As a child, he attended only traditional Islamic schools. At age 15, he attended Fata Provincial Arabic School in Zaria to study Arabic and completed his studies ahead of schedule. He has the distinction of being a *hazif* (one who has memorized the **Koran**). He continued his education at the School of Arabic Studies in **Kano** and **Ahmadu Bello University** from 1976 to 1979, obtaining an advanced degree in economics. As a student, he was active in the Muslim Students Society until he was expelled from the university in 1979. Al-Zakzaky called for the rejection of Nigeria's **constitution** and the start of an Islamic revolution. For over a decade, as the founder and leader of the **Islamic Movement of Nigeria**, he has campaigned for the establishment of Nigeria as an Islamic state. Between the mid-1970s and late 1990s, al-Zakzaky was in prison. His arrests were based on his recorded speeches calling for the total Islamization of Nigeria and declaring "there is no government except that of Islam," which successive Nigerian governments considered treasonous. Hundreds of his supporters have been murdered, arrested, or harassed by the **police**. *See also* KORANIC SCHOOLS; SHARI'A.

**ZAMFARA STATE.** A state created out of **Sokoto State** in 1996. It is one of Nigeria's current 36 states. Zamfara is located in northwestern Nigeria, bordering **Niger**. The capital is Gusau, and the state slogan is "Farming Is Our Pride." Before the arrival of the British, Zamfara was one of the thriving **Hausa Kingdoms** from about the 10th to the 18th centuries. In 1804, it became part of the **Sokoto Caliphate**. In 2000, Zamfara State was the first of several northern states that incorporated **Shari'a** into their criminal law. The dominant **ethnic group** in Zamfara is the **Hausa**, and the **languages** spoken include Hausa and **Fula**. *See also* STATE CREATION.

**ZANGON-KATAF.** A town in **Kaduna State**, it is inhabited by Kataf and **Hausa** people, who have a history of tension over land ownership and the location of marketplaces. The dispute centers on who are the settlers and who are the original people of the town. In February and May 1992, there were clashes between Hausa (predominantly Muslim) and Kataf (predominantly **Christian**) students over the relocation of a **market**. The killing of Hausa people by members of the Kataf sparked a broader Muslim–Christian clash. The federal government set up a tribunal to try those involved. The tribunal was criticized for having a Muslim-favored composition lacking any Kataf members. Also, those involved were denied the right to appeal any decision made by the tribunal. The tribunal's verdict was death by hanging for six of the accused men. In 1995, after national and international pressure, the accused were pardoned and released. The Zangon-Kataf crisis is one of many faith-based eruptions of violence in Kaduna State since the late 1980s.

**ZARIA.** Zaria was founded as Zazzau in the 11th century by Queen Bakwa Turunku, the 22nd ruler, and became one of several **Hausa Kingdoms**. Queen Turunku built strong walls around the city. Following her example, several other Hausa Kingdoms constructed walls to protect their cities. Zazzau was renamed Zaria in 1536 in honor of Turunku's granddaughters. The *Zaria Chronicle* lists 60 rulers of Zaria before the **Fulani jihad** led by **Usman dan Fodio**

in 1804. The city of Zaria is in **northern Nigeria**'s **Kaduna State**. During the colonial period, Zaria served as a British military post and favorite location for playing polo. Zaria is Nigeria's center for **cotton** ginning and creating the distinct *babban riga* style cloth, worn by wealthy citizens to display their (and the designer's) taste. Zaria is also the home of **Ahmadu Bello University**. Its population is approximately 400,000. *See also* TEXTILES.

**"ZIK MUST GO."** The rallying cry in a crisis in 1959 within the **National Council of Nigeria and the Cameroons** (NCNC) in the weeks running up to **independence**. Thirty-one members of the NCNC, which **Nnamdi Azikiwe** had founded, called on him to resign from his posts as **premier** of the **Eastern Region** and president of the party. They accused him of dividing, and then abandoning, the party. This movement was orchestrated by K. O. Mbadiwe, the minister of commerce, and **Chief Kolawole Balogun**, the minister of information. Although weakened, the party did not disband, and the opponents of Azikiwe were dismissed. Azikiwe went on to become president of the Senate and president of Nigeria.

**ZIKIST MOVEMENT.** Also referred to as Zikism, it was the radical nationalist wing of the **National Council of Nigeria and the Cameroons** (NCNC). In 1946 young men and women, including **Nnamdi Azikiwe** and **Chief Melie Ajuluchuku**, dissatisfied with the slow pace of decolonization, started the Zikist Movement. **Chief Adeniran Ogunsanya** served as its president-general. Based in **eastern Nigeria**, the movement served as the **Igbo**-dominated radical wing of the NCNC. The movement gained strength after the British realized that **independence** for the Gold Coast (present-day **Ghana**) was imminent. The Zikists proposed an alternative political economy for independent Nigeria. They used the economic instability of the post–**World War II** period as an avenue for activism. In 1949, the Zikists organized mass protests in cities such as **Onitsha**, Aba, and **Port Harcourt** in response to the death of striking **coal** miners. Their activism also took the form of refusing to pay taxes to the government and instead investing that money in anticolonial activities. They launched military training programs for Nigerians and intimidation campaigns against British officials. Members of the

Zikist Movement were imprisoned and often killed by the colonial government. The fall of the Zikist Movement resulted from the collaboration of moderate nationalists and the colonial government.

**ZUNGERU.** A town located on the Kaduna River in **Niger State**. During the colonial period, Zungeru was the administrative capital of the **Protectorate of Northern Nigeria** from 1902 until 1917. Zungeru was chosen by the British for this purpose because it was the northernmost location accessible by **water** transport. In 1917, the colonial government moved the headquarters from Zungeru to **Kaduna**. The town is the birthplace of several of Nigeria's nationalist leaders, including **Nnamdi Azikiwe**. It was also the original site of **Sir Frederick Lugard**'s footbridge, constructed in 1904. In 1954, the bridge was relocated to Kaduna Gardens. Today, Zungeru is a relatively quiet town and is home to Niger State Polytechnic.

**ZUNGUR, SA'ADU (1915–1958).** Born in **Bauchi State**, Zungur studied at **Yaba Higher College** in **Lagos** in the 1930s as the first northern student. He was a popular **Hausa** poet and political activist. Zungur worked as a community health inspector and teacher between 1938 and 1948. In the 1940s, he helped form the Zaria Friendly Society. In 1943, he cofounded the **Bauchi General Improvement Union**. He was a key member of the **Northern Elements Progressive Union**, starting in 1954, and gave the **Northern People's Congress** (NPC) its name. He also worked with **Nnamdi Azikiwe** and the **National Council of Nigeria and the Cameroons** (NCNC). From 1948 to 1950, Zungur served as secretary of the NCNC. He is recognized as having a strong influence on **Alhaji Muhammed Aminu Kano**. Zungur also influenced the general population through his anticolonial and secular poetry. His most famous poem focuses on the return of Nigerian soldiers from fighting in Asia during **World War II**. *See also* LITERATURE.

# Bibliography

**CONTENTS**

# INTRODUCTION

In comparison to other African countries, Nigeria has attracted a great deal of academic interest, particularly in the fields of politics, religion, and economics. Much of Nigeria's popularity comes from its place in world history. The field of Nigerian studies is relatively young and tied to Nigeria's independence, gained in 1960. Scholars at that time promoted the study of Nigeria as part of a broad nationalist project. In addition, because of Nigeria's size and political clout, it has also been of increasing interest as an essential part of Africa (and occasionally world) history.

The literature ranges from thoroughly researched topics to areas in need of further investigation. One of its strength is studies on the era of colonialism in Nigeria. There are several excellent works, particularly those included in the Ibadan History Series published by Longman in the 1960s and 1970s, which provide in-depth analyses of colonial Nigeria. A. E. Afigbo, *The Warrant Chiefs* (London: Longman, 1972); Murray Last, *The Sokoto Caliphate* (London: Longman, 1967); and J. F. Ade Ajayi, *Chris-*

*tian Missions in Nigeria, 1841–1891* (London: Longman, 1965) are among the most frequently referenced titles in this series. Other notable works are Lisa A. Lindsay, *Working with Gender: Wage Labor and Social Changes in Southwestern Nigeria* (Portsmouth, N.H.: Heinemann, 2003) and G. O. Olusanya, *The Second World War and Politics in Nigeria 1939–1953* (Lagos: University of Lagos/Evans Brothers, 1973).

Another strong area of research is the anticolonial, nationalist movements that developed after World War II. Valuable works are Paul E. Lovejoy and J. S. Hogendorn, "Revolutionary Mahdism and Resistance to Colonial Rule in the Sokoto Caliphate, 1905–6," *Journal of African History* 31, no. 2 (1990): 217–244; and Susan M. Martin, *Palm Oil and Protest: An Economic History of the Ngwa Region, South-Eastern Nigeria, 1800–1980* (Cambridge: Cambridge University Press, 1988). There are several fine publications on the role of women during this vibrant moment in Nigeria's history. They include Nina Emma Mba, *Nigerian Women Mobilized: Women's Political Activity in Southern Nigeria, 1900–1965* (Berkeley, Calif.: Institute of International Studies, 1982) and Cheryl Johnson, "Grassroots Organizing: Women in Anticolonial Activity in Southwestern Nigeria," *African Studies Review* 25, nos. 2/3 (June–September 1982): 137–157. Several works on nationalism also focus on the formation of political parties and regional alliances for Nigeria's first-ever round of general elections. Indeed, several scholars have identified this messy process as the start of Nigeria's struggle with ethnic- and region-based politics. Notable works on this subject include J. S. Coleman, *Nigeria: Background to Nationalism* (Berkeley: University of California Press, 1963) and Toyin Falola and Ann Genova, eds. *Yoruba Identity and Power Politics* (Rochester, N.Y.: University of Rochester Press, 2006).

Within the past 20 years, religious tension and the Niger Delta Conflict have attracted scholarly attention, but they need further analysis. Both pose an immediate threat to Nigeria's social, political, and economic fabric because they are complicated and difficult to resolve. In both cases, spontaneous riots and premeditated acts of violence have destroyed valuable property, communities, and infrastructure as well as tarnishing Nigeria's international reputation and posing serious challenges to Nigeria's development and democracy. Several works provide historical context, illuminate each side's arguments, and provide possible solutions. In the case of religious tension between Christians and Muslims, Toyin Falola, *Violence in Nigeria* (Rochester, N.Y.: University of Rochester Press, 1998); Carina Tertsakian, *"Political Shari'a?"* Human Rights and Islamic Law in Nigeria 16, no. 9A

(New York: Human Rights Watch, September 2004); and Matthews Ojo, *The End-Time Army: Charismatic Movements in Modern Nigeria.* (Trenton, N.J.: Africa World Press, 2006) are important works. The best works on crisis in the Niger Delta are Jedrzej George Frynas, *Oil in Nigeria: Conflict and Litigation between Oil Companies and Village Communities* (Berlin: Lit Verlag, 2000); Sarah Ahmad Khan, *Nigeria: The Political Economy of Oil* (Oxford: Oxford University Press, 1994); Bronwen Manby, *The Price of Oil: Corporate Responsibility and Human Rights Violations in Nigeria's Oil Producing Communities* (New York: Human Rights Watch, 1999); and Kenneth Omeje, *High Stakes and Stakeholders: Oil Conflict and Security in Nigeria* (Burlington, Vt.: Ashgate Publishing Publishing, 2005). New research on these topics has become difficult in the face of escalating violence and political oppression.

Generally, the literature on Nigeria unfortunately lacks thorough works on cultural practices and daily life after the 1970s. There are several excellent studies on Yoruba music, which has been popular with Nigerian adults and Western consumers, including Christopher Alan Waterman, *Juju: A Social History and Ethnography of an African Popular Music* (Chicago: University of Chicago Press, 1990) and Tejumola Olaniyan, *Arrest the Music! Fela and His Rebel Art and Politics* (Bloomington: Indiana University Press, 2004), but not on hip-hop, which young Nigerians listen to almost exclusively. The same can be said for other aspects of Nigerian popular culture, such as Nigeria's booming film industry, literature, cuisine, and family dynamics. However, several scholars have made a good start with regard to literature, including Norman Whitsitt, "Islamic-Hausa Feminism and Kano Market Literature: Qur'anic Reinterpretation of the Novels of Balaraba Yakubu," *Research in African Literature* 33, no. 2 (Summer 2002): 119–36 and Karin Barber, "Popular Reactions to the Petro-Naira," in *Readings in African Popular Culture*, edited by Karin Barber, 91–99 (Bloomington: Indiana University Press, 1997).

For scholars and students interested in doing research on Nigeria, there are several good libraries and archives in and outside of Nigeria. In the United States, the New York Public Library and the Center for Research Libraries in Chicago have extensive collections of out-of-print books, government publications, newspapers, and journals from Nigeria. The G.I. Jones Photographic Archive of Southeastern Nigerian Art and Culture (at Southern Illinois University) holds photos taken by the late scholar during his research trips in the 1930s. The Museum of African Art in Washington, D.C., boasts an extensive collection of art and artifacts from Nigeria. In

Great Britain, the best places to find archival material on Nigeria are the National Archives, which houses documentation on almost all aspects and time periods of Nigeria; and the Rhodes House Library of Oxford University. For materials covering Nigeria's early history, art, and archeology, the British Library and British Museum are excellent places to start.

For those traveling to Nigeria, the Nigerian nationalist scholar J. F. A. Ajayi has opened his private collection for use in Ibadan. All of Nigeria's major university libraries have books and journals devoted to Nigerian studies. The Nigerian Institute for International Affairs and the Nigerian Institute of Social and Economic Research provide researchers with locally published newspapers, journals, books, and unpublished conference papers. For archival research, Nigeria has three branches of its National Archives—Ibadan, Enugu, and Kaduna—that house primarily colonial era documents and some postindependence materials such as newspapers. The Ibadan branch houses most of the general colonial records in addition to local colonial materials; Enugu's and Kaduna's holdings include primarily regional documents. Umuahia is home to the National War Museum, which displays relics from the civil war and the short-lived Republic of Biafra. In its library are Biafran newspapers and pamphlets as well as international pro-Biafran propaganda. One of the most impressive research libraries in Nigeria is the Arewa House, the former residence of Sir Ahmadu Bello, maintained by Ahmadu Bello University, in Zaria. This research center holds rare Arabic manuscripts and colonial era documents. Almost every major town in Nigeria has a museum that may cover early history, culture, and ecology. However, visitors may find the collections incomplete, with most of the artifacts on loan to European museums and limited information available.

The Internet resources available on Nigeria are constantly expanding. The most reliable websites are the online editions of daily newspapers from Nigeria. *This Day* (www.thisdayonline.com) and *The Guardian* (http://www .ngrguardiannews.com) are the most popular and informative. In addition, several comprehensive websites offer news, weather, online chatting, and basic information about Nigeria. They include Nigeriaworld (http://nigeria world.com), E-Nigeria (http://www.e-nigeria.net), and Online Nigeria (http://onlinenigeria.com). On the subject of Nigerian art, the Metropolitan Museum of Art (http://www.metmuseum.org/toah/hi/te_index.asp?i=3) posts articles about its precolonial collections. The Sacred Groves of Osogbo art movement maintains a website with pictures from its collection. (http://www.geocities.com/adunni1/sg.html). For information on health and illness, USAID (http://www.usaid.gov/our_work/global_health/aids/

Countries/africa/nigeria.html) and the World Health Organization (http://www.who.int/countries/nga/en/) provide up-to-date statistics and information about government and nongovernment improvement programs.

## I. BIBLIOGRAPHIES AND DICTIONARIES

Akinyotu, Adetunji. *Who's Who in Science and Technology in Nigeria.* Akure: Federal University of Technology, 1989.

Ekpiken, A. N. *A Bibliography of the Efik-Ibibio-speaking Peoples of the Old Calabar Province of Nigeria, 1668–1964.* Ibadan: Ibadan University Press, 1970.

Emezi, Herbert O. *Nigerian Population and Urbanization, 1911–1974: A Bibliography.* Los Angeles: University of California, 1975.

Ihonvbere, Julius. *The Oil Industry in Nigeria: An Annotated Bibliography.* Montreal: McGill University, 1983.

Kelly, Bernice M. *Nigerian Artists: A Who's Who and Bibliography.* London: Hans Zell, 1993.

Ogbondah, Chris W. *The Press in Nigeria: An Annotated Bibliography.* New York: Greenwood Press, 1990.

Oluronke O. Orimalade. *Bibliography of Labour in Nigeria, 1910–1970.* Lagos: National Library of Nigeria, 1974.

Osinulu, Clara, and Oluremi Jegede, eds. *Who's Who of Nigerian Women.* Lagos: Allison & Co., 1985.

Osso, Nyaknno. *Who's Who in Nigeria.* Lagos: Newswatch, 1990.

Shaw, Thurstan. *A Bibliography of Nigerian Archaeology.* Ibadan: University of Ibadan, 1969.

Stanley, Janet. *Nigerian Government Publications, 1966–1973: A Bibliography.* Ile-Ife: University of Ife Press, 1975.

Stanley, Janet, et al. *Ife: The Holy City of the Yoruba: An Annotated Bibliography.* Ile-Ife: University of Ife Press, 1982.

## II. HISTORY

### A. General

Adamu, M. *The Hausa Factor in West African History.* Zaria: Ahmadu Bello University Press, 1978.

Ajayi, J. F. A., and Michael Crowder, eds. *History of West Africa,* Vols. 1 and 2. New York: Columbia University Press, 1972.

Crowder, Michael. *The Story of Nigeria.* London: Faber and Faber, 1962.

Falola, Toyin. *The History of Nigeria.* Westport, Conn.: Greenwood Press, 1999.

——. *Nigeria in the Twentieth Century.* Durham, N.C.: Carolina Academic Press, 2002.

Falola, Toyin, and Matthew M. Heaton. *A History of Nigeria.* Cambridge: Cambridge University Press, 2008.

Ikime, O., ed. *Groundwork of Nigerian History.* Ibadan: Ibadan University Press, 1980.

Isichei, Elizabeth Allo. *A History of Nigeria.* New York: Longman, 1983.

Osaghae, Eghosa E. *Crippled Giant: Nigerian since Independence.* Bloomington: Indiana University Press, 1998.

Osuntokun, Akinjide. *Nigerian Peoples and Cultures.* Ibadan: Davidson, 1997.

## B. European Accounts

Bovill, E. W., ed. *Denham, Clapperton, and Oudney, Narrative of Travels and Discoveries in Northern and Central Africa in the Years 1822, 1823, 1824.* Cambridge: NOK, 1964.

Burns, A. C. *History of Nigeria.* London: G. Allen & Unwin. 1929.

Crowther, Samuel. *Journal of an Expedition up the Niger and Tshadda Rivers, Undertaken by Maegregor Laird in Connection with the British Government in 1854.* 2nd ed. London: Frank Cass, 1970.

Hallett, Robin. *The Niger Journal of Richard and John Lander.* New York: Praeger, 1965.

Johnston, H. A. S., and D. J. M. Muffett. *Denham in Bornu: An Account of the Exploration of Bornu between 1823 and 1825 by Major Dixon Denham, Dr. Oudney, and Commander Hugh Clapperton, and of Their Dealings with Sheik Muhammad El Amin El Kanemi.* Pittsburgh, Pa.: Duquesne University Press, 1973.

Lockhart, Jamie Bruce, and Paul E. Lovejoy. *Hugh Clapperton into the Interior of Africa: Records of the Second Expedition, 1825–1827.* Boston: Brill, 2005.

Lord Lugard. *The Dual Mandate in British Tropical Africa.* 5th ed. London: Archon Books, 1965.

Miller, Ronald, ed. *Travels of Mungo Park.* Rev. ed. New York: Dutton, 1954.

Palmer, Herbert. *The Bornu Sahara and Sudan, by Sir Richmond Palmer, Sometime Resident of the Bornu Province, Nigeria.* London: J. Murray, 1936.

Perham, Margery. *Native Administration in Nigeria.* London: Oxford University Press, 1937.

## C. Early Kingdoms and Peoples

Adamu, Mahdi. *Confluences and Influences: The Emergence of Kano as a City-State.* Kano: Munawwar Books Foundation, 1999.
———. *The Hausa Factor in West African History.* Zaria: Oxford University Press, 1978.
Adekunle, Julious O. *Politics and Society in Nigeria's Middle Belt: Borgu and the Emergence of a Political Identity.* Trenton, N.J.: Africa World Press, 2004.
Agbaje-Williams, Babatunde. *Archaeology and Yoruba Oral Tradition.* Ibadan: African Notes, 1987.
Ajayi, J. F. A., and Robert Smith. *Yoruba Warfare in the Nineteenth Century.* Cambridge: Cambridge University Press, 1964.
Alagoa, Ebiegberi Joe. *A History of the Niger Delta: An Historical Interpretation of Ijo Oral Tradition.* Ibadan: University of Ibadan Press, 1972.
———. "Long-distance Trade and States in the Niger Delta." *Journal of African History* 11, no. 3 (1970): 319–329.
Baier, Stephen, and P. Lovejoy. "The Tuareg of the Central Sudan: Gradations in Servility at the Desert Edge (Niger and Nigeria)." In *Slavery in Africa: Historical and Anthropological Perspectives,* edited by S. Miers and I. Kopytoff, 391–411. Madison: University of Wisconsin Press, 1977.
Biobaku, S. O. *The Egba and Their Neighbors.* Oxford: Oxford University Press, 1957.
———. *The Origin of the Yoruba.* Lagos: Government Printer, 1955.
Bradbury, R. E. *The Benin Kingdom and the Edo-Speaking Peoples of South-Western Nigeria.* London: International African Institute, 1957.
Connah, Graham. *Three Thousand Years in Africa: Man and His Environment in the Lake Chad Region of Nigeria.* Cambridge: Cambridge University Press, 1981.
Cookey, S. J. S. *King Jaja of the Niger Delta.* New York: Nok Publishers, 1974.
Dike, K. O. *Trade and Politics in the Niger Delta, 1830–1885.* Oxford: Clarendon Press, 1956.
Dike, K. O., and Felicia Ekejiubu. *The Aro of Southeastern Nigeria, 1650–1980.* Ibadan: University of Ibadan Press, 1990.

Ekeh, Peter, ed. *History of the Urhobo People of the Niger Delta.* Buffalo, N.Y.: Urhobo Historical Society, 2007.

Ekejiuba, Felicia Ifeoma. "Omu Okwei, the Merchant Queen of Ossomari: A Biographical Sketch." *Journal of the Historical Society of Nigeria* [Ibadan] 3, no. 4 (1967): 633–646.

Equiano, Olaudah. *The Interesting Narrative and Other Writings.* Rev. ed. New York: Penguin Books, 2003.

Falola, Toyin, ed. *Igbo History and Society: The Essays of Adiele Afigbo.* Trenton, N.J.: Africa World Press, 2005.

———. *The Political Economy of a Precolonial African City: Ibadan, 1830–1893.* Ile-Ife: University of Ife Press, 1984.

Falola, Toyin, and G. O. Oguntomisin. *Yoruba Warlords of the Nineteenth Century.* Trenton, N.J.: Africa World Press, 2001.

Heussler, Robert. *The British in Northern Nigeria.* London: Oxford University Press, 1968.

Hiskett, M. "The 'Song of Bagauda': A Hausa King List and Homily in Verse—III." *Bulletin of the School of Oriental and African Studies, University of London* 28, no. 2 (1965): 363–385.

———. *The Sword of Truth: The Life and Times of the Shehu Usman dan Fodio.* New York: Oxford University Press, 1973

Ikime, Obaro. *Merchant Prince of the Niger Delta: The Rise and Fall of Nana Olomu, Last Governor of the Benin River.* London: Heinemann, 1968.

Isichei, Elizabeth. *A History of the Igbo People.* London and New York: Macmillan Press, 1976.

Johnston, H. A. S. *The Fulani Empire of Sokoto.* London: Oxford University Press, 1967.

Johnson, Samuel. *The History of the Yorubas from the Earliest Times to the Beginning of the British Protectorate.* Reprint. Lagos: CSS, 2001.

Johnston, Sir Harry Hamilton, and Rudyard Kipling. *The History of a Slave.* London: Kegan, Paul, and Trench, 1889.

Jones, G.I. *The Trading States of the Oil Rivers.* London: Oxford University Press, 1963.

Last, Murray. "Historical Metaphors in the Kano Chronicle." *History in Africa* 7 (1980): 161–178.

Law, Robin. "The Constitutional Troubles of Oyo in the Eighteenth Century." *Journal of African History* 12, no. 1 (1971): 25–44.

———. *The Oyo Empire, c 1600–1836: A West African Imperialism in the Era of the Atlantic Slave Trade* Oxford: Clarendon Press, 1977.

———. "Trade and Politics behind the Slave Coast: The Lagoon Traffic and the Rise of Lagos, 1500–1800." *Journal of African History* 24, no.3 (1983): 321–348.

Low, Victor N. *Three Nigerian Emirates: A Study in Oral History.* Evanston, Ill.: Northwestern University Press, 1972.

Morton-Williams, Peter. "The Oyo Yoruba and the Atlantic Trade, 1670–1830." *Journal of the Historical Society of Nigeria* 3, no.1 (1964): 25–45.

Nachtigal, Gustav. *Sahara and Sudan. Volume II: Kawar, Bornu, Kanem, Borku, Ennedi.* Translated by Allen G. B. Fisher et al. New York: Barnes & Noble, 1975.

Nadel, S. F. *A Black Byzantium: The Kingdom of Nupe in Nigeria.* London: Oxford University Press, 1942.

Njoku, Raphael Chijioke. *African Cultural Values: Igbo Political Leadership in Colonial Nigeria, 1900–1966.* New York: Routledge, 2006.

Ogundiran, Akinwumi. *Precolonial Nigeria: Essays in Honor of Toyin Falola.* Trenton, N.J.: Africa World Press, 2005.

Ohadike, Don C. *The Ekumeku Movement: Western Igbo Resistance to the British Conquest of Nigeria, 1883–1914.* Athens: Ohio University Press, 1991.

Ojo, Samuel. *Short History of Ilorin.* Oyo: Atoro Print Works, 1957.

Okoro Ijoma, J., ed., *Arochukwu History and Culture.* Enugu: Fourth Dimension Publishers, 1980.

Palmer, H. R. "The Kano Chronicle." *Journal of the Royal Anthropological Institute* 38 (January–June 1908): 58–98.

Peel, J. D. Y. *Ijeshas and Nigerians: The Incorporation of a Yoruba Kingdom.* Cambridge: Cambridge University Press, 1983.

Ryder, A. F. C. *Benin and the Europeans 1485–1897.* London: Longman, 1969.

Smith, R. S. *Kingdoms of the Yoruba.* 3rd ed. Madison: University of Wisconsin Press, 1988.

———. "The Lagos Consulate, 1851–1861: An Outline." *Journal of African History* 15, no. 3 (1974): 393–416.

Stilwell, Sean. *Paradoxes of Power: The Kano Mamluks and Male Royal Slavery in the Sokoto Caliphate, 1804–1903.* Portsmouth, N.H.: Heinemann, 2004.

Talbot, P. A. *The Peoples of South-Western Nigeria.* London: Frank Cass, 1969.

Tamuno, T. N. *The Evolution of the Nigerian State: The Southern Phase, 1898–1914.* London: Longman, 1972.

Usman, Y. B. *Studies in the History of the Sokoto Caliphate*. Zaria: Ahmadu Bello University Press, 1979.

Usman, Y. B., and Nur Alkali, eds. *Studies in the History of Pre-Colonial Borno, Zaria*. Zaria: Northern Nigeria Publishing, 1983.

——. *The Transformation of Katsina, 1400–1883: The Emergence and Overthrow of the Sarauta System and the Establishment of the Emirate*. Zaria: Ahmadu Bello University, 1981.

Wesler, Kit W. *Historical Archaeology in Nigeria*. Trenton, N.J.: Africa Press, 1998.

## D. Colonial

Adeleye, R. A. *Power and Diplomacy in Northern Nigeria, 1804–1906*. New York: Humanities Press, 1971.

Afigbo, A. E. *The Warrant Chiefs: Indirect Rule in Southeastern Nigeria, 1891–1929*. London: Longman, 1972.

Asiwaju, A. I. *Western Yorubaland under European Rule, 1889–1945*. London: Longman, 1976.

Atanda, J. A. *The New Oyo Empire: Indirect Rule and Change in Western Nigeria 1894–1936*. London: Longman, 1973.

Chuku, Gloria. *Igbo Women and Economic Transformation in Southeastern Nigeria, 1900–1960*. New York : Routledge, 2005.

Coleman, J. S. *Nigeria: Background to Nationalism*. Berkeley: University of California Press, 1963.

Curtin, Philip D. *Death by Migration: Europe's Encounter with the Tropical World in the Nineteenth Century*. Cambridge: Cambridge University Press, 1991.

Dusgate, R. H. *The Conquest of Northern Nigeria*. London: Frank Cass, 1985.

Ekundare, R. Olufemi. *An Economic History of Nigeria 1860–1960*. London: Methuen, 1973.

Falola, Toyin, ed. *Nigerian History, Politics, and Affairs: The Collected Essays of Adiele Afigbo*. Trenton, N.J.: Africa World Press, 2005.

Flint, John E. *Sir George Goldie and the Making of Modern Nigeria*. London: Oxford University Press, 1960.

Haywood, A., and F. A. S. Clark. *The History of the Royal West African Frontier Force*. Aldershot: Gale and Polden, 1964.

Ikime, Obaro. *The Fall of Nigeria: The British Conquest*. London: Heinemann, 1977.

Johnson, Cheryl. "Grassroots Organizing: Women in Anticolonial Activity in Southwestern Nigeria." *African Studies Review* 25, nos. 2/3 (June–September 1982): 137–157.

Kazenga Tibenderana, Peter. "The Role of the British Administration in the Appointment of the Emirs of Northern Nigeria, 1903–1931: The Case of Sokoto Province." *Journal of African History* 28, no. 2 (1987): 231–257.

Lovejoy, Paul E., and J. S. Hogendorn. "Revolutionary Mahdism and Resistance to Colonial Rule in the Sokoto Caliphate, 1905–6." *Journal of African History* 31, no. 2 (1990): 217–244.

Malami, Shehu. *Sir Siddiq Abubakar III, 17th Sultan of Sokoto*. Lagos: Evans Brothers, 1989.

Mann, Kristin. *Marrying Well: Marriage, Status, and Social Change among the Educated Elite in Colonial Lagos*. Cambridge: Cambridge University Press, 1985.

Mba, Nina Emma. *Nigerian Women Mobilized: Women's Political Activity in Southern Nigeria, 1900–1965*. Berkeley, Calif.: Institute of International Studies, 1982.

Marjomaa, Risto. *War on the Savannah: The Military Collapse of the Sokoto Caliphate under the Invasion of the British Empire, 1897–1903*. Helsinki: Academia Scientiarum Fennica, 1998.

McEwen, Alec C. "The Establishment of the Nigeria/Benin Boundary, 1889–1989." *Geographical Journal* 157, no. 1 (March 1991): 62–70.

Miles, William F. S. *Hausaland Divided: Colonialism and Independence in Nigeria and Niger*. Ithaca, N.Y.: Cornell University Press, 1994.

Ofonagoro, W. I. *Trade and Imperialism in Southern Nigeria, 1881–1929*. New York: Nok, 1979.

Olusanya, G. O. *The Second World War and Politics in Nigeria 1939–1953*. Lagos: University of Lagos/Evans Brothers, 1973.

Oyemakinde, Wale. "The Pullen Marketing Scheme: A Trial in Food Price Control in Nigeria, 1941–1947." *Journal of the Historical Society of Nigeria* 4 (June 1973).

Tayler, F. W. "The Word 'Nigeria'." *Journal of the Royal African Society* XXXVIII (1939): 154–159.

Umar-Buratai, Mohammed Inuwa. *Durbar as Performance of Power in Nigeria and India under the British Empire and after 1876–1972*. Zaria: Ahmadu Bello University, 2003.

## E. Contemporary

Adamolekun, L. *The Fall of the Second Republic*. Ibadan: Spectrum Books, 1985.

Adejumobi, S., and A. Momoh, eds. *The Political Economy of Nigeria under Military Rule: 1984–1993*. Harare: SAPES Books, 1995.

Ademoyega, A. *Why We Struck: The Story of the First Nigerian Coup*. Ibadan: Evans, 1981.

Ajayi, Adegboyega Isaac. *The Military and the Nigerian State, 1966–1993: A Study of the Strategies of Political Power Control*. Trenton, N.J.: Africa World Press, 2007.

Akinyemi, A. B. *Foreign Policy and Federalism: The Nigerian Experience*. Ibadan: Ibadan University Press, 1974.

Amuta, C. *Prince of the Niger: The Babangida Years*. Lagos: Tanus Communications, 1992.

Aniagolu, A. N. *The Making of the 1989 Constitution of Nigeria*. Ibadan: Spectrum Books, 1993.

Apter, A. "Things Fell Apart? Yoruba Responses to the 1983 Elections in Ondo State, Nigeria." *Journal of Modern African Studies* 25, no. 3 (September 1987): 489–503.

Arikpo, O., ed. *TheDevelopment of Modern Nigeria*. Harmondsworth, UK: Penguin Books, 1967.

Bretton, Henry L. *Power and Stability in Nigeria: The Politics of Decolonization*. New York : F.A. Praeger, 1962.

Clarke, P. B., and I. Linden. *Islam in Modern Nigeria: A Study of a Muslim Community in a Post-Independence State, 1960–1983*. Mainz, Germany: Grünewald, 1984.

Diamond, L. *Class, Ethnicity, and Democracy in Nigeria: The Failure of the First Republic*. Syracuse, N.Y.: Syracuse University Press, 1988.

———. "Cleavage, Conflict and Anxiety in the Second Nigerian Republic." *Journal of Modern African Studies* 20, no. 4 (1982): 629–668.

Edozie, Rita Kiki. *People Power and Democracy: The Popular Movement against Military Despotism in Nigeria, 1989–1999*. Trenton, N.J.: Africa World Press, 2002.

Falola, Toyin, and Ann Genova, eds. *Yoruba Identity and Power Politics*. Rochester, N.Y.: University of Rochester Press, 2006.

Falola, Toyin, and Julius Ihonvbere. *The Rise and Fall of Nigeria's Second Republic: 1979–1983*. London: Zed Books, 1985.

Gana, Aaron T., and Yakubu B. C. Omelle, eds. *Democratic Rebirth in Nigeria: Volume One, 1999–2003*. Plainsboro, N.J.: African Centre for Democratic Governance, 2005.

Igbokwe, J. *Igbos: Twenty-Five Years after Biafra*. Lagos: Advent Communications, 1995.

Joseph, R. *Democracy and Prebendal Politics in Nigeria: The Rise and Fall of the Second Republic*. Cambridge: Cambridge University Press, 1987.

Kirk-Greene, A., and D. Rimmer. *Nigeria since 1970.* London: Hodder and Stoughton, 1981.

Maier, Karl. *This House Has Fallen: Midnight in Nigeria.* New York: PublicAffairs, 2000.

Nwachuku, Levi A., and G.N. Uzoigwe, eds. *Troubled Journey: Nigeria since the Civil War.* Lanham, Md.: University Press of America, 2004.

Onyejekwe, Okey. *The Role of the Military in Economic and Social Development: A Comparative Regime Performance in Nigeria.* Washington, D.C.: University Press of America, 1981.

Oyediran, O. ed. *Nigerian Government and Politics under Military Rule, 1966–1979.* London: Macmillan, 1979.

Soyinka, Wole. *The Open Sore of a Continent; a Personal Narrative of the Nigerian Crisis.* New York: Oxford University Press, 1996.

Schwarz, Frederick, *Nigeria: The Tribes, the Nation, or the Race; The Politics of Independence.* Cambridge, Mass.: MIT Press, 1965.

Smythe, H. H., and M. M. Smythe. *The New Nigerian Elite.* Stanford, Calif.: Stanford University Press, 1971.

## F. Nigerian Civil War: 1967–1970

Abiodun, Adekunle. *The Nigeria Biafra War Letters: A Soldier's Story.* Atlanta, Ga.: Phoenix Publishing Group, 2003.

Achuzie, Joe. *Requiem Biafra.* Enugu: Fourth Dimension Publishers, 1986.

Akpan, Ntieyong U. *The Struggle for Secession, 1966–1970: A Personal Account of the Civil War.* London: Frank Cass, 1972.

Clarke, John D. *Yakubu Gowon: Faith in a United Nigeria.* London: Frank Cass, 1987.

Cronje, Suzanne. *The World and Nigeria: A Diplomatic History of the Biafran War.* London: Sidgwick and Jackson, 1972.

De St. Jorre, John. *The Brothers' War; Biafra and Nigeria.* Boston: Houghton Mifflin, 1972.

Elaigwu, J. I. *Gowon: The Biography of a Soldier-Statesman.* Ibadan: West Books, 1986.

Kirk-Greene, A. H. M. *Crisis and Conflict in Nigeria: A Documentary Sourcebook 1966–1970.* Vol. 2. London: Oxford University Press, 1971.

Madiebo, Alexander A. *The Nigerian Revolution and the Biafran War.* Enugu: Fourth Dimension Publishers, 1980.

Niven, Sir Rex. *The War of Nigerian Unity, 1967–1970.* Ibadan: Evans Brothers, 1970.

Nzimiro, I. *The Nigerian Civil War: A Study in Class Conflict*. Enugu: Fourth Dimension Publishers, 1979.

Obasanjo, Olusegun. *My Command: An Account of the Nigerian Civil War, 1967–70*. London: Heinemann Books, 1981.

Odogwu, Bernard. *No Place to Hide (Crises and Conflicts inside Biafra)*. Enugu: Fourth Dimension Publishers, 1985.

Okpaku, Joseph, ed. *Nigeria: Dilemma of Nationhood: An African Analysis of the Biafran Conflict*. New York: Third Press, 1974.

Onyegbula, Godwin Alaoma. *The Nigerian-Biafran Bureaucrat: An Account of Life in Biafra and within Nigeria*. Lagos: Spectrum Books, 2005.

Stremlau, John J. *The International Politics of the Nigerian Civil War, 1967–1970*. Princeton, N.J.: Princeton University Press, 1977.

## III. POLITICS

### A. Government

Adedeji, Adebayo, and Onigu Otite. *Nigeria: Renewal from the Roots? The Struggle for Democratic Development*. London: Zed Books, 1997.

Akpata, Tayo. *In Pursuit of Nationhood: Selected Writings on Politics in Nigeria*. Lagos: Malthouse Press, 2000.

Blitz, L. Franklin. *The Politics and Administration of Nigerian Government*. New York: Praeger, 1965.

Diamond, Larry, Anthony Kirk-Greene, and Oyeleye Oyediran, eds. *Transition without End: Nigerian Politics and Civil Society under Babangida*. Boulder, Colo.: Lynne Rienner Publishers, 1997.

Dudley, Billy J. *An Introduction to Nigerian Government and Politics*. Bloomington: Indiana University Press, 1982.

Falola, Toyin, and Julius Ihonvbere. *The Rise and Fall of the Second Republic, 1979–84*. London: Zed Books, 1985.

Ihonvbere, Julius. "Are Things Falling Apart? The Military and the Crisis of Democratization in Nigeria." *Journal of Modern African Studies* 34, no.2 (1996): 193–225.

Ikpuk, John Smith. *Militarisation of Politics and Neo-Colonialism: The Nigerian Experience 1966–90*. London: Janus Publishing, 1995.

Johnson-Odim, Cheryl, and Nina Emma Mba. *For Women and the Nation: Funmilayo Ransome-Kuti of Nigeria*. Urbana: University of Illinois Press, 1997.

Kirk-Green, Anthony, and Douglass Rimmer. *Nigeria since 1970: A Political and Economic Outline.* New York: Africana Publishing, 1981.

Makintosh, John P. *Nigerian Government and Politics.* London: Allen & Unwin, 1966.

Momoh, Abubakar, and Said Adejumobi, eds. *The National Questions in Nigeria.* Hampshire, UK: Ashgate Publishing, 2002.

Moore, Jonathan. "The Political History of Nigeria's New Capital." *Journal of Modern African Studies* 22, no. 1 (1984): 167–175.

Nicolson, Ian. *The Administration of Nigeria, 1900–1960.* Oxford: Clarendon Press, 1969.

Nnadozie, Uche O. *The State, Civil Service and Underdevelopment in Nigeria: An Analysis of Policy-Making Process in a Neo-Colonial Society.* Enugu: Johnkens and Willy, 2004.

Nwankwo, Arthur A. *National Consciousness for Nigeria.* Enugu: Fourth Dimension Publishers, 1985.

Oluleye, J. J. *Military Leadership in Nigeria, 1966–1979.* Ibadan: Ibadan University Press, 1985.

Omar, Faruk Ibrahim. *The Prince of the Times: Ado Bayero and the Transformation of Emir Authority in Kano.* Trenton, N.J.: Africa World Press, 2002.

Oyediran, Oyeleye, and Adigun A. B. Agbaje, eds. *Nigeria: Politics of Transition and Governance, 1986–1996.* Dakar: Council for the Development of Social Science Research in Africa, 1999.

Panter-Brick, S. K., ed. *Nigerian Politics and Military Rule: Prelude to the Civil War.* London: Athlone Press, 1970.

Post, Kenneth, and Michael Vickers. *Structure and Conflict in Nigeria, 1960–1966.* London: Heinemann, 1973.

Reynolds, Jonathan T. *The Time of Politics (Zamanin Siyasa): Islam and the Politics of Legitimacy in Northern Nigeria, 1950–1966.* San Francisco: International Scholars Publications, 1999.

Tseror, T. *Democracy in Nigeria.* Jos: Greenwood Press, 2002.

Whitaker, C. S., Jr. *The Politics of Tradition: Continuity and Change in Northern Nigeria, 1946–1966.* Princeton, N.J.: Princeton University Press, 1970.

## B. Foreign Policy

Akiba, Okon. *Nigerian Foreign Policy towards Africa: Continuity and Change.* New York: Peter Lang, 1998.

Akinyemi, A. Bolaji. "Nigerian Foreign Policy in 1975: National Interest Redefined." In *Survey of Nigerian Affairs,* edited by Oyeleye Oyediran. Ibadan: Oxford University Press, 1981.

Aluko, Olajide. *Essays on Nigerian Foreign Policy.* London: George Allen & Unwin, 1981.

——. "Nigeria and Britain after Gowon." *African Affairs* 76, no. 304 (July 1977): 303–320.

——. "Nigeria, the United States and Southern Africa." *African Affairs* 78, no. 310 (January 1979): 91–102.

Aluko, Olajido, Olawiyola Abegunrin, and Olawoji Akonolafe, eds. *Nigeria in Global Politics: Essays in Honor of Professor Olajide Aluko.* New York: Nova Science Publishers, 2006.

Gambari, Ibrahim A. *Theory and Reality in Foreign Policy Making: Nigeria after the Second Republic.* Atlantic Highlands, N.J.: Humanities Press International, 1989.

Oyediran, O., ed. *Survey of Nigerian Affairs, 1975.* Ibadan: Oxford University Press, 1978.

——. *Survey of Nigerian Affairs, 1976–1977.* Lagos: Macmillan Nigeria Publishers, 1981.

——. *Survey of Nigerian Affairs, 1978–1979.* Lagos: Macmillan Nigeria Publishers, 1988.

Polhemus, James H. "Nigerian and Southern Africa: Interest, Policy, and Means." *Canadian Journal of African Studies* 11, no. 1 (1977): 43–66.

Saliu, Hassan A. *Essays on Contemporary Nigerian Foreign Policy.* Ibadan: Vantage Publishing, 2006.

Shaw, Timothy, and Olajide Aluko, eds. *Nigerian Foreign Policy: Alternative Perceptions and Projections.* New York: St. Martin's Press, 1983.

Shaw, Timothy. "The State of Nigeria: Oil Crises, Power Bases and Foreign Policy." *Canadian Journal of African Studies* 18, no. 2 (1984): 393–405.

Spiliotes, Nicolas J. "Nigerian Foreign Policy and Southern Africa: A Choice for the West." *Issue: A Journal of Opinion* 11, nos.1/2 (Spring-Summer 1981): 41–45.

Tijani, Hakeem Ibikunle. *Britain, Leftist Nationalists and the Transfer of Power in Nigeria, 1945–1965.* New York and London: Routledge, 2006.

## C. Specific Institutions

Adekeye Adebajo. *Liberia's Civil War: Nigeria, ECOMOG, and Regional Security in West Africa.* Boulder, Colo.: Lynne Rienner Publishers, 2002.

Akinterinwa, Bola A. *Nigeria and the Development of the African Union.* Ibadan: Vantage Publishers, 2005.

Asante, S. K. B. *The Political Economy of Regionalism in Africa: A Decade of the Economic Community of West African States (ECOWAS).* New York: Praeger, 1986.

Ezenwe, Uka. *ECOWAS and the Economic Integration of West Africa.* New York: St. Martin's Press, 1983.

Falola, Toyin, A. Ajayi, A. Alao, and B. Babawale. *The Military Factor in Nigeria, 1966–1985.* Lewiston, N.Y.: Edwin Mellen Press, 1994.

Miners, N. *The Nigerian Military: 1956–1966.* London: Methuen, 1971.

Shaw, Timothy M., and Julius Emeka Okolo, eds. *The Political Economy of Foreign Policy in ECOWAS.* New York: St. Martin's Press, 1994.

Vogt, M. A., ed. *Liberian Crisis and ECOMOG: A Bold Attempt at Regional Peace-Keeping.* Lagos: Gabumo Publishers, 1992.

## D. Law

Adewoye, Omoniyi. *The Judicial System in Southern Nigeria: 1854–1954.* Atlantic Highlands, N.J.: Humanities Press, 1977.

Ahire, Philip Terdoo. *Imperial Policing: The Emergence and Role of the Police in Colonial Nigeria.* Philadelphia: Open University Press, 1991.

Alao, Akin. *Statesmanship on the Bench: The Judicial Career of Sir Adetokunbo Ademola (CJN), 1939–1972.* Trenton, N.J.: Africa World Press, 2007.

Elias, T. O. *The Nigerian Legal System.* London: Routledge & Paul, 1963.

Harunah, Hakeem B. *Shari'ah under Western Democracy in Contemporary Nigeria: Contradictions, Crises and the Way Forward.* Ikeja: Perfect Printers, 2002

Okonkwo, C. O. *Introduction to Nigerian Law.* London: Sweet and Maxwell, 1980.

Tertsakian, Carina. *"Political Shari'a?": Human Rights and Islamic Law in Nigeria* 16, no. 9 (A). New York: Human Rights Watch, September 2004.

## E. Political Alliances and Elections

Albin-Lackey, Chris. *Politics as War: The Human Rights Impact and Causes of Post-Election Violence in Rivers State, Nigeria* 20, no. 3 (A). New York: Human Rights Watch, March 2008.

Amdi, I. E. S., and L. Hinjari Wilberforce. *Party Systems, Democracy, and Political Stability in Nigeria.* Zaria: Nigerian Political Science Association, 1990.

Anifowoso, Remi, and Tunde Babawale, eds. *2003 General Elections and Democratic Consolidation in Nigeria.* Lagos: Friedrach Ebert Stiftung, 2003.

Awolowo, Obafemi. *Awo: The Autobiography of Chief Obafemi Awolowo.* Cambridge: Cambridge University Press, 1960.

Azikiwe, Nnamdi. *My Odyssey: An Autobiography.* London: C. Hurst and Company, 1970.

Bah, Abu Bakarr. *Breakdown and Reconstitution: Democracy, the Nation-State, and Ethnicity in Nigeria.* Lanham, Md.: Lexington Books, 2005.

Balewa, Sir Abubakar Tafawa. *Nigeria Speaks: Speeches Made between 1957 and 1964.* Ikeja: Longman, 1964.

Bello, Ahmadu. *My Life.* Cambridge: Cambridge University Press, 1962.

Bratton, Michael. *Democratic Experiments in Africa: Regime Transitions in Comparative Perspective.* Cambridge: Cambridge University Press, 1997.

Dudley, J. B. *Parties and Politics in Northern Nigeria.* London: Frank Cass, 1968.

Enahoro, Chief Anthony. *Fugitive Offender: The Story of a Political Prisoner.* London: Cassell, 1965.

Eleazu, Uma O. *Federalism and Nation-Building: The Nigerian Experience, 1954–64.* Ilfracombe: Arthur H. Stockwell, 1977.

Ibrahim, Jibrin. *Nigeria's 2007 Elections: The Fitful Path to Democratic Citizenship.* Washington, D.C.: United States Institute of Peace, 2007.

Koehn, Peter. "Prelude to Civilian Rule: The Nigerian Elections of 1979." *Africa Today* 28, no. 1 (1981): 17–46.

Kukah, Matthew Hassan. *Democracy and Civil Society in Nigeria.* Oxford: Africa Books Collective, 1999.

Ogunbiyi, Yemi, and Chidi Amuta. *Legend of Our Time: The Thoughts of M. K. O. Abiola.* Lagos: Tanus Communications, 1993.

Olurode, 'Lai, and Remi Anifowose, eds. *Issues in Nigeria's 1999 General Elections.* Ikeja: John West Publishers, 2004.

Otite, O. *Ethnic Pluralism and Ethnicity in Nigeria.* Ibadan: Shaneson, 1990.

Oyediran, O., ed. *The Nigerian 1979 Elections.* London: Macmillan, 1981.

Rotberg, Robert I. *Nigeria: Elections and Continuing Challenges.* New York: Council on Foreign Relations, 2007.

Sklar, Richard. *Nigerian Political Parties: Power in an Emergent African Nation.* Princeton, N.J.: Princeton University Press, 1963.

Stauss, Karen, and Carina Tertsakian. *Testing Democracy: Political Violence in Nigeria.* 15, no. 9 (A). New York: Human Rights Watch, April 2003.

——. *Nigeria's 2003 Elections: The Unacknowledged Violence.* New York: Human Rights Watch, June 2004.

Takaya, B. J., and S. G. Tyoden, eds. *The Kaduna Mafia: A Study of the Rise, Development and Consolidation of a Nigerian Power.* Jos: Jos University Press, 1987.

Tokoya, 'Yomi. *General Ibrahim Babangida: A Patriotic Leader of Our People.* Ikeja: People's Publications, 1988.

Udogu, Emmanuel. *Nigeria in the Twenty-first Century: Strategies for Political Stability and Peace Coexistence.* Trenton, N.J.: Africa World Press, 2005.

West, Deborah L. *Governing Nigeria: Continuing Issues after the Elections.* Cambridge, Mass.: World Peace Foundation, 2003.

Williams, David. *President and Power in Nigeria: The Life of Shehu Shagari.* London: F. Cass, 1982.

Yakubu, Alhaji Mahmood. *An Aristocracy in Political Crisis: The End of Indirect Rule and the Emergence of Party Politics in the Emirates of Northern Nigeria.* Brookfield, Vt.: Ashgate Publishing Company, 1996.

## IV. ECONOMY

### A. Agriculture

Berry, Sara S. "The Concept of Innovation and the History of Cocoa Farming in Western Nigeria." *Journal of African History* 15, no. 1 (1974): 83–95.

Clarke, Julian. "Households and the Political Economy of Small-Scale Cash Crop Production in South-Western Nigeria." *Africa* 51 (1981): 807–823.

Idachaba, Francis Sulemanu. *The Effects of Taxes and Subsidies on Land and Labour Utilization in Nigerian Agriculture.* East Lansing: Michigan State University, 1973.

Ijere, Martin Ohaeri. *New Perspectives in Financing Nigerian Agriculture.* Enugu: Fourth Dimension Publishers, 1986.

Ite, Uwem E. "Small Farmers and Forest Loss in Cross River National Park, Nigeria." *Geographical Journal* 163, no. 1 (March 1997): 47–56.

Korieh, Chima J. "The Invisible Farmer? Women, Gender, and Colonial Agricultural Policy in the Igbo Region of Nigeria, c. 1913–1954." *African Economic History* 29 (2001):117–162.

Lovejoy, Paul E. "Plantations in the Economy of the Sokoto Caliphate." *Journal of African History* 19, no. 3 (1978): 341–368.

Martin, Susan M. *Palm Oil and Protest: An Economic History of the Ngwa Region, South-Eastern Nigeria, 1800–1980.* Cambridge: Cambridge University Press, 1988.

Nwosu, A. C. *Structural Adjustment and Nigerian Agriculture.* Washington, D.C.: Department of Agriculture, 1992.

Okere, L. C. *The Anthropology of Food in Rural Igboland, Nigeria.* Lanham, Md.: University Press of America, 1983.

Okolie, Andrew C. "Oil Rents, International Loans, and Agrarian Policies in Nigeria, 1970–1992." *Review of African Political Economy* 22, no. 64 (June 1995): 199–212.

Ottenberg, Simon. *Farmers and Townspeople in a Changing Nigeria: Abakaliki during Colonial Times (1905–1960).* Ibadan: Spectrum Books, 2005.

Russell, T. A. "The Kola Nut of West Africa." *World Crops* 7 (1955): 221–225.

Wallace, Tina. "Agricultural Projects and Land in Northern Nigeria." *Review of African Political Economy* 17 (January–April 1980): 59–70.

Watts, Michael. *Silent Violence: Food, Famine, and Peasantry in Northern Nigeria.* Berkeley: University of California Press, 1983.

## B. Petroleum

Aminu, Jibril. "Nigeria and the World of Oil." In *Nigerian Petroleum Business: A Handbook*, edited by Victor E. Eromosele, 19–38. Lagos: Advent Communications Limited, 1997.

Eberlein, Paul. "On the Road to the State's Perdition? Authority and Sovereignty in the Niger Delta, Nigeria." *Journal of Modern African Studies* 44, no. 4 (2006): 573–596.

Frank, Lawrence. "Two Responses to the Oil Boom: Iranian and Nigerian Politics after 1973." *Comparative Politics* 16, no. 3 (April 1984): 295–315.

Frynas, Jedrzej George. *Oil in Nigeria: Conflict and Litigation between Oil Companies and Village Communities.* Berlin: Lit Verlag, 2000.

Gelb, Alan H., and Henry Bienen. "Nigeria: From Windfall Gains to Welfare Losses?" In *Oil Windfalls: Blessing or Curse?* edited by Alan H. Gelb and Associates, 227–261. Washington, D.C.: World Bank, 1988.

Ihonvbere, Julius O. "The Foreign Policy of Dependent States: The Impact of Oil on Nigerian Foreign Policy 1960–1982." *The Indian Political Science Review* 18, no. 1 (January 1984): 81–106.

———. *The Oil Industry in Nigeria: An Annotated Bibliography*. Montreal: Centre for Developing-Area Studies, McGill University, 1983.

———. "Resource Availability and Foreign Policy in Nigeria: The Impact of Oil." *India Quarterly* 39, no. 2 (April–June 1983): 109–136.

Ike Okonta, Oronto Douglas. *Where Vultures Feast: Shell, Human Rights, and Oil in the Niger Delta*. San Francisco: Sierra Club Books, 2001.

Ikein, Augustine A. *The Impact of Oil on a Developing Country: The Case of Nigeria*. New York: Praeger, 1990.

Ikein, Augustine A., and Comfort Briggs-Anigboh. *Oil and Fiscal Federalism in Nigeria: The Political Economy of Resource Allocation in a Developing Country*. Aldershot: Ashgate Publishing, 1998.

Khan, Sarah Ahmad. *Nigeria: The Political Economy of Oil*. Oxford: Oxford University Press, 1994.

Lewis, Peter. *Growing Apart: Oil, Politics, and Economic Change in Indonesia and Nigeria*. Ann Arbor: University of Michigan Press, 2007.

Manby, Bronwen. *The Niger Delta: No Democratic Dividend* 14, no. 7 (A). New York: Human Rights Watch, October 2002.

———. *The Price of Oil: Corporate Responsibility and Human Rights Violations in Nigeria's Oil Producing Communities*. New York: Human Rights Watch, January 1999.

———. *The Warri Crisis: Fueling Violence* 15, no. 18 (A). New York: Human Rights Watch, December 2003.

Mayall, James. "Oil and Nigerian Foreign Policy." *African Affairs* 75, no. 300 (July 1976): 317–330.

Na'Allah, Rasheed, ed. *Ogoni's Agonies: Ken Saro-Wiwa and the Crisis in Nigeria*. Trenton, N.J.: Africa World Press, 1998.

Nnadozie, Emmanuel U. *Oil and Socioeconomic Crisis in Nigeria*. Lewiston, N.Y.: Edwin Mellen University Press, 1995.

Ogezi, Agbaji E. *Mineral Raw Materials and Nigerian Industry*. Jos: University of Jos, 1985.

Okome, Onookome, ed. *Before I Am Hanged: Ken Saro-Wiwa—Literature, Politics, and Dissent*. Trenton, N.J.: Africa World Press, 2000.

Olayiwola, Peter O. *Petroleum and Structural Change in a Developing Country: The Case of Nigeria*. Westport, Conn.: Praeger, 1987.

Omeje, Kenneth. *High Stakes and Stakeholders: Oil Conflict and Security in Nigeria*. Burlington, Vt.: Ashgate Publishing, 2005.

Omoweh, Daniel A. *Shell Petroleum Development Co., the State, and Under Development of Nigeria's Niger Delta*. Trenton, N.J.: Africa World Press, 2005.

O'Neil, Tom, and Ed Kashi. "Curse of Black Gold: Hope and Betrayal in the Niger Delta." *National Geographic* 211, no. 2 (February 2007): 88–117.

Onoh, J. K. *The Nigerian Oil Economy: From Prosperity to Glut*. New York: St. Martin's Press, 1983.

Osha, Sanya. "Birth of the Ogoni Protest Movement." *Journal of Asian & African Studies* 41, nos. 1–2 (2006): 13–38.

Panter-Brick, K, ed. *Soldiers and Oil: The Political Transformation of Nigeria*. London: Frank Cass, 1978.

Saro-Wiwa, Ken. *Genocide in Nigeria: The Ogoni Tragedy*. London: Saros International Publishers, 1992.

Soremekun, Kayode, ed. *Perspectives on the Nigerian Oil Industry*. Lagos: Amkra Books, 1995.

Sote, Kayode. *Beyond the Crude Oil and Gas Reserves*. Lagos: Lubservices Associates, 1993.

Turner, Terisa. "Multinational Corporations and the Instability of the Nigerian State." *Review of African Political Economy* 3, no. 5 (Spring 1976): 63–79.

———. "Oil Workers and the Oil Bust in Nigeria." *Africa Today* 33, no. 4 (1986): 33–50.

———. Nigerian Refining Industry." *World Development* 5, no. 3 (1977): 235–256.

## C. Finance and Revenue Allocation

Aboyade, Ojetunji, and Bolanle Awe. *Footprints of the Ancestor: The Secret of Being Ojetunji Aboyade*. Ibadan: Fountain Publications, 1999.

Adebayo, A. G. *Embattled Federalism: History of Revenue Allocation in Nigeria, 1945–1990*. New York: P. Lang, 1993.

Adedeji, Adebayo. *Nigerian Federal Finance: Its Development, Problems, and Prospects*. New York: African Publishing, 1969.

Okigbo, P. N. C. *Nigerian Public Finance*. Evanston, Ill.: Northwestern University Press, 1985.

Onoh, J. K. *The Foundations of Nigeria's Financial Infrastructure*. London: Crown Helm, 1980.

Sanusi, J. O. *The Nigerian Economy: Growth, Productivity, and the Role of Monetary Policy*. Ibadan: Development Policy Centre, 2001.

Yekini, Salisa. *The Politics of Revenue Allocation.* Lagos: Bantam Press, 1992.

## D. Trade

Ekechi, F. K. "Aspects of Palm Oil Trade at Oguta (Eastern Nigeria), 1900–1950." *African Economic History* 10 (1981): 35–65.

Harris, Rosemary. "The History of Trade at Ikom, Eastern Nigeria." *Africa* 42 (1972): 122–139.

Hopkins, A. G. *An Economic History of West Africa.* New York: Columbia University Press, 1973.

Johnson, Cheryl. "Madam Pelewura and the Lagos Market Women." *Tarikh* 7, no. 1 (1981).

Latham, A. J. H. *Old Calabar, 1600–1891: The Impact of the International Economy upon a Traditional Society.* Oxford: Clarendon Press, 1973.

Lovejoy, Paul E. *Caravans of Kola: The Hausa Kola Trade, 1700–1900.* Zaria: Ahmadu Bello University Press, 1980.

———. "Interregional Monetary Flows in Precolonial Trade of Nigeria." *Journal of African History* 15, no. 4 (1974): 563–585.

———. *Salt of the Desert Sun: A History of Salt Production and Trade in the Central Sudan.* Cambridge: Cambridge University Press, 1986.

Martin, Susan M. *Palm Oil and Protest: An Economic History of the Ngwa Region, South-Eastern Nigeria, 1800–1980.* Cambridge: Cambridge University Press, 1988.

Northrup, David. "The Compatibility of the Slave and Palm Oil Trades in the Bight of Biafra." *Journal of African History* 17, no. 3 (1976): 353–364.

———. "The Growth of Trade among the Igbo before 1800." *Journal of African History* 13, no. 2 (1972): 217–236.

Nwabughuogu, Anthony I. "From Wealthy Entrepreneurs to Petty Traders: The Decline of African Middlemen in Eastern Nigeria, 1900–1950." *Journal of African History* 23, no. 3 (1982): 365–379.

Olukoju, Ayodeji. "'Buy British, Sell Foreign': External Trade Control Policies in Nigeria during World War II and Its Aftermath, 1939–1950." *International Journal of African Historical Studies* 35, nos. 2/3 (2002):363–384.

———. *The "Liverpool" of West Africa: Maritime Trade in Lagos, 1900–1500.* Trenton, N.J.: Africa World Press, 2004.

Oyejide, T. Ademola. *Nigerian Trade Policy in the Context of Regional and Multilateral Trade Agreements.* Ibadan: Development Policy Centre, 2001.

Soule, Bio G., and C. I. Obi. *Prospects for Trade between Nigeria and Its Neighbours.* Paris: Organisation for Economic Co-operation and Development, 2001.

## E. Development

Bauer, P. T. *Nigerian Development Experience: Aspects and Implications.* Ile-Ife: University of Ife Press, 1974.

Dibua, Jeremiah. *Modernization and the Crisis of Development in Africa: The Nigerian Experience.* Aldershot: Ashgate Publishing, 2006.

Ekundare, R. Olufemi. *An Economic History of Nigeria 1860–1960.* London: Methuen, 1973.

Essien, Efiong. *Nigeria under Structural Adjustment.* Ibadan: Fountain Publications, 1990.

Falola, Toyin, ed. *Britain and Nigeria: Exploitation or Development?* London: Zed Books, 1987.

——. *Development Planning and Decolonization in Nigeria.* Gainesville: University Press of Florida, 1996.

——. *Economic Reforms and Modernization in Nigeria, 1945–1965.* Kent, Ohio: Kent State University Press, 2004.

Falola, Toyin, and Julius O. Ihonvbere. *Nigeria and the International Capitalist System.* Boulder, Colo.: Lynne Rienner Publishers, 1988.

Forrest, Tom. *Politics and Economic Development in Nigeria.* Boulder, Colo.: Westview Press, 1995.

Ihonvbere, Julius O. *Nigeria: The Politics of Adjustment and Democracy.* New Brunswick, N.J.: Transaction Publishers, 1994.

Jega, Attahiru, ed., *Identity Transformation and Identity Politics under Structural Adjustment in Nigeria.* Uppsala, Sweden: Nordiska Afrikanstitutet, 2000.

Kalu, Kelechi Amihe. *Economic Development and Nigerian Foreign Policy.* Lewiston, N.Y.: Edwin Mellen Press, 2000.

Moser, Gary G., et al. *Nigeria: Experience with Structural Adjustment.* Washington, D.C.: International Monetary Fund, 1997.

Nnoli, Okwudiba. *Ethnicity and Development in Nigeria.* Aldershot: Ashgate Publishing, 1995.

——. *Path to Nigerian Development.* Westport, Conn.: L. Hill, 1981.

Nwoke, Chibuzo N. "Towards Authentic Economic Nationalism in Nigeria." *Africa Today* 33, no. 4 (1986): 51–69.

Odetola, T. O. *Military Politics in Nigeria: Economic Development and Political Stability.* New Brunswick, N.J.: Transaction Books, 1978.

Olinger, John Peter. "The World Bank and Nigeria." *Review of African Political Economy* 13 (September–December 1978): 101–107.

Olukoshi, Adebayo O. *The Politics of Structural Adjustment in Nigeria.* London: James Currey, 1993.

Onimode, B. *Imperialism and Underdevelopment in Nigeria.* London: Zed Books, 1982.

Osaghae, E. E. *Structural Adjustment and Ethnicity in Nigeria.* Uppsala, Sweden: Nordiska Afrikainstitutet, 1995.

Usman, Y. B. *Nigeria against the IMF: The Home Market Strategy.* Kaduna: Vanguard Publishers, 1986.

Williams, Gavin, ed. *Nigerian Economy and Society.* London: Rex Collines, 1976.

## F. Labor

Ananaba, Wogu. *The Trade Union Movement in Nigeria.* New York: Africana Publishing Corporation, 1970.

Blyfield, Judith. *The Bluest Hands: A Social and Economic History of Women Dyers in Abeokuta (Nigeria), 1890–1940.* Portsmouth, N.H.: Heinemann, 2002.

Brown, Carolyn A. *"We Were All Slaves:" African Miners, Culture, and Resistance at the Enugu Government Colliery.* Portsmouth, N.H.: Heinemann, 2003.

Burfisher, Mary. E., and Nadine R. Horenstein. *Sex Roles in the Nigerian Tiv Farm Household.* Westport, Conn.: Kumarian Press, 1985.

Freund, Bill. *Capital and Labour in the Nigerian Tin Mines.* London: Routledge and Kegan Paul, 1981.

Guyer, Jane I. "Food, Cocoa and the Division of Labor by Sex in Two West African Societies." *Comparative Studies in Society and History* 22, no. 3 (1980): 355–373.

Lindsay, Lisa. *Working with Gender: Wage Labor and Social Change in Southwestern Nigeria.* Portsmouth, N.H.: Heinemann, 2003.

Okeke-Ilejirika, Philomina E. *Negotiating Power and Privilege: Igbo Career Women in Contemporary Nigeria.* Athens: Ohio University Press, 2004.

Otobo, Dafe. *Foreign Interests and Nigerian Trade Unions.* Oxford: Malthouse, 1987.

Panford, Martin Kwamina. "State-Trade Union Relations: The Dilemmas of Single Trade Union Systems in Ghana and Nigeria. *Labour and Society* 13, no. 1 (January 1988): 37–53.

## G. Transportation

Adeniji, Kunle. *Transport Dubsidies in Nigeria*. Ibadan: Freidrich Ebert Foundation, 1993.

Gavina, Juan, et al. *The Rural Road Question and Nigeria's Agricultural Development*. Washington, D.C.: World Bank, 1989.

Falola, Toyin, and S. A. Olanrewaju. *Transport Systems in Nigeria*. Syracuse, N.Y.: Syracuse University Press, 1986.

Ogunremi, Gabriel Ogundeji. *Counting Camels: The Economics of Transportation in Pre-Industrial Nigeria*. New York: NOK Publishers International, 1982.

Orakomaiya, S. O. *Highway Development in Nigeria: A Review of Policies and Programmes, 1900–1980*. Ibadan: NISER, 1980.

Pollitt, H. W. W. *Colonial Road Problems: Impressions from Visits to Nigeria*. London: Her Majesty's Stationery Office, 1950.

# V. SOCIETY

## A. Anthropology

Afigbo, A. E., and Toyin Falola. *Myth, History and Society: The Collected Works of Adiele Afigbo*. Trenton, N.J.: Africa World Press, 2006.

Apter, Andrew. *Black Critics and Kings: The Hermeneutics of Power in Yoruba Society*. Chicago: University of Chicago Press, 1992.

———. *The Pan-African Nation: Oil and the Spectacle of Culture in Nigeria*. Chicago: University of Chicago Press, 2005.

Barber, Karin. "Popular Reactions to the Petro-Naira." In *Readings in African Popular Culture*, edited by Karin Barber, 91–99. Bloomington: Indiana University Press, 1997.

Chambers, Douglas B. "'My Own Nation': Igbo Exiles in the Diaspora." *Slavery and Abolition* 18, no.1 (1997): 72–97.

Falola, Toyin. *Culture and Customs of Nigeria*. Westport, Conn.: Greenwood Press, 2001.

Falola, Toyin, and Matt D. Childs, eds. *The Yoruba Diaspora in the Atlantic World*. Bloomington: Indiana University Press, 2006.

Honey, Rex, and Stanley I. Okofor, eds. *Hometown Associations: Indigenous Knowledge and Development in Nigeria*. London: Intermediate Technology Publications, 1998.

Okehie-Offoha, Marcellina Ulunma, and Matthew N. O. Sadiku, eds. *Ethnic and Cultural Diversity in Nigeria.* Trenton, N.J.: Africa World Press, 1996.

Onwurah, Ngozi, dir. *Monday's Girls.* DVD. California Newsreel.

Smith, M. G. "The Hausa System of Social Status." *Africa* 29, no. 3 (1959): 239–252.

Smith, Mary. *Baba of Karo: A Woman of the Moslem Hausa.* New York: Praeger, 1964.

Tseayo, P. *Conflict and Incorporation in Nigeria: The Integration of the Tiv.* Zaria: Gaskiya, 1975.

## B. Education

Ajayi, J. F. A. "Higher Education in Nigeria." *African Affairs* 74, no. 297 (October 1975): 420–426.

Akinkugbe, O. O. *Betwixt and Between: Higher Education and Tertiary Health.* Ibadan: Mosor Publishing, 2003.

Akpan, Philip A. "The Role of Higher Education in National Integration in Nigeria." *Higher Education* 19, no. 3 (1990): 293–305.

Fafunwa, A. Babs. *History of Education in Nigeria.* London: George Allen & Unwin, 1974.

Mitchell, Robert Edward, James M. Seymour, and Howard F. Tuckman. *Northern Nigeria Teacher Education Project.* Washington, D.C.: Agency for International Development, 1981.

Nwagwu, Cordelia C. "The Environment of Crises in the Nigeria Education System." *Comparative Education* 33, no. 1 (March 1977): 87–95.

Okafor, Nduka. *The Development of Universities in Nigeria.* London: Longman, 1971.

Oriaifo, S. O., and Uche B. Gbenedio. *Towards Education in Nigeria for the Twenty-first Century.* Benin: University of Benin, 1992.

Peshkin, Alan. *Kanuri Schoolchildren: Education and Social Mobilization in Nigeria.* New York: Holt, Rinehart & Winston, 1972.

## C. Religion

Adesogan, E. Kayode. *Faith, Politics, and Challenges: A Christian's First-hand Account.* Ibadan: HEBN Publishers, 2007.

Ajayi, J. F. A. *The Christian Missions in Nigeria, 1841–1891: The Making of a New Elite.* Evanston, Ill.: Northwestern University Press, 1965.

Atanda, J. A., G. Asiwaju, and Y. Abubakar, eds. *Nigeria since Independence: The First 25 Years.* Vol. 9, *Religion.* Ibadan: Heinemann, 1989.

Ayandele, E. A. *The Missionary Impact on Modern Nigeria.* London: Longman, 1966.

Bascom, William. *Ifa Divination: Communication between Gods and Men in West Africa.* Bloomington: Indiana University Press, 1969.

Birks, J. S. *Across the Savannas to Mecca: The Overland Pilgrimage Route from West Africa.* London: C. Hurst & Co., 1978.

Bivins, Mary Wren. *Telling Stories, Making Histories: Women, Words, and Islam in Nineteenth-Century Hausaland and the Sokoto Caliphate.* Portsmouth, N.H.: Heinemann, 2007.

Bunza, Mukhar Umar. *Christian Missions among Muslims: Sokoto Province, Nigeria 1935–1990.* Trenton, N.J.: Africa World Press, 2007.

Crampton, E. P. T. *Christianity in Northern Nigeria.* London: Geoffrey Chapman, 1975.

Danfulani, Umar Habila Dadem. "Exorcising Witchcraft: The Return of the Gods in New Religious Movements on the Jos Plateau and the Benue Regions of Nigeria." *African Affairs* 98, no. 391 (April 1999): 167–193.

De La Torre, Miguel A. *Santeria: The Beliefs and Rituals of a Growing Religion in America.* Grand Rapids, Mich.: Eerdmans Publishing, 2004.

Enwerem, I. M. *A Dangerous Awakening: The Politicization of Religion in Nigeria.* Ibadan: IFRA, 1995.

Falola, Toyin. *Violence in Nigeria.* Rochester, N.Y.: University of Rochester Press, 1998.

Falola, Toyin, and Ann Genova, eds. *Orisa: Yoruba Gods and Spiritual Identity in Africa and the Diaspora.* Trenton, N.J.: Africa World Press, 2005.

Haskett, Rosalind. *Religion in Calabar: The Religious Life and History of a Nigerian Town.* New York: Mouton de Gruyter, 1989.

Hiskett, Mervyn. *The Development of Islam in West Africa.* London: Longman, 1984.

Hogben, S. J. *An Introduction to the History of the Islamic States of Northern Nigeria.* Ibadan: Oxford University Press, 1967.

Ilesanmi, Simeon O. *Religious Pluralism and the Nigerian State.* Athens: Ohio University Center for International Studies, 1997.

Jell-Bahlsen, Sabine, dir. *Mammy Water: In Search of the Water Spirits in Nigeria.* DVD. Tadem Film and Nigerian Television Authority, 1989.

Korieh, Chima J., and G. Ugo Nwokeji. *Religion, History, and Politics in Nigeria: Essays in Honor of Ogbu U. Kalu.* Lanham, Md.: University Press of America, 2005.

Lavers, John. "Islam in the Bornu Caliphate." *Odu* 5 (1971): 27–53.

Loimeier, Roman. *Islamic Reform and Political Change in Northern Nigeria.* Evanston, Ill.: Northwestern University Press, 1997.

MacLean, Una. *Magical Medicine: A Nigerian Case Study.* London: Allen Lane, 1971.

Makanjuola, J. D. A., A. O. Odejide, and O. A. Erinosho. *The Integration of Mental Health into Primary Health Case in Nigeria.* Lagos: Federal Ministry of Health, 1990.

Nadel, S. F. *Nupe Religion.* New York: Schocken Books, 1954.

Ojo, Matthews. "The Contextual Significance of the Charismatic Movements in Independent Nigeria." *Africa: Journal of the International African Institute* 58, no. 2 (1988): 175–192.

——. *The End-Time Army: Charismatic Movements in Modern Nigeria.* Trenton, N.J.: Africa World Press, 2006.

Olupona, Jacob K., and Toyin Falola. *Religion and Society in Nigeria: Historical and Sociological Perspectives.* Ibadan: Spectrum Books, 1991.

Orde Browne, G. St. J. "Witchcraft and British Colonial Law." *Africa* 8, no. 4 (October 1935).

Paden, J. *Religion and Political Culture in Kano.* Berkeley: University of California Press, 1973.

Peel, J. D. Y. *Aladura: A Religious Movement among the Yoruba.* Suffolk, UK: University of Oxford, 1968.

——. *Religious Encounter and the Making of the Yoruba.* Bloomington: Indiana University Press, 2000.

Reynolds, Jonathan T. *Stealing the Road: Colonial Rule and the Hajj from Nigeria in the Early 20th Century.* Boston: African Studies Center, Boston University, 2003.

Tasie, G. O. M. *Christian Missionary Enterprise in the Niger Delta, 1864–1918.* Leiden: E.J. Brill, 1978.

Tertaskian, Carina. *Revenge in the Name of Religion: The Cycle of Violence in Plateau and Kano States* 17, no. 8 (A). New York: Human Rights Watch, May 2005.

Trimingham, Spencer. *A History of Islam in West Africa.* Oxford: Oxford University Press, 1962.

Usman, Y. B. *The Manipulation of Religion in Nigeria, 1977–1987.* Kaduna: Vanguard Publishers, 1987.

Uwazie, Ernest E., Isaac O. Albert, and Godfrey N. Uzoigwe, eds. *Inter-Ethnic and Religious Conflict Resolution in Nigeria.* Lanham, Md.: Lexington Books, 1999.

Webster, James Bertin. *The African Churches among the Yoruba, 1888–1922.* Oxford: Clarendon Press, 1964.

Williams, Pat, and Toyin Falola. *Religious Impact on the Nation State: The Nigerian Predicament.* Brookfield, Vt.: Ashgate Publishing, 1995.

Works, John A., Jr. *Pilgrims in a Strange Land: Hausa Communities in Chad.* New York: Columbia University Press, 1976.

## D. Crime and Corruption

Albin-Lackey, Chris. *Chop Fine: The Human Rights Impact of Local Government Corruption and Mismanagement in Rivers State, Nigeria* 19, no. 2 (A). New York: Human Rights Watch, January 2007.

——. *Criminal Politics: Violence, "Godfathers," and Corruption in Nigeria* 19, no. 16 (A). New York: Human Rights Watch, October 2002.

Kelly, Robert. J. "Slicing Nigeria's 'National Cake.'" In *Menace to Society: Political-Criminal Collaboration around the World*, edited by Roy Godson, 137–174. New Brunswick, N.J.: Transaction Publishers, 2003.

Marenin, Otwin. "The Anini Saga: Armed Robbery and the Reproduction of Ideology in Nigeria." *Journal of Modern African Studies* 25, no. 2 (June 1987): 259–281.

Sindzingre, Alice. "The Cultural Dimensions of Corruption: Reflections of Nigeria." In *Civil Society and Corruption: Mobilizing for Reform*, edited by Michael Johnston, 61–73. Lanham, Md.: University Press of America, 2005.

Smith, Daniel Jordan. *A Culture of Corruption: Everyday Deception and Popular Discontent in Nigeria.* Princeton, N.J.: Princeton University Press, 2007.

Tertsakian, Carina. *The Bakassi Boys: The Legitimization of Murder and Torture* 14, no. 5 (A). New York: Human Rights Watch, May 2002.

——. *The O'odua People's Congress: Fighting Violence with Violence* 15, no. 4 (A). New York: Human Rights Watch, February 2003.

## VI. CULTURE

## A. Archeology

Bivar, A. D. H., and P. L. Shinnie. "Old Kanuri Capitals." *Journal of African History* 3, no. 1 (1962): 1–10.

Connah, Graham. *The Archaeology of Benin*. Oxford: Oxford University Press, 1975.

———. "The Daima Sequence and the Prehistoric Chronology of the Lake Chad Region of Nigeria." *Journal of African History* 17, no. 3 (1976): 321–352.

Darling, P. J. *Archaeology and History in Southern Nigeria*. Oxford: B.A.R., 1984.

Shaw, Thurstan. *Nigeria: Its Archaeology and Early History*. London: Thames and Hudson, 1978.

———. *Unearthing Igbo-Ukwu: Archaeological Discoveries in Eastern Nigeria*. Ibadan: Oxford University Press, 1977.

Swartz, B. K., and Raymond E. Dumett. *West Africa Cultural Dynamics: Archaeological and Historical Perspectives*. New York: Mouton, 1980.

Wesler, Kit W., ed. *Historical Archaeology of Nigeria*. Trenton, N.J.: Africa World Press, 1998.

## B. Architecture

Agbola, T. *The Architecture of Fear: Urban Design and Construction Response to Urban Violence in Lagos, Nigeria*. Ibadan: IFRA, 1997.

Carroll, Kevin. *Architectures of Nigeria*. London: Ethnographica, 1992.

———. *Church Art and Architecture in Nigeria*. London: Clergy Review, 1968.

Cunha, Mariaanno, and Pierre Verger. *From Slave Quarters to Town Houses: Brazilian Architecture in Nigeria and the People's Republic of Benin*. Sao Paulo, Brazil: SP, 1985.

Dmochowski, Z. R. *The Work of Z.R. Dmochowski: Nigerian Traditional Architecture*. London: Ethographica, 1988.

Izomoh, Samuel. *Nigerian Traditional Architecture*. Benin: S.M.O. Aka and Brothers Press, 1994.

Kirk-Green, A. H. M., and Michael Crowder. *Decorated Houses in a Northern City*. Kaduna: Baraka Press, 1963.

Moughton, Cliff. *Hausa Architecture*. London: Ethnographica, 1985.

## C. Studio Art and Film

Barnes, Sandra, ed. *Africa's Ogun: Old World and New*. Rev. ed. Bloomington: Indiana University Press, 1997.

Beier, Ulli. *Luckless Hands: Paintings by Deranged Nigerians*. Bremen, Germany: CON Medien-und Vertriebsgesellschaft, 1982.

Berns, Marla. "Decorated Gourds of Northeastern Nigeria." *African Arts* 19, no. 1 (November 1985): 28–87.

Brockway, Merrill, dir. *Duro Ladipo's National Theatre of Nigeria: Oba Kò So.* VHS. WCBS-TV, 1975.

Cardew, Michael. "Ladi Kwali." *Craft Horizons* 32, no. 2 (April 1972): 34–37.

Dark, P. J. C. *An Introduction to Benin Art and Technology.* Oxford: Oxford University Press, 1973.

Drewal, Henry John, and Margaret Drewal. *Gelede: Art and Female Power among the Yoruba.* Bloomington: Indiana University Press, 1983.

Drewal, Margaret. *Yoruba Ritual: Performers, Play, Agency.* Bloomington: Indiana University Press, 1992.

Fagg, Angela. "Thoughts on Nok." *African Arts* 27, no. 3 (July 1994): 79–103.

Fagg, William Butler. *Living Arts in Nigeria.* New York: Macmillan, 1972.

Highet, Juliet. "Five Nigerian Artists." *African Arts* 2, no. 2 (Winter 1969): 34–41.

Holy Trinity Cathedral. *Christian Arts in Nigeria.* Nsukka: University of Nigeria at Nsukka, 1979.

jegede, dele. *Kole the Menace.* Lagos: Times Press, 1986.

Kelani, Tunde, dir. *Thunderbolt.* DVD. Mainframe Productions, 2000.

Lawal, Babatunde. "*Ori*: The Significance of the Head in Yoruba Sculpture." *Journal of Anthropological Research* 41 (Spring 1985): 91–103.

Odutokun, Gani. "Art in Nigeria since Independence." In *Nigeria since Independence: The First 25 Years,* vol. 7, *Culture,* edited by Peter P. Ekeh and Garba Ashinwaju, 139–151. Ibadan: Heinemann Educational, 1989.

Okeke, Chukwuanugo. "Tradition and Change in Igbo Woven Fabrics." *Nigeria Magazine* [Lagos] 121 (1976): 32–45.

———. "Wrapper Designs for the Nigerian Market: Design Features for Igbo Women's Wrapper." *Nigeria Magazine* [Lagos] 140 (1982): 29–43.

Ottenberg, Simon. *New Traditions from Nigeria: Seven Artists of the Nsukka Group.* Washington, D.C.: Smithsonian Institution Press, 1997.

Plankensteiner, Barbara. *Benin Kings and Rituals: Court Arts from Nigeria.* Vienna: Kunsthistorisches Museum, 2007.

Poynor, Robin. "Traditional Textiles in Owo, Nigeria." *African Arts* 14, no. 1 (November 1980): 47–88.

Sacchi, Franco, and Robert Caputo, dirs. *This Is Nollywood.* DVD. Eureka Film Productions, 2007.

Ukadike, N. Frank. "Booming Videoeconomy: The Case of Nigeria." In *Focus on African Films,* edited by Françoise Pfaff, 173–185. Bloomington: Indiana University Press, 2004.

Willet, F. *Ife in the History of West African Sculpture.* London: Thames and Hudson, 1967.

Winston Blackmun, Barbara. "Obas' Portraits in Benin." *African Arts* 23, no. 3 (Special Issue: Portraiture in Africa), pt. I (July 1990): 61–104.

## D. Literature, Theater, and Oral Tradition

Achebe, Chinua. *Anthills of the Savannah.* London: Heinemann, 1987.
——. *No Longer at Ease.* London: Heinemann, 1960.
——. *Things Fall Apart.* London: Heinemann, 1958.
Abdulkadir, Dandatti. *The Poetry, Life, and Opinions of Sa'adu Zunger.* Zaria: Northern Nigerian Publishing, 1974.
Akinde, David, dir. *Chinua Achebe: Africa's Voice.* VHS. Films for the Humanities and Sciences, 1999.
Baldwin, Claudia. *Nigerian Literature: A Bibliography of Criticism, 1952–1976.* Boston: G.K. Hall, 1980.
Booth, James. *Writers and Politics in Nigeria.* London: Hodder and Stoughton, 1981.
Boyd, Jean, and Beverly B. Mack. *Collected Works of Nana Asma'u, Daughter of Usman dan Fodiyo, (1793–1864).* East Lansing: Michigan State University Press, 1997.
Carnochan, J. "The Coming of the Fulani: A Bachama Oral Tradition." *Bulletin of the School of Oriental and African Studies* 30, no. 3 (1967): 622–633.
Clark, John Pepper. *Casualties: Poems 1966–1968.* New York: Africana Publishing, 1970.
——. *A Reed in the Tide.* London: Longman, 1965.
Emicheta, Buchi. *In the Ditch.* Portsmouth, N.H.: Heinemann, 1972.
——. *Joys of Motherhood: A Novel.* New York: Braziller, 1979.
——. *The Rape of Shavi.* New York: Braziller, 1985.
——. *Second Class Citizen.* New York: Braziller, 1974.
Ekwensi, Cyprian. *African Night's Entertainment.* Lagos: African Universities Press, 1962.
——. *Burning Grass: A Story of the Fulani of Northern Nigeria.* London: Heinemann, 1962.
——. *Gone to Mecca.* Lagos: Heinemann, 1991.
——. *People of the City.* London: Dakers, 1954.
Ezenwa-Ohaeto. *Chinua Achebe: A Biography.* Oxford: James Currey, 1997.
Fagunwa, Daniel. *Ogboju Ode Ninu Igbo Irunmale.* Reprint. London: Nelson, 1959.
Imam, Alhaji Abubakar. *Magana Jari Ce.* Zaria: Gaskiya 1960.

——. *Ruwan Bagaja* [*The Water of Cure*]. Zaria: Northern Nigeria Publishing, 1971.

Garuba, Harry, ed. *Voices from the Fringe: An ANA Anthology of New Nigerian Poetry*. Lagos: Malthouse Press, 1988.

Ladipo, Duro. *Moremi: A Yoruba Opera*. Ibadan: University of Ibadan Press, 1973.

——. *Oba Kò So: The King Did Not Hang*. Rev. ed. Ibadan: University of Ibadan Press, 1972.

Ladipo, Duro, Wale Ogunyemi, and Obotunde Ijimere. *Three Plays*. London: Longman, 1967.

Larson, Charles. *The Emergence of African Fiction*. Bloomington: University of Indiana Press, 1972.

Lindfors, Bernth. *Early Nigerian Literature*. New York: Africana Publishing, 1982.

Mack, Beverly B., and Jean Boyd. *One Woman's Jihad: Nana Asma'u, Scholar and Scribe*. Bloomington: Indiana University Press, 2000.

Merrick, G. *Hausa Proverbs*. New York: Negro Universities Press, 1969.

Monye, Ambrose Adikamkwu. *Proverbs in African Orature: The Aniocha-Igbo Experience*. Lanham, Md.: University Press of America, 1986.

Na'Allah, Abdul-Rasheed. *The People's Poet: Emerging Perspectives on Niyi Ogundare*. Trenton, N.J.: Africa World Press, 2002.

Ngozi, Adichie Chimamanda. *Half of a Yellow Sun*. New York: Alfred P. Knopf, 2006.

Ngumoha, Emma. *Creative Mythology in Nigerian Poetry*. Enugu: Jemezie Associates, 1998.

Nwapa, Flora. *Efuru*. London: Heinemann, 1966.

——. *Never Again*. Enugu: Nwamife Publishers, 1975.

——. *This Is Lagos and Other Stories*. Enugu: Tana Press, 1971.

Nwoga, Donatus. "Onitsha Market Literature." In *Readings in African Popular Fiction*, edited by Stephanie Newell, 37–44. Bloomington: Indiana University Press, 2002.

Obiechina, Emmanuel. *An African Popular Literature: A Study of Onitsha Market Pamphlets*. Cambridge: Cambridge University Press, 1973.

Ogali, Ogali A. *Veronica, My Daughter and Other Onitsha Plays and Stories*. Washington, D.C.: Three Continents Press, 1980.

Okigbo, Christopher. *Heavengates*. Ibadan: Mbari Publications, 1962.

——. *Labyrinths with Path of Thunder*. New York: Africana Publishing, 1971.

Onwueme, Osonye Tess. *Shakara: Dance-Hall Queen: A Play about Mothers and Daughters*. San Francisco: African Heritage Press, 2000.

——. *Tell It to Women: An Epic Drama for Women*. Detroit: African Legacy Plays, 1995.

Osofisan, Femi. *Aringindin and the Night Watchman: A Play*. Ibadan: Heinemann, 1991.

——. *The Chattering and the Song*. Ibadan: University of Ibadan Press, 1977.

——. *The Oriki of a Grasshopper and Other Plays*. Washington, D.C.: Howard University Press, 1995.

Osundare, Niyi. *Select Poems*. Oxford: Heinemann, 1992.

——. *Songs of the Marketplace*. Ibadan: New Horn Press, 1983.

——. *Two Plays*. Ibadan: University Press, 2005.

——. *Village Voices: Poems*. Ibadan: Evan Brothers, 1984.

Pachocinski, Ryszard. *Proverbs of Africa: Human Nature in the Nigerian Oral Tradition*. St. Paul, Minn.: Professors World Peace Academy, 1996.

Quayson, Ato. *Strategic Transformations in Nigerian Writing: Orality and History in the Work of Rev. Samuel Johnson, Amos Tutuola, Wole Soyinka and Ben Okri*. Bloomington: Indiana University Press, 1997.

Rotimi, Ola Emmanuel. *The Gods Are Not to Blame*. London: Oxford University Press, 1971.

——. *Kurunmi: An Historical Tragedy*. Ibadan: Oxford University Press, 1971.

——. *Our Husband Has Gone Mad Again: A Comedy*. Ibadan: Oxford University Press, 1977.

Saro-Wiwa, Ken. *A Month and a Day: A Detention Diary*. London: Penguin Books, 1995.

——. *Sozaboy: A Novel in Rotten English*. Port Harcourt: Saros International Publishers, 1985.

Soyinka, Wole. *Aké: The Years of Childhood*. New York: Random House, 1981.

——. *Collected Plays*. New York: Oxford University Press, 1973.

——. *A Dance in the Forests*. London: Oxford University Press, 1963.

——. *Five Plays: A Dance in the Forests, The Lion and the Jewel, The Swamp Dwellers, The Trials of Brother Jero, and The Strong Breed*. London: Oxford University Press, 1984.

——. *Idanre and Other Poems*. London: Methuen, 1967.

——. *The Interpreters*. New York: Africana Publishing, 1965.

——. *Madmen and the Specialists: A Play*. New York: Hill and Wang, 1971.

——. *A Play of Giants*. New York: Methuen, 1984.

Tutuola, Amos. *The Brave African Huntress*. New York: Grove Press, 1958.

——. *My Life in the Bush of Ghosts*. New York: Grove Press, 1954.

——. *The Palm-Wine Drunkard and His Dead Palm-Wine Tapster in the Dead's Town.* London: Faber and Faber, 1952.

——. *Yoruba Folktales.* Ibadan: Ibadan University Press, 1986.

Whitsitt, Norman. "Islamic-Hausa Feminism and Kano Market Literature: Qur'anic Reinterpretation of the Novels of Balaraba Yakubu." *Research in African Literature* 33, no. 2 (Summer 2002): 119–136.

Whitting, C. E. J. *Hausa and Fulani Proverbs.* Lagos: Government Printers, 1967.

Wren, Robert M. *Achebe's World: The Historical and Cultural Context of the Novels of Chinua Achebe.* Washington, D.C.: Three Continents Press, 1980.

Yakubu, A. M. *Sa'adu Zungur: An Anthology of the Social and Political Writings of a Nigerian Nationalist.* Kaduna: Nigerian Defence Academy Press, 1999.

Yakubu, Balaraba Ramat. "Excerpts from Balaraba Ramat Yakubu's Alhaki Kwikwiyo." In *Readings in African Popular Fiction*, edited by Stephanie Newell, 33–37. Translated by William Burgess. Bloomington: Indiana University Press, 2002.

## E. Linguistics

Bowen, T. J. *Grammar and Dictionary of the Yoruba Language.* Washington, D.C.: Smithsonian Institute, 1858.

Crozier, D. H., and R. M. Blench, eds. *An Index of Nigerian Languages.* Dallas, Tex.: Summer Institute of Linguistics, 1992.

Emenanjo, E. Nolue. *Multilingualism, Minority Languages and Language Policy in Nigeria.* Agbor: Central Books, 1990.

Nwachukwu, Akujuoobi. *Tone in Igbo Syntax.* Nsukka: Igbo Language Association, University of Nigeria at Nsukka, 1995.

Nwachukwu, Akujuoobi, and Ozo-mekuri Ndimele. *Trends in the Study of Languages and Linguistics in Nigeria: A Festschrift for Peter Akujuoobi Nwachukwu.* Port Harcourt: Grand Orbit Communications & Emhai Press, 2005.

Williamson, Kay. *The Pedigree of Nations: Historical Linguistics in Nigeria.* Port Harcourt: University of Port of Harcourt, 1988.

## F. Media, Communications, and Publishing

Agbaje, A. B. *The Nigerian Press, Hegemony, and the Social Construction of Legitimacy, 1960–1983.* Lewiston, N.Y.: Edwin Mellen Press, 1992.

Anamaleze, John. *The Nigerian Press: People Conscience?* New York: Vangate Press, 1979.

Duyile, Dayo. *Makers of Nigerian Press: An Historical Analysis of Newspaper Development, the Pioneers, Heroes, the Modern Press, and New Publishers from 1859–1987.* Lagos: Gong Communication, 1987.

Jose, Ismail Babatunde. *Walking a Tight Rope: Power Play in Daily Times.* Ibadan: University of Ibadan Press, 1987.

Ladole, Olu Adefale, V. Olufemi, and Olu Lasekun. *History of the Nigerian Broadcasting Corporation.* Ibadan: University of Ibadan Press, 1979.

Larkin, Brian. *Signal and Noise: Media, Infrastructure, and Urban Culture in Nigeria.* Durham, N.C.: Duke University Press, 2008.

MacKay, Ian. K. *Broadcasting in Nigeria.* Ibadan: University of Ibadan Press, 1964.

Mgbejume, Onyero. *Film in Nigeria: Developments, Problems and Promise.* Nairobi: Africa Council for Communication Education, 1989.

Odunlami, Idowu Samuel. *Media in Nigeria's Security and Developmental Vision.* Ibadan: Spectrum Books, 1999.

Ogbondah, Chris W. *Military Regimes and the Press in Nigeria, 1966–1993: Human Rights and National Development.* Lanham, Md.: University Press of America, 1994.

Okwilagwe, Oshiotse Andrew. *Book Publishing in Nigeria.* Ibadan: Stirling-Horden Publishers, 2001.

Oloyede, I. Bayo. *Press under Military Rule in Nigeria, 1966–1993: An Historical and Legal Narrative.* Lewiston, N.Y.: Edwin Mellen Press, 2004.

Olukotun, Ayo. *Repressive State and Resurgent Media under Nigeria's Military Dictatorship, 1988–98.* Uppsala, Sweden: Nordiska Afrikainstitutet, 2004.

Olunlade, Taiwo. "Notes on Yoruba Newspapers, 1859–2002." In *The Yoruba in Transition: History, Values, Modernity*, edited by Toyin Falola and Ann Genova. Durham, N.C.: Carolina Academic Press, 2006.

Omu, Fred. *Press and Politics in Nigeria, 1880–1937.* Atlantic Highlands, N.J.: Humanities Press, 1978.

## G. Music

Akpabot, Samuel. "African Instrumental Music." *African Arts* 5, no. 1 (Autumn 1971): 63–84.

———. *Ibibio Music in Nigerian Culture.* East Lansing: Michigan State University Press, 1975.

Ames, David. "Professionals and Amateurs: The Musicians of Zaria and Obimo." *African Arts* 1, no. 2 (Winter 1968): 40–84.

Boyd, Raymond, and Richard Fardon. "Bìsíweéérí: The Songs and Times of a Muslim Chamba Woman (Adamawa State, Nigeria)." *African Languages and Cultures* 5, no. 1 (1992): 11–41.

Holender, Jacques, dir. *Juju Music*. DVD. Hendring, 1987.

jegede, dele. "Popular Culture and Popular Music: The Nigerian Experience." *Présence Africaine* [Paris] 144 (Fourth Quarter 1987): 59–72.

Kiel, Charles. *Tiv Song*. Chicago: University of Chicago Press, 1979.

Klein, Debra L. *Yorùbá Bàtá Goes Global: Artists, Culture Brokers, and Fans*. Chicago: University of Chicago Press, 2007.

Mack, Beverly B. *Muslim Women Sing: Hausa Popular Song*. Bloomington: Indiana University Press, 2004.

Marre, Jeremy, dir. *Konkombe: Nigerian Music*. DVD. Harcourt Films, 1988.

Olaniyan, Tejumola. *Arrest the Music! Fela and His Rebel Art and Politics*. Bloomington: Indiana University Press, 2004.

Omojola, Olabode F., and Ayo Bankole. "Contemporary Art Music in Nigeria: An Introductory Note on the Works of Ayo Bankole." *Africa: Journal of the International African Institute* 64, no. 4 (1994): 533–543.

Waterman, Christopher Alan. *Juju: A Social History and Ethnography of an African Popular Music*. Chicago: University of Chicago Press, 1990.

## VII. SCIENCE

### A. Geography and Geology

Buchanan, Keith M., and John Charles Pugh. *Land and People in Nigeria: The Human Geography of Nigeria and Its Environmental Background*. London: University of London Press, 1955.

Kogbe, C. A. *Geology of Nigeria*. Lagos: Elizabethen Publishing, 1976.

Thomas, David H. L., and William M. Adams. "Space, Time and Sustainability in the Hadejia-Jama'Are Wetlands and the Komodugu Yobe Basin, Nigeria." *Transactions of the Institute of British Geographers* new series 22, no. 4 (1997): 430–449.

Watson, George Derek. *A Human Geography of Nigeria*. London: Longman, 1960.

## B. Public Health and Medicine

Adeloye, Adelola. *African Pioneers of Modern Medicine: Nigerian Doctors of the Nineteenth Century.* Ibadan: University of Ibadan Press, 1985.

Asuni, Tolani. "Community Development and Public Health: By-Product of Social Psychiatry in Nigeria." *West African Medical Journal* 13, no. 4 (1964): 151–154.

——. "Psychiatry in Nigeria over the Years." *Nigerian Medical Journal* 2, no. 2 (April 1972): 54–58.

Boroffka, Alexander. "The History of Mental Hospitals in Nigeria." *Psychiatry* 8 (1985): 709–714.

——. "Mental Illness in Lagos." *Psychopathologie africaine* 9 (1973): 405–417.

Buckley, Anthony. *Yoruba Medicine.* Oxford: Clarendon Press, 1985.

Eze, Osita C., and Eze Onyekpere. *Study on the Right to Health in Nigeria.* Lagos: Shelter Right Initiative, 1998.

Falola, Toyin, and Matthew M. Heaton, eds. *Traditional and Modern Health Systems in Nigeria.* Trenton, N.J.: Africa World Press, 2006.

Klein, Axel. "Nigeria & the Drugs War." *Review of African Political Economy* 26, no. 79 (March 1999): 51–73.

Mume, J. O. *Traditional Medicine in Nigeria.* Agbarho: Jom Nature Cure Center, 1973.

Opara, Victor Nnamdi. "Emerging Issues in Nigerian Abortion Jurisprudence." In *Endangering Bodies: Women, Children, and Health in Africa,* edited by Toyin Falola and Matthew M. Heaton, 19–74. Trenton, N.J.: Africa World Press, 2006.

Peace, Tola Olu and Toyin Falola. *Child Health in Nigeria: The Impact of a Depressed Economy.* Brookfield, Vt.: Avebury, 1994.

Popoola, Solagbade S. "Abiku: The Recurring Birth-Mortality Syndrome." *Orunmila* 2 (June 9, 1986): 22–25.

Sadowsky, Jonathan. *Imperial Bedlam: Institutions of Colonial Madness in Southwestern Nigeria.* Berkeley: University of California Press, 1999.

Schram, Ronald. *A History of the Nigerian Health Services.* Ibadan: University of Ibadan Press, 1971.

Simpson, George E. *Yoruba Religion and Medicine in Ibadan.* Ibadan: University of Ibadan Press, 1980.

Stock, Robert. "Environmental Sanitation in Nigeria: Colonial and Contemporary." *Review of African Political Economy* 42 (1988): 19–31.

## C. Science and Technology

Andah, Bassey W. *Nigeria's Indigenous Technology*. Ibadan: Ibadan University Press, 1992.

Emeagwali, Gloria T. *The Historical Development of Science and Technology in Nigeria*. Lewiston, N.Y.: Edwin Mellen Press, 1992.

Nwachuku, Michel A. *Computers for Industrial Management in Africa: The Case of Nigeria*. Vienna: United Nations Industrial Development Organization, 1989.

Nwoko, Matthew I. *The Philosophy of technology and Nigeria*. Nigeria: Claretian Institute of Philosophy, 1992.

# VIII. INTERNET RESOURCES

## A. General

Arewa-online. http://www.arewa-online.com/index.html

BBC. "BBC Hausa." www.bbc.coo.uk/hausa/

Central Intelligence Agency. "The World Factbook: Nigeria." https://www.cia.gov/library/publications/the-world-factbook/geos/ni.html

E-Nigeria. http://www.e-nigeria.net

Embassy of the Federal Republic of Nigeria. http://www.nigeriaembassyusa.org/f_index.html

*The Guardian*. http://www.ngrguardiannews.com

*Nigerian Tribune*. www.tribute.com.ng

Nigeriaworld: All about Nigeria. http://nigeriaworld.com

Online Nigeria. http://onlinenigeria.com

*This Day Online*. www.thisdayonline.com

*Vanguard Online*. www.vanguardngr.com

## B. Politics

Benjamin M. Cahoon. "World Statesman: Nigeria." http://www.worldstatesmen.org/Nigeria_native.html

*Biafra Nigeria World*. http://www.biafranigeriaworld.com

Economic Community of West African States. www.ecowas.int

Roberto Ortiz de Zárate. "Leaders of Nigeria." http://www.terra.es/personal2/monolith/nigeria.htm

## C. Economy

International Monetary Fund. "Nigeria and the IMF." http://www.imf.org/external/country/NGA/index.htm
New Partnership for African Development. http://www.nepad.org
Nigerian National Petroleum Corporation. http://www.nnpcgroup.com
World Bank. "Nigeria." http://worldbank.org/nigeria

## D. Society

Church of Nigeria Anglican Communion. http://www.anglican-nig.org
Human Rights Watch. "Africa: Nigeria." http://hrw.org/doc?t=africa&c=nigeri
Russell D. Schuh. "UCLA Hausa Home Page." http://www.humnet.ucla.edu/humnet/aflang/hausa
Toyin Falola. www.toyinfalola.com

## E. Culture

Adunni Olorisha. "The Sacred Groves of Oshogbo." http://www.geocities.com/adunni1/sg.html
Egbe Omo Yoruba. www.yorubanation.org
Google Group. "Yoruba Affairs." http://groups.google.com/group/yorubaaffairs
Metropolitan Museum of Art. "Thematic Essays: Africa: Western Africa." http://www.metmuseum.org/toah/hi/te_index.asp?i=3

## F. Science

Nigeria Health Watch. http://nigeriahealthwatch.blogspot.com/
USAID. "USAID Health: HIV/AIDS: Nigeria." http://www.usaid.gov/our_work/global_health/aids/Countries/africa/nigeria.html
World Health Organization. "WHO African Region: Nigeria." http://www.who.int/countries/nga/en/

# About the Authors

**Toyin Falola** is a Nigerian, born in Ibadan. He earned his Ph.D. in Nigerian history from the University of Ife. Currently he is the Frances Higginbotham Nalle Centennial Professor in History at the University of Texas at Austin. He is also a fellow of the Nigerian Academy of Letters. Falola is the author and editor of numerous books on Nigerian and African history. His most celebrated works on Nigeria include *History of Nigeria* (Greenwood, 1999), *Economic Reforms and Modernization in Nigeria, 1945–1965* (Kent State University Press, 2004), *Violence in Nigeria* (University of Rochester Press, 1999), and the coauthored *Yoruba Warlords of the 19th Century* (Africa World Press, 2001). In 2002, Nigerian scholars compiled a comprehensive three-volume festschrift in his honor on Nigeria's culture and history. Falola's most recent works include his memoir, *A Mouth Sweeter Than Salt* (University of Michigan Press, 2004), *Christianity and Social Change in Africa: Essays in Honor of J. D. Y. Peel* (Carolina Academic Press, 2005), and the coauthored *Migrations and Creative Expressions in Africa and the African Diaspora* (Carolina Academic Press, 2008).

**Ann Genova** is an assistant professor of African history at Roanoke College. Her research interests include petroleum, nationalism, and development in Nigeria. She received her Ph.D. from the University of Texas at Austin. Her publications include the coauthored *Politics of the Global Oil Industry* (Praeger, 2005) and the coedited *Yoruba Identity and Power Politics* (University of Rochester Press, 2006).